The IAF Handbook of Group Facilitation

BEST PRACTICES FROM

THE LEADING ORGANIZATION

IN FACILITATION

Sandy Schuman
Editor

JOSSEY-BASS
A Wiley Imprint
www.josseybass.com

Published by Jossey-Bass
A Wiley Imprint
989 Market Street, San Francisco, CA 94103-1741   www.josseybass.com

Jossey-Bass books and products are available through most bookstores. To contact Jossey-Bass directly call our Customer Care Department within the U.S. at 800-956-7739, outside the U.S. at 317-572-399386 or fax 317-572-4002.

Jossey-Bass also publishes its books in a variety of electronic formats. Some content that appears in print may not be available in electronic books.

Library of Congress Cataloging-in-Publication Data

The IAF handbook of group facilitation : best practices from the leading organization in facilitation / Sandy Schuman, editor.
    p. cm.—(The Jossey-Bass business & management series)
    Includes bibliographical references and index.
    ISBN 0-7879-7160-X (alk. paper)
    1. Group facilitation—Handbooks, manuals, etc. 2. Group decision-making—Handbooks, manuals, etc. 3. Consensus (Social sciences)—Handbooks, manuals, etc. 4. Conflict management—Handbooks, manuals, etc. 5. Management—Employee participation—Handbooks, manuals, etc. I. Title: International Association of Facilitators handbook of group facilitation. II. Title: Handbook of group facilitation. III. Schuman, Sandy, 1951- IV. International Association of Facilitators. V. Series.
    HM751.I24 2005
    302.3'5—dc22

                          2004026722

Printed in the United States of America
FIRST EDITION
HB Printing   10 9 8 7 6 5 4 3 2

The Jossey-Bass
Business & Management Series

CONTENTS

What is group facilitation? A short answer: *Helping groups do better.* A long answer: *Read this book!* Many views are represented in this book. Although most of them are consistent with each other, they emphasize different aspects of group facilitation, and some present interesting differences. We have not attempted to present a singular view but rather a diversity of credible perspectives.

For a midrange answer, start with Chapters Twenty-Six and Thirty, "Facilitator Core Competencies as Defined by the International Association of Facilitators," by Lynda Lieberman Baker and Cameron Fraser, and "Facilitator Values and Ethics," by Dale Hunter and Stephen Thorpe. Together these two chapters convey a sound foundation for understanding group facilitation.

While you may choose to read this book cover to cover, it was designed as a handbook or desktop reference to which you might refer as needed. Each part corresponds to one of the major areas of facilitator competencies, and each chapter was placed in the part to which it most closely relates. Nevertheless, recognizing that each chapter addresses more than one competency, we have provided a Matrix of Contents to help you find chapters pertinent to your needs. The matrix, which follows this Preface, shows each chapter and the competencies it substantially addresses.

One hundred fifteen authors contributed to this book and CD. This is an extraordinary demonstration of the willingness of practitioners and scholars to contribute to the expanding practice and developing theory of group facilitation.

Another sixty people were engaged in reviewing the articles contributed to *Group Facilitation: A Research and Applications Journal*, the first five issues of which appear on the CD, and in reviewing the chapter proposals for this book. Furthermore, references are made to the work of authors—more numerous than I would like to tally—on which the current work builds and expands. To these many hundreds of individuals who have graciously shared their knowledge and wisdom, we owe our gratitude and respect.

Without the long-term determination and support of the volunteer leaders and professional staff of IAF, the *Journal* and *Handbook* never would have been conceived, much less implemented. Mark Adkins, Robin Bailey, Lynda Baker, Mark Fuller, Beret Griffith, Laura Hayter, Dale Hunter, Jon Jenkins, Kerri McBride, Dan Mittleman, Cookie Murphy/Pettee, Jo Nelson, Wayne Nelson, Ned Ruete, Peggy Runchey, Marieann Shovlin, Jim Spee, Bill Staples, David Vukovic, Sunny Walker, Jean Watts, and Vicki Wharton all played critical roles. So, too, our thanks go to the editorial and production professionals at Jossey-Bass who have made this book possible: Rob Brandt, Mary Garrett, Tamara Keller, Beverly Miller, Carolyn Miller, Debbie Notkin, Kathe Sweeney, Akemi Yamaguchi, and others yet to be involved as of this date, as the book enters its final stages of production. In addition, thanks to Reinhard Kuchenmüller, who graciously provided illustrations for each part of the book, and Kevin Kuhne, whose illustrations complement this Preface.

My hope is that writing these chapters and articles was worthwhile for the authors, and reading them will be valuable to you, but it has been no more beneficial to anyone than me. My personal thanks to all who contributed, and my apologies for any omissions or errors.

The work of this book is not done. Your reactions, questions, and suggestions will add value and contribute to the growth and development of group facilitation. Please feel free to contact me as indicated below.

January 2005

Sandy Schuman
Center for Policy Research
University at Albany, SUNY
Albany, New York
sschuman@albany.edu

MATRIX OF CONTENTS

This matrix identifies which chapters provide information related to the IAF Foundational Facilitator Competencies.

Chapters

IAF Foundational Facilitator Competencies	1	2	3	4	5	6	7	8	9
A. Create Collaborative Client Relationships									
1. Develop working partnerships	X	X	X	X		X			
2. Design and customize applications to meet client needs	X		X	X					X
3. Manage multisession events effectively			X	X					X
B. Plan Appropriate Group Processes									
1. Select clear methods and processes			X	X		X	X	X	X
2. Prepare time and space to support group process		X		X	X		X		
C. Create and Sustain a Participatory Environment									
1. Demonstrate effective participatory and interpersonal communication skills	X	X	X			X		X	X
2. Honor and recognize diversity, ensuring inclusiveness	X			X	X	X		X	X
3. Manage group conflict		X	X			X		X	
4. Evoke group creativity							X		
D. Guide Group to Appropriate and Useful Outcomes									
1. Guide the group with clear methods and processes	X	X	X				X	X	X
2. Facilitate group self-awareness about its task		X			X			X	
3. Guide the group to consensus and desired outcomes		X					X	X	X
E. Build and Maintain Professional Knowledge									
1. Maintain a base of knowledge	X	X		X					
2. Know a range of facilitation methods		X	X						X
3. Maintain professional standing									
F. Model Positive Professional Attitude									
1. Practice self-assessment and self-awareness	X	X	X	X					
2. Act with integrity	X	X	X			X			
3. Trust group potential, and model neutrality		X	X			X			

10	11	12	13	14	15	16	17	18	19	20	21	22	23	24	25	26	27	28	29	30	31	32	33
		X							X	X						X				X			
			X	X						X			X	X	X	X	X						X
			X					X								X							
				X	X	X				X			X	X		X	X					X	X
X			X	X	X				X	X	X					X						X	
X	X	X	X	X		X	X	X	X	X		X	X			X						X	
	X	X		X	X	X	X	X	X	X			X	X	X	X						X	X
		X		X					X				X			X						X	
X		X	X	X	X	X	X			X				X		X							X
X			X	X	X			X	X	X	X					X							
X	X	X	X		X		X	X	X			X				X							X
X		X	X		X	X		X			X	X	X	X	X	X						X	
				X	X				X					X		X	X	X	X				
	X		X	X		X	X		X					X		X	X	X	X				
				X												X	X	X	X	X			X
	X	X		X	X	X		X					X	X	X	X		X	X	X	X	X	X
X	X	X	X		X			X	X				X	X	X				X	X	X	X	X
X		X	X		X	X	X	X	X	X			X	X		X				X	X		X

Sandy Schuman has been helping organizations work more effectively to solve complex problems and make critical decisions for more than thirty years. He facilitates problem-solving and decision-making processes for a wide variety of public management and policy issues; works with organizations to develop a more collaborative culture; and provides training in group facilitation, decision making, communication, systems thinking, conflict management systems, public involvement, and information management. He is qualified on the National Roster of Environmental Dispute Resolution and Consensus Building Professionals and Sub-Roster of Transportation Mediators and Facilitators of the U.S. Institute for Environmental Conflict Resolution and the Roster of REDRESS Mediators of the U.S. Postal Service.

Schuman is a research associate of the Center for Policy Research, University at Albany, SUNY, and president of Executive Decision Services LLC, a consulting firm in Albany, New York. He moderates the *Electronic Discussion on Group Facilitation* and is the editor of *Group Facilitation: A Research and Applications Journal.* He helped found the *International Decision Conferencing Forum* and the *New York State Forum on Conflict and Consensus* and is cochair of the Ethics and Values Think Tank of the International Association of Facilitators.

He holds a Ph.D. in organization behavior from the University at Albany, SUNY, where he also earned his M.P.A., and a B.S. in natural resources management from Cornell University. His work has been published in *Interfaces, Information and Management, Journal of Policy Analysis and Management, Quality Progress, Government Technology, Fisheries, Journal of Extension, The Search for Collaborative Advantage* (Sage Publications), *Organizational Decision Support Systems* (North-Holland Press), and *New York State in the Year 2000* (SUNY Press).

Kristin J. Arnold, president of Quality Process Consultants, specializes in facilitating executives and their leadership, management, and employee teams as well as training others to facilitate teams to higher levels of performance. She is the author of several professional articles and books, as well as a featured columnist in the *Daily Press.* She earned her M.B.A. from St. Mary's College in California.

Lynda Lieberman Baker is founder and president of MeetingSolution, an organization development consulting practice based in Austin, Texas. She specializes in values-based facilitation, strategic organizational planning and alignment, and personal strengths and styles assessments. Prior to founding the firm in 1994, she worked with the internationally recognized technology business incubator for technology businesses and at the Graduate School of Business at the University of Texas at Austin. She is an accredited assessor for the International Association of Facilitators' Certified Professional Facilitator programs and a member of the association's coordinating team (its board of directors). MeetingSolution's clients are primarily corporate, professional, and trade associations and nongovernmental social service agencies.

Nadine Bell has over twenty years of experience in working with clients in the private and public sectors and the United Nations Development Program. She facilitates them to plan strategically, communicate effectively, and work collaboratively to achieve their goals. Bell builds her customized facilitations around participative processes that are designed to promote dialogue, transform conflict, develop consensus, expand creative problem solving, and enhance productivity. A mentor trainer of several facilitation courses and founding member of the International Association of Facilitators (IAF), Bell is a member of the Southwest Facilitators Network and the Dallas–Fort Worth Organization Development Network. The first North American to become a Certified Professional Facilitator and one of the first four Certified Master Facilitators, Bell, an assessor and a process manager, has assessed facilitator candidates globally. A past chair of IAF and coordinator of Conference 2002 Texas, she has also served as a cochair of IAF's 1996 Conference in Dallas and IAF's Professional Development Task Force.

Terry D. Bergdall is a founding member of IAF with extensive international experience. In the early 1980s, he facilitated planning events with dozens of municipal governments and public agencies in suburban Chicago. In the late 1980s, as country director of an international nongovernmental organization in Kenya, he initiated and facilitated a highly participatory process of internal restructuring and "indigenization." He has designed facilitation processes and trained numerous facilitators in Kenya, Tanzania, Zambia, and Ethiopia. Facilitation work has taken him to the Balkans, the Caucasus, the Middle East, Southeast Asia, and East Africa. He is the author of *Methods for Active Participation.* He earned his Ph.D. at the University of Wales.

Michael Beyerlein is director of the Center for Collaborative Organizations and professor of industrial/organizational psychology at the University of North Texas. His research interests include all aspects of collaborative work systems, organization transformation, work stress, creativity and innovation, knowledge management and the learning organization, and complex adaptive systems. He has published in a number of research journals and has been a member of the editorial boards for *TEAM Magazine, Team Performance Management Journal,* and *Quality Management Journal.* Currently, he is senior editor of the Elsevier series Advances in Interdisciplinary Studies of Work Teams and the Jossey-Bass/Pfeiffer Collaborative Work Systems series. He has authored or edited fifteen books. His most recent are *Guiding the Journey to Collaborative Work Systems: A Strategic Design Workbook* (2003), *The Collaborative Work System Fieldbook* (2003), and *Team-Based Organizing* (2003).

Jeff Bracken is an organizational effectiveness consultant specializing in organizational survey-feedback-action planning processes, group facilitation, change management consulting, and leadership development and coaching. Since founding Bracken and Associates in 1993, he has served over 250 client organizations in diverse industries. Prior to that, he held key human resource management positions with Fortune 500 corporations and other leading organizations. He is a past examiner, senior examiner, and process observer for the Texas Award for Performance Excellence and has been a member of the board of overseers with the Quality Texas Foundation since 2001. Bracken was named a member of the board of examiners for the Malcolm Baldrige National Quality Award in 2003 and 2004. He is a member of the International Association of Facilitators, the Southwest Facilitators Network, and the Dallas–Fort Worth Chapter of the International Society for Performance Improvement, and is a founding member of the Dallas–Fort Worth Organization Development Network. He earned a B.B.A. in general business and an M.S. in manpower and industrial relations at the University of North Texas, and is a mentor trainer of the Technology of Participation Group Facilitation Methods of the Institute of Cultural Affairs.

Lori Bradley recently completed doctoral course work in industrial/organizational psychology at the University of North Texas and is researching a dissertation on virtual collaboration and virtual leadership. She is currently a strategic learning principal with Raytheon Learning Institutes and a current and founding member of the Virtual Collaboration Research Group at the Center for Collaborative Organizations. Her research and practice areas include virtual collaborative systems and technology, leadership development, and strategic learning solutions. She has worked as a consultant in the medical, banking, real estate, aviation, and information services industries.

Joe Chilberg is a professor of communication at the State University of New York at Fredonia whose work emphasizes helping others understand and excel as human communicators. His work ranges from the classroom to the boardroom as a consultant, trainer, meeting facilitator, and researcher for communication assessments in educational and corporate settings. He has contributed several publications and presentations on group communication, group process designs, and creative problem solving. His current work emphasizes the use of dialogue and appreciative inquiry as approaches for creating participatory, change-responsive cultures.

Mary Eggers is a consultant with Dannemiller Tyson Associates. She has worked in education, government, health care, information technology, banking, and manufacturing, helping her clients tap the wisdom, heart, and energy of those in the organization to achieve desired results. Her work has focused on team development strategic planning, culture change, and redesigning business processes and organization structures. She earned her M.S. in organization development from American University. She is a member of the National Training Labs and the Organization Development Network.

John Epps has conducted seminars and consultations on an in-house basis for organizations in Southeast Asia, the United States, and Europe. As director of LENS International in Malaysia and Singapore, he consults with groups on the subjects of strategic thinking, facilitation methods, customer service, and leadership development. Clients include companies in banking, insurance, manufacturing, and petroleum industries. Epps is a contributing author of the book, *Participation Works: Business Cases from Around the World.* He has published articles in *IMAGE,* the *Journal of Personal and Organisation Transformation,* the *Journal of Quality and Participation,* and *Facilitator.* He is a founding member of the International Association of Facilitators and is currently an adjunct professor at the University of Maryland University College. Epps received his B.A. from the Citadel and his Ph.D. from Southern Methodist University.

Cameron Fraser has worked as a facilitator and trainer for clients throughout North America and in Europe since 1993. His facilitation and consulting services include custom process design in strategic and operational planning and stakeholder consultations. He has facilitated large and small group workshops at and across all organizational levels, designed and installed the delivery structure for organizations, and designed and implemented facilitated processes for team building. He serves as president and CEO of RANA International, based in Ottawa, Ontario, Canada, and is director of operations for the International Association of Facilitators Certified Professional Facilitator Program.

Kathy Free has over thirteen years facilitating experience and seven years teaching and mentoring facilitators by employing her self-developed twenty-week instructional program. She serves as a senior examiner for the Malcolm Baldrige National Quality Award Program and has been appointed to the Executive Guidance Board of the U.S. Senate Productivity and Maryland Excellence Awards. Free is a featured speaker for professional organizations, conferences, and colleges and universities on a variety of topics, including facilitation techniques and performance excellence. She is currently employed at the U.S. Social Security Administration.

Izzy Gesell has a B.A. in psychology and an M.S. in education. He began facilitating while teaching in the graduate school of education at Hunter College in New York. Since then, his facilitation clients have included NASA, Hewlett-Packard, Microsoft, and the Internal Revenue Service. He has run training workshops in improvisation at regional and national gatherings of, among other groups, the International Association of Facilitators, Organizational Development Network, National Speakers Association, and American Society for Training and Development. He is the author of *Playing Along: Group Learning Activities Borrowed from Improvisation Theater,* numerous articles, and a training video, *Humor Works with Izzy Gesell.*

Dennis S. Gouran is professor of communication arts and sciences and labor studies and industrial relations at the Pennsylvania State University. He is the author or coauthor of numerous books and articles dealing with communication in decision-making and problem-solving groups, has served as editor of both *Communication Monographs* and *Communication Studies,* and has been president of both the National Communication Association and the Central States Communication Association. He received his Ph.D. from the University of Iowa.

Randy Y. Hirokawa is dean of the College or Arts and Sciences at the University of Hawaii at Hilo. A specialist in the study of communication in decision-making and problem-solving groups, as well as former editor of *Communication Studies,* he has published extensively in the area. He is chair of the of Group Communication Division of the National Communication Association. Hirokawa received his Ph.D. from the University of Washington.

Christine Hogan is a professional facilitator and educator. She is committed to helping people to learn how to facilitate and to fostering innovations in facilitation through reflective practice, networking and research. Her extensive consultancy work (Bhutan, Lao PDR, Malaysia, Hong Kong, Nepal, Mongolia, the United Kingdom, and Australia) focuses on personal, organization, and community development. Previously, she taught as a senior lecturer in human resource development at Curtin University of Technology, Perth, Australia. She specialized in the education of facilitators and supervision of student research into the field. She is now an adjunct associate professor with the Centre for Research and Graduate Studies in the Division of Humanities at Curtin University. She has published four books and over thirty journal articles and conference papers. She has facilitated workshops in the United States, Canada, Malaysia, Mongolia, and Laos. She has recently been working with SNV Netherlands in the Kingdom of Bhutan in the Himalayas as a training and decentralization adviser.

Marsha Hughes-Rease has over twenty years of leadership experience and worked nine years as an internal consultant prior to joining Dannemiller Tyson Associates. She has provided consultative services, facilitation, and training in diverse organizational settings, including the government, military, health care, education, and manufacturing. Consultative services have included strategic planning and management, organizational restructuring, work process redesign and improvement, conflict management, team development, and leader succession planning. She is also an adjunct faculty member at George Mason University in Fairfax, Virginia. She has graduate degrees in nursing administration and organization development. Her professional affiliations include the American College of Healthcare Executives, American Society for Quality, the Society for Organizational Learning, Chesapeake Bay Organization Development Network, and the Mid-Atlantic Facilitators Network.

Dale Hunter is a group facilitator and author in the field of facilitation. She is a director of Zenergy Ltd. a New Zealand–based company providing facilitation, mediation, and coaching services. The Zenergy Diploma of Facilitation, codesigned by Hunter, has taken more than twelve hundred people to various levels of its eight-module program. She is the principal coauthor (with Anne Bailey and Bill Taylor) of *The Art of Facilitation, The Zen of Groups, Co-operacy—A New Way of Being at Work,* and *The Essence of Facilitation* (also published under the title *Handling Groups in Action: The Use of Distinctions in Facilitation*). Hunter's doctoral thesis, "Facilitation of Sustainable Co-Operative Processes in Organisations," includes a survey of facilitator values and ethics and the monitoring of the IAF code of ethics process. She is vice chair international on the board of directors of the International Association of Facilitators.

Sylvia James has twenty years of experience using whole system, large-scale change methods in high-tech, service, manufacturing, government, and education systems around the world She has designed and facilitated large group interactive meetings involving over a thousand participants in creating and implementing strategy, redesigning work processes and organizational structures, integrating diverse cultures, building multicontractor teams, and planning and launching major programs. She is a partner in Dannemiller Tyson Associates and in the mid-1980s pioneered Whole-Scale Change processes in aerospace. She is coauthor of *Whole-Scale Change: Unleashing the Magic in Organizations* and *The Whole-Scale Change Toolkit* and a chapter contributor to *Flawless Consulting Fieldbook* and *The Change Handbook*. She has also written a number of articles and presented at conferences and workshops around the world. James approaches all her work with a passion for enabling individuals and groups to realize their hopes.

Sandra Janoff worked in public education from 1974 to 1984, helping organize one of the first team-based high schools in the United States. Her research on relationships among organization structure, behavior, and gender led to her doctoral dissertation, "The Influence of Legal Education on Moral Reasoning," published in the *Minnesota Law Review* and in *Feminist Jurisprudence: Taking Women Seriously—Cases and Materials.* She consults with Fortune 500 companies, small businesses, communities, and nonprofits on whole systems redesign and leadership coaching. She also has run training workshops on systems-oriented group dynamics and is coauthor of "Systems Thinking and Small Groups" for the *Comprehensive Textbook of Group Psychotherapy* (1993). She codirects Future Search Network, a worldwide voluntary nonprofit service organization and is a member of the European Institute for Transnational Studies. Together with Marvin Weisbord, she has facilitated future searches in many countries and given seminars in facilitation and future search.

Jon Jenkins has more than thirty-five years of experience in facilitating social and organizational change in developing and developed countries and in training in the fields of short- and midterm planning, community development, team building, motivation, and methods of education. He facilitated or helped facilitate participative month-long consultations in nineteen comprehensive community development projects in eleven countries. He was project director or assistant project director involving one- to two-year on-site residencies in three communities. He has taught over one hundred two- to three-day modules on individual and social change, community development, facilitation, and training methods. He has designed and facilitated a wide variety of events for Shell International Exploration and Production, KPN Telecom, Netherlands, the Community Revitalization through Democratic Action project in Western Serbia, and the Institute of Cultural Affairs, among many others. He has written or edited a number of articles and books on facilitation, training, and social problems. He is on the International Association of Facilitators' ACT, the board of directors, with responsibility for communications and publications. Also, he serves on the board of directors for the Union of International Associations, Brussels. He is one of the co-owners of Imaginal Training, a Netherlands-based international training and facilitation company.

Sam Kaner has been writing and practicing in the field of organization development since the early 1980s. He is the senior author of *Facilitator's Guide to Participatory Decision-Making.* He has made presentations on his concepts and models at the annual conferences of several professional associations, including the International Association of Facilitators, the National Organization Development Network, the American Society for Quality, and the Association for Quality and Participation. His corporate clients have included Hewlett-Packard, VISA International, Charles Schwab, PricewaterhouseCoopers, and many other Fortune 500 companies. His public service clients have included the California Supreme Court, March of Dimes, Special Olympics, Omidyar Foundation, and many community-based organizations and government agencies. Since 1986, he has been executive director of Community At Work, a San Francisco-based consulting firm that specializes in designing and facilitating cross-sector, multistakeholder collaboration.

Miki Kashtan conducts public workshops in nonviolent communication (NVC) and offers mediation, meeting facilitation, coaching, and training for organizations and businesses throughout the United States. She directs the Social Change Project for the Center for Nonviolent Communication (CNVC), a global organization offering NVC training and materials worldwide. In 2002, she cofounded Bay Area Nonviolent Communication (BayNVC). BayNVC is part of CNVC's international network of trainers and local organizations committed to the creation of a world where everyone's needs are met peacefully through compassionate giving and receiving. She holds a doctorate in sociology from the University of California in Berkeley. She has published articles on the theory and applications of nonviolent communication in *Tikkun, Encounter,* and *Communities* magazines.

Lisa Kimball is the founder and executive producer of Group Jazz, a consulting and services company that supports the work of purposeful groups—teams, communities, task forces, organizations—that meet face-to-face or on-line or both.

Clients have included Pfizer, Merck, IBM, USDA, NTL, California Institute of Integral Studies, and City University of New York. She serves on the board of the Plexus Institute, an organization dedicated to promoting organizational and community health through the applications of ideas from complexity science. She has deep experience in facilitating on-line groups and training moderators on multiple networks. She also coaches facilitators and team leaders. Prior to founding Group Jazz, she was a principal consultant in Metasystems Design Group and a cofounder of Caucus Systems. She received her Ph.D. in educational psychology, cognition, and learning from the Catholic University, a master's in social science from Wesleyan University, and a B.A. from Sarah Lawrence College.

Reinhard Kuchenmüller: Having worked as an architect for thirty-five years, my main theme was facility programming, that is, detecting, developing, and communicating human needs as a basis for the design process, including research and consultancy in this field. In 1992, I was fortunate enough to come across a method using hand-drawn pictures to visualize people's statements, originally developed by the architectural firm CRSS from Houston, Texas. This method of visualization soon revolutionized my work. The method matured and became the source of a new profession, visual facilitation, which spread into all fields of business. In 1998, I founded *VISUELLE PROTOKOLLE* in Munich, Germany, a company that offers visual facilitation using hand-drawn images. My holistic approach integrated all my professional, emotional, and spiritual dimensions and brought me into contact with the same dimensions in organizations.

Roland Loup has engaged in whole system consulting with a variety of profit and nonprofit organizations, state and national governments, and universities in the United States, Canada, Europe, India, and Australia for the past twenty years. Specific applications include strategy development and implementation, mergers and acquisitions, culture change, and quality systems implementation. He has codesigned and cofacilitated workshops on the Whole-Scale change process in the United States, Europe, Canada, and India and is cofounder and copresenter of "Intentional Interventions—Diagnosis and Design for Consultants and Trainers" and "The Whole Systems Practicum—An Experience in Laboratory Learning." He has written numerous articles on the practice of organization development and is coauthor of *Whole-Scale Change: Unleashing the Magic in Organizations* and *Whole-Scale Change Toolkit.* He is now partner emeritus of Dannemiller Tyson

Associates after serving as partner for over fifteen years. He holds a master's in mathematics and a doctorate in statistics.

Larry Meeker is a founder and president of Advanced Team Concepts, which specializes in training and support for organizations that are working to improve the human dynamics within their groups. An area of specialty is leadership development programs. He has been involved in the development and delivery of training courses and workshops for Christian-based organizations including World Vision, Habitat for Humanity, federal government agencies, and many private sector organizations such as Dell Computer, Texas Instruments, Ericsson, and Motorola. Previously he was a manager at Texas Instruments. He is a graduate of the University of Arkansas and author of two books on training.

Toshihiko Nakui is a doctoral candidate in the Department of Psychology at the University of Texas at Arlington. He graduated from Kanto Gakuin University in Yokohama, Japan, and received a master of counseling psychology degree from the College of Notre Dame, California. He has been studying group creativity and decision making in collaboration for four years. His primary interest is in the influence of group composition and type of communication system on group work.

Fred Niziol is a full-time facilitator specializing in collaborative Joint Application Development and other information technology–specific sessions, as well as interest-based bargaining negotiations. He is a member of the International Association of Facilitators and the Mid-Atlantic Facilitators Network. Niziol is currently employed by the U.S. Social Security Administration, working in the information technology area.

Susan Nurre, a Certified Professional Facilitator and Certified Master Facilitator, has designed and facilitated sessions for over fifteen years. In 1993, she created and continues to publish *The Facilitator,* a quarterly professional publication with international readership. Nurre has worked with a variety of clients to determine and satisfy their needs from systems requirements to organizational change readiness. In addition to facilitation, Nurre has experience in assessing organizational culture, soliciting customer feedback, developing and implementing communication strategies, managing projects and team members, and the development and delivery of training, including several facilitation courses. Prior to starting her own practice, Nurre worked for Arthur Andersen, American Airlines, and Computer

Sciences Corporation. She is a member of the Southwest Facilitators Network and has been a member of the International Association of Facilitators for nine years. She served as program chair for the 1996 IAF Conference and the logistics chair for the 2002 IAF Conference.

Paul B. Paulus is professor of psychology and interim dean of the College of Science at the University of Texas at Arlington. He has published in the area of group dynamics for over thirty years, including publication of five scholarly books and a textbook devoted to effectiveness in the workplace. For the past fifteen years, he has been studying group creativity employing the brainstorming paradigm and has published over thirty papers and chapters on this topic. He edited *Group Creativity: Innovation Through Collaboration,* which was published in 2003. His research has uncovered many factors that influence the effectiveness of brainstorming that are relevant facilitator practice.

Steven N. Pyser is a principal in a consulting firm that provides dialogue, strategic planning, conflict management, and synergy services to educational institutions, corporations, and nonprofit organizations. He is a member of the faculty at the University of Phoenix, Greater Philadelphia (Pennsylvania) Campuses, where he teaches undergraduate, graduate business, and management courses. Pyser facilitates public conversations and dialogues and conducts workshops on diversity, issues of public importance, group facilitation skills, and conflict management. He serves on the editorial board for *Conflict Resolution Quarterly* and as a staff editor for *Journal of Legal Studies Education.* He received his J.D. from Temple University School of Law.

Maria Begoña Rodas-Meeker has been a facilitator and trainer for the past eight years. She is a founder and principal of Amauta International, which specializes in training and mentoring leaders and facilitators for organizational and social change. She has been involved in the development and delivery of training courses and workshops for groups in corporate settings, government agencies, and a wide range of nonprofit organizations, including Christian-based organizations such as World Vision International, Habitat for Humanity, and Lutheran Church of Colombia. Previously, she was organization development director at Alpina, headquartered in Bogotá, Colombia. She is a graduate of Pontificia Universidad Javeriana, Bogotá, Colombia, and a Certified Professional Facilitator.

John Rohrbaugh earned his Ph.D. in social psychology at the University of Colorado and currently serves as full professor in the Department of Public Administration and Policy and director of the Office of International Education, University at Albany (SUNY). His research has focused on the problem-solving processes of management groups, executive teams, and expert task forces in an effort to identify methods that would improve both the efficiency and effectiveness of organizational decision making. His work, ranging from brief laboratory studies to a ten-year demonstration project in a field setting, has been published as articles in more than twenty journals and as chapters in nearly as many books. As a consultant and facilitator, he has worked with over thirty agencies of federal and state government in the United States, as well as participating on project teams working with governments in Chile, Egypt, Somalia, Lebanon, and Hungary.

Roger Schwarz is an organizational psychologist and president of Roger Schwarz & Associates, a consulting firm that helps people think and act differently so that they can create powerful results and productive relationships in ways they did not think possible. Since 1980, he has served as facilitator, consultant, trainer, and coach to Fortune 500 corporations, governments, and nonprofit organizations, helping them develop effective work groups and facilitative leaders, and create organizational change. He is the author of *The Skilled Facilitator: A Comprehensive Resource for Consultants, Facilitators, Managers, Trainers and Coaches, New and Revised Edition* (Jossey-Bass, 2002), considered a standard reference on facilitation. He is coauthor of *The Skilled Facilitator Fieldbook* (Jossey-Bass, 2005). Formerly an associate professor of public management and government at the University of North Carolina at Chapel Hill, in 1996 he founded Roger Schwarz and Associates. He earned his B.S. degree from Tufts University, an M.Ed. from Harvard University, and an A.M. and Ph.D. in organizational psychology from the University of Michigan.

Beverly Seiford has over twenty-five years of experience as an organization development consultant, project director, and educator. She has facilitated strategic planning, process improvement, leadership development, conflict resolution, and team-building initiatives for Fortune 100 corporations, federal and state governments, medical centers, educational institutions, and nonprofit agencies. The focus of her work is helping clients create a culture that supports superior organizational performance, ongoing individual employee development, and the effective use of available resources in the context of a constantly changing environment. She is a partner in Dannemiller Tyson Associates. She has a master's degree and an advanced graduate studies certificate in foundations of management from the University of Massachusetts. In addition, she is a certified administrator and trainer for the Myers-Briggs Type Indicator.

David Sibbet is a facilitator, organizational consultant, and communications designer. He is founder and president of the Grove Consultants International, a full-service organization development consulting firm and publishing company located in San Francisco. He and his team design and lead strategy, visioning, creativity, future-forces, leadership development, and large-scale system change processes for clients throughout the world. In addition, he and the Grove's Design Solutions Group provide documentation and communication design services that help move insight to action. He is the author and designer of many of the Grove's process consulting tools and guides. Sibbet received a master's degree in journalism from Northwestern University and a B.A. in English from Occidental College. He is a long-time affiliate with the Institute for the Future in Menlo Park and a member of the Global Business Network in Emeryville.

Trish Silber is president of Aliniad Consulting Partners, a consulting firm focused on leadership, team, and organization development. She works with clients in executive coaching, strategic alignment, and corporate learning in leadership, productive reasoning, and communication. Prior to forming Aliniad, she was a senior partner with Catalyst Consulting Team, a national consulting firm known for its work in strategic alignment, leadership development, and experiential learning and served on its board of directors from 1996 through 2002. Prior to joining Catalyst, she held several internal human resource positions at Apple Computer. She earned a master's degree in business from the University of Santa Clara and a bachelor's degree in behavioral psychology from Connecticut College, and has done graduate work in organizational behavior at George Washington University. She has completed numerous certificate programs in the fields of human resources, organization development, and coaching. She is an assistant professor at George Washington University in Washington, D.C., where she teaches in the Leadership Coaching graduate program.

Marianne Stifel: People have always interested and fascinated me. For this reason, I studied medicine and, after receiving my doctorate, specialized in family practice.

I pursued further education in psychotherapy and systemic organization and team development. My professional background consists of twenty years of medical experience and knowledge, with a special focus on psychosomatic medicine, psychotherapy, and art therapy. For a long time, the fine and performing arts have been a personal source of inspiration, regeneration, and intense encounters for me. Art therapy has been particularly fascinating in offering me the possibility of healing by means of creative media. Working with images presents a wonderful opportunity of comprehending people and their needs, their sensitivities and interwoven relationships, and communicating with them on this basis. Since 2000, I have been dedicated to the continued development of this field of work as a partner in *VISUELLE PROTOKOLLE.*

David Straus founded Interaction Associates in 1969 and over the years has served as president, CEO, and chairman of the board. Interaction Associates works in the areas of organization development, group process facilitation, training, and consulting. He guided the development of Interaction Associates' consulting practice and training programs. He was also responsible for major change efforts in a variety of organizations, including the health care and service industries, and has worked with social action partnerships in Newark, New Jersey, and Palm Beach County, Florida. Straus earned a bachelor's degree from Harvard University and a master's degree in architecture from Harvard's Graduate School of Design. Under grants from the National Institute of Mental Health and the Carnegie Corporation, he conducted research in creativity and developed training programs in problem solving. Straus coauthored *How to Make Meetings Work* (1976) and is the author of *How to Make Collaboration Work: Powerful Ways to Build Consensus, Solve Problems, and Make Decisions* (2002).

Glyn Thomas is a lecturer at La Trobe University, Bendigo, Australia. He teaches in the area of outdoor leadership with a particular focus on facilitation, and his research interests lie in the area of facilitator education. He has eighteen years of experience facilitating groups in a broad range of educational and organizational contexts and seeks to help individuals and groups with their development.

Stephen Thorpe works with Zenergy, a New Zealand-based company providing facilitation, mediation, and coaching services. He is an information technology consultant and researcher and a part-time lecturer at the Auckland University of Technology, New Zealand. He holds a bachelor of business degree in information technology from the Auckland University of Technology and is currently undertaking doctoral work on the opening of cross-cultural vistas through on-line storytelling.

James P. Troxel is a founder and partner in Millennia Consulting in Chicago and serves on the adjunct faculty for DePaul University's School for New Learning. His career in community and organization development and leadership training spans thirty years and a dozen countries. He is a facilitation and training expert with specialties in the field of citizen and employee participation, strategic planning, change management, organizational learning, and long-term systemic change. He has published and lectured widely. He edited *Participation Works: Business Cases Around the World* and *Government Works: Profiles of People Making a Difference* and contributed a chapter to *Beyond Prince and Merchant: Citizen Participation and the Rise of Civil Society* (edited by John Burbidge). He is a founding member of the International Association of Facilitators.

Patricia Tuecke, an international facilitator and trainer, has over twenty years of experience in organization and community development, meeting facilitation, and multisector collaboration in the United States, Europe, and Asia. President of Sierra Circle Consulting in Reno, Nevada, she specializes in strategic planning and facilitative leadership development of skills required in participatory organizational cultures and collaborative projects. She works with business, government, education, nonprofit, and community groups to deliver solutions and skills in organizational effectiveness. She is an editor, curriculum designer, published author on facilitative leadership and planning, and a founding member of the International Association of Facilitators.

David Wayne has been involved in facilitation and organization development efforts for over twenty-five years, working in the United States and Canada, as well as internationally through TAPESTRIES International Communications, where he is one of two principals working with a team of one hundred contracted consultants around the world. He has a Ph.D. in psychology, master's degrees in sociology and counseling, and a postgraduate diploma in psychiatry. He has coauthored books on leadership, special education, and peer helping, plus countless journal articles and received the top writing/research award in Canada from the Hilroy Foundation. He is currently incoming chair of the board of the International Association of Facilitators. He teaches part time at Arizona State University and was formerly associate clinical professor of psychiatry at McMaster University in Canada.

Nedra Weinstein is a principal with Arden Consulting, an organization development consulting firm specializing in strategic planning and implementation, leadership and team development, and small and large group facilitation. As an internal consultant working within organizations for seventeen years, as well as an external consultant for the past ten years, she is sensitive to the realities of organizational life and the challenge of instituting meaningful, productive, and lasting changes. Past clients have included Fleishman-Hillard, Maryland-National Capital Park and Planning Commission, WashingtonPostNewsweek Interactive, T.RowePrice, NASA, the Department of Defense, and the Environmental Protection Agency. She is a frequent presenter in professional programs as well as an adjunct professor for American University and George Washington University. She has an M.S. in organization development from American University, an M.S. in administration of justice from Southern Illinois University, and a B.A. in philosophy from the University of Connecticut.

Marvin Weisbord was a business executive and author for many years before becoming an organization development consultant in 1969. Until 1992, he worked with business firms and medical schools as a partner in the consulting firm Block Petrella Weisbord. For many years, he was an associate editor of the *Journal of Applied Behavioral Science* and a member of NTL Institute. He is a fellow of the World Academy of Productivity Science and honorary lifetime member of the Organization Development Network. He also is author of *Organizational Diagnosis* (1978), *Discovering Common Ground* (1992), *Productive Workplaces* (1987), and *Productive Workplaces Revisited* (2004) and the coauthor of *Future Search: An Action Guide to Finding Common Ground in Organizations and Communities* (2000). He codirects Future Search Network, a worldwide voluntary nonprofit service organization, and is a member of the European Institute for Transnational Studies. Together with Sandra Janoff, he has facilitated future searches in many countries and given seminars in facilitation and future search in Africa, Asia, Australia, Europe and North America. He has coauthored *Future Search: An Action Guide to Finding Common Ground in Organizations and Communities* (2000).

Michael Wilkinson is the managing director of Leadership Strategies, which specializes in facilitating executive meetings and providing training in facilitation skills.

He is the primary author of the firm's course, "The Effective Facilitator," which teaches the ten fundamental principles of facilitation from preparing for success to consensus building and managing disruptive behavior. Wilkinson is one of the nation's leaders in the facilitation industry. He is a board member of the National Institute for Facilitation, past president of the Southeast Association of Facilitators, and founder of the National Facilitator Database. He is a Certified Master Facilitator and one of the first five people in North America granted the Certified Professional Facilitator designation by the International Association of Facilitators. In the past decade, he has directed hundreds of facilitated sessions around the world. His first book, *The Secrets of Facilitation,* was recently published.

Paul T. P. Wong received his doctorate in psychology from the University of Toronto. His research ranges from psychology to management, with more than one hundred publications. He has expanded Frankl's logotherapy into meaning-centered counseling and narrative therapy. His current interest is to apply the meaning-centered approach to several cognate disciplines, such as management, leadership, education, occupational therapy, nursing and medicine. He is the founding director of the graduate program in counseling psychology of Trinity Western University. He is also the founding president of the International Network on Personal Meaning, the International Society for Existential Psychology and Psychotherapy, and editor-in-chief of the *International Journal of Existential Psychology and Psychotherapy.* He has extensive experience in group work, from life review groups, to seminars, to board meetings. As a registered clinical psychologist in Ontario, he has many years of experience in counseling individuals and couples.

The IAF Handbook
of Group Facilitation

A Superlative Task

Sandy Schuman

One can hardly contemplate the passing scene of civilized society without a sense that the need of balanced minds is real and that a superlative task is how socially to make mind more effective.

Chester Barnard, *The Functions of the Executive* (1938)

While some might say that group facilitation is just an ordinary task, I believe that group facilitators tend to think of it as an important task, or even an extraordinary task. But who among us has the chutzpah—the self-righteousness—to assert that group facilitation is a *superlative* task? Better to turn to a venerated and impartial authority who can issue this bold proclamation!

Chester Barnard is such a person, a preeminent mid-twentieth-century corporate executive often called the Father of Organization Theory. His classic *The Functions of the Executive* was required management school reading for many decades following its 1938 publication. Although the book is still in print, Barnard's occasionally impenetrable prose has limited its use to only the more rigorous graduate

Note: An earlier version appeared in *Group Facilitation: A Research and Applications Journal,* Spring 2001, p. 1.

programs, replaced elsewhere by more recent and easily read authors. Nonetheless, Barnard still challenges us with pertinent ideas that have retained, if not increased, their relevance. In the concluding paragraph of this renowned book, Barnard highlights four salient points:

- *Society is increasingly complex and organizations are more elaborate.* Even more true than in 1938, the idea that society is increasingly complex now is accepted axiomatically. Organizations are greater in number, size, and geographical scope. We are more dependent than ever before on elaborate technologies and the equally elaborate organizations that create and rely on them. We are interconnected and interdependent yet distinct and diverse.

- *The increasing specialization necessitated by such a society brings with it a diversity of methods and purposes that may be inconsistent and foster misunderstandings.* To manage our complex, technological world, people must be specialized—in roles, expertise, and skills. This makes effective communication, sharing of knowledge, and interpersonal understanding more difficult. This difficulty occurs not only at the level of substantive issues but also at the underlying levels of method (*how* people think about issues) and purpose (*why* they think about them). Misunderstandings occur between individuals, of course and, even more crucial, between large groups of people.

- *What is needed are balanced minds that integrate feeling with reasoning, sense the net balance, and perceive the parts as well as the whole.* The difficulties brought on by the effects of complexity and specialization can be addressed. How? By incorporating the views of multiple stakeholders with diverse interests and perspectives; perceiving the specific parts of the system, as well as the system as a whole; and clarifying the expected results and desired ends. We need to integrate analysis and intuition, facts and values, objective and subjective, thinking and feeling.

- *Meeting these challenges—which will help groups to be more effective cognitively and socially—is a superlative task.* To meet these challenges, we must address the intellectual, analytical, and cognitive demands of the situation. This is necessary but not sufficient. At the same time, we must help groups engage interpersonally, politically, emotionally, and spiritually. As group facilitators, we must, in Barnard's words, strive "socially to make mind more effective." Toward this accomplishment, we devote ourselves and dedicate *The IAF Handbook of*

Group Facilitation. Working together, we aim to strengthen our understanding—in organizations, communities and societies—of group facilitation, a superlative task.

Here is Barnard's full quotation:

> One can hardly contemplate the passing scene of civilized society without a sense that the need of balanced minds is real and that a superlative task is how socially to make mind more effective. That the increasing complexity of society and the elaboration of technique and organization now necessary will more and more require capacity for rigorous reasoning seems evident; but it is a super-structure necessitating a better use of the non-logical mind to support it. "Brains" without "minds" seem a futile unbalance. The inconsistencies of method and purpose and the misunderstandings between large groups which increasing specialization engenders need the corrective of the feeling mind that senses the end result, the net balance, the interest of all, and of the spirit that perceiving the concrete parts encompasses also the intangibles of the whole [p. 322].

PART ONE

Create Collaborative Client Relationships

1. Develop working partnerships.

   - Clarifies mutual commitment

   - Develops consensus on tasks, deliverables, roles, and responsibilities

   - Demonstrates collaborative values and processes such as in cofacilitation

2. Design and customize applications to meet client needs.

   - Analyzes organizational environment

   - Diagnoses client need

   - Creates appropriate designs to achieve intended outcomes

   - Predefines a quality product and outcomes with client

3. Manage multisession events effectively.

   - Contracts with client for scope and deliverables

   - Develops event plan

   - Delivers event successfully

   - Assesses or evaluates client satisfaction at all stages of the event or project

The Big Picture

Creating an Ongoing Client Relationship

Nadine Bell
Susan Nurre

We received a call from Judith, an information technology (IT) executive in search of facilitation training for her team of project managers. We explored in general terms what she was seeking and arranged a meeting to talk in more detail about her needs.

Arriving at the meeting prepared with materials and questions, we began our discussion with the specifics of the requested facilitation class. We then asked Judith how her team would use the facilitation tools that we would be teaching and what problems she hoped these skills would address. During our meeting, Judith and we exchanged ideas, experiences, and methodologies as we established rapport and began to build a foundation of credibility and trust. It became clear through the interview that besides general facilitation, Judith wanted her team to learn how to apply those skills to specific IT sessions.

When we asked about our competition, we learned that we knew both of the other candidates since we were all part of the local facilitator network. We told Judith that although we wanted her to choose us, she would not go wrong with any of her choices.

Later that afternoon, Judith called requesting some information on mind mapping. We quickly pulled together and e-mailed some resources, then followed up with a telephone call.

We delivered our proposal to her within a few days, recommending two classes and follow-on coaching for maximum success. Shortly after, she accepted our proposal, and we delivered the classes. Two weeks later, we met with Judith to debrief the classes, review the evaluations, and discuss next steps.

At a celebratory dinner, Judith shared that she had received many positive comments about the training. She had told a number of people, both inside and outside the company, that she thought our training would be of great benefit to them. Judith also recommended opportunities to showcase our services, such as speaking at the local Project Management Institute meetings. During the course of the conversation, we also explored her current challenges. We brainstormed a variety of solutions, identified where we could provide assistance, and recommended other resources for services that were beyond our expertise.

At a subsequent luncheon meeting, we agreed that our interactions were so rich that we wanted to take our collaboration to a new level. We discussed submitting a proposal to deliver a joint session on facilitation and project management at the 2004 IAF conference.

Since that time, Judith has referred colleagues to us and asked us to submit another proposal for both a repeat of the course we delivered and two additional courses.

As we continue to keep in touch with follow-up telephone calls, e-mail, and occasional lunches, we offer Judith assistance in defining issues and brainstorming solutions. We also serve as a sounding board for her ideas and make referrals to resources to meet her specific needs. When other managers ask her for assistance with their challenges, she does not hesitate to recommend us because our continued, productive contacts have kept our name and services fresh in her mind.

CREATING THE BIG PICTURE

Developing a relationship with clients based on trust and collaboration goes beyond working with them to prepare for a single workshop or series of sessions. The skills we use to design and facilitate sessions—clarifying mutual commitment, customizing the session to meet the client's needs, emphasizing collaborative values and processes, deciding which participants to include, and reaching understanding on scope, deliverables, roles, and responsibilities—do not merely result in successful sessions.

We use these same skills to establish rapport, credibility, and trust with our clients as we help them look beyond the current engagement to the big picture in which they define their problems from a comprehensive organizational point of view. It is through this process that we establish mutually beneficial partnerships that provide our clients with a trusted adviser to help them define their problems, explore possible solutions, and refer to appropriate resources (books, courses, and other people). These partnerships provide us a source of repeat business as well as positive referrals to other potential clients.

As we use our facilitation skills to help our clients broaden their view and fit their immediate needs into their Big Picture, we make it a point to:

Be prepared.

Interview effectively.

Gain trust.

Practice empathetic listening.

Invest in quality.

Communicate intentionally.

Think about clients.

Understand needs.

Recognize challenges.

Evaluate satisfaction.

BE PREPARED

Preparation is the backbone of our facilitation. (See Chapter Four.) The preparation we do at the front end of a facilitation session—understanding the objectives, interviewing the client and participants, crafting sample deliverables, and designing a suitable agenda—lays the foundation necessary to achieve the desired results.

That same focus on preparation is important in managing client relationships and helping clients to see their challenges within the context of the Big Picture. Being prepared for client interactions before and after the session is as important to creating an ongoing client relationship as being prepared for all that we do during the session. Being prepared builds trust, nurtures the client relationship, and develops clients' confidence in our ability to meet their needs.

As we prepare for each interaction with our clients, we determine the objective of the client meeting and design a suitable agenda for accomplishing the objective. For some of our interactions, we may conduct research on the Web, review periodicals, read company materials, and talk with others in order to learn about their company and industry; identify legislative, economic, and environmental issues affecting their business; and become aware of what their competitors are doing.

Just as preparation pays off in a facilitated session, there are many dividends to the preparation we do to nurture client relationships. The better prepared we are, the easier it is to ensure that we achieve the objectives we set for our client relationships: ongoing partnership, additional work, and positive referrals.

INTERVIEW EFFECTIVELY

When we ask facilitators what their most versatile tool is when facilitating a session, they often answer, "Questions." We ask questions of potential clients to obtain the information we use to determine whether to accept an assignment and, if we do accept it, how to proceed. During the session, we ask questions to get information, clarify what was said, elicit more detail, and determine if we have consensus.

Well-phrased questions assist clients to identify issues, concerns, and goals that are broader than our current assignment. By taking a Big Picture view, we encourage clients to explore both the scope of a single engagement and the way it fits into the organization's initiatives for the year. In addition, questions are excellent tools to learn about circumstances that currently exist elsewhere in the company and explore in what other ways we may be of service.

We have found that using the journalist's questions—who, what, when, where, and how—is the most effective way to help clients identify issues because these questions provide data with which we can work. We tend not to ask "why" questions because they are likely to put people on the defensive and often produce one of two nonproductive answers: "I don't know" or "Because."

We ask questions to determine what is in place to support the successful integration of the product of the session. Questions that explore obstacles to success, bottlenecks, and emerging problems reveal information that will assist us in maximizing the results of the session and surface additional areas in which our services can provide valued assistance.

Questions designed to explore the likely impact of industry trends and practices on our client expand the perspective to the Big Picture. Through our questions, we can discern if it is important to the client to be on the cutting edge in his or her industry, what it would take to achieve that end, and how we might assist in reaching that goal. By enlarging our clients' perspective to the industry as a whole, we help them to anticipate and plan rather than react.

Many of the same questions that we use to ask clients about a specific engagement can be broadened to help them focus on the Big Picture. Examples of Big Picture questions include:

- What are the key issues and problems with which your company is dealing?
- How do these affect your department?
- Who are the stakeholders outside your department who are affected?
- How will the resolution of these issues affect other teams, departments, and divisions in your company?
- What are your competitors doing regarding these issues?
- What is a trend in your industry that you believe will affect your company? When did it emerge?
- What areas need improvement to stay abreast of the developments in your industry?

A good resource for session-related questions that could be broadened into Big Picture questions is *The Skilled Facilitator* (Schwarz, 2002). Schwarz identifies four areas—process, structure, organizational context, and behaviors—for which he has developed a series of questions to help diagnose the client's issues and determine whether to work together. For the Big Picture, we can identify which of Schwarz's questions are appropriate for the particular client's situation and broaden their perspective beyond asking about a specific engagement. Asking about a session, Schwarz uses the question, "In what ways does the organization help or hinder the group?" (p. 279). The Big Picture question, "What is it about our organizational culture that has a negative impact on our people and puts them at risk?" could help a floor covering company focus on what is happening within the entire company that results in the manager of every one of their stores suffering a heart attack.

Whether exploring a single engagement or managing a productive client relationship, effective questions assist us in putting clients in touch with information we can use to support them in achieving their objectives.

GAIN TRUST

In our facilitated sessions, we strive to build trust in order to maximize the people, the process, and the product. (See Chapter Six.) Trust creates a safe environment that enables the participants to open up and share freely without criticism. We build trust by providing operating agreements on communication, respect, and confidentiality, as well as using inclusive techniques to encourage broad participation.

When we have created a relationship that is built on trust, clients are more willing to explore their problems and challenges with us as we address their Big Picture.

We establish our trustworthiness by demonstrating reliability, interacting openly, being authentic, respecting confidentiality, honoring our commitments, and operating with our clients' best interests in mind.

When we share highlights of similar engagements, we demonstrate a successful track record and build credibility. Additional ways to build trust and show clients that we value them and their time include these:

- Maintain regular contact during all assignments with frank and periodic communications on progress.
- Return calls and e-mails promptly.
- Be punctual for meetings and telephone calls.
- Meet without interruptions from our cell phones and pagers.

While it takes time to build our clients' trust, it can be destroyed very quickly. If we find that we have made a mistake, cannot meet a deadline, or have a problem in fulfilling a commitment, we do not ignore it. We have an honest and timely discussion on how we will remedy the situation.

Trust grows as we demonstrate our commitment to the client's success in ways that do not benefit us financially, such as suggesting an alternative to a facilitated session or recommending another consultant for a particular service we do not offer. Although it might seem as if we are "losing the work," we are actually strengthening our client relationship and potentially setting ourselves up for future opportunities.

In the Big Picture, when both the client and the facilitator bring trust, shared respect, and understanding to the table, a long and mutually beneficial relationship will result.

PRACTICE EMPATHETIC LISTENING

When we are facilitating, we listen with our ears and our eyes for both the spoken and the unspoken communication. By paying attention to the words, tone of voice, body language, and gestures, we enhance our understanding of what is being said, how the client feels about it, and what lies beneath the words.

Empathetic listening, a structured form of listening and responding, is a powerful tool that we use as successful facilitators and client relationship managers. Empathetic listening has several benefits:

- It requires people to listen attentively to each other.
- It avoids misunderstandings as people confirm that they understand what the other person has said.
- It focuses the listeners on the feelings and needs beneath the words.
- It encourages the clients to open up and say more.

Our questions not only evoke answers about the specifics of the assignment, they also produce information on issues that are important to their Big Picture. Thus, we broaden our scope as we listen for potential areas of difficulty as well as for departments, divisions, or allied operations that could potentially use our services.

In effective relationship management, we not only listen for information that will heighten our effectiveness with the specific engagement, we also listen for those things that relate to the Big Picture. We created the empathetic listening model for use in our course, "The Consciously Competent Facilitator," because it provides the means for facilitators to address the needs and the feelings behind the words used by the participants (see Exhibit 1.1):

Listen. Put all attention on what the client is saying, and listen for statements that relate to the company, the industry, and the latest trends. *Example:* The participant says, "Why are we bothering to work on this plan? It's just like all the other plans we've done. It won't get implemented, and we'll just have wasted all this time!"

Paraphrase. State in different words what the client has said. This avoids misunderstanding because we know immediately if we both understand what was said. *Example:* We might respond, "It sounds as if you think we're wasting time working on this plan because the company is unlikely to put it into operation."

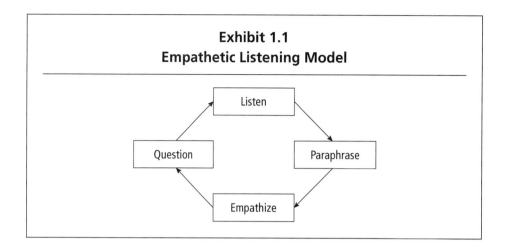

Exhibit 1.1
Empathetic Listening Model

Empathize. Identify and reflect the needs and feelings heard beneath the words. *Example:* We might ask, "Are you frustrated because you feel this is just one more plan that management will ignore?"

Question. Formulate a question that probes for more information or leads to action that will address the issues we heard identified. *Example:* We might ask, "What can we do to help get this plan implemented?"

Marshall Rosenberg (2003, p. 127) underscores the power of empathetic listening in his book, *Nonviolent Communication:* "Empathy lies in our ability to be present." This ability to be fully present with clients and hear the needs and feelings behind their words takes our interaction to a deeper level through which we build partnerships.

INVEST IN QUALITY

When we facilitate during a project, we commit to doing what needs to be done with excellence. Our investment in a quality product includes meeting the session objectives and deliverables as well as being honest with the client about what we can and cannot do within the constraints of time, budget, and resources.

Clients are more inclined to explore their Big Picture with us when they have already benefited from the quality products we have delivered. Producing with excellence what the clients have requested is a springboard to repeat business with these clients, as well as their referrals to other potential clients.

To build our clients' confidence in us and strengthen our relationships with them, we do what we promise within the agreed-on time and budget and deliver a quality product each and every time.

Delivering a quality product includes providing suggestions to our clients for ways to effectively implement the results of a session as well as minimize or eliminate barriers that may have surfaced during the session. Quality produces satisfied clients. Performing with excellence positions us for trusted adviser status and can lead to additional work and referrals.

COMMUNICATE INTENTIONALLY

When we facilitate, we communicate with intention. We have a clear purpose in mind, use terms that are part of our client's culture, ask well-phrased questions, listen empathetically, and accommodate different thinking and operating styles.

The ability to communicate intentionally with clients is essential to building dynamic, ongoing relationships. When our communication is clear and mutually understood, we minimize the chances of misunderstanding and maximize the possibility of achieving the desired results. Since all people do not send or receive information in the same way, we adapt our thinking and operating styles to those of our clients.

We understand, respect, and appreciate diverse thinking patterns and respond to each appropriately. By listening to our clients' words and watching their behavior, we learn whether the way they process information is auditory, visual, or kinesthetic. We then speak in terms to match their thinking style. Auditory thinkers engage in the exchange of ideas and typically say something like, "I hear what you are saying." Visual thinkers use illustrations and graphics and are likely to say, "I see what you mean." Kinesthetic thinkers prefer to take action and may say, "Let's get this done" (NLP Learning Systems, 1993, p. 7).

In addition to using different thinking styles to process information, clients have different operating styles. Although they may demonstrate characteristics from several operating styles, one of the following four styles will be dominant (Wilson Learning, 1987):

Driver. Action oriented, brief, and gets right to the point. Drivers do not like detail and consider small talk and personal exchanges a waste of time. They cut to the chase, make decisions quickly, and get things accomplished. Adapt to this style by talking in bulleted points and quickly getting to the bottom line.

Expressive. Articulate, enthusiastic, high energy, and influences others easily. They are people centered and do not like a lot of detail or working alone. They think out loud and are constantly revising as they speak. Adapt to this style by being friendly and focused and keeping the conversation on track. Otherwise, they are likely to take it in a different direction.

Amiable. Responsible, reserved, logical, cooperative, patient, and persistent. They take all the responsibility on themselves and will not delegate. These good listeners do not like fast change and want to be treated fairly. Adapt to this style by drawing them out and allowing time for ideas to incubate.

Analytical. Organized, methodical, quantitative, critical thinkers who want all the facts and great detail. They are perfectionists who seek detailed answers. They are precise, controlled, and reserved, and they resist change. Adapt to this style by giving them information in writing and providing time for them to analyze and process information.

Effective communication with clients requires clarity on what we plan to accomplish during our client interactions, awareness of the information our clients are seeking, and knowledge of how to deliver it to match their thinking and operating styles.

THINK ABOUT CLIENTS

In addition to conducting specific research for an engagement, we keep the session objectives in mind as we review literature, engage in professional discussions, and attend sessions at conferences. This helps us recognize and apply new facilitation techniques to address issues effectively, make the session more participative, and create positive results.

As our clients see that we are continually thinking about their Big Picture needs, they are more likely to remember us when an opportunity arises for facilitation or other consulting services.

We keep our clients' Big Picture needs in mind as we read newspapers and professional magazines, peruse conference flyers and book reviews, participate in meetings and other networking experiences, and engage in activities that could provide information pertinent to our clients.

We use this information in a variety of ways to enhance our clients' operations and maintain our connection. One way is simply to forward the information, such as telling them about a conference. Another is to customize the information to meet client needs, such as recommending specific workshops within the conference. A third is to use this information to help them expand their thinking such as recommending we copresent at the conference.

We use other techniques as well to demonstrate that we continue to think about our clients:

- Create a short newsletter with information pertinent to their needs. Include contact information and a listing of our services. Use success stories with quotations from satisfied clients, especially if these emphasize new or different services. Consider an e-newsletter that is cheaper and faster than printed newsletters.

- Send article clippings, book reviews, and copies of white papers with a personal note. As appropriate, highlight certain portions or add comments and suggestions.

- Offer to speak, or help identify speakers, for company meetings or company-sponsored events.

- Write specific articles or white papers for a group of clients. One consultant commissioned a bimonthly article aimed at her CEO clients; another sent a more general article to all clients.

- Send a regular e-mail with tips or quotes that apply to our client base.

- Send birthday or holiday cards. With a preprinted company name, a note and hand-addressed envelope adds a personal touch.

Taking the initiative to stay in touch can include any or all of these techniques, as well as other approaches such as taking clients to lunch or dinner, making periodic telephone calls, and forwarding relevant e-mails. The question is not, "Which of these techniques shall we use?" but rather, "How can we most effectively demonstrate to our clients that we're thinking about them and their Big Picture?"

UNDERSTAND NEEDS

As facilitators, one of our main tasks is to help the group achieve a common understanding of issues and resolutions. Some of the things we do to accomplish this are paraphrase, probe for more detail, and document for clarity. We also invite participants to write their own concerns, ideas, and issues on cards and then group the cards to identify common themes.

In effective client relationship management, understanding our client's immediate needs and how they fit into the company's Big Picture enables us to help them address both. With this information, we are not only able to be more effective on our current project, we can also identify other areas where our services can provide added value to the client.

We stimulate our clients' thinking when we ask them about their immediate, long-term, and Big Picture needs, using questions such as these:

- What problems are you experiencing that led you to believe you need a facilitator?
- Imagine you have addressed these problems. What has changed as a result? How does the department work now?
- What conditions exist in the company that must be addressed to keep from interfering with the success of this undertaking?

The answers to these questions enable clients to understand that by focusing only on the immediate situation, they resolve the pressing issue yet run the risk of not adequately addressing issues that have a broader scope. For example, a client who is problem-solving an issue may be too narrowly defining the problem by looking only at his or her own department without considering the interdepartmental impact.

As we come to understand the full extent of our clients' needs, we are able to suggest services that would best meet them. Some of these services we will deliver ourselves, and others will be provided through our network of consultants. To build our referral base of consultants, it is important that in addition to networking with facilitators, we build solid relationships with people in related services.

When we recommend a colleague to provide services for our client, we make a point of debriefing that person following the completion of the work. The focus of this discussion is to identify issues that emerged that require attention and might result in additional work for us.

Taking a Big Picture view means that we have our client's total needs in mind, understand the long-term objectives, and provide the vehicles to achieve them.

RECOGNIZE CHALLENGES

When we interview clients or participants about a session we will be facilitating, we ask if there are any issues that might surface, such as hidden agendas, turf conflicts, or individual or organizational challenges. By getting this information in advance of the session, we avoid surprises and are able to deal more effectively with dysfunctional behavior that may arise from these issues.

Being aware of potential challenges facing our clients can help us better understand their Big Picture and provide alternatives for minimizing or eliminating those challenges.

We use the journalistic questions with our clients to encourage conversations that focus on where they are, where they want to go, and possible barriers they may encounter.

We stimulate their thinking about potential challenges with information gathered from our research on their company, industry, and competition. We also reference our experience with similar engagements and identify the similarities and differences in the challenges.

During a session, we listen for companywide or departmental issues that could sabotage the work that is being done. We communicate these potential issues to our client and encourage that they be addressed to maximize the chances that the work will be successfully implemented. In addition, we share what we have heard about challenges outside the scope of the session and suggest ways in which they can be dealt with in a timely fashion.

This approach instills confidence in our clients that we are committed to uncovering their challenges, able to meet their needs, and prepared for the unexpected.

EVALUATE SATISFACTION

Having participants evaluate our performance at the end of each session provides us valuable information. We learn if the participants thought we achieved the session's stated objectives, if the process worked for them, and if we were effective in managing the group. We use this information to note our strengths so we repeat them and identify our areas for improvement so we can modify them.

Satisfied clients produce additional work and positive referrals. Monitoring our clients' level of satisfaction on an ongoing basis positions us not only to exceed our clients' expectations on a specific engagement, it also demonstrates our interest in helping them succeed at the Big Picture level. Their feedback provides us with a realistic picture of the opportunities for additional work and their level of willingness to be a referral source.

While client satisfaction for a specific engagement is measurable through the use of evaluation forms, relationship satisfaction is more informal and not as easily measured. Actions and behaviors provide clues to the level of our clients' satisfaction with the relationship. We conclude that our clients are satisfied when they:

- Seek us out for additional guidance and support.
- Use us as trusted advisers to brainstorm solutions to challenging issues.
- Respond positively to suggestions for collaborative work.
- Are responsive to periodic invitations to lunch or dinner.
- Initiate telephone calls and get-togethers.

By providing a listening ear, exchanging ideas, and operating with their best interests in mind, we work toward becoming a trusted adviser—the person to whom our clients come when they are in need.

When clients are pleased with our work, they are excellent sources for future business. By maintaining contact with clients following our successful engagement, we stay abreast of their issues and problems. This information helps us determine what additional services to offer to them.

CONCLUSION

Developing relationships with our clients that are built on trust and collaboration is vital to our continued success as facilitators. As we use our facilitation skills to assist clients to operate effectively in their Big Picture, we strengthen our relationship and position ourselves to provide service beyond a single engagement. By partnering with clients, we maximize the likelihood of achieving success, both theirs and ours.

The Skilled Facilitator Approach

Roger Schwarz

The Skilled Facilitator approach is a values-based, systemic approach to facilitation. It is designed to help groups increase the quality of decisions, increase commitment to decisions, reduce effective implementation time, improve working relationships, improve personal satisfaction in groups, and increase organizational learning. It accomplishes this in a way that creates collaborative relationships between the facilitator and the group and within the group itself. In this chapter, I identify the key elements of the approach and explain how they fit together.

WHAT IS GROUP FACILITATION?

Group facilitation is a process in which a person whose selection is acceptable to all members of the group, is substantively neutral, and has no substantive decision-making authority diagnoses and intervenes to help a group improve how it identifies and solves problems and makes decisions, to increase the group's effectiveness.

Note: This chapter is adapted from *The Skilled Facilitator: A Comprehensive Resource for Consultants, Facilitators, Managers, Trainers, and Coaches, New and Revised Edition* by Roger Schwarz, Jossey-Bass Publishers, 2002.

The facilitator's main task is to help the group increase its effectiveness by improving its process and structure. *Process* refers to how a group works together. It includes how members talk to each other, how they identify and solve problems, how they make decisions, and how they handle conflict. *Structure* refers to stable and recurring group processes, such as group membership or group roles. In contrast, *content* refers to what a group is working on. For example, the content of a group discussion may be whether to enter a new market, how to provide high-quality service to customers, or what each group member's responsibilities should be. Whenever a group meets, it is possible to observe both its content and process. For example, in a discussion about how to provide high-quality service, suggestions about installing a customer hot line or giving more authority to those with customer contact reflect content. However, members responding to only certain members' ideas or failing to identify their assumptions are facets of the group's process.

Underlying the facilitator's main task is the fundamental assumption that ineffective group process and structure reduces a group's ability to solve problems and make decisions. While research findings on the relationship between process and group effectiveness are mixed (Kaplan, 1979), the premise of facilitation is that by increasing the effectiveness of the group's process and structure, the facilitator helps the group improve its performance and overall effectiveness. The facilitator does not intervene directly in the content of the group's discussions; to do so would require the facilitator to abandon substantive neutrality and would reduce the group's responsibility for solving its problems.

To create the collaborative relationship between the facilitator and group, ensure that the facilitator is trusted by all group members, and see to it that the group's autonomy is maintained, the facilitator needs to be acceptable to all members of the group (and seen as impartial toward individual members or parties), be substantively neutral—that is, display no preference for any of the solutions the group considers—and not have substantive decision-making authority. In practice, the facilitator can meet these three criteria only if he or she is not a group member. While a group member may be acceptable to other members and may not have substantive decision-making authority, the group member has a substantive interest in the group's issues. By definition, a group member cannot formally fill the role of facilitator. Still, a group leader or member can use the Skilled Facilitator principles and techniques to help a group. Effective leaders regularly use facilitation skills as part of their leadership role.

To *intervene* means "to enter into an ongoing system" for the purpose of helping those in the system (Argyris, 1970, p. 15). The definition implies that the system—or group—functions autonomously—that is, the group is complete without a facilitator. Yet the group depends on a facilitator for help. Consequently, to maintain the group's autonomy and develop its long-term effectiveness, the facilitator's interventions ideally should decrease the group's dependence on the facilitator. The facilitator accomplishes this, when appropriate, by intervening in a way that teaches group members the skills of facilitation.

KEY ELEMENTS OF THE SKILLED FACILITATOR APPROACH

The Skilled Facilitator approach is an approach to facilitation that I have been developing since 1980 when I began teaching facilitation skills. Often facilitation approaches represent a compilation of techniques and methods without an underlying theoretical framework. The Skilled Facilitator approach is based on a theory of group facilitation that contains a set of core values and principles and a number of techniques and methods derived from the core values and principles. It integrates the theory into practice to create a values-based, systemic approach to group facilitation. Exhibit 2.1 identifies the key elements of the Skilled Facilitator approach.

Exhibit 2.1
Key Elements of the Skilled Facilitator Approach

The Group Effectiveness Model

A Clearly Defined Facilitator Role

Useful in a Wide Range of Roles

Explicit Core Values

Ground Rules for Effective Groups

The Diagnosis-Intervention Cycle

Low-Level Inferences

Exploring and Changing How We Think

A Process for Agreeing on How to Work Together

A Systems Approach

The Group Effectiveness Model

To help groups become more effective, you need a model of group effectiveness as part of your approach. To be useful, the model needs to be more than descriptive-that is, it needs to do more than explain how groups typically function or develop because many groups develop in a way that is dysfunctional. To be useful, the model needs to be normative-that is, it should tell you what an effective group looks like. The group effectiveness model identifies the criteria for effective groups, identifies the elements that contribute to effectiveness and the relationships among them, and describes what these elements look like in practice. The model enables you and the group to work together to jointly identify when the group is having problems, identify the causes that generate the problems, and begin to identify where to intervene to address the problems. When you are helping to create new groups, the model helps you and the group jointly identify the elements and relationships among the elements that need to be in place to ensure an effective group.

A Clearly Defined Facilitator Role

To help groups, you need a clear definition of your role as facilitator so that you and the groups you are helping have a common understanding about and agree on the kinds of behaviors that are consistent and inconsistent with your facilitator role. This has become more difficult in recent years as organizations have used the word *facilitator* to define many different roles. Human resource experts, organization development consultants, trainers, coaches, and even managers have sometimes been referred to as "facilitators." The Skilled Facilitator approach clearly defines the facilitator role as a substantively neutral person who is not a group member and works for the entire group.

The Skilled Facilitator approach distinguishes between two types of facilitation: basic and developmental. In basic facilitation, the facilitator helps a group solve a substantive problem by essentially lending the group his or her process skills. When the facilitation is complete, the group has solved its substantive problem but, by design, it has not explicitly learned how it improves its process. In developmental facilitation, the facilitator explicitly helps a group solve a substantive problem and learn to improve its process at the same time. Here the facilitator also serves as teacher, so the group can eventually become self-facilitating. Developmental facilitation requires significantly more time and facilitator skill, and it is more likely to create fundamental change.

Useful in a Wide Range of Roles

Although I described the Skilled Facilitator approach as having a substantively neutral third-party facilitator, the approach also recognizes that everyone needs to use facilitative skills even if they are not neutral third parties or not working in groups or teams. The Skilled Facilitator approach introduces roles in addition to facilitator: facilitative consultant, facilitative coach, facilitative trainer, and facilitative leader. All of these roles are based on the same underlying core values and principles as the role of facilitator. In addition, many of my clients have told me that they have used the core values and principles outside the workplace, including with their families and friends, and with positive results. The approach is broadly applicable because it is based on principles of effective human interaction. Consequently, if you use this approach across your roles, you are likely to be viewed by others as acting consistently and with integrity across situations.

Explicit Core Values

All approaches to facilitation are based on some core values. Core values provide the foundation for an approach and serve as a guide. They enable you to craft new methods and techniques consistent with the core values and to continually reflect on how well you do in acting congruently with the values. If you are to benefit most from the core values, they need to be explicit. The Skilled Facilitator approach is based on an explicit set of four core values—valid information, free and informed choice, internal commitment, and compassion—and principles that follow from them. (The first three core values come from Argyris and Schön, 1974.)

Valid information means that you share all the relevant information that you have about an issue in a way that others can understand it, as well as the reasoning by which that information is integrated. Ideally, valid information is specific enough so that others can confirm for themselves whether the information is valid. With free and informed choice, members make decisions based on valid information, not on pressure from inside or outside the group. With internal commitment, each member feels personally responsible for the decision and is willing to support the decision, given his or her role. With compassion, you temporarily suspend judgment to understand others who have differing views. When you act with compassion, you infuse the other core values with your intent to understand, empathize with, and help others in a way that still ensures that each person is accountable for his or her behavior. Together, the core values provide the foundation for the group to collaboratively develop a common understanding of a situation and to make decisions and take actions to which it is fully committed.

As a facilitator, you need not only a set of methods and techniques but also an understanding of how and why they work. By using an explicit set of core values and the principles that follow from them, you can improvise and design new methods and techniques consistent with the core values. Without this understanding, you are like a novice baker who must either follow the recipe as given or make changes without knowing what will happen.

Making the core values explicit also helps you work with groups. You can discuss your approach with potential clients, so that they can make more informed choices about whether they want to use you as their facilitator. When clients know the core values underlying your approach, they can help you improve your practice, identifying when they believe you are acting inconsistently with the values you espoused. In this way, the core values provide a basis for a collaborative relationship in which facilitators learn with clients rather than the client's simply learning from the facilitator. Because the core values for facilitation are also the core values for effective group behavior, when you act consistently with the core values, not only do you act effectively as a facilitator, but you also model effective behavior for the group you are working with.

Ground Rules for Effective Groups

As you watch a group in action, you may intuitively know whether the members' conversation is productive even if you cannot identify exactly how they either contribute to or hinder the group's process. Yet a facilitator needs to understand the specific kinds of behaviors that improve a group's process. The Skilled Facilitator approach describes these behaviors in a set of ground rules for effective groups. The ground rules (see Exhibit 2.2) make specific the abstract core values of facilitation and group effectiveness.

The ground rules serve several functions. First, they serve as a diagnostic tool. By understanding the ground rules, you can quickly identify dysfunctional group behavior—which is inconsistent with the ground rules—so that you can intervene on it. Second, the ground rules are a teaching tool for developing effective group norms. When groups understand the ground rules and commit to using them, the members set new expectations for how to interact with each other. This enables the group to share responsibility for improving its process, often a goal of facilitation. Finally, the ground rules guide your behavior as facilitator.

Together, the ground rules enable group members to collaborate productively, exploring their different points of view, and develop a common course of action. For example, testing assumptions and inferences enables members to make sure that they are working together based on valid information about each other and the situation. Share relevant information, explain your reasoning and intent, focus on interests rather than positions, and ensure that members have a common base of information. By combining advocacy and inquiry, group members both share their views and encourage others to share different views and identify gaps in members' thinking. Jointly designing next steps and ways to test disagreements enables group members to collaborate on testing out their differing points of view rather than each member's gathering information to prove the other is wrong. Discussing undiscussable issues enables group members to address underlying issues that hinder group members from working together effectively.

The behavioral ground rules in the Skilled Facilitator approach differ from the more procedural ground rules ("start on time, end on time"; "turn off your beepers and cell phones") that many groups and facilitators use. Procedural ground rules can be helpful, but they do not describe the specific behaviors that lead to effective group process.

The Diagnosis-Intervention Cycle

The group effectiveness model, the core values, and the ground rules for effective groups are all tools for diagnosing behavior in groups. But you still need a way to implement these tools. Specifically, you need to know when to intervene, what kind of intervention to make, how to say it, when to say it, and to whom. To help put these tools into practice, the Skilled Facilitator approach uses the diagnosis–intervention cycle, a six-step process:

1. Observe behavior.
2. Infer meaning.
3. Decide whether, how, and why to intervene.
4. Describe behavior, and test for different views.
5. Share your inference, and test for different views.
6. Help the group decide whether to change its behavior, and test for different views.

The cycle is a structured and simple way to think about what is happening in the group and then to intervene consistent with the core values. It serves to guide the facilitator (and group members) into effective action.

Low-Level Inferences

As a facilitator, you are constantly trying to make sense of what is happening in a group. You watch members say and do things and then make inferences about what their behavior means and how it is either helping or hindering the group's process. An inference is a conclusion you reach about something that is unknown to you based on what you do know. For example, if you see someone silently folding his arms across his chest in a meeting, you may infer that he disagrees with what has been said but is not saying so.

The kinds of inferences you make are critical because they guide what you will say when you intervene, and they affect how group members will react to you. To be effective, you need to make these inferences in a way that increases the chance that you will be accurate, enables you to share your inferences with the group to see if they disagree, and does not create defensive reactions in group members when you share your inferences.

The Skilled Facilitator approach accomplishes this by focusing on what I refer to as low-level inferences. Essentially, this means that facilitators diagnose and intervene in groups by making the fewest and the smallest inferential leaps necessary. Consider two facilitators with different approaches, working with the same group simultaneously and hearing this conversation:

Tom: I want to discuss the start time for the new project. Next week is too soon. We need to wait another month.

Sue: That's not going to work. We need to do it right away. We can't wait.

Don: I think you're both unrealistic. We will be lucky if we can start it in ninety days. I think we should wait until the next quarter.

A facilitator making a low-level inference might privately conclude, and then publicly point out, that members have stated their opinions but have not explained the reasons for their opinions or asked other members what leads them to see the situation differently. Observing the same behavior, a facilitator making a high-level inference might privately conclude that the members do not care about others' opinions or are trying to hide something. Making high-level inferences such as this creates a problem when you try to say what you privately think. Higher-level inferences are further removed from the data that you used to generate them and so may be less accurate. If the inference also contains negative evaluations about others' motives, sharing the inference can contribute to the group members' responding defensively. By learning to think and intervene using low-level inferences, you can increase the accuracy of your diagnosis and your ability to share your thinking with others, and reduce the chance that you will create defensive reactions when you do so. This ensures that your actions increase rather than decrease the group's effectiveness.

Exploring and Changing How We Think

Facilitation is difficult work because it is mentally demanding—cognitively and emotionally. It is especially difficult when you find yourself in situations you consider potentially embarrassing or psychologically threatening. The research shows that if you are like almost everyone else, in these situations, you use a set of core values and think in a way that seeks to unilaterally control the conversation, win the discussion, and minimize the expression of negative feelings (Argyris and

Schön, 1974). This is called the unilateral control model. (I have adapted the unilateral control model from the work of Argyris and Schön, 1974, who developed the model and called it Model I, and from Robert Putnam, Diana McLain Smith, and Phil McArthur at Action Design who adapted Model I and refer to this as the unilateral control model.) You think of yourself as knowing all we need to know about the situation while thinking others who disagree are uninformed, you think of yourself as being right and others as being wrong, and you think of yourself as having pure motives while others' motives are questionable.

It is not possible to create collaborative relationships if you are thinking this way. Consequently, this thinking leads you to act in ways that create the very results you are trying hard to avoid: misunderstanding, increasing conflict, defensive reactions, and the strained relationships and lack of learning that accompany the results. To make matters worse, you are usually unaware of how your thinking leads you to act ineffectively. Rather, if you are like most other people, you typically attribute the cause of these difficult conversations to how others are thinking and acting.

The same problem that reduces your effectiveness as a facilitator reduces the effectiveness of the groups you are seeking to help. Like the facilitator, the group members are also unaware of how they create these problems for themselves.

The Skilled Facilitator approach helps you understand the conditions under which you act ineffectively and understand how your own thinking leads you to act ineffectively in ways that you are normally unaware of. It provides tools for increasing your effectiveness, particularly in situations you find emotionally difficult. This involves changing not only your techniques, but also how you think about or frame situations and the core values that underlie your approach. This shift to the mutual learning model means thinking that you have some information and others have other information, that others may see things you miss and vice versa, that differences are opportunities for learning rather than for proving others wrong, and that people are trying to act with integrity given their situation. (I have adapted the mutual learning model from the work of Argyris and Schön, 1974, who developed the model and called it Model II, and from Robert Putnam, Diana McLain Smith, and Phil McArthur at Action Design who adapted Model II and refer to this as the mutual learning model.) This shift in thinking makes it possible to use the ground rules appropriately for effective groups and reduce the unintended consequences that stem from the unilateral control model. Making this shift is difficult but rewarding work, and it is essential for creating authentic collaborative relationships. By doing this work for yourself, you increase your effectiveness. Then you can help groups learn to reflect on and change the ways they think in difficult situations so that they can work more effectively together.

A Process for Agreeing on How to Work Together

Facilitation involves developing a relationship with a group—a social-psychological contract in which the group gives you permission to help them because they consider you an expert and trustworthy facilitator. Building this relationship is critical because it is the foundation on which you use your facilitator knowledge and skills; without the foundation, you lose the essential connection with the group that makes your facilitation possible and powerful. To build this relationship, you need a clear understanding and agreement with the group about your role as facilitator and how you will work with the group to help it accomplish its objectives. I have found that many of the facilitation problems my colleagues and I have faced stemmed from a lack of agreement with the group about how to work together.

The Skilled Facilitator approach describes a process for developing this agreement that enables the facilitator and the group to make an informed free choice about working together. The process begins when someone first contacts the facilitator about working with the group and involves a discussion with group members. It identifies who should be involved at each stage of the process, the specific questions to ask, and the type of information to share about your approach to facilitation. The process also describes the issues on which you and the group need to decide to develop an effective working agreement. The issues include the facilitated meeting objectives, the facilitator's role, and the ground rules that will be used. By using this process, you act consistently with your facilitator role and increase the likelihood that you will help the group achieve its goals.

A Systems Approach

Facilitators often tell me stories of how, despite their best efforts to help a group in a difficult situation, the situation gets worse. Each time the facilitator does something to improve things, the situation either deteriorates immediately or temporarily improves before getting even worse. One reason this occurs is that the facilitator is not thinking and acting systemically.

In recent years, the field of systems thinking has become popular in part through the work of Peter Senge (1990) and his colleagues. The Skilled Facilitator approach uses a systems approach to facilitation. It recognizes that a group is a social system—a collection of parts that interact with each other to function as a whole—and that groups generate their own system dynamics, such as deteriorating trust or continued dependence on the leader. As a facilitator, you enter into this system when you help a group. The challenge is to enter the system, complete with its functional and dysfunctional dynamics, and help the group become more effective without becoming influenced by the system to act ineffectively yourself. The Skilled Facilitator approach recognizes that any action you take affects the group in multiple ways and has short-term and long-term consequences, some of which may not be obvious. The approach helps you understand how your behavior as facilitator interacts with the group's dynamics to increase or decrease the group's effectiveness.

For example, a facilitator who privately pulls a team member aside who, she believes, is dominating the group may seem to improve the team's discussion in the short run. But this action may also have several unintended negative consequences. The pulled-aside member may feel that the facilitator is not representing the team's opinion and may see the facilitator as biased against him, thereby reducing the facilitator's credibility with that member. Even if the facilitator is reflecting the other team members' opinions, the team may come increasingly to depend on her to deal with its internal process issues, thereby reducing rather than increasing the team's ability to function independently.

Using a systems approach to facilitation has many implications, a number of which are central to understanding the Skilled Facilitator approach. One key implication is treating the entire group as the client rather than only the formal group leader or the member who contacted you. This increases the chance of having the trust and credibility of the entire group, which is essential in serving as an effective facilitator.

A second implication is that effective facilitator behavior and effective group member behavior are the same thing. Excepting that the facilitator is substantively neutral and not a group member, the Skilled Facilitator approach does not have different sets of rules for the facilitator and group members. Just as you use the core values and ground rules to guide your own behavior, you use them to teach group members how they can act more effectively. Consequently, when you act consistently with the core values and ground rules, you serve as a model for the group. The more that group members learn about how you work, the better they understand how to create effective group process. Ultimately, as group members model effective facilitator behavior, they become self-facilitating.

A third key implication is that to be effective, your system of facilitation needs to be internally consistent. This means that the way you diagnose and intervene in a group and the way you develop agreements with the group all need to be based on a congruent set of principles. Many facilitators develop their approach by borrowing methods and techniques from a variety of other approaches. There is nothing inherently wrong with this, but if the methods and techniques are based on conflicting values or principles, they can undermine the facilitator's effectiveness as well as that of the groups they work with. For example, a facilitator who states that his client is the entire group and yet automatically agrees to individual requests by the group's leader may soon find himself in the middle of a conflict between the group and its leader rather than helping to facilitate the entire group. By thinking and acting systemically, you increase your long-term ability to help groups.

THE EXPERIENCE OF FACILITATION

Facilitation is challenging work that calls forth a wide range of emotions. Part of this work involves helping group members deal productively with their emotions while they are addressing difficult issues. It is equally important to deal with your own emotions as facilitator. Because your emotions and how you deal with them profoundly determine your effectiveness, the Skilled Facilitator approach involves understanding how you as a facilitator feel during facilitation and using these feelings productively.

These feelings are about yourself and the group you are working with. Throughout the facilitation, various events trigger your own reactions. You may feel satisfied having helped a group work through a particularly difficult problem or proud to see the group using some of the skills they have learned from you. Yet when your work goes so smoothly that the group does not recognize your contribution, you may feel unappreciated. When the group is feeling confused and uncertain about how to proceed in their task, you may be feeling the same way about the facilitation. If your actions do not help the group as well as you would like, you may feel ashamed because your work does not meet your own standards. You may be frustrated by a group's inability to manage conflict even if you have been asked to help the group because they are having problems managing conflict. You may feel sad watching a group act in ways that create the very consequences they are trying to avoid, feel happy that you can identify this dynamic in the group, and feel hopeful seeing that the group's pain is creating motivation for change.

At one time or another, I have experienced each of these feelings as a facilitator; they are part of the internal work of facilitation. The Skilled Facilitator approach enables you to become more aware of these feelings and increases your ability to manage them productively—what some refer to emotional intelligence (Goleman, 1995; Salovey and Mayer, 1990). I have found that my ability to develop these emotional skills is both distinct from and related to my larger set of knowledge, skills, and experience as a facilitator. Although there are many ways to improve my facilitation skills that do not focus on dealing with my emotions, my use of any of these skills becomes more powerful if I am attuned to my feelings and to others' feelings and deal with them productively.

Through facilitating groups, you also come to know yourself by reflecting on how you react to certain situations, understanding the sources of your feelings, and learning how to work with your feelings productively. In doing so, you not only help yourself but increase your ability to help the groups with which you work.

CONCLUSION

The Skilled Facilitator approach is based on a set of core values. Using a systems thinking approach, it enables you to clearly define your facilitator role and develop explicit agreement with a group about how you will work together. Together, the core values, the group effectiveness model, the ground rules, and the diagnosis-intervention cycle help you identify functional and dysfunctional aspects of the group and intervene to help the group increase its effectiveness. The approach enables you to explore and change how you think and improve your ability to facilitate difficult situations. It also helps groups explore and change their thinking to help them create fundamental change. All of the elements in the Skilled Facilitator approach are integrated to enable both group members and the facilitator to create collaborative relationships in which they can learn with and from each other. The core values, principles, and methods of the Skilled Facilitator approach are equally applicable to facilitative leaders, consultants, coaches, and trainers.

Facilitation

Beyond Methods

David Wayne

You cannot step twice into the same river;
for other waters are ever flowing in upon you.

Heraclitus of Ephesus

There is one constant for the facilitator: no matter how elegant the methods used or the skill of the practitioner, each group we work with is unique. In this chapter, we examine a few of these properties of groups and see how the effective facilitator's awareness of them can create the best results for all participants.

All of us have been at meetings where hidden agendas, interpersonal issues, or group dynamics have had an impact on accomplishments. These process issues, as they are often called, occur in every group, and they are obvious to the effective facilitator. They include recognizing and understanding the different personality and learning strengths that each individual, including the facilitator, brings to the facilitation experience. Process issues include the group's stage of development, cultural norms, agreements by group members that take place outside the group but are unstated, and the relationship of the group to its larger organization and community. The effective facilitator integrates methods (the philosophy of the facilitator and specific tools in achieving a set objective) with process (the important dynamics of how we all function as individuals and as groups). The facilitator's goal is to ensure that the group stays balanced on both important tracks of facilitation and does not risk derailing (see Exhibit 3.1). Placing all of our emphasis on one or the other track can have serious implications for success. For example, if we ignore the emotions and feelings of the group, they will often surface and interrupt the flow, despite the good methods being used. Similarly, with a total focus on process, facilitators could be accused of doing therapy, not facilitation. Both are essential for success, although the distinction between these two tracks is often blurred.

The premise for the facilitator recognizing these issues goes back to what is arguably one of the earliest roots of modern facilitation, the field of psychology. Research into individual and group practice, as well as organizational psychology, has given us clues to effective facilitative practice. This chapter examines these clues with a focus on what they are and techniques for individual and group empowerment.

HISTORICAL OVERVIEW

From early psychology, Jung's work on personalities provided us with an understanding of different preferred ways of acting (Jung, 1961). Slightly later, William Moulton Marston, a physician (and, incidentally, the creator of Wonder Woman),

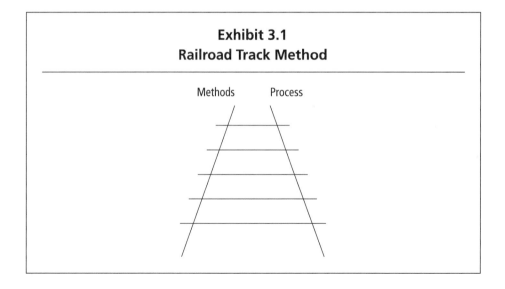

Exhibit 3.1
Railroad Track Method

Methods   Process

wrote *The Emotions of Normal People* (1928), in which he described different personality types. Out of Jung's work emerged the well-known Myers-Briggs Type Indicator. From Marston's writing, the DISC Profile was eventually created. Both personality inventories served as foundations for many other abbreviated or different personality assessments now on the market. Each has the capacity to shed light on functional and dysfunctional behaviors of individuals in groups that are being facilitated. In addition, most effective ways of relating to individuals and groups evolved from the work of Carl Rogers, the founder of humanistic psychology, in what became known as a client-centered approach (Rogers, 1995). Characteristics such as empathy, warmth, and genuineness, plus giving people unconditional positive regard, became regarded as hallmarks of successful therapeutic interaction. We have come to understand that these characteristics, plus the awareness of individual personality styles and behavior, are just as important to the successful facilitator as they are to the therapist.

A more recent development has come from a new, broader approach to the psychology of intelligence and learning. The work of Howard Gardner, trained in both developmental and neurological psychology, has provided more insight into the needs of groups (Gardner, 1999). Applying his work on multiple intelligences has helped us understand that any facilitation method that does not take into account the different abilities and learning patterns of all participants is unlikely to be as successful as one with a broader range. Similarly, Daniel Goleman, with his strong background in clinical psychology and personality development, has broken ground by describing emotional intelligence, a new perspective on interpersonal functioning and some behaviors that facilitators need to be aware of in groups (Goleman, 1995).

From the earliest writings on group psychology, we have learned the complexity and the dynamics of bringing any collection of people together. Wilfred Bion, in his pioneering work (Bleandonu, 1998), wrote of three issues that may arise in groups. The first, dependency, is often acted out toward a person or persons in the group with more perceived power than the others. The second issue, pairing and grouping, often leads to alliances that appear within the group and have an impact on the transparency of group functioning. Finally, Bion spoke of fight-or-flight responses that arise when a group is under stress. All three issues have a significant impact on the process part of facilitation.

Adding to these insights on group behavior, in the mid-1960s Tuckman published his stages of group development which he characterized as *forming, storming, norming, performing* (Tuckman, 1965). Later he added *adjourning* as a fifth stage (Tuckman and Jensen, 1977). This window into evolutionary group development expanded our understanding of group behavior and ultimately provided facilitators with a rough road map that explains functional dynamics in groups.

In the last half of the twentieth century and now into the twenty-first, the work in individual, group, and even family psychology has been integrated into a new field that started as organizational psychology. As it has evolved, it has brought in a heritage from many other disciplines, including natural science, business, economics, and sociology, and has come to be known more commonly as organization development. From biology, engineering, and later from family therapy, it has recognized that groups are similar to complex, dynamic systems (Katz and Kahn, 1978). They have a balance such that the impact on any part of a system has an effect on other parts of the system. We have learned that groups and organizations, like everything else in nature, have a life cycle and develop a distinct culture. From pioneers with roots in psychology, like Edgar Schein, we have learned the significance of understanding organizational culture as an important issue in our work.

APPLICATIONS

From this foundation in psychological theory and practice come techniques that can assist facilitators in maintaining the important balance between the delivery of methods and the awareness of human dynamics that we are referring to as process. Probably the best place to start is with ourselves—our personality and how it affects our facilitation.

The Individual Personality

I know of no research that shows that any particular personality style is likely to produce better facilitators than another. At the same time, it is clear that our nature, whatever it is, has the potential to have a group mirror or react to a facilitator's behavior. In other words, considering an axiom from quantum physics that says, "The observer changes the observed," so too does the facilitator have the potential to change the facilitated. To do this in a positive and constructive fashion, facilitators need to be aware of their own personality and key components of those in the group. Using a cofacilitator with a different personality style broadens the facilitation team's appeal and balance. Complementing this balance can come through awareness of Rogers's work. The conscious demonstration by the facilitator of warmth, empathic understanding, and genuineness goes a long way in making this job easier and the outcomes more successful. The group becomes more engaged and open, and the members feel cared for, progressing to a performing stage of development faster than with a facilitator who does not display these characteristics.

Understanding personality styles has other potential benefits as well: facilitators can judge whether they are a suitable match for a client. Despite the notion of maintaining a balance, clashes of personality, in conjunction with other issues of power and culture, make it much harder to have an effective ongoing relationship. Understanding personality acts as a measure to the facilitator on whether to proceed.

Finally, an understanding of personality can help a facilitated group move forward effectively. If all those in the group know their particular strengths and those of their colleagues, they can develop their planning accordingly. For some personalities, working with people with similar temperaments is ideal. Others want to network with a variety of people with different styles. Some are natural idea people but get impatient if action does not occur quickly. Others are excellent at looking at how decisions made in the group will fit with priorities in the larger organization. Having these ways of operating made transparent to all often improves group functioning and helps build cohesiveness and ability to function positively as a team.

The issue of personality inventorying raises two important questions. Is there time in a facilitation to add yet another item to the agenda? And if the facilitator is not a psychologist or does not have a background in personality assessment, what can she use? My experience with the first question is that taking thirty minutes at the beginning of work with a group saves more time than it uses, based on later group effectiveness. The second answer is a little more complicated. The Myers-Briggs Type Indicator and the DISC are wonderful instruments, but both can be time-consuming to administer, score, and use the results for the purposes described, including generating an applied understanding by participants. In addition, the instruments should be administered by someone trained and certified in their use. If I facilitate a group that will be together for a long period and if time is not a limiting factor, I will choose one of these. However, most often I do not have that luxury.

As a result, when a group will be together for only a short time, the facilitator might use a simple and quickly administered instrument. There are many commercial ones available that fit these criteria. Among those most readily available are the *Keirsey Temperament Sorter* (Keirsey and Bates, 1984) based on the Myers-Briggs,

True Colors (Miscisin, 2001), and *What Color Is Your Personality?* (Ritberger, 1999). In addition, Linda Vogelsong and I have created an easily used instrument, *Four Seasons,* which appears in Appendix 3A at the end of this chapter. Although it does not claim to assess personality types, it is useful for helping a group understand the resources that members bring to it.

Difficult Behaviors

When working with individuals, every facilitator is likely to see difficult behaviors emerge. Some go as far as to say that all of us have a "difficult person" hiding inside waiting to emerge. That being said, individual problem behavior poses serious challenges and opportunities for the facilitator. The challenges are to identify what has triggered the behavior, understand the form it is taking, and not be exploited by it. The opportunity is to respond in a way that provides for growth of the individual and the group. There are many descriptions of these archetypal problem behaviors in the literature and of ways of dealing with them (see Exhibit 3.2). The problem is that the behaviors tend to be more complex than the overt behavior would indicate and are inherently difficult for facilitators.

Where possible, identifying the situation that is triggering the behavior is a first step. In many cases, it is the facilitation experience itself. Since facilitation often leads to change, it may be perceived as threatening. Some personality types have more difficulty with change than others. However, a person's response to change goes beyond personality; it involves the person's expectations regarding survival within the organization and imagined outcomes. Consider the following case study:

> An organization hires a facilitator to assist in what they regard as needed change. In the group is Sally, a senior executive who pays lip-service to the change effort but through her behavior in the group continually blocks efforts to plan the change. She pressures subordinates who wish to move forward with changes to maintain the status quo, does not complete work she has agreed to do for the group, and disrupts group meetings with whispered conversations to peers.

Picture a meeting with Sally as a participant. For the facilitator, the first action should be internal, that is, he should not allow himself to be triggered by Sally's behavior by varying his facilitation efforts or in focusing on one individual's behavior. The key to dealing successfully with the problem behavior is formulated action as opposed to reaction or ignoring the behavior.

Exhibit 3.2
Describing and Addressing Difficult Behaviors

Behavior	Description	Facilitator Approach
Hostile Aggressives	Although these people seem to be loud and angry, they fall into three categories. These include the Tanks, who are characterized by being loud and aggressive, attacking both behavior and people. Next are the Snipers, who take aim at an issue and shoot at it, but often behind the backs of others so they can hide. Finally, there are the Rockets. These are people who totally explode, often burning a fuse for awhile and then flying off into outer space.	The Tanks respond best to "I" messages and use of their names. This means that the facilitator starts almost each sentence with their name and says, "I'm really concerned with [whatever the behavior is and its impact on the group]." Saying, "You did this," is a challenge to this behavioral type, but having the facilitator own the problem often makes for good outcomes. Snipers, once identified, need to have specific examples of their behaviors described and, if culturally appropriate, often respond well to eye contact. Finally, regarding Rockets, all the facilitator can do is to listen and let the fire go out. No amount of discussion is likely to help until the upset is expressed, and then the facilitator can work by getting clear facts and then offering concrete help.
Clams	Unlike Hostile Aggressives who exhibit overt action, Clams use silence and non-participation. Sometimes it is just shyness, but other times it may be a way of acting out. They are often	Ask specific questions and wait for an answer, even if it takes several minutes. Unfortunately, the group may feel uncomfortable and answer for this person. When talking with the Clam alone,

Behavior	Description	Facilitator Approach
Clams (continued)	unresponsive to questions and may use the discomfort of others to control the group.	the facilitator can describe the lack of participation and ask the Clam about his feelings about the process. Again, it is important to wait for an answer. If the problem is shyness, the individual might be encouraged to run a movie in his or her mind and then describe it. This often takes some of the pressure off and increases this person's comfort. However, if the same quiet symptoms indicate a passive-aggressive behavior, it is important to have a full discussion of the behavior and the potential implications for the group.
Super Agreeables	Facilitators often love having Super Agreeables in a group. They promise to do whatever is needed and praise the results of the group. Unfortunately, they rarely follow through on what they promise but do come up with pleasant excuses for their lack of action.	These people need to be called on their behavior and held accountable. However, it will depend on the nature of the role of the facilitator if they are the appropriate person to take on the task. Some groups will have team leaders or people hierarchically responsible for the group's performance, and this is behavior that should be turned over to them. At the same time, depending on the maturity of the group, pressure may come up within the group. The facilitator's role then is to ensure that any upset is directed to performance and does not become personal.

Behavior	Description	Facilitator Approach
Super Agreeables (continued)		Again, depending on the group's maturity, this is often an excellent time to visit or revisit group norms
The Carcinogens	Carcinogens are people who complain all the time. They not only decry the people and the process involved, but they have the skill and ability to spread their negativity to other members of the group.	Although discussing the situation in private with the individual may be helpful, this is the single most destructive type of behavior a group can experience. It is often best for all concerned if the person be encouraged or asked to leave the group. Too often, people put up with the behavior despite the negative impact. (As we will discuss below, even this apparently difficult behavior can have a positive effect on the group and the organization in terms of learning and growth.)
The Experts	As the name implies, this individual puts on the appearance that he or she already has the knowledge and expertise to solve whatever problems or tasks the group is dealing with. Sometimes they do, in fact, have a lot of knowledge; other times they have little but use it strategically to look good.	The way to deal with the expert depends on the subcategory of behavior. For the "expert" who is like a hot air balloon, it is easy to stick in a pin by asking for detailed expansion of what he or she is talking about and making it available to the group. That type of expert deflates easily; this behavior is often just a way of responding to personal insecurity. The Expert who

Behavior	Description	Facilitator Approach
The Experts (continued)		really does know a great deal is much more difficult. Building on this knowledge as a foundation, putting him or her in charge of gathering more information, or channeling the existing knowledge productively for the group is a challenge.
The Indecisives	These are people who cannot or will not make a decision, something very difficult in a group where participation and agreement are often keys to success. Behind the indecisiveness is a desire to avoid hurting other people's feelings and/or low self-esteem, which makes sitting on a fence an easier choice than making the wrong decision.	First, find out what is on the Indecisive's mind, and then facilitate a conversation on both possibilities and implications. Once a decision is reached, give personal support.

Next, the source of the behavior needs to be investigated. Since this was a long-term planning effort, the facilitator was able to talk to Sally individually and to her boss. It turned out that Sally had a combination of issues that had grown because her company had not acted on them. Her behavior originated from the belief that her organization did not need to change and that she was concerned that she would lose power if it did. When she started showing blocking behavior in other arenas, which had been reported to the CEO, it turned out that her company had no history of confronting personnel problems among executives. Some people were afraid of Sally, and the CEO was concerned about losing a valued contributor, so nothing had been done.

When the facilitator has some understanding of the problem, he has the responsibility to take action. The action can take several forms. The first needs to be expressing concerns about the behavior directly to Sally. From psychology, we can apply transactional analysis (Berne, 1961), where we learn that the conversation must be an Adult-Adult transaction. To get a reasoned and nondefensive response from Sally, the facilitator needs to be as objective as possible in reporting observations and concerns and encourage responses and agreement. The facilitator should use "I" messages in reporting his observation to avoid blame, and this can take a couple of forms.

From an appreciative inquiry approach (Cooperrider and Dutton, 1999), the facilitator might take Sally through the following steps:

1. Ask Sally when in the past she had been in a similar situation and felt that it had gone well.

2. Ask her to examine her role and how she contributed to the success. Inquire about her wishes for this facilitation process if it could be as successful.

3. Get her to come up with her wishes for how she would be able to both help the facilitation effort in the future and deal with the identified difficult behavior.

From a mediation point of view, the same situation might proceed differently beginning with an objective overview of the concern, moving to an identification of the facilitator's feelings about the situation, and inviting the same from Sally. Next, the facilitator could ask what is needed to overcome the identified issue and share his view. Finally, Sally is asked to identify her needs and desired outcomes, with the goal of reaching agreement.

If the behavior does not change, the next step is to discuss the concerns in as objective a way as possible within the group. This will provide the members with an opportunity to set norms to overcome the concerns. The group needs to feel safe for this to occur. The same format for discussion as was illustrated for use with Sally can be used with the group. If this is viewed as too risky or if it is done and does not change behavior, the facilitator's responsibility may be to describe the behavior to the person to whom he is reporting, depending on agreements made with the client when the facilitation is contracted for.

In each of these interventions, there is the opportunity for change and growth starting with the individual, moving to the group, and eventually to the organization.

Essentially, the facilitator has to check his own reaction, identify the difficult behavior and its cause, if possible, and then act discreetly and objectively, beginning at the source.

Group Development

We have thus far examined personality and behavior that affect the group but come from the individual. Group dynamics are separate issues that have a potential impact on the process track. In this section, we look at some of those dynamics as well as techniques that will help smooth the journey of the group.

Three of Bion's principles can affect the facilitation: dependency, pairing, and fight or flight. Dependency is what can happen when a group believes that it cannot function without the facilitator. Instead of being seen as someone who gives power to the group, the group tries to pass the power to the facilitator. This is not surprising since so many people are used to a hierarchical structure, where the power does in fact reside with the person who wields the pen (or marker). Pairing and grouping do not refer to relationships that people had prior to their participation in the group but rather develop as a product of the group work. More often than not, the pairing or grouping is by gender and, at least in theory, is about alliances being formed to define positions of power. Finally, fight or flight is about our natural response to stress. When pressure builds in the group, some would rather leave; others turn on members of the group or the facilitator.

In each of these naturally occurring conditions, the facilitator has a chance to move the work of the group forward by raising them as a basis for discussion. That transparency builds trust and understanding and provides reassurance in the group's development. Dependency issues can be lessened by beginning the facilitation with a discussion of the role of the facilitator. This can be reinforced if the issue reemerges or seems problematic. In addition, since there are times when a facilitator may step out of that role, some symbolic gesture that shows it happening (such as, "I'm now removing my facilitator's hat for a moment") will help the group. Simply being aware that pairing and grouping will occur is usually all that is needed by the group unless its appearance creates difficulties. If a fight-or-fight response shows itself in the group, it is important to diagnose its source. One potential source is the progression into Tuckman's storming stage that certain individuals have discomfort with. Alternatively, it may have to do with pressures that the group is experiencing, such as time or task completion. Regardless, spending a few minutes paying attention to it—asking the group how they see their behavior, what feelings have been generated because of it, why they see it occurring, and what they want to do about it—lessens the pressure significantly.

Group Stages

Another aspect of group process that involves a natural cyclical flow are the stages of development of the group. Shown in Exhibit 3.3, they should be seen less as a progression from beginning to end and more a continuing and sometimes revolving cycle.

Exhibit 3.3
Tuckman's Stages of Group Development and Some Corresponding Facilitation Techniques

Stage	Description	Facilitation Techniques
Forming	Group members are often overly polite. They are learning about their task, the process, and the role of the facilitator. They are beginning to develop bonds and establish ways in which the group will operate.	Set operational ground rules, such as starting and ending meetings on time. Focus on the task, and draw a rough map of the group's schedule. Collective agreement on how to function effectively overall will come later, but the facilitator should begin the discussion with clear expectations.
Storming	A product of the three areas described in Bion's work relative to dependency, pairing, and fight-or-flight, almost every group that is successful will go through this stage and for some, such as our "Spring" personality types (see Appendix 3A), it is particularly uncomfortable.	This is a time for the group to reflect on what is going on, to examine the process track. It is also a time for the facilitator to give reassurance that the difficulties are normal. Finally, it is the catalyst for the third stage, norming.

Stage	Description	Facilitation Techniques
Norming	It is the group's choice to go beyond initial procedural and ground rules created in the forming stage in order to enhance performance. The group is maturing, and they truly begin to own their uniqueness.	As in storming, taking time away from task to deal with the process development is one of the most important contributions a facilitator can make at this stage.
Performing	Work gets done, the group is productive, and the parts work well together. It is easy for the group to slip from this stage or devolve into storming.	Less needs to be done on process and more on task except to appreciate and celebrate the group's performance.
Adjourning	There is often a feeling of sadness and impending loss, particularly in groups that have functioned well and been together over some time.	A celebratory event, encouraged by the facilitator, can become an important passage for the group by providing acknowledgment of what has been produced and as a signal for the future.

Source: Based on Tuckman (1965) and Tuckman and Jensen (1977).

The Group Newcomer

Tuckman's work was meant to describe group functioning, but there are other considerations that should be accounted for. A group does not methodically go from the first stage through the last. It is a continuous evolution, which may mean going back to earlier stages or progressing to new ones. If a group is mature, it has developed its own equilibrium. That balance is potentially disrupted by the addition of a newcomer entering the mix. Much has been written about how the group may then have to go back through its earlier stages in order to create a new balance (Cini, 2001). The facilitator may help the group by having the newcomer go through some small rites of passage, such as completing a personality inventory, if that had been done, and having the newcomer and the group briefly revisit the personality preferences of all members. While new group members may cause some minor readjustment in functioning, they may also bring in new energy and ideas and speed up the group's accomplishments. While some facilitators prefer groups to remain intact, research shows that this new vitality may prove useful in the facilitation process (Cini, 2001).

Group Culture

Another area on the process track that has emerged from psychology and with deeper roots in anthropology and sociology is the importance to the facilitator of understanding the culture in which she is operating. Groups, like organizations and societies, possess a culture. Taking a cue from anthropology, we are defining culture as the system of shared beliefs, values, customs, and behaviors that the members of a group use to cope with their world and with one another. Once developed, that culture is transmitted to each new member. It may reflect a way of being within an organization or the broader values of the group members or even the culture from which they come. If the facilitator comes from outside the organization or is not from the larger culture that it reflects, he or she needs to begin to identify and honor the culture in which the facilitation work is taking place.

The culture of the organization begins at its inception with what is referred to in appreciative inquiry as its positive core. This consists of its values, mission, and purpose. Over time, this culture may become invisible, turning into a taken-for-granted set of assumptions that are held by the majority of members of an organization (Schein, 1996).

According to Schein (2003), in order to understand culture, the newcomer must examine several diverse areas, such as language, customs, traditions; norms, standards, and values; formal philosophy and mission; rules of the game; climate; embedded skills; habits of thinking and acting; shared meanings; and metaphors or symbols. Although Schein addresses these concerns to the organization development consultant, they are no less important to the facilitator who is brought in to work in the organization. In fact, the facilitated change process recommended in the more recent writings of management guru Peter Drucker begins with uncovering the culture through what he refers to as an internal summary (Stern, 1999).

Organizational culture may grow from societal culture (and vice versa). Following is an example from modern Japanese business culture attributed to more ancient relationships, in this case between rice farmers and samurai warriors. The samurai were dependent on the rice farmers for food, and the rice farmers were dependent on the samurai for protection. Although this relationship no longer exists, the cultural values it represented provided a natural bridge to the present. Today, management depends on its workers to produce products or services, and workers depend on management to take care of them. Scholars argue that the cultural foundations made it easier for the Japanese to embrace this codependency and the team concept it represents compared to other cultures without similar historical roots. By better understanding the historical culture, the facilitator has the potential to be more effective by honoring the underlying or core values.

Group Intelligence

Yet another component of working with groups are the many new theories on intelligence. Howard Gardner (1993) posited seven and then eight forms of intelligence. Each type brings a different and useful way of thinking to the group. Exhibit 3.4 lists the intelligences and posits the implications for the group facilitator.

Exhibit 3.4
Multiple Intelligence Theory and the Facilitator

Intelligence	Implications for Facilitation
Linguistic	People in this group learn through reading. Ensuring that work is displayed in written form (as on flip charts) is vital, as is capturing their words as spoken.
Logical/ mathematical	Good at patterns and relationships, these participants can be called on to see how ideas cluster and relate to the external environment.
Bodily kinesthetic	Learning through sensation and the body, group activities that call for movement or skits maximize participation and involvement.

Intelligence	Implications for Facilitation
Spatial	The use of drawing or creation of symbols will help these individuals, who are great with images and pictures.
Musical	While music is less likely than the other intelligences to be focused on in facilitation, having music before the meeting and at breaks sets a positive tone for this group.
Interpersonal	Picking up on mood and the feelings of others, this is the group best able to help look at process issues and the sensitivities in the larger group.
Intrapersonal	More internal, reflective, and self-motivated, these individuals can be counted on to gather information or work on projects that are brought back to the group.
Naturalist	The environment is most important in the learning of this group. Having a comfortable ambience and harmony with that environment is vital for them to use their skills.

As with understanding and using personality profiles, facilitation that draws on multiple intelligences is likely to produce more valuable outcomes than if the work was based on the particular intelligence of the facilitator alone.

CONCLUSION

This chapter has examined a few of the many psychologically based practices important to the art and practice of facilitation. I hope it entices readers to search out other areas that go beyond methods of facilitation to help the individuals and groups involved.

APPENDIX 3A: FOUR SEASONS PERSONALITY PROFILE

Instructions to the facilitator: Provide a copy of the quadrants to all participants. Ask them to select which quadrant contains the words that they are most nearly like. While some individuals will be able to choose one quadrant quickly, others may have a hard time. The facilitator can give the group a couple of minutes, and if they are unable to choose, ask individuals to arbitrarily select one quadrant.

FALL	SPRING
• Dependable • Prepared • Loyal	• Personal • Warm • Compassionate
• Sensible • Punctual • Organized	• Sympathetic • Communicative
• Caring • Concrete • Clear Values	• Sincere • Spiritual • Enthusiastic
• Value Home/Family/Tradition	• Imaginative • Romantic • Flexible
• Follow Rules and Respect Authority	• Authentic • Nurturer • Empathic
• Proud to Serve • Concerned	• Harmonious • Sensitive
WINTER	**SUMMER**
• Logical • Innovative • Analytical	• Impulsive • Witty • Bold
• Global • Conceptual • Abstract	• Spontaneous • Generous
• Cool • Calm • Investigative	• Optimistic • Eager • Need Fun
• Perfectionistic • Nonconformist	• Charming • Immediate • Restless
• Problem Solver • Visionary	• Hate Routine • Competitor
• Insightful • Inner Directed	• Trouble-Shooter • Adventurous

Divide the group into four subgroups based on which "season" the participants identified. Assign the following task:

Create a perfect meeting environment for the stereotypical person described by your quadrant. Include a description of: the layout of the room; how the meeting would be run, led, or facilitated; how decisions would be made and implemented; and what role you see people from your quadrant playing in a group with mixed personalities. You are to come up with a catchy slogan that describes your own quadrant. All of this is to be presented back to the larger group in whatever creative form you choose. You might do a skit, lecture, song, or rap, but it must be performed by all the quadrant members.

Give the following warning (tongue-in-cheek):

"Springs: Do not spend all your time getting agreement, participation, and buy-in, as that might hold you back."

"Summers: Do not put off the task until the very end. Allocate your time so the task gets done."

"Falls: "Leave time to practice your presentation, as it's important for you to get things as perfect as possible."

"Winters: Focus on the task at hand; do not get diverted by discussions on world affairs and social issues."

This process can be completed in less than thirty minutes. It is followed by a facilitated discussion, which might take another thirty minutes, on how each seasonal personality type can add to the workings of a group.

The facilitator might ask the participants to guess his preferred "season." This question can be used before or after the groups divide into the four subgroups. In any case, if the group is not familiar with the facilitator, they might be given the opportunity to ask questions that might give clues.

For more comprehensive details, contact the author at info@wovenstory.com.

PART TWO

Plan Appropriate Group Processes

1. Select clear methods and processes.

- Fosters open participation with respect for client culture, norms, and participant diversity
- Engages the participation of those with varied learning and thinking styles
- Achieves a high-quality product / outcome that meets the client needs

2. Prepare time and space to support group process.

- Arranges physical space to support the purpose of the meeting
- Plans effective use of time
- Provides effective atmosphere and drama for sessions

Eight Ps of Effective Facilitation Planning and Preparation

Jeff Bracken

You are at the front of the room facilitating a group. Suddenly something is wrong. You have the group's complete attention, but you cannot remember the next step in the process. Or the group does not understand your instructions for an exercise and responds with blank stares. Perhaps there is an unexpected shift in group dynamics that throws the meeting off track, and you cannot seem to bring it back. Maybe you cannot locate a handout or a prepared flip chart. Or the process you designed is not producing the results you expected. These seemingly unrelated problems often share a common root cause: ineffective facilitation planning and preparation.

In response to these challenges, I have developed an approach that has consistently worked for me in successfully facilitating hundreds of groups over the past ten years. It works particularly well in planning and preparing for complex, high-stakes facilitation projects, where the situations and issues are complicated, and personal relationships and organizational performance are at stake. Specific examples of these types of projects include leading the design, development, and delivery of an organizational survey-feedback-action planning process, and designing and facilitating a multiday event with fifty or more participants to address a critical business issue.

The level of facilitation involved with this kind of work demands that you delve deeper in planning and preparation than simply reviewing a checklist of things to do before facilitating. You need to reach a fairly sophisticated level of shared understanding, support, and acceptance with the client regarding a variety of important issues.

This approach is not a linear, generic cookie-cutter template that applies to all facilitation situations. However, it does provide a clear process and useful guidelines that professionals can customize to their unique requirements.

The Eight Ps in this chapter and the dozens of practical tips and techniques that they include will help make the task of facilitation planning and preparation easier and increase your personal effectiveness as a facilitator.

Following is an overview of the approach:

- Perspective—developing an understanding of the client's organization and operating situation to provide a context for your facilitation project

- Purpose—clarifying the needs and expectations of the client and their stakeholders

- People—considering stakeholder demographics and dynamics

- Product—defining the specific work product, content, and format to meet client requirements

- Place—anticipating and managing the details and logistics of the physical meeting space

- Process—customizing the facilitation process design, materials, and evaluation to the client's perspective, purpose, people, product, and place

- Practice—reviewing process documentation and materials and rehearsing your delivery

- Personal preparation—being mentally, emotionally, and physically ready to perform and paying attention to your long-term personal and professional development

PERSPECTIVE

It is critically important to gain perspective about your client's organization and operating situation at the outset of a project. A fact-based context helps you make informed decisions and eliminates guesswork and faulty assumptions about what the client needs and how to best meet those needs.

Developing perspective involves a systematic process of gathering and assessing relevant information. It entails exploring your client's Web site, reviewing annual reports and other written material, meeting face-to-face with the client and asking open-ended questions, and paying attention to the themes, patterns, and nuances that emerge.

The Organizational Profile within the Baldrige National Quality Program's Criteria for Performance Excellence (U.S. Department of Commerce, 2004) is the most useful framework I have found for developing an in-depth perspective about a client organization. I have used these criteria for several years as an examiner for both the Texas Award for Performance Excellence and the Malcolm Baldrige National Quality Award processes. There are separate criteria for business, education, and health care industry sectors that are researched and updated every two years. The criteria for each sector contain industry-specific terminology, but the content is quite similar across industry sectors. I developed the following series of questions based on the organizational profile in the business criteria.

Begin by developing a picture of your client's organization, operating environment, and key relationships:

- What are their primary products and services?
- What are their stated values, purpose, vision, and mission?
- How would you describe their workforce?
- What is the employee turnover rate?
- What are their technologies, equipment, and facilities?
- Where are their major locations?
- What government regulations do they need to comply with?
- What is their public reputation?
- What legal or adverse publicity issues are they dealing with?
- What is their organizational structure?
- What management changes have taken place?
- When did those changes occur, and what influenced them?
- How would you describe their major customers and markets?
- Who are their major suppliers, partners, and distributors, and what roles do they play?

Next, consider the important challenges that your client is facing:

- What is their competitive position in the marketplace?
- What is the size of their overall market or industry?
- Is it growing, stable, or declining?
- Who are their major competitors?
- What are the key factors that have determined your client's success?
- What changes are taking place in their marketplace?
- How would you describe their performance in key areas such as customer satisfaction, product and service performance, financial and market results, human resource results, organizational effectiveness, and governance and social responsibility?
- How does their performance compare to industry averages and leading organizations in their industry?
- What are their most important strategic challenges?
- What are their major goals for the future?
- How do they evaluate and improve their processes and performance?
- How do they learn and share knowledge throughout the organization to improve performance?

You will want to scale back the level and amount of information you gather for smaller, short-term projects or one-time events. However, this information can be an invaluable resource in meeting the challenges of larger, more complex projects and in building long-term relationships with clients.

PURPOSE

It is essential to understand what your client views as a successful project, meeting, or event before determining the detailed requirements, specific deliverables, and how to measure results.

In *The Performance Challenge* (1999), Gilley, Boughton, and Maycunich offer practical definitions of needs and expectations: "Needs are the problems or issues that must be resolved before an organization can reach its business goals and objectives. They are the gaps that must be filled in order for an organization to function effectively and provide value to all stakeholders." They add, "Expectations are outcomes desired by stakeholders, while needs are requirements that stakeholders must have to maintain satisfactory performance" (pp. 27–28).

These definitions highlight the importance of considering both the needs and expectations of the entire organization and all major stakeholder groups. The Baldrige Criteria for Performance Excellence define *stakeholders* as "all groups that are or might be affected by an organization's actions and success. Examples of key stakeholders include customers, employees, partners, investors and local/ professional communities" (U.S. Department of Commerce, 2004, p. 35).

There are several questions you can ask to determine your client's needs and expectations:

- What are their current results or outcomes?

- What are their ideal desired results or outcomes?

- When do they hope to achieve them?

- What is happening now? What should be happening?

- How can this project, meeting, or event help fill the gap between what is happening and what should be happening?

- What do we need to achieve in this meeting or event in order to meet their needs?

- What is a realistic expectation of what they hope to accomplish through this event?

- What kind of atmosphere do we need to create in order to accomplish the results they want?

- What kind of tone do we want to set for this event?

The Institute of Cultural Affairs (ICA) Technology of Participation Group Facilitation Methods provides a particularly effective way to develop a practical purpose for a facilitated event. Resources for learning this approach include Laura J. Spencer's book, *Winning Through Participation* (1989), and the course participant manuals for ICA's *Group Facilitation Methods* (2000) and *Participatory Strategic Planning* (1996). ICA methodology guides you to work with clients to identify a focus question and then develop a supporting rationale and experiential aims. This approach can be useful in a variety of situations and applications.

A focus question is an open-ended question that draws the group's attention and creativity to a specific subject or issue. It is helpful to think of this as an overarching question that must be answered through the course of the facilitated event or process. It should include all stakeholders who will be affected by the results. When you are developing a plan, it is important to include a specific time frame. Two examples of focus questions are, "How can we build effective teamwork among all departments throughout our business unit?" and "How can we reduce our division operating costs by 20 percent over the next three years?"

A rational aim refers to the results or outcomes the client is seeking—for example, "a prioritized list of specific strengths and opportunities for improvement with actionable feedback for each department" or "a documented action plan for the entire organization."

An experiential aim speaks to the experience the group will have during the event and how they will be different at the end of the session. Think in terms of the atmosphere you need to create. For one type of application, you might want to set a tone of thoughtful reflection and constructive problem solving. In another situation, you may need to create a sense of camaraderie and teamwork to build consensus.

During the meeting or event, be sure to keep the focus question visible to the group at all times. If the group gets stuck or off track you can ask them, "How does that help answer our focus question?" That usually refocuses their attention and energy.

PEOPLE

You need to determine who your client's key stakeholders are and clarify their needs and expectations in order to develop a practical purpose for the meeting or event. It is equally important to understand the unique demographics and dynamics of the groups you will be facilitating. Resist the temptation to gloss over this step and rely too much on your professional experience and personal charisma. Sometimes you can get lucky through guesswork. However, it is important to recognize that you are risking failure if you do not understand what you are getting yourself into.

A common mistake is failing to identify and include the important stakeholders who need to participate in the event. Another is assuming that the people at the top of an organization understand the depth and breadth of issues at the level of detail needed to represent the interests of their respective business units, functions, or departments effectively. In many cases, a better approach is to include a diagonal slice of the organization's participant population in the process, ensuring that all levels of stakeholder communities throughout the organization are represented. If you want to understand a complex issue, get information from a variety of vantage points, including the people who are directly dealing with it.

With all stakeholder groups defined, you are ready to consider demographics: the factual data that describe the population characteristics of the organization or group that you are working with. It is helpful to develop a profile of the types of positions, levels of experience, age ranges, educational levels, professional designations or certifications, years of experience with the organization, gender and racial diversity, nationalities, languages spoken, and related characteristics that are important to the client. Having a sense of the demographics can help you design a process that is appropriate to their organizational culture.

Asking candid questions about group dynamics can pay rich dividends when you are facilitating. Every group has a history together. You need to know what that history is and take it into consideration:

- What are the conflicts?

- Where are the sensitivities?

- Given the issues being addressed and past experiences, how does the client expect certain people or groups of people to react?

- What are the biases, preconceived ideas, and other potential barriers to success?

- What are the group's emotionally charged issues?

- What have been their experiences with other facilitators or consultants?

- What are their clear likes and dislikes?

- What advice does your client have for you regarding what to do or what not to do, and why?

PRODUCT

It is essential to clarify and define the desired work product and the practical content and format that meet your client's requirements. After the project or event is completed, there must be sufficient documentation so that the client knows what the next steps are and how to take action. In *Flawless Consulting* (1981), Peter Block emphasizes the importance of being very specific in determining what will be delivered. A lack of specificity can create misunderstandings with clients.

As you are defining the work product, consider the client's viewpoint. Your clients are looking for results. They want to be able to take action, not just explore interesting theories or discuss vague generalities. You need to be up to the task of determining and documenting a clear, concrete, specific, descriptive work product that is relevant and important to their needs. Otherwise, you may end up producing meeting documentation that is a boring recitation of buzzwords, boilerplate, catchy phrases, and slogans. When participants walk out of the room, they need to be saying, "I understand the issue, and I know what to do," not, "Why did we waste our time on that again? I don't know any more now than when I walked in!"

There are several practical questions that can help you clarify and define your client's specific work product requirements:

- What is the most important thing they need to accomplish?
- What documentation do they want to walk out of the room with?
- What specific information do they need and in how much detail?
- Who will use the information, and how will it be used?
- Who else will see the information?
- When will the information be needed?
- What format do they want it in?
- What specific day, date, and time do they want it?
- How do they want it delivered?

Answer these questions, and you will know what your client's real requirements are.

PLACE

An often overlooked step is taking the time to see the planned physical meeting space firsthand. (See Chapter Five.) This is your opportunity to discover its strengths and limitations and whether you will be able to create the atmosphere you need. You may find that it does not meet your requirements and need to suggest alternative meeting space. That is not something you want to find out on the day of the event.

THE FACILITATOR HAD BEEN *ASSURED*
THE ROOM HAD AMPLE WALL SPACE

Determine your requirements before you begin the process of finding meeting space:

- How many participants will be attending?
- What kind of seating, tables, physical work space, and room setup will be needed?
- What exercises and materials will be used?
- What special equipment is needed, such as flip charts, markers, wall mountings, overhead projectors, personal computers, screens, microphones, VCRs, DVDs, or Internet access?
- Will all the work be done in one room, or will you also need breakout rooms?
- What are your requirements for water, coffee, tea, soft drinks, meals, and snacks?
- What travel and lodging accommodations are needed?

Have all of your requirements well documented before you begin looking for appropriate meeting space.

When you visit the meeting room, first visualize yourself facilitating in the space. Then visualize your participants working in the space. Physically walk around and sit in participant chairs at several different locations around the room. Then consider these questions:

- How is the visibility from their perspective?
- How is this area going to work for you and for the participants?
- Are you being energized or deenergized in this space?
- What is causing your reaction?
- What are the problems or obstacles you are encountering?
- What changes need to be made in order to make the space work?
- What are the strengths of the space?
- What are some creative ways to use the space that might add value to the meeting experience of the participants?

There are several more factors to consider:

- Is the size of the room appropriate for what you are planning?
- How do you rate the overall lighting, acoustics, ventilation, and cleanliness?
- Is the condition of the furniture and audiovisual equipment acceptable?
- Are there enough rest room facilities?
- Is there enough parking?
- Can participants effectively use telephones and get messages during breaks?
- Is the wall space what you need, and can you mount things on the walls as you require?
- Can you serve meals and refreshments in a way that will not be a distraction to the participants?
- How are you going to handle getting more water when you run out in the middle of the meeting?
- Can you control the temperature and lighting?

- Can you control room access and privacy as needed?

- What is the noise level from adjacent rooms?

- Can you create the overall atmosphere you desire in this physical space?

Often, it is the ability to anticipate and manage the details and logistics of the physical meeting space that can make or break an event.

PROCESS

Armed with knowledge of your client's perspective, purpose, people, product, and place, you are in a solid position to design a process that is custom-tailored to their unique situation and requirements. You can now make informed decisions about choosing or creating methods, developing supporting process documentation and materials, and evaluating the process.

Process design is extremely important. The more complex the situation is, the more emphasis you need to place on process. The Baldrige National Quality Program Criteria for Performance Excellence define *process* as "linked activities with the purpose of producing a product or service for a customer (user) within or outside the organization." The criteria add, "Generally, processes involve combinations of people, machines, tools, techniques and materials in a defined series of steps or actions" (U.S. Department of Commerce, 2004, p. 34).

Documenting the facilitation process is a way to integrate and synchronize everything you have learned about the perspective, purpose, people, product, and place into a cohesive, focused approach. The act of writing it down creates clarity of thought. It allows you to visualize the entire process and all its parts, and get a sense of the transition of each part into the next.

An effective technique is to reduce an entire day's agenda to a single sheet of paper, breaking it down into blocks of time for each key part of the agenda, with time increments ranging from ten minutes to two hours. In each time block, document key words or phrases you are going to say; the specific exercise or activity you will do; and the materials needed for each exercise or activity, such as flip charts, handouts, overheads, PowerPoint slides, participant manuals, or images to post on a wall. Indicate the title of each flip chart, exercise, or handout. It is particularly helpful to have the openings, key points, transitions, and closings for each time block at your fingertips.

The payoff comes when you are in the middle of delivering your facilitation, and an unpredictable group dynamic throws the group off course. After you handle the situation, you can refer to your one-page detailed agenda and quickly identify where you are in the process without fumbling around. This is especially helpful when you are working as part of a team of facilitators, in which case everyone must be on the same page. You will also find that using process documentation as a reference point throughout the day will improve your time management.

A word of caution is appropriate: a planned process and agenda should not be viewed with a straitjacket mentality. Facilitation is a dynamic process, and situations vary. Professional judgment is required to strike an appropriate balance between the degree of structure needed to achieve the result with adaptability and responsiveness to what emerges through the course of facilitating a group process. We need to be open to the possibility that changing or even abandoning a planned approach may be exactly what is needed to help a group achieve an important breakthrough.

At this point, you will have enough information to develop an approach for measuring and evaluating the effectiveness of the facilitation project. It is good practice to provide the opportunity for participants to complete a brief evaluation form at the end of your session. (See Chapter Twenty-Five.) You will want to measure their immediate reaction to the content, process, materials, facilitator, facilities, and the usefulness, or "take-away" value. It is best to limit this form to a single page. Include items or questions for participants to rate on a standard five-point scale and adequate space for written comments. In this manner, you will capture both the quantitative data and qualitative information needed to assess the effectiveness of your project or event.

PRACTICE

This step can mean the difference between success and failure. By *practice,* I mean doing a dry run of the process, reviewing the documentation and materials that you will use at each stage, visualizing and rehearsing the event, anticipating potential problems, and preparing appropriate contingency plans.

Review the agenda, process documentation, and materials, and make sure that everything is ready in finished format. Rehearse by standing up, speaking out loud, and experimenting with gestures that you plan to use. Hearing yourself say something aloud can help you better connect with your meaning and intentions.

As you are doing your dry run, consider what is missing. Sometimes this will lead you to make significant improvements to your process and materials. It is a lot easier to make needed improvements in advance of a session rather than trying to improvise in front of a group.

On the day of the event, arrive before the participants. For large events, it is a good idea to bring a final preparations checklist with you. Test the equipment, and make sure that backup equipment is ready in case of an emergency. Spare bulbs, extension cords, additional handouts, and a backup computer diskette or CD containing your original documentation can come in handy during an emergency. Make sure that your materials are properly staged and ready. See that the refreshments are in place. When you are sure everything is in order, take a few moments for yourself. Visit the rest room, check your personal appearance, and visualize yourself facilitating a successful event. You are now prepared to facilitate with confidence.

PERSONAL PREPARATION

Personal preparation encompasses being mentally, emotionally, and physically ready to perform each time you facilitate, as well as paying attention to your long-term personal and professional development.

If you are not personally ready to perform, it may have a negative impact on how you relate to participants and the client culture, the quality of the overall participant experience, and the ultimate work product and results achieved.

When you facilitate, you are a role model for the group. At any given time, someone will be watching your every move, listening to your every word, and forming impressions. This holds true not only when you are at the front of the room, but also while you are performing room setup, on breaks, and cleaning up after an event.

Personal readiness begins with mental focus. Being mentally focused involves paying attention to the complexities of your role as a facilitator. The primary role of a facilitator is to help the group; it is not to lead, manage, entertain, present, lecture, or train it. You are not the center of attention; the participants are. Your focus needs to be on the context of the client's situation, the process you are facilitating, the group dynamics, how you are affecting the group, and the results you seek to achieve.

Being emotionally ready means being aware of your own emotions and attitudes and leaving any personal problems and agendas behind. You need to be in a neutral and objective zone when you facilitate. When you operate in this zone, you keep your personal emotions in neutral gear. You are aware of the feeling or mood of the group but not drawn into it. You are empathetic with the group, but do not overly identify with the group's emotions and lose your objectivity.

Physical readiness entails being sufficiently rested and having plenty of energy. When you are tired, you lose your mental and emotional edge. A good night's rest can make a big difference in your effectiveness.

Beyond being ready to perform for a specific event or project, it is imperative to maintain a disciplined approach to your long-term personal and professional development:

- What is your overall professional image?
- Are you creating a distraction through your personal appearance, energy level, physical fitness, personal hygiene, dress, attitude, eye contact, voice tone, body language, or mannerisms?
- Are you in tune with the times and the cultures of your clients?
- How do you really come across to others?
- How knowledgeable and skilled are you?
- What are you learning and improving right now?

In his book *The Fifth Discipline* (1990), Peter Senge eloquently captures the essence of personal and professional development. Senge states that "personal mastery is the phrase my colleagues and I use for the discipline of personal growth and learning. People with high levels of personal mastery are continually expanding their ability to create the results in life they truly seek." He adds, "When personal mastery becomes a discipline—an activity we integrate into our lives—it embodies two underlying movements. The first is continually clarifying what is important to us" and "the second is continually learning how to see current reality more clearly." He goes on to say that "people with a high level of personal mastery live in a continual learning mode. They never arrive." His view is that "personal mastery is not something you possess. It is a process. It is a lifelong discipline. People with a high level of personal mastery are acutely aware of their ignorance, their incompetence, their growth areas. And they are deeply self-confident. Paradoxical? Only for those who do not see that the journey is the reward" (pp. 141–142).

In your journey of mastering facilitation skills, it is essential to obtain objective feedback from your clients and professional peers on a regular basis. Be keenly aware of your own barriers to receiving and accepting feedback. It is a natural human tendency to minimize feedback and rationalize away the need to change, grow, and improve. Challenge your complacency, and be open to change. A good rule of thumb is to focus on improving one or two key areas of your facilitation at a time. Work on those areas that will make the biggest positive difference in your facilitation. When you reach your improvement goal in an area, take it off your list, and add another one. Just as we advise our clients, we need to develop written goals and action plans, measure progress, and manage our own continuous improvement process.

CONCLUSION

When I was in human resource management and learning the skills of stand-up training and public speaking, one resource that I turned to was the *Creative Training Techniques Handbook* (1989) by Robert Pike. In his chapter on presentation preparation, Pike offered "six P's of an effective presentation": "Proper Preparation and Practice Prevent Poor Performance" (p. 7). I have found that the fundamental truth in his memorable slogan is as applicable to facilitation as it is to training. Just as Pike's work helped me learn how to train and do public speaking many years ago, it also stimulated the idea for developing my Eight Ps model for effective facilitation planning and preparation.

We face an increasingly competitive world. Our time, energy, and discretionary effort are becoming even more precious commodities. In many organizations, there appears to be a growing cynicism about the very idea of attending meetings, conferences, and events. In the push for efficiency and economy, we hear the continuing drumbeat to meet less and use more technology to minimize the need for people to meet face-to-face. High-tech communications and meeting tools have their place, but there are practical limits to their applications and what can be effectively accomplished with them.

Situations and issues related to organizational, leadership, and team effectiveness are complex. Because personal relationships and organizational performance are involved, the stakes are high. In these complex, high-stakes arenas, there is a clear need for people to meet face-to-face, fully engage in an effective process, and do the hard work required to achieve meaningful results. We need to fully use our marvelous human capabilities of rational thinking, logical analysis, expression of authentic feelings, and intuitive creativity. This is high-touch work that high tech cannot replace.

As professionals committed to this challenging work, we encounter emergencies, last-minute changes, unpredictable shifts in group dynamics, and other surprises. We are expected to respond to these situations in a fluid, flexible way. A systematic approach to facilitation planning and preparation can help us deal with these realities, continuously improve our performance, and increase the value we provide clients.

The Architecture of Participation

Patricia Tuecke

I have always had a strong sense of space, developed perhaps as my family moved from place to place as my father's job required. We always fixed up our new space, making it reflect our family values and needs, and creating a pleasant space in which to live. In my first job after graduate school, I worked with a dynamic woman who was passionate about the role that space arrangement played in the learning environment. Our job was to transform a drab building into an inviting space for children. As we painted chairs, hung pictures, arranged tables, and planted flowers, I learned about the importance of intentional space arrangement to the effectiveness of an overall learning environment. I have never forgotten those lessons. They have served me well as a facilitator of group meetings. In this capacity, I have continued to travel and work in many different locales around the world. In Asia, Europe, and South and North America alike, the yin-yang of skillful facilitation and responsible participation was enhanced or hindered by the space I was working in.

Participative meetings take place in many kinds of spaces. I have facilitated meetings in school cafeterias, dining rooms, penthouses, courtrooms, boardrooms, ballrooms, porches, under tents, in club lounges, offices, training rooms, storefronts, libraries, living rooms, and village meeting halls. In all of these, it took forethought and preparation to make the energy of the space work for participation, not against it.

Every space conveys a certain atmosphere and climate. Reflect on the different feelings you get when you enter a cathedral, a factory, a forest glen, a courtroom, a boardroom, a meditation room, or a gymnasium. Some spaces have a sense of calm and harmony, others of purposeful activity, some of chaotic energy, and others a sense of awe. Every space has a particular energy that those who enter feel. The design and arrangements of meeting spaces convey a message about the kind of activity and demeanor that are appropriate to it and have a noticeable effect on those who enter it.

FENG SHUI: ANCIENT CHINESE WISDOM ABOUT SPACE

The ancient Chinese had a strong sense of place and use of space. Well over three thousand years ago, the practice of feng shui emerged to help people live their lives in harmony and dynamic balance with the forces of energy of the earth and nature in their environment. To do so made practical sense given their interdependence on the land and their agricultural livelihood. To do so seemed to bring happiness, prosperity, good health, and good luck. The practice of feng shui works to create harmony and balance in one's surroundings. It is built on the belief that the "breath of life, or Chi, fills and flows through all people, places, and things, bringing life and fullness" (Bender, 2003, p. 1). Feng shui experts advise people how to optimize the beneficial energy flow in the spatial decisions of buildings and work and living spaces and how to avoid a negative flow of energy. To this end, feng shui experts advise on the placement of furnishing, seating arrangements, decorative elements, and overall design of the work or living space.

In the five years I worked with organizations in Hong Kong and China, I became aware of how much the practice of feng shui continues today as new interpretations and applications emerge from the still relevant foundational principles. It is well known that the Hong Kong and Shanghai Bank considered advice from feng shui masters when they built a new forty-seven-story headquarters in the Central District of Hong Kong (Wydra, 1995). Growing interest in and application of feng shui is evident in professional offices (Williams, 2003) and in other geographical locations. It is possible today, in Reno, Nevada, where I live, to take classes in feng shui at the local community colleges and engage a feng shui practitioner to give advice about your home or place of business. "Feng shui posits that our accomplishments in life are influenced by the places where we live and work" (Wydra, 1995, p. 6). In meetings where people work together to solve problems, hold discussions, make decisions, and plan, I find that the design, arrangement, and feel of the physical environment of meeting rooms contribute greatly to the quality of the outcomes of the meeting or detract from accomplishing the desired outcomes. In their preparation for a meeting, leaders often overlook this factor.

Much of feng shui is based on what we call common sense, a sense of the appropriateness of design to achieve a certain purpose along with a feel for color and shape. Architects apply their knowledge of the dynamics of color, shape, lighting, position, and movement in their designs to create harmonious place for people to live and work. Mediators are quite aware of the importance of equalizing the power between parties with the seating arrangements in their session (Williams, 2003). Intuitively perhaps, or through practice, effective facilitators are aware of and use similar dynamics of space design to beckon group participation and enhance the positive energy flow in meetings as much as they use effective techniques for dialogue and decision making.

THE CHANGING FORM OF MEETINGS

One of the fundamental shifts in our time is that people are demanding to participate in the decisions that affect their lives. Organizational leadership is becoming more facilitative as leaders explore ideas together with staffs and ask for the ideas of those closer to the customer. In these participative meetings, people work together to problem-solve, improve procedures, discover more effective ways to serve customers, and deal with complex issues that have no obvious, simple solutions. The outcome is not imposed by the boss but emerges from the group's discussions and decisions. This requires the whole group to think and work together in new interactive ways.

Most meeting rooms block participation rather than beckon it by the arrangement of the furnishings. Winston Churchill said "We shape our buildings; thereafter they shape us." Mainstream images and standard operating procedures of a previous time influenced meeting room design, with all seating facing the front of the room, where the expert or the boss is expected to tell the others what do to or how to do something. The focus is on the speaker or leader in the front of the room. There is little or no interaction between participants, and they do not need eye contact with one another. Verbal interaction with the leader is most often limited to participants sitting near the front of the room. It is difficult for people in the rear to hear and see, as well as to be heard and seen. Discussion among small groups of participants is difficult to arrange in venues like auditoriums where the seats are fixed to the floor. The implication of the theater- or classroom-style arrangement is that someone up front has something to tell or teach the audience, with little participation expected. A panel arrangement in front conveys that the wisdom resides in a few experts, not the audience. A boardroom arrangement, typically around a long, narrow table, indicates that somewhat equal participation is expected; however, the person who can be seen and heard best by the others is the one who sits at the head of the table, usually the chair of the board.

These space arrangements indicate that the action will take place up front where the group's attention and energy are directed, and primarily around one person, the leader, and that communication will be one way: from the leader to the audience. These conditions make these settings inappropriate for participative meetings. The energy or focus of many meetings has shifted with the times, and the physical space arrangements need to reflect this shift

In contrast, a participative meeting spreads its attention to everyone in the group rather than focusing it solely on the leader, and the physical setup of the room supports this. Participative meetings require seating arrangements that level the playing field and indicate that the participants as well as the leader have experience and expertise that will be shared. The seating arrangements also indicate that in the meeting, no one participant has more power or status than another. The seating arrangements need to be flexible and easily moved, as a participative meeting usually includes activities that require people to move out of their seats and into small subgroups or teams for periods of time. The focus shifts from the leader's words to the group's work. The front of the room becomes the space where the group's ideas and decisions are scribed, usually on flip chart pages, whiteboards, or, increasingly, electronically. This record becomes the group memory. It may also consist of visual images such as charts, graphs, and templates, which may be drawn or projected. These are displayed on what I call a "front working wall," a large, flat, uninterrupted wall space on which to attach chart paper or to project images.

MEETING ROOM ARRANGEMENTS THAT BECKON PARTICIPATION

Three key physical elements must be considered and carefully arranged to beckon participation in a meeting:

- The size and shape of various kinds of spaces in relationship to the group size
- The physical arrangement of the furniture
- The "feel" of the space as people walk into the room

Size and Shape of Meeting Rooms

Some architectural elements such as walls, windows, doors, ceilings, and flooring are not changeable and therefore must be taken into account in the selection of the meeting location. Facilitators learn how to work with or around elements that block participation and cannot be changed or to avoid venues with unworkable space. In every instance, the facilitator needs to take into consideration the group size, the room size, the purpose of the meeting, and the activities that will take place. The front of the room is of great importance in this type of meeting and is usually the first aspect of a proposed meeting space that a facilitator evaluates. In some rooms, the most appropriate wall may not be the one usually considered the front of the room. Sometimes a side wall provides the best unobstructed working space and becomes the "front working wall," with the seating arranged to face it.

Everyone needs to be able to visually access the information recorded and displayed at the front working wall of the room. The room should be clear of pillars, permanent dividers, or structural aspects that jut out into the room and interrupt this line of sight. Participants need to be able to hear all the dialogue around the topic being discussed in order to participate fully in the meeting. Therefore, the seating arrangements need to minimize the maximum distance between participants and minimize visual disruptions between any two people and between any person and the shared record. Sometimes the facilitator will use a corner of the room as the front of the meeting space if the two side walls are unobstructed and provide better wall space. This arrangement also works when the space is too large for the size of the group, putting the large, empty space behind the group. For a small group in a large room, the amount of empty space is overwhelming and can give a sense of insignificance to the work they are doing. If the room is too small in proportion to the number of participants, a group may feel crowded and therefore edgy or uncomfortable being elbow to elbow, especially with people they do not know, which can stifle creativity; some might find it claustrophobic. Physical and emotional comfort comes first in the minds of most meeting participants. Safety concerns and fire regulations have to be factored in figuring out room capacity.

In addition to appropriate room size and a workable front wall, factors that must be considered are table and chair style and arrangements; acoustics; climate; lighting; electrical, electronic, and audiovisual capabilities; refreshments; data display capabilities; decor; and breakout spaces. Experienced facilitators can look at a potential meeting space and know in a glance what will work well for the meeting and what will need to be adjusted or modified.

Allen Hickling (1990), a facilitator working with an architect-designer, drew up the following design brief for an ideal meeting room or decision space. It can be used as a list of factors to consider when evaluating the space for a participative meeting:

- Clear space, free of columns and changes of level is needed for groups of six to thirty people—must allow for a wide variety of seating configurations—mostly semi-circular, focused on a wall, but also more conventional—square plan format will serve most layouts best—choice of size varies from 5m × 5m for small groups (say six to ten) to 10m × 10m for larger groups (say twenty-five to thirty)....

- Easy access to "alternative" space (ideally interior and exterior)—interior "alternative" space could be a very wide hallway outside the room (also accommodating coffee supply?)—exterior could be terrace or balcony (in either case access should be as direct as possible).

- As much uninterrupted wall space as possible—large, flat, with durable surface—should be minimum 2.5m high—if possible one "working" wall big enough to accommodate up to twenty flip chart sheets in two rows—about 7m long with doors in other walls.

- Windows are desirable—where possible opposite the "working" wall—none actually on the "working" wall—views out to avoid claustrophobia, but beware of glare—high-level or roof lights.

- Subdividing partition system must be acoustically effective and provide a hard, flat, rigid working surface, probably heavy but needs to be easily handled.

- Artificial lighting must provide an even all-over basic level of light, but at the same time a focus on the walls—arrangements should be very flexible (with dimming capability?)—must cover walls evenly—floods, no spots. . . .

- Furniture should be reasonably comfortable (but not too much so)—easy to move around (lightweight)—suitable for a wide variety of arrangements—modular system of tables (could be 0.75m × 0.75m or 0.75m × 1.5m)—no "specialty" shapes, but with specially designed resilient edges to avoid damage when they are moved frequently—seating for four or six per table.

- Wide variety of technical support (for example projectors of various types, and perhaps computer aid) to be provided without obstruction of the process—multiple options for access to power supply—no fixed technical apparatus.

- Easy access to a continuous supply of refreshments, and to toilets and other services—communications, data, copying and stationery supplies, secretarial, etc. [pp. 172–173].

Physical Arrangement of Furnishings

Just as there is no one right way to facilitate meetings, there is no one right room arrangement that works for all meetings. Each facilitator discerns how the space can be used to support the outcome of that particular meeting and his or her facilitation style. For example, some facilitators prefer round tables for the more informal, small group work atmosphere they convey. These usually seat six (at a five-foot diameter table) to ten (at an eight-foot diameter table) persons. The ten-person size places people too far apart to converse easily except with those seated on either side of them. In any case, always leave one or two places vacant at round tables so that no one sits with his or her back to the front of the room. Some prefer a living room or lounge type of arrangement for the type of meeting they facilitate. They feel that tables create a barrier between the facilitator and participants or between participants. Others want tables for serious working meetings, especially those that use information in documents and need table space for those items as well as the ubiquitous and important coffee cups.

In a participative meeting, the communication, focus, and energy flow from the facilitator to the participants swirl around the group in their discussion or dialogue, back to the group memory, and out again to the participants many times over. The seating arrangements must enable this flow, not block it. Some sort of semicircular seating arrangement best enables this energy flow. Exhibit 5.1 shows three common seating arrangements (lecture, boardroom, and theater) that block participation for the reasons mentioned. It also shows arrangements that beckon participation. These are all somewhat semicircular in shape, and the working wall is at the open end of these arrangements, which allows all participants to see it. It also allows the participants to have eye contact with the facilitator and all (if not, then a majority) of the other participants, and to read facial expressions and body language so important in discussions leading to consensus.

Many meetings need space for the whole group to be together for some portion of the meeting, with other space arranged for small group work. Seating needs to be flexible and easily moved into different configurations, such as small sub-groupings for certain activities. These spaces can be in separate but convenient breakout rooms, or if the meeting space is large enough and the acoustics are good, groups can meet around small tables or in chair circles in the rear of the larger room without disturbing each other (see arrangement h in Exhibit 5.1). Sometimes the energy generated with lots of creative activity in the same large space is preferred to dispersing the group. Especially in long meetings, facilitators may have the group meet in a different space or rearrange the existing space for a change of pace. Like feng shui experts, they rearrange furnishings and decor to enable the positive energy to flow freely in the meeting and support the planned activities.

Often clients who decide to involve staff or constituents in facilitated planning or decision making book space in a favorite venue, unaware of how the physical setting affects the style of this new type of meeting. The importance of the meeting location and room arrangements in participative meetings needs to be part of the client conversation and contracting process from the beginning rather than tacked on just prior to the meeting date. Experienced facilitators know this often entails educating the client in advance of the meeting about the importance of space dynamics to support the outcomes of the meeting.

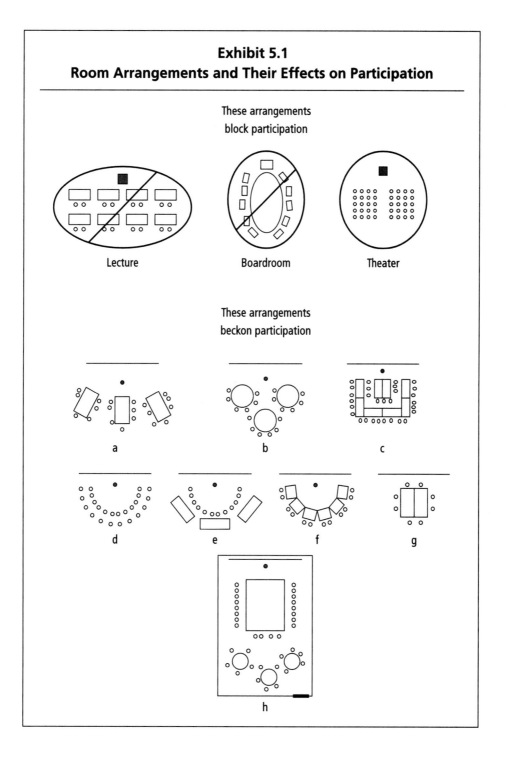

Exhibit 5.1
Room Arrangements and Their Effects on Participation

These arrangements
block participation

Lecture   Boardroom   Theater

These arrangements
beckon participation

a   b   c

d   e   f   g

h

Create a page of your meeting room specifications with setup diagrams to give to and discuss with the client and the person designated to handle the logistics of the meeting. Exhibit 5.2 shows such a list, developed for use with clients. Yours need not be as detailed, but your conversations about the space along with your room specs page are important ways to care for your clients and prevent problems.

Exhibit 5.2
Meeting Room Specifications

Selection and arrangement of the meeting room is critical. Any questions regarding the selection or arrangement of the room should be referred to the lead facilitator. Many factors come into play, such as the following:

Floors should be flat.

Floor space of 30 feet by 30 feet is needed for twelve to fifteen participants (40 feet by 40 feet for a larger group of fifteen to twenty-five).

Ceiling should be at least 10 feet high.

Lighting should be controllable, varying from bright (as you would have for working at a desk) to dark (as you would have in a movie theater). Indirect lighting is preferred. Unacceptable is lighting that emanates from eye level (such as wall sconces) or overhead spot lights. The lighting over the projection screen must be able to be controlled independently (even if that means unscrewing bulbs). No light should shine directly on the screen.

Acoustics should be evaluated to ensure that voices carry well within the room. Noises from other meeting rooms, hallways, public address systems, machinery, ventilation systems, and other areas are unacceptable.

Chairs should be comfortable, executive-style chairs (but not with high backs). They should be movable, preferably on casters, and should swivel. They should have adjustments for height and back support. They should be arranged in a U-shaped curve (not in a straight line) in a single tier (only one row).

Tables should be small snack tables, one per chair or one for two chairs, located between and slightly in front of the chairs. If snack tables are unavailable, larger tables may be placed behind the chairs. Unacceptable are large tables that dominate the room, put distance between participants, or require that chairs are arranged in a straight line. If you insist, narrow tables arranged in a U-shaped curve may be placed in front of participants.

Wall space. A large expanse of unobstructed wall space is needed to hold flip chart paper. Check to make sure that the wall surface is smooth, so that masking tape will stick to it, and that there is no prohibition against using masking tape on the walls. The walls may be covered with a fuzzy, carpet-like material or may be textured. If this is unavoidable, we can still manage by using adhesive Velcro tape or sticky tack, but we have to know this in advance.

Two flip chart easels with solid rectangular backs that support a pad of chart paper. Unacceptable are triangular easels that do not provide a solid backing for the entire rectangular easel pad. Also supply easel chart pads.

Breakout rooms should be available. If the group will be working in smaller subgroups, separate breakout rooms are preferable. If the subgroups are sharing a large room, adequate space is critical to avoid noise problems. The main meeting room should be large enough to hold all the work groups with their flip chart papers on the walls.

Projection screen should be 8 feet (6 feet is okay for a smaller group; 4 feet is unacceptable). The surface should be white; gray is unacceptable. A specialized screen for LCD computer projection is preferred.

Electricity should be available with a grounded three-prong outlet near the open end of the C (the way the room is arranged; see below).

Copier should be available to make copies of materials.

Room setup

- Chairs arranged in a curved C-shape (no straight lines) and single row (chairs should not be one behind the other).
- Open end of the C should face the unobstructed wall space.
- Projection screen and flip chart easels at open end of C. No light should fall on the screen.
- The open end of the C cannot be backlighted, such as backed by a window.
- Table for staff behind or to side of the C near the doorway and near an electrical outlet.
- Coffee setup well off to side or in the hallway or outer room.

Room access and security

- Access to the room the night before is necessary to inspect the room setup and ensure that the facilities are adequate.
- Access to the room is needed one hour prior the start of the meeting.

- The room should be available for use even after the meeting is over (to 9:00 P.M. or later).
- The room should be able to be secured so that participants' materials and conference equipment can be left overnight.

Catering

- Continental breakfast: Coffee, tea, juices, breakfast rolls, bagels, rolls with butter, cream cheese; must be set up a half-hour before conference starting time and located in an adjoining room or hallway or off to the side
- Coffee: available at all times; refresh at midmorning and midafternoon
- Lunch buffet: include dairy or vegetarian selections; no sweet or heavy desserts

Large Group Participative Meetings   Very large groups of fifty to two hundred participants move space requirements to another level. All of the factors already addressed must still be considered. Much has been learned in the past fifteen years about how to work with large groups in large spaces by those engaged in large group conferences such as Future Search (Weisbord and Janoff, 1995), Real-Time Strategic Change (Jacobs, 1994), and Participative Strategic Planning (Spencer, 1989). The space must convey the unity of the whole group as well as provide smaller spaces for breakout work groups. Both the space design and the processes used must create the physical, emotional, and work environment important for the group to stay engaged, focused, comfortable, and productive in a large setting. One solution is to have smaller simultaneous working meetings bracketed by whole group plenary sessions for the opening context and focus and the closing reports and reflection.

Electronic Meeting Support Arrangements   The rising popularity of electronic meeting support systems brings another factor into meeting space design. Many facilitators are beginning to use available systems and programs for capturing ideas, opinions, votes, and decisions electronically. A number of designs and arrangements of such meeting spaces can be found in Bostrom, Watson, and Kinney (1992). The room setup needs to allow the facilitator to move around the room rather than being stuck in one spot to use the equipment. The following optional arrangements support participation:

- Peripheral, with tables and computers around the edge of the room facing the walls. During group discussions, participants can move their chairs facing into the center of the room or in smaller groups around tables.
- Workstations with two or four computers in clusters to support small group discussions.
- All computers along one wall, as a sort of data-input section, with room for group discussion in another area of the room, or all terminals clustered around the technographer in a space separate from the discussion and decision making area.

Important considerations for all arrangements are the number and location of cables and power outlets.

Feel of the Space

In addition to the physical arrangements, facilitators can create an inviting environment that is noticeable upon walking into the meeting room. Be sure the room is prepared before participants arrive. The space must be clean. If the room has not been cleaned or straightened by the maintenance staff, the facilitator needs to see that this happens, even doing it herself or himself when necessary. Arrange for wastebaskets to be included; too often, they are overlooked. Chairs should be evenly spaced and, if tables are used, aligned with the tables. Make sure materials are set out on tables in an orderly manner to communicate that care has gone into the meeting preparation. If folders or notebooks are used, arrange the bottom edges parallel with the edge of the table, not haphazardly placed. Attractive covers add a colorful note in the room.

I often place posters with quotations on the walls. They help fill the space in colorful and intriguing ways, especially helpful in claiming undesirable aspects of a room such as structural posts or permanently attached distracting mirrors or pictures. They also provide an indirect focus on the topic or process or occasion, and give another place for wandering eyes and minds to settle. I print a few quotations that highlight some aspect of the session in a large-size, easy-to-read font and attach them to large, colorful construction or poster paper with a glue stick or mounting spray. An eleven-by-fourteen-inch size fits in the top of a suitcase when I fly. Larger ones go into a portfolio. I have also had a copy shop enlarge the quotations to poster size on colored paper to use in ballroom settings with large groups. A quotation I often use is this statement of Peter Senge: "Each person's view is a unique perspective on a larger reality. If I can look out through your view and you through mine, we may both see something we might not see alone" (Senge, 1990, p. 248). It supports the spirit of participation that I try to enable in a meeting.

An inviting refreshment area, fresh flowers, interesting three-dimensional decor appropriately placed, and music playing softly in the background indicate that care has gone into the preparation for this meeting and that someone has taken time and effort to make this a pleasant space in which to meet. A greeting from the leader as people come into the meeting adds to the inviting feel of the space. During breaks, pick up discarded paper cups, napkins, and crumpled paper to keep the space free of unnecessary clutter, so that when people return, the space continues to communicate an invitation to creative work and a profound respect for the participants, and it lets good energy flow through the room.

Jo Nelson, former president of IAF, has a sculpture of three figures, arm-in-arm in a circle, that she often uses in the middle of the table or on a table in the middle of the room. She says, "We don't always talk about it, but when people get distracted, it is there to bring their attention back to the group. It also symbolizes the circle that is the group" (e-mail to the author, May 28, 1998).

ASSESSING AND ADAPTING SPACE

Part of the responsibility of a facilitator is to assess the space ahead of time and decide whether it will support the meeting under consideration. Always check out the space ahead of the meeting, at least by the night before the meeting. Often the space has been reserved and travel arrangements made before a facilitator is hired. If the meeting is in another locale, you need to communicate with the client about your space needs, sending a list of requirements and a floor plan for the meeting you will facilitate. Rarely is everything to your liking, so do not leave this until the hour before the meeting. In a hotel, convention center, or public space, talk with the meeting coordinator or the facilities staff person in charge of your space. Enlist that person's help to rearrange whatever will optimize a productive meeting. Explain graciously what is needed and why, but stand your ground as to its importance.

Most times it is not possible to work in an ideal space. When assessing a space, the first aspect I consider is the front working wall and other useable wall space. Almost simultaneously I consider the seating arrangement of tables and chairs in relationship to that wall that will work for optimal inclusion, participation, and focus. Then I consider lighting, acoustics, climate, and equipment. If it appears that the space will not enable participation, there are alternatives: decline the job, get agreement to change the venue to a better space, modify activities in the agenda design, or adjust some of the most distracting factors.

For example, in rooms with less than adequate wall space, I have found a number of ways to create a working wall in an otherwise useable room. I have used six eight-foot tables with legs folded and leaned side by side up against the wall to provide a flat space for the flip charts and group memory. I have used large pieces of foam-core board with their long sides taped together on the back with masking tape, to make a smooth wall. In small meetings, I have arranged several flip chart stands with solid backs side by side to create a "front wall" or placed foam-core board horizontally across the flip chart stands. I have had moveable partitions built that created flat wall space and also blocked off unneeded space, creating a wonderful working area. Cheryl Kartes (personal communication to the author, 2003), a facilitator in Minneapolis, has developed a moveable easel that consists of a framework made of aluminum tubing that is collapsible, lightweight, and transportable. It holds a large sheet of foam core or plywood board that becomes the "wall." As shown in the photo in Exhibit 5.3, it creates a useable "front working wall" in a room with no uninterrupted wall space. This kind of flexibility allows a facilitator to divide up a large space or to hold meetings in places like libraries that have few accessible walls. Like feng shui practitioners, we can bring balance and harmony into less than optimal venues.

As I prepare a room for a meeting, I think about the group that will be working with me as I begin to create the place where we will spend our time and energy in collaborative work. I adjust or even rearrange tables and chairs and flip chart stands to invite participation. I create a visual focus on the front wall of the room with a quotation, create small group space if needed, put colorful poster quotations on other walls, and place a small plant or flowers on the registration or refreshment table if there is one. Markers, sticky notes, and other materials may go into in colorful containers such as baskets made of plastic or natural materials placed on the tables for participants to use. I might place a piece of three-dimensional decor on

a table to fill an otherwise large empty space. Doing these activities has become almost a ritual for me, helping me center myself before the participants arrive. As the room takes shape, it is filled with an inviting energy.

CONCLUSION

The facilitator is responsible for creating the environment that evokes participation. Long before the session begins, decisions about the physical setting, the emotional climate, and purposeful agenda design are made to achieve the targeted outcomes of the meeting. Space arrangements, together with appropriate group processes and facilitator style, can bring a vibrant energy, wholeness, and balance into group deliberations and dialogue by honoring all participants, making it easy for them to hear and see everything, and not letting one position adversely dominate the discussion. The physical setting becomes a comfortable and safe container in which the facilitated discussions, consensus decision making, and win-win solutions occur that engender ownership and commitment and move a group into action. Its importance is such that effective facilitators should always take the time needed to pay detailed attention to it.

Building Trust

The Great Enabler

Maria Begoña Rodas-Meeker
Larry Meeker

> *Trust is a supremely important element in relationships between people.*
> *To trust someone makes a statement of faith about the other human being.*
> *It means you believe in the person, that you are willing to rely on his/her*
> *integrity, strength, ability and surety. It rings of confidence. Relationships*
> *strong in trust have a feeling and sense of security and strength.*
>
> Larry Meeker, Steve Fischer, and Beth Michalak (1994)

For organizations, teams, and groups both large and small, trust is one of the great enablers of actions and behaviors that are important to achieve success. It is not a skill and cannot be learned by intellectual study. It is learned, or more appropriately built, based on our experiences one with each other.

In the profession of facilitation, this could not be more true. As with many other professions—medical, legal, and financial, to name a few—successful outcomes depend largely on interpersonal relationships. Trust is a key ingredient in strong working relationships.

89

Three critical areas regarding trust demand the facilitator's attention:

- Trust between the facilitator and the hiring manager client
- Trust between the facilitator and the group or groups being facilitated
- Trust within and between groups or organizations that will be critical to the implementation and execution of their desired outcomes and actions

We will examine each, explaining the importance of each to effective facilitation, proposing indicators of levels of trust, and considering facilitation practices and techniques appropriate to build trust.

For each of these critical areas, it is vital to have effective relationships among members that are based on trust. When this exists, the participants and facilitators can find success in processes and activities important for achieving success: communication, effective coordination of processes, timely decision making, successful problem solving, cooperation among members, and commitment to decisions and results.

Success in these areas enables progress toward business goals. Absence of trust has an extremely negative impact on groups, and at a very high organizational cost. Such a lack can be far more serious than simply a lack of confidence between people. (Confidence is a product of trust. It pertains to our faith in each other's trustworthiness to behave and take actions in a manner that contributes.) It can have much deeper consequences and even result in loss of progress toward business objectives. When trust is absent, negative emotions and actions, such as suspicion and blaming, can steal from an organization's productive energy and undermine the positive work that people should be attending to. "The dynamics of trust and betrayal in the workplace are complex. That is why people have difficulty understanding them" (Reina and Reina, 1999, p. 1). It is critical that the facilitator understands these dynamics, facilitates processes that increase knowledge about trust and mistrust, and stimulates group members to behave in ways that have the potential to cultivate and nurture high levels of trust.

The importance of this appears to be universal, spanning cultures around the globe. We have observed the critical role of trust while working with diverse teams in the United States and Europe. The United States is perhaps the most diverse nation on the planet. Working with organizations and teams in the United States requires an appreciation and understanding of processes that can build trust among diverse participants. In work with multinational corporations in Europe as well as the United States, the stimulation of trust across cultures is similarly important.

We have had similar experience in other parts of the world. In Latin America, team members commonly wait until they can see the actions and results of a new team member in order to start building trust. In the past year, important multicultural facilitation experience in countries such as South Africa further demonstrated that important alliances and partnerships can be built when people feel they are in a safe environment where they can participate, learn, and trust in each other to find ways to cooperate and build together sustainable development agreements.

TRUST BETWEEN THE FACILITATOR AND CLIENT

Levels of trust, whether great or small, start to take shape in the initial discussions and interactions that a facilitator has with a potential client. This is true whether it is a process that will use a facilitator internal to the organization or a professional consultant from outside the company. The client has some need. There may be serious pain in the organization. The decision to take action to resolve those needs to some extent involves whether the client has confidence and trust in the facilitator (or facilitation team) to help with the issues.

The qualities and values critical to forming trust are important in those initial discussions between client and facilitators. A lot is at stake for both, depending on the trust that they can establish in their relationship. To achieve the results the client expects, it will be very important for the facilitator to be honest, responsible, and professional. To build and maintain the relationship with the client, it is important to reach agreement on ground rules and to be clear about what can be negotiated and what cannot. Finally, it will be important to talk honestly about any possible conflict of interest. This will help the client make informed decisions regarding the facilitation services. (These issues are discussed as well in Chapter Thirty.)

Gaining the trust of the client is equally important for internal facilitators. In particular, in Latin America (but also in North America and other countries), it is common practice to place more trust in external and "expert" facilitators rather than in the inner resources of the organization. The early work of an internal team of facilitators is critical for their future credibility and continuity; when positive results are evident, the leadership will increasingly ask for the internal rather than external facilitators. The internal processes are then perceived to be more effective and trusted and can achieve results more quickly. In addition, there is a double gain in the process because members of the facilitation team begin to feel that the organization has more trust in them. Because of this shift in trust and confidence, the use of the internal resources becomes common: the leaders trust in the internal facilitators more than the external resources for certain special activities. The facilitator can aid this process of creating strong levels of trust in several ways:

- Listening and understanding. There is nothing more important in the beginning of an intervention process than for the facilitator to listen authentically, asking questions that reveal the issues to be addressed and displaying genuine interest throughout the process of fact finding.

- Client needs. The facilitator aids the process of creating strong levels of trust when he or she has in mind the needs of the client and shows that he or she can help the client to achieve the objectives.

- Ethics and values. The facilitator should serve as a role model in terms of ethics and values. When the client observes that the facilitator's behavior reflects a strong commitment to values and ethics, he or she will trust more that the group will obtain what they need. Personal integrity is critical to building trust with the client.

TRUST BETWEEN THE FACILITATOR AND THE GROUP

Throughout facilitated interventions, levels of trust have an impact on the capacity for success. From the introductions at the very beginning of a meeting, the members of the group judge the safety of the environment in which they are being asked to contribute. Their perceptions of safety bear on many factors—for example:

- Their level of participation

- The ultimate results

- Their commitment to outcomes

- Their belief about the possibilities that the results will be implemented

- The continuity of the processes

Trust internal to the group is an important factor in each event. Some individuals and groups bring a lot of baggage with them into meetings—for example, perceptions and experiences involving past commitments what were not kept, past disagreements, or a variety of relationship challenges. It is important for the facilitator to be prepared for the work ahead. The preconsultation process steps provide the facilitator important information and stories of previous circumstances where trust could have been damaged, such as projects that did not achieve their full potential. This type of background information and insight can aid the facilitator in creating an environment where the participants may share more openly their thoughts, feelings, and perceptions and create the appropriate processes where those conflicts and baggage can be handled.

It is important to address the issue of preparation and responsiveness of facilitators. The manner in which the facilitator prepares for and executes the events will increase the client's confidence and trust in the technical ability of the individual to do the work involved. (See Chapter Four.)

Preparation to facilitate is critical. This engages the facilitator in the business or mission of the group. It illustrates where challenges are likely to be encountered during the facilitation processes. It enables the facilitator to design interventions appropriate for the specific group to achieve the outcomes important to the company or organization. It will provide the opportunity to create adequate processes that will enable the group to build trust.

Responsiveness means the ability of the facilitator to "be in the moment" with the group. For all of the preparation that a good facilitator can perform prior to an event, it is critical that he or she be tuned in to what is occurring with the group during the facilitated processes. Almost always, the attentive facilitator will discover new information that he or she should respond to as it emerges from within the group.

Flexibility is the key to responding to what emerges during the facilitated intervention. It is these skill areas in combination that can enable great outcomes and results—great preparation combined with great sensitivity and responsiveness to those things that occur during a facilitation process. When a group sees these together in a facilitator, the level of trust between the group and the facilitator grows rapidly, and better results can be achieved.

There are additional keys for a facilitator to understand and enhance trust when working with a group:

- Flexibility to provide better processes to help a group or to reconcile emerging needs with the initial need that had been stated.
- Processes that are aligned with the group needs and style

- Permanent feedback and follow-up of the process

- Rapport that is built with the group from the first moments

- An understanding of the development stage of the team, with the facilitation type chosen accordingly

- Management of the information that the group shares during the sessions in order to guarantee that what they say remains in the room and will not be shared with other people unless this has been agreed to beforehand

TRUST WITHIN AND BETWEEN GROUPS

Ideas and plans developed during a facilitated intervention are great, but the pay-off comes later, when the individuals and groups within the organization set out to implement their ideas.

Many times facilitation activities are connected to organizational changes, whether they are painful changes, such as restructuring following a downsizing, or processes essential to examine changes necessary to facilitate growth in the organization or marketplace. "Trust among organizational members increases the likelihood of successful change" (Shaw, 1997, p. 3). Facilitation processes related to organizational change must comprehend the important dynamics of trust if they are to have a chance of succeeding. Without attention to this facet of change, much is at risk relative to the ultimate outcomes of the change initiatives and the levels of commitment and participation that can be achieved among the members of the organization.

Sometimes specific efforts must be facilitated to help groups overcome difficulties from their pasts and to create solid working relationships that will enable the implementation of their ideas and plans. This ongoing and enduring trust will be essential to:

- Enhance organizational performance by implementing changes and improvements

- Break down silos between organizational groups that may have been holding back progress

- Improve the total effort toward accomplishing their mission rather than sub-optimizing with improvements at the individual team level

- Communicate the needs clearly

- Evaluate the performance, recognizing the mistakes and learning from them
- Manage conflict effectively
- Engage the teams that will be working to plan and implement the changes

MEASURING TRUST

In some settings, as illustrated in Exhibit 6.1, we have measured change in the level of trust with survey instruments. Most often this was done in the context of measuring outcomes from facilitated learning and development processes, such as experiential team-building programs. The data displayed in the exhibit are an example. They reflect the perceptions of changes in team dynamics by approximately four thousand employees of a major electronics company located in Texas. The data were collected sixty to ninety days following the experiential team development processes for each team. Trust was the second most improved aspect of team dynamics.

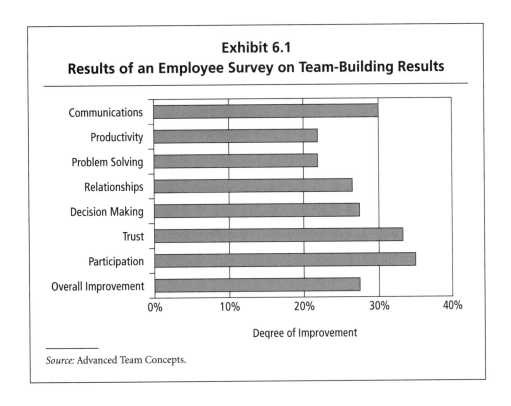

Exhibit 6.1
Results of an Employee Survey on Team-Building Results

Source: Advanced Team Concepts.

Attitude surveys are administered in some organizations on an annual basis. In South America, it is very common for well-known and successful organizations to survey their employees annually to measure and evaluate how they perceive and value the organizational culture. One of the key factors that is monitored with these surveys is trust among the members of the organization, the level of trust that the employees have toward the leadership, and trust in the future of the company. These are examples of another type of history that may tell the facilitator how the people of the organization perceive trust levels within the enterprise.

More often than not, the greatest evidence of trust, lack of trust, or mistrust will be anecdotal: stories and experiences communicated to the facilitator while preparing for or delivering the facilitated programs. A critical skill for facilitators is the ability to ask questions that invite the stories and experience through which he or she can encounter and recognize important symptoms of key issues in a group. A single question usually is not sufficient to get to core problem areas such as mistrust. The facilitator must develop the skill to press for examples that will illuminate the areas that need attention. That skill must be combined with great listening and observation skills to discern what might not be said, interpret the stories, and develop a good sense of a group's health in areas such as trust.

KEYS TO UNDERSTANDING THE LEVEL OF TRUST IN AN ORGANIZATION

It is important to be on the lookout for behaviors and practices that are indicators of the level of trust that exists within an organization. Examination of the following areas can be useful in preparing for facilitation processes:

- Does the organization's top management empower employees or tend to micromanage?

- How open is communication? Are people informed?

- Are there honesty and congruency with the core values of the organization? Do behaviors reflect those values?

- Does leadership create spaces where people can participate and make decisions? Is leadership supportive, so that employees can implement those decisions?

- Are roles designed where people have the space to be creative and participate?

In addition, levels of empowerment and delegation at all levels can be a significant indicator of the levels of trust that prevail in a group or organization.

TRUST AND EMPOWERMENT

A useful way to view the relationships and dynamics we have outlined is with an eye to levels of empowerment, that is, vesting people with the responsibility to take actions to make the organization succeed. It is a major enabler in the interactions among individuals and groups. Is the facilitator empowered to use his or her expertise to help? Is the group empowered to create ideas and opportunities?

An important caution must be noted here. Empowerment and empowering styles of leadership should develop over time. There is no magic formula to have empowered people instantly. It is important for leaders to apply the proper measures of both direction and support that are appropriate based on the maturity of the group, as well as the levels of confidence and trust. Leaders should not abdicate their responsibilities in the name of empowerment. Instead, they should commit to facilitate the development processes that will lead to greater levels of empowerment and trust.

Are the people and groups in the organization empowered to take the actions necessary to succeed? Empowerment means trusting people to take the actions that will help serve the enterprise and make the business successful. The process of increasing empowerment, whether to an individual or a team, occurs over time. It is not an instantaneous change. The change involves two parties: the person or team receiving increased empowerment and responsibility and the party giving up some responsibility or authority. At the heart of this giving and receiving of empowerment is trust. It requires trust on the part of the one doing the empowering and trustworthiness on the part of those receiving the increased scope of work and responsibility. It requires both time and experience for this trust to evolve.

The scope and freedom in each of these areas of interaction may be increased in small ways at first. When these are handled successfully, an increasing level of action and authority may be enabled. It is important for both parties to understand the dynamics of building trust, so that they will know what is at stake in their activities as empowerment is increased. Knowledge of this will accelerate the process, because everyone will be expecting an outcome that moves the process forward.

COVEY'S EMOTIONAL BANK ACCOUNT

Stephen Covey, in his famous book, *The Seven Habits of Highly Effective People* (1989), refers to an emotional bank account that we all have with each other. Our actions toward each other make either deposits to or withdrawals from these accounts. Covey states that if we make deposits through courtesy, kindness, honesty, and keeping commitments, trust levels increase. The opposite effect occurs if we are not courteous or are disrespectful or dishonest. When this is how we treat people, these emotional withdrawals reduce or eliminate levels of trust.

Some organizations find tremendous value in Covey's metaphor of the emotional bank account, so much so that they develop experiential techniques to bring this principle to life in their classes and facilitated events. We recently developed a curriculum for the graduate-level leadership education program of World Vision and Habitat for Humanity. World Vision's leadership programs has created this giving and taking from the "emotional bank" in forms of actual feedback between students during the residency portions of the education. The students get real-time feedback on how their personal behaviors are being perceived and how they are affecting trust and confidence in the group.

Important lessons can be woven into the processing that accompanies many types of experiential exercises. Experiential exercises create a safe arena for the group to hold a discussion about trust and confidence and the related consequences. The focus is on what just occurred in the activity, but the lessons stick because they pertain to the group's real mission.

TECHNIQUES FOR BUILDING TRUST

Trust cannot be taught. It is not a skill that can be acquired intellectually. You cannot gather team members into a classroom one day and say, "Folks, today we are going to learn to trust each other." It simply does not work that way.

Trust develops over time and is based on our experiences with each other. It takes time, but this important topic should not be left to chance. There is too much at stake not to try to create relationships that are strong and based on trust. If trust is absent, the result will likely not be neutral; it will probably be negative.

Eliciting Stories and Experiences from the Group or Organization

There is much power in the stories and experiences within a group. These reveal the important history that has resulted in the current levels of trust, whether they are good or bad. A great place to look for the stories, history, and examples is in the preconsultation, before facilitated events. When interviewing individuals one-on-one, the facilitator can invite stories rich in history that will reveal the issues that affect organizational trust.

In the setting of group events, the facilitator must use caution when inviting stories and examples that reveal the organizational baggage that has damaged the level of trust in the group. The facilitator must be skilled at guiding groups from what can be painful past examples to planning for more positive behaviors and activities that will repair damage and restore trust. Depending on the culture of the group, this can be a real challenge. There are countries and regions where people have very strong feelings related to the past and tend to see only the negative things. They have sometimes lost hope of beneficial change and will not believe very easily that they can participate in building a different process or structure. Then, a good process to rebuild those levels of trust will be needed.

Appreciative Inquiry

We often take an "appreciative" approach to examining the history of the group. Appreciative inquiry (AI) is a powerful facilitation process for examining the history and stories of an organization. It has a very positive focus. The purpose of the tool is to facilitate the identification, recognition, and appreciation of the positive influences and experiences of a group in order to develop propositions and plans to use those elements for greater organizational success in the future. (See Chapter Thirty-Three.)

The keys to AI are the facilitative techniques that help the group identify the behaviors and actions that in the past resulted in major positive outcomes and success, for example, superior levels of trust and confidence. The AI process then facilitates the discovery of the key enablers within those shared stories and experiences. This is followed by specific facilitation steps that promote the group to develop provocative propositions that can enable similar successes in their current and future work.

It is a powerful technique to illuminate the possible actions that can be taken to move the group in a positive direction. As with many other facilitation processes, ultimate success can depend on follow-up and follow-through so that the great ideas—those "provocative propositions" created by the group—are implemented and brought to life by the organization or team.

Experiential Learning

A good way to engage and involve people about the processes of building trust, through demonstration of trustworthiness, is by using experiential facilitation and learning processes.

With experiential learning processes, people experience firsthand the impact of trust. They experience that trust is essential to accomplishing training activities successfully. The impact and importance are usually quite vivid. The experience in the activity provides a safe and comfortable platform for discussing the issues related to trust in the workplace. Facilitators can often weave powerful learning activities into the sessions with their client groups, provoking important thought and consideration about individual and group actions critical to building trust.

Experiential learning processes can accelerate the development of trust. It is the most powerful way to educate and stimulate the building of trust, first within individual team members and then within the team. We examine two types of experiential activities.

Outdoor and Adventure Training and Ropes Courses   These types of experiences are employed by many facilitators in their work to improve levels of trust, cooperation, and teamwork within organizations. Many excellent experiential learning activities exist that can help groups experience the issues related to trust. (for example, see Meeker, Fischer, and Michalak, 1994).

Often the issues related to trust emerge from the discussions that take place after the activities, in the context of how the group makes decisions, solves problems, and executes programs, for example. The ability of these types of experiential activities to lead to improved levels of trust is a function of facilitators' skills in helping the group relate the experience of the activity to the real work setting and issues that the group contends with on a day-to-day basis. If this is facilitated well, the group understanding of trust and their commitment to behaviors important to building trust can be significant. Without facilitation focused on the group's actual work challenges, this type of event can simply be a fun (or not-so-fun) exercise.

Classroom-Based Experiential Activities   These are a powerful alternative to the outdoor team building and ropes courses. They often are quite simple and can be woven into the design of many types of facilitated events and programs. Vision planning, strategic planning, mission development, problem solving, and many more types of facilitated sessions can often be greatly enhanced by adding some experiential activities to the session. For example, a problem-solving exercise can be used to facilitate the recognition of key principles that a group needs to apply in solving their immediate issues and challenges. Important lessons related to trust, confidence, honest communication, and cooperation can be revealed to the group members using the activity as the vehicle of discover. The key to success is the facilitation that helps the group associate what happened in the exercise to what needs to happen in their real work. That is the heart and soul of experiential learning.

THE BOTTOM LINE

High levels of trust within any group are a clear advantage. There is a lot to be gained by investing in facilitation processes to help individuals and groups understand and build their levels of trust. It is the key to effective relationships that will result in effective teamwork that works toward the objectives of the organization.

Many organizations recognize the importance of building commitments. It is common to hear talk of "creating ownership," "increasing empowerment," and "raising empowerment," for example. This has a positive impact on a company's bottom line. High levels of trust with your customers can improve loyalty, resulting in more business. Strong levels of trust with your employees increases motivation and your ability to retain the talent in your organization.

In the profession of facilitation, from the beginning steps of creating a good relationship with a potential client to the implementation and follow-up of facilitation programs, building trust is the great enabler.

Facilitation of Group Brainstorming

Paul B. Paulus
Toshihiko Nakui

Most meetings or group interactions involve an exchange of ideas among two or more individuals in order to develop some solutions to a problem or make a decision. It seems a reasonable presumption that an effective interaction would involve a full exchange of the relevant information or ideas so that the parties involved could make their best decisions or develop their most creative solutions. Although there may be some groups or pairs of individuals who develop very productive creative exchange relationships (John-Steiner, 2000; Sutton and Hargadon, 1996), much evidence suggests that groups often have a difficult time reaching their creative potential (Paulus and Nijstad, 2003; Taylor, Berry, and Block, 1958). There has been an explosion of interest in the past fifteen years in ways to overcome the various factors that hinder group functioning in information exchange processes. We summarize the basic factors that hinder effective group functioning and empirically based means of overcoming them (see Brown and Paulus, 2002; Paulus and Brown, 2003, for detailed reviews).

103

FACTORS THAT HINDER EFFECTIVE GROUP FUNCTIONING
Social Loafing

Whenever groups gather to perform a task or make a decision, there is an tendency for individuals to have a lower of level of task motivation in comparison to situations in which people are individually responsible for their tasks and decisions. This tendency toward social loafing or free riding leads to low levels of productivity (Karau and Williams, 1993) or poor decisions (Lerner and Tetlock, 1999). To counteract this motivation loss problem, it is important to increase the accountability of individual group members for group performance (for example, to make sure that each person's contribution is identifiable) or ensure that the task has a high level of intrinsic interest to all members of the group.

Common Information Bias

Group members typically differ in their expertise on particular topics. They are likely to overlap in some domains of knowledge but have no overlap in others. So it is important for group members to fully share relevant knowledge in order to make the best decisions. Unfortunately, groups are more likely to share and repeat information or knowledge that is common rather than unique (Stasser and Birchmeier, 2003). This bias appears to be difficult to reverse completely, but clearly defining areas of expertise and using procedures that increase effective information sharing (such as nominal group technique or computer-based communication support systems) can reduce the effect.

Groupthink

Group members have a tendency toward conformity or consensus. That is, there is often a premium on reaching a quick agreement and the avoidance of conflict. This has resulted in some rather famous examples of groupthink (Janis, 1982)—the tendency of groups to come to a premature consensus without a full exchange of information or perspectives. Groupthink may be a problem in everyday group decision making as well (Paulus, 1998). It has been demonstrated that conflict in groups helps them develop more creative solutions (Nemeth and Nemeth-Brown, 2003). Effective group decision making may be aided by the use of a facilitator who effectively manages the conflict and leads the group in effective decision-making strategies such as exposure to outside perspectives, the use of subgroups, and second-chance meetings to reexamine decisions (Janis and Mann, 1977).

Production Loss

Many group meetings may involve some degree of brainstorming. That is, there may be period of creative idea exchange without regard to evaluation of those ideas. The aim is to generate a lot of ideas for later evaluation by saying all ideas that come to mind and building on the ideas of others. This approach was apparently used by Walt Disney and championed by Osborn in various books (Osborn, 1957). The general presumption was that group brainstorming was an excellent way of increasing the production of creative ideas. However, research has demonstrated that for face-to-face brainstorming groups, this is not the case. These groups generate fewer ideas than comparable sets of individual brainstormers. The larger the group, the greater is the production loss relative to comparable numbers of individual brainstormers (Diehl and Stroebe, 1987). The production loss of interactive groups seems to be due in part to a broad range of factors, such as concern about group evaluation, competition of time for idea expression, negative influence of low performers, and cognitive interference (Paulus and others, 2002).

FACTORS THAT IMPROVE EFFECTIVE GROUP FUNCTIONING

Our research has focused on ways of overcoming the production losses that brainstorming groups experience. We believe these techniques will be useful for all idea exchange sessions, whether or not they use a brainstorming approach. In addition, they address some of the other hindering factors we have discussed.

A number of approaches can be used to enhance the performance of various groups. Certain group compositions may be more optimal than others for specific tasks. Group performance may also be improved by using motivational or cognitive stimulation strategies. The way the group interaction process or the task approach is structured may also be important. Specific facilitator behaviors may be useful in promoting effective ideation and decision making. We highlight each of these alternatives.

Group Composition

It is not very profound to suggest that not all groups will function equally well. A key issue, of course, is to match a group with its appropriate task. This requires knowing something about the task, the task-relevant characteristics of potential group members, and how these influence task performance. Although there has been some progress in this area, much remains to be learned. We do know that the ability of group members is an important predictor of group performance (Devine and Philips, 2001). For example, in brainstorming tasks, intellectual skill or orientation as measured by grade point average or openness to experience is related to higher levels of idea generation. However, social and personal characteristics are also important. Groups composed of individuals low in social interaction anxiety tend to perform well in group ideation sessions apparently because of low levels of concern about social evaluation (Camacho and Paulus, 1995). Individuals who are highly agreeable also tend to perform well in group settings (Bouchard, 1969), although this characteristic may also enhance the tendency toward groupthink. The ideal person in a group is one who is comfortable with honest exchange and feedback in group settings and can maintain positive group interactions while engaged in intellectual conflicts with other group members. So far, no one has investigated groups whose members have this composite of characteristics to see if these indeed would be "supergroups." Also, it is not clear whether unselected groups can be trained to function in such a way.

With the current emphasis on the importance of teamwork in business and industry, corporations are trying to select individuals who will function well in teams and spend considerable time training individuals for effective teamwork. The success of these strategies remains to be demonstrated convincingly (Bradley, White, and Mennecke, 2003). One implication of the research cited is that one should compose groups that are similar in their group-relevant characteristics (for example, agreeable, low anxious, open to experience). This certainly makes sense for group tasks that require much open exchange of information or ideas. Yet it may also be important to have group members who complement each other in the critical skills needed for effective functioning and performance in problem-solving groups. A group in which all members are highly extraverted and want to dominate the discussion may be counterproductive (Berry and Stewart, 1997). It may be best to have a group that is composed of people who take on somewhat different roles. For example, in a group concerned with innovation, one person may play the role of encouraging all group members to contribute. Another may have a high level of cognitive ability and dominate the idea-sharing process. Another member may be more reflective and challenge the group's premature consensus toward some alternatives. A fourth person may have the ability to integrate the shared ideas into an organized and coherent product.

It is also important for group members to have diverse areas of expertise relevant to a particular problem in order to develop novel and effective solutions. Although there is some evidence for this presumption, much evidence suggests that groups that are diverse in terms of expertise and background may have difficulty working together effectively in part because of different biases and the difficulty of appreciating or understanding conflicting perspectives (Milliken, Bartel, and Kurtzberg, 2003). A similar problem exists for demographic diversity. There is increasing emphasis on the importance of this type of diversity in the workplace. Yet diverse groups tend to be characterized by negative emotional reactions and difficulties working together effectively. This may be primarily because of lack of familiarity with those "different others." Increased experience in diverse groups may overcome these types of problems (Watson, Kumar, and Michaelson, 1993), at least if the interactions are in a positive context and are reasonably successful (Milliken, Bartel, and Kurtzberg, 2003). It is interesting in that light that gender composition of brainstorming groups has little impact, possibly in part due to the increased levels of interaction of both sexes in all different domains of life (a reduction in traditional gender roles). However, since almost all published brainstorming research has been done in Europe and the United States, the generality of this result (and other potentially culturally based findings) remains to be determined.

What are the implications of these findings for facilitator practice? In most cases, facilitators will have little control over group composition or little prior information about group-relevant personal characteristics. So they will need to be sensitive to the potential benefits and drawbacks of group composition. In concert with group or organizational goals, groups may be composed for certain aims. Selection of group members for specific tasks may make it easier for groups to function effectively. For example, agreeable people may be selected for consensus tasks, those high in openness to experience for creativity tasks, and diverse groups for tasks requiring diverse task and interpersonal skills.

Motivation

One the main problems of groups is a low level of motivation. Therefore, it is important for facilitators to be able to help group members motivate themselves to high levels of performance and set high goals. Groups tend to set low standards for success (Larey and Paulus, 1995) and tend to have the illusion that they are performing well when they are actually underperforming (Paulus, Larey, and Ortega,

1995). However, providing periodic feedback about individual and group performance appears to motivate higher levels of group ideation (Paulus and others, 1996). Knowledge that one is individually accountable seems to limit the tendency to loaf. Competition with other groups can also motivate high levels of performance, especially if there is a strong level of group identification (Coskun, 2000). It helps if the group task is a highly involving one in which the group members have a strong interest. Most laboratory studies have involved assigned tasks. Allowing groups some choice in their task and the task process (self-management) may motivate them to perform at a higher level.

Cognitive Stimulation

Much of the work done by groups today is knowledge work. It involves the exchange of knowledge and the development of new knowledge or innovations. The basis for new knowledge development is the cognitive stimulation process that is associated with knowledge exchange. Exposure to the ideas of others can stimulate new ideas or lead to novel combinations of ideas. However, exchanging ideas with others can also be distracting. The interaction process may hinder the ability of individuals to experience their own cognitive flow of ideas since others repeatedly interrupt them. Individuals may tune out during the exchange process while they focus on mentally constructing or preparing their own contributions. Ideas from others may also lead individuals to limit their thinking and creative processes to the initial domains or perspectives that are shared. Therefore, they may not fully tap their own relevant knowledge or that of the other group members. The daunting task of facilitators is to develop a group interaction pattern that optimizes the stimulation aspect and minimizes the distraction aspect. There are two general approaches that have been successful: changing the form of the interaction and changing the structure of the interaction.

Form of Interaction   The most natural way for groups to interact is face-to-face. This may have evolutionary significance since this is the type of interaction we have experienced since the origin of our species. With the advent of computers, virtual groups are now feasible. Recent developments in group decision support systems now enable group members to exchange ideas with one another and make decisions on computer networks. The advantage of such exchange systems is that individuals can exchange ideas as they occur and access ideas from others whenever they choose, so there is not the inevitable competition for time or distraction. Research has found that computer-based groups do not suffer the same production loss as face-to-face groups (Dennis and Williams, 2003). However, there is also no special motivation to attend to the ideas of others under those circumstances. Unless group members are motivated to attend to these ideas, they may show little benefit of the group interaction. Facilitators need to develop procedures that ensure that group members do process the exchanged ideas at some time in the session. We have done this by instructing participants that we would test their memory for exchanged ideas (Dugosh, Paulus, Roland, and Yang, 2000). However, other strategies may also be useful, such as asking participants to note ideas from others that they think are particularly useful for later discussion.

It is not necessary to use computer networks to facilitate idea exchange. Similar benefits can be obtained by precomputer-era techniques for strengthening individual efforts such as the nominal group technique, in which group members work individually during certain stages (Delbecq, Van de Ven, and Gustafson, 1986), and brainwriting, in which individuals exchange ideas on pieces of paper (Geschka, Schaude, and Schlicksupp, 1973; Paulus and Yang, 2000; Siegel, 1996). (For additional examples, see Van Gundy, 1988.) It may also be useful to use multiple modalities for interaction. Some preliminary interaction by means of computer or writing may make a subsequent face-to-face interaction session more productive.

Structure of the Interaction   Formal or informal brainstorming in organizations is typically done with groups, even though individual brainstorming may be more effective. It is true that individuals enjoy group interaction and may find individual brainstorming a bit awkward. This may be in part a cultural bias based on the expectations that brainstorming should be a group activity. It turns out that the most effective strategy may be a combination of group and individual brainstorming. It might be useful to have individuals generate ideas individually (possibly by writing ideas on a piece of paper) prior to sharing those ideas with the group to allow each individual to have a pool of highly available ideas to share in the group process. However, there may be a tendency to focus on these prior ideas rather than becoming fully engrossed in the idea flow of the group (so it might be best if the prior ideas were not written down).

Another option is to have individuals continue to brainstorm individually after group interaction. The group interaction may generate a lot of associations that do not have an opportunity to develop fully during the group interaction. A subsequent "incubation session" in which individuals reflect individually on the exchanged ideas and relate them to their own knowledge structure may allow the generation of a considerable number of additional ideas (Paulus and Yang, 2000). In our experience, such sessions are relatively rare in structured group sessions. Group information exchange sessions are typically followed by decision-making sessions or movement to unrelated activities (for example, going back to one's regular work activities). Unfortunately, much of the intellectual gain of the interaction process may be lost by switching prematurely to such other activities. It should be noted that research on the nominal group technique has typically used an individual writing procedure followed by an exchange of the written ideas without comment and then a subsequent discussion (Van Gundy, 1988). However, this process is different from our suggestion of continued brainstorming with a variation of individual and group approaches. Unfortunately, evidence is mixed as to the differential benefits of various orders of individual and group brainstorming (Paulus, Larey, and Ortega, 1995).

Task Structure

Most brainstorming experiences are generally structured in the following manner. Group members typically focus on a general problem, discuss it until they feel they have depleted their ideas, and then try to come to a decision about the best alternatives. Although this seems a natural approach, minor changes in this procedure can greatly enhance the number of ideas generated.

Focusing on a broad issue or problem may sometimes be overwhelming. There are many different aspects to the problem to be considered and it is difficult to know how to allocate time effectively. We have found that one useful strategy is to decompose a problem into its basic subelements and have the group consider each element in turn (Coskun, Paulus, Brown, and Sherwood, 2000). This allows the group to focus its intellectual energies on each aspect of the problem in isolation. This technique is more likely to lead to a full tapping of the relevant group knowledge for each of these subareas. Also, it may allow group members to more clearly see connections among the different subelements (Brown and Paulus, 2002).

Another tendency of groups is to slow their idea generation process over the course of their allotted time. This slowing process appears to be used as a cue that they are reaching the bottom of their pool of ideas. However, we have found that simply giving the group a short break and then instructing them to continue the task often leads them to generate a large number of additional ideas. Brief breaks in the ideation process may also help dissipate the cognitive inhibition or overload that group members may experience during the exchange process (Smith, 2003).

Another strategy for counteracting a reduction in ideation during the group process is to prime the group with key ideas or categories. This is often a strategy that facilitators use (Osborn, 1957). We have found that exposure to experimenter-presented ideas during the brainstorming process increases the number of ideas generated during both the exposure process and a subsequent session in which individuals continue to brainstorm without external priming. In a sense, the cognitive potential of groups should be very high as long as we keep priming them with relevant ideas or categories of ideas. This is especially true for groups that consist of experts in diverse fields relevant to the problem.

Active Facilitators

Each of the previous sections suggests strategies that facilitators can use to optimize the potential of their creative groups. We believe that each of these strategies can be quite useful. In addition, facilitators may want to intervene in the group process to make sure that the groups are following the best practices or rules for group interaction. They may intervene if groups are becoming prematurely critical or to encourage low contributors to increase their participation.

Several studies have examined the utility of such facilitator interventions and have found that they can improve group brainstorming (Kramer, Fleming, and Mannis, 2001; Offner, Kramer, and Winter, 1996; Oxley, Dzindolet, and Paulus, 1996), especially if the facilitators have considerable group experience. However, we have found that to some extent, groups can become self-facilitating. If brainstorming groups are trained to follow rules of effective group interaction, they can greatly increase the number of ideas generated. In our studies, these rules included the typical brainstorming rules of not criticizing, focusing on quantity, saying all ideas that come to mind, and building on the ideas of others. In addition, groups were trained to avoid discussing irrelevant issues, present ideas in an efficient manner (without unneeded elaboration or stories), encourage others to participate, and go back to old categories of ideas during lulls in the brainstorming session. We have found that groups can effectively use these additional rules of effective brainstorming without the active participation of a facilitator (Paulus, Nakui, and Putman, forthcoming).

Facilitation of Group Decision Making

Although it may be fun to generate a lot of ideas, the basic goal of most brainstorming sessions is to come up with some subset of useful solutions or strategies. This involves some type of evaluation and selection process. This selection process can be done by outsiders, as when employees brainstorm new ideas that are then passed on to management for further evaluation and possible selection of some of the ideas for implementation. Sometimes the same group that brainstorms is involved in the subsequent selection and evaluation process.

We are just beginning to understand the connection between the ideation and decision phase of creative group interaction. It is quite possible that groups that generate ideas may not be good at selecting the best ideas since they may have personal and social biases that could influence those decisions. Objective outsiders might be able to evaluate the ideas based on their merits more effectively. However, in some high-level groups, such as scientific or industrial groups, only the group members have the expertise to evaluate the generated alternatives. Also, it is possible that some people are better at ideation and others at evaluation. Facilitators need to be aware of all of these possibilities. One useful strategy would be to have the ideas evaluated by both the group that generated them and an outside group. It is important to train evaluators in an effective selection process. It is of little benefit to have a highly trained brainstorming group's output evaluated by a group that is not trained to make effective decisions.

THEORY VERSUS PRACTICE

The various recommendations we have made are based on empirical data from controlled studies and are consistent with the social and cognitive information processing model (Paulus and others, 2002). How well do these fit with practices of those who actually do brainstorming sessions with organizations? We have not found a comprehensive summary of typical practices. A casual survey of articles by facilitators about brainstorming suggests than many use some of the suggested procedures (Paulus, Nakui, and Putman, forthcoming). We have found none that appear to have a broad theoretical grounding for their work or base their work on the empirical literature. For example, one common suggestion is that multisensory experiences will enhance group creativity. Yet we know of no empirical evidence for this. Another common suggestion is that making the creative experience fun will enhance creativity. There is some evidence that positive moods can enhance creativity (Grawitch, Munz, and Kramer, 2003), but there is no evidence that such moods have an impact on group processes. Obviously, what is needed is a careful assessment of the benefit of the procedures suggested by empirical research and practicing facilitators in a variety of real-world settings.

Our review and analysis of the brainstorming literature suggests the following best practices:

Ten Best Practices for Group Brainstorming

1. If possible, select group members who are suited for the brainstorming task. This selection can be based on the factors we have highlighted but can also be based on facilitator experiences with these individuals in group situations. A similar approach might be used to select group members for the decision process.

2. Selecting diverse group members can enhance creativity but also create problems for interaction. Facilitators should train group members in skills required to function effectively in diverse groups, such as conflict management and empathy. Diverse groups are more likely to reach their potential if they have considerable experience working with one another.

3. Group members who believe that their contributions really matter and are intrinsically interested in the problem are likely to perform at higher levels. Facilitators should emphasize the contextual and task-related features that provide both extrinsic and intrinsic motivation for the task.

4. Cognitive stimulation in the group can be enhanced by priming the groups with additional ideas or categories of ideas that they have not yet considered. Such ideas can be derived from a survey of experts in a particular idea domain.

5. The use of a variety of interaction modalities may optimize the ability of the group to have a full exchange of ideas. Facilitators should seek opportunities for mixing computer-based, written, and oral exchange of ideas by group members.

6. Effective group brainstorming can be overwhelming in terms of information overload and mental demands. Combining group sessions with individual brainstorming or reflection sessions may be optimum.

7. The group task should be decomposed into its basic elements, and the facilitator should guide the group to deal with each element in turn. After many

ideas have been generated for each of these elements, facilitators may lead groups to consider possible connections among them.

8. Facilitators should intersperse the brainstorming process with brief rest periods or alternative activities. Our research suggests that it is probably best if those activities are in the same general cognitive domain. However, other research suggests that contrasting activities and exposure to nature can be most helpful in overcoming mental fatigue or inhibition.

9. Although facilitators should be active in developing an optimum environment and structure for group brainstorming, it is important for the facilitator not to dominate the interaction. This may distract the creative process and reduce intrinsic motivation.

10. Facilitators should train groups in effective procedures for both brainstorming and decision making so that they can use these skills in other contexts. Research suggests that such training is most effective if all members of such future groups are trained together.

Promoting Mutual Understanding for Effective Collaboration in Cross-Functional Groups with Multiple Stakeholders

Sam Kaner

One of the intriguing aspects of being human is that each of us organizes our experience of life into a unique, personal set of perceptions, categories, assumptions, and meanings. In other words, subjective construction of reality is an inescapable feature of the human condition.

This leads directly to one of the toughest, and deepest, challenges in participatory, collaboration-based decision making: the problem of intersubjectivity. The problem is that everyone who participates in a given discussion interprets it differently. It is hard not to hear what we want to hear or, rather, what we have programmed ourselves to hear. (For more information regarding intersubjectivity, see Rogers and Roethlisberger, 1991.)

In a multiple-stakeholder collaboration, the problem of intersubjectivity has huge significance. Diverse stakeholders often arrive at a given collaboration with very different starting positions. Furthermore, participants are not only stakeholders;

115

they are also human beings. Their individual frames of reference, influenced by their education, culture, gender, age, upbringing, and countless other factors, will inevitably create substantial communication obstacles, over and above the surface-level differences in their stakeholder positions.

As facilitators, how seriously should we take these obstacles? How can we understand the problem constructively and engage with it effectively? These are the questions I address in this chapter.

INTRODUCTION TO CASE STUDY

The following depiction of a multiple-stakeholder collaboration is typical of numerous cases we see at my consulting firm, Community At Work. The central narrative is based on an actual case: a success story of a school-based collaborative that got off to a rocky start but was able to adjust and grow into a broad community-supported coalition. (Today, more than ten years after its inception, the collaborative is still functioning effectively.) All identifying information, including the specifics of the presenting request and the details that portray the individual characters and their conversations, has been disguised to preserve confidentiality, and the narrative flow has been simplified and fictionalized in places to bring key points into focus. Nonetheless, the overall trajectory and character of this depiction remain loyal to the realities of the actual case.

The collaboration began with the formation of a simple committee, convened by the local junior high school to develop a policy on student discipline. The members were two teachers, a parent, the school principal, and an elected member of the school board. Partway through the committee's first meeting, the following interchange took place:

Parent: We need a clearly structured disciplinary system, with severe consequences for misbehavior. Students who get into fights should be suspended immediately.

Teacher: Children misbehave because they have low self-esteem or problems at home. Our disciplinary system should emphasize activities that build self-esteem and prevent misbehavior.

Parent: That's well and good, but safety must come first. Suspend them for fighting. Let the problem students get the message loud and clear. Once they learn to play by the rules, then we can think about their self-esteem.

Teacher: Suspension is often not the answer. These kids are facing some really challenging situations at home and on the streets. Forcing them out of school will only aggravate their problems.

Parent: I'm more concerned about protecting children who don't have problems.

Teacher: But teachers are paid to be responsive to the needs of our entire community.

This interchange was typical of what happened at the meeting, and participants went home feeling frustrated and stuck. They could not figure out why they had not been able to make better progress. After all, everyone had acted in good faith, and they sincerely wanted to produce a policy that worked for everyone. "That's why we created the committee in the first place," said one of the teachers.

Despite their good intentions, they did not have a grasp on the fundamentals of effective collaboration. In the snippet of conversation shown above, both the parent and the teacher stood up for their own ideas, but neither of them made any effort to understand the other's reasoning. They behaved as if they were in a debating competition.

Effective Collaboration

Here's what the participants did not understand: that solutions that work for everyone are solutions that have incorporated everyone's point of view. Effective collaboration means thinking together. And that means being able to think not only from one's own point of view but also from another person's different point of view. That's how common ground is discovered.

Effective collaboration, in other words, means thinking within a framework of mutual understanding. And mutual understanding, in this sense, means more than merely understanding what someone says in words out loud; it also means taking the time to understand what that person means, wants, and needs. In other words, it means understanding someone's perspective well enough to be able to think from that person's point of view, with or without affinity for that perspective.

To the junior high school committee, all of this was invisible. The committee members had no training to understand the structure of an inclusive win/win solution, and they had no awareness that this type of solution emerges from a group's ability to incorporate one another's perspectives. As one member put it, they were "just trying to set a policy that everybody could sign onto."

Membership of the Committee

It is easy to see how this group could become stuck (see Exhibit 8.1). Indeed, it is hard to imagine how this group would *not* become stuck.

Exhibit 8.1
Student Discipline Committee

PARENT
"Troublemakers should be sent home at once."

TEACHER 2
"Problem children need support, not punishment."

TEACHER 1
"The problem is in the home life. I was trained to teach, not be a counselor, a nurse, and a police officer! Parents need to discipline their own children."

PRINCIPAL
"Teachers need to deal with discipline in their classrooms, not send every minor offender to the office."

SCHOOL BOARD MEMBER
"What's wrong with the way we used to handle discipline when I was a kid? Everyone knew the rules: you got your knuckles rapped on your first offense, and spanked on the second. It worked just fine!"

Adapted from Kaner, Lind, Toldi, Fisk, and Berger, 1996.

And then what? Well, they could continue debating and miscommunicating until they finally exhausted the goodwill of the group.

And then? They could just stop coming to meetings, and eventually disband without reaching an agreement. Or they could agree to set up an altogether different committee ("because the issue needs further study.") Or they could hand the problem back to the school principal, as in, "You're in charge, so *you* deal with it." Or they could come up with a watered-down, lowest-common-denominator compromise.

The Pseudo-Solution

Sure enough, the committee's deliberations followed one of the predictable pathways. After four meetings of going around in circles, they nominated the school board member and teacher 2 to form a subcommittee and draft a proposal. Their charge was to come up with a plan that met two objectives: (1) it would cover everyone's concerns, and (2) it would be acceptable to all parties. Exhibit 8.2 shows what they came back with.

Exhibit 8.2
The Pseudo-Solution

Policies for Improving Discipline at Lincoln Junior High School

- Extreme student misbehavior will not be tolerated at this school.

- A quarterly newsletter, stressing the importance of discipline at home, shall be mailed to parents.

- Every teacher and administrator will be expected to read two books or articles on positive methods of child discipline during the next year.

- Teachers shall try harder to handle student misbehavior within their classrooms.

Adapted from Kaner, Lind, Toldi, Fisk, and Berger, 1996.

At Community At Work, we call this type of outcome a pseudo-solution: innocuous, noncontroversial, and entirely ineffectual. Yet when it was submitted to the other participants for their endorsement, it was almost adopted. The parent and the school principal made it known that they were willing to approve it. It was blocked only because one of the teachers held out, insisting that this proposal, if implemented, would have no effect on student discipline and would be regarded by the faculty with cynicism and scorn. The school principal then realized that the proposal had the potential to lower teacher morale and undermine the school's credibility with the broader community. After a few more rounds of discussion, the group decided to hire a professional facilitator. Thus, a Community At Work facilitator became engaged in this case.

Enter the Facilitator

The facilitator began her work by interviewing each person separately. She did this for two equally important reasons: so she could spend quality time with each of them as individuals in order to begin building positive relationships with them and so she could begin to learn about each person's subjective reality as it influenced his or her thinking about student discipline. In this regard, she was interested not only in their stakeholder positions but also anything else—background, core values, assumptions—that might be meaningfully related to the task at hand, in the mind of the person being interviewed.

Exhibit 8.3 shows a small sample of what she learned from the interviews regarding the participants' frames of reference.

As the exhibit makes clear, each participant's opinions on student discipline were shaped by his or her own life experience. This provides a perfect illustration of the classic problem of intersubjectivity. The problem is that everyone who participates in a given discussion interprets it quite differently. If those participants do not know each other well (and often, even when they *do* know each other well) their discussions will be laced with misinterpretations and misunderstandings—sometimes explicit and sometimes unnoticed.

The challenge for the student discipline policy-setting group, as for any other multistakeholder group that comes face to face with the problem of intersubjectivity, was this: What will it take for group members to transcend their individual frames of reference and build a shared framework of understanding.

DYNAMICS OF GROUP DECISION MAKING

To prepare the group to move toward effective collaboration based on mutual understanding, the facilitator began by teaching the group about the dynamics of group decision making. She wanted to give participants the ability to communicate objectively about the experiences they were having. This meant teaching them a few simple principles that would provide them with shared points of reference and shared language.

Exhibit 8.3
Frames of Reference

PARENT

- Last month, her son had to get stitches because he got caught in the middle of a playground fight.

- There have been two burglaries recently in her neighborhood.

- She grew up in a small town where they left their houses unlocked day and night.

TEACHER 2

- He has a master's degree in child psychology and has attended intensive summer training seminars about self-esteem-based behavior programs.

- He had a rough home life as a child and often misbehaved at school to get attention.

- He feels alienated from his peers, who often accuse him of taking the kids' side too often. He feels hurt by teachers who hint that he needs kids to like him.

TEACHER 1

- She is nearing retirement and doesn't want to stay up nights changing lesson plans that worked fine for years.

- The principal gave her a bad evaluation last year, and she's afraid she'll be put on a performance review.

PRINCIPAL

- As her budget has been further cut each year, she has had to assume increasing responsibility for jobs that were previously done by resource teachers and an assistant principal.

- She constantly feels under the gun with deadline pressures and feels blamed from all sides. She wants people to help shoulder the responsibilities, but she doesn't know how to get them to help her.

SCHOOL BOARD MEMBER

- He went to grammar school in the 1940's. His teachers were strict disciplinarians.

- He served with distinction in the Korean War. Then he started his own business. He believes strongly in the value of self-reliance.

- He was elected to the school board on a campaign of fiscal responsibility, so he has not paid close attention to academic matters.

Adapted from Kaner, Lind, Toldi, Fisk, and Berger, 1996.

First, she explained the principles of divergent thinking and convergent thinking, and gave them examples of each type of process in action. "When a group is in a divergent phase," she explained, "the members are tossing out their thoughts and beliefs without even trying to understand one another. People are just 'putting it out there.' In a convergent phase, in contrast, people are more naturally focusing, narrowing, simplifying—coming together as they move toward agreement." (See Exhibit 8.4.)

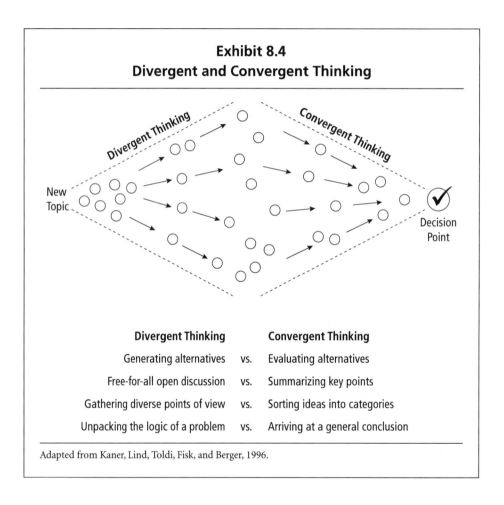

Exhibit 8.4
Divergent and Convergent Thinking

Divergent Thinking		Convergent Thinking
Generating alternatives	vs.	Evaluating alternatives
Free-for-all open discussion	vs.	Summarizing key points
Gathering diverse points of view	vs.	Sorting ideas into categories
Unpacking the logic of a problem	vs.	Arriving at a general conclusion

Adapted from Kaner, Lind, Toldi, Fisk, and Berger, 1996.

Then she introduced the key problem, intersubjectivity (though she never used that term). To her audience of participants, she posed the problem as "the struggle to understand one another, the struggle to integrate each other's points of view."

Thus, the facilitator proceeded to show the group how difficult it is for people in any group to put their own opinions aside while they focus on one another's perspectives. To help group members see this, she led them through a three-step activity. First, she asked them to generate but not discuss some examples from their own interactions with one another. Second, they generated a related list using examples from previous experiences in different groups entirely. Third, they discussed the new thoughts and insights that were now surfacing.

In the ensuing discussion, the facilitator validated the obvious: in the throes of misunderstandings and under time pressure, group members can be impatient, repetitious, insensitive, defensive, short-tempered, or worse. Building mutual understanding is a frustrating process. It can be draining and confusing. Still, it's not a bad thing to go through that struggle; it's perfectly normal. In fact, it's actually a healthy thing—much healthier, indeed, than cranking out an ineffectual pseudo-solution and calling it quits as a group.

At Community At Work, we have given this difficult period of group process a name: the Groan Zone (Kaner, Lind, Toldi, Fisk, and Berger, 1996). The goal of hanging in there and working through the Groan Zone is to achieve a shared framework of understanding, an ability to think from one another's points of view. This capacity to think from the perspectives of other members is essential for developing an inclusive win/win solution.

The entire model, which was developed by several colleagues at Community At Work, is presented in Exhibit 8.5.

When the facilitator explained the dynamics of group decision making to the members of this group, they responded with a huge outpouring of relief. They said things like, "So you mean we're normal?" and "I am so glad there are words to describe what I've been feeling."

Yet despite the fact that their new insights strengthened their determination to persevere, it did not (and could not) prevent them from getting stuck in their own Groan Zones.

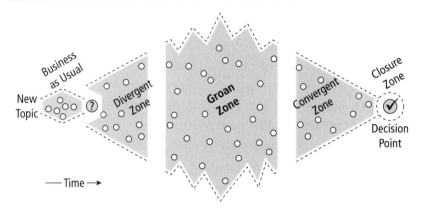

Exhibit 8.5
Diamond of Participatory Decision Making

This is the *Diamond of Participatory Decision Making*. It was developed by Sam Kaner with Lenny Lind, Catherine Toldi, Sarah Fisk, and Duane Berger. Facilitators can use this model in many ways: as a diagnostic tool, a road map, or a teaching tool to provide their groups with *shared language and shared points of reference*. But fundamentally it was created to validate and legitimize the hidden aspects of everyday life in groups.

Most people have trouble communicating in groups, especially when the issues are complex. But how often is this acknowledged? Blaming and complaining are more typical. This is self-defeating. Group dynamics can be awkward, but they are natural and normal nonetheless. Only when this is accepted can people succeed in tapping the enormous power of group decision making. These beliefs are at the very heart of *Community At Work's* philosophy of group facilitation.

Source: The Diamond of Participatory Decision-Making was originally published in S. Kaner, with L. Lind, C. Toldi, S. Fisk, and D. Berger, *Facilitators' Guide to Participatory Decision-Making*, Gabriola Island B.C., Canada: New Society, 1996.

A TYPICAL GROUP DISCUSSION IN THE GROAN ZONE

Exhibit 8.6 is an illustration of "no listening." Each person has spoken, but only superficially on the same topic. When "no listening" occurs, the group has no chance to build a shared framework. People are instead operating from their own points of view, disconnected from one another, driven for the most part by preexisting, fixed positions.

TEACHER 1
"Perhaps your son needs professional help. We are teachers, not psychiatrists."

TEACHER 2
"I'm sorry you had to deal with the break-in. But suspending our students for misbehavior will not change what happened to your son."

PARENT
"Our house was broken into last year–my son still has nightmares."

PRINCIPAL
"Sounds like you want to hold the school responsible for the conditions in your neighborhood."

SCHOOL BOARD MEMBER
"I think we are *all* responsible for the safety of our neighborhoods. It's terrible that your son is still having nightmares. If we spent less tax money on our bloated school bureaucracy, we'd have more to spend on police, and people's homes would be better protected."

Adapted from Kaner, Lind, Toldi, Fisk, and Berger, 1996.

Yet at the same time, these participants were beginning, bit by bit, to reveal their individual contexts. For the facilitator, the challenge was to tease out these personal frames of reference and, by using careful, effective listening skills, help the group members begin to listen better too. A facilitator's skill at listening can have an enormous effect on participants' capacity for transcending their fixed positions.

BUILDING MUTUAL UNDERSTANDING THROUGH
EFFECTIVE LISTENING

Mutual understanding requires taking the time to understand. This means taking time to listen. To ask. To wonder. To draw someone out. To show support and empathize.

All of these activities could conceivably be done by the members themselves, without the aid of a facilitator. Yet so often, it seems as though the facilitator is the only person in the room who is willing and ready to make the attempt to understand.

Why is this so? The obvious answer is that a facilitator is a trained listener who has been authorized to bring those skills to the group. But the question remains: Why *only* the facilitator? Why don't the other members of a group use their own skills and talents to draw each other out and enhance mutual understanding?

Part of the answer resides in one's capacity to tolerate discomfort and stay detached. A facilitator who can tolerate the discomfort of the Groan Zone will be able to keep listening, keep inquiring, keep trying to learn more about what really matters to each participant. Conversely, facilitators who feel uncomfortable and impatient will find themselves pushing their groups, not flowing with them. Under those circumstances, a group may arrive at the Convergent Zone, but the resulting agreements will likely be shaped by compromise and acquiescence, rather than by both/and thinking, in the service of a commitment to find inclusive solutions.

This, of course, does not relieve the facilitator of the duty to transfer the responsibility for effective listening to the group members. The more that participants listen to one another actively rather than through the mediating presence of a facilitator, the more quickly and capably they will grasp each other's views.

In Exhibit 8.7 the behavior of effective listening is being done by the facilitator. This representation was deliberate, and it accurately reflects what was done by the real facilitator in the actual case, during periods when no one else was willing to pay more than superficial attention to the views and feelings of the others.

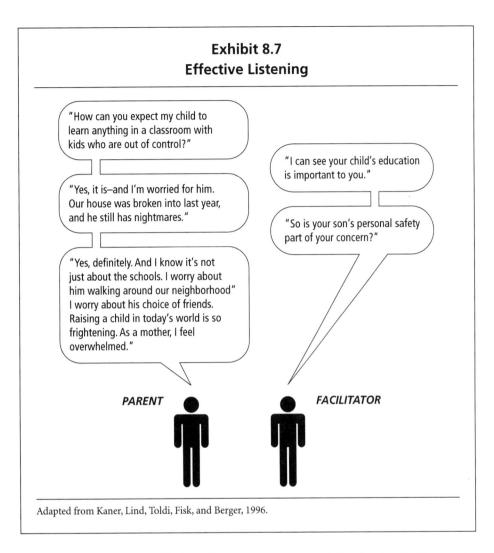

Exhibit 8.7
Effective Listening

"How can you expect my child to learn anything in a classroom with kids who are out of control?"

"Yes, it is—and I'm worried for him. Our house was broken into last year, and he still has nightmares."

"Yes, definitely. And I know it's not just about the schools. I worry about him walking around our neighborhood" I worry about his choice of friends. Raising a child in today's world is so frightening. As a mother, I feel overwhelmed."

"I can see your child's education is important to you."

"So is your son's personal safety part of your concern?"

PARENT   *FACILITATOR*

Adapted from Kaner, Lind, Toldi, Fisk, and Berger, 1996.

Later, as the case unfolded, and with consistent modeling by the facilitator, the group members became increasingly able to listen and therefore to understand and then to collaborate. They broke free of their pattern of making speeches, complaints, and veiled accusations (Exhibit 8.8).

Exhibit 8.8
The Diamond Necklace

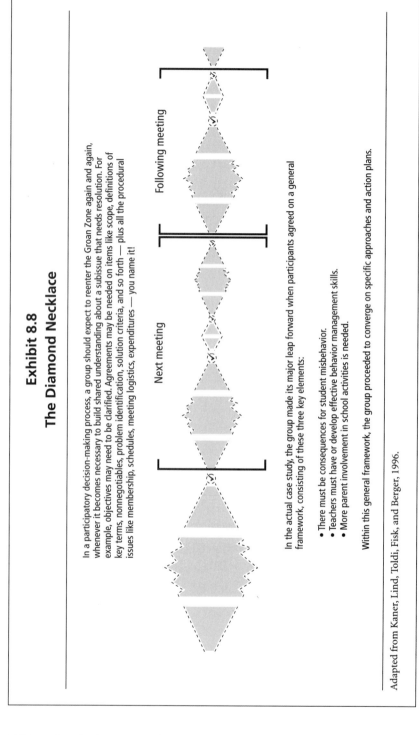

In a participatory decision-making process, a group should expect to reenter the Groan Zone again and again, whenever it becomes necessary to build shared understanding about a subissue that needs resolution. For example, objectives may need to be clarified. Agreements may be needed on items like scope, definitions of key terms, nonnegotiables, problem identification, solution criteria, and so forth — plus all the procedural issues like membership, schedules, meeting logistics, expenditures — you name it!

In the actual case study, the group made its major leap forward when participants agreed on a general framework, consisting of these three key elements:

- There must be consequences for student misbehavior.
- Teachers must have or develop effective behavior management skills.
- More parent involvement in school activities is needed.

Within this general framework, the group proceeded to converge on specific approaches and action plans.

Adapted from Kaner, Lind, Toldi, Fisk, and Berger, 1996.

SUBSEQUENT DEVELOPMENTS

Ten years after the original committee was formed, effective collaboration is still very much alive in this community, with many tangible results to show for the work. The facilitator from Community At Work has remained involved to some degree, but to a large extent the many groups and subgroups of this school-based community have taken matters into their own hands.

The evolution has been gradual. For the first two years, the process unfolded in fits and spurts. With each small success, a new layer of deeper obstacles was revealed, leading to new rounds of misunderstanding and frustration. For example, a new policy regarding student violence was indeed put into place, but the policy-setting discussion introduced a new controversy about classroom management and the competence of certain teachers. Thus, with each forward step, the group found itself once again returned to the Groan Zone.

In order to overcome those recurring dynamics of miscommunication and impatience, the group repeatedly had to slow down and focus on rebuilding mutual understanding. Gradually, by learning from experience with support from their facilitator, the group became better at moving through the Groan Zone and coming out the other side, into a convergence of views. As they gained the ability to recognize the Groan Zone for what it was, they became less resistant, each time a new context arose, to listening nonjudgmentally to one another's biases and interpretations and subjective conclusions. They became better and better, in other words, at thinking from each other's point of view.

A turning point occurred in the third year. What had begun as a discussion of a discipline policy had by then morphed into a much broader analysis of the relationship between school district policies and parent involvement in school governance. An official from the school district then secured funding for a facilitated steering committee mandated to strengthen neighborhood-based collaboration on school-related issues of importance to the entire community.

This model was hugely effective. Over the following two years, the steering committee created several operating procedures that made the collaborative friendlier to parents. More meetings were scheduled to fit the timetables of working parents. Child care during meetings was provided. Bilingual facilitation was introduced and, later, translation equipment was purchased to give those who spoke little English a more meaningful opportunity to participate.

As more time passed, the collaborative continued to evolve, turning its efforts toward a broader community improvement agenda. As of this writing, the

Exhibit 8.9
A Framework for Action

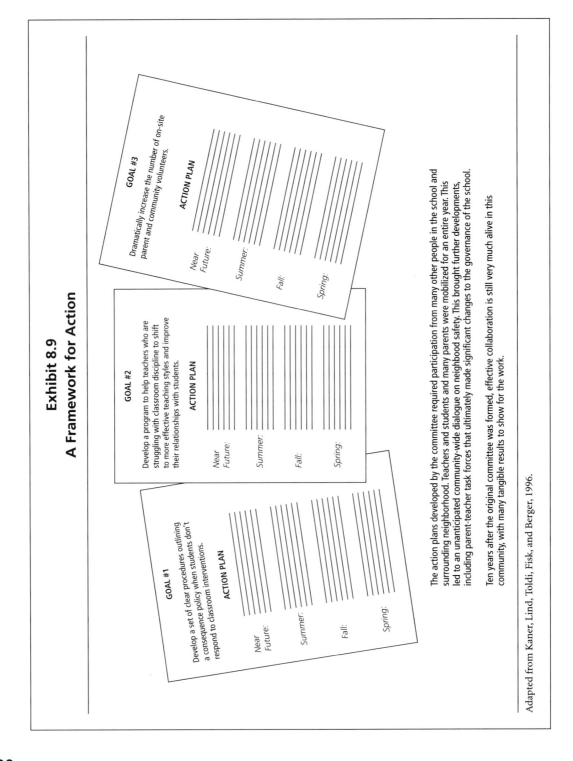

GOAL #3

Dramatically increase the number of on-site parent and community volunteers.

ACTION PLAN

Near Future:

Summer:

Fall:

Spring:

GOAL #2

Develop a program to help teachers who are struggling with classroom discipline to shift to more effective teaching styles and improve their relationships with students.

ACTION PLAN

Near Future:

Summer:

Fall:

Spring:

GOAL #1

Develop a set of clear procedures outlining a consequence policy when students don't respond to classroom interventions.

ACTION PLAN

Near Future:

Summer:

Fall:

Spring:

The action plans developed by the committee required participation from many other people in the school and surrounding neighborhood. Teachers and students and many parents were mobilized for an entire year. This led to an unanticipated community-wide dialogue on neighborhood safety. This brought further developments, including parent-teacher task forces that ultimately made significant changes to the governance of the school.

Ten years after the original committee was formed, effective collaboration is still very much alive in this community, with many tangible results to show for the work.

Adapted from Kaner, Lind, Toldi, Fisk, and Berger, 1996.

collaborative has created, developed, and secured funding for two fully operational community-based organizations that provide health care and other human services to the family members of school-aged youth. What began as a simple issue-focused collaboration has resulted in many sustained improvements, not only at the original school site but also at other schools throughout the district.

INTEGRATION OF THEORY AND PRACTICE

This case provides a classic example of the problem of intersubjectivity and how to relate to it effectively.

As I stated earlier, the problem of intersubjectivity derives from a basic feature of the human condition: that each human being creates his or her own idiosyncratic, subjective construction of reality, grounded in unique personal life experience. Given this fundamental chasm of meaning, what does it take for a roomful of individuals with diverse perspectives to communicate effectively, especially when the issues are complex and the stakes are high?

To answer this question, many contemporary writers and thinkers have focused on the role of the facilitator. After all, a facilitator can treat individual differences seriously and yet still work effectively toward integration of those differences.

The case of the school-based collaborative demonstrates clearly the enormous contribution a facilitator can make. Here are some of the specific actions taken and judgments made by the facilitator in this case:

- Before conducting an actual meeting, she interviewed group members to understand their individual frames of reference. For many consultants, this is a routine step to take when beginning an engagement with a multistakeholder group.

- She was fully committed to using effective listening skills consistently and to fostering a listening attitude in others.

- She understood group dynamics and conveyed her understanding to the participants. She gave them language and shared points of reference to understand and communicate about the process dimensions of their experience together.

- She drew from a model that normalizes and validates, not one that pathologizes and prescribes. Specifically, she used the Diamond of Participatory Decision Making. This model is grounded in the belief that human beings should not be seen as dysfunctional for doing what comes naturally. Using the diamond, she normalized the difficulties that are inherent in collaboration and gave the group permission to relax and become honest about their frustration, without resorting to pseudo-solutions or giving up altogether.

- And most important to see: underlying all her behavior, she drew from her authentic, heartfelt commitment to tolerating the foibles and anxieties of group life in order to support the emergence and development of genuine warts-and-all collaboration.

This type of facilitation is a genuinely enabling process, helpful and supportive and grounding. But does that mean facilitation is the essential key to successful collaboration? I think not.

Whether a facilitator is present or not, the problem of intersubjectivity, in my opinion, has a profound underlying influence on a group's capacity to collaborate. In other words, it is a primary phenomenon and should be dealt with as a primary phenomenon, not as a nuisance that can be disregarded unless it pops up here and there. To put it another way, the fundamental imperative of collaboration is to build mutual understanding.

Here are four principles that are particularly helpful in bringing this viewpoint into focus:

- *Principle 1: For multistakeholder collaboration, building mutual understanding is not optional; it is mandatory.* So long as participants in a collaboration have not acquired sufficient mutual understanding, their chance of success will be painfully low. Constrained by their own individual interpretations, trapped in their own individual frameworks of meaning, what more than a pseudo-solution should they expect to achieve? To be effective cothinkers participants have to be able to think from each other's points of view, even when they disagree. By necessity, a serious collaboration has to transcend the problem of intersubjectivity, not be limited by it.

- *Principle 2: The existence of the Groan Zone is a normal fact of life; making it visible to participants is a powerful, grounding intervention.* It does not matter what you label it. If you prefer, you can use the term *storming* (Tuckman, 1965) or *chaos* (Peck, 1987), or a term of your own. But whatever one calls it, this period of struggle and impatience and frustration—this period, fundamentally, of poor communication—is a natural, normal, recurring phase of multi-stakeholder collaboration. When its existence is left unrecognized, participants frequently misdiagnose and misattribute their frustrations, which lead generally to ineffective interventions. By contrast, when the existence of the Groan Zone can be acknowledged and normalized, its effects can be observed and discussed and managed.

- *Principle 3: It takes careful, effective listening to build mutual understanding.* The subjective construction of meaning may be a problematic fact of life, but to an extent, careful listening can serve as its antidote. Under most circumstances, participants in a collaboration will probably never be able to know the private depths and crevices of one another's inner worlds. But that level of intimacy is rarely required by the demands of collaboration. What does matter is whether participants can understand each another well enough to think from each other's points of view. Careful listening is the behavior that enables that level of comprehension. A facilitator can be a great role model for this behavior and a workshop on listening skills can be a fine method of instruction; but in the final analysis, the key is to enable the participants to acquire and practice those skills. When people chronically are not listening, they are not collaborating.

- *Principle 4: Collaboratives, and the skillfulness of the participants, develop over time.* Building mutual understanding is not accomplished at a single sitting. Genuine mutual understanding unfolds and emerges, analogous to the peeling of the proverbial onion. For all participants, learning how to persevere, in good faith and with tolerance, is not merely a good practice. It is essential.

CONCLUSION

Exploring the problem of intersubjectivity—its nature, its extent, and its power—has been the purpose of this chapter. Building mutual understanding is the fundamental imperative of collaboration. If the purpose of convening and investing in multistakeholder collaborations is to develop bold, inclusive solutions that produce sustainable outcomes—if, in other words, the purpose of collaboration is to promote collective responsibility for our projects and our visions—then mutual understanding must be held as an ongoing, unflinching intention—as "true north" on the compass of effective facilitation.

A Procedural Analysis of Group Facilitation

A Communication Perspective

Joe Chilberg

Group facilitation is a communication-based intervention since it prescribes and guides group member interaction and message behaviors. Understanding and recognizing the functions of communication for group facilitation can aid effective group facilitation. A communication perspective establishes the task and social functions of message behaviors and the role of the procedural function in initiating and managing productive group decision-making communication. The procedural function, the domain of group facilitation, is to engender participative and collaborative practices that enhance the quality of decisions and promote constructive and satisfying group relationships. This procedural function must consider the constructive nature of message behaviors in both the task and relational dimensions of communication.

This chapter presents a macro- and microlevel scheme of procedural communication for analysis of process designs to illustrate the procedural, task, and social functions of communication. The scheme is then applied using three process designs (interaction method, nominal group technique, and synectics). The scheme offers facilitators, consultants, and group members a way of seeing decision-making events, activities, episodes, and acts through a communication schematic to enhance adopting, implementing, and monitoring formal or informal decision-making practices.

COMMUNICATION: THE HEART OF GROUP DECISION MAKING

The ideal outcome for task groups is to arrive at decisions that are acceptable and satisfying to group members. There are a host of techniques and practices offered to guide groups toward such ends. Regardless of the practice or technique, they all have one thing in common: they require groups to focus and coordinate group communication. They more or less provide a group process design that shapes communication toward particular ends. Communication is the common denominator of process designs.

When group process designs are used, they require guidance; they need to be facilitated. The central job of group facilitation is to guide and monitor the communication behaviors required by the process design. Whether the facilitator is a manager of a team meeting, chairperson of a committee, or a neutral third party leading a brainstorming session, this person's job is communication.

A communication perspective offers a practical schema for understanding and facilitating group decision making. It provides the facilitator a way of "seeing." That is, understanding the roles and functions of group communication can aid in the development, selection, and implementation of a process design. Furthermore, it offers a way to develop the facilitator's eye, that is, to guide and monitor the message behaviors required for a process design.

MESSAGES AND THEIR DIMENSIONS

The central focus of communication studies is "the relationship between messages and people" (Zarefsky, 1993, p. 2). A major emphasis of communication research investigates how the characteristics of message structures and content affect communicators. Communication researchers seek to understand and explain how messages work—what influences the sources of messages and how messages influence receivers. It is widely accepted that messages have two dimension of information: content or task and socioemotional or relational information (Watzlawick, Beavin, and Jackson, 1967; Keyton, 1999). Message behaviors can be understood as performing task and relational functions coextensively. Thus, all member message behaviors have implications for decision-making tasks as well as individual and group relationships. While the task dimension of messages provides information and critical activities such as idea generating and evaluation, the relational dimension establishes members' identities and intragroup relationships (Keyton, 1999) and moderates matters of power and self-esteem that can support or inhibit effective task communication (Collins and Guetzkow, 1964; Hackman, 1990; Poole, 1999).

The above perspective makes clear that effective group decision making is attained by communicating to develop effective group relationships that in turn support effective task communication. What may not be so obvious are the task and relational implications and requirements of a process design selected to facilitate decision making. The facilitator who understands and internalizes the task and relational dimensions of communication will have a critical advantage in selecting, guiding, monitoring, and intervening in the process of group decision making.

PROCEDURES AND THE FUNCTIONS OF GROUP COMMUNICATION

Benne and Sheats's influential study (1948) on group communication identified three main functions of message behaviors—task, maintenance (social and relational), and self-serving—and the types and purposes of message behaviors associated with each. Procedural message behaviors were minimal and folded into the task and relational functions, giving them an incomplete treatment and subordinate status (Chilberg, 1989). Although task and relational functions of communication are inherent in the procedural function, the importance of the procedural function for effective group decision making has gained attention. There is a significant body of research on the influences of formal procedures on group process, member relationships, and task outcomes that indicate procedures for discussion, decision making, and problem solving to enhance group performance. "At the same time 'which procedure(s) should be used, and under what circumstances, remains unclear'" (Sunwolf and Seibold, 1999, p. 395). Off-the-shelf process designs provide more or less adequate information for their implementation, but the facilitator is frequently left to his own devices in advocating and guiding procedural choices, monitoring group members' performance, and intervening with regard to group members' task and relational message behaviors. Facilitators should be concerned with more than monitoring the step-by-step procedures of a process design; they should also attend to the relational implications of the procedures and actual members' communication behaviors.

The facilitator who is cognizant of the task and relational functions of message behaviors required by procedures achieves a more critical understanding of process designs. Such understanding is an aid in selecting and facilitating a process design that fits a group's task and relational circumstances. It helps the facilitator discern the fit of a process with a particular group and its decision goals, establishes task and relational message requirements, and provides a basis for monitoring compliance with or need for adaptation of the process design.

For example, a multistakeholder steering committee for a group decision forum established the problem to be solved by a group. When the facilitator stated the problem to establish the focus for the next step, an influential member expressed dissatisfaction with the problem statement. The facilitator solicited the objections of the member and soon recognized that the objection was based in a power issue: whose interests were going to define the problem to be solved. The facilitator offered a more inclusive phrasing of the problem that satisfied the objector and was acceptable to all present. The facilitator's ability to read the messages of the dissatisfied member at both the task and relational levels contributed to her ability to resolve the dispute without a protracted discussion or additional process in an already time-constrained meeting.

A process design is valuable, but being able to "see" from a communication perspective can be useful. It is not enough to know if members are off-task or following the rules of good group citizenship. Communication is more than a conduit of information or just performing decision-making tasks. It also constructs, or "makes," the group's reality of itself, decisions, and the context in which it is embedded. "Group decisions [are] social products emerging from and embedded in a 'social milieu' (or 'reality') that is both created and sustained through communication" (Poole and Salazar, 1999, p. 172). Group communication can reproduce or alter group reality and decisions. The consummate facilitator maximizes constructive and productive interventions by providing and facilitating procedural messages that address both the decision-making tasks and the relational aspects of group communication.

LEVELS OF ANALYSIS FOR GROUP COMMUNICATION

The following conceptualization provides a comprehensive scheme for understanding group decision-making communication. The schema provides a basis for examining the task and relational attributes of a process design that can aid in identifying the task and relational communication needs for group decision-making procedures.

Group decision making, among other types of social gatherings, operates at four nested levels that can help in selecting and monitoring process design procedures: the event, activity, episode, and act (see Exhibit 9.1). The event level is the social gathering for the purpose of communicating to make decisions: the meeting. Activities are phases or steps designed to organize the task and support constructive member relationships. The episode level involves the specific types of activity message behaviors (for example, idea generating and solution evaluation) to fulfill selected decision-making activities in a manner that promotes participation and productive relational outcomes. The act level involves the specific message behaviors that enact the task messages in a relationally supportive and confirming manner.

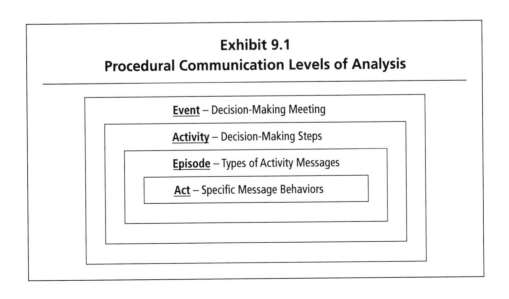

Exhibit 9.1
Procedural Communication Levels of Analysis

<u>Event</u> – Decision-Making Meeting

<u>Activity</u> – Decision-Making Steps

<u>Episode</u> – Types of Activity Messages

<u>Act</u> – Specific Message Behaviors

Event Level of Group Communication

The first level of analysis for selecting a process design or procedures to maximize effective group decision making requires assessing the task demands and the relational circumstances of the group. The facilitator needs to know the purpose and goals of the meeting, number of participants, decision background, information needs, and task complexity. From a relational perspective, the facilitator needs to know the group's history, participation norms, communication climate (defensiveness, cohesiveness, morale, or commitment, for example), and intergroup or organizational issues such as social conformity pressures, competition, power relations, or cultural diversity. This front-end analysis will help a facilitator discern the group's task and relational needs to aid in selecting a procedural intervention appropriate for the meeting and group culture (Chilberg and Riley, 1995).

Activity Level of Group Communication

The event-level analysis establishes the nature and requirements of facilitation to achieve the goal of decision making and the relational status of the group and its members. It provides a basis from which the facilitator can identify or create the types of activities to optimize effective task and relational results. From the task perspective, activities establish a sequence of focused communication to accomplish decision-making tasks: goal setting, decision and problem analyzing, idea generating, idea evaluating, and choice making. The procedures for each activity can incorporate relation-building practices that promote involvement, equal participation, consensus, and creativity, all of which can contribute to task effectiveness while enhancing individual and group satisfaction.

Episode Level of Group Communication

Each activity may involve one or more communication episodes to operationalize the activity. The episode level involves the specific types of message behaviors that are required to enact a specific activity or fulfill a technique used for decision making. That is, episode communication involves task messages that either give or seek instruction, ideas, information, judgments, or choices. For example, a solution assessment activity may have two episodes, identifying the merits of a choice followed by an episode to identify and ideas to improve a choice. The relationship aspect of episode communication can support broad participation and coordinate interaction in ways that lead to creative ideas, high levels of participation, and group satisfaction. For instance, a more coordinated and noninteractive approach to generating and sharing ideas used in the nominal group technique can enhance the diversity and creativity of ideas while promoting involvement and the equalization of participation. In contrast, episodes characterized by open or free discussion have been found to undermine participation, task performance, decision quality, and member satisfaction (see Fox, 1987; Sunwolf and Seibold, 1999).

Act Level of Procedural Communication

It is at the act level that the facilitator completes a communication analysis of a process design. Specific message behaviors are required to enact the task and relational dimensions of an episode. The typical task message behaviors associated with episodes are to describe, explain and elaborate, evaluate (pros and cons), and support (reasons and evidence). Message behaviors to enact constructive relational outcomes are typified by supportive and confirming message behaviors (Gibb, 1961; Sieberg, 1976). For instance, having members participate in an evaluation episode using proactive descriptive language to phrase negative judgments (that is, what they would like to see or wish for) may improve the initial idea and minimize defensive reactions. Such approaches to evaluation can also enhance the solution advocates' feeling of inclusion and contribution while supporting group morale and satisfaction.

Using the Four Levels

The analysis of group process needs using the four levels of procedural communication offers a comprehensive way to identify, plan, and implement facilitative interventions. The event and activity levels provide a macro analysis that then set up the microlevel analysis necessary for the episode and act levels. These levels can then be reviewed for their task and relational fit with the event and the individual and interpersonal needs of the group (see Exhibit 9.2). The identification of activities, episodes, and acts can (1) provide the facilitator with a way to critically develop, plan, and implement processes, keeping in mind both the task and relational aspects of group decision making; (2) aid in instructing and guiding group members in expected message behaviors for activity episodes; (3) provide the facilitator with a way to monitor members' acts for compliance with an episode activity; and (4) help the facilitator detect task or relational problems while facilitating a group.

Exhibit 9.2
Procedural Levels of Group Decision-Making Communication

Level	Task	Relationship
Event	Meeting needs (goal, objectives, complexity, constraints, expertise, and information management)	Group size, involvement and collaboration needs, communication climate, social pressures, power relations, cultural diversity, and others.
Activity	Steps, phases, sequence of activities to fulfill decision-making functions (such as problem identification, analysis, idea generation, and evaluation and selection) to increase decision quality	Promote participation, consensus, morale, individual and group creativity, and satisfaction
Episode	Give and seek instruction, ideas, information, judgment, and choices to fulfill activity content function	Establish who gives or seeks what and when; coordination of individual communication for participation and constructive interaction climate
Acts	Specific communication behaviors (such as describing, explaining, evaluating, and supporting) to enact episode	Supportive and confirming message behaviors (such as listening and acknowledging ideas and feeling, seeking understanding) versus defensive and disconfirming (such as competitive, personal attacks, inflexibility, and domination)

PROCEDURAL COMMUNICATION ANALYSIS OF PROCESS DESIGNS: THREE EXAMPLES

The most common problems associated with decision-making meetings are directly related to communication practices that limit or obstruct member participation and minimize or neglect the treatment of matters that enhance the quality of decisions. The use of open or free discussion approaches to group decision-making poses a recognized problem to promoting member participation (see Fox, 1987; Sunwolf and Seibold, 1999) and critical treatment of decision-making communication (see Hirokawa and Salazar, 1999). The process designs selected for this analysis were developed to minimize these problems by providing procedures that support participation and focus communication on the requirements of critical, effective decision making. They do so by establishing meeting procedures, norms, and rules to establish and guide who can say what, and when, during decision-making communication. (See Chilberg, 1989, on the degree to which process designs vary in terms of controlling meeting communication behaviors.) The procedures and rules are typically organized in steps or sequences of activities that involve one or more episodes that establish opportunities for communication acts appropriate to the task and development of productive member relationships.

Using three distinctly different process designs developed for decision-making meetings—interaction method, the nominal group technique, and synectics—the following analysis will identify the task and relational dimensions of each of the four levels of procedural communication.

Interaction Method for Conducting Meetings

The interaction method developed by Michael Doyle and David Straus (1976) was designed to promote effective group meetings by designing several rules for preventing communication-based problems and four meeting roles to enact the process design. The method was developed to arrest problems commonly observed across a variety of groups and meetings: the wandering discussion, inappropriate discussion procedures, obstructions to participation and consensus, and ineffective information management. Although Doyle and Straus's work covered numerous issues relevant to effective meeting facilitation, these problems were central to the process design.

Process Design Overview   The interaction method process designates four roles to prevent the typical meeting problems; the facilitator, the recorder, member, and member/manager. The facilitator's job entails having members identify and maintain a discussion focus that includes a desired outcome. In addition, the facilitator makes sure all members have an opportunity to participate in discussion and weigh in on all decisions concerned with selecting the focus, focus procedures, and substantive decisions. Consensus decision making is recommended for all decisions unless the group decides otherwise (for example, to use majority voting), and a "no-attack rule" is enforced to promote participation and prevent "flight-or-fight" meeting behaviors. The designated recorder manages meeting information by providing a group memory that visually displays before the group the meeting foci, information, and outcomes. This practice supports maintaining foci and procedures, provides access to meeting information and a meeting record for future reference, and allows meeting participants and the facilitator to concentrate on the business of the meeting.

The members and manager/member are responsible for following the process rules and together have control of meeting content. They are also responsible for seeing that the facilitator and recorder perform their duties and maintain their roles as neutral third parties unless members agree to permit them to offer content or procedural suggestions. The manager/member may establish meeting goals and provide substantive guidelines or constraints for decision making. Otherwise, the manager/member is treated as any other participant and held to the same process rules.

Procedural Communication Analysis   At the event level, the process design is meant to address the most common problems of meetings: member involvement and participation. Meetings are notorious for uneven participation (see Fox, 1987; Sunwolf and Seibold, 1999) and ineffective and inefficient practices that have a negative impact on meeting communication and undermine decision quality and member satisfactions. Jensen and Chilberg (1991) derived four rules to operationalize the procedural guidelines of the interaction method; the focus rule, tool rule, consensus rule, and the no-attack rule.

The focus rule requires that members establish and state a focus for discussion that establishes the topic, purpose, and desired result or outcome. Topical agenda items tend to include numerous issues that are hidden or not recognized, thus leading to discussion that wanders (Doyle and Straus, 1976). For example, "discussion of fundraising" is too general and open-ended, whereas a procedural agenda item such as "generate a list of fundraising ideas" is more definitive and directive. The former could allow all sorts of messages on fundraising, whereas the latter would limit discussion to ideas for fundraising and require making a list in some manner. The focus rule can help a group recognize that a decision goal may involve numerous foci. For example, a discussion on fundraising ideas can be separated into generating ideas, selecting a few promising ideas, judging the pros and cons of each selected idea, and deciding on the most promising idea, among others. The focus rule can aid groups in effective, critical decision making by decomposing complex agenda items that have numerous distinct but related procedural tasks and establishing the desired result for each. Task process effectiveness may also contribute to group satisfaction by reducing the frustration created from cross-task communication where no task gets critical or thorough treatment.

Meeting events that involve complex tasks and open discussions that become unproductive and dissatisfying are candidates for the focus rule. The first activity is to establish the first focus. This activity requires the facilitator to guide two episodes: soliciting ideas on foci and choosing a focus. The soliciting episode would require acts that produce ideas comprising a clear topic, purpose, and desired outcome. The choosing episode would require acts of narrowing choices, explanation, evaluating, and supporting (for example, reasoning, pros and cons, and evidence).

Although the interaction method provides a clear and useful guideline to support effective decision making, it leaves some implementation details up to the facilitator. A facilitator's effectiveness could be enhanced by recognizing what episodes and acts are involved in conducting the focus activity. A facilitator of a group that is contentious, diverse, faced with complex tasks, and accustomed to unbridled discussion could establish more elaborate rules. For example, when soliciting ideas for a focus, the facilitator could require a brief rationale for the focus or list all foci followed by seeking members' needs for elaboration, followed by pros and cons for first choice preferences.

The focus rule sets up the second rule and activity of the process design, the tool rule. This rule asks group members to consider the best way to handle a focus and implicitly questions the tendency and efficacy of open discussion for all and any foci. It is a procedural rule that poses some requirements on the communication practices appropriate for conducting the focus. For example, if the focus establishes that an outcome will be a list of ideas, the selected procedure must attend to it in some manner. The interaction method leaves this decision to the group and offers the facilitator an opportunity to make a recommendation. This poses an opportunity to address the participatory and relational circumstances of the group by advocating procedures that incorporate activities to increase participation, reduce domination, or ease tension. The tool rule activity is similar to the focus rule activity in that it requires idea seeking and giving and idea selection episodes. The acts needed for both of these episodes would be similar to those identified for the focus rule, with one exception: tools could require an instructional episode involving explanatory acts to instruct members on the required activities, episodes, and acts to use the tool. For instance, the facilitator could suggest a comprehensive approach to a decision-making task, such as nominal group technique, which has its own set of activities, episodes, and acts, or recommend a timed round robin to attain a quick sense of members' opinions on decision options. In concert with the focus rule, the tool rule can enhance task effectiveness by resulting in the selection of practices that promote more critical and thorough decision-making activities. It offers relational payoffs by avoiding the participatory liabilities of an inappropriate use of open discussion while choosing practices that can support diverse and equitable participation.

The last two rules of the interaction method, the consensus and no-attack rules, further member participation by promoting involvement, commitment, and sense of collective action. The consensus rule is implemented when there is a choice-making situation (including the focus and tool selection choices). It is intended to keep the group together and prevent domineering members from hijacking the meeting. Where decision options are already established from previous episodes, the consensus rule enacts a judgment and choosing episode. The facilitator engages the group in consensus decision making by having members engage in evaluative and supporting acts of communication over preferred options. Members are asked to agree to a choice only if they can genuinely accept or live with it. In addition, the no-attack rule asks members to avoid personal criticism and permits the facilitator to remind members when they do. This reinforces the importance of a positive, confirming relational communication, and reinforces a constructive and productive communication climate.

Nominal Group Technique for Idea Generating

Process Design Overview   André Delbecq and Andrew Van de Ven (1986) developed this process design to aid groups in idea generation and consensus. It is suited for meeting events where collective involvement is needed to identify problems and solutions among members who vary in personal interests, expertise, culture, and ideology (Ulschak, Nathanson, and Gillan, 1981). Research indicates that nominal approaches to idea generating outperform interactive approaches in the quantity and quality of ideas. Nominal group technique (NGT) is most helpful in situations where social pressure, evaluation, or social loafing hinders idea generation, creative thinking, task emphasis, and participation (Sunwolf and Seibold, 1999).

Procedural Communication Analysis At the activity level of procedural communication, NGT emphasizes individual work and minimizes interaction through six major steps: silent idea generating, round robin reporting, discussion for clarification, ranking by importance, and repeating the last two steps to finalize a decision choice (Ulschak, Nathanson, and Gillan, 1981). Each step requires instructional episodes followed by the requisite activity episodes. From the communication perspective offered here, NGT has two main activities: idea generating and idea selection. The idea-generating activity has three episodes: silent idea generation, idea giving, and soliciting clarification. The first episode requires members to write short statements on the session focus (for example, identify problems with X or solutions to problem Y). This is followed by an idea-giving episode using a round robin technique where members take turns presenting one idea at a time until all ideas are recorded verbatim by the facilitator. Members are invited to silently hitchhike on others' ideas and report them at the end of the round robin.

This episode is characterized by descriptive acts. Members are not to explain or evaluate, just report. The discussion and clarification of ideas is held off until the information-seeking episode. From a task perspective, these episodes contribute to maximizing the quantity and diversity of ideas by preventing the loss of ideas due to premature discussion or evaluation. From a relational perspective, these episodes promote personal and collective ownership of the decision-making event and reinforce constructive member relationships through equalizing member participation, emphasizing supportive acts, coordinating interaction, and encouraging members to build on each other's ideas.

The information-seeking episode for idea clarification is the only time when members interact. The facilitator reviews each idea one at a time and asks participants "to ask one another the meaning of words and phrases. . . . Discussion can and should convey the meaning, logic, and thought behind an idea" (Ulschak, Nathanson, and Gillan, 1981, p. 87). Discussion is to focus on seeking clarification; thus, communication acts are descriptive and explanatory—evaluative acts are not permitted. The clarification episode directs interaction toward descriptive and explanatory acts, thus minimizing the potential for ideational or interpersonal conflict while emphasizing clarity and understanding.

The next step of NGT is an idea selection activity requiring members to engage in a silent evaluation episode by rank-ordering a specified number of ideas based on importance or preference. The silent ranking is meant to promote independent judgments by reducing social pressures (Ulschak, Nathanson, and Gillan, 1981). Once this step is completed, the ranked ideas are listed on a master chart for review. The remaining steps of NGT can be implemented if the ranking episode reveals inconsistencies, ambiguous consensus, or preferences for a questionable option. A second round of discussion similar to the clarification-seeking episode can be conducted to ensure the initial ranking was not due to misunderstandings or incomplete information. A final round of ranking follows.

The main communication features of NGT are its emphasis on pooling individual ideas, limiting interaction to descriptive and explanatory acts, and sharing personal choices. It has a strong task emphasis and notable emphasis on intragroup relationship management. It is well suited for gathering ideas and preferences regarding contentious decisions; it avoids complications arising from highly interactive meetings where differences of views can undermine both task and relational outcomes.

Synectics for Creative Problem Solving

Process Design Overview   The George Prince (1970) version of synectics is a solution-centered process design used to solve difficult problems creatively. It is a completely scripted process involving a client with a problem, participants who serve as the generators of creative perspectives and potential solutions, and the facilitator who orients and guides members through the meeting process. Synectics is an atypical approach to group decision making in that the only person invested in the problem is the client, who is the problem owner and expert who offers problem background and evaluates solutions developed by the participants. Participants have no vested interest in the problem and perform their creative idea-generating role based on the client's problem background. The facilitator ensures that the client and participants perform the prescribed activities, episodes, and acts of group members to create tenable solutions for the client.

Unlike other process designs where event analysis is multifaceted and fundamental to selecting a process design, the synectics meeting is relatively eventless. It is meant to help a client with a solution-resistant problem. The facilitator and participants are neutral parties whose concern is with performing their respective roles employing creative practices. The creative promise of this process design is cultivated by minimizing constraints to group creativity and maximizing divergent thinking (see Jarboe, 1999).

Procedural Communication Analysis   The activities, episodes, and acts of synectics are well detailed from the sequence of steps to specific language used in performing communication acts (see Jensen and Chilberg, 1991 or Ulschak, Nathanson, and Gillan, 1981, for more detailed summary). There are three activities: problem analysis, solution development, and solution planning. The second two activities can be repeated in efforts to generate additional solutions. Each activity has several episodes with specific communication protocols that can be repeated as needed to develop tenable solutions. The problem analysis activity begins with an episode that occurs prior to the group meeting when the facilitator works with the client using several scripted questions to discern the problem background, unworkable solutions, and desired results and establish the problem in a how-to form (for example, how to make a frame for a portable solar mirror). When the group is assembled, this analytic episode is repeated; the participants sit together listening to the client's answers to the facilitator's questions. While listening, the participants are instructed to engage in an information-seeking episode to acquire additional information or clarification. At the same time, participants engage in a solution development activity by generating ideas silently in the form of metaphorical how-to statements (for example, how to use a sky hook, how to use a spoon). They use the problem analysis information along with the client's implied wishes and needs to reframe the problem regardless of how strange or unusual the reframing might be.

The participants' how-to statements set up the beginning of the solution development activity. First, the facilitator initiates an idea-seeking episode by soliciting and listing the participants' how-to ideas for the client's review. Second, the facilitator engages the client in a choice-seeking episode and explanatory act by selecting a how-to statement that stands out and explains why it was chosen. Third, for the selected statement, the facilitator solicits ideas for solutions from the client and then the participants. This idea-giving episode calls for descriptive and explanatory communication acts where the facilitator coaches participants to work on one idea at a time, build on an initial idea, and credit the previous person for the contribution. This approach to solution development promotes both task and relational features of the group process by encouraging attention to one idea at a time while acknowledging participants' contributions. Creative behavior, preventing negative judgment of others, and acknowledgment of ideas can promote group morale and member satisfaction (see Jarboe, 1999).

Once an idea is formed, an evaluation-seeking episode ensues where the client in asked to engage in evaluative acts using the spectrum policy (Prince, 1970). Solution evaluation involves three steps, which require the client to paraphrase the solution, describe all of its positive features, and then state what, if anything, he would wish to see added to it. This approach to evaluation reinforces productive task and supportive relational outcomes by first checking on the client's understanding of the idea, followed by identifying what works for the client while confirming the contributions of the participants. In addition, the client's concerns with the solution are not stated in a negative manner but posed as additional features for a viable solution. These desired features set up a feedback loop where the participants are asked how to modify the initial solution to make it more workable for the client, followed by a reevaluation of the modified solution with additional cycles of how-to's and reevaluation as needed. This process avoids the problems associated with the emphasis on negative aspects of a solution that can lead to dropping it prematurely. It also prevents the dampening of enthusiasm and creativity associated with evaluation and negative criticism (see Jarboe, 1999).

Once the client perceives a possible solution, the process moves into the solution development activity where the client is asked to determine if the solution is a new idea, next steps for implementation, and if there are any residual concerns with the solution. If there are any residual concerns, the facilitator asks the client and participants for how-to's that could resolve the concern, followed by a cycle of the client evaluation and solution planning activities. When a possible solution is developed, or should a cycle fail to provide a possible solution, the facilitator asks the client to pick another metaphoric how-to and the process, activities, and episodes are repeated.

Synectics, unlike most other process designs, not only identifies process activities and episodes but also establishes the specific phrasing of key communication acts to promote fruitful task and relational results. The design promotes the task aspects of group problem solving in many ways, most notably through structuring and coordinating problem-solving interaction, separating the creative and evaluative roles, and employing feedback loops to develop viable solutions. The most notable relational features are associated with the consistent opportunities for participation, acknowledgment of participants' ideas, and elimination of negative idea evaluation. These features can motivate participation and support creative thinking that can contribute to productive and satisfying problem-solving events.

ENHANCING FACILITATION EFFECTIVENESS

Effective group facilitation is not solely dependent on the process design but is determined by selecting a process design that fits the task demands, builds constructive relationships, and considers group circumstances. Regardless of the procedures used to facilitate group decision making, consideration of the interrelated and interdependent nature of the task and relational dimensions of communication can help maximize decision-making effectiveness. The analytical scheme presented here provides a means for examining a process design for its inherent activities, episodes, and acts for fit with the meeting event. Conducting a procedural communication analysis also aids with preparing for implementation by detailing the communication requirements of the facilitator and group members. The facilitator is better able to rehearse the communication demands of the process design and prepare instructional episodes for group members. Most important, a communication perspective sensitizes the facilitator to message behaviors and the message-person relationship. Being able to see the task and relational functions of messages inherent in the procedural activities, episodes, and acts helps in identifying when members are off-procedure and why. It promotes critical awareness of messages in the unfolding process of group communication. It can help in recognizing when interventions are needed to bring communication back on track or what element of a process design needs modification. The more one is aware of the implications of messages and acts in the moment, the more one is able to respond in ways that maximize the benefits of task and relational communication, the main ingredients of effective group facilitation.

 **PART THREE**

Create and Sustain a Participatory Environment

1. Demonstrate effective participatory and interpersonal communication skills.

- Applies a variety of participatory processes
- Demonstrates effective verbal communication skills
- Develops rapport with participants
- Practices active listening
- Demonstrates ability to observe and provide feedback to participants

2. Honor and recognize diversity, ensuring inclusiveness.

- Encourages positive regard for the experience and perception of all participants
- Creates a climate of safety and trust

- Creates opportunities for participants to benefit from the diversity of the group
- Cultivates cultural awareness and sensitivity

3. Manage group conflict.
- Helps individuals identify and review underlying assumptions
- Recognizes conflict and its role within group learning and maturity
- Provides a safe environment for conflict to surface
- Manages disruptive group behavior
- Supports the group through resolution of conflict

4. Evoke group creativity.
- Draws out participants of all learning and thinking styles
- Encourages creative thinking
- Accepts all ideas
- Uses approaches that best fit needs and abilities of the group
- Stimulates and taps group energy

Graphic Facilitation

The Art of Drawing Out the Best in People

David Sibbet

Facilitation is the art of leading group process toward agreed-on outcomes in ways that elicit participation, creativity, and ownership from everyone involved. At its heart is the art of calling out the wisdom in groups and guiding individuals into fully participating and collaborating in creating solutions and results for themselves.

Graphic facilitation has become especially effective at achieving these kinds of facilitative results reliably. It is most commonly distinguished by large visual displays used to interactively record and visualize group thinking. Because everything is recorded publicly and open to feedback and correction, it is one of the most direct ways to make group processes explicit and accessible. The conscious employment of imagery, graphic metaphor, and structured group displays lets people literally see what they mean. Practitioners find that this way of working predictably increases participation, systems-level thinking, memorability, and group ownership.

While good facilitation practice is similar across different styles, the effects of working with panoramic visuals are dramatic and worth understanding. The demands on a facilitator when working graphically are different from nongraphic facilitation options in important respects. There are initial challenges of simply figuring out how to use the trademark tools of markers, wall space, and large white

155

paper or graphic templates. The discipline involves helping people make visual sense out of their information by listening for and reflecting the mental models and patterns of understanding that guide the process of making meaning out of what is being said.

This chapter introduces the tools and best practices of graphic facilitation. It begins by describing a meeting that epitomizes the promise in graphic facilitation as a way to support multisector meetings and almost any group facing complex communication challenges. (There is also a growing field of graphic recording, to support large meetings and other processes where the graphics are not always front and center but used for rich documentation. This chapter is not intended to treat graphic recording, although many of the observations are relevant.)

UNDERSTANDING SUSTAINABILITY: A VISIONARY CHALLENGE

The forty-five environmental and foundation leaders coming to the first Roots of Change (ROC) advisory board meeting in the spacious Irvine Foundation conference center in downtown San Francisco were greeted by two panoramas. One was a wall of windows facing the San Francisco Bay. The other was a thirty-foot-long mural with a big title, "What Is a Sustainable Food System?" Across the chart at the bottom was a suggestive map of California, drawn in bird's-eye view with markers and chalk. In the middle was a smaller poster with an image of a large wheel of influences. A large U-shaped conference table faced the nearly blank mural.

This first ROC advisory board meeting was convened by a small consortium of funders frustrated with their attempts to support more sustainable approaches to agriculture in California. They decided to pool their efforts to tackle projects that might help change the entire system of thinking surrounding sustainable food systems. Because the topic was immensely complex and out of the general public's focus of attention, success would depend on expanding their core group to include a larger network of advisers experienced in environmental and agricultural matters. These advisers would help shape the giving policies of their ROC Fund and help stimulate projects.

The Challenge of Engaging Participation and Understanding

The funders faced a classic set of challenges. They had already met for months refining their own understanding of the need. They knew that any change needed to be systemic, because farmers, wholesalers, retail stores, agriculture policymakers, bankers, and other players are very interdependent. They also needed to engage the public imagination. And they had to convey the complexity and think about the subject within the context of a one-day meeting.

Need for a Map of the Larger Context

The funders already had an image of the system, in the form of a wheel with peapod spokes. The rim was a series of factors that make up the food system. But the image was very abstract. "Why don't we work with this image, but begin this first advisory board meeting with a more free-form mapping of what everyone in attendance thinks a sustainable food system is?" I suggested. "This will engage everyone, prime them for listening, and honor the breadth of experience you are bringing to the table. Instead of pushing information at people, let's draw it out." I described the possibility of creating a thirty-foot-long display across the shorter end of the conference room.

The idea of creating a California-wide map across the whole front of the room was accepted and came to be the opening activity at the advisory board meeting. It proved to be a perfect choice.

The Power of Large Group Dialogue

A member of the funder's group used the chart showing the peapod wheel to share the reasons for expanding the scope of the ROC effort. This introductory chart was then moved aside, and we revealed the larger map that would be used for the morning deliberations.

I initially framed the exploration with a review of the reason for picking a graphic format and the key question that would drive the drawing and the question: What Are Sustainable Food Systems? People were encouraged to begin identifying some of the constituent elements, stimulated by the peapod chart, and talk about their relation to the larger picture.

An initial contribution described the primary system as it stands today, with production, processors, buyers, and retailers linked in a commonly understood supply chain. I focused in on that which addressed the explicit theme and its implicit components—in this case, elements involved in a sustainable food system and a characterization of the relationship between these elements. I wrote "PRIMARY SYSTEM" on the chart, picking a red color that would be used only for the other elements of a sustainable food system so they would stand out when the chart was more complete. In another color, I diagrammed the value chain being described.

Because we were working visually, the group members could literally see what they were discussing. They could choose to add comments or make changes in order to achieve a shared understanding.

As others spoke, I repeated the process of listening for constituent elements, using people's actual words, and leaving space for them to have confidence that their perspective was visible for all to see.

The chart grew in complexity as categories and data were added in different places. Since everyone watched the process unfold, they could follow the pattern. At strategic times, I reviewed the chart and asked for more detail and other elements. Everyone was completely engaged. The give and take, communication, and instant feedback took on a rhythm and direction.

Although this meeting was unique, we experienced the excitement and engagement that I have come to expect from cocreating a single, huge, panoramic map of the relevant environment. The group was stimulated by the increasing array of data that they could now remember, revisit, compare, and find patterns within.

Results for the ROC Advisory Board

This context map, when completed, was transferred to the window side of the room, where it remained visible as a reminder of the larger system the ROC Fund was supporting. The meeting continued for a full day, surfacing suggestions for initial focus of the fund, polling to narrow choices, further discussion, and initial agreements. All these exchanges were recorded graphically on new charts. The initial session succeeded in involving everyone.

After the meeting, everyone received a full-color set of chart reproductions and photos of the session, in eleven- by seventeen-inch format, made possible by digital photography and some technical enhancement of the photos by the consulting team. Short captions and headlines were added to guide people through the photographs, creating a storybook that everyone could use to brief others about the meeting.

RESULTS BEGINNERS CAN EXPECT

There is a very predictable pattern in this graphic way of working:

- The built-in intention of "seeing things whole" implicitly honors everyone's contribution and makes room for visionary and skeptic alike. This same intent can express itself in a process that is not graphically facilitated, but having ideas literally written next to each other on the same chart makes the point incontrovertibly. This becomes critical with participants who are chronically discounted.

- Participation and creativity soar as everyone is acknowledged immediately for contributing, sees their ideas supported with imagery, and has a chance to add and correct whatever they say. The audible sound of the pen on paper becomes a reinforcing drumbeat of sound at an unconscious level that I believe directly influences people's sense of being heard.

- Big pictures support panoramic, system-level thinking at a group level—a near impossibility without this medium. Comparing and contrasting, linking and juxtaposing are all cognitive activities that imply display making of some sort. Making these pictures explicit has the added value of making them open to challenge and improvement, unlike the pictures we form in our imaginations without explicit displays.

- Groups can remember what they have done, both in the meeting and afterward when they see the charts reproduced or visible in a later meeting. Groups that watch a large display being created will find their memories triggered at much deeper levels when they see the same display photographically reproduced in a meeting report. Typing up or summarizing information after a meeting changes it and can lose the mnemonic power of the original displays.

These four results happen from the beginning of working with this visual medium and are inherent biases, as long as the facilitator's intent is to truly listen and mirror what is happening and not manipulate the charts to reflect his or her own purposes.

A BRIEF HISTORY OF GRAPHIC FACILITATION

Many influences are shaping this rapidly growing field of practice.

In the 1970s, several West Coast architects left the field of design and applied their visualization techniques to guide other kinds of planning and creative thinking efforts. Joe Brunon was using his generative graphics at SRI International in Palo Alto to support brainstorming. An early article shared his thinking (Brunon, 1971). Lawrence Halprin, a well-known landscape architect with offices in San Francisco, used his junior designers to support planning workshops that he conducted with his colleague Jim Burns (Halprin and Burns, 1963). Michael Doyle and David Straus, both trained architects, teamed up to make facilitation an accepted third-party intervention strategy through their firm, Interaction Associates. They subsequently published their work in *How to Make Meetings Work* (1976). Many of the current visual practitioners owe their start to Interaction Associates, which almost single-handedly created a market for graphic recorders, by teaming them with facilitators using their method.

Not all the influences were from the West Coast. In St. Louis, Nancy Margulies (2002) applied graphics to capturing the essence of people's communication in much more illustrative drawings and trained a growing number of people who are active practitioners. Jim Channon applied his design background to graphic briefings in the U.S. Army and articulated what he called "advanced visual language" when he retired into full-time facilitation. He had reframed it as "Adventure Learning" by the time of the ROC history mapping. Robert Horn (1998), in the Boston area, was defining methodologies for "chunking" information, based on the work of psychologist George Miller (1956), and visually organizing information, using these methods as a basis for his firm Information Mapping.

In 1977, I created an organization development consulting practice devoted to exploring graphic facilitation, combining the roles of facilitator and recorder in the use of large blank or partly preformatted displays. In 1988, I created Graphic Guides, Inc., to begin publishing tools to support this way of working, and in 1994 renamed this company The Grove Consultants International, which continues to explore graphic solutions to all kinds of process consulting challenges.

The International Forum of Visual Practitioners, begun by Leslie Salmon Zhu, Susan Kelley, Jennifer Hammond Landau, and Karen Stratford, all full-time graphic recorders, formally incorporated as an association in 2002. The International Association of Facilitators began supporting graphic facilitation and recording tracks in its conferences in the late 1990s.

Although this field is in its infancy, it has been greatly stimulated by an information economy that is increasingly visual, computing tools that allow for graphic and multimedia authoring in every conceivable way, and cultures around the world that relate easily to image, metaphor, and storytelling.

TYPES OF PROCESSES BENEFITING FROM GRAPHIC FACILITATION

There are a range of meetings and processes where graphic facilitation is especially powerful and useful. Here are a few of the many applications:

- Visioning, planning, and design meetings of almost any kind, where many factors and forces need to be appreciated as a whole from past, present, and future perspectives.

- Process improvement and organizational change efforts, where seeing stated changes and mapping and analyzing processes almost always require a visual display.

- Diagnosing customer needs in critical sales situations and large projects of all kinds.

- Team start-up and problem-solving meetings, where pulling together everyone's thinking is an asset.

- Information design, with overviews of complex information supported by graphic facilitation to generate the key ideas.

- Leadership strategy communications, where big pictures support big picture thinking and graphic facilitation can be used to solicit feedback and input.

- Café processes and multistakeholder dialogues. The World Café, a growing network of people using small group dialogue to support deep engagement of people, often uses table graphics to capture ideas and graphic facilitators to reflect larger group discussions.

- Teaching interactively. The use of text and image on blackboards should probably be considered the original source of this approach.

THE FOUR FLOWS OF FACILITATION

What began as an experience of having groups come alive with graphic facilitation has evolved into a broad practice. Meetings are a set of complex flows of activity that happen on multiple levels, only one of which is obviously graphic.

The Grove Facilitation Model (2002) illustrates the four flows of facilitation: attention, energy, information, and operations (Exhibit 10.1). The model is a framework that guides our approach to teaching graphic facilitation and applies to single meetings or a whole series of meetings and the work in between. Each of these flows can be managed in the service of groups as they work to reach their desired goals. They are like the different parts that make up a full musical composition. As in music, skill can be evaluated in terms of the breadth of the repertoire a person brings to each flow of activity.

We have identified four sets of strategies for directing a group through the four flows in the early stages of group process and three sets of strategies for empowering the group once it is running on its own. (For more information on this model, go to www.grove.com/about/model_facilitation.html) or Sibbet, 2002.)

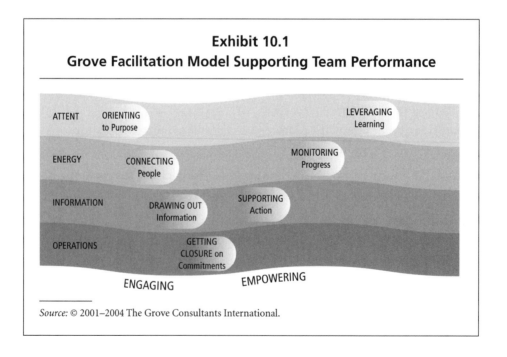

Exhibit 10.1
Grove Facilitation Model Supporting Team Performance

ATTENT ORIENTING to Purpose LEVERAGING Learning

ENERGY CONNECTING People MONITORING Progress

INFORMATION DRAWING OUT Information SUPPORTING Action

OPERATIONS GETTING CLOSURE on Commitments

ENGAGING EMPOWERING

Source: © 2001–2004 The Grove Consultants International.

Operations Flow

Exhibit 10.1, the operations flow of activity, is the foundation for the others. It represents the metaphorical ground on which a facilitator stands and the tools that a facilitator uses and provides a group. It includes the process mechanisms like agendas and procedural agreements that allow control over time, the number of people, and agreements about starting and stopping by which a facilitator establishes control. It also includes the physical tools needed for facilitation: the walls, the pens, tables, chairs, food, equipment, and so forth. Because these elements are the most objective aspects of group process, they allow control when mastered but challenge when not. A conscious graphic facilitator uses procedural and structural mechanisms to reflect and support the more dynamic elements of the process reflected in the upper flows. Handouts, food, props, and the arrangement of the room, for instance, are visual statements as well as tools.

Attention Flow

The attention flow is as open as the operational flow is constrained. It includes people's expectations, purposes, intentions, imagined outcomes, and other invisible elements that are the fruits of our conscious awareness. In a literal sense, it is what each person is attending to—his or her point of view. In a more comprehensive sense, the attention flow includes the entire field of awareness in which the meeting or process is being held. Imagination, not mechanism, rules in this domain and has a very different character from operations. While invisible and imaginary, it is of equal, if not more, importance. Graphic facilitation makes one especially aware of the power of inner imagery—how metaphor and story suggest different orientations and how the images and intentions the facilitator holds directly influence the group.

Energy and Information Flows

Energy and information are the middle flows. Energy is placed above information because it is less objective. It includes all the movement and dynamics of a meeting or process; emotion and feelings, morale and momentum are all in this flow. These share the common property of being in motion and being constrained by the direction in which they are moving. Energy is felt directly. It is the dancing part of facilitation. It includes the pacing; the way in which the graphic facilitator uses line, color, and movement to mirror emotion; and the literal dance of response.

Body movement communicates directly to that sense in people that feels things directly. A skilled graphic facilitator reflects this emotion and movement with color and line quality and works to align visual expression with group energy. For instance, physical excitement translates directly into how a line is drawn on a chart with more intensity and boldness of color. Hesitation becomes thin, wavering, and less bold. The movement of the graphic facilitator's own person is a form of mime that is itself a language.

Information, the content of what is being said and recorded, is more objective than energy and the most obvious part of what a graphic facilitator uses to help guide the group. The informational flow includes the symbols, words, and images that are shared in speech and recorded on the charts. This flow includes all the forms in which information is recorded—the templates, formats, frameworks, and models. The informational flow is the most conspicuously visible layer of group process when it is being graphically facilitated. Because the graphic facilitator is completely exposed in the way in which he or she listens and organizes information, most graphic facilitators become very attentive to underlying frameworks and archetypes with which people make sense out of things.

PUTTING IT ALL TOGETHER

Walking through the facilitation model step by step serves as a lens for understanding how to put graphic facilitation into practice, using the seven strategies illustrated in Exhibit 10.1. Although I treat the different aspects sequentially, in practice they integrate much like different voices in music blend together. It is best to start simply and then build a repertoire.

Step 1: Orienting to Purpose

At the very heart of graphic facilitation is the purpose of visual listening: helping other people literally see what they say. This is distinguished from public presentation, in which the intent is to have others understand what *you* are saying.

This shift in intention from "pushing out" to "drawing out" information is fundamental, and far more important than the icons and visual words used in the method. Drawing out immediately shifts the attention and intention of the whole group from intake to participatory exploration. This was the immediate message at the ROC council meeting inferred from the large, blank mural.

Because the attention and intention of a facilitator are so visible, from the moment a graphic facilitator picks up a pen, working this way becomes a practice in self-awareness for both the group and the practitioner. Since it is impossible to graphically record everything that is happening in a meeting, especially a highly interactive one (even the fastest graphic recorders can get only 15 to 20 percent of what is said in terms of words), everyone wonders about what is driving a graphic facilitator's selection process.

Ideally, a facilitator's selection process should be informed primarily by whatever purpose or outcomes have been set for the meeting. In reality, of course, it is a reflection of what the individual facilitator hears, which in turn is driven by what he or she is listening for and thinks is important. In the case of the ROC context map, the purpose of the display was explicit and reflected in the title. We were identifying elements in a sustainable food system and describing the relationship between those elements and the larger system.

Sometimes the purpose in a meeting is not clear. This will show up in the recording and provide an opportunity for everyone to move attention to this initial, fundamental aspect of group process. There is much that a graphic facilitator can do to align a team to its purposes simply by creating the title posters and theme charts that frame the meeting or engaging participants in identifying what to put on these kinds of charts.

Step 2: Connecting People

Soon after orienting, people in groups focus on how much they are going to trust the process, whom they know, whom they do not know, and the consequences of participating. At this point, the graphic facilitator helps to connect people with each other at an energetic level by creating a context of immediate acknowledgment for everyone who speaks. It helps to record participants' names and introductory material on a seating chart, creating, in effect, a group portrait. People might be asked to add their names to a map or a history chart to show when they got involved. They also can be asked to create posters about themselves.

Immediate feedback feels good. An unrelenting acceptance of the worth of each person's contribution, metered out in the steady beat of recording, is a drumbeat of acknowledgment that directly fuels group participation. When people begin to truly hear each other, they connect more deeply.

Step 3: Drawing Out Information

When people begin to open up and trust each other, the focus moves to what they need to learn and communicate. This process always begins somewhat slowly and can be confusing as people work to make connections and see patterns. Here is where recording comments on charts that are matched to the purpose of the meeting helps immensely. Graphic facilitation literally draws out people's ideas. It works whether or not the drawing or recording is initially accurate. If it is, people feel heard. If it is not, they will move to correct the drawing or add more. Either way, more gets shared.

The informational flow is more visible and objective than the flows of attention and energy. Information can be wrong. Spelling can be right or wrong. The facilitator's screen for listening might not be aligned correctly. The choice of graphic format or framework may be dissonant with the purpose of the meeting (as in trying to sort out roles and responsibilities with a free-form cluster diagram instead of a matrix).

In smaller groups, where the charts are integral parts of the process, such as a planning session with a management team, everyone can see immediately if the recording is working. In such cases, the process is self-correcting. This does not happen so much in a larger meeting, and not at all if the graphic record is created off to the side. Recording that is not directly observed while being created is not really graphic facilitation in the sense I am writing about it, and is usually called graphic recording. Such displays can be used facilitatively if the recording is reviewed and integrated into the process. If it is shared afterward only as documentation, a good deal of the power of the visual work is lost. Graphic recorders, teamed with nongraphic facilitators, can achieve the same effects as a graphic facilitator working alone if the facilitator uses the display as a tool for facilitation. In fact, in the case of larger groups, the team approach is preferable so that one party can stay facing the group and calling on people.

Knowing something about the content of a meeting helps to manage the informational flow, although preconceptions can get in the way of listening. In technical meetings, it is essential to know key terms, core concepts, and other background ideas.

In smaller groups, the ability of the graphic facilitator to learn very quickly is more important, using his or her natural curiosity as a driver to pull out more information. In fact, the facilitator's ignorance of the subject can provide a stimulus for everyone explaining important ideas that the group may be taking for granted or leaving unreviewed.

It is especially important when working with imagery to have the group involved in tight feedback loops. Creating imagery from spoken language is an act of translation and is limited by the imagery and drawing ability of the graphic facilitator, which may or may not accurately correspond to the imagery in a speaker's mind. This may be why using imagery is so stimulating: a very creative dissonance sets up between peoples' internal imagery and the external image on the display. Struggling to get this right is part of what draws people out.

Step 4: Getting Closure on Commitments

The pinch point in group process comes when people need to make decisions and commitments. The constraints of other commitments, time, money, and other resources all become factors. Learning and mastering the various techniques for polling, ranking, sorting, and refining choices is more demanding than learning how to record expectations in a free flow of discussion. Yet mastering this level is the key to groups' taking ownership themselves and moving to implementation and action, usually a more dynamic and flexible stage.

It is at the point of closure and commitment that the overall arrangement of charts becomes most important, and choices of frameworks and templates for organizing information become critical. If the various steps taken to get to that decision point are clearly titled and the displays arranged logically so they can be visually scanned and understood in a panoramic mirror of the larger meeting, then the way forward will often be discovered by the group. When the structure of the meeting is well designed to support the attention, energy, and information flows, groups can focus on finding the patterns of meaning and feeling, and not be tied up procedurally.

A good example is the Graphic Gameplan, shown in Exhibit 10.2, a strategic visioning template designed to help teams get their plans into one big picture. It reflects an archetypal metaphor people use to understand planning—that of the journey and destination—and graphically demonstrates the need for a sequence of activities to reach a particular target. It also introduces sequencing and timing, an essential element in taking action as a group. When it is introduced into a discussion that up to that point has not involved timing, it will precipitate action awareness. If the group cannot commit to a set of objectives, then it will be very difficult to do an action plan.

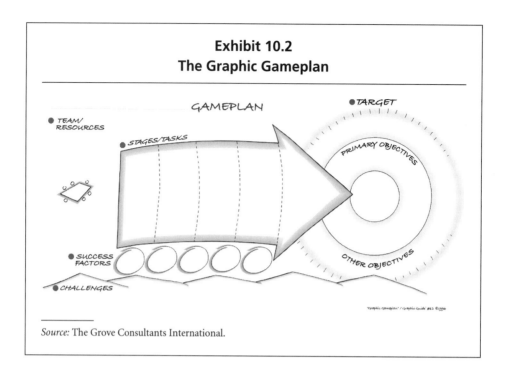

Exhibit 10.2
The Graphic Gameplan

Source: The Grove Consultants International.

Step 5: Supporting Action

As a group moves to action, the role of the graphic facilitator shifts from directing people toward closure and commitments toward supporting the agreements in action. Much of this is done by managing the informational flow, including clear schedules, progress review charts, and communications that graphically indicate the way forward. For this reason, the Graphic Gameplan works not only for closure but also for staying aligned. Some facilitators hand out a highlighted Graphic Gameplan every few weeks, marking off progress as a way of giving feedback to everyone.

Step 6: Monitoring Progress

The more high performing a group is, the more it begins to focus back on the energetic level, rising above objective plans to take advantage of breaking opportunities and flexibly adapting with new developments. A graphic facilitator at this stage mirrors this by using special murals and charts to commemorate the special visions and agreements that thread through all the changes. These maps serve as a kind of software for groups, and we put version numbers on them. As they change, the charts get new numbers, and people can see how their thinking evolves.

Step 7: Leveraging Learning

Because of the intense amount of attention a graphic facilitator is paying to group process, the facilitator learns a huge amount. Over longer processes, it becomes important to share this bounty with the larger group by providing time for everyone to review and digest what has happened. Reviewing projects and processes with graphic history sessions provides strong support for group learning. Reviewing charts periodically with gallery walks and verbal summaries helps people reflect and think about where they have come. One of the great benefits of graphic facilitation is how it generates clear evidence of what is usually a large amount of work that people put into critical meetings.

CONCLUSION

Graphic facilitation is a rich and versatile way to support effective group process. It goes well beyond drawing images and recording words, to the larger purpose of making everything that happens as explicit and accessible as possible.

Creating a Positive Participatory Climate

A Meaning-Centered Counseling Perspective

Paul T. P. Wong

I cannot think of any work more important than that of a group facilitator. Whether the task is adjudicating a family dispute, leading a seminar, chairing a board meeting, presiding over a large gathering, running a training camp, managing a company, or heading up a task force, whenever a group is involved in reaching decisions, the process can be helped by a group facilitator.

Not all situations require the service of an external, professional group facilitator. CEOs, managers, trainers, professors, coaches, and even parents from time to time need to play the role of a group facilitator. However, when the issues are very complex, opinions are strongly divided, and the meetings are emotionally charged, an outside group facilitator can make the difference between success and failure (Schuman, 1996).

AN ILLUSTRATIVE STORY

In the heyday of campus gender politics, antiracism activism, and radical student movement, the president of my former university put together a task force on human rights. The president wanted to bring together representatives of different constituents of the university, especially various minority groups, to make recommendations regarding principles and processes that would protect the university and its members from human rights violations. The task force members included one representative from each of the following: administration, faculty, staff, student council, ethnic minority students, gay and lesbian students, and students with disabilities.

The vice president for student life, a mild-mannered administrator who truly tried to accommodate student needs, chaired the task force. Taking advantage of his concern, the four student representatives claimed that they did not feel safe and requested that they each needed a partner to attend the meeting. Therefore, there were eight students, one faculty representative (that was me), one staff representative, and the vice president. The composition of the task force and the dynamics of the group clearly favored students. Since the vice president had to chair all the meetings and the staff representative was busy taking minutes, I became the only nonstudent member who was able to get actively engaged in the meetings.

At the outset, the student representatives demanded that an external professional facilitator be brought in to chair all meetings of the task force. Their rationale was that they would trust only an outside person to chair the task force in spite of their overwhelming majority. Their proposal was not acceptable to the president, who did not think it proper to bring in an outsider to chair an important task force that dealt with internal affairs of the university. (I think at that time the administration did not have the faintest idea about what a group facilitator did.) The meetings proceeded without a facilitator and with the vice president as chair.

In the first semester, the meetings went quite smoothly. Each week we simply discussed some relevant documents and brought in an expert on a particular human rights issue, such as sexual harassment, violence against women, and racism and discrimination. Student representatives recommended most of these external experts. However, even then, one problem, which proved to be undoing of the task force, became increasingly troublesome: none of the representatives of ethnic minorities stayed on the task force longer than two or three weeks. It became very disruptive to bring in new members who did not have the knowledge of what had already been covered in the meetings. The main stated reason for the high turnover rate was that these students of color did not feel comfortable sitting with the white folks. (Apparently my presence as a Chinese did not help make them feel at home.) (For a look at the role of newcomers in groups, see Cini, 2001.)

In the second semester, another problem developed: none of the student representatives would take part in the process as individuals because they stated that they needed to report back to the group and find out what their group wanted. They were neither socially nor intellectually engaged. They functioned only as the mouthpieces for some powerful individuals who were not part of the task force. Therefore, nothing could be decided before it was approved by some external groups. The vice president who chaired the meetings did not realize that by allowing these faceless external groups to dictate both the process and the decisions, the task force actually existed in name only.

The inevitable end came abruptly. One day the student representatives were unusually quiet. Shortly after the meeting started, about fifty people stormed into the boardroom, most of them nonstudents. Their leader, an angry and aggressive person of color, claimed he was president of the Rainbow Coalition, consisting of the Student Council, Antiracism Coalition, Gay/Lesbian/Bisexual Coalition, and others. He declared that the task force was illegitimate because it did not have any representation from persons of color and demanded that it dissolve itself immediately. When I pointed out that I represented visible minorities, the Rainbow Coalition leader walked up to me and threatened me with physical violence. Under duress, all members (except me) signed a prepared document declaring that the task force no longer existed because of its lack of legitimacy. I simply resigned from the task force.

After scoring this easy victory, the invaders stormed into the president's office demanding that the university hire four human rights officers to be responsible for four human rights areas: sexual harassment, gender equity, racial equity, and sexual orientation. They demanded that these four officers develop all principles and procedures pertaining to human rights. Thus, they fully revealed their political strategy and agenda after they had succeeded in killing the task force.

I have often wondered what would have happened had we engaged an external group facilitator. The complexity of the issues and the lack of trust among members of the task force clearly justified the need. However, several questions have lingered. Since students were so keen to appoint one of their favored facilitators, could that facilitator have been completely neutral and objective? What would this person have done to ensure that all task force members, especially the student representatives, put aside their group loyalties, ideologies, and politics so that they could have fully participated in the process? How could the facilitator have prevented the task force from being hijacked by external groups with a different agenda?

These are some of the tough questions facing facilitators. From my perspective, an effective group facilitator needs some of the same skills and competencies of counselors and group therapists. More specifically, the theoretical perspective of meaning-centered counseling can enhance the efficacy of facilitation. In this chapter, I outline the development of my theoretical framework, highlight the process, competencies, and characteristics needed to create a positive participatory climate, and outline the conditions for success from a meaning-centered counseling perspective.

DEVELOPMENT OF THEORETICAL FRAMEWORK

Meaning-centered counseling (MCC) is an extension of Carl Rogers's person-centered counseling (1951, 1957, 1986), Abraham Maslow's existential/humanistic psychology (1968, 1970), and Viktor Frankl's logotherapy (1985; Wong, 2002a). MCC (Wong, 1998, 1999) is integrative, because it integrates several theoretical models around the pivotal role of personal meaning. Personal meaning is an individually construed but socially constructed cognitive system that makes sense of events and endows life with a sense of purpose and significance. It consists of three components: cognitive, affective, and motivational. Feelings of fulfillment typically accompany coherent belief systems and the purposeful pursuit of meaningful goals.

Contribution of Carl Rogers

Rogers laid the foundation for nondirective counseling. His client-centered counseling (Rogers, 1951), which evolved into person-centered counseling (Rogers, 1986), posits that the main function of the therapist is to create a climate of safety and trust. Given a supportive, empowering environment, people can resolve their own problems without the direct intervention of a therapist. The necessary and sufficient conditions for successful therapeutic outcomes (Rogers, 1957) are the following:

- Unconditional positive regard. The therapist treats others with dignity and respect and accepts others in a nonjudgmental manner. The therapist also demonstrates a positive attitude of trust in the client's agency and ability to make the right choices.
- Empathy. The therapist shows a genuine interest in the client's phenomenological world of meaning, demonstrates the ability to understand the client's internal frames of reference, and reflects an attitude of caring and concern for his or her well-being.
- Congruence. The therapist demonstrates genuineness or authenticity. It is important that the therapist be seen as the same person in and out of the clinic and that there is congruence between his or her words and deeds.

These attitudes or characteristics are essential in creating a positive, therapeutic environment, in which the clients will become less defensive and more open to self-exploration and the quest for meaning. The therapist empowers the client by creating a supportive climate; the primary responsibility in deciding on therapeutic direction and life goals rests with the client.

It does not take any stretch of imagination to see the importance of Rogers's contribution to group facilitation. When a facilitator demonstrates the same kind of trust in the group and creates a supportive climate through positive regard, empathy, and congruence, the likelihood of achieving successful outcomes is increased.

However, there is one caveat: What will happen when the facilitator finds the values and attitudes of some group members offensive? If she expresses such negative feelings, she will violate the facilitator's cardinal tenet of neutrality. (For additional perspectives on neutrality, see Chapter Thirty.)

How could the facilitator be authentic and neutral at the same time? It seems to me that the only way to maintain strict neutrality is to perform the role of a facilitator as an actor, thus creating a safe distance between one's own value judgments and feelings and the task one must perform.

Certainly, the facilitator must remain genuine as a person, but when it comes to cherished values and beliefs, she needs to be authentic and compelling in the role of facilitator by not allowing personal feelings to get into the way. This does not mean that the facilitator becomes diminished as a person. It means that the best way to ensure neutrality and thus fulfill her professional duty is to adopt the stance of an actor by temporarily putting aside her own feelings and values and letting the character of facilitator take over. Otherwise, her biases will be betrayed unconsciously through facial expressions, tone of voice, and other nonverbal communication.

The absolute imperative of neutrality cannot be overstated. Since it is almost inevitable that the facilitator will encounter individuals who are antagonistic, offensive, destructive, or seductive and that transference and countertransference may take place, the only way to ensure neutrality is for the facilitator to remain an authentic actor of the professional role.

Contributions of Maslow and May

Maslow and May share Rogers's view that inherent in each person is the tendency toward purposefulness and growth. People will move toward self-actualization when their needs for acceptance and respect are met. According to Maslow (1968, 1970), self-actualizing persons welcome acceptance, spontaneity, creativity, and an open attitude toward life and exhibit a genuine caring for others.

Rollo May believed that "the creative person can affirm life in its three dimensions—affirm himself, affirm his fellow-men and affirm his destiny" (1940, p. 19). Also, he emphasized the importance of self-acceptance and the courage to maintain individuality as ways of experiencing authenticity and meaning (May, 1953, 1967).

The same positive psychological forces operate in group situations. Therefore, a facilitator who creates a climate of acceptance, affirmation, caring, openness, and authenticity unleashes creative energies for problem solving as well as personal and social transformation.

Contribution of Viktor Frankl

Frankl (1985) emphasized meaning actualization rather than self-actualization (Wong, 1998, 2002a); the focus is shifted from self-fulfillment to social responsibility. Frankl's logotherapy has three basic tenets:

- The freedom of will. This is the fundamental human capacity to choose, to take a stand, regardless of the predicaments confronting one. Since individuals have the freedom to make choices, they are responsible for the consequences. In exercising their freedom, they need to be concerned about the needs of friends, family, and society. They must ask what life demands of them rather than what they can get from life.

- The will to meaning. The primary and basic human motive is to discover and fulfill meaning and purpose. The will to meaning gives people hope and sustains them in their struggle for survival.

- The meaning of life. The discovery of meaning is possible even in the most appalling circumstances. The emphasis is not on why bad things happen to us, but on what we can do to find a meaningful solution. Meaning can be found only in responding to one's calling or mission toward community, humanity, and a higher power.

These tenets provide not only positive motivation but also helpful guidelines in group facilitation. By emphasizing the freedom of will, the facilitator reinforces the need for group members to be free from party loyalty and situational constraints in order to make responsible choices and decisions. By framing the group task in terms of the will to meaning, the facilitator can encourage the group to persist in spite of setbacks. By adopting the criteria of meaningfulness and responsibility, the facilitator can encourage the group to evaluate the quality and ethical concerns of their decisions.

Wong's Meaning-Centered Counseling

Wong (1998, 1999, 2002a, 2002b) has incorporated the major themes of existential-humanistic psychology with cognitive-behavioral therapy and narrative therapy. He defines personal meaning as an individually construed, socially constructed cognitive system that makes sense of events and endows life with a sense of purpose and significance.

One's cognitive meaning consists of both the construed meaning of a specific event and the discovered meaning and purpose of one's life goals. The meaning of a situation often takes on added significance from the perspective of one's meaning of existence.

Consistent with Gergen (1994), Wong considers personal meaning as based on a unique set of personal history, temperament, and life circumstances, as well as social construction through language, culture, interactions, and dialogues. (For a more detailed analysis of the definition of meaning, see Wong, 1998.)

The facilitator has a twofold task: to understand and clarify the unique meaning each member individually construes from the situation and to guide the process of achieving a shared, or socially constructed, understanding.

This shared reality may emerge as members suspend their preconceived views and cherished beliefs, and seek to truly understand what each one has to say. Although the group can come up with amazing results, we should always be aware of the potential harm of groupthink. Janis and Mann (1977) have shown that groupthink may lead to risky and wrong decisions because of pressure for conformity and the illusion of unanimity. Schuman (2002) has wisely advised that facilitators need to trust the group process but also believe in doubt. (For additional information about groupthink, see Chapter Seven.)

That is why the facilitator needs to be vigilant about consensus reached through groupthink or through the undue influence of some charismatic and prominent group members. The facilitator not only encourages cooperative problem solving (Maier, 1967), but also creates a supportive climate that favors open inquiry and the quest for meaning. She would encourage members to express objections and doubts, consider unpopular alternatives, and evaluate each decision with respect to shared objectives.

A meaning-centered facilitator will use a technique that helps the group study the implications of its decisions, such as the fast-forwarding technique (Wong, 1998), which asks clients to imagine and anticipate likely scenarios and consequences given a particular choice. Then she will challenge members to evaluate the choice: Do you all feel comfortable with the decision? Are you sure that this is what you really want? Where will it get you? Is it consistent with your long-term goal?

Sibbet (2002) points out that facilitators need to make sense of all the interactions, expectations, emotions, and exchanges of information in order to facilitate the group process. Therefore, they need to manage the complex flow of meanings from individuals and the group, as well as from their own understandings. Facilitators manage the group process well to the extent that they succeed in sorting out and clarifying the various meanings.

A meaning-centered facilitator is interested in both the journey and the destination, because no matter how smooth the process is, the group members will not go very far if they do not understand both the nature of the problem and what they really want to achieve. The meaning-centered approach facilitates the problem-solving process because it seeks to accomplish the following:

- A deeper understanding of the nature of the problem. "What might have contributed to the problem? What can we learn from it? What purpose does it serve? What is the meaning of the situation? What are the main issues involved?" The group not only needs to describe the problem accurately, but also understand the nature and causes of the problem.

- A clearer understanding of group goals and objective. "What do you really want to achieve? What is the significance and purpose of the goal? Why is this goal preferable to alternative ones? How important is this goal with respect to the larger picture and your long-term plan?" Once this understanding is achieved, the group can quickly move to resolution or terms of settlement.

- A better understanding of the self. "What are the bases for your strong feelings about this issue? What are your concerns? What is preventing you from changing your view on this issue? Are you excited about finding a solution that everyone can be proud of?" Self-understanding can contribute to personal growth and positive group dynamics.

The meaning-centered approach will facilitate the problem-solving process because it helps to clarify the main issues and empowers the group to move forward. In the following sections, the benefits of a meaning-centered orientation to group facilitation will become clearer.

CREATING A POSITIVE PARTICIPATORY CLIMATE

To create a positive, participatory climate, the facilitator needs to avoid the following common errors:

- Saying the wrong thing at the wrong time
- Saying nothing when intervention is needed
- Saying the same thing repeatedly

- Saying things that favor one subgroup or coalition
- Saying things that are confusing or contradictory
- Saying too much
- Saying too little

Any combination of these mistakes can derail the entire process. In the story at the start of this chapter, the vice president who chaired the task force committed several mistakes, especially the first two errors.

The facilitator needs to avoid the trap of yielding to the tyranny of the majority or the tyranny of a few powerful members. He needs to pay special attention to what the minority has to say, and empower the passive and inarticulate members and ensure that their views are expressed.

At times, the facilitator becomes so preoccupied with the cognitive or analytical aspects of the group process that he overlooks the emotional undercurrents and the affective components of interactions. The facilitator needs to pay the same amount of attention to the exchange of emotions as the exchange of information, because an emotionally wounded group member can be very destructive.

While avoiding these common mistakes, the effective facilitator needs to attend to the following key steps.

Build Rapport

Introduce yourself and your role as a facilitator. Explain your philosophy and approach to group facilitation. Demonstrate your unconditional positive regard, empathy, and genuineness. Assure the group of your strict adherence to the cardinal rule of neutrality.

Explain the Facilitation Process

Explain the decision-making process and procedure of finding a solution to make sure that everyone knows exactly how things will be done. This common understanding will ensure that the meeting will focus on issues that have been mandated or agreed on and will not allow any party to take over the meeting with its own agenda. Let everyone know that the procedures, meeting format, and agenda are not set in stone, for two reasons. First, a change in the seating plan, meeting place, or format may help create a fluid situation, in which participants may become more open to change and more creative in finding a solution. Second, the process is only as good as it is moving effectively to a successful solution. When the process is stalled, an experienced facilitator will be flexible and wise enough to make the necessary adjustment to get the process going again. These adjustments may involve breaking the group up into smaller subgroups, bringing a consultant in to address some thorny content issue, or having a weekend retreat, for example.

Emphasize That the Process Is Result Oriented

Explain that to achieve successful outcomes, the process needs to focus on issues and solutions rather than politics or personalities. If the discussion is not regulated and focused, some individuals may wander all over the map, go around in circles, or get bogged down in trivial side issues, and then the process may become unproductive. It may be helpful to focus on one issue at a time, because that allows the facilitator to jot down the various contributions, summarize the best ideas, and reach some consensus before moving to the next issue. Also, small, incremental steps of success can boost morale and enhance trust in the process. It is important that the facilitator not rush things to make sure that he has a good understanding of how everyone feels about an important issue and whether the solution is shared by most of the group.

Establish Ground Rules

Keep the meetings on time, and follow the agreed-on agenda and objectives. Emphasize the importance of avoiding accusatory, inflammatory, and injurious statements and the need to express opinions clearly. Ensure that everyone has the right to speak, question, disagree, change one's views, be heard, and treated with respect. No one is allowed to insult others or sabotage the process through nonparticipation or passive aggression.

Clarify the Objectives and Goals

It is important to identify and clarify the objectives and goals of the group. The process cannot move forward unless the parties involved can agree on what they need to accomplish. In the story at the start of the chapter, the students did not agree to the objectives of the task force, as mandated by the university president. They wanted the university to hire human rights officers to develop human rights principles and procedures rather than have the task force do this directly.

Manage Meaning Systems

It is essential that the facilitator, through a variety of skills, such as empathizing, reflecting, and summarizing, help the group create a system of shared meanings by grasping each individual meaning system and their similarities and differences. The rapid exchange of information needs to be synthesized and crystallized to manageable building blocks in order to construct shared meanings.

Manage Group Dynamics

Observe the group dynamics, dominating personalities, and patterns of interactions. Make sense of the emotional undercurrents, and monitor the emotional intensity from moment to moment. The facilitator has the skills to manage potential conflicts and emotional levels to ensure that group dynamics remain positive and constructive.

Teach Some Basic Skills

Depending on the needs of each group, the facilitator may provide instructions on basic skills, such as active and proactive listening, empathy, and dialogue. Dialogue has emerged as a valuable tool (Burson, 2002) in conjunction with learning organizations (Senge and others, 1994) and community building (Wong, 2003). When the situation involves racial and cultural conflict, it also is helpful to teach some basic cross-cultural counseling skills (Sue and Sue, 1999).

Provide Feedback

After each session, there needs to be some time for feedback and reflection. This exercise serves two important functions: it is a self-corrective process, and it demonstrates a spirit of openness and the desire to improve.

Identify and Celebrate Progress

Identifying and celebrating each small victory along the way helps maintain a positive climate and create the momentum toward success.

Debrief

At the conclusion of the process, debriefing will help evaluate what has been accomplished and create a sense of closure. It will also be a time for healing, repairing, and consolidating.

COMPETENCIES NEEDED TO CREATE A POSITIVE PARTICIPATORY CLIMATE

Competencies in Communication Skills

Communication skills are important. Basic counseling skills such as feedback, reflecting, and summarizing can play a vital part in facilitating dialogues and discussion. The ability to grasp and integrate diverse ideas and the ability to summarize and communicate what they have in common are also important in enhancing participation. Finally, group members need to learn how to be assertive without being aggressive and how to express dissent without resorting to negative or accusatory words.

Competencies in Cognitive Skills

The facilitator needs to have a well-educated mind. It takes years of learning and cultivating of one's intellectual ability to be able to grasp complex issues quickly and accurately. A person who does not have a sharp, analytical mind and does not possess a rich deposit of knowledge and experience will have difficulty following the arguments and counterarguments and teasing out the essentials from trivial side issues. The cognitive skill of synthesis is equally important to make sense of the myriad pieces of information and summarize the main points.

Competencies in Leadership Skills

A facilitator is by definition a leader. A great deal of leadership skill is needed for keeping the group together and motivating them to work through difficulties to arrive at some destination. These skills include team building, conflict resolution, maintaining discipline, vision casting, and delegating. It also important for the facilitator to have the ability to read people and situations and sense the underlying dynamics at work. She needs to understand the developmental nature of any group process and possess the necessary skills to help a group transform itself from uncertainty and mistrust to a cohesive work team.

As a group leader, the facilitator needs to understand and manage different kinds of diversity in order to transform tensions and conflicts into creative energies. This means that the facilitator should possess a certain level of knowledge and understanding of individual differences in ethnicity, culture, beliefs, values, temperaments, and learning style.

Competencies in Maintaining Neutrality

It is essential that the facilitator be a fair-minded, honest broker and a well-trained group process expert. It is not easy to maintain neutrality when some group members violate your moral sensitivity or try to get under your skin. Our sympathy tends to lie with those who share our values and are like us. Often our partiality surfaces in subtle and unconscious ways. However, even the slightest hint of bias can rob the facilitator of effectiveness and even derail the entire process. That is why the facilitator should not even hint which solutions are better or whose approach holds the best promise, even when his own expertise wants to cry out: "Look, I think so and so has got the best answer!" It takes a great deal of self-discipline to maintain self-control and not let one's own feelings and biases get in the way.

Competencies in Managing a Positive Climate

Climate management involves a set of skills such as gentle confrontation, unearthing hidden feelings, reframing negative events, and translating emotional outbursts into objective statements. To create and maintain a positive participatory climate, the facilitator needs to set the tone and standard for the meetings, and have the courage and wisdom to moderate and modulate the climate. It is important that she demonstrates and cultivates a climate of openness, acceptance, honesty, trust, respect, and professionalism (Wong, 2002b; Wong and Gupta, 2004). The facilitator also inspires confidence and optimism that the group can work together to find a solution.

To maintain a positive climate, the facilitator must not allow any individuals to disrupt the group process. He needs group skills to manage this, such as gently reminding people of the ground rules, turning to other members of the group for support to reinforce the ground rules, and talking to difficult members privately and soliciting their cooperation.

Competencies in Meaning Management

From the perspective of MCC, the key to effective facilitation is meaning management, because we live in the world of meanings, and problems and conflicts are most often due to:

- Misunderstanding each other's beliefs and values

- Misconstruing each other's statements and positions

- Mistrusting each other's motives and intentions

- Misreading each other's emotions
- Misattributing the causes of the problem
- Misconceived projects
- Misguided ambitions
- Misplaced priorities
- Misdirected objectives

To facilitate the problem-solving process in a complex and conflictual situation, the facilitator focuses on meaning clarification. Primarily, this involves clarifying the nature of the problem or dispute, clearly defining the objectives and goals, and identifying major issues and obstacles. In addition, it involves the ability to grasp the meanings of verbal and nonverbal communications, keep things in proper perspective, and view problems within a larger context of social responsibilities and humanistic concerns. Finally, it aims at cultivating a deeper understanding of the self as well as the group process.

In addition to meaning clarification, meaning management involves the ability to make sense of chaos, paradoxes, ambiguities, uncertainties, conflicts, and confusions. This requires the ability to analyze and synthesize multiple pieces of conflicting information and weave them into meaningful patterns. It entails the process of deconstruction and reconstruction of arguments and stories. It demands the creation of a new meaning system that incorporates diverse viewpoints and reflects a shared reality. This becomes more challenging in working with members from different ethnic backgrounds, because the facilitator needs to be knowledgeable of cultural differences in values and orientations (Leong and Wong, 2003; Triandis, 1995).

Finally, meaning management involves the ability to manage the group process to ensure that it moves purposefully toward a successful conclusion. The facilitator needs to possess the ability to keep one eye on the ball and another eye on the goal post. He is able to move the group forward by managing the moment-to-moment turbulence caused by the cross currents of conflicting ideas and clashing directions.

CHARACTERISTICS OF EFFECTIVE GROUP FACILITATORS

Based on all the characteristics set out already, what would be the generalized portrait of an effective, meaning-centered group facilitator? Note that the following characteristics are quite different from those of negotiators from the traditional adversary system.

Attributes and Attitudes

The following attributes and attitudes are vital for a meaning-centered group facilitator:

- Being a compassionate and caring individual
- Being a growing and self-actualizing person
- Being a wise and mature person capable of good judgment
- Understanding human nature and the human condition
- Understanding universal existential anxieties
- Understanding individual struggles with existential issues
- Being a world citizen who respects people from different nations
- Trusting in the individual's ability to overcome and grow
- Trusting in the group and the group process
- Remaining optimistic even when things are not going well
- Being enthusiastic, engaging, and inspiring in working with people
- Being purposeful and focused in carrying out the responsibility
- Being open to new ideas and flexible to adapt to new situations
- Being supportive, accepting, and warm toward others
- Demonstrating authenticity and integrity to engender people's trust
- Being strictly neutral and objective in order to facilitate the process
- Demonstrating empathy and understanding as a good counselor
- Having a genuine interest in people and being willing to enter into their worlds
- Being professional and confident and not taking offense easily
- Being generous in validating others and giving of oneself in serving others
- Being willing to put aside one's ego and self-interests in order to facilitate group success

Roles and Responsibilities

By definition, a facilitator has the expertise to manage the processes of information exchange and interpersonal dynamics toward an appropriate or desired goal.

From the perspective of MCC, the facilitator not only focuses on the process but also plays an important role in helping to clarify the objective to make sure that it is attainable and agreed on by all group members. More important, the facilitator is responsible for creating a positive, supportive participatory climate that is conducive to problem solving and positive transformation.

To summarize, the facilitator fulfills the following roles and responsibilities

A counselor—to facilitate clarification of the issues and discovery of meanings and purpose

A mentor—to cultivate unconditional positive regard, empathy, and genuineness

A teacher—to guide and challenge group members to come up with the best answers to their problems

An honest broker—to facilitate some resolution of conflicting positions; to take a neutral and detached pragmatic view of disputed issues

A moderator and referee—to facilitate the process and enforce the ground rules, maintain order, ensure all members are treated equally, and control problem people

A model—to demonstrate how to keep cool and focused even in an emotionally charged situation

A leader—to motivate and inspire creative, cooperative problem solving and create a team from diverse individuals

A consultant—to provide some guidelines or insight to get the process moving forward

A manager—to manage time and resources effectively and create and maintain a positive, participatory climate

An actor—to put aside personal feelings and biases in performing the role of facilitation with authenticity and neutrality

CONDITIONS FOR SUCCESS

Given the complexity of the task and the important responsibilities of the facilitator, the precondition for success is that the facilitator has received quality graduate education and professional training and has resolved most of her debilitating personal issues and achieved a certain level of maturity.

From the perspective of MCC, success is measured not just by the efficiency of the process, but also by the positive impact the process has on the individual members and the group as a whole. Successful meaning-centered facilitation is transformational.

Therefore, this approach is appropriate in the following situations:

- Resolving conflicts and impasse between two groups or members within a group
- Reducing the level of mistrust and conflict in an organization
- Facilitating the decision-making process to achieve organizational goals
- Brainstorming sessions
- Mediation between two parties
- Focus groups
- Community agency planning
- Community development projects
- Strategic planning and visioning
- Retreats for management and staff
- Task forces involving different stakeholders
- Commission with expert members
- Bridge building and peacemaking
- Corporate training to transform organizational culture and climate
- Membership meetings
- Alternative dispute resolution
- Board meetings

More often than not, CEOs or presidents want to control the agenda and process of meetings in order to secure maximum board support for their projects. This approach is not applicable to such situations. However, a CEO who prefers a responsible and active board that participates in the decision-making process needs to adopt the role of a facilitator in chairing board meetings. Furthermore, CEOs may take on the role of facilitator to empower staff members to participate.

It may not be most appropriate to use the meaning-centered approach in times of emergency, when tough decisions need to be made quickly. In such situations, individuals given the responsibility, expertise, and position to make decisions should be allowed to do so without the elaborate exercise of team building and consensus building among all members. This approach may not be effective in electronic meetings, because it would be difficult for the facilitator to create a climate of trust, caring, and safety through digital media.

How to Build a Collaborative Environment

David Straus

How do facilitators build a collaborative environment—a lasting culture of collaboration? This challenge rests on the cutting edge of our profession as facilitators. To support a client to build a culture of collaboration involves a significant expansion of the role of facilitator and most likely requires forming a partnership with other consulting professions. I believe that creating collaborative organizations and communities will be one of the most important challenges society will face in the twenty-first century, a challenge that as facilitators are well positioned to embrace.

COLLABORATIVE ORGANIZATIONS AND COMMUNITIES

I believe we are witnessing the evolution of a new kind of organization that I call collaborative. Collaborative organizations are a direct response to forces both external (increasing complexity of issues, marketplace uncertainty, customer demands for better-quality and integrated services, and increased competition to reduce time to market and costs) and internal (workforce demands for more involvement in decision making and access to information). Collaborative communities are also evolving in response to the need to reinvigorate deliberative democracy through increased, meaningful public involvement in resolving complex issues (Chrislip, 2002).

191

Once you make a commitment to three fundamental values and beliefs (respect for human dignity, appropriate stakeholder voice, and a belief in the power of collaborative action) everything changes: how you lead, how you organize, how you reward employees, how you use technology, and what new skills and competencies are required. (For the case for collaborative organizations and communities, see Straus, 2002.) For the purposes of this chapter, collaborative organizations have the following characteristics:

- Aligned around shared purpose and meaning as expressed in vision, mission, values, and strategic direction
- Organized collaboratively across a number of dimensions
- Dependent on core skills of facilitative leadership, teamwork, and collaborative problem solving
- Committed to supporting and rewarding lifelong learning and teamwork
- Socially responsible
- Enabling collaboration and access to information by using new technologies
- Reliant on a new social contract of rights and responsibilities between the organization and employee

A successful systemic change effort must address all aspects of an organization. In addition to culture, you must bring into alignment the reward systems, technology systems, and organizational structure. That is why an effective organizational change effort will likely have to involve other disciplines in addition to facilitation. In this chapter, I address only the cultural aspects of change and focus on organizations, although most of these approaches apply to communities as well. By *culture*, I mean the norms, values, beliefs, and basic assumptions of an organization (Schein, 1985). In a collaborative culture, the expectation is that everyone will work collaboratively with the maximum appropriate level of stakeholder involvement. A collaborative environment has been built when the following conditions exist:

- Leadership has made an explicit commitment to the core values of collaboration and is demonstrating this commitment through its actions.
- Critical issues throughout the organization are being resolved successfully through collaborative action.

- Managers and employees throughout the system have acquired and are successfully applying collaborative attitudes, skills, and behaviors within their normal work environments.

- A corps of internal change agents with the necessary skills of training, facilitation, conflict resolution, and change management has been developed, and its services are widely used.

CONDITIONS FOR SUCCESS

In my experience, organizations come to understand the strategic importance of a collaborative culture and consciously commit to building it only after completing several successful and significant collaborative efforts. First comes the problem: how to build alignment around a new strategic plan, how to downsize with maximum employee support, or how to increase customer satisfaction, for example. Next, the organization experiences a measure of success in tackling a number of these strategic issues collaboratively. This leads it to realize that cultural change is a necessary and efficient way of institutionalizing collaborative capabilities. Leaders begin to ask how to make collaboration the norm, how to spread collaborative capabilities through the organization, and how to become less dependent on outside process consultants and trainers.

If you want to be in a position to support an organization to change its culture, there are some important implications for you as a consultant and facilitator. First, you and your colleagues must have been lead consultants in the design and facilitation of one or more collaborative efforts involving top management. You must have facilitated some strategic meetings with the leadership team and have worked closely with the CEO. Moreover, the CEO must see you as a respected adviser and coach, and you must trust each other. Undertaking a cultural change effort requires a huge leap of faith on the part of a leader. This person will need to trust that you will be there when needed, can offer honest feedback, and possess the experience and credibility to provide the required consulting and training services.

Indeed, you must be seen as more than a facilitator or trainer. You can support an existing change effort from below, but to partner in the leadership of change process, you must be working with the top team. The internal human resource (HR) department staff should be allies but not, as so often happens, gatekeepers to the top. This is a difficult triangular relationship to manage. You need to have open access to the CEO and top leadership and be included in strategic meetings, an access the director of HR may not have. At the same time, you need a good working relationship with the internal training and organization development departments, which should see this effort as a way of increasing their strategic impact and role in the organization.

THE CHALLENGES OF SYSTEMIC CHANGE

At some point, you must answer the inevitable question: How do we institutionalize collaboration throughout the organization? Systemic change is incredibly difficult. In times of stress, organizational systems tend to snap back to old behaviors unless new norms are deeply ingrained. Ask fellow consultants how many clients have successfully implemented some change that is still in place five years after the intervention was completed. Usually it does not take many fingers to count. This has been true in my career as well. Therefore, I offer the following ideas with great humility, realizing what a difficult task it is to build a truly collaborative culture.

I work from a few basic assumptions about systemic change:

- You cannot consult or train your way to change. You must do both. *Doing* and *learning to do* feed off each other and must go hand in hand. You learn a great deal by participating in a well-facilitated collaborative effort. And when you learn new collaborative skills, you become a more effective leader and participant.

- Change must occur simultaneously in many parts of an organization. Otherwise, the system at large will seal itself off from the innovation as if from an infection. If one part of an organization is getting all the attention and resources, resentment can build elsewhere. If the intervention is seen as being focused only on the top or bottom of the organization, other parts will discount it.

- The change must be seen as a strategic response to some internal or external challenge, the so-called burning platform phenomenon, where standing still is not an option.

- Dealing with the problem must be seen as critical to survival and growth.

- Top leadership must model the values and behaviors of the new culture.

- Other organizational systems—rewards and recognition, technology, and structure—must be aligned to support the cultural change.

A FIVE-PRONGED APPROACH TO BUILDING A COLLABORATIVE ENVIRONMENT

Based on these principles and mindful of the difficulty of the tasks, I offer a five-pronged approach to building a collaborative environment.

Link the Change to the Organization's Mission and Strategy

The first prong is to *build leadership and ownership at all levels of the organization by linking the change to the mission and strategy and forming a cross-functional, multilevel team to guide and own the change effort.*

A basic principle of collaboration is that if you do not agree on the problem, you will never agree on the solution. Building a collaborative environment must be seen as a solution to a strategic issue, not just a good thing to do. There must be some pressing business reason to become more collaborative and cross-functional. Otherwise the change effort will fail as soon as economic hard times hit.

In general, a cultural change effort should be preceded by a strategic planning process. Fortunately, the need to increase collaboration is a strategic issue for many organizations today as they try to respond to escalating customer demands. In industries such as health care, manufacturing, financial services, and energy, customers expect integrated solutions delivered globally. Teamwork across disciplines and geographies is essential. However, an organization must arrive at this conclusion itself. The logic and rationale for increased collaboration must be clear to all, and this usually means an effective process of strategic thinking, which itself should be conducted with maximum stakeholder involvement.

The cultures of organizations are finely crafted systems—even in their dysfunctionality. Everyone colludes in maintaining the existing culture, even though many may complain vociferously. Everyone gets something out of maintaining the way things are, even if it is just predictability. Therefore, the first phase of a cultural change process should begin with describing and acknowledging responsibility for the current norms, values, and behaviors. People in the organization must look at how things actually work—not at the professed values and procedures but at the unwritten rules of the road. To get at the current norms, we often ask the question this way: "If you were briefing a new member of your team about how to get along, how to fit in, what would you tell him or her about how to succeed— how not to rock the boat?" This often elicits smiles from the group and makes it okay to discuss matters that are usually left unsaid.

Some of the norms and values may be positive, and the organization may want to hold on to them. Others may be clearly destructive and inappropriate for the culture it wants to build. Leaders must make it comfortable for people to discuss the current culture but, more important, to acknowledge their role in keeping things the way they are. It is important for leaders to model openness and vulnerability, to take responsibility for how they collude in the negative aspects of the current culture. If leaders cannot do these things themselves, they cannot expect them of their direct reports.

A good example of this kind of leadership comes to mind. Hospitals are notorious for adversarial relationships between administrators and physicians. In one hospital where I did consulting work, everyone (president, physicians, administrators, nurses, even the board) complained about a very autocratic, command-and-control culture and open warfare between the president and the division chiefs, who were physicians. After some coaching and the creation of an appropriate setting, the president openly admitted to his physician chiefs that he rather liked the fighting—that it kept him in control and kept the chiefs from developing too much power. Besides, he had to meet with them only for two hours each month.

The division chiefs admitted that they too colluded in the system. By conducting one-on-one budget negotiations with the president, each division chief thought he could make a better deal for his division and did not have to worry about trade-offs with other divisions. Both the president and the division chiefs confessed to each other that they would have to give up these perceived benefits if they were to move to a more collaborative culture, one they agreed they needed to survive in a rapidly changing, competitive external environment.

In another example, the administration of a large private school I worked with wanted to become less paternalistic and more collaborative in its decision making. The breakthrough occurred when the vice president realized that she treated the president very formally and never confronted him directly when she disagreed with him. She (and he) saw that this behavior communicated to the management team and the rest of the school that openness and directness were not welcomed or permitted. Real progress was not possible until they acknowledged that their actions sent the wrong message and then changed their behavior.

It is important to balance the top team's ownership of the effort with involvement from other levels of the organization. A senior leadership team can easily become insulated and may not be the best judge of what is going on in other parts of the organization. Even if the senior leaders are working very hard on their own teamwork and collaboration, they may assume the rest of the organization is equally engaged in this effort when it is not.

You can resolve this dilemma through the structure of the strategic planning process itself. While the senior leadership team should be responsible for the overall strategic planning process, it should charter cross-functional, multilevel teams to plan and oversee the implementation of specific strategies. One of these strategies would be concerned with the need to build a more collaborative culture. While the team responsible for this strategy, sometimes called a key result area (KRA), should include one or more members of the senior leadership team, it should also include relevant stakeholders from different parts and levels of the organization— a diagonal slice. Members might include staff from the HR and training departments, middle managers, and employees from the front line of the organization. In this way, the KRA team can provide a reality check on the effects of the change effort. The KRA team should report regularly to senior management and advocate for the necessary resources to support the change effort.

Demonstrate the Power of Collaborative Action

The second prong of the approach is to *demonstrate the power of collaborative action throughout the organization by addressing and resolving issues collaboratively.*

A powerful feedback loop links facilitating and teaching facilitation. When you facilitate, you are subtly teaching participants about collaborative problem solving; when you are training, you are providing opportunities for participants to practice their skills on work-related problems, as well as showcasing your skills as a facilitator. To put it another way, the change you want is the change you begin with. If you want to build a collaborative culture, you must work collaboratively from the beginning. There is no better way to build credibility for the effectiveness of multistakeholder collaborative problem solving than to resolve a strategic business issue by means of a highly visible collaborative planning process.

Often managers resist trying a new idea or process with their own direct reports until they have experienced it somewhere else. For example, after a manager participates in a facilitated meeting convened by someone else, he or she may be willing to try facilitation in his or her own meetings. A theory of change that emerged in the 1980s maintained that rather than targeting your existing organization, you should create a parallel informal organization that models the behaviors and skills that you want and then let the formal organization begin to absorb these new behaviors. In other words, rather than demanding that all managers become more facilitative, top leadership should involve these managers in collaborative planning efforts. Managers can witness that their leaders are serious about stakeholder involvement and that consensus can be developed efficiently around strategic issues. Then, if offered training and consulting support, these managers can introduce more collaborative management practices in their own work groups and organizational units. While at some point senior leadership must make clear that facilitative leadership and appropriate stakeholder involvement are expected to become the norm, these parallel collaborative efforts can be an effective front-end phase of building a more collaborative environment.

Build the Collaborative Capability of the Workforce

The third prong is to *increase the number of people at all levels of the organization who have internalized collaborative skills and applied them to real issues.*

Collaboration requires an integrated way of looking at the world. It involves new mind-sets and skill sets as well as heart sets. While your heart may learn through experience, your mind and skills can be trained. The collaborative capability of a workforce can be built through an integrated curriculum of skill training in such areas as facilitative leadership, facilitation, teamwork, process design and management, strategic thinking, and coaching. The challenge is to determine who needs what training and when. Not everyone needs to be an expert facilitator or process designer. Only a few need to be good process trainers. People need different but related skills depending on their role or function. What is important is building a common language about collaboration and problem solving, and ensuring that different training modules easily integrate and build on each other. It is very helpful if everyone means the same thing when using terms such as *process, content, strategy, vision, strategic moment, stakeholder, solution space, facilitation,* and *sponsor.*

The best learning moment is when you have a need to know but have not struggled so long that you are frustrated and want to give up. Training is most effective when it is delivered just-in-time and can relate to a specific need. This usually implies that training is delivered on-site by internal resources. It is important that collaborative skills training is available when needed and can be delivered to intact teams. This kind of training is powerful because real work issues can be used, and the skills transferred are directly related to the task at hand.

Training is best conceived as a learning process rather than a specific event or workshop. Participants need to be supported after classroom workshops in order to integrate and use their new skills effectively. Therefore, an important ingredient to the transfer of collaborative capabilities is the availability of follow-up coaching and process consulting services. Trainees should have access to skilled people who can assist them in designing effective involvement processes, as well as facilitate difficult meetings. Increasingly, these support services should be offered by internal consultants. This point leads to the fourth approach to building a collaborative culture.

Transfer Collaborative Capacity to the Organization

The fourth prong is to *develop and deploy internal training, facilitation, consulting, and coaching capability.*

A truly collaborative culture must be self-sustaining. It cannot be dependent on external intervention. Our job as facilitators and change agents is to work ourselves out of a job. Ultimately our goal should be to transfer as much collaborative capability as possible to client organizations. This transfer process usually has three phases.

In the initial phase, you and your colleagues provide most of the consulting and training services externally. The client organization may be testing the effectiveness of large-scale collaborative planning and not be ready to invest in the internalization of the collaborative capabilities.

Even so, you should be identifying internal resources, especially in the HR and training departments, to work with you as allies and members of your team. They should understand the implications for their role if this intervention is successful. The transformation from a more command-and-control culture to a more participatory one creates a legitimacy and demand for people with process skills. This demand is usually met by the HR and training departments, whose role expands to include a more strategic, task-oriented role of process consultants and facilitators. It is essential to build a partnership with these internal resources from the beginning of an intervention so they do not see you as a threat and sabotage the effort.

Often a large collaborative effort requires a dedicated, internal process manager to coordinate the project, manage the logistics and staffing of the various committees, and serve as liaison with external consultants. The process manager needs advanced training in process skills and will become a strong advocate for the change process.

As the intervention proceeds and other collaborative projects spin off, the question of the availability and cost of external consultants eventually arises. A good response is to advocate for the creation and training of an internal corps of process consultants and trainers. The rationale is that an increasing amount of facilitation, process management, and training services can be delivered more conveniently and at a lower cost by internal personnel. This is the time to begin to co-envision what a more collaborative environment might consist of, including such elements as better meeting spaces, support technology, and just-in-time training in process skills.

Therefore, the second phase of the transfer of advanced collaborative capabilities involves actively partnering with internal people to plan and facilitate meetings and deliver training programs. In the same way as you would train a new associate, you will gradually and deliberately move into the background, allowing internal consultants to lead new interventions. This transfer of responsibilities can happen only if you are very clear in your own mind that success means having the client prefer to have someone else lead a new intervention. It is natural for a client to "love the one they're with." You can easily justify your indispensability by saying, "They insist on my doing this work." Often this means that you are not willing to let go and are somehow communicating to the client that you are the better choice. Sometimes the weaning process may involve just saying that you are not available (when you really are) or even not showing up at the last moment so that your internal partner must take the lead. This process is very hard for both sides but necessary. However, if your client is going to own and sustain the change, this process of letting go and transferring responsibilities must take place. Many change efforts flounder at this point.

The third phase involves indirect support where you are less or not at all involved in delivering direct services, but instead are supporting internal consultants to deliver the services themselves. This support may consist of a range of activities, including on-site meetings with internal consultants, advanced training, and a support hot line. It is also very helpful to create a support network, or community of practice, by linking internal change agents from different organizations involved in similar interventions. Sustaining a change effort requires a tremendous output of leadership energy. It can be reinvigorating to talk with others who have completed a similar effort successfully or are struggling with similar issues.

Measure and Monitor Progress

The final prong is to *measure and monitor progress of the change effort.*

Evaluation is an essential component of the heuristic cycle of problem solving. We need to know if our strategy is working. If it is not, we need to try something else. One of the advantages of facilitation is that it is immediately clear to all participants that it works in the three dimensions of results, process, and relationship. Formal evaluation instruments do not seem necessary. However, the benefits of creating a collaborative culture take longer to become evident and are harder to assess quantitatively. While we may believe intuitively in the value of collaborative cultures, there have been very few formal studies of the benefits of collaborative organizations and few validated assessment tools to measure progress in the development of collaborative cultures. (Examples of assessment instruments can be found at the Management Research Group Web site, http://www.mrg.com, 2003, and Vroom, 2003. A cross-cultural card game is described in Chapter Sixteen.) Naturally, clients want to know that they will recoup the costs and reap the bottom-line benefits of large-scale change efforts. They want to know, step by step, the progress they are making. I believe the lack of validated, easy-to-administer assessment tools is a serious deficit in our profession. Evaluation is important to a successful change effort, but I do not have many tools to offer. (For related information on evaluation, see Chapters Twenty-Four and Twenty-Five.)

The closest tool I have found, but have not applied in an intervention, is the Denison Organizational Culture Survey. Using a validated assessment instrument, Daniel Denison at the University of Michigan tested and scored twelve hundred companies in relation to four cultural traits: mission, involvement, adaptability, and consistency. Caroline J. Fisher (2000), a student of Denison's work, describes these traits as follows:

> *Mission:* The degree to which the company knows why it exists and what its direction is. This is not about your company having a mission that the executive team designed which is framed nicely on the wall over the copier. It is about shared understanding, alignment, and ownership of that vision throughout your company—with line of sight from job to mission.
>
> *Involvement:* The degree to which individuals at all levels of the company are engaged in and hold that direction as their own. This is not about how involved your managers "say" your front-line workers are. This is about how involved your front-line workers say *they* are. And how well people at all levels are positioned, through personal responsibility, authority, accountability, skills, and team orientation, to achieve goals that support the company's mission.

Adaptability: The ability of the company to know what customers want, and the degree to which it can respond to external forces and demands. True customer focus is not just knowing what the customer wants—it is also knowing what you have to learn to provide it, and infusing your organization with that learning.

Consistency: The company's systems and processes which support efficiency and effectiveness in reaching goals. This is not about having a nice set of values that are printed on coffee mugs. This is about a defined set of behavioral standards that allow the organization to move beyond restrictive policies and procedures and move to general guidelines for effective interaction. It is about walking the talk from the top to the front lines. It is about creating a shared language which helps everyone work more smoothly together—increasing speed in movement and efficiency in achieving results [p. 4].

These four traits do a good job of describing a collaborative culture. Indeed, collaborative action is essential to scoring highly in all four dimensions. And what Denison discovered is that companies with high performance (an average return on investment of 30 percent) scored well on all four traits, compared with companies with low performance (an average return on investment of 9 percent), which scored poorly in these four areas. The survey consists of sixty questions scored on a five-point Likert scale, which can be administered on-line. There is also a leadership development instrument.

Using whatever assessment tools are available, including employee surveys and focus groups, the KRA cultural change committee should attempt to assess and measure the progress of the cultural change effort. Ideally, baseline measurements should be taken at the beginning of the intervention and administered annually thereafter. Not only do you need to see progress on the way to becoming a more collaborative environment, you should also check to see if there is any slippage or regression after the new norms have been established. Our collective mission of building collaborative organizations will be greatly enhanced if new tailored, validated assessment tools are developed, and the linkages to the bottom-line benefits can be clearly established.

CONCLUSION

It is possible to build collaborative cultures. I have experienced the joy and productivity of having led and worked in a collaborative environment for more than thirty years. And I have witnessed client systems become more collaborative and reap the rewards. All it takes is a facilitative leader who believes in the power of collaborative action and is willing to model and promote the essential values, behaviors, and skills. With this leadership commitment and by following the five-pronged approach I have presented, collaborative environments can be built and sustained. I believe organizations that know how to collaborate across functions and geographies will have a competitive advantage in the future. I believe our ultimate mission as professional facilitators should be to assist people to build collaborative environments through demonstrating the power and transferring the skills of collaborative action.

Effective Strategies for Designing and Facilitating Dialogue

Steven N. Pyser

*D*iversity initiatives in American corporations have created opportunities and challenges. Not all executives, managers, or employees have embraced cultural differences and workplace programs or understand the benefits of learning and working with a diverse community.

Managers and labor representatives of a public transit agency are scheduled to negotiate a new collective bargaining agreement. There is a history of conflict, strikes, misunderstanding, and intractable conflict. Each team does not believe the other will negotiate in good faith.

Multiple communities and business stakeholders have different visions for redeveloping the World Trade Center site after September 11, 2001. All parties are concerned that government is not responsive to their concerns.

These vignettes contain comparable themes involving disagreement and conflict among stakeholders—anyone with some form of interest or a share. Each person is unique and holds viewpoints developed through divergent life events. Each thus brings to these scenarios identities comprising "ideas, beliefs, opinions, feelings, desires, patterns, hopes and fears" (Hunter, Bailey, and Taylor, 1995, p. 5). Fortunately, these situations are not deadlocked, and there are potential opportunities for facilitators to use dialogue to help uncover interests and needs, build understanding,

205

and find common ground. "Dialogue is a structured form of communication which emphasizes respectful and attentive listening about deep-rooted feelings, beliefs and experiences" (Conflict Research Consortium, 1998a). Many participants emerge from dialogue with compelling stories of powerful, life-altering experiences that motivate personal growth and mutual action.

One interpretation of these fact patterns is that the stakeholders are concurrently trying to occupy (and perhaps control) the same physical, psychological, and political space to achieve their goals. Their histories and manner of contact and communication (or miscommunication) are factors that can influence or decide the outcomes. The reader might relate to these vignettes to personal circumstances or professional facilitation experiences where adversarial interactions unraveled into blame or similar negative and unproductive behaviors. Unfortunately, these exchanges often present as blocked communication channels and can quickly intensify in conflict. Too often, many people employ these tactics as unspoken default modes of conduct during interpersonal encounters. Dialogue is a viable and productive alternative way to communicate, build understanding, and be understood by others. As facilitators, we can use dialogue to help clients (and ourselves) understand different stakeholders' viewpoints and create a collaborative environment in which to work out ideas and alternatives for collective action.

Noted physicist and Nobel laureate Albert Einstein once stated, "No problem can be solved from the same level of consciousness that created it." What if a process existed where the goal is not to change the views of the participant but rather to listen deeply with other unique individuals and a personal intention to gain understanding in a nonjudgmental, emotionally, and physically safe environment? What if as a facilitator you could help create and apply guidelines for group behavior to encourage respect and keeping an open mind? Assume further that you can guide a process where each participant is recognized, valued, and allowed to share his or her stories without interruption, ask difficult questions, engage in conversation, present viewpoints, and talk about issues of concern. Finally, what if this process provided structure that allowed participants to examine the basis of their opinions and perceptions of other stakeholders in a different light? Would you be interested in learning about these benefits and potential uses of dialogue?

This chapter examines foundational skills for designing and moderating a dialogue. A story binding different facilitation skills and an example from actual practice are presented through a diversity vignette drawn from business, management, law, and organizational ethics. These lessons can help readers develop services for clients by learning to facilitate conversations that can change a focus from continuing problems involving stubborn disagreements to opportunities to explore opposing opinions, positions, and interests. A list of support organizations and resources for designing and facilitating dialogue is provided at the end of this chapter.

WHAT IS DIALOGUE?

The *Oxford English Dictionary* defines *dialogue* as "a conversation carried on between two or more persons; a colloquy, talk together." It has been suggested the ancient meaning of the word *dialogue* (*dia* and *lagos*) is a "flow of meaning" (Jaworski, 1998, p. 13). "This stands in stark contrast to the word 'debate,' which means 'to beat down,' or even 'discussion,' which has the same root as 'percussion' and 'concussion'—'to break things up'" (Jaworski, 1998, p. 110). Discussion occupies a different location in the communication continuum. Gerard and Ellinor (2004) suggest that people use discussion "to tell, sell, persuade; to gain agreement on one meaning; to evaluate and select the best; to justify/defend assumptions."

It is important to recognize that dialogue is a process where participants commit to listen, challenge, reflect, and continue to talk over time; it is not an event (Schoem and others, 2001, p. 6). "Dialogue . . . is about a shared inquiry, a way of thinking and reflecting together. It is not something you do *to* another person. It is something you do *with* people" (Isaacs, 1999, p. 9). Participants seek a shared understanding to find meaning in dialogue. "During the dialogue process, people learn how to think together—not just in the sense of analyzing a shared problem or creating new pieces of shared knowledge, but in the sense of occupying a collective sensibility, in which the thoughts, emotions, and resulting actions belong not to one individual, but to all of them together" (Isaacs, 1994, p. 358).

Dialogue can play an important role in the facilitator's toolbox. Sandy Heierbacher (2004), convener of the National Coalition for Dialogue and Deliberation, has assembled quotations and descriptions from expert practitioners and researchers about the dynamic processes of various models and methods of dialogue and deliberation. In this collection of quotations, Harold Saunders has artfully described dialogue as a "process of genuine interaction through which human beings listen to each other deeply enough to be changed by what they learn. Each makes a serious effort to take others' concerns into her or his own picture, even when disagreement persists. No participant gives up her or his identity, but each recognizes enough of the other's valid human claims that he or she will act differently toward the other."

An Ethiopian proverb that reflects the power and spirit of dialogue states: "When spider webs unite, they can halt even a lion." From this wisdom, it becomes apparent that even small and focused efforts have far-reaching consequences among interdependent people. There are untapped intellectual, emotional, and spiritual energies that can be revealed and used through dialogue. Through talking and listening to other individuals, dialogue affords an opportunity to grasp and identify our experiences and disclose our beliefs and opinions.

The current dialogue movement can be traced to the pioneering work of physicist David Bohm and philosopher Martin Buber and more recent innovators such as William Isaacs, Peter Senge, Daniel Yankelovich, Ambassador John W. McDonald, Ambassador Harold Saunders, and Deborah L. Flick. We are now at an important crossroad in the evolution and development of applications for dialogue. Commentator Tom Atlee (2003) has suggested, "In the midst of all of the challenges and difficulties we're facing, I believe that we are witnessing the emergence of the larger culture of dialogue. The phenomenon includes many forms of dialogue—from therapy sessions to open space conferences, from Internet chat room to conflict resolution work, from workplace team meetings to private heart-to-heart talks, from interracial dinners to creative radio interviews to weekly salons and café conversations" (p. 218).

The terms *dialogue* and *deliberation* are often mentioned together. Deliberation is associated with dialogue and is a method with a different emphasis. "Deliberation promotes the use of critical reasoning and logical argument in decision-making. Instead of decision-making by power, coercion or hierarchy, deliberative decision-making emphasizes the examination of facts and arguments and the weighing of pros and cons of various options" (Heierbacher, 2004). This chapter is limited in scope to the topic of dialogue. Exhibit 13.1 compares and contrasts debate and dialogue and the benefits of using a dialogue process.

Dialogue as Possible Agent of Change

Dialogue is an important emerging method of facilitation and holds enormous promise as a versatile and successful communication process. It offers unlimited possibilities for transforming the manner in which we communicate and share knowledge. In addition, it has the potential to resolve differences and clashes of interests between individuals, organizations, and communities. Various models and techniques of dialogue are in worldwide use and are affecting the lives of people, workplaces, and society.

A review of the current literature on dialogue reveals a multitude of practices, methods, and definitions with a confusing range of characteristics, terms, and models. In fact, a Google search "what is dialogue" on April 1, 2004, returned over eight hundred responses. In response to the profusion of practices, techniques, and definitions, it has been suggested that "none of these [dialogue] approaches can lay claim to being the 'correct' view, it is indeed possible to distinguish the various views, and to clarify what is intended by each" (Bohm, 2003, p. vii). The following are representative examples of models or terms describing dialogue and deliberation: "civic engagement, public participation, study circles, community conversations, public discourse, honest conversations, deliberative discourse, and community cafes. Some of these are 'brands' that are developed and promoted by particular organizations, and some are terms that are used within certain constituencies" (Heierbacher and Fluke, 2001/2002).

Collective Inquiry

Among the models of dialogue that Zuniga and Nagda (2004) have identified is the Collective Inquiry Model, which emerged from the highly influential work of Bohm. "Collective inquiry models posit that suspending judgments and assumptions is essential to finding shared meaning among dialogue participants. The Collective Inquiry Model focuses on nurturing participants' abilities to engage in collective thinking and inquiry for the development of synergistic and meaningful relationships" (Zuniga and Nagda, 2004, p. 307). Another example of the Collective Inquiry Model is the research and applications on organizational learning by William Isaacs and his colleagues at the Dialogue Project at the Massachusetts Institute of Technology. Organizations and communities throughout the United States have put this model into service (Zuniga and Nagda, 2004). A facilitator using the Collective Inquiry Model will move through several stages (Zuniga and Nagda, 2004):

1. Establish an environment for dialogue. Clarify the purpose of the dialogue. Build a container for dialogue for safety and trust issues to emerge. Develop group consensus on purpose, mission, and structure.

2. Develop a common base of knowledge—conceptual and personal. Explore beliefs and assumptions by sharing information leading to public suspension of judgments. Engage in dialogue about personal, work-related, or general topics.

Exhibit 13.1
Distinguishing Debate from Dialogue

Debate	Dialogue
Premeeting communication between sponsors and participants is minimal and largely irrelevant to what follows.	Premeeting contacts and preparation of participants are essential elements of the full process.

Debate	Dialogue
The atmosphere is threatening; attacks and interruptions are expected by participants and are usually permitted by moderators.	The atmosphere is one of safety; facilitators propose, get agreement on, and enforce clear ground rules to enhance safety and promote respectful exchange.

Debate	Dialogue
Participants speak as representatives of groups.	Participants speak as individuals from their own unique experience.

Debate	Dialogue
Differences within sides are denied or minimized.	Differences among participants on the same side are revealed as individual and personal foundations of beliefs and values are explored.

Debate	Dialogue
Participants express unswerving commitment to a point of view, approach, or idea.	Participants express uncertainties as well as deeply held beliefs.

Debate	Dialogue
Participants listen in order to refute the other side's data and to expose faulty logic in their arguments. Questions are asked from a position of certainty. These questions are often rhetorical challenges or disguised statements.	Participants listen to understand and gain insight into the beliefs and concerns of the others. Questions are asked from a position of curiosity.

Debate	Dialogue
Statements are predictable and offer little new information.	New information surfaces.
Success requires simple impassioned statements.	Success requires exploration of the complexities of the issue being discussed.

Source: Excerpted and adapted from "Distinguishing Debate from Dialogue: A Table." Reprinted with permission from the Public Conversations Project (1992).

3. Explore questions, issues, or conflict. Focus the dialogue on one or more questions, issues, or specific conflicts, and deepen the dialogue. Increase suspension of judgment (when people judge, stereotype, and characterize) and trust in the dialogue process while inquiry and creativity flow in the container. Engage in dialogue about personal, work-related, or general topics.

4. Move from dialogue to action. Assess experiences, and engage in dialogue about transferring learning and skills to daily life.

Under the Collective Inquiry Model, "the goal of dialogue is to open new ground by establishing a 'container' or 'field' for inquiry: a setting where people can become more aware of the context around their experience, and of the processes of thought and feeling that created that experience" (Senge and others, 1994, p. 353). Virginia M. Swain, in her work through the Institute for Global Leadership, suggests that dialogue occurs within the confines of a container or holding environment that is "a metaphoric structure, created by participants, to share resources and power, withdraw projections of the unconscious, and dissipate emotional reactions in such a way that the outcome of the conversation is owned by everyone present" (Swain, 2001). "A container can be understood as the sum of the collective assumptions, shared intentions, and beliefs of the group" (Senge and others, 1994, p. 360). In addition, Senge and others describe different phases of the container as the dialogue moves through different stages.

DESIGNING THE DIALOGUE: AN EXAMPLE

You have been asked by the CEO of a national manufacturer of children's clothing to design and facilitate a dialogue on diversity for a small group of fifteen employees. All levels of the organization chart are represented in this sample. They have accepted an invitation to take part in a one-day dialogue.

The CEO recognizes the strength of a diverse workplace. Under her leadership, the corporation has cultivated an image of sensitivity to recruiting and hiring a diverse workforce. The company has been able to attract minority employees; however, they have been unable to retain and promote these individuals despite commitment to diversity from top management. The turnover of minority employees is four times that of nonminorities. Exit interviews reveal that the educational diversity programming, tracking, and in-house training have failed to create an organizational culture where all employees have embraced cultural differences and workplace programs or understand the benefits of learning and working with a diverse community.

You met separately with the CEO and the entire group of fifteen individuals. Before accepting this assignment, you made a determination if this situation was appropriate for dialogue. Threshold design questions for convening a dialogue were asked (Study Circles Resource Center 2001):

- What brings us together? "Create a dialogue to foster shared meaning. People work better together and achieve more when they are aligned around a shared purpose, value and goals. Shared meaning leads to cooperative action, mutual understanding and respect" (Whitney, Cooperrider, Trosten-Bloom, and Kaplin, 2002, p. 2).

- Why is this issue important? Business, social, and moral imperatives: "Diversity initiatives can improve the quality of your organization's workforce and can be the catalyst for a better return on investment in human capital . . . [and] to capitalize on new markets" (Society for Human Resource Management, 2004).

- How would dialogue help? "Increased Creativity. . . . Customer bases are becoming even more diverse than the workforce. . . . Flexibility ensures survival. . . . Diversity initiatives and diversity results will attract the best and the brightest employees to a company" (Society for Human Resource Management, 2004).

- Is this topic compelling to many different kinds of people? All participants have personal, political, and professional stakes in the outcome.

When naming and framing the issues, consider these additional questions:

- Is the issue a concern, challenge, opportunity, or recurring problem that is becoming more troublesome (Scott, 2002)? Yes. It is likely to continue in this manner.

- Why is it significant? What's at stake? How does this affect dollars, income, people, products, services, customers, and family (Scott, 2002)?

The answers to the first five questions are all applicable to this question.

DIALOGUE PROCESSES: GENERAL CHARACTERISTICS AND PROTOCOLS

There is not an exact formula for facilitating dialogue. A Statement of Values and Code of Ethics (2002) has been adopted by the International Association of Facilitators (IAF). (See Chapter Thirty.) And the IAF core facilitation competencies required for skillful facilitation of meetings and workshops provide guidance. (See Chapter Twenty-Six.) Nevertheless, the context and nature of the dialogue coupled with the individuality and personal style of the facilitator make each dialogue one of a kind.

The governing principles for dialogue success are simple and begin with building and preserving a vessel where the integrity of group process will perform without disturbance (Davis, 2003). Dialogue participants then "become the sounding boards, the graveyards, and the launching platforms of our thoughts . . . [and] dialoguing is crucial to test our thoughts" (Kirby, Goodpaster, and Levin, 2003, p. 9). From that point in dialogue, a facilitator can move participants through dialogic processes, described in the diversity vignette, and guide them to listen, appreciate one another's positions, and try to reach some common understanding. The techniques and protocols for leading a dialogue differ from model to model and facilitator to facilitator.

Who Is Present at the Dialogue?

People are extended invitations to participate in a dialogue; however, it is their choice whether to join. All participants are granted an opportunity to speak once the invitation is accepted and the dialogue begins. A list of invitees should include as many stakeholders as possible to ensure a representative group. A more productive and complete dialogue occurs when all necessary parties are present to contribute. At the time of the dialogue, if not raised by participants, the facilitator should identify stakeholders essential to the topic who are not in the room. Possible perspectives of the unavailable individuals should be questioned and revealed to the group.

A facilitator and sometimes a cofacilitator lead the dialogue. There is a discipline necessary to design and lead a dialogue. Anyone can learn the dialogue process, but the techniques to design and lead a dialogue properly require practice, training and experience.

If possible, a competent individual is selected and attends the dialogue as a recorder to capture information in real time on an easel pad. If a recorder is unavailable, this role can be filled by the facilitator or cofacilitator. Recording content can keep the group on task and provide a contemporaneous record of what has transpired. It can provide visual feedback that balanced views are presented and reference materials for debriefing or future dialogues. It can also be shared with stakeholders who did not attend the dialogue.

Basic Structure of Dialogue

There is no verbatim script in dialogue. It is important to be flexible in approach and facilitation. The process is adaptable to nearly all circumstance with proper investigation, analysis, and design. Learning and discovery can occur when the process includes participants' respect, there is deep listening, assumptions are questioned, and judgment is suspended. Dialogue is not recommended where participants will not act in good faith, have not accepted the invitation, or are compelled to attend. Remember to honor the adage to trust the process.

Framework and Dialogic Functions

According to Edwards (2002), managing an on-line dialogue about public issues falls within a framework of three functions, which I view as equally applicable to the design and facilitation of face-to-face dialogues: "The strategic function: establishing the boundaries of the discussion and embedding it in the political and organizational environment; the conditioning function: taking care of conditions and provisions for the discussion (for example, obtaining participants, seating arrangements, tables, chairs, coffee and bagels); and the process function: managing the discussion (social) process as a collective purposeful activity" (p. 5). It is incumbent on the facilitator to include each of these elements in the dialogue design plan and to monitor carefully and modify these processes, as dictated by the circumstances.

Process Leadership

As facilitators, we support through process leadership both the group's social and cognitive processes while respecting the group's need to understand and learn from the problem-solving process (Schuman, 1996). When we actively listen, respect, and value the group, our behavior serves as a model that we wish the group to emulate. At the same time, facilitators must recognize that people communicate in a multiprocess way verbally and nonverbally. Reading the subtext of these nonverbal messages requires attention and knowledge. These nonverbal elements include gestures, facial expressions, and defensive postures (Madonik, 2001; Nierenberg and Calero, 2003). These nonverbal actions are meters of our states of mind and are real-time perceptions of the status of the dialogue. Facilitators should be cognizant of the importance of process leadership and develop competences for managing process as well as understanding, analyzing, and using nonverbal communication, including sensitivity to subtle messages.

Ground Rules

The use of ground rules, guidelines, or agreement assists the facilitator in keeping a dialogue from becoming an adversarial debate. This approach also allows the introduction of an agenda that enables the balancing time and content of the dialogue while maintaining the energy of the group members. Establishing norms for individual and group behavior supports maximum contributions and yields a receptive and respectful dialogue. Positive relationships and information exchange spring from a safe setting in which to explore difficult subjects and relationships (Pyser and Figallo, 2004).

Critical Thinking

A facilitator needs to search for understanding and formulate and ask interrelated questions at fitting times. During dialogue, it is essential that the facilitator use critical thinking skills to simultaneously evaluate, listen, and process the event. "The ideal critical thinker is habitually inquisitive, well-informed, trustful of reason, open-minded, flexible, fair-minded in evaluation, honest in facing personal biases, prudent in making judgments, willing to reconsider, clear about issues, orderly in complex matters, diligent in seeking relevant information, reasonable in the selection of criteria, focused in inquiry, and persistent in seeing results which are as precise as the subject and the circumstances of inquiry permit" (Aretz, Bolen, and Devereux, 1997).

Framing and Asking Questions

The ability to frame and ask questions of participants is an essential facilitator skill for beginning and sustaining a dialogue (see Exhibit 13.2). When properly phrased, well-crafted questions can engage participants, stimulate thoughtful reflection, and energize conversation through sharing of personal and valuable insights. Questions are one of the essential elements of a productive and balanced dialogue. Facilitators should continue to practice and hone the skill of developing and posing questions. The quality and success of the dialogue will turn in large part on this facilitator skill.

Exhibit 13.2
Framing and Asking Dialogue Questions

Effective Techniques	Ineffective Techniques
Prepare and write out your questions.	Trust fate, and fly by the seat of your pants.
Know your identity and act with integrity to cultivate a "capacity for connectedness" (Palmer, 1998, p. 13).	Pretend to be someone you are not to gain group approval or advantage or to preordain a dialogue result.

Effective Techniques	Ineffective Techniques
Ask questions.	Make statements; present solutions or offer advice ("Why don't you . . ." or "My brother had this situation once before, and he . . .").
Who is in your group? Seek to invite participation. Prepare stimulating questions that people can relate to, are important and relevant to group, and attract their attention.	Ask safe questions—those for which you know the expected response.
Be brief with your question.	Ask compound questions with multiple subparts and choices.
Use exploratory questions that call for discussion.	Use rhetorical questions that require no answer.
Deliver questions in a tone that invites contributions.	Mandate that participants respond. Select a person to speak.
Customize questions that reveal motivations for points of view and perspectives.	Pose questions that might degrade, threaten, or marginalize participants to create controversy.
Craft questions to reveal information, feelings and interests, opinions, and personal experiences and insight.	Ask assumptive questions (a form of leading question) where the question assumes a fact ("How much will taxes go up next year?").

Effective Techniques	Ineffective Techniques
Ask open-ended questions that allow a wide range of possible responses.	Ask closed-ended questions (usually answered with a yes or no), and interrupt the flow or end the conversation.
Use questions beginning with "What" and "How."	Avoid questions that start with, "Why do you . . . " as these will elicit a self-judgment or generate an "I don't know" response.
Challenge assumptions and views not yet considered by the group.	Maintain the status quo, and avoid asking the question that needs to be posed and answered.
Listen before asking questions.	Substitute your judgment before hearing the entire response.
Be spontaneous. (For information on spontaneity in facilitation see Chapter Seventeen.)	Engineer every moment for the dialogue, and do not deviate from the plan.
Stay calm, and defuse contentious situations.	Respond with anger, sarcasm, and strong-arm tactics to control group behaviors.

Duration of Sessions

The nature of the dialogue and the complexities of the issues control the length of the session. "Some processes are just a few hours long, while others last a week or more. Many continue over a period of time, for example having week-long meetings once or twice a year for several years. Usually, for these long-lasting meetings, an effort is made to have as much continuity in participants as possible, although sometimes considerable turn-over in participation occurs" (Conflict Research Consortium, 1998b).

Tone

The tone should be informal, with questions delivered in a manner that invites contributions.

Purpose and Focus

Guide the group toward an open, respectful, and free conversation. The focus is not on reaching a solution or decision but rather to suspend judgment and gain insights into how others might feel toward the subject of the dialogue. Look at the big picture, but do not stray too far way from the purpose of the dialogue.

DIALOGUE USING THE CONVERSATION CAFÉ PROCESS

A Conversation Café is a facilitated process and dialogue with agreements that encourage a meaningful exchange of thoughts, opinions, and feelings; it is held in cafés and other public places. This open, hosted model of dialogue was created in Seattle, Washington, and has gained more exposure and use since the September 11, 2001, terrorist attacks. It offers people a forum to deal with their concerns and feelings on unlimited topics.

The Conversation Café model is related to the Collective Inquiry Model. The design elements are similar, with a call for inquiry and an opportunity to provide engagement for participants. In addition, the stages of dialogue described by Zuniga and Nagda (2004) are implicit elements and processes in the Conversation Café model. The essence of the Conversation Café approach is the suspension of judgment, assumptions, and movement toward building shared meaning. "It is a one-and-a-half hour hosted conversation, held in a public setting like a café, where anyone is welcome to join. A simple format helps people feel at ease and gives everyone who wants it a chance to speak" (Conversation Café, 2002). The Conversation Café process is described in Exhibit 13.3.

The simple structure and minimal rules of a Conversation Café made it a logical choice to demonstrate a representative working dialogue model for this chapter. One need not master complex dialogic theory to conduct a dialogue using Conversation Café. It also provides a beginning point to gain a sense of the many benefits of facilitating a dialogue and offers a gateway to other more complex theories and models of dialogue.

This method can be used by facilitators of all experience levels and provides a dialogic structure that has a beginning, middle, and end, and it can meet the conditions and needs of a multitude of participants.

DIALOGIC CONVERSATION STARTERS

Communication is central to well-designed and implemented dialogue. At all stages of dialogue, facilitators face the challenge of exploring challenging issues with participants. The main road map for dialogue is through the question. Returning to the diversity vignette, questions should be crafted to probe the awareness of personal and business benefits of a varied workforce, acceptance of the intermingling of cultures, and whether there has been an affirmation of cultural diversity. What are the values of the stakeholders who are present or absent? Is there conflict between these values and the different categories of stakeholders? What is the value of diversity to each of the stakeholders? Following are some example conversation starters (Whitney, Cooperrider, Trosten-Bloom, and Kaplin, 2002):

- Describe a time when you were part of a diverse team that really benefits from its diversity.

- How did you learn about each other's unique gifts and differences?

- What was special about what this group achieved?

Exhibit 13.3
Conversation Café Process

Preparation

Conversation Café "hosts" provide nametags, paper and pencil (for note taking), a centerpiece (candle, flower) and a talking object (something symbolic or just handy) that is held by the person speaking.

Welcome

The host welcomes everyone, states the theme . . . reads the agreements, sets an ending time, and calls for a moment of silence to relax, reflect and become open.

Round one

Each person speaks in turn, going around the circle once. Each person holds the talking object while they speak. During this round, everyone says their name and speaks briefly about what is on their minds regarding the theme. Anyone may pass if they don't want to speak. Everyone is asked to express themselves fully yet succinctly, allowing time for others to speak. No feedback or response.

Round two

Now that everyone has been introduced, the group goes around the circle again. If someone wants to respond to another's remarks, they can do so in their own turn. Each person holds the talking object. To allow more time for conversation, keep remarks brief, possibly just naming the theme or subjects you want to delve into more deeply. Again, no feedback or response.

Spirited Dialogue

Now the conversation opens up and people can speak in no particular order. This conversation will take up most of the time. If there is domination, contention, or lack of focus, the host may suggest that the group again use the talking object. Keep in mind the agreements.

Closing

A few minutes before the end of the Café, the host will ask everyone to go around the circle again, giving each a chance to say briefly what they are taking away from the conversation.

Source: Reprinted with permission from Conversation Café and the National Coalition for Dialogue and Deliberation. Excerpted from http://www.conversationcafe.org/hosts_agree.html and http://www.thataway.org/resources/understand/models/concafe.html.

- Tell me about a time you had a wonderful working relationship with someone different from yourself. What was the high point of the relationship? What did you learn from this relationship?

CONCLUSION

Dialogue is an effective and promising tool for transforming the manner in which people learn, communicate, share knowledge, and address vital issues affecting individuals, businesses, and communities. The hallmarks of dialogue are open communication and commitment to common purpose. In dialogue, well-trained facilitators interact with participants to create a safe place where everyone can trust and then think, talk, and gain insights and understanding to resolve challenges. Participants learn from one another in an environment where individuality, diversity, and creativity are not repressed. The dialogue process fosters deep listening and enables participants to connect, communicate, and bond.

Dialogue exists as an open source where facilitators are not married to using a particular approach. The existence of multiple models of dialogue allows selection from a wide catalogue of models with the possibility for unlimited customization and use across a wide range of communities. Rational solutions develop from inquiry and sharing other perspectives of participants. Dialogue is a worthy alternative to debate and other unproductive modes of adversarial interpersonal interactions. The possibilities for dialogue practice are limitless.

RESOURCES

National Coalition for Dialogue and Deliberation (http://www.thataway.org). A network of organizations and individuals who regularly engage millions of Americans in dialogue around critical issues. A resource section (http://www. thataway.org/resources/practice/index.html) provides tools and information for practicing dialogue and deliberation. The Models and Techniques section (http://www.thataway.org/resources/understand/models/models.html) describes many dialogue and deliberation models in use throughout the world. In addition, sample ground rules for dialogue and deliberation are available (http://www.thataway.org/resources/practice/rules.html).

Conversation About Conflict (http://www.sfcg.org/resources/training/resources_conversation.html). Conversation About Conflict was established by Search for Common Ground and encourages participants to develop a new awareness of conflicts in our lives: how we currently respond to them, what they cost us, and alternative approaches that can be used. The Conversations are currently hosted in different cities in the United States for diverse audiences with no previous exposure to the conflict resolution field.

Let's Talk America (http://www.letstalkamerica.org). Politics does not have to polarize. Let's Talk America is a new nationwide nonpartisan movement to revitalize our democracy by bringing together thousands of people each week to bookstores, cafés, churches, and living rooms for open-hearted dialogue in search of higher ground. The Web site contains downloadable discussion guides and information about how to host a conversation.

Penn's Landing Public Forum (http://www.philly.com/mld/inquirer/news/special_packages/penns_landing/.com). A face-to-face citizen dialogue on redeveloping the waterfront at Philadelphia, Pennsylvania.

Public Conversations Project (http://www.publicconversations.org). A nonprofit facilitation, consultation, and training group focused on divisive values-based conflicts. Many of these materials are available on-line at no cost.

Study Circles Resource Center (http://www.studycircles.org). Dedicated to finding ways for all kinds of people to engage in dialogue and problem solving on critical social and political issues.

Western Justice Center (http://www.westernjustice.org/orgs.cfm). Features an on-line database of more than fourteen hundred community groups, educational institutions, and professional associations that provide resources or experience in the skills of dialogue, cross-cultural collaboration and conflict resolution.

Dynamic Facilitation

Design Principles from the
New Science of Complexity

Lisa Kimball
Trish Silber
Nedra Weinstein

> *Complexity is where we are going in the 21st century.*
> *It is the future of science.*
>
> Edward O. Wilson

In major universities around the world, in government laboratories, and in interdisciplinary think tanks, scientists have made stunning progress in characterizing the properties of complex, dynamic systems. At its core, this intellectual revolution known as complexity science is transforming our understanding of life, while providing new principles for making sense of what is most fundamental in our lives: our relationships with other people and our environment. This chapter connects and applies learning from this new science to the practice of facilitation.

One way of thinking about complexity science is as science's most recent attempt to explain how order and novelty emerge in the world. Many of the concepts are extensions of ideas from systems and chaos theory. Until recently, most people thought about the natural world as a kind of machine that could be understood by taking it apart and examining the parts. This approach enabled scientists to discover a great deal about diverse phenomena. But this kind of analysis failed to explain some of the most interesting and important things about our world. The reason is that most of nature is not a well-ordered machine but rather is made up of what complexity scientists call nonlinear, complex, adaptive systems.

We make a distinction between complex and complicated systems. An airplane is complicated, with many different components. However, anyone who understands each of the individual parts can figure out, and even predict, how the whole plane will work in practice. A complex system is greater than the sum of the parts because the whole emerges dynamically from the interactions of all the components. Feedback loops exist at many levels, which influence and change how individual parts will behave over time. Such systems are constantly adapting and evolving, creating unpredictability. Examples of large complex systems are the weather, economies, and rain forests.

This new science is influencing researchers in many fields. For example, medical researchers are looking at new diagnostic methods that shift away from history's dominant reductionist approach to prediction and control toward more holistic and participatory methods. The mathematics of complexity is being used to model patterns of fluctuations in human heartbeats to discover ways an individual can improve the chances of healing after a heart attack (Cole and others, 1999).

Economists have been exploring how the complexity-based study of social networks can be applied to economic development strategies in the Appalachian region. Using new ways of mapping relationships among and between businesses in the community, the group has begun to identify where and how to build the most productive alliances (Appalachian Center for Economic Networks, 1998).

Facilitators also work with complex systems: organizations, large groups, and change processes with networks of stakeholders. Meetings are themselves complex systems, involving the interplay of individuals, ideas, processes, and time. Complexity science offers an exciting new framework to inform facilitation practice.

We have been designing and facilitating groups for more than twenty years and have been looking at many of the facilitation practices that work through this new lens of complexity science. Using this new perspective, we have started to define some ways to make deliberate design choices based on complexity principles. We considered how we could use this thinking to create a new set of design principles for meetings that work—that flow, promote creativity, and allow new understanding to emerge.

We noticed that many of the ideas informed by complexity do not sound particularly new. Rather, they validate some of the best practices that have emerged from experience. But we believe an awareness of complexity-based design principles can help facilitators create and choose better processes by deepening their consciousness of how and why certain practices work (and others do not). This deeper understanding will also make it easier to be more adaptable. For example, rather than using favorite designs as is (in cookbook style), we can make choices more flexibly based on an understanding of the principles that underlie these practices.

In this chapter, we describe the characteristics of complex adaptive systems, describe three design principles that facilitators can use to inform their work, and share the experience of one facilitator by describing how these principles changed her original meeting design and how the process worked for her client organization.

CHARACTERISTICS OF COMPLEX ADAPTIVE SYSTEMS

At the heart of complexity science is a set of essential characteristics of complex adaptive systems that we can directly apply to organizations and our work as facilitators. It is always risky to take scientific principles developed in one context and apply them to another. Some researchers (Stacey, 2001) have objected to treating organizations as complex adaptive systems and point to the many ways in which human organizations differ from the models developed by complexity theorists. However, we believe that treating organizations as if they are complex adaptive systems can yield many valuable insights.

Systems are composed of agents—molecules, termites, plants, or people, for example. In complex systems, multiple agents interact with each other, each agent unique and different from the next, such that no agent's behavior will be the same in all conditions. Each of these agents changes and adapts over time and has an impact on the other agents because of the mutual context of the system they share.

Complex adaptive systems have the following characteristics:

1. *Order is emergent and self-organizing.* One characteristic of a complex system is that order emerges as it flows from the interactions among the individuals. This process is called self-organization because there is no central

control over the behavior of the individual agents. Think about how teams and organizations pull together in crises: they are often able to achieve astonishing results and later reflect on how rewarding the experience was. There is no time in a crisis to mandate or centrally control action. Relationships are the coordinating mechanism in these situations as order emerges from the interactions and relationships among individuals.

A common puzzle in organizations is why groups work together so well and achieve so much during a crisis, yet everyone reverts back to poorly coordinated, territorial behavior on an everyday basis. Complexity science explains that our everyday desire to centrally control activities and behavior in organizations actually stifles individuals' ability to interact, take coordinated action, and achieve desired results. This explains why micromanagers tend to foster precisely what they do not intend—either stagnation or chaos, actually preventing the organization from being able to perform.

2. *A small set of simple rules generates purposeful, complex, and dynamic behavior.* Flocking birds are exquisite examples of another essential characteristic of complex adaptive systems because they exhibit a kind of self-organization where a small set of rules generates complex behavior. A computer simulation developed by Craig Reynolds in 1987 demonstrates this concept (Zimmerman, Plsek, and Lindberg, 1998). In this simulation, autonomous agents (called *boids*) are placed in an on-screen environment full of obstacles and are governed by three rules: (1) maintain a minimum distance from all other boids and objects, (2) match the speed of neighboring boids, and (3) move toward the center of the mass of boids in your vicinity. Although the boids are not instructed to flock, the simulation generates complex, dynamic flocking behavior. In the same way, many organizations today (among them, Yahoo! Dell, Miramax, and Lego) successfully navigate uncertain and chaotic business environments by using a small set of rules and strategic processes to guide themselves (Eisenhardt and Sull, 2001). There is no time to wait for guidance from top management or lengthy strategic plans in such a rapidly changing business environment. These simple rules and strategic processes help individuals (and business units) quickly decide what kinds of opportunities to pursue, when a project should be dropped, and how to rank priorities.

3. *The whole is greater than the sum of its parts, with its own distinct identity.* As each unique individual takes independent action, changes, and interacts with

other individuals, a complex system emerges as a whole greater than the sum of its parts. Unlike the airplane example described above, by studying each of the individuals, we achieve only an incomplete understanding of the whole. When we think about great team experiences, the team typically exhibits a unique identity, and great ideas or achievements cannot be attributed to only one or a few individuals, but rather to the whole team. The same is true when we reflect on great meetings or the culture of great organizations such as Disney, Herman Miller, or Cirque de Soleil.

4. *At the edge of chaos is where systems are most adaptable and creative.* Complexity scientists describe complex adaptive systems as moving among three states: stability at one end of a continuum, chaos at the other, and a state called the *edge of chaos* in between. When systems are in this zone between stability and chaos, they are most adaptable and creative. The elements of the system do not lock into place but do not dissolve into anarchy. There is a balance between order and disorder. This is where innovations happen.

In organizations, the edge of chaos is that space where new ideas and unexpected directions emerge and flourish. When skunk works became popular in research and development organizations, it was an attempt to provide an environment that would create and protect this edge of chaos. The features of skunk works typically include guidance by a set of simple rules and freedom from most of the organization's policies and procedures and provision of resources and an environment (physical and cultural) that fuel the creative interaction among team members.

5. *Small changes can generate big effects.* The relationships and connections between the parts of a complex system can be the underlying cause for changes and new ideas to accelerate and multiply throughout the system. This produces another key characteristic of complex adaptive systems: small changes or ideas might create big effects (which is precisely what happens in skunk works). This phenomenon represents a very different notion from the Newtonian view that actions and reactions are equal and opposite. In organizations, we typically assume that it takes big change efforts to create big change, but we have found that many of these huge efforts failed. However, on any given day, a rumor can spread like wildfire and have a huge impact on careers, business decisions, or Wall Street at lightning speed.

These five characteristics of complex adaptive systems provide a general framework for facilitation. We think facilitators can go even further and define a set of design principles to inform specific design choices. In the remainder of this chapter we focus on three such design principles:

1. Engage the whole system first.
2. Use simple rules.
3. Create an edge.

DESIGN PRINCIPLES FOR FACILITATING DYNAMIC MEETINGS
Principle 1: Engage the Whole System First

This design principle derives from the characteristic that the whole of a complex adaptive system is greater than the sum of its parts. This principle suggests the importance of keeping the system perspective present in the minds of all participants. This system frame sets the stage for all of the discussions that emerge and allows participants to see how their particular perspective both contributes to the overall result and is affected by the interplay between the various groups and stakeholders within the system.

To garner this synergy during a meeting, especially with a group of people grappling with a contentious or complex issue, first engage the group of attendees with a system perspective of the issue at hand rather than kick off the meeting with specific stakeholders focusing on their individual perspective on the situation. There are several ways to do this in a meeting or multiple meetings.

One tactic is to begin the meeting with small, heterogeneous groups, that is, groups comprising five to seven participants who have different perspectives or allegiances, to focus on the whole system that they represent rather than on their particular stake or position. These minisystems (in complexity science terms, *fractals*) contain the diversity of views, opinions, hopes, and concerns that are inherent in the larger system.

There have been a number of large change approaches that have developed over the last fifteen years, such as Janoff and Weisbord's Future Search Conferences (Weisbord, 1992), Dannemiller-Tyson's Real Time Strategic Change (Dannemiller and others, 1994), and Axelrod and Axelrod's Conference Model (1993). Although each of these has its own unique approach, one common denominator is that they all bring the whole system into the room.

Another approach that is used to put the whole system first is the World Café process, which was conceived by Juanita Brown (World Café Community Foundation 2003). This approach, described in Exhibit 14.1, allows the entire group, even a large group of over a hundred people, to have one conversation in which ideas, questions, and themes around an issue can begin to be linked and connected.

Graphic recording on a large wall or chart is another method that can be used to put the whole system first. A combination of text and graphics is created that allows each small group or individual to see their ideas merged with others' ideas in a single, shared picture of the whole, resulting in a systemic view of the issue at hand.

Principle 2: Use Simple Rules

Understanding that a small set of rules or guidelines can generate complex and dynamic behavior and useful results leads to a design principle to use simple rules. A completely open process without structure or rules generates chaos, and too long or narrow a list of rules stifles a group. For example, as facilitators, our desire to ensure that a group has a rich, deep, and fruitful conversation can sometimes lead us to overstructure a session with too many ground rules, instructions, and expectations. In these instances, it is not uncommon for groups to be confused and raise many questions and for the session as a whole to fall flat.

**Exhibit 14.1
World Café Process**

The World Café uses multiple small groups (approximately six to nine people in each) that are arranged around the room. There are progressive rounds of conversation (usually three) of approximately fifteen to thirty minutes each, and everyone is in a new group for each round of discussion. To kick off each round, the facilitator poses a provocative question to engage the group in a discussion around the presenting systemic issue facing the larger group or organization. One person at each table is asked to be the recorder or note taker during the round. After the round, everyone except the recorder is asked to move to a different table. The recorder shares with the new group the key ideas that were generated by the first group. A new recorder emerges for each successive round. After all of the rounds, the larger group may engage in a discussion outlining the major themes that emerged. (For more information on the World Café process, see http://www.theworldcafe.com.)

Complexity science tells us as facilitators that our simple rules must provide minimum specifications and no more. Each simple rule should be just that: simple and a rule. Groups should be provided with a short list of rules that refer to how individuals should interact with each other. Too many detailed instructions will burden and stall the group.

Implementation of the rules should be tightly managed, but what the rules produce should be loosely held, allowing as much self-organization to emerge as possible. Think of simple rules as liberating structures for groups that allow individuals and groups to safely step up to the edge of chaos, where they can be most creative, adaptive, and productive. Exhibit 14.2 provides some examples of simple rules.

Simple rules guide the interaction between individuals and the system and are not focused on any one individual. The simplicity of the rules gives freedom to individuals to behave in adaptive, creative, surprising ways, which create complexity.

We have noticed that groups, organizations, and cultures have so many unwritten rules and norms that one way to liberate the natural performance of a complex system is to explicitly confirm or reshape these unwritten rules. We recently facilitated a meeting in which we invited small groups to discuss a set of issues. In this organization, an implicit rule was that small group conversations must generate a consensus view. We told the small groups that we did not expect them to provide a consensus view; instead, we were curious to hear what they naturally agreed on, any patterns in their views, and any differences of opinions they held. We noticed that the input of the small groups was particularly creative and powerful. At the end of the meeting, many participants shared with us how ecstatic they were to be freed from the expectation of consensus; they found it refreshing and believed the freedom to disagree encouraged them to explore ideas and views with more vigor and rigor.

Principle 3: Create an Edge

In nature, the edge of chaos is a called a *verge*—a rich mixture of ecosystems that happens when two distinct regions border each other and begin to overlap and interact. All living things in these regions are forced to engage in adaptation, cooperation, and competition that cause them to differentiate and create new forms. Costa Rica is an example of an area where two continents met and created a verge in which there is extraordinary biological diversity. Although it makes up less than three ten-thousandths of the earth's landmass, Costa Rica is home to 5 percent of its species. How can we create this zone of creativity where ideas can emerge and develop in human systems?

Exhibit 14.2
Simple Rules for Groups

Brainstorming, dialogue, and Open Space are all examples of methodologies guided by simple rules. Consider the rules we use with each methodology:

Brainstorming

- Quantity counts at this stage, not quality.
- Encourage wild and exaggerated ideas.
- Postpone and withhold your judgment of ideas.
- Build on others' ideas.

Dialogue

- Hold positions lightly; suspend judgment.
- Identify own assumptions; respect differences.
- Listen for shared meaning.
- Ask questions with the intention to gain insight and perspective.

Open Space (Owen, n.d.)

- Four Principles:
  - Whoever comes are the right people.
  - Whatever happens is the only thing that could have.
  - Whenever it starts is the right time.
  - When it is over it is over.
- One Law
  - The Law of Two Feet—"If, during the course of the gathering any person finds him or herself in a situation where they are neither learning nor contributing, they can use their own two feet and go to some more productive place" (Owen, 1992, p. 72)

Most organizations and groups operate with multiple boundaries, including those between organizations, functions, roles, and areas of expertise. To create an edge, we need to find ways to engage people in and around these boundaries. We want to put participants in the zone where they grapple with the differences among or transitions between their familiar patterns.

One approach to creating an edge in a meeting is to work with the physical environment. Dixon (2000) writes about the hallways of learning, making the point that much of the juicy learning and knowledge exchange within an organization takes place in the hall rather than within the formal structure of offices and meetings. Although most of us recognize the value of these informal exchanges, we have not thought consciously about how to make explicit use of the "hall" within the context of a meeting. Hewlett Packard convened a series of Work Innovation Network (WIN) meetings where they tried to do this. The goal of the WIN meetings was to bring people from different parts and levels of the company together to share learning. They provided the typical opportunities for people to make presentations and facilitate discussions about projects. But they also created what they called white space in the meeting by placing comfortable sofas, plants, and coffee tables in defined areas between the conference rooms where sessions took place. The configuration of the furniture was inviting and attracted people to sit down in small groups. This space enabled conversations among people who would not necessarily have encountered each other in the course of their work and conversations that were not defined by the formal agenda of the meeting.

Another approach to creating an edge is to introduce disruptive agents to the system. A product development group from a consumer products company convened an off-site meeting to develop new ideas for reaching customers. They had experienced frustration in previous meetings where it seemed that the ideas were limited to unimaginative extensions of current offerings. In the past, they had invited outside experts in different fields to make presentations that they hoped would trigger new thinking, but the strategy had not paid off as they hoped. The presenter's new ideas had not become integrated with the discussions around projects. This time, they invited professionals from another field to come to the meeting as full participants rather than as outsiders. Their different perspectives, language, and frameworks were surprising and challenging and took the conversations in new directions.

One of the most effective ways facilitators can create an edge is to introduce challenges to the group's standard mode of operating. This can be done by providing advice about who should be invited to a meeting, who could be added to the group, or where the meeting could be held. It can also be done by posing provocative questions that cause participants to stop and think before responding with their standard reply. These questions can put participants literally on edge, where they experience just enough discomfort to generate new ideas.

The following story describes one of Nedra Weinstein's experiences in beginning to think about design using these principles.

ONE FACILITATOR'S EXPERIENCE

I participated in a learning group with the other authors of this chapter created to explore new and emerging trends within the organizational development field. The group was discussing complexity science and its application to facilitation at a time when I was designing an off-site meeting for a long-standing client.

The meeting was to focus on a historic and complex issue that affected a variety of stakeholders within the organization. The issue involved the core functions of planning, designing, constructing, and maintaining their key product. As happens frequently in organizations, the construction and maintenance functions felt they did not have sufficient input into the final product. The planners and designers, who were being pushed to complete their tasks more quickly and efficiently, felt they were receiving adequate feedback from their construction and maintenance colleagues.

I had been thinking of starting off the meeting with each of the functional groups meeting by themselves to discuss their perspective of the situation. I was planning on having each group present this information to the whole group, and then collectively they would identify common themes and issues. They would then form into smaller groups (consisting of different functional areas) for analysis and problem solving.

During the learning group discussion on complex adaptive systems, it occurred to me that some of the principles we were exploring could apply to my upcoming meeting, so I began to rethink my design.

Put the Whole System First

Rather than begin the meeting with each functional group focusing in on its views, I decided to use the World Café exercise. I divided the larger community into twelve smaller groups, each consisting of a mix of the functional stakeholders. Many of these individuals had never had a direct discussion on this issue with some of the people who were in their groups. Later in the day, I again divided the larger group into different mixed functional groups for further analysis and discussion on these issues. Each of these small groups was formed as a minisystem and incorporated stakeholders from all of the functional areas. After this meeting, another small group of mixed functional stakeholders was created from this larger group to serve as a project team to further address the issue.

Use Simple Rules

For the World Café exercise (see Exhibit 14.3), I provided simple instructions and guidelines on what to do. At first, I was concerned that the World Café would seem too odd and chaotic to this client system. However, the simplicity of the instructions allowed the participants to move ahead with the next steps of the exercise even before I repeated the instructions for the next round. The quality of the World Café dialogue was enhanced by the initiative the groups took during the exercise. This helped them see the issues more systemically and recognize they had the power to make changes.

Exhibit 14.3
World Café Opening Exercise

When switching groups, sit with people whom you normally don't work with. You will have 90 seconds to create these groups.

For each round, choose someone to be a recorder who will keep notes on the key themes and highlights of discussion. The recorder will stay in that group for the following round and will spend a few minutes reviewing his or her notes at the beginning of the round.

Discussion questions:

Round one: **What are the core issues around this issue that have been playing themselves out over the years?**

Round two: **What are the dilemmas and paradoxes inherent in this process? How do you see what you are up against as being either a dilemma or a paradox?**

Round three: **What's the part you play in the recurring story you have been describing and hearing about in the two earlier rounds? What is it that you, your team, or department does that keeps the issues in place and keeps this story continually being retold?**

Create an Edge

I knew that this meeting had to be different from the many discussions that had occurred over the years to address this issue. As many of the participants had been in their jobs for several years, they were somewhat locked into their thinking. Not surprisingly, they had strong views about how *others* were the cause of the problems. I realized that for real progress to occur, they needed to shift collectively to a new frame or paradigm for the issue. I needed a relatively profound and simple mechanism to gently push them to the edge of chaos.

I used an exercise called "Circles in the Air" (described in Exhibit 14.4), designed to explore the premise that our particular perspective in a system colors our view of that system. In addition, it is an exercise that can be done with a large group of people (in this case, ninety participants). The experience of the exercise suggests that by changing our vantage point mentally or physically, we may discover new insights and new leverage points.

The majority of the participants understood the intent of the exercise. In fact, during the meeting, when there was a need to get out of one perspective and into another, I would twirl my finger to symbolically suggest the need to change perspective. At various points in the meeting, participants twirled their fingers to invite others to consider the point of view that was being presented rather than to keep advocating their point.

In addition to this exercise, I knew that the group needed to have a very different kind of conversation with each other—one in which they were seeing both the systems view and their own. I thought the key to moving them there was the use of provocative questions in the World Café exercise, with each question adding an increased level of complexity. It was not until the session was concluded, and we debriefed it, that I knew I had hit the jackpot with these questions. During the debriefing, participants commented that they had not realized the similarity of their concerns and frustrations around this issue. When asked if they had learned anything new from the discussion, one man stood up. He was seen by the group as having strong opinions and unlikely to concede to others. He said he had not realized how he and his division had been contributing to the problem. The larger community applauded.

The mood of the large group shifted from one of resignation to a sense of hope. During the small group problem-solving sessions during the afternoon, many individuals expressed a cautious sense of optimism that perhaps these issues could be resolved.

Results: What Has Happened Since

Approximately two weeks after this meeting, a project team was formed. It met over the course of the next five months, building on the data generated at the kickoff meeting. One project team member said it was the most exciting work in which he had been involved during his twenty years with the organization. Several significant recommendations have been made and agreed to by the senior managers of the organization. As one project team member said, "Our key recommendation is quite simple but profound."

Other significant positive shifts took place throughout the organization. The political entity that directs this organization requested a meeting with the organization's management to talk about the planning and delivery process. Neither an off-site meeting nor a discussion between these groups has ever occurred during the history of the organization. Employees from different offices (who are geographically separate and report to different divisions) initiated discussions to explore how they can operate more in sync with each other. Most important, a number of issues previously deemed undiscussable were talked about openly.

It is hard to pinpoint the exact cause of many of these initiatives, and I am certainly not claiming that they all stem from the success of this particular meeting. What I am convinced of, though, is that small changes in organizations can produce large effects. Complexity science and the design principles we can derive from it have a lot to offer in generating these small changes.

CONCLUSION

Complexity science offers an exciting new framework to inform facilitation practice. Facilitators can use this thinking to create a new set of design principles for meetings that flow, promote creativity, and encourage new understanding to emerge. An awareness of complexity-based design principles can help facilitators create and choose better processes by deepening their consciousness of how and why certain practices work.

RESOURCES

In addition to the works referenced in the chapter, we recommend the following to practitioners interested in exploring the field:

Allison, M. A. "Enriching Your Practice with Complex Systems Thinking." *OD Practitioner,* 1999, *31*(3), 11–21.

Arrow, H., McGrath, J., and Berdahl, J. *Small Groups as Complex Systems: Formation, Coordination, Development and Adaptation.* Thousand Oaks, Calif.: Sage, 2000.

Arthur, W. B. "Increasing Returns and the Two Worlds of Business." *Harvard Business Review,* 1996, *74*(4), 100–109.

Ashmos, D., Duchon, D., McDaniel, R. R., and Huonker, J. W. "What a Mess! Participation as a Simple Managerial Rule to 'Complexity' Organization." *Journal of Management Studies,* 2002, *39*(2), 189–206.

Dooley, K. "A Complex Adaptive Systems Model of Organizational Change." *Nonlinear Dynamics, Psychology, and Life Sciences,* 1997, *1*(1), 69.

Olson, E. E., and Eoyang, G. *Facilitating Organization Change: Lessons from Complexity Science.* New York: Wiley, 2001.

Osborn, A. *Applied Imagination: Principles and Procedures of Creative Problem Solving.* New York: Scribner, 1957.

Owen, H. "A Brief User's Guide to Open Space Technology." N.d. [http://www.openspace world.com/users_guide.htm].

Shaw, P. *Changing Conversations in Organizations: A Complexity Approach to Change.* London: Routledge, 2002.

Tower, D. "Creating the Complex Adaptive Organization: A Primer on Complex Adaptive Systems." *OD Practitioner,* 2002, *34*(3).

Facilitating the Whole System in the Room

A Theory, Philosophy, and Practice
for Managing Conflicting Agendas,
Diverse Needs, and Polarized Views

Sandra Janoff
Marvin Weisbord

Every time I intervene I deprive a group member
of the chance to do something important.

Jim Elliott

For thirty years, we have been developing a philosophy, theory, and practice of facilitating based on differentiation-integration (D/I) theory. Sandra embraced D/I theory working with systems-centered training groups and facilitating Tavistock conferences. Marvin first applied it while consulting to business firms and medical schools and facilitating workshops at the NTL Institute. For more than a decade, our mutual learning laboratory has been a strategic planning meeting called "future search." From scores of these sessions lasting two and a half days, we have evolved an effective practice based on D/I principles from which we have derived a few simple techniques. We have employed these repeatedly in strategic planning and systems design conferences. Dozens of colleagues have adapted our methods to meeting formats of a few hours to several days.

In large, diverse groups, it is not possible to diagnose group needs or provide conceptual frames that every person will understand. Thus, we manage at the group level and make structural interventions. Rather than try to change any one person's behavior, we seek to enable the whole to become more effective. This way of working has proved especially useful when we count diversity, group cohesion, and commitment as inseparable from good outcomes. The results have been amply documented in many cultures (Weisbord and Janoff, 2000). Although we believe there are many other effective ways to facilitate, this is the way we have found most satisfying.

We define facilitating as a form of leadership that helps work groups increase their cooperation, satisfaction, and productivity. We are talking here about interdependent groups—those where people meet to pursue a goal that none can realize alone. For us, facilitating has three equally essential objectives:

- Designing meetings so that the right people are in the room, they explore every aspect of the task at hand, they discover their common ground, and they accept responsibility for acting.

- Managing meetings so that the task stays front and center. Our key role is helping people contain their discomfort with differences enough to keep working. We get out of the way unless people are at risk of fighting or abandoning the task.

- Managing ourselves by containing our thoughts, feelings, and judgments long enough to allow meeting participants to find their way out of sticky situations with minimum intervention from us.

WHY A PHILOSOPHY AND THEORY?

Having a philosophy and theory of action can be very comforting when you wish, in Rudyard Kipling's memorable line from his poem "If," "to keep your head when all about you are losing theirs and blaming it on you." We take comfort from having internalized a framework that helps us choose certain procedures and avoid others. Years ago, working with groups of ten or twelve, we invested much energy in diagnosing a group's needs and prescribing the right corrections. In those years, we died a thousand deaths when people abandoned the task and clashed over differences. We sometimes found ourselves working harder than the people we were facilitating. Leading larger and more diverse groups for the past twenty years, we have had to rethink what we were doing. We found it impossible to foresee every person's learning needs or to frame people's outputs in ways every person could accept.

Fortunately, we have had a rich tradition to draw on. The umbrella for our work is biologist Ludwig von Bertalanffy's general system theory (1960), which has informed the biological and social sciences for half a century. We also see ourselves in the direct line of descent from Kurt Lewin, the "practical theorist" (Marrow, 1977), and Ronald Lippitt, who together with Lewin coined the term *group dynamics* (Lewin, Lippitt, and White, 1939) and helped found NTL Institute for Applied Behavioral Science in 1947. We also count as a key ancestor Wilfred Bion, a founder in 1945 of the Tavistock Institute of Human Relations (Trist with Murray, 1990), who evolved a parallel theory of group development to NTL's. We have also adapted to our practice the work of friends and colleagues we have known for years. In this chapter, we introduce a few of them: Paul Lawrence and Jay Lorsch on D/I theory in organizations, Yvonne Agazarian on subgroups, and John Weir and Joyce Weir on self-differentiation.

A Philosophy of Facilitating

We owe our philosophy of facilitating to the Weirs, who trained thousands of people in self-differentiation workshops over forty years (Weir, 1971). Self-differentiation means exploring the many parts of oneself. We resonate to the Weirs' conviction that all of us do the best we can with what we have every minute of every day. Whatever people are ready, willing, and able to do now is what they *are* doing. We do our best to work with people the way we find them, not the way we wish they were. This philosophy has had profound implications for our practice. We no longer mix the teaching of meeting skills with work on consequential matters. We no longer train facilitators to work with small groups in a large group meeting, inadvertently creating multiple centers of dependency. People are capable of managing their own work when they consider it important. Natural leaders abound in every gathering.

We set out to create conditions under which people will do their best using what they already have. This means structuring meetings so that people can bring in their experience, learn from each other, and take responsibility for themselves, their goals, their flip charts, and their results. When we structure a meeting correctly and maintain functional structures throughout, participants do all the rest for themselves.

A Theory of Facilitating

We start with biology, a description of the glue that binds every living thing to every other. A cell is the basic unit of life. At conception, the first cell divides in half, then in half again and again. Groups of cells differentiate, become specialized, and develop into organ systems. Plants and animals become complex entities. As organisms develop, they increasingly integrate their differentiated parts. Our psychological development follows a similar path. From seed to infant to adult—from playpen to boardroom—we learn and grow from a single cell to organisms capable of increasingly more complex tasks. As newborns, we experience the world as an undifferentiated mass. Soon we recognize others outside ourselves. As we mature, we make ever clearer distinctions between our internal states and our environment. The better our ability is to differentiate our feelings, impulses, ideas, and needs from those of others, the better equipped we become to form integrated organizations and communities.

Differentiation, in *Webster's Dictionary*, means "to distinguish, classify, define, and separate," which implies grouping like with like. The word also means "to isolate, exclude, ostracize, and segregate." *Integration* means "to make one, harmonize, and blend," the essence of unity. It also means "to centralize and orchestrate." In purposeful meetings, we are faced with a variety of people seeking to integrate their stakes for a shared benefit. Our task is helping people differentiate without excluding anyone and integrate without forcing unity.

Organizational Implications

We notice parallels between the way nature spontaneously manages development and the way people choose to manage work groups, task teams, boards, and committees. We can consciously differentiate and integrate roles, functions, goals, and decisions by making choices based on what we are trying to do. Good results are not automatic. Lawrence and Lorsch (1967), in their seminal studies of organizations in various task environments, showed significant differences between more and less successful organizations. The best ones maintained appropriate differences among functions in such areas as goal focus, interpersonal requirements, and time horizons. In such cases, conflict among functions like manufacturing (short feedback loops, moderate interpersonal needs), sales (longer time horizons, high interpersonal needs), and research (long time spans, low interpersonal needs) are inevitable. The greater an organization's required functional differences are, the greater is the potential for conflict. The best performers accepted conflict as natural and provided useful integrating mechanisms. The worst performers ignored conflicts or reduced differentiation to avoid them, thus frustrating people in all functions.

Task-focused processes largely succeed or fail based on the quality of people's ability to manage differentiation and integration. Thus, people in integrating roles—project managers, for example—become more critical to success. Skilled integrators learn to validate the range of differences they encounter. They develop a midpoint orientation, seeing the value in a wide spectrum of beliefs and practices, and they create forums in which people can cooperate to reach their goals. We see facilitating, whether by line managers or specialists, as a major integrating role.

PRACTICAL USES OF D/I THEORY
Organizing and Designing Meetings

We always start by matching the goal with the right people. We have never developed enough skill to facilitate our way out of meetings where key people are missing. Who are the right people? That depends on the purpose. For meetings where action is called for, we advocate "the whole system in the room." This we define as those with authority, resources, expertise, information, and need. We want in the same dialogue those who, if they chose, could act without having to ask permission from anyone not present. Although it is not always possible to have them, this principle helps our clients know what they are giving up when key people are absent.

Next, we want a meeting agenda that enables all participants to experience the whole issue through one another's eyes before seeking to work on any aspect. D/I theory tells us that to integrate, we must first differentiate, so we devise a plan where participants can make public their points of view and create a shared picture of the whole that no one had coming in. Only then do we seek to integrate what is learned into a joint action plan.

Three structures describe most of our repertoire. When differentiation is wanted, we have people speaking individually or working in affinity groups. For example, if the task is strategic planning in a school, we want to hear from teachers, administrators, staff, parents, and pupils, all clarifying their respective stakes. Our second structure calls for the same people to work in mixed groups that replicate the whole, giving them an opportunity to integrate their diverse perspectives. We always ask small groups, affinity or mixed, to report to the whole. Our third structure is the large group. Much integrating takes place in large group conversations following small group or individual reports. We use these D/I-based practices to design and manage task-focused meetings for any purpose (see Exhibit 15.1).

Exhibit 15.1
Principles Applicable to Many Kinds of Meetings

Get the "whole system" in the room. The quotation marks imply that we never get everybody. It is possible, though, to have in the same room people with authority, resources, expertise, information, and need. Simply calling such a meeting is often a radical change, making possible many others.

Explore the whole before seeking to fix any part. Each person has a part of the whole. When all have put in what they know, every person has a picture none had coming in, and they can plan together in a shared context.

Put the future and common ground front and center. You cannot chew gum and whistle, so problems and conflicts become information to be shared, not action items.

Invite self-management and personal responsibility for action. Groups are capable of doing a great deal more than they customarily are asked to do. Each time a facilitator does something for a group, he or she deprives others of a chance to be responsible.

Managing Meetings: Applying D/I Theory to Task Groups

Assume that the right people are in the room and the purpose is clear. (Should there be any doubt, we ask people to talk over the goal in small groups and raise their concerns immediately.) Once underway, we focus most attention on enabling every person who has something to say to speak. We ask each person to make an opening comment related to the task. We let people know that we will manage whole group conversations so that anybody who wants to speak can do so in the time available. We suggest that people manage small groups the same way. If a meeting becomes sticky, we ask people to differentiate their views. When all have a sense of where everyone else stands, prospects for integration increase.

Our facilitating methods emerged as we gave up years of more complex interventions. We now focus on a central concern that we believe is the key to managing large groups. We intend to keep the group whole and working together with commitment no matter what tensions are present. When a group knows its goal and knows where others stand, it will go where it needs to go regardless of members' skills, motives, or idiosyncrasies. When the meeting is structured so that everybody contributes to a view of the whole before anybody tries to fix any part, we have very little to do. We believe our main job is to ask a simple question on rare occasions when a member may be at risk of becoming isolated, usually as the result of saying something others consider impolite, wrong, inappropriate, or divisive. Such incidents, if ignored, will immediately fragment a group and divert it from its task. The intervention goes like this: "Who else feels that way?"

There is a long theoretical rationale for this deceptively simple question that we will get to in a moment. The point is that when we focus on validating differences to keep a group whole, we make very few interventions. When we first realized this, we were startled by the implications. What about those years of pressuring ourselves to know what groups need? Using those diagnostic categories and stages of development? Pressing for hidden assumptions? Surfacing resistance and denial? Reframing statements the way we wished they had been made? At one time, we thought we earned our keep by showing off how insightful we were. Now we earn it by enabling the validation of all views, no matter how deviant, and getting out of the way. When we see what the groups we work with are accomplishing with minimal help from us, we know that this is a path we always wanted to be on.

We believe that group members develop their ability to solve increasingly complex problems as they discover new skills, insights, creative ideas, feelings, or points of view. All of these are potential resources. When a group can discover and contain its differences (even those some may not initially like) and do this repeatedly, we call it a mature working group. Mature groups can solve both task and process problems, moving forward consciously, reflecting on how they are doing, turning either-or dilemmas into both-and integrations. Our structures serve to maximize each person's discoveries. We intervene to keep people's attention off us and on each other and the task at hand. When a mature group gets stuck, it takes very little to keep people working through differences and moving toward common ground. That describes applied D/I theory—when everything is going the way we like best.

Managing Differences: A Theoretical Rationale for Doing Very Little

Alas, rare is the work group that starts out managing itself in a mature way. For millennia, our species has been haunted by difference. Through the ages, people have stereotyped others—from another family, tribe, or village—in an eyeblink. It is our nature to judge people on characteristics we like or despise and to act accordingly. Whether this behavior is innate or learned is beside the point. Think how various societies dichotomize men and women, rich and poor, old and young, fat and thin, light skin and dark, physically able and disabled, short and tall, sick and healthy, housed and homeless, employers and employees—the list is unending. We tend to be emotional, not neutral, about differences. We move toward people who seem similar to us and away from those who do not. We do this unconsciously and nearly always based on the psychological phenomenon of projection.

Projection is the act of unconsciously attributing to others impulses or traits that we like or dislike in ourselves. We may engage in projection when we encounter hidden aspects of ourselves reflected back to us by those around us. "I can't stand speeders!" says the envious inner-speeder watching a reckless driver whiz by. The process is as natural as breathing and often harmless. It can also be deadly, as anyone who has lived in Ireland, the Middle East, Africa, and inner cities the world over can relate. You need not go to exotic places. The tip of this iceberg can be observed in practically any meeting. Every get-together provides a forum for infinite mutual projections of the best and worst parts of ourselves (Weir, 1971).

That is the situation we find ourselves in each time we run a meeting. No matter what formal structures we have arranged, group members, from the first moment, organize into unconscious, unspoken, stereotypical, invisible subgroups. People have no way of knowing which subgroups they are part of, for they keep most projections to themselves. Every meeting, smooth and orderly to the naked eye, in no time becomes a jumble of unspoken judgments, wishes, energies, and frustrated impulses. Every statement anybody makes is a focal point for new, invisible subgroups. On the surface, we have a board, committee, or task force doing what it always does. Under the surface, each person is aligning with, distancing from, or ignoring every statement anybody else makes. These subgroups form and re-form from moment to moment. If a meeting were a cartoon panel, you would see little cloudlike balloons over each person's head with unspoken statements like, "That's the dumbest thing I ever heard." Or, "*I'd* never say anything like *that* out loud." Or, "This is a huge distraction." Or "I'm glad she had the guts to speak up."

Rarely do people say these thoughts aloud. Many people sit on ideas, feelings, or views that might violate a group's norms (unwritten rules). Nearly anybody who has ever talked up in a meeting knows the psychic risks of going against the group. When somebody heeds the impulse to do that, tension rises. Some people manage their discomfort by waiting, indeed expecting, the leader to do something. Others ask challenging questions. Others patiently explain how the "deviant" missed the point. Still others practice a firm, friendly coercion toward their own view. In twenty-first-century meetings, such archetypal behavior no longer serves us.

A central job for us in managing meetings is to interrupt this behavior. The practice is simple, easy, fast, and effective. We interrupt potentially divisive behavior by helping people form what we call *functional subgroups*. We use the adjective *functional* here to suggest "contributing to growth," not to describe people's jobs. These subgroups transcend the stereotypical, potentially stultifying subgroups that form and re-form in people's heads. We owe our insights into the power of functional subgrouping to Yvonne Agazarian (1997) and her innovative systems-centered group theory. In her way of working, people continually differentiate their thoughts, feelings, and ideas. This builds the capacity of the whole group for increasingly rich integrations.

When We Intervene with a "Who Else?" Question

So long as each person has a home in a functional subgroup that includes at least one other person, a large group will stay connected and working on its task. Our minimal job is helping people experience functional differences when stereotypes might prevail. If we do this job right, group members take care of the rest. That is our core theory. The practice is stunningly simple. We act when we hear people make statements so emotionally charged that they put themselves at risk of being isolated or labeled. Such statements can be as simple as, "I don't agree," and as complex as,

"I'm bored, and unless we get to the point, I'm leaving." Or, "This is not working. Why don't you tell us what we should do?"

We judge a statement's impact by the extent to which tension rises in us and in the group. Sometimes people confront the statement head on, raising the group's anxiety by several degrees. Sometimes they change the subject. Either way, the statement functions like the proverbial elephant in the room: nobody knows what to do with it, so they pretend it is not there. At such moments, we neither ignore nor escalate the impact. Instead, we invite an informal subgroup to support the apparently deviant group member. This is the least intervention that will permit people to keep working without having to deny their own or anyone else's feelings:

Group member: I don't agree with what's being said here.

Facilitator: Who else doesn't agree with something that's been said?

Group member: I'm bored, and unless we get to the point, I'm leaving.

Facilitator: Are there others feeling bored?

When the content includes negative comments about another subgroup, we seek a subgroup for the emotion, not the judgment about others—for example:

Group member: I am so sick of businesspeople thinking only of their bottom line.

Facilitator: Is anyone else frustrated that another group has concerns different from theirs? [Note that we don't say, "Who else is frustrated with the business group?" Our question is intended to head off the potential isolation of the person stereotyping the business group.]

Nearly always one or more people will acknowledge that they have the same or a closely related issue. Oddly enough, it takes only one other to form a subgroup, validate a person's right to his or her opinion, and keep the meeting on track. As people learn that there is a subgroup for every issue that matters to them, they are more likely to join the conversation, add to the spectrum of views, and create a more complete and realistic portrait of the issue. Note that we do not organize subgroups. We discover what already exists. So long as each person who takes a risk has an ally, the group will continue to work. A person who knows he or she has support is more likely to listen to other views. Moreover, people with allies are less likely to cave in to group pressure (Asch, 1952).

Most of the time, all we need to keep a group on track is a show of hands and a supporting comment or example from other group members. Sometimes we run several meetings in a row without having to resort to another step. In rare cases, people become deeply polarized and stuck. In those instances, we draw on another insight from Agazarian: when people talk with others who are ostensibly similar, they nearly always discover differences. When they can listen in on conversations among those they consider different, they nearly always find similarities. People who make these finer distinctions develop a more grounded sense of what is possible. They can suspend for the time being their stereotypes and projections and get on with the business at hand.

In a business meeting, people split over what they believed were the principles underlying effective decisions in their company. Fact-based decision making ranked high for one vociferous participant. A vice president hesitantly noted that feelings and intuition often entered into decisions. The first speaker was surprised by this and heatedly defended the centrality of facts. We asked her to pause for a moment and find out who else shared her view. Several raised their hands. Next, we asked who believed intuition and feelings entered in. More hands went up. People had considerable passion for their positions.

Two functional subgroups had become visible. Rather than confront their differences, we asked each subgroup to explore their feelings among themselves while the other subgroup listened. Members of both soon found differences in their apparent similarities. One woman, for example, admitted that to stay fact based, she had to struggle to keep feelings and intuition out. On the other side, one man said, "Of course, I pay attention to data, and I also use information that is not based on hard numbers." The subgroups integrated their views by validating each other's stand under certain conditions. People later said they appreciated hearing the other subgroup's thought processes. They were astonished that no confrontation was necessary. The whole exchange took less than ten minutes.

Even in meetings lasting two or three days, we will ask a "Who else?" question only once or twice and sometimes not at all. We attribute this to the fact that we seek from the start to validate all views and every person's experience. Even rarer is the occasion—maybe once every year or two—that one of us will ask a "Who else?" question and be greeted by silence, even after waiting an interminable twenty seconds or so. In that case, there is nothing for us to do but see whether we can authentically join the person who has gone out on a limb:

Participant: This has been a big waste of time for me.
Facilitator: I've had moments here when I thought I was wasting my time too.

Listening for the Integrating Statement

How do we know that groups are ready to move from one topic to the next or to move toward action? One clue is when a whole spectrum is on the table and people start recycling earlier statements. Perhaps the most dependable sign that a group has all it needs to move on is what we call an integrating statement. In groups polarized by either-or conversations, the rising tension can be a debilitating meeting stopper. An integrating statement takes the form of a both-and comment, recognizing that each side of a polarity has validity. During a meeting on affordable housing, for example, one subgroup fought for more low-cost housing. Another equated low cost with high density in single-family neighborhoods. As the issue heated up toward confrontation and before either of us could say anything, a group member said, "There are some people here who want low-cost housing for all, others who say they fear high rises. We don't have to resolve this in order to treat these as two legitimate goals to be considered in our plan." Tension drained away as people released themselves to the creative work that followed. Fortunately, we find many natural integrators in groups we work with. Moreover, in a pinch, we can always say, "We hear two points of view, A and B. What would you like to do with these?" When all else fails, we consult group members on what they want to do.

To summarize, we manage fight, flight, dependency, avoidance, scapegoating, and other dysfunctional behaviors indirectly by creating conditions under which functional subgroups can form. So long as we encourage functional differentiation and interrupt stereotypical differentiation, we enable a group to integrate its many parts and do richer, more complex work.

MANAGING OURSELVES

Waiting, asking instead of telling, shutting up when a group is working, finding subgroups when tension is high, consulting the group when we are not sure what to do, are relatively simple acts. Anybody should be able to learn them. Yet it has taken each of us years of self-discovery to get to a place where we can confidently work this way. We grew up with high expectations for ourselves, having internalized the need to do things right and look good. We also learned group dynamics in that heady time when the meeting management tool kit expanded exponentially. Anything that could be done in groups, from force-field analysis to finger-painting, would be done, if for no other reason than to see what happens. If you got a new diagnostic concept in those years, it would be a shame not to use it. Perfectionism wed to infinite techniques can be an exhausting combination. Perhaps the most valuable step we have taken for untangling ourselves from this self-made morass was learning to internalize John and Joyce Weir's philosophy of self-management. We have also spent a good deal of time practicing the Weirs' theory and method for owning our own projections and separating ourselves from the projections people make on us. Their system calls for recognizing how we filter our experiences through a murky amalgam of genes, gender, age, history, fears, hopes, ethnicity, parentage, birthplace, health, and a thousand other factors. What starts with the neutral evidence of our senses—sight, smell, hearing, touch, and so on—becomes a filtered set of unique beliefs, judgments, and assumptions that we call our reality. Each of us acts as if this reality, constructed entirely in our own heads, is the only real one.

Our filters are as unique as fingerprints. We dredge the characteristics we impute to others from the depths of our own psyches. When we label a person as resistant, passive-aggressive, or rebellious, when we identify groups as overly dependent, lazy, or in denial, we are projecting parts of us on others to reduce our own discomfort. If we are so good at what we do, why don't *they* live up to our expectations? Whatever labels we put on others must be parts of us. Were they not, how could we recognize them in others? We have come to accept that the world is the way it is. Each of us makes up his or her own version. We make up percepts to maximize our comfort and minimize our pain. Each of us has a reality no other can share. Knowing this makes it easier to help people differentiate their views and avoid imposing ours, whether as conceptual models, interpretations, or prescriptions for change.

Inevitably, we have had to confront our own projections on authority. Every meeting includes authority figures. Bosses and chairpeople represent one kind, experts another. Facilitators are considered experts, else why would we be there? How we wear the cloak of the authority that others invest us with has profound impact on a group. In new groups, some people—filtering a lifetime of experiences—move naturally to dependency on the leader. Others—also filtering like mad—automatically challenge the leader's authority. Faced with uncertainty, the most mature among us can regress to childhood fantasies that the leader will make everything okay, or conversely, that the leader represents a threat to be resisted.

We have come to expect these authority projections. We recognize them in ourselves. We know they come our way each time we stand in front of a group. Our practice is to do whatever we can to minimize them, so we never pretend we have no authority. We repeat the meeting's goals at the start and differentiate our roles from the group members'. We ask people to share leadership and self-manage their small groups. We try to avoid doing anything for people that they could readily do for themselves. We keep our instructions to a minimum. We ask people if they are ready to move. We check out our assumptions and judgments with the group before acting on them. When somebody lobs an annoying projection at us, we do our best to pause, breathe, and avoid acting defensively. We do not interpret people's motives or statements or judge the relevance of somebody's comments. When people are in dialogue, we stay out. When people risk becoming scapegoats, we find them subgroups. If people start to fight, we ask them to differentiate their positions. Above all, we seek to shift attention away from us and on to the task. Sometimes none of this is enough. When all else fails, we default to our most secure position: we consult the group. The less we intervene, the more compliments we get. "I really appreciated the way you guys let us do the work" is for us a practical validation of our theory and a great payoff for self-restraint.

Successfully Facilitating Multicultural Groups

Christine Hogan

> *Difference just is. It is a fact of life.*
>
> Distefano and Maznevski (2000)

The purpose of this chapter is to assist facilitators to prepare and facilitate workshops and training sessions where participants come from diverse cultural backgrounds. It provides a selection of tools and a checklist for designing workshops, models, strategic devices, and processes that have proved helpful in designing workshops, presentations, and conferences for multicultural groups. In addition, it provides some sources so that readers can follow up on specific points of interest.

Participants from different cultures have different perspectives and implicit ground rules for interaction. Culture is a set of values, beliefs, and assumptions

Note: I express warm thanks to the many people who made contributions and gave feedback on this chapter: Asma Abdullah, Colin Beasley, Gilbert Brenson-Lazán, Laura Hsu, Lawrence Philbrook, Peter Shepherd, Richard West, and Kati and John Wilson.

255

that influence our thoughts, perceptions, behaviors, and customs. These assumptions are implicit and taken for granted, much like breathing. The advances in the human genome research tell us that out of the thirty thousand known genes in the human body, we are similar to other races across the planet in 99 percent of these; that is, genetically we have much in common. It is wise, however, to assume differences in values and behaviors until similarities emerge (Adler, 1997). Many of us are hybrids of many different cultures through studying, living, and traveling abroad. Every group has a culture, and no group has any one culture (G. Brenson-Lazán, e-mail to the author, Dec. 14, 2003).

Throughout history and in all cultures, there have been wise people with outstanding communication, mediation, and facilitation skills. The roots of facilitation have their origins in the helping professions—for example, teaching, counseling, social work, and development work. Elements of facilitation permeate history and different cultures (Hogan, 2002). For example, Socrates encouraged people to question ideas; shamans used talking sticks and talking stones to encourage people to speak the truth from the heart; holy leaders and sages like Gautama Buddha, Muhammad, Christ, Lao-tzu, Mahatma Gandhi, Rabindranath Tagore, Sri Aurobindo, and Swami Vivekananda used, among other techniques, storytelling, questioning, metaphors, and self-reflection to engage people in changing their mind-sets and psychological states in order to encourage new ways of thinking about their lives (Chakraborty, 1998). The Inca people in South America built an empire of 13 million in just one hundred years due partly to the Mitimaes, facilitators of "agro teamwork" (G. Brenson-Lazán, e-mail to the author, Dec. 14, 2003).

Participants from different cultures have different perceptions about the roles of facilitators, facilitation processes, and desirable behavioral norms in workshops (Verghese, 2003). Just because some processes may be unknown to people from some cultures does not mean these processes are not useful. Extra care may be needed to build trust and give clear verbal and written explanations of why you are using a process and the ground rules.

If the cultural background of the facilitator is different from that of the group members, there may some impact on group norms. For example, Lawrence Philbrook (personal communication to the author, Nov. 30, 2003) observed that some Chinese facilitators working with Chinese groups in Taiwan had to work much harder to get participants to interact than some Western facilitators did. He reasoned that Chinese participants returned to their usual "respect for teachers" norm, whereas they expected something different to happen with Western facilitators.

DIVERSITY CHECKLIST FOR WORKSHOP DESIGN

The cultural composition of a group is one aspect of diversity. The checklist in Exhibit 16.1 contains questions for facilitators to think about when planning and evaluating workshops with regard to the gender, race, age, disability, sexual orientation, and cultural background of participants. It is not necessary to address all of these points, but it is useful to be aware that they exist and check through them from time to time as a reminder of issues that may need attention. A rule of thumb that is useful to remember is that "no *one* facilitative process or technique will work in all cultures or with all groups" (G. Brenson-Lazán, e-mail to the author, Dec. 14, 2003).

Exhibit 16.1
Diversity Checklist for Workshop Design

1. **Workshop Design**
   - **Consider the participants' gender, cultural background, learning, thinking and communicating styles, age range, health and disability status, English language proficiency, values, and past experiences.**
   - **Who should be invited? For community-based workshops, identify the formal and informal leaders and power holders.**
   - **Check workshop dates and religious calendars. For example, religious festivals like Ramadan, when Muslim participants are fasting, may have an impact on attendance and energy levels.**
   - **Check prayer times. In many cultures, it is useful to have meetings after prayers, when everyone is already together.**
   - **Contact participants in advance (perhaps by e-mail) to ascertain cultural and dietary needs or concerns.**
   - **Include opportunities for a positive engagement with people from other cultures, practices, and life expectations.**
   - **Seek assistance in workshop design from facilitators or cultural advisers who are knowledgeable about the culture you will be working with.**
   - **Include examples and readings that reflect a diversity of perspectives.**
   - **Check the metaphors and teaching stories you will use. For example, attributes of animals vary across cultures. If you use an exercise in which you ask individuals to identify with certain animals, remember that dogs are regarded as unclean in some Muslim societies, as food in many parts of China, and as pets and working animals in many Western societies. Cows are regarded as holy by Hindus. A white elephant is considered very positively in Thailand and Lao PDR, but in many Western societies, "white elephant" refers to something of little or no value that nobody wants.**

- Check the visuals to ensure they are inclusive, that is, include examples of people from the different ethnic groups in the workshops.

- Think about warm-up activities. Is physical touch involved? For some groups, touching or close proximity to members of the opposite sex may be embarrassing, so you may wish to use single-sex groups for some activities.

- Think about ground rules that will include all groups—for example, "Your comfort in the workshops is important so please make your needs known," and invite participants to discuss ways in which they may value differences.

- Cater to a range of learning styles and left- and right-brain activities by mixing group processes (such as using different turn-taking procedures), modes (verbal, written, picture, story), and size of groups (such as pairs, triads, up to a maximum of seven people; Gardenswartz, Rowe, Digh, and Bennett, 2003). For example, explain and negotiate ground rules verbally, and display them on flip charts.

- Check your nonverbal communication. For example, what are appropriate dress codes? What are the attitudes of participants to sitting on the floor? Some groups are more at ease sitting on mats on the floor, whereas others regard the floor as unclean or unsuitable because of their clothing or status. Some older people or people with back trouble may find the floor uncomfortable.

This is not an exhaustive list, but illustrates the sorts of things that are useful in terms of learning about the cultural practices and preferences of the people you will be working with. Don't be overly confident. Be prepared for surprises.

2. Content
   - Acknowledge the diversity of knowledge and experience of participants.
   - Help participants to map their different perspectives. (See the suggestions later in this chapter.)
   - Use examples, case studies, and stories that are free of negative stereotypes or assumptions.
   - Use participants' examples, case studies, and stories as a basis for discussion.
   - Examine the implications of diversity as part of the organizational issues being examined.
   - Encourage participants to recognize and understand different ways of knowing and perceiving the world.

3. Delivery
  - Provide opportunities for members of different cultural groups to explore their differing perceptions of both the goals of the workshop and the processes to achieve them.
  - Provide participants with learning opportunities to stimulate different learning styles, for example, activist, reflector, theorist, and pragmatist (Honey and Mumford, 1986, 1992).
  - Encourage participants to get to know and actively listen to each other.
  - Avoid negative or potentially offensive stereotypes or assumptions.
  - Encourage participants to use their backgrounds and experiences as learning tools.
  - Speak in plain English, explain acronyms, and avoid using colloquialisms and jokes that are culturally specific or difficult to explain.
  - Actively discourage language or behavior that is racist, sexist, or homophobic.
  - Actively watch and listen for any cross-cultural issues that may be influencing group dynamics, communication, and learning.

4. Evaluation
  - Provide participants with opportunities to give you feedback early on in a workshop regarding your pace, volume, use of language, and clarity of explanations.
  - Provide participants with a range of anonymous or informal feedback mechanisms.
  - Provide participants with the opportunity for one or more group representatives to act as a messenger to give you informal verbal feedback.

Source: Adapted from a handout from the Teaching and Learning Committee (2003).

WARM-UPS AND ENERGIZERS

It is useful to have a range of nonverbal activities as warm-ups and energizers for cross-cultural groups so that participants who are not fully fluent in the language of the meeting are not immediately disadvantaged.

Forming Cross-Cultural Subgroups

It is useful to be able to form cross-cultural groups quickly and easily without causing embarrassment. Ask the participants to line up according to their places of birth. Start on the left side of the room, and tell the participants that the area on the far right represents the farthest place from the workshop venue. Some chaos will ensue while people try to sort themselves out. Then ask participants to introduce themselves and give a little information about where they were born.

To form subgroups, start at the left end of the continuum (those born closest to the workshop venue) and ask individuals to number off from, say, one to five if you want five subgroups in a room of twenty-five people. Ask all the number ones to raise hands and spot each other, then number twos, and so on. Ask people to form into groups, and you will have a mix of ethnic backgrounds in each group.

Having formed cross-cultural groups, the facilitator needs to help these groups explore and value their differences and similarities and develop ground rules to enable them to work together.

Pass the Blob

A useful icebreaker is "Pass the Blob" in which the facilitator explains that she has a blob that needs to be passed around the group. (A "blob" is an imaginary shape held in one or both hands; it may change size and substance depending on the creativity of the person holding it.) Participants quickly catch on to how they can carefully, playfully, or carelessly pass on the blob (or even drop it and scrape it up together). This exercise causes laughter and can lead to later discussion on how we pass information and new ideas around an organization.

Remember that laughter may indicate embarrassment rather than enjoyment. If individuals in the group appear embarrassed, the facilitator can retrieve the situation by diverting the focus away from them and moving on.

Clapping Exercise

Another quick activity is a clapping exercise. A facilitator claps once and passes it on to another person who must clap at the same time as the facilitator. Once "caught," she turns and claps to the next person in line. The next person receives the clap by clapping exactly at the same time as the sender. When everyone has the idea, a single clap can be passed across the group. Everyone must pay attention in order to be ready to clap together. Many variations can be developed along these lines.

Check out the culture you are going to work with. For example, this exercise was very popular in Lao PDR with women's groups and nongovernmental organizations, but members of the Guambian Indian tribe, descendants of the Inca in southern Columbia and northern Ecuador, do not react well to nonverbal activities that they perceive as "child's play." They consider it to be demeaning (G. Brenson-Lazán, e-mail to the author, Dec. 14, 2003).

Learning Names

It is often quite hard to learn names with which you are unfamiliar, that use different sounds, and are written with characters different from your own language. It helps to have large labels on which participants write their preferred names or nicknames and how they are pronounced (rather than Anglicized names, unless they choose to use them). For more formal settings, large place cards may be drawn up with participants' names in English facing the front and their names in their own language and characters facing them. If the spelling is incorrect, rewrite the name cards as necessary.

Name Meanings

It is useful if individuals can introduce their names and the names that they prefer to be called (and their pronunciation). Many people from South, East and Central Asia, South America, and Africa have names that have a meaning, so you can help them feel at ease by asking them to tell the group the meaning behind their names. The names of some Westerners have meanings, but for those who do not know their name meanings, you can add an alternative request: explain how their parents chose their names.

Singing Songs

In many Asian and African cultures, singing songs is a pleasant way to start a workshop. Not only is singing an integral part of many of these cultures, but the rise of karaoke in many cultures has increased the popularity of singing in public. (For an in-depth discussion on using music with groups, see Hogan, 2003b.)

CREATING VALUE WITH DIVERSE TEAMS: THE MAPPING, BRIDGING, AND INTEGRATING MODEL

This section focuses on a three-stage model and processes to enable multicultural groups to focus on diversity and maximize the potential of individual members of the group.

Research by Adler (1997) and Distefano and Maznevski (2000) concluded that diverse teams tend to perform either better or worse than homogeneous teams, with more of them performing worse than better. Distefano and Maznevski divided multicultural teams into three categories:

- Destroyer teams. These teams were dysfunctional because the formal leaders made decisions without genuine discussion among members. As a result, they destroyed the potential value of these multicultural teams.
- Equalizer teams. These team members smoothed, compromised, and suppressed any differences in ideas and perspectives. Distefano and Maznevski's research led them to believe that most culturally diverse teams that thought of themselves as doing well were equalizers.
- Creator teams. These teams did more than use platitudes like, "We value diversity." They actively explored their differences and took advantage of their diversity like a jazz ensemble. Brenson-Lazán (e-mail to the author, Dec. 14, 2003) calls this the "humongous paradox of synergy," that is, the greater the diversity, the greater the potential for synergy and the greater the difficulty in achieving it. The less diversity there is, the lower is the potential for synergy and the greater the ease of achieving it.

Distefano and Maznevski concluded that the key to being successful was the quality of the interaction processes rather than the team membership. As a result, they developed the mapping, bridging, and integrating (MBI) model as shown in Exhibit 16.2. In their research they observed that creator teams actively mapped and tried to understand their differences, bridged their communication and took differences into account, and integrated team-level ideas by carefully monitoring participation patterns, solving disagreements, and creating new perspectives.

The MBI model is a set of principles for helping teams to develop their own best ways to perform well. It may be applied to debriefing a meeting or for analyzing a videotape of a team meeting. A facilitator may take a group through each stage in turn; if there is confusion, it may be necessary to revert to a previous stage:

- Mapping to understand differences. The important aspect of mapping is identifying which differences will affect interactions and decision making, for example, cultural values, thinking styles, and ways of achieving goals. Most multicultural teams do not take the time to map cultural differences openly; they instead rely on broad generalizations (stereotypes) that they have heard (Distefano and Maznevski, 2000).

There are many different methods that use different senses that may be used to map cultural differences. Among them are learning basic words in the languages

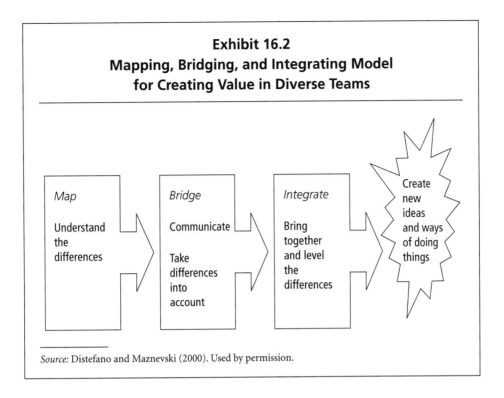

Exhibit 16.2
Mapping, Bridging, and Integrating Model
for Creating Value in Diverse Teams

Map

Understand the differences

Bridge

Communicate

Take differences into account

Integrate

Bring together and level the differences

Create new ideas and ways of doing things

Source: Distefano and Maznevski (2000). Used by permission.

of group members (Reese, 1997), discussing the cultural iceberg (after Brislin, 1991), developing cultural suitcases, and playing the cross-cultural card game (Abdullah and Shepherd, 2000):

• Bridging to communicate across differences. This requires trust building, development of ground rules, and motivation and confidence to discuss differences openly. Team members need to learn decentering, a skill similar to empathy and role reversal, which requires individuals to suspend judgment and value differences using the information from the mapping stage as a "translation key" (Distefano and Maznevski, 2000).

• Integrating and leveling differences. Participants need to recenter and build new ground rules and processes based on what they have learned during the mapping and bridging stages in order to manage participation, resolve disagreements, and build on ideas.

People with different cultural backgrounds often have very different norms for participating and turn taking, so Distefano and Maznevski (2000) provide some suggestions:

- Rotating a process leader or observer, provided this is not a threat and is culturally appropriate. In very hierarchical societies, it may be almost impossible for a participant of low rank to take the role of process leader.
- Varying modes of meeting and sharing information—for example, solicit ideas by e-mail before a meeting, talk to staff in hallways to gather ideas, have paired-group discussions during meetings, and have frequent breaks in meetings.
- Map ideas on flip charts as lists, mind maps, or drawings.

If conflict occurs, go back to basics to understand more fully what cultural perceptions and values are underpinning problems. (For further exercises on cross-cultural conflict resolution, see Blainey, Davis, and Goodwill, 1995, and Brenson-Lazán, 2003.)

PROCESSES AND STRATEGIES TO MAP DIFFERENCES

This section describes a variety of processes that facilitators may use at the various stages in the MBI model.

Learning Basic Words in the Other Languages of Group Members

This exercise is based on the work by Reese (1997) to encourage face-to-face active engagement between participants in multicultural groups by encouraging everyone to make the effort to learn basic greetings of their coparticipants—for example:

Hello.

How are you?

What is your name?

Can I help you?

Can you help me?

Thank you.

Please.

Excuse me.

Goodbye.

In addition, it is useful to learn the meanings and differences in usage or nonusage of a term (for example, in some cultures, "thank you" is used only for a major gift, not for a basic service in a shop) and other aspects of communication, such as tone of voice, body language, types of eye contact, and interpersonal space. It is useful for facilitators to develop a basic vocabulary of these key phrases in the languages of people they work with. Participants are usually very appreciative of these efforts.

The interactions that result give an advantage to the bilingual participants who become teachers. It does not matter whether participants develop perfect pronunciation; it is the attempt that counts. Indeed, it is the mistakes that generate laughter and are the hooks that encourage further dialogue. During the learning process shown in Exhibit 16.3, participants start to engage with one another: one person is teaching and another is being taught, and everyone is engaged in the dialogue of learning (Reese, 1997; Burson, 2002). Laughter and humor develop, which is productive provided that participants are laughing with and not at each other, and participants can learn, with guidance, to give one another positive as well as constructive feedback.

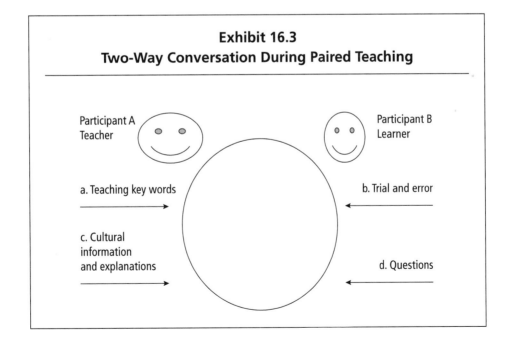

Exhibit 16.3
Two-Way Conversation During Paired Teaching

Participant A
Teacher

Participant B
Learner

a. Teaching key words

b. Trial and error

c. Cultural
information
and explanations

d. Questions

Discuss the Cultural Iceberg

The cultural iceberg model is a useful tool to stimulate discussions and map similarities and differences. The iceberg as a metaphor is useful since only a small percentage of an iceberg is seen above the surface. This is similar to cultures, in that we can observe some food, ceremonies, and dress codes, but there may be many attitudes and beliefs that underpin these customs that are not obvious at first (and that we may not learn for many years, if ever). As depicted in Exhibit 16.4, the level of the water line varies from culture to culture, and what aspects of culture appear above and below the waterline will vary between cultures and individuals.

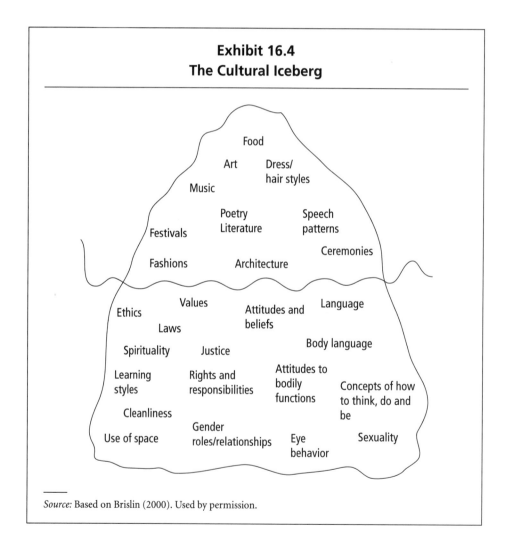

Exhibit 16.4
The Cultural Iceberg

Source: Based on Brislin (2000). Used by permission.

Develop Cultural Suitcases

Another cultural mapping exercise is to ask participants to join groups of similar cultural background and discuss what participants from other countries should pack in their "cultural suitcases" to enable them to live and work in their respective cultures. The suitcase can be packed with basic do's and don'ts, as well as songs, sayings, and proverbs. Issues and contradictions that arise may then be used as starting points for developing bridges and integrating the views of participants from different cultures who are present.

Learn About Your Own and Other Cultural Dimensions

Scholars in the area of intercultural communication have advanced many different classifications or dimensions in order to help us make sense of other cultures and our own (Hall, 1990; Hofstede, 1980, 1991; Trompenaars, 1993; Trompenaars and Hampden-Turner, 2000; Abdullah, 2001). Different cultural dimensions or patterns may affect the values, attitudes, learning, and thinking styles of participants and facilitators. We should be careful not to stereotype one another, as within each culture there are subcultures and individual variations that vary widely. The dimensions, however, do help us to be more aware of the assumptions that underlie both our own and conditioning and that of others, and provide us some vocabulary with which to analyze diversity.

One exercise is to invite participants to show where they fit on the continuum shown in Exhibit 16.5. Quickly you will find that there is great diversity and also that people often say, "It depends on the circumstances," that is, styles of behavior are "situational."

Exhibit 16.5
Eight Cultural Dimensions and Explanations

Culture A	Culture B
1a Harmony with nature and society **Disagreements must be overcome. Politeness, respect, and emotional restraint.**	1b Control over nature and society **Harness and challenge nature and society to achieve own goals. Show initiative.**

Culture A	Culture B
2a Relationships Building and maintaining relationships are more important than tasks.	**2b Task** Getting the task done is more important than buildings and maintaining relationships.
3a Hierarchy (high power distance) Large distance between people with status and those without it. Formality and protocol in dress and behavior toward people in authority.	**3b Equality (low power distance)** Low distance between people with status and those without it. Less formality in dress and behavior toward people in authority.
4a Shame Fear of making mistakes and bringing shame on the group and loss of face.	**4b Guilt** Individuals and internal sense of right and wrong.
5a High context Circular and indirect speech. What you see is not necessarily what you get. Indirect and spiral logic. There are many implicit messages in nonverbal communication patterns.	**5b Low context** Direct, open speech. Say it as it is. What you see is what you get. Linear, direct logic.
6a Polychronic time Time is regarded as circuitous, nonsequential, and flexible. Less attention to ranking and sequencing of tasks. Deadlines flexible.	**6B Monochronic time** Time is linear. Attention to ranking and sequencing of tasks from important to less important. Deadlines less flexible, time management.
7a Collectivism ("We") Loyalty to the group above personal goals. Enjoyment of being in and working together as a group.	**7b Individualism ("I")** Pride in being different and setting own goals. Privacy and individual space important.
8a Spiritual/Religious Time at work allocated to prayer or attending religious festivals and rituals. Dress codes according to religious laws.	**8b Secular** Work seen as most important and not to be interrupted by religious rituals.

Abdullah and Shephard (2000) developed a colorful and useful cultural card pack comprising the sixteen cultural dimensions shown in Exhibit 16.5. There are three cards with a sentence to describe each of the sixteen dimensions, giving a total of forty-eight cards. (There are more dimensions, but space does not allow discussion here. For further information see Samovar and Porter, 2004.)

In this cross-cultural card sort, participants form groups with others from the same culture. They are asked to pick out cards that best describe their own culture. While doing this, they become familiar with a list of cultural concepts that they can use to differentiate others—not as "good" or "bad," but just different from their own. The objective of this game is for players to become aware of and acknowledge cultural differences and acquire a neutral language to describe cultural differences and similarities.

The facilitator may use the card sort to help participants address questions such as these:

- How and why are people different?
- Why do people go about achieving goals differently?
- How and why do some people like to work in groups and others alone?
- Why do some people build relationships before getting the task done?
- What are our hidden cultural dimensions and underlying assumptions?

At the end of the exercise, the facilitator can gather data on a flip chart in a table of cultural dimensions like the one in Exhibit 16.6 as a tool for mapping cultures and then developing integrating strategies. You should acknowledge that terms like *Chinese* and *European* are gross generalizations and that all cultures have many differences, such as those between individuals, age groups, regions, and urban-rural settings.

The example in Exhibit 16.6 shows the results of a workshop in which six cultural groups (six to seven people per group) played the card game. The cultural groups are identified at the top of the table. On the right side of the table, under the heading "groups," is a column for each group. The numbers in the column indicate the number of cards that each group selected to describe itself for each of the eight dimensions. This information may then be used to stimulate discussion on how to build bridges and communication flows across the groups.

Exhibit 16.6
Results of a Cross-Cultural Card Sort

Each group was asked to select the cards that best described their own culture. There was a maximum of three cards for each cultural dimension. The number of cards chosen by each group are shown on the right. The groups were:

Group 1 Anglo-Australian   Group 4 Western European

Group 2 Malaysian (Bumiputra)   Group 5 Anglo-African

Group 3 Chinese   Group 6 Indian

Relationships	Dimensions	Number of Cards Chosen by Groups					
		1	2	3	4	5	6
With nature and society	1a. Harmony	0	3	3	2	0	3
	1b. Control/mastery	3	0	1	1	3	0
	2a. Relationships	2	3	3	2	1	3
	2b. Task	0	0	0	0	1	0
	3a. Hierarchy	0	3	3	0	0	3
	3b. Equality	3	2	2	2	2	0
With other people	4a. Shame	0	3	3	2	3	2
	4b. Guilt	2	2	0	1	2	0
	5a. High context	1	3	3	1	1	0
	5b. Low context	3	0	0	2	2	0
	6a. Polychronic time	2	3	3	2	1	3
	6b. Monochronic time	2	0	0	0	2	0
	7a. "We" collective	1	1	3	2	2	3
	7b. "I" individual	3	0	0	2	2	1
With God and spirituality	8a. Religious	0	3	0	0	1	1
	8b. Secular	2	1	2	3	3	2

Processes and Strategies to Building Bridges and Integrate Across Cultural Dimensions

Building bridges and integrating processes and strategies may be used by groups to discuss ways of overcoming difference and maximizing the inputs of everyone in a group. For each of the eight dimensions in Exhibit 16.5, I illustrate divergent participant perspectives followed by some bridge building and integrating ideas for facilitators. It is also useful to ask participants to develop their own bridging and integrating strategies. (The ideas for this section have been developed and adapted from Beasley and Hogan, 2003; Chang, 2002; and Verghese, 2003.)

Harmony

I don't like to disagree too much in a workshop or seem to be in conflict with other participants. . . I'll just go with the flow.

It's hard to be friends with participants in the workshop who think so differently from me.

I won't speak out as it's better if I let others have the opportunity to gain face.

Control

I like to have an argument in workshop and then carry on our debate over lunch or even later over a few drinks.

I like to volunteer in workshops or lead discussions because that's how I learn.

I like to challenge ideas in a workshop just to see what happens.

Some Bridge Building Ideas

• Explain to participants at the beginning of your workshop the differences between dialogue and debate (Bohm, Factor, and Garrett, 1995).

• Show participants how to look at all sides of an issue to gain the whole picture, for example, the six thinking hats process (de Bono, 1985, 1987).

• Encourage reticent participants to express their ideas and responses and make sure that each participant is given the opportunity to contribute something to the discussion. A round robin process takes away the need for participants to think about interrupting, and turn taking is highly structured.

• Build in written processes to enable quieter participants and participants whose English is their second or third language to reflect. Writing gives everyone time to think and reflect. This equalizes participation and generates many ideas quickly. For example, with card sorts (Schnelle, 1979) or brainwriting (Geschka, Schaude, and Schlicksupp 1973; Hogan 2003a), participants write one idea per card; the facilitator collects them and redistributes them anonymously so that individuals can add positive ideas. Eventually, all cards are displayed, clustered, and discussed. This is an equalizing process, as everyone is participating at the same time, there is no turn taking, and people whose first language is other than the language being used in the workshop have a chance to think and write (it is far less stressful for them than having to think and speak on their feet). In contrast, brainstorming is spoken, slows idea generation as only one person can speak at a time, and favors the participants with good verbal skills who can think on their feet and are not afraid to verbalize what may at first be considered as ideas far out of the mainstream. Brainwriting allows for paradoxical ideas to be generated anonymously. (See Hogan, 2003a, for further analysis of creative processes.)

• Working in pairs maximizes verbal participation and builds confidence. Pairing together the power holders and more dominant participants ensures that quieter participants have an opportunity to voice their ideas and opinions.

Relationships	Tasks
I need to get to know my fellow group members before we get down to work.	Icebreakers are a waste of time.
I work best with people I trust and feel comfortable with.	I'm really busy, so I just want to get the work done in the minimum amount of time and with the least amount of fuss.
It's more important to be able to work well with my colleagues than to show how clever I am.	I like to know exactly what to do and complete it in the time.
I like to have specific ground rules about how we should relate to one another in workshops.	I like to have specific ground rules about what we have to do in workshops.

Some Bridge Building Ideas

• Build in warm-up activities that are related to the goals of the workshop so that participants can get to know one another but do not feel they are doing activities without a purpose.

• Ensure that preworkshop refreshments, lunch, and breaks are provided adjacent to the workshop room so that participants mingle and chat and do not return to their offices.

• Arrange tasks and group activities so that participants who do not already know each other work together and have to discuss and share different perspectives and experiences.

• Change the composition of groups regularly for different tasks.

Hierarchy: High Power Distance	Equality: Low Power Distance
Mmm . . . ok. You are the facilitator, but what are your qualifications and areas of expertise?	The facilitator can't expect respect just by being a facilitator. I hope she knows what she's doing!
The facilitator has been employed by the company and deserves some respect. How should I address you: Mr. Steve or Ms. Chris or Ms. Hogan?	Well, what do you mean, and why do you want us to use this process?
The facilitator is the expert and should provide the answers or tell us what to do.	The facilitator is here as a guide and should be there to provide a service to me and the group.
	Everyone should offer their ideas and exchange information.

Some Bridge Building Ideas

• Make your own roles as a facilitator clear (for example, that as facilitator, you are not going to enter into content or when you are going to go into content that you are putting on your "trainer" hat).

• Ensure the participants are clear about their roles. Information about roles may be sent by e-mail with the workshop outline to prospective human resource development staff and participants before the workshop and then explained or renegotiated at the workshop itself.

• In some hierarchical cultures, it may be useful to ask a senior executive to introduce you and indicate your qualifications and experience (for example, if you are a female facilitator in a male-dominated culture or workshop).

• Write about your experience, qualifications, and interests in the workshop handout. This saves your having to give a long introduction about yourself. You can show it to participants so they can refer to it.

• Take an interest in the participants, and show that you are flexible. Recognize the participants as individuals who may have very different backgrounds.

• Be patient with participants from societies that are different from your own, and remember that it may take them more time to feel at ease if you are from a culture different from theirs.

• Participants from low power distance societies may feel quite happy to speak out, so build in equalizing processes such as round robins to give opportunities for people from hierarchical societies to speak out.

- With participants who show low power distance behaviors and are too familiar or show lack of respect, you may need to draw the line in a friendly but firm manner. (This comment may be more applicable to female facilitators.)
- Do not take personal questions as an affront, but encourage participants to ask questions related to the workshop.
- Strongly hierarchical societies may not value participation and facilitation.

Shame	Guilt
My family members will all feel so shamed if I make a mistake or if I fail.	If I speak out and upset someone in the workshop, I would feel guilty.
I feel nervous about speaking out in the workshop in case I get it wrong and lose face.	As long as my conscience is clear, I will do whatever it takes to succeed, even if it means using the ideas of others and claiming them as my own.
I am concerned with what others (especially the boss) may say about me if I say something stupid.	
As the boss, I will lose face if I do not say something (even if I have nothing to say).	

Some Bridge Building Ideas

- Explain to participants that with many processes designed to generate creative ideas, for example, brainstorming and brainwriting, there is no such thing as a right or wrong idea.
- Be supportive, and encourage others to support shy participants who do speak out.
- Generate awareness that some people in every society feel nervous to speak out.
- Explain that it is important to attribute information or an idea to its source, to honor an authority, be professional as a scholar, and so that others know where they can obtain additional information.
- Teach participants how to paraphrase, quote, and reference correctly (both in-text and end-of-text) according to Western disciplinary conventions. Provide models, examples, and practice exercises and activities.
- In training situations, allow participants the opportunity to retake tests and resubmit reports to avoid stress and fears of failure, which may inhibit their thinking processes.

High Context	Low Context
I find it hard to express how I really feel in a workshop. Anyway, surely they can see how I feel from my body language.	I just like to say it as it is.
They will know I disagree because I'm remaining silent.	It's important to stick to the point and not beat around the bush.
It's my job to build my case by giving all the background circumstances, but not to tell someone else what to think.	It's my job to make my case clearly and directly and to back it up with facts and sound arguments.

Some Bridge Building Ideas

• Present good models of report structure and oral presentations to illustrate the framework required for expressing opinions and arguments in the context in which you are working.

• Acknowledge that different cultures and languages have different ways of agreeing, disagreeing, and expressing opinions.

• Examine examples of cultural variations of styles of thinking (Ballard and Clanchy, 1991).

Polychronic Time	Monochronic Time
I like it when a workshop develops, and we can explore different ideas on a topic as they arise.	I expect to start and finish on time.
I like to have the time to be able to explain the context of an example.	I like a detailed workshop agenda.
I think that facilitators should be more flexible over deadlines and schedules.	I dislike it when some participants jump in rather than wait their turn.
We all like to talk at once. So what?	We should elect a timekeeper to keep everyone on schedule.

Some Bridge Building Ideas

• Acknowledge different cultural perspectives of time and punctuality.

• Help the group to reach an agreement regarding issues such as punctuality, turn taking, and the structure of the meeting agenda.

• At the end of a break, play a piece of music that is a signal to everyone that you will restart in five minutes. This enables participants who have been chatting to take care of needs they have put off.

• Explain the rationale behind turn taking and one person speaking at a time.

Collectivism

Group discussions are a chance to work together and draw on others' expertise and viewpoints. However, it would be annoying if people do not contribute, as the whole team will suffer.

Should I contribute? Only if I am adding value and have something worthwhile to say. Otherwise, I might waste everyone's time.

I like doing group work as long as we share the kudos equally.

Individualism

Group activities are a nuisance because there are bound to be people who will not put in their fair share of the work.

It should be up to me whether I want to contribute in the workshop. It's my problem, and I should be able to do what I am comfortable with.

I'm a high achiever, and if I have to do group work, my marks may suffer.

I don't like writing things on cards so ideas are anonymous. If I have a good idea I want the kudos.

Some Bridge Building Ideas

• Invite participants to contract for desirable group norms by asking questions like, "How can we all get the most out of our time together?" Ensure these ideas are written up and clearly visible in case you wish to refer to them later. I usually add "the right to say no and participate by observing." People can participate in a group in many different ways—by listening, thinking, and supporting nonverbally as well as by talking. This ground rule is very freeing for participants who feel shy. It also often results in everyone joining in everything.

• Explain, or invite participants to discuss, the advantages and disadvantages of individual and group activities and competition and cooperation. Ask participants to raise their concerns at the beginning and invite them to develop ways of dealing with "social loafers," language constraints, poor timekeepers, and dominating and dysfunctional behaviors.

• Invite members of small discussion groups to present their ideas together, with everyone saying something. At other times, ask for a representative to report back to the whole group; at the end, ask if any other group members want to add anything.

• Ensure there are face-saving mechanisms in place for mediation if a group is dysfunctional. Some highly individualistic people find it very hard to work productively in a group environment.

Religious/Spiritual

I feel embarrassed when people swear using the name of God.

Secular

I think religious ideas and beliefs are a private matter and should play no part in workshops.

I feel that my spiritual beliefs should be treated as seriously as the facilitator's views.

I feel awkward on the occasions when I should go to prayers and we have a workshop.

I wish they had gone to the trouble of finding out my dietary needs.

I don't see why we should have to finish workshop early so a small number of participants can go to prayers.

Some Bridge Building Ideas

• Ensure that the workshop venue can cater to the particular religious and other dietary needs of your participants (for example, kosher, halal, as well as low salt, vegetarian, vegan, low carbohydrate, no gluten).

• Build in a break or tangential discussion activities for secular participants when others are at prayers. Check to see that those who are at prayers do not feel left out.

The Mirroring Process

The mirroring process (Satir, 1983) is a useful multisensory exercise including role-play, drawing, and singing for groups that have been working together for some time but want to improve communication between them. Participants from "culture A" are asked to hold up a metaphorical mirror to the participants from "culture B" (and vice versa) so that everyone can learn more about how they behave and communicate (Hogan, 1996, 2003). There need to be high levels of trust for this exercise.

It is important to focus participants on issues, not people. If some team members cannot attend, it is very important to discuss with those present how they will brief the absentees later. This is because some of the participants' behaviors may change as a result of the workshop.

An explanation of the mirroring process might be presented as follows: "This is your opportunity to learn a great deal about one another, so that you can improve communication and interactions in the future. Please be as open, honest, and sensitive as you can in the way you express your feedback. Do not mention names of individuals. Please illustrate ideas and behaviors."

Participants are asked to form groups of four to five people of homogeneous cultures. Provide them with flip chart paper, felt pens, and masking tape. Props like scarves, local cloth and clothing, hats, and musical instruments are useful to make this fun.

Give participants the list that follows, and explain that each group will be asked to illustrate the characteristics of the "other" culture using drawings, poems, songs, storytelling, skits, or role play. Among the things to illustrate are these:

- Aspects of the other culture that they like, appreciate, or admire
- Aspects of communication with the other culture they find difficult to understand or appreciate
- Suggestions for improving communication between members of the respective cultures

Allow groups twenty minutes for preparation and five minutes to show each skit to represent the other culture. Allow at least one hour for debriefing and discussion.

This activity leads to increased awareness of the "other" and may take a group to a new level of understanding. This process helps to open up communication between cultural groups, to raise issues to the surface in a playful way.

Issues are presented in a variety of creative ways using role plays with props of clothing and objects and drawings, songs, stories, poems, chants, or even rap. Skits produce a lot of laughter (sometimes from the humorous situations and sometimes tinges of embarrassment). The humor and costumes allow people to take on the roles of court jester and in some instances enable groups to move from the norming (smoothing) to the performing stage of group development (Tuckman and Jensen, 1977), that is, where discussions of differences and bridging and integration are more likely to occur.

Where role play is used, the facilitator later asks each group to state verbally the points they are trying to get across to check for accuracy. From these issues, the group generates a list of hints for improved communication between "culture A" and "culture B."

The process could lead to polarizing the two groups into "them" and "us" if time is not spent in debriefing to highlight how the information gained can be used to enable the participants to work better as a team. (For a more detailed example of this process used in Nepal between development workers, see Hogan, 1996.)

CONCLUSION

Facilitating multicultural groups can provide wonderful learning experiences and fun. We all make cultural faux pas at some time or another. But for the most part, in my experience, people are understanding of "foreigners" and make allowances provided that we approach them with respect and interest in their traditions and ways of seeing the world. Here are some final practical hints for facilitating multicultural groups:

- Be aware that all facilitation strategies contain a cultural imprint, whether implicit or explicit. Facilitation is not value free. In some cultures, participation of people from all levels is neither wanted nor valued, and as a result, a workshop may not be the most appropriate way of gathering ideas. A better choice may be shuttle diplomacy, that is, talking with individuals separately or in groups of people from similar levels.

- Note the danger that group facilitation techniques may submerge individual differences, and you are likely to need strategies to overcome this. Nonconformist or divergent views may throw up some really interesting aspects of an issue. Paradoxes or seemingly absurd or contradictory statements are often important and help participants to think about ideas from different angles (see brainwriting described above).

- The choice of processes and techniques needs to be compatible with the aims of the workshop and the cultures of the participants.

- It is important to involve the participants in evaluation of the processes used as well as feedback on the overall success factors of the workshop.

- Learn about your own culture and where it fits in the cultural dimensions.

- Discover the truth and wisdom in every culture, and concentrate on acknowledging and understanding specific behaviors rather than judging them (Brenson-Lazán 2003).

- Use your mind, body, and spirit to integrate what is happening.

- Avoid stereotyping and generalizations—for example, that an individual represents a culture, that all age groups have the same cultural values, and that city and rural dwellers have the same values.

- Be curious. Investigate differences in perceptions and understandings.

- Ask questions.

- Be aware that sometimes you do not know what questions need to be asked.

- Be aware that sometimes participants do not know what questions to ask. They may not know what they don't know.

- Be aware that some questions may cause offense, so you may need to preface them with, "I'm not sure if I should ask this question . . ." and wait for a response.

- Be sensitive to possible differences as well as similarities.

- Actively listen with empathy.

- Learn to be comfortable with silence as well as everyone talking at once.

- Establish comfortable contexts for interaction.

- Develop a high tolerance for ambiguity. Be flexible and open.

- Look for ways of building bridges with two-way and multiway interactions. Invite participants to identify bridges.

- Look for examples of music from different cultures, and play music that represents different cultures represented in your workshop. Invite participants to sing their songs, and teach them to others.

- Do not swear.

- Show genuine interest in learning about other cultures; read books on diversity and watch movies like *Bend It Like Beckham, Japanese Story, Farewell My Concubine, Madam Sowztka, Mississippi Masala, The Wedding Banquet, Wild Swans, Iron and Silk, The Scent of the Green Papaya, My Beautiful Launderette, Gung Ho, A Tale of O, Blue Eyes, Brown Eyes, Himalaya, Travellers and Magicians, Spring, Summer, Autumn, Winter and Spring,* and *The Other Final.*

- Step out of your own space in your own community and participate in multicultural events and celebrations.

- Develop friendships with people from other cultures.

- Travel overseas and try to learn other languages or at least key phrases. The people you meet will appreciate your efforts.

Improvisation in Facilitation

Izzy Gesell

Improvisational theater dates from the Italian Renaissance in the 1500s, when touring groups of actors performed theater pieces that consisted of a fixed story line, stock characters, and a mere framework of a script. Today, the conventional definition of improvisation, or Improv for short, is "acting without a script." The building blocks of this modern form of Improv are variously known as structures, games, or activities. The objective of any Improv activity is to give the person or persons participating a task to complete. These players then engage in solving the challenge while operating within given simple guidelines.

Improv games are wonderful resources for facilitators because they call for participants to respond to an experience as it happens. This moment of involvement and spontaneity sparks discovery, creative expression, shared laughter, and behavior change. Improv is exciting, scary, challenging, immensely enjoyable, and paradoxical.

The skills that make Improv participants successful have direct relevance to the skills that make all relationships successful. These include listening, agreement, acceptance of what one is given, partnering, helping others succeed, letting go of the need to know outcome in advance, letting go of the drive for personal recognition, trust, spontaneity, believing in oneself, dealing with fear, and knowing you do not have to do it all by yourself.

Disguised as simple learning activities, these positive, participative processes also function as microscopes, allowing participants to see beneath the surface of their individual and group behaviors. They are effective at identifying behavior because they call for participants to respond to an event as it occurs. This moment

281

of unplanned commitment reveals much about the players' beliefs and attitudes because they are responding in an honest way. Writing in the introduction to Keith Johnstone's *Impro* (1989), Irving Wardle says, "Open the book to any of the exercises and you will see how the unconscious delivers the goods" (p. ii). In other words, the way people respond in a game is similar to the way they respond in real-life situations with similar emotional content.

THE FOUR STEPS TO SUCCESSFUL IMPROV

To the audience, improvisers seem to create orderliness out of disorder, reason out of nonsense, and harmony out of discord. In truth, there is a method to the madness that Improv seems to be. Yes, something is created from nothing, but the process to make it happen has to be learned and practiced. In Improv, the framework that defines the structure actually serves to expand possibilities rather than constrict them by allowing the participants to focus on the process rather than the outcome. This process consists of four steps that build toward success in Improv:

Focus
- Stay present. Resist the urge to plan ahead, evaluate, or anticipate what other players will do.
- Remain within the structure's guidelines. The simplicity of the framework makes it easy to adhere to.

Accept
- Receive everything you are given by others without question or denial.
- You need not agree with everything offered, but you need to accept it. This is a foundational concept in making Improv successful.

Build
- Once you accept an idea, add to it. Support it, and help it move forward.
- Avoid trying to make the "right" or best contribution. Whatever you offer will have to be accepted by the others.

Release
- It is futile to try to control the outcome of an Improv structure. Contribute and let go.
- Practice improvising with high involvement and low attachment."

Exhibit 17.1 shows an example of an Improv structure.

Exhibit 17.1
Example of an Improv Structure: "One Word at a Time"

Description: Team tells a story with each player speaking in turn only one word at a time.

Number of players: Two to six (this example uses two players)

Time, including debriefs: Ten to fifteen minutes

Process: Demonstrate the game first before asking others to do it. Ask for one volunteer to come to the front of the room to help you demonstrate it. (Encourage the group to applaud the volunteer.) Then review the instructions for everyone.

- Introduce the game as one where you and the volunteer together will tell a story that has never been told before. (I coach the player by saying, "The key to success here is to keep from thinking ahead, trying to tell a specific story or attempting to be creative, funny, or helpful. Each of us has a role, and that is to speak one word at a time.")

- Inform the player that using the words *period* or *question mark* is allowed to indicate the end of a sentence. However, they are not substitutes for a turn.

- Suggest that the goal is to use sentences and correct grammar, but this is a game and the primary purpose is to have fun.

- Ask the rest of the group to call out the name of a story that has never been told before.

- Repeat the title you are going to use, and ask the volunteer if she would like to go first or second. (Most players will defer to you. I usually begin with "Once" which leads the other player to say, "upon.")

- Continue back and forth for a few minutes until a logical ending place is arrived at in the story. The volunteer is likely to occasionally use two words instead of one or pause to come up with a "perfect" or "creative" word. I let these go unless audience members offer the opportunity for a teachable moment.

- Of more concern is the player who does not understand the rules. Responding as if the activity is a word association game usually signals this. It is always possible to stop the game and review the rules. Getting a new title and moving forward from there is very simple in Improv. My goal is always to have the player up front leave after a successful experience.

- Once you have decided the story is at an end distinctly say, "the end." Thank the volunteer, elicit applause for her, and begin the debrief.

After demonstrating the structure, have the entire group pair up. If there is an odd number, allow a group of three.

- Have each duo self-select which of them will go first. Inform them that they will be playing the same game, "One Word at a Time." Each team will tell the same story and will have about two minutes to do so.
- Ask if there are any questions, and again ask for a suggestion of a story that has never been told before.
- Repeating the title for all to hear, have them begin.
- Mark the time for them after one minute, and at the ninety-second mark, I say, "Please begin to wrap up your story. You each have the power to come to the perfect conclusion."
- Announce the two-minute mark, and give those that need it, some extra time.

Adapted from Gesell (1997, pp. 62–64). Used with permission.

THE CORNERSTONE OF SUCCESSFUL IMPROVISATION

Just as a facilitator helps groups to engage in dialogue about a situation instead of the personalities within that situation, successful improvisers' dialogue is with the material, not with the other player or players in the game. Successful improvisers are not concerned whether what they are doing is right or wrong. They are taught to accept and use whatever is offered to them within a given Improv structure. This concept of unconditional acceptance, a universal model taught in all Improv theater classes and commonly referred to in Improv as "yes . . . and," is also useful for facilitators as they debrief an Improv activity.

Improv encourages understanding and acknowledging divergent points of view, The "yes" indicates acceptance, and the "and" is the buildup on the acceptance. In my experience, the simplest and perhaps the most practical way to incorporate Improv techniques into facilitation is by understanding and adopting the concept of "yes . . . and." For improvisers, "yes . . . and" serves the same purpose as the North Star does for sailors: that of a guiding light and a way to keep moving forward even when outcome of the journey is uncertain.

This fundamental Improv principle is based on the difference between the concepts of acceptance and agreement. It trains us to take what we are given and develop it. Brought into our everyday lives, "yes . . . and" allows us to deal with things as they are, not as we wish they were. We may not agree with what is said or done, but we need to accept it because that is reality. Because of "yes . . . and," improvisers never seem stuck or off-balance. They do not spend time judging what they have been given or evaluating their response. They simply accept what they are given and act on it. In other words, improvisers not only understand the distinction between acknowledgment and approval, but act on it in a way that keeps them focused on what is important.

Begin to develop this skill yourself by paying attention to all the times you or others use "yes . . . *but.*" Develop the habit of substituting "yes . . . and" whenever you can. By encouraging the substitution of "yes . . . and" for the more common, and almost reflexive, "yes . . . *but,*" it is easy to see how a difference of opinion transforms from a zero-sum game, where someone has to be right and another has to be wrong, into a dialogue where complementary, different, and even opposing opinions can coexist. We become better able to cocreate with others and also better able to stay in dialogue with someone we disagree with. This gives us a better shot at a mutually satisfactory outcome.

Here is an illustrative story:

A manager worked under a department head that took any difference of opinion as a criticism of his ability. The manager was tasked with interpreting data and making recommendations for an important project. The department head reviewed the manager's report and dismissed it as unacceptable, claiming that his own analysis of the data proved the manager's calculations were wrong.

The manager requested a meeting with the department head to see where the difference of opinion originated. "I know you found my work to be incorrect," began the manager, "*and* I'd like to know where my error was." "I had to do the whole thing over and you were way off," replied the boss. "We did come up with very different conclusions *and* I wonder if we could go over it together so I might see where we diverged." Not once did the manager defend his position or try to show the other to be wrong. Eventually, working together, the pair saw that each had been given different data, accounting for the different outcomes.

DEBRIEFING IMPROVISATIONAL GAMES

Improvisational theater games are wonderful resources for facilitators because they call for participants to respond to an experience as it happens. Viola Spolin, one of the creators of modern Improv, wrote that "we learn through experience and experiencing and no one teaches anyone anything" (Spolin, 1963, p. 3).

Learning from Self-Discovery

Using Improv in facilitation means that an examination of the process is more important than of the outcome; there is no correct or incorrect response, so all there is left to examine is the process. Each person tells his or her experience or opinion. All are valid because each is true in each person's understanding. As different truths and realities are offered, group members see how fluid truth can be and how their own preconceived ideas or firmly held beliefs might be obstacles to the achievement of their desired results. Improv brings behavior from the unconscious level up to where it can be seen.

The debriefing of an Improv activity holds ideas up for an airing and possible reassessment. Beliefs that no longer serve a purpose can then be removed and replaced by more useful ones. As former Visa International chairman Dee Hock has noted, "The problem is never how to get new, innovative thoughts into your mind, but how to get the old ones out" (Waldrop, 1996, p. 79).

Being told by others that one should change and how it should be done often leads to defiance, defensiveness, and denial. Guidance to self-discovery about the benefits of change as well as seeing different ways of being and behaving through the Improv debriefs are much more effective ways of modifying behavior.

For some suggestions on debriefing "One Word at a Time," see Exhibit 17.2.

Examples of debriefing questions that can be used with almost any Improv game can be seen in Exhibit 17.3.

A model for connecting insights gleaned from general debrief questions to an understanding of the relevance of those insights to participants' lives can be seen in Exhibit 17.4.

Exhibit 17.2
Debriefing Questions for "One Word at a Time"

- Ask the group if they think you and the volunteer were successful in reaching your goal.

- Follow up their reply with a query about what criteria they used. Sample comments are, "It was fun," "I was surprised at the way it went," and "[name of volunteer] did a great job." I usually ask for clarification of their answers: "What made it fun?" "What made it surprising?" and "Could you have done the same great job if you were there?"

- Another line of questions focuses on behavior. I may ask, "If you felt it was successful, what did we do to achieve that effect?" Common responses are, "It was teamwork," "You listened to each other," and "Cooperation."

For a large group, use the following questions:

- "How many of the teams felt they had a successful experience?"

- "What made it successful in your estimation?" Common replies are "We made something out of nothing," "It was fun," and "We had no idea where we were going, and suddenly it came together."

- "For those who didn't have a successful experience, what made it that way?" Typical responses are, "She didn't follow my story line," "I tried to influence his choice of words," and "We were telling two different stories."

- "What behavior made for a successful story?" Common replies are, "Focus," "Surrendering my desires to a common story," and "The feeling of shared creation."

- Open the floor to a general discussion.

- End with a summary of points made that are relevant to the group.

```
┌─────────────────────────────────────────────────────────────┐
│                                                             │
│                      Exhibit 17.3                           │
│        General Debriefing Questions for an Improv Game      │
│   ─────────────────────────────────────────────────────     │
│                                                             │
│   • Were we successful in achieving the objectives of the   │
│     game?                                                   │
│                                                             │
│   • What behaviors made it successful [or unsuccessful]?    │
│                                                             │
│   • What states—physical, mental, and emotional—did you go  │
│     through during the experience?                          │
│                                                             │
│   • How did your thinking or beliefs before and during the  │
│     game affect the result of the game?                     │
│                                                             │
│   • Would a different approach result in a different        │
│     outcome? How?                                           │
│                                                             │
│   • Where does the opportunity to change present itself?    │
│                                                             │
└─────────────────────────────────────────────────────────────┘
```

```
┌─────────────────────────────────────────────────────────────┐
│                                                             │
│                      Exhibit 17.4                           │
│            A Model for Debriefing Questions                  │
│   ─────────────────────────────────────────────────────     │
│                                                             │
│   • Was the objective achieved?                             │
│                                                             │
│   • Why or why not? What behaviors led to this outcome?     │
│                                                             │
│   • What would you do differently to get a different        │
│     outcome?                                                │
│                                                             │
│   • Is there relevance to your work and the rest of your    │
│     life?                                                   │
│                                                             │
└─────────────────────────────────────────────────────────────┘
```

Benefits to Observers as Well as Players

One advantage Improv games have over other kinds of linking activities is that the lessons of the game are as clear to the observers as they are to the players. Watching an Improv game is as interesting for the audience as it is for those playing the game. Many spectators play along as the game unfolds. They experience a level of intensity and involvement similar to the participants, so the feelings are as powerful for onlookers as for the participants. Observer and the observed are thus both transformed through the same experience. This means those who choose not to "play" can still be included in the debriefing and therefore in the session learnings. It also means the facilitator need not engage in a power struggle over who participates and who does not.

Exploring Behaviors Before and After a Game

In my experience, very few people are indifferent to an invitation to become part of an Improv structure. Ask for a volunteer to help demonstrate an Improv exercise, and a facilitator is often faced with a group that is nervously silent. Asking a question like, "What is keeping the rest of you from volunteering?" can start a fertile discussion. Even if someone does volunteer, the investigation may begin, "How did the rest of you feel when you saw that someone had finally volunteered?" Knowing that you can use whatever happens frees you from the need to have anyone volunteer. (Do not fear, though; someone always volunteers.)

Debriefing allows us to use personal stories as data gathering. As we listen to others, we start to see common themes and patterns. Following a game, the explorations might include, "On reflection, were the beliefs you held before the activity accurate?" or "There seems to be more energy in the group. If you experience that also, how do account for it?"

> The members of a rowing team had just finished a game in which players, working in groups of five, attempted to design a creative campaign under the following restrictions: it had to be completed in five minutes *and* there could be no discussion among the players about the choices that were made. Whatever was suggested first *had* to be immediately and enthusiastically accepted by the rest of the group.
>
> During the debriefing, I asked for opinions about the experience. One woman hated it: "I'm very introverted and need to process things for a long while before speaking up in a group," she explained, "and just like in my real life, I'm never quick enough to get my thoughts out before someone else gives theirs." Another woman raised her hand and said, "I'm very introverted also, and I *loved* this exercise! Unlike my real-life experience, when I did say something in this group, no one could object or revise my contributions. I loved the feeling!" The result was a keen awareness by all that similar experiences may have radically different interpretations by those involved.

Instructional Moments

Often during the games, players or observers reveal their thinking about important beliefs they hold. These revelations, sparked by something about the Improv game or the way it is being played, are invitations to facilitators to halt the action temporarily and bring the group into a dialogue. I refer to these pauses as instructional moments. These revelations usually present themselves in the form of a judgment, which may be masked by an overt or implied emotion. They are fruitful times for powerful learning and are one of the greatest gifts that Improv offers a facilitator because the involving nature of Improv means most of the observers have been playing along and are alert to the stoppage. Any questions, comments, or discussions at the instructional moment will thus be relevant to a large portion of the group.

A volunteer and I were at the front of the room playing "The Alphabet Game." In this game, each of the players is conversing with the other on a topic suggested by the audience. Whoever started the conversation had to begin with a word whose first letter was "A." The second player's reply had to kick off with a "B" word, and so on, back and forth. The goal was to continue the conversation in that way until we had reached the end of the alphabet. During the course of the game, my partner skipped the letter "D" and began her segment with an "E" word. Immediately, someone from the group called out, "You skipped a letter!"

I recognized the opportunity for an instructional moment, stopped the game, and asked the person who had called out to explain why he did so. "She made a mistake," he answered.

"Who else noticed a letter was skipped?" I asked.

Some raised their hands. Others did not. I invited those who noticed the skip and had not pointed it out to tell us why they chose to remain silent. "It wasn't a big deal," "The game was fun to watch," and "I didn't want to interrupt the flow" were three of the responses.

I then queried those who had not noticed the oversight to comment on how they reacted to the stoppage in play. "It was frustrating" and "He should have let it go" were the most common replies from that group. Learnings that came from this simple instructional moment included the notion that all actions have consequences, some of which may not be evident at the time, not everyone watching an event sees the same things, monitoring someone too closely may inhibit that person's creativity, and people have differing notions about how closely some rules need to be followed. Following the discussion, I asked the group for another topic, and the player and I started the game again. This time we were able to finish.

FACILITATING IN LIMINAL SPACE

The *Merriam-Webster's Collegiate Dictionary* defines *liminal* as an adjective meaning "of or relating to a sensory threshold, barely perceptible." It defines *hybrid* as "something heterogeneous in origin or composition" and *hybridity* as "causing things to blend together and become something new and not realized until some time has passed."

I believe Improv works as it does because it operates in players' psychological liminal space. This is where the different aspects of the Improv experience come together. I am referring to the conflicting thoughts, the paradoxical ideas, the surprising results, and the clash between the players' desire to think or act in one way while trying to think or act in a different way. These incongruous facets coincide and rub up against each other until they begin to evolve into a new behavior. This hybrid behavior displays a new energy, derived from a new way of seeing the world. Not only can participants see ways to change their behavior, they also are able to change how they feel and thereby change how others act and feel toward them. Hybridity is evolutionary change. It is the result of the transformational nature of Improv.

THE FACILITATOR AS ENERGY DIRECTOR

Among the many roles a facilitator must play is one that reads "energy director." Improv activities are vehicles that help to transform thought, action, belief, and feeling. They do this through the distribution and charging of energy. The redirection is from blocking, or imploding energy to flowing or expanding energy. One of the most common descriptions of what it feels like to be in a successful Improv game is, "I felt we were flowing." Conversely, difficult or frustrating Improv experiences are often described as "being stuck."

The participants in a program, when not engaged in an activity, regularly experience one of two states of energy flow: they are either being energized or being drained of their liveliness. Whether the participants remain alert and engaged depends on many things, not the least of which is how we understand and direct the flow of their energy, particularly that which runs between the participants and ourselves. To that end, Improv games are quick, hold the interest of player and observer, and are mentally stimulating to all, so the attention of the group does not have time to sag.

Consider that the energy level of the participants defines the emotional state of the group in the same way lighting sets the tone in a theater production, where changing lights indicate a shift in mood. In the theater, the illumination fills in the holes and occupies the spaces between characters, events, and sets. In facilitation, which consists of sets of human relationships (between us and the participants, among the participants themselves, connecting the participants with the people who are on their minds), the energy illuminates the dynamics of the group. Energy is what fills the space linking the people who are present in the room. The way we manage the energy in a room more or less has the effect of working like a thermostat, controlling the emotional climate among the attendees.

THREE PARADOXES OF IMPROV

To help groups grasp the underlying principles of Improv, I have found it useful to provide them with the following seemingly contradictory notions. Also, they are foundational concepts for developing confidence in using the games.

Practice Spontaneity

Spontaneity, like other cognitive skills, can be developed through practice. For example, fluency in a new language is achieved through practice. Practice is actively responding or doing something over and over. Since Improv encourages spontaneity, it can be practiced.

Experience Freedom Through Structure

The myth about Improv is that it has no structure and is anarchical in its unfolding. The truth is that each Improv game has a simple structure to it. It is this structure that allows for the tremendous amount of freedom in the playing of the game. For example, "One Word at a Time" is described as a game where the players must create a story that has never been told before. They must do this by speaking one word at a time, in turn. For instance, one hundred groups of three persons each can be playing at the same time, with each group starting with the same title. Every group will come out with a different story using this simple structure.

Feel in Control by Giving It Up

Most times, it is impossible to predict what a person will say or do next in a game. Trying to produce a particular response or control a destination is futile. The key to success in Improv is to let go of the need to know where you will end up and just go along following the structure. The most frustrated players in "One Word at a Time" are the ones who have an opinion on how well the story is progressing or the value of the partner's contributions. Once the need for control of process and outcome is relinquished, frustrations turn to relaxed feelings. Trusting the process and knowing it will be okay no matter how it turns out is a very powerful way of being.

CONCLUSION

Improv is the absolute and unconditional acceptance of what your partner is offering you. It teaches how to listen without prejudging, how to share control, and how to accept what others offer. Also, Improv is about making your partner look good and developing trust in others by showing that a dilemma represented by the Improv activity can be solved by joint collaboration and trust in self by embracing risk-taking.

Using Improv games is helpful in dealing with resistance to change and exploring the anger, resentment, withdrawal, and cynicism that infect organizations. It sparks people's belief in their own creativity, and it is a safe way to question one's beliefs about what others are going through. Improv clearly shows that the weapons you use against others are the ones you use against yourself.

When using Improv theater activities in facilitation, you are inviting participants to enter and embrace the unknown, live each moment without an agenda, exist in a state of absolute and unconditional acceptance of what is offered, relish process, and remain relaxed about outcome. It is applied mindfulness in action. All this is done while enjoying and valuing working with others. (Exhibit 17.5 has tips for facilitators.)

For facilitators, the benefits of games do not come without risk. Because no one can predict exactly how an Improv game will turn out, facilitators using these games step into the uncertainty with confidence in their ability to make use of whatever comes up. In other words, they have to experience exactly what is asked of their participants: trust, vulnerability, spontaneity, and willingness to being uncomfortable in public.

In a sense, the work becomes a practice, a way of being. The concepts and techniques that you offer participants are gifts to you also. You learn to be very present while facilitating with Improv, exuding a calm confidence that comes from your trust of the process. You become comfortably spontaneous as you learn how Improv instills the ability to handle surprise and enjoy the unexpected. Mostly, you

---
Exhibit 17.5
Tips for Facilitators

- Become as familiar with a game as possible before using it with a group. Try it out on friends, family, or peers. Each time you play the game, it is a bit different than other times.

- Just because a group has played a game already does not mean the same group cannot use it again.

- See as much Improv as you can, whether on television or live.

- Improv games can be stopped and resumed at almost any time. They also can be stopped and restarted with new endowments. An *endowment* is the information given to the players to help them with the game. Examples of endowments are the title of the story being told, the secret the character brings to the scene, or the relationship of the characters to each other.

- I use only volunteers in activities. You may decide to choose players other ways.

- I always use the first suggestion I hear when soliciting endowments. You may choose to do it differently.

---

learn to believe in yourself, and as e. e. cummings said, "Once we believe in ourselves we can risk curiosity, wonder, spontaneous delight or any experience that reveals the human spirit."

RESOURCES

AppliedImprov.net—the Web site for the Applied Improvisation Network, an organization for those using Improv as a facilitation, training, or learning tool

Humanpingpongball.com—home to the Improv encyclopedia

Learnimprov.com—has descriptions of hundreds of Improv games

Yesand.com—an extensive source of Improv information

Facilitation of the Future

How Virtual Meetings Are Changing the Work of the Facilitator

Lori Bradley
Michael Beyerlein

Many meetings today occur across boundaries of geography, company, and culture rather than face-to-face. The situation has changed, and that means that facilitation has changed. Or has it? That is the topic that this chapter discusses: how facilitation changes when the meeting is virtual.

Today's organizations exist in a complex climate of intense competition and fast-paced, quickly changing global markets. It has become imperative for organizations to adapt quickly in order to thrive. Business reorganizations, large-scale change projects, and mergers and acquisitions have become the norm rather than the exception as companies struggle to maintain the flexibility required to succeed. Given the events of September 11, 2001, the downturn in the economy, and the rapid advances in communication and information technology, many organizations have begun to outsource a number of organizational functions. Outsourcing has created networks of loosely connected organizational entities (LeMay, 2000). These networks, with their resulting porous boundaries, have become a popular response to the challenging business environment as a way for organizations to maximize intellectual capital, employee talent, and synergy and minimize

295

travel costs, relocation expenses, and disruption to employees' lives (Bal and Teo, 2001). Also, networks allow organizations to (LeMay, 2000):

- Share facilities and resources
- Share core competencies and expertise
- Share risk and infrastructure costs
- Respond more quickly to opportunities
- Share markets, customers, and market loyalties
- Create synergies that result in innovative solutions

Virtual networks assume many forms. They may be temporary networks of independent companies, suppliers, customers, even rivals (LeMay, 2000). They may range from a quickly deployed response team formed around a problem or issue and then just as quickly disbanded, to a stable and enduring team that works together regularly and over longer periods of time. Virtual networks are creating a new corporate model that is fluid, flexible, and adaptable—able to come together quickly to respond to business opportunities and morph itself into the best configuration possible (LeMay, 2000).

People involved in a virtual collaborative enterprise are often referred to as virtual teams (VTs). A virtual team is usually made up of members separated by geographical distance, sometimes sufficiently distant as to be in different time zones. Team members may also be from different organizational departments or even different organizations (Duarte and Snyder, 2001). Success depends on the ability of the group to communicate and collaborate effectively, and in a VT, that communication takes place using technology. Much of this collaboration takes place in virtual meetings, defined here as any meeting in which the participants are not all physically present in the same location, but may be connected through videoconferencing, teleconferencing, or Web conferencing (Internet) technology. Geographical and time zone differences often present significant barriers for effective communication and can be especially challenging when high levels of collaboration are sought. According to LeMay (2000), flatter organizational structures may enhance organizational efficiency, but having employees dispersed geographically and organizationally makes collaboration and management much more difficult.

The power of collaboration comes from inclusion—specifically, including all relevant stakeholders (Straus, 2002). Research has shown that teams that effectively use the knowledge and resources of a number of organizational units are more creative than teams working within a limited and defined functional area (Creighton and Adams, 1998). When the full range of existing interests and varied points of view is involved in solving problems or making decisions, the solution is likely to be more comprehensive and creative than if a small group of like-minded individuals acted on its own (Straus, 2002). Increased support for decisions and increased likelihood of implementation are fortunate by-products of effectively involving all appropriate stakeholders.

As organizational management focuses more on teams rather than individuals, ensuring that the organization has an effective system of collaboration becomes a survival factor. Historically, much of the collaborative process took place in face-to-face meetings where two or more people worked together on their shared project. Creighton and Adams (1998) found that meetings are the most frequent form of collaboration and that both meetings and collaboration are crucial to project success. Yet effective collaboration is made more complex when the virtual meetings substitute for face-to-face meetings.

According to Attaran and Attaran (2002), companies in the United States were turning to videoconferencing, teleconferencing, and Web conferencing to reduce travel costs even before the 2001 terrorist attacks; since then, the adoption rate of these virtual tools has dramatically increased. The Web conferencing market especially has seen aggressive growth, with vendors reporting interest levels up more than 50 percent since the attacks. For example, immediately after September 11, 2001, PlaceWare saw a 40 percent increase in business. It was subsequently acquired by Microsoft Corporation, and its Web conferencing software is the core of its new product, Office Live Meeting, which displaced NetMeeting. Recognizing the emerging importance of virtual collaboration, Microsoft created a business division, the Real-Time Collaboration Business Unit, dedicated to marketing and developing tools to support virtual collaboration.

While organizations are attracted to the concept of working virtually for the convenience and savings in time and travel costs, the challenges in maintaining expected levels of performance and supporting virtual collaboration are considerable. Some of the most commonly cited frustrations related to working virtually involve technology and the inability to hold efficient and productive virtual meetings (Anderson, Ashraf, Douther, and Jack, 2001; Fels and Weiss, 2000; Whittaker, 1995). With the recent and rapid advances in technology capable of connecting large numbers of globally dispersed people, meetings can take on various forms and a daunting new level of complexity. Here are a few examples from our experience:

- A group of eight regional managers for an airline conduct a weekly conference call to share updates and review performance statistics for each of the airline's regions.
- A staff of human resource executives located at corporate headquarters conducts a virtual interview with a job candidate by videoconference. The job candidate is at a videoconference facility at a branch office.
- A team of industry professionals that is creating a presentation for an upcoming conference e-mails drafts to each other for editing and holds weekly teleconference meetings. They will meet each other in person for the first time thirty minutes before their joint presentation.
- Forty-five credit card company application designers, dispersed among four different international sites, edit and review a document that outlines business system requirements for a new project. They use group editing software to view and make changes to a document that they view simultaneously. They use videoconferencing technology to communicate with each other as they work on the document.
- A project team made up of engineers from three aviation companies meets to discuss the design and manufacture of an airplane component. They are connected by a videoconference except for the employees of company A, who must teleconference into the meeting. They cannot share documents because of company B's firewall. Company C's employees cannot be present when certain details of the project are discussed due to competition on an unrelated project.

These examples should make it obvious that while no two situations are identical, what most VTs have in common is the complexity of their meetings, their topics, and their infrastructures. Traditional meeting skills may not be enough for successful virtual meetings.

Connell (2002) suggests that technology has evolved so rapidly that organizations are challenged to catch up with the human factors. The challenge becomes the ability to perform at the level the technology will allow without compromising the quality of the interaction and the work of the team members. The bulk of a VT's real-time interaction happens during virtual meetings; thus, it is critically important that these go well. It is in the best interest of any organization using VTs to design and conduct virtual meetings as effectively as possible.

The fastest route to improved virtual meetings may be with a skilled virtual meeting facilitator who has the requisite knowledge, skill, and experience. However, there is a dearth of research specifically investigating virtual meeting effectiveness. Organizational leaders, meeting participants, and facilitators currently depend on their general knowledge of organizational theory, group facilitation, and an understanding of group dynamics to support them in managing virtual employees and projects (Connell, 2002). Clearly, this is an area ripe for study.

BEST PRACTICES

It is generally accepted that face-to-face meetings benefit from skillful facilitation. The advantages that effective facilitation can provide are well known and well documented. Furthermore, there exists a set of commonly accepted best practices on which meeting facilitators agree. While many of these commonly accepted practices are applicable for the virtual facilitator (for example, setting agreed-on ground rules and seeking consensus), some new techniques are required for virtual meetings.

Although it is relatively early in the research process, it appears that facilitation does add value to virtual meetings. Because there is less social presence and more challenging technology in virtual meetings, we predict that studies will find facilitation to be as critical in virtual settings as in face-to-face ones, and possibly even more critical. Which existing facilitation practices can be adapted to the new venue, and what new facilitation techniques should be created to meet the new demands of these meeting environments? We are still early in the process of discovering a set of best practices, and it is unlikely that any one set will ever generalize to all possible virtual scenarios. However, we can draw on experience to make suggestions and practical recommendations to guide facilitators who are interested in expanding their facilitation practice to include virtual settings.

Before the Meeting

Scheduling   Scheduling can be one of the more daunting tasks for virtual groups. It is common to have to deal with two or more time zones, and finding a time that works for everyone can be a challenge. As is the advice for so many things, it is important to overcommunicate when collaborating virtually. Send scheduling information to everyone well ahead of the meeting; then send it again the day before and even the morning of the meeting. It may sound like overkill, but it is easier to forget a meeting that happens in cyberspace than it is to forget a face-to-face meeting with the memory pegs of the physical space or passing a fellow meeting attendee in the hallway, among other things.

Have a standard protocol for contacting group members who are absent at the appointed meeting time. It is important to have accurate contact information on everyone scheduled to attend the meeting. In face-to-face settings, one has the option of running down the hall to someone's office to remind the person of a meeting. This is not the case with virtual meetings.

The success of the meeting is heavily dependent on the quality of the preparation for it. A meeting checklist can be helpful to ensure that nothing is overlooked. Example checklists are shown in Exhibits 18.1 and 18.2 and are included on the CD accompanying this book. Also, see Exhibit 18.3 for an overview of premeeting facilitator actions.

Contracting   As in traditional facilitation, a contracting process with the meeting owner is very valuable. The facilitator and meeting owner should discuss, at a minimum, the agenda and the desired meeting outcomes. Answers to the following questions should help ensure that the facilitator and meeting owner are in alignment as to how the meeting should go (this list is not exhaustive):

- What technology is available?
- What are the equipment requirements?
- Who will attend?
- How will everyone be attending? All present? Some on teleconference or video-conference?
- Are there any hot spots that will need to be dealt with carefully? For example, are particular topics likely to spark heated dialogue? Or perhaps there is a history of animosity between particular members, and this knowledge will help the facilitator manage any conflict that might arise.

It is the job of the facilitator to ensure an appropriate task-technology match. This means that all available technology that could be useful for the tasks of a specific meeting is being used appropriately and, furthermore, that no inappropriate technology is being used. Just because a company has access to sophisticated Web conferencing tools does not mean the tools are appropriate in every situation. Perhaps a simple teleconference would suffice. The general rule of thumb is to keep the meeting as simple as possible. Remember that the more technology that is added, the greater is the opportunity for costly (in terms of both time and money) technology failures.

Exhibit 18.1
Virtual Meeting Setup Checklist

Project name:

Meeting date(s):   Time:

Lead facilitator: Cofacilitators:

Meeting rooms: Premeeting due date:

Phone number (conference line):

Tech support phone number/pager number:

TASK	ASSIGNED TO	DATE COMPLETED	COMMENTS
Scheduling			
Schedule meeting dates, times, resources.			
Send meeting confirmation to meeting owner.			
Determine which equipment will be used, and schedule delivery if necessary.			
Preparation			
Conduct premeeting with meeting owner.			
Provide information and results of premeeting with cofacilitators.			
Day Before			
Contact meeting owner to confirm that necessary people will be in attendance. (If not, does meeting need to be rescheduled?)			
Upload documents, if necessary.			
Confirm LAN connections are active and equipment is functioning in room you will be using.			

TASK	ASSIGNED TO	DATE COMPLETED	COMMENTS
Day of the Meeting			
Set up and/or coordinate setup of laptop, software, and screen and/or projector if needed (one hour prior to meeting).			
Activate bridge line or video connection fifteen minutes prior to meeting, if applicable.			
After the Meeting			
Send copy of meeting documents to meeting owner.			
Conduct debriefing with meeting owner and other facilitators. Discuss possible future commitments.			
Verify that checklist is completed.			

During the Meeting

Cofacilitation   One company that conducts frequent multisite videoconferences with large groups opted to train in-house facilitators from each site rather than continue to hire costly outside facilitation resources. Facilitators were brought together for an intensive two-week virtual facilitation training course. Their time together was vital in not only developing and honing facilitation skills and establishing a standard protocol, but in familiarizing the group members with each other so they could function as a team once they were back at their respective sites. Cofacilitation allows a facilitator to monitor his or her local room and also ensure that the participants at that site are getting adequate opportunity to take part in the meeting.

The facilitator in each site serves as an advocate for the participation of the individuals at that site. Cofacilitation, with one facilitator in each site, has proven especially valuable for this client. The savings in travel costs alone quickly offset

Exhibit 18.2
Premeeting with Meeting Owner

PREMEETING TASK	COMMENTS	DATE COMPLETED
Discuss objectives of the meeting.		
Review role of lead facilitator and cofacilitators.		
Review documents to be used during the meeting.		
Discuss how to handle last-minute changes to documents.		
Obtain name and contact information of person who will be providing meeting documentation.		
Determine delivery time of the documents.		
Discuss equipment needed.		
Obtain bridge line number, host code, and participant code.		
Determine dress code (if held off site or during nonbusiness hours).		
Confirm that audiovisual request includes split screen if desired.		
Confirm that additional equipment not provided by the facilitator has been ordered (for example, flipchart, tables, chairs, food).		
Schedule debriefing meeting.		

Exhibit 18.3
Facilitator Premeeting Actions

As Soon as Meeting Is Scheduled
- Determine the specific purpose and type of meeting (for example, sharing information, consensus building, problem solving).
- Schedule and meet with cofacilitators (if needed).
- Reserve room and equipment.
- Create and circulate agenda for feedback and input.
- Set deadline for receipt of documents (if using collaborative software to work on a document).

Two Days Prior to Meeting
- Distribute documents and agenda.
- Verify room and equipment reservations.
- Verify technical support availability.

Day Before the Meeting
- Load documents and set up and test equipment.
- Ensure that you have phone numbers on critical contacts (for example, project manager, cofacilitators, technical assistant).

Day of the Meeting
- Arrive at least an hour early for the meeting.
- Ensure optimal room and equipment configuration (for example, U-shaped tables and the number of video cameras and monitors).
- Establish contact with other sites.
- Discuss last-minute details with cofacilitators.

---

the investment in training and technology, and new product development cycle time at this company has been shortened by 400 percent. The intangible benefits of less time away from the home office and less disruption to employees' personal lives brought about as a result of excessive travel time is hard to assess in dollars but very valuable nonetheless.

While this company was willing to make the training investment that would ensure facilitation was a success, most cofacilitators do not have the luxury of joint training, but are thrown together at the last minute or simply informed that another site will have a facilitator in the room. If this situation arises, it is important to contact the other facilitator ahead of time to discuss how you will work together.

Other questions should be answered as well:

- How will differences be handled?
- What is the facilitation style of each facilitator?
- What roles will each facilitator play in the meeting?
- Will one be the lead facilitator and the other an assistant?
- Will the facilitators be coleaders?
- How will the facilitators signal to each other if one room would like the floor?
- Is it acceptable to intervene on behavior in the other's room?

Questions such as these should be discussed before the facilitators are in front of the group (Bradley, Wagner-Johnson, and Ballantine, 2002). It is usually worth the time investment to delay the meeting for a few minutes and get on the phone with each other to discuss the game plan quickly rather than having this discussion, with its possible points of disagreement, in front of the group. Having cofacilitators in virtual meetings can be a valuable addition for the group as long as they work well together.

Introductions   Once everyone is present or accounted for, the meeting should begin with introductions. In established groups, it is tempting, but unwise, to skip this step. If the group is familiar with everyone present, then the introductions become more identifications. Virtual meetings may have a few members attending by videoconference, a few members present in the room, and some connected by telephone. Members may be scattered across continents and communication technologies. It will help orient the meeting participants if they know who else is attending the meeting, where they are, and how they are connected. A visual display of this information, even on a flip chart, can remind the participants of the who and where.

Every meeting should begin with going around the meeting space and having everyone identified—for example, "I'm in Atlanta with Charles and Joe. We've got Rob, Scott, and Jennifer on the video link from Dallas, and we have several people on the telephone—Todd, Lana, and Robin. Have we accounted for everyone?" Another option is to have everyone introduce themselves. This can prove tricky in the virtual sphere without eye contact within a room. It is easier on videoconference when one can say, "England, please introduce yourselves." The group there will tend to naturally go around the table and introduce themselves in an organized order. On teleconference, this is difficult without people awkwardly stepping on each other, since they cannot use visuals to structure who speaks in turn. It is better in that situation for the facilitator to name everyone known to be joining by teleconference or bridge line and then ask if anyone has been missed. When someone joins the call late, the facilitator should take an appropriately timed moment to introduce that person. As should be apparent, the value of having a facilitator to structure the meeting begins from the first moment of the meeting.

Agenda Review and Meeting Process   Once introductions have been made, as in a face-to-face meeting, the facilitator should clearly go over the purpose of the meeting and the agenda and seek confirmation that everyone is in agreement on these facts. Then the facilitator should suggest a process for accomplishing the goals of the meeting within the constraints (or with the assistance, to frame it in a more positive light) of the technology that is being used. It is usually best for the facilitator to explain that he or she is recommending a certain process, because it has been found to be effective in this particular virtual setting in the past. The facilitator should make the suggestion if the group needs it but should always seek agreement from the group. The group may have existing process norms with which the members are comfortable. Above all, it is important for the group to own its process.

The beginning of the meeting is also the time to discuss the process for relinking if the connection is lost. Will the meeting stop until everyone is reconnected? Will it continue? Will the facilitator contact the other sites by telephone? The process for relinking will be different based on the structure of the meeting, but the important thing is to have a plan in place.

Setting Ground Rules   Next, the facilitator should discuss how members will gain the floor or otherwise be recognized in their various settings. On videoconference, it may be a wave or just speaking up. The facilitator should explain that his or her job is to make sure that everyone is able to participate. The group should be asked to signal the facilitator if they would like the floor or if they feel stepped on or cut off. In a face-to-face meeting, facilitators often use eye contact to signal to someone that they are aware that he or she wants the floor and to acknowledge that they will help get the meeting participant into the discussion. This can be difficult or impossible to do virtually. While trying to minimize any interruption of the flow of the meeting, it is sometimes necessary for the virtual facilitator to make a statement such as, "That's a good point, Tom. I think Joe on the bridge line was trying to say something earlier, and it also looks as if the group in Boise may have some input on this topic. So, Joe, let us hear from you. Then Boise, you follow up on Joe. Okay?" Often all that is needed is just a bit of structure to help the group stay organized and to enhance flow and the sense of inclusion.

Facilitating the Process   Once the meeting is underway, the virtual facilitator's job is much like it is in a face-to-face meeting, with these responsibilities:

- Providing structure to the VT meeting
- Encouraging participation
- Keeping the group on task
- Ensuring balanced participation
- Encouraging different points of view
- Encouraging effective decision making
- Dealing with conflict or an impasse
- Asking questions to help the group think through key issues
- Encouraging meeting participants to listen actively, creating an atmosphere of openness and trust
- Organizing and summarizing input from team members
- Moving the team though the stages of group decision making to consensus

In addition to these traditional facilitator tasks, the virtual facilitator must make sure all equipment is in place and in working order, monitor the meeting equipment, check in with individuals at other sites or on the telephone line (avoiding the out-of-sight, out-of-mind syndrome), make sure that people are comfortable and are not being shut out by technology anxiety, and ensure that meeting archives and other documents are captured for later dissemination.

Technology   It is important that facilitators are comfortable with the meeting technology and that they project this confidence. A facilitator who is confident and competent with the technology will help put at ease any meeting participants who are inhibited or intimidated by the technology. The facilitator should always take the time to explain or demonstrate how to operate the technology (preferably on a break) if someone expresses interest. The more demystified the technology is, the more the group's comfort level will be increased. People fear what they do not understand. The facilitator can help the group understand the technology to the extent that it does not slow the progress or interfere with the process of the meeting. It is also nice to have others in the room who can troubleshoot if equipment malfunctions or temporarily operate the equipment if the facilitator needs to give his or her attention to other needs of the group.

Technology represents a challenge not just to groups but also to facilitators. Most facilitators are "people people." This is often what drew them to facilitation in the first place. They tend to be comfortable with and enjoy working with people and not necessarily with machines. And they are not immune from the same apprehension about technology as the groups they are being asked to help. Nevertheless, it is important that virtual facilitators familiarize themselves with the technology to be used and become very comfortable with it. The group takes its cues from the facilitator, and it can distract or interfere with the functioning of the group if the facilitator seems anxious about technical glitches or projects a negative attitude toward the technology. Knowing who can help with technology breakdowns and how to contact those people can also save time when meetings that are difficult to schedule wait on hold until the link is reestablished.

It is best to accept that technological malfunctions or glitches are inevitable. The best defense is to have a plan for how to deal with them when they happen. If possible, ask for a tech support person to be on call. The facilitator should then keep that person's pager number close by and should not hesitate to call if needed. The main thing for a facilitator to remember when there is a technology problem is to keep calm. If efforts to correct the problem are not successful, then it is usually best to suggest that the group take a short break while the facilitator gets the equipment working again. This approach allows the facilitator to move out of the spotlight as he or she tries to fix the problem. Once the problem is corrected, the facilitator should call the group back together, apologize for the delay, and pick up where the group left off. Most people have been frustrated with technology at some point and are usually understanding of short delays due to technology failure.

Part of good virtual facilitation, like all other facilitation, is the ability to think on one's feet, and this often involves coming up with workarounds. The facilitator should always know what to do if the meeting loses the video feed, how to review the document if the group editing software fails, and what backup communication system to shift to until the main system is working again. Facilitators must expect the unexpected and be ready with suggestions when the unexpected happens. Ultimately, it should be the group's decision if something is a large enough problem to warrant rescheduling the meeting or if a workaround is acceptable.

One particular anxiety-provoking medium is videoconferencing, which is becoming increasingly popular as the technology becomes more affordable. Videoconferencing is beneficial in that it provides more social presence to the participants and gives more contextual cues about the other participants, but it also seems to provoke a lot of stress about the proper way to communicate. It can feel awkward at first, especially if there is not sufficient bandwidth. This can result in a lag time after comments, which sometimes causes people to speak "on top" of one another. However, most of the newer technology has full duplex sound capabilities, so this is becoming rare. With practice and experience, people will become more comfortable in this environment. Facilitators help by reminding participants to ensure that someone has finished speaking before beginning to speak, to keep unnecessary movements to a minimum, and to remember that the microphones can sometimes pick up and amplify undesired sounds (such as a pen tapping on the table or someone unwrapping a piece of candy). Some general guidelines for videoconferencing are included in Exhibit 18.4.

Ending the Meeting The virtual facilitator should make sure that required follow-up actions to the meeting are made explicit and that responsibilities for each task are clearly assigned (Bradley, Wagner-Johnson, and Ballantine, 2002). It is also helpful to solicit feedback from the group and any cofacilitators on how they felt the technology and facilitation process served them and what might be improved in the future.

After the Meeting

If working with one or more cofacilitators, the facilitator should debrief immediately following the meeting. The facilitators should discuss what did and did not go well and what changes should be made if they work together again. They should also decide who will be responsible for any follow-up documentation. The debriefing captures lessons learned, solidifies best practices, and establishes the groundwork for more successful subsequent meetings.

Exhibit 18.4
Videoconferencing Do's and Don'ts

Do

- Introduce yourself when you join a conference. Announce your name and location. Avoid embarrassing situations when people are not aware of your presence. Remember that the microphone and camera are always on.

- Let the other person finish speaking before you start talking. Make new users aware of the delay in video and audio switching. Be conscious of side noises (such as pencil tapping or coughing).

- Remember to maintain eye contact with the camera when you are speaking.

- Speak at a normal volume. Many early participants in videoconferences feel that they must speak loudly. Let the equipment do its job.

- Zoom the camera in as much as possible without cutting anyone out of the picture.

- Consider using the feature that will zoom the camera in on whoever is speaking. Caution: This feature can become annoying if the conversation is lively. You may want to reserve this for more presentation-type meetings.

- Control the size of your audience.

Don't

- Wear shirts or blouses that are checked, striped, have busy patterns, or are all white. Busy patterns can blur or "buzz" on camera. White shirts can appear too bright or can blend in with white walls, creating a "floating head" effect. A solid color, preferably blue, works best.

- Wear large, dangly jewelry. It can reflect light and cause a glare on camera or create noises on the speakers.

- Make repetitive, fast movements, such as tapping a pen on the table, drumming fingers, or other nervous habits. These can cause the camera to freeze or jump and cause sound distortions.

- Engage in sidebar conversations. They are distracting in any circumstances, but in a videoconference with multiple microphones, they can drown out the main conversation.

- Wear bright red lipstick. Bright colors of red can appear to bleed on camera.

Follow-up with the client or meeting owner ensures that he or she was satisfied with the meeting. Changes that might make future meetings go more smoothly should be discussed with the meeting owner as well. Any problems with the equipment should be reported. If the facilitator feels that there was not a good technology-task match, this is an opportunity to educate the client about the importance of this match.

Finally, keeping a facilitation journal in order to document experiences and growth as a facilitator can be a valuable practice. By making notes about what that should be changed or remembered and then reviewing those notes before the next virtual facilitation event, the facilitator can expedite his or her improvement.

CONCLUSION

Advances in technology are creating exciting new opportunities for facilitators. Virtual facilitators are in the enviable role of helping people learn new ways of collaborating. An understanding of group dynamics, conflict resolution, and meeting effectiveness makes facilitators uniquely qualified for this task. Virtual facilitation draws on many of the same skills and abilities and much of the same knowledge that traditional group facilitation does, with the additional necessity of some technological proficiency and an understanding of how being virtual changes a group's interaction.

It can be challenging for facilitators to keep up with all the available technology on the market today, but those who are willing to venture into virtual facilitation will be rewarded with the knowledge that they are part of building the foundation for a new way of working. Facilitators may find it very rewarding to expand their practices to include virtual facilitation. Furthermore, virtual facilitators can help advance the field by writing about their experiences, joining listservs, and making presentations at conferences in order to share critical success factors and elevate this emerging area of expertise.

PART FOUR Guide Group to Appropriate and Useful Outcomes

1. Guide the group with clear methods and processes.
   - Establishes clear context for the session
   - Actively listens, questions, and summarizes to elicit the sense of the group
   - Recognizes tangents and redirects to the task
   - Manages small and large group process
2. Facilitate group self-awareness about its task.
   - Varies the pace of activities according to group needs
   - Identifies information the group needs and draws out data and insight from the group
   - Helps the group synthesize patterns, trends, root causes, and frameworks for action
   - Assists the group in reflection on its experience
3. Guide the group to consensus and desired outcomes.
   - Uses a variety of approaches to achieve group consensus
   - Uses a variety of approaches to meet group objectives
   - Adapts processes to changing situations and group needs
   - Assesses and communicates group progress
   - Fosters task completion

The Team Start-Up

A Scripted Approach to Facilitating the Start of an Effective Work Team

Fred Niziol
Kathy Free

The Start-Up is a scripted process that assists facilitators serving a team in its early development. Our definition of *team* is "a small number of people with complementary skills who are committed to a common purpose, performance goals, and approach for which they hold themselves mutually accountable" (Katzenbach and Smith, 1993, p. 45). In the Start-Up, when we use the word *group,* we are referencing the team.

To give the Start-Up a theoretical context, if it is viewed from the classic linear theory of development—forming, norming, storming, and performing (Tuckman, 1965)—the Start-Up would occur during the forming stage. It is the point at which the team is becoming oriented to the task it will be performing and defining some of the basic roles and responsibilities of its members.

In the context of the cyclical or pendular models of group development (Smith, 2001), the Start-Up, or activities selected from it, would occur when needed to help the team resolve the developmental issues that these models suggest the groups will revisit. This revisiting occurs both at the beginning of the team's existence and during the team's life as a reaction to issues that arise in order to define or revise their task, problem, or direction.

315

The immediate objective of conducting a Start-Up is to define the project's purpose and scope. The Start-Up will establish a healthy foundation for the team's work. It attends to "team basics . . . size, purpose, goals, skills, approach and accountability. . . . A deficiency in any of these basics will derail the team, yet most potential teams inadvertently ignore one or more of them" (Katzenbach and Smith, 1993, p. 3).

At the completion of the Start-Up, the team will have created and agreed on:

- A clear and common understanding of the team's charter
- Meeting ground rules and operating procedures
- Defined roles for the team members
- An identification and understanding of the team's interests
- A vision of the desired outcome
- A mission statement and a draft work plan

Each team member will also be able to confidently answer the following questions:

- What is the project's purpose?
- What problem or gap is the team addressing?
- What impact will closing this gap have on customers?
- What other reasons exist for addressing this gap?
- How will the team know it is succeeding?
- What is the team's plan for this project?

We have already defined the term *team.* Here are some additional definitions that will be useful in reading about and using the Start-Up:

Chartering body—the organization or individual that is the core initiator of the project. The chartering body describes the performance challenge that must be met. Often it is an executive or executive committee.

Team sponsor—the person, normally a manager responsible to the chartering body, who is tasked with answering the performance challenge.

Team leaders—the persons, usually designated by the team sponsor, with the responsibility for organizing and directing the development of the solution to the performance challenge.

Facilitator—a neutral servant of the group whose purpose is to help the team become more effective. (See Chapter Two for a detailed discussion of the facilitator's role.)

Throughout the Start-Up, the team establishes how it will tackle and resolve issues, and practices doing so. Trust, common understanding, mutual accountability, and group ownership will begin to develop among team members; we call this group of feelings *teamness*. The Start-Up has been used effectively with information technology development work teams. It is also used with diverse work teams such as labor-management partnership teams. The Start-Up allows the team leaders to fully participate in the session, while the facilitator introduces the use of meeting skills and models appropriate meeting behaviors that should improve later meetings, whether or not they are facilitated.

From our experiences, we recommend that a block of time (three or four hours) be set aside for this activity when a team begins its initial meeting.

PLANNING THE START-UP MEETING

The team leaders, the team sponsor, if possible, and the facilitator should meet in advance to discuss the team, its makeup, and its tasks and how the Start-Up will be conducted. As part of the planning meeting, the facilitator should ask about potential problem areas or sensitive issues that the team is to tackle and discuss how best to approach them.

The facilitator should begin the planning meeting by asking the leader, "Tell me about your team," or "Tell me about your project." The answer to these inquiries will give the facilitator a sense of the scope of the team's task. It will help the facilitator gain a sense of what the leader may require in terms of additional coaching or support. This meeting also forms the basis of the relationship between the facilitator and the team leader. (See Chapter One for more information on these relationships.)

The facilitator should review this guide with the team leader and explain what is expected to occur during the Start-Up. Based on this discussion, the facilitator and team leader together develop and select the statements to use for the data-gathering exercise.

During this meeting with the team leader and team sponsor, the facilitator learns about the project, the team, its history, its members, potential problems, and how clearly they understand their charter.

The facilitator discusses the procedural agenda with the team leader concerning methods, tools, and responsibility for materials, setup, and leadership of the Start-Up. The topical agenda will be developed after these procedural items are addressed. He or she explains that the Start-Up will produce a number of flip chart pages that will need to be transcribed and ensures that the team leader understands that it is his responsibility to arrange for someone to transcribe the flip charts after the meeting. The facilitator and team leader should establish ground rules for how they will work together. For example, the facilitator and leader may agree to a ground rule that they will meet two days before each team meeting to assess group progress and review the expected outcomes or, when working with a new leader, the facilitator may enter into a ground rule covering leadership coaching sessions with the leader (see Chapter Two for a discussion of other facilitative roles such as trainer or coach).

The facilitator should identify which chartering body members should attend the Start-Up to launch the project. Ideally one or more should attend to say a few words to inspire and encourage the team. The chartering body members should also be prepared to answer questions from the group.

The facilitator explains the data gathering exercise to the leader and sponsor. The exercise is used to elicit information, ideas, and opinions that the team will use as the basis for the team process: a clear and common understanding of the charter, mission statement, ground rules, member roles, vision statement, interests, and draft work plan. Also, this exercise reinforces positive meeting behavior in that it causes all team members to participate mentally and physically. The facilitator should go over the questions in the data gathering exercise and decide with the leader and sponsor which will be most useful and appropriate.

Occasionally, a team leader will request team training for his or her group. When this occurs, we still use the Start-Up, but we refer to it as "team training," during which the team learns by working through their tasks.

Developing a Meeting Agenda

Working with the team leader, the facilitator creates an agenda for the Start-Up. Exhibit 19.1 presents a sample agenda that employed multiple facilitators.

Preparing the Meeting Room

The room for the Team Start-Up should be large enough to hold the team and several flip charts, and still allow enough open space for team members to move around. It is important that the room have adequate wall space to post flip chart

Exhibit 19.1
Sample Team Start-Up Agenda

Time	Content	Facilitator	Recorder	Process
12:30	Arrive training room 9 and set up	All		
1:00	Opening/housekeeping Introduce facilitator	Team leader		Presentation
1:10	Icebreaker/introductions of team members	Fred	Christina, Kathy	
1:30	Chartering body member	Leslie	Kathy	Presentation Q&A
1:50	Gathering data	Kathy	Christina	Round-robin elicitation
2:20	Explain consensus	Kathy		Presentation
2:30	TEN MINUTE BREAK			
2:40	Ground rules and operating procedures	Nikki	Kathy	Elicitation
2:55	Interests	Kathy	Fred	Elicitation
3:15	Draft vision	Kathy	Nikki	Elicitation
3:30	Draft mission	Nikki	Kathy	Elicitation
3:45	Draft work plan	Fred	Nikki	Elicitation
4:10	Process check	Kathy	Fred, Claire	
4:15	Adjourn			

pages because the team will be working from a number of them at a time. (See Chapter Five for more information about arranging meeting space.)

The following materials are needed:

- Flip chart easels (at least four) and at least one pad of flip chart paper for each
- Enough water-based markers in a variety of colors (water-based markers do not bleed through paper) to allow all team members to be writing on flip chart pages at the same time
- Masking tape or push pins for posting flip chart pages to the wall
- Name tags or tent cards (optional)

- Copies of the team's charter or other documentation that explains the team's task or provides background information

The facilitator hangs flip chart pages on the walls of the room for the data gathering exercise and writes one of the selected questions on each sheet. In order to preserve the spontaneity of the individual's answers, he or she does not write the purpose on these pages because that could lead some participants to give answers that they think are expected. The facilitator then folds and tapes the paper to cover the question until it is time to conduct the data gathering exercise. Additional blank sheets should be handy for questions that may require longer or many answers. In addition, one page that is hung should be titled "Parking Lot" (or whatever title is appropriate to the group, such as "Issues") for potential solutions, future action items, and other concerns.

If the agenda requires the group to break into small groups, breakout rooms or areas should also be prepared with flip charts, markers, and tape.

CONDUCTING THE TEAM START-UP MEETING

At the beginning of the Start-Up, all in attendance introduce themselves. The team members learn what is expected of them from the sponsor or team leader. Support personnel explain their relationship to the team, and general housekeeping is done.

Opening, Housekeeping, and Introduction of Facilitator

The Start-Up begins with a self-introduction and welcome from the team sponsor or the team leader, and preferably both. The team leader should provide a quick review of necessary logistic information—for example:

- Handouts everyone should have, such as a copy of the team's charter
- Name or tent cards to be completed and displayed
- Rosters or forms that group members need to complete
- Start time, stop time, and break times
- Location of the cafeteria and rest rooms
- Location of telephones for participants' use
- Transportation and hotel information, if appropriate

The team leader introduces the facilitator to the group. The facilitator should explain her role (as agreed in the initial meeting with the team sponsor and team leader) and the purpose of the Start-Up—for example, "At today's start-up session, we will get to know each other a little better, clarify our group's purpose, and make decisions about how we'll work together."

The facilitator explains that during team discussions, issues may arise that are important but inappropriate for the discussion at hand. These items will be posted on the Parking Lot and reviewed periodically for appropriate action. Other Parking Lot items include questions and concerns that need to be brought to the attention of people outside the team and ideas for potential solutions and recommendations that arise during team meetings.

When the Start-Up is being referred to as team training, the facilitator explains to the group that training will be "just-in-time" and team members will learn team skills by working together through their tasks.

Introducing Team Members

The facilitator should ask everyone present to introduce themselves briefly (a structured icebreaker can be useful here). The purpose of the introductions is not only to learn names but to bring out common interests that help promote teamness. For example, each team member can be asked to state his or her name, organization, and some personal comments—for example:

"Tell us about a hobby or special interest you pursue outside the workplace."

"If you could be doing anything in the world at this moment, having unlimited resources, what would it be?"

"Tell us something surprising about yourself, something people in this room might not guess about you."

The goal of these introductions is to introduce common ground and have members begin to know each other on a personal level before they reveal their own, or their organization's, positions.

Launching the Project

A member, or members, of the chartering body should attend the Start-Up to launch the project and inspire the team. This person should explain the history of how the team became chartered, show support, provide encouragement at the start of this work, and provide any documentation or other resources the team may need. He or she can answer any questions team members have, especially regarding the charter and, if possible, remain on call during the team's early meetings to help clarify issues or concerns that may arise. If a member of the chartering body is unavailable, the team leader should perform this function.

Gathering Data

The facilitator explains to the team that the purpose of this exercise is to bring out information, ideas, and opinions that the team will use to develop their processes: a clear and common understanding of the charter, mission statement, ground rules, member roles, vision statement, interests, and draft work plan. This exercise models and reinforces participation by all team members.

The facilitator then reveals the questions on the preposted flip chart pages and reads each of the questions aloud. He or she asks the team member and team leader to take a marker, go to the flip charts, silently complete each statement, then silently read all answers, and return to their seats when they are finished. If their idea has already been recorded by another team member, they simply place a check mark next to it. The statements and questions used for this exercise are a product of the initial planning for the Start-Up meeting. We have found the following statements to be the most useful (the items in parentheses after each statement indicate the purpose addressed by the question):

I believe our team has been tasked to . . . *(mission)*

I volunteered for this team because . . . *(interests and commitment)*

It's important to me that this team succeed because . . . *(interests)*

The concerns I have about this group and our tasks are . . . *(interests, issues to be addressed)*

We'll know this team has succeeded when we see or hear . . . *(vision and criteria for success)*

During meetings I hate it when . . . *(ground rules and operating procedures)*

I expect our team to complete our charter in _____ months. *(operating procedures, mission)*

I can spend _____ hours per week doing our team's work . . . *(mission— how much the team can take on)*

The skills, knowledge, and experience I bring to this team are . . . *(tasks, data collection)*

Tasks I prefer to perform as a team member include . . . *(tasks, data collection)*

The best thing about this project is . . . *(used to break open negative paradigms and set a positive tone at the outset)*

In today's meeting, I hope this team . . . *(agenda)*

Some people may be reluctant to leave their seats. The facilitator's preparation and encouragement for their participation will help. In order to get the team members up and writing during the Start-Up, the facilitator can arrange for the team leader and some others in attendance to enthusiastically get up and begin writing when the facilitator asks the team to do so.

During the exercise, there should be an occasional reminder to everyone to complete all statements and read all answers. It is important that everyone in the room remain silent, including the team sponsor and facilitator (except when reminding the group), because the goal in this exercise is to have the individual members list their ideas and concerns with as little distraction as possible. Be sure to allow enough time for all participants to complete their statements and read all the completed flip chart pages.

When all statements have been completed and all flip charts have been read, the facilitator asks and very briefly discusses, "What can we learn about this group from the data we see here? Are there common themes that appear throughout?" The themes are recorded on a flip chart.

During any of the discussions, the facilitator should be sure to ask the team for their opinions, but refrain from giving his or her own. If a common theme is identified that the group did not discover, the facilitator can ask a question such as, "I noticed XYZ mentioned in several places. How might this affect your team and its work?"

Again, the purpose of this brief discussion is to identify common interests and understandings. The discussion should be kept in a positive light, because it will set the tone for the team's time together.

The team should be aware of flip chart pages that show potential problems, such as conflicting ideas, because these will probably be areas for future discussion.

There should be a review of the responses to the statement, "Why I volunteered . . ." If it is answered, "I didn't," the facilitator can initiate a brief discussion of how this affects the team. There should also be a review of the answers to, "In today's meeting, I hope this team . . ." to affirm the expectations that will be met and identify items outside the scope of the day's activities.

Consensus

The purpose behind introducing consensus decision making (see Exhibit 19.2) at this time is threefold. First, some teams need to establish ground rules about what they will do in situations when consensus cannot be reached. Second, the team will use consensus decision making to discuss and accept the ground rules they are developing. Third, by using formal consensus decision making during the team Start-Up, the team gets practice in using the technique on smaller issues so that the use of the decision-making technique becomes automatic when dealing with difficult issues.

The facilitator now explains consensus decision making and entertains questions about it. Consensus is used to ensure that everyone has a part in the decision-making process and all issues are addressed before conclusions are drawn. It ensures that all team members can support the team's decisions and have ownership in them.

The facilitator then demonstrates the practice of formulating questions for consensus by having one person clearly state the question while the recorder writes it on a flip chart. He or she asks another team member (usually the one who appears to understand the least) what she believes the question means and then asks the team if that is correct. If it is not, the facilitator then gets clarification from the team, and again one person clearly states the question while the recorder posts it. When the team reaches consensus, the facilitator acknowledges this by writing "agreed by consensus" and the date next to the item on the flip chart. (See Chapter Twenty-Two for a more extensive treatment of consensus decision making.)

Ground Rules and Operating Procedures

The purpose of establishing ground rules and operating procedures is to establish roles, responsibilities, meeting schedules, and logistics for future meetings. There are a number of ways to accomplish this—for example:

- Using the flip chart page titled, "During meetings I *hate* it when . . .," explain that the team can establish ground rules to help prevent these events from occurring. Work down the list, asking the team to combine duplicate items and ask them to propose rules that might prevent each unwanted event. (Some rules may handle more than one event.)

- Ask the group, "In your experience, what kind of rules have worked for you?"

- Ask the team if they understand each rule, and have team members clarify any rules they do not understand.

Exhibit 19.2
Consensus Decision Making

Consensus is group decision making at its purest. It means arriving at a decision each member of the group can accept and support. The decision may not be everyone's first choice. It may not even be anyone's first choice, but it's a decision everyone can live with.

When a team uses consensus:

- All members of the group fully participate in the decision-making process.
- The group arrives at a decision that every member can accept and support.
- The decision may not be the outcome each person favored, but each person, based on logic and feasibility, decides he or she can accept and support it. When each member of the group has reached this point, the group has reached consensus, sometimes known as 100 percent buy-in.

Good consensus decision making takes conscious effort and practice. Understanding group process and effective communication skills helps enormously.

Steps for Reaching Consensus

1. Clearly define the issue.
2. Discuss the issue. Put all ideas on the table; focus on interests, not positions. Put forward all ideas without criticism, and discuss each of the ideas, considering pros and cons. Use decision-making techniques such as prioritization and multivoting to aid the process.
3. Test for consensus. Can each group member live with the decision?
4. Make the decision.

Reminders When Using Consensus

- Allow sufficient time for active discussion and participation by all team members.
- Maintain an open mind, and demonstrate skills in providing feedback, listening, and conflict resolution.
- Use a visual sign, such as "thumbs up" (or any other culturally acceptable action, for example, head nodding or raising a hand), to clearly demonstrate group members' preference on the issue.

The facilitator needs to be careful during this exercise. There may be a temptation to lead the team to what seems to be an apparent answer. Keep in mind that the goal is to ensure that the team members have understanding and ownership. They gain this by working through the issues themselves.

The facilitator encourages the team to determine when they meet, for how long, and how often. Then they define appropriate team roles, such as meeting leader, team leader, minute taker, timekeeper, recorder, and liaison to the chartering body. The team needs to develop and understand the responsibilities of each role, who will serve in that role, and the term of office. It is also very helpful to brainstorm on what should be included in the team's minutes. (For more information on brainstorming, see Chapter Seven.)

The facilitator checks for consensus on all rules and roles, and discusses the issue until consensus is reached. If there is no consensus on ground rules, one strategy is to check for consensus on each rule. This approach reveals areas of common understanding and isolates those that require more discussion. By beginning with small areas of agreement, many times the group will discover that their disagreements on other issues can be resolved. The ground rules exercise sets a tone of collaboration, and the team demonstrates to itself that it can reach agreement. The ground rules should be posted at all team meetings. (For another discussion of ground rules, see Chapter Two.)

Establishing the Team's Interests

The facilitator establishes what is important to team members by bringing out their interests and getting them away from positions. This process develops common understanding, commitment, and trust and helps focus the team's work. The output may be used as criteria for testing the team's solutions.

If defining the team's interests is done well, this exercise alleviates much of the anxiety people can bring to the group. They may be apprehensive that their concerns and fears will not be addressed. This is an important activity because it promotes listening and understanding of team members' deepest concerns. The team members learn that they will be heard, which allays any of their fears and helps to create an environment in which team members feel freer to focus on the issues.

This step of the Start-Up will bring out concerns about this team and its work. The facilitator can explain the difference between interests and positions by telling a story such as this one:

Two students were studying across the table from each other in a library. One went over to a window, opened it, and returned to his seat. After a few minutes, the other student got up, closed the window, and sat back down. Looking rather annoyed, the first student rose, reopened the window, and took his seat. The second student once again got up and closed the window.

After several minutes of watching this battle continue, the librarian walked over to the table and confronted the two.

"What is going on here?" she asked the first.

"I want to feel the fresh air," the student replied.

The second asserted, "But when the window is open, my papers blow around. I want the window closed."

The librarian went into the next room and opened a window. This allowed the first student to enjoy the fresh air, without causing the second student's papers to blow around.

What someone wants, having the window open or closed, is a *position*. *Why* someone wants it is an *interest*. Interests define the issue or problem. For every interest, there are several positions that could satisfy that interest. Behind positions lie shared as well as conflicting interests (Fisher, Ury, and Patton, 1992).

By addressing positions, the students in the library were in a win-lose situation (when I win, you lose). But by addressing interests, not positions, the librarian provides a win-win solution. The facilitator should explain to the group that it is important to understand everyone's interests so that they can work to develop solutions and recommendations that are win-win.

Later, the facilitator can refer to the story of the window when a team member makes hear a position statement. This simple story serves as a reminder to work from interests, not from positions.

Identifying Interests: The Process

Following is a more detailed description of a process that can be used to help group members identify their interests.

1. Review with the team the flip chart pages that reflect interests or positions, for example, "It's important to me that this team succeed because . . ." or "Concerns about the tasks and/or team . . ."

2. Brainstorm for additional ideas. It is often helpful to ask several different questions to stimulate thinking, such as, "What are your concerns about this project?" "Why is it essential that we solve this problem or make good recommendations?" "Why is this team's work important to you?" "What are your concerns about this team?"

3. Record the ideas on flip chart paper as they are presented.

4. Ask the team to clarify the brainstormed items, if appropriate.

5. Ask the team to combine similar or duplicate items. Do not waste time searching for a word or phrase that captures all the ideas. Just clump these together.

6. Encourage full discussion on each interest grouping so that each team member has the same understanding of the interest and what it means to the team. Based on the discussion and with the team's help, list the underlying interests. Since some of these interests may be similar, ask the group if they see common themes and, with the group's permission, combine them.

7. Have the team multivote (Bens, 1999) to decide which interests are most important to them. As a rule of thumb, divide the total number of items by three. This is the number of votes each person is given. Allow team members to cast more than one of their votes on an item if they feel strongly about that interest. Using different colored markers, chart the results using a visually meaningful representation that separates the group's significant issues from those of less importance (A good source of charts for this purpose is Brassard and Ritter, 1994.) By multivoting and charting the interests, all can clearly see what is most important to the team.

8. Discuss the interest diagram. Check for consensus by asking the group if they agree that these are the *team's* interests. After all the work and discussion, there should be consensus.

9. Post the interest diagram at all future meetings as a reminder and guide. When appropriate, refer to it during future team meetings.

Creating a Vision

"A vision, simply defined, is a picture that captures in vivid, concrete detail what things could be like. As it is currently used in the context of organizations, vision also implies contribution. It's a possible dream about realizing opportunities and living out values. . . . A vision, by appealing to people's longings and capturing their imaginations, taps a motivation for work that surpasses contractual obligations and makes the work its own reward. Doing what you are told often breeds mere compliance. Pursuing a vision engenders involvement and commitment" (Napolitano, 1992).

The facilitator reads the answers on the flip chart to the question, "We'll know this team has succeeded when we see or hear . . . " and then asks the group what this means to them. He or she then asks for more ideas, and adds them to the list as they are expressed. Here are some group energizing questions:

"We overhear someone talking about the great job you did on your project. Who is saying what about your project? Who else is talking about what we accomplished?"

"People seek out your group to congratulate us on your great success. What did you do to create this success?"

"A front-page story in your city's newspaper raves about your great accomplishment. What does the article say?"

"Fifty years from now, you fondly remember this group and project as the best time of your career. What do you remember that made this so memorable?"

Each answer is recorded on the flip chart.

Creating a vision should be energizing and invigorating. The group should stretch their imaginations, and the facilitator should be sure to smile and offer his or her own energy when leading this exercise.

When the list of items is exhausted, the group summarizes their vision for their task. This raw information can serve as a rough vision statement or a reminder of the discussion that you may use, if time allows, to assist the group in developing a formal vision statement.

Reviewing the Charter

In preparation for developing a mission statement, the team reviews their charter for clarity and understanding. Any of their unresolved questions or concerns are noted on flip chart paper. When the list is complete, a member from the chartering body should come in to address their questions and concerns.

Developing a Mission Statement

A mission statement is used to articulate the team's purpose to its members and to others. It also forces the team to set the boundaries of their project. The facilitator explains that the next step in the Start-Up is to discuss the following questions and answer them by developing a mission statement:

- What is our purpose?
- What is our scope? What will we take on? What won't we take on?
- How much time can we devote to this project per week?
- How often and when do we present our interim findings to the chartering body?
- Do we have all the skills and resources we need?

The facilitator discusses the flip charts relating to time commitments and how this relates to the team charter. The team discusses and agrees on when they expect to complete their project. Then they review the flip charts representing all of the work the team has accomplished so far.

As an example of a good mission statement, the facilitator can distribute the Star Trek mission statement in Exhibit 19.3, and ask each team member (or in a large group, small groups of team members) to develop a similar mission statement for the team. They should consider all of the work the team has done to date and also any time and resource constraints that exist, write their mission statements on sheets of flip chart paper, and post them on the wall. Then all team members should stroll around the room and review all the mission statements.

Based on the multiple mission statements, the facilitator leads the group in developing a combined team statement. If there is one mission statement that captures most of the team members' ideas, the facilitator can modify it with the team's suggestions. If there is not, he or she can ask the team to identify the key words and phrases in each mission statement, marking or circling those words and phrases as they do so. Then he or she can assist the team in organizing the key words and phrases to create a fresh mission statement. The facilitator uses consensus to ensure that the team agrees on the mission statement and then asks the team to post the mission statement at all team meetings.

Some teams will not be able to complete the mission statement at this session. If this appears to be the case, a small group of volunteers can develop a draft mission statement that the team can discuss at their next meeting.

Drafting a Work Plan

A work plan is developed to identify tasks that need to be carried out by the team and to assign responsibility and schedules for each of these tasks. The plan can be considered only a draft at this early stage of the team's development, but as the team progresses, the plan should be revised to include additional tasks and details.

Several methods can be used, but the following method is quick and easy, and works well with a large group. It uses the format of a cause-and-effect/fishbone diagram (Brassard and Ritter, 1994). The facilitator posts a large sheet of flip chart paper (six to ten feet long) on the wall (or several pieces of regular flip-chart paper placed together so they appear as one large sheet) and draws the "bones" of the fish (see Exhibit 19.4).

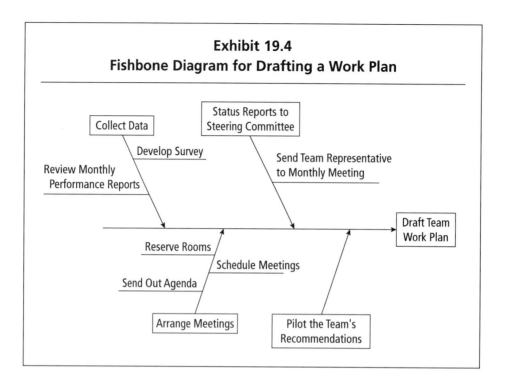

Exhibit 19.4
Fishbone Diagram for Drafting a Work Plan

The group brainstorms what categories of products or tasks would appear on the work plan. Examples include reports to the chartering body, data gathering, making arrangements for meetings, and piloting solutions or recommendations. The facilitator clarifies items and combines any duplicates. This is the process:

1. Place one category of product or task on each bone of the fishbone diagram.

2. Ask the team what tasks need to be accomplished for each category, filling in the fishbone as they offer ideas.

3. Ask the team to identify any missing tasks.

4. When the diagram is complete, request volunteers to further develop and format the work plan after the team meeting.

Planning for the Next Meeting

The facilitator assists the team in planning the agenda and logistics for the next team meeting. It is a good idea to establish this habit now so that it is repeated at every meeting.

Process Check

The team members brainstorm on what is going well or what they liked about the Start-Up, as well as what did not go well or needs improvement. Each item is recorded on the flip chart using a plus sign for what they liked and a minus sign for what did not go well. As an alternative, the team members could brainstorm the various parts of the process and use a grading of 1 through 5 of how well or poorly a process went with 1 meaning "needs reworking" and 5 meaning "outstanding; don't change it." The facilitator briefly reviews each list and asks the team what could be done to improve the items on the "what did not go well/needs improvement" list.

It is a good idea to conduct a process check at the end of each meeting. This allows the team to identify areas that need to be adjusted in their meeting process.

Closing

The facilitator congratulates the team for their hard work and wishes them well on their task. The flip chart pages are recorded for the team's reference and pages to be posted at future meetings are prepared for the next meeting.

CONCLUSION

At the beginning of this chapter, Katzenbach and Smith's team basics were noted as well as their caution that if these basics are not addressed, it would harm the team's efforts. The Start-Up addresses those basics. Once a team completes the Start-Up, all members know more about their colleagues in the effort. They have a shared understanding of what it is they are supposed to accomplish: knowledge of the various skills and abilities they have to accomplish the task along with a general idea of how the task will be approached. The team learns about itself and demonstrates to itself that they can work together.

From our viewpoint as facilitators, the Start-Up is a repeatable method for organizing and effectively helping a team form. It affords a consistency of approach to working with clients, whether as an internal facilitator or an outside consultant. The consistency fosters efficiency, which is always a concern in today's world.

Facilitating Large Group Meetings That Get Results Every Time

Sylvia James
Mary Eggers
Marsha Hughes-Rease
Roland Loup
Bev Seiford

Large group meetings can be powerful accelerators when an organization or community wants to build alignment, deploy strategy, get work done (budget planning, project management, or exchanges of practice, for example), accelerate the way work gets done in communities and organizations, or accelerate and deepen organizational transformation. At the same time, facilitating groups of one hundred or more participants can seem a daunting task.

This chapter presents ten principles for the design and facilitation of large group meetings based on our twenty years of experience designing and facilitating large group meetings in all sizes and types of organizations and communities around the world. By applying these ten principles, the large group facilitator will feel more confident that the meeting will achieve its intended results. In addition, participants will leave energized to act because their voices were heard, they acted wisely, and they saw the meeting as worthwhile for themselves and for the group as a whole.

335

THE PLANNING TEAM PROCESS

The meeting participants and sponsor are the best sources to ensure that the meeting has clear purpose and outcomes, the right participants, and the right conversations and activities to accomplish the meeting's purpose. Throughout the planning and facilitation of the large group meeting, we work with a planning team that is a microcosm of the whole group that will participate in the meeting (Dannemiller Tyson Associates, 2004). This microcosm represents the diverse levels, roles, locations, experiences, viewpoints, attitudes (especially the cynics and skeptics), and cultures that characterize the meeting participants. The size of a planning team can vary from six to twenty-five, as long as it is representative. This team works together to ensure that the large group meeting produces the results that the organization needs to achieve.

Our experience is that the process of working with a planning team ensures success by creating participation, meeting ownership, predictability that the meeting agenda will lead to the desired outcomes, and energy (not only for the planning team members, but for all participants) around the large group meeting and the actions that come out of it.

In working with planning teams, we have learned to consider the following:

- Facilitate a design meeting with the planning team, up to two days in duration, to clarify the purpose and outcomes of the large group meeting and create the agenda.

- During the planning meeting, include the quiet voices and the voices of the fringe. These fringe voices make valuable contributions because they espouse views that are controversial and help break paradigms and make the undiscussable discussable. When they believe the agenda for the meeting will really work, there is a high probability that it will.

- Build the microcosm as a team. Help them to create a shared picture by first listening to each other for understanding, honoring that each person's truth is true.

- After the design meeting, develop a detailed design including logistics, specific task assignments, and related handouts. Review the detailed design with the planning team, and revise as needed.

- Some organizations are so resource constrained that they will not give up people for two full days. Nonetheless, find creative ways to use whatever time you do have to combine the microcosm's thinking and inform the design.

- If you cannot sit down with a planning team that truly represents the organization in a microcosm, do the best you can. Repeatedly ask the group questions like, "If the people from X department were here, what would they be saying?" The group often does a good job of representing the perspectives of those not present.

The flow of the planning meeting moves like an accordion. The meeting starts with gathering as many data as possible to allow the team to create a common database that reflects the richness of all their perspectives. Then the meeting narrows to agree on a specific purpose for the session being planned, expands again to identify all the possible chunks of the agenda, and narrows again to specify next steps needed for a successful meeting.

The planning team process is a key ingredient and underlies each of the ten principles for design and facilitation of large group meetings.

TEN PRINCIPLES AND THEIR PRACTICE
Principle 1: Develop a Compelling Purpose Statement to Guide the Meeting Design

A fundamental design principle that contributes greatly to the success of large group meeting facilitation is having a compelling statement of purpose for the meeting. This statement not only reflects the interests of the diverse stakeholders who will be attending the meeting but conveys an optimistic prediction about the result of bringing these stakeholders together for conversations that "unleash widespread creativity and inspire new levels of motivation" (Gerard and Ellinor, 2001, p. 2). Without a clear and succinct purpose statement, we find that it is almost impossible to create an intentional design for the right conversations and activities.

Developing a compelling purpose statement is a generative process involving the exploration of a wide range of possibilities for addressing complex and sometimes controversial issues. First, the planning team members work together to surface different perspectives and interests of the groups they represent and offer their own desires for the future. With data coming from many sources to inform the team, the facilitator's challenge is to enable the planning team members to see the interconnectedness among diverse perspectives and create shared meaning. Based on the results of this discussion, the planning team is ready to agree on the meeting outcomes. As a microcosm of all the participants who will attend the large group meeting, these outcomes will reflect the interests of the whole group.

Once the planning team has agreed on the desired outcomes for the meeting, the next step is to agree on the purpose of the large group meeting by asking, "If these outcomes are met, what will be different at the end of this meeting?" Bunker and Alban (1997) suggest that many large group meetings fail because the purpose "is unclear, too broad, or too narrowly focused" (p. 218). Cady and Dannemiller (2004) advise that the purpose needs to be "broad enough to allow for flexibility and innovation while providing focus and direction for the identified objectives" (p. 560).

Developing a compelling purpose statement for a large group meeting can take a long time, and the struggle to agree on the purpose is vital to the success of the planning. Here are some tips for keeping the group moving toward the purpose statement:

- Let the design team brainstorm as a whole group any words or phrases or ideas that anyone thinks should belong in the purpose statement.

- Divide the team into subgroups, and have each group draft a purpose statement. If there is not one draft that the whole team accepts as a first draft, find and circle words and phrases common to all drafts. Ask them to use those to create a common draft.

- Explain consensus, and describe behavior that will help the group move to consensus—for example, "Instead of saying what you don't like about the purpose draft, suggest what you want to add, change, or delete and why."

- Be patient. People will drop out, come back in, get bored, and get frustrated. Stay positive, and keep encouraging.

- Be mindful to facilitate to consensus, not advocate for particular words or a purpose. The power of purpose comes from the planning team reaching consensus on the statement.

Principle 2: Think Converge/Diverge as a Design Framework Toward Consensus and Action

A large group meeting involves a series of conversations that allow people to come together and move apart to create and sustain change. Managing the flow of these conversations is a critical element of design. A critical design component is having the participants sit in groups at round tables, usually eight people at a table; each table group is a mix of diversity in the whole group (for example, location, function, and length of service with the organization).

The converge/diverge principle provides a model for planning a sequence of conversations that enables participants to identify and express their individual thoughts to their table group (diverge) and share their group's collective thoughts with everyone in the room so all are aware of the diverse views in the room (converge). Table groups develop options for next steps (diverge) and make decisions for systemwide action (converge). The goal of the diverge step is to get everyone's best thinking out on the table, generating as many ideas as possible. This usually creates a new reality for people as they begin to gain a broader perspective of issues facing the whole system or possibilities for ways to address issues. The goal of the converge step is to build a common whole system picture and then gain agreement on the best way to proceed to reach the desired outcomes.

Keep these points in mind when planning divergent and convergent conversations in large groups:

- Make sure everyone knows the purpose of every conversation and activity, whether it is at the table or across the whole room (large group). Diverge in table groups to broaden understanding, brainstorm ideas, and provide input.

- Converge in the whole room (large group) to build common understanding of the whole system view and make decisions on next steps.

- The most effective small group conversations to gain greater understanding of the issues facing the whole system take place within the table groups. By hearing the viewpoints of other participants, everyone builds a broader picture of the current state of the whole and the potential for the future.

- The timing of conversations is critical for ensuring active participation throughout the meeting. The flow is usually from the individual to the tables to the whole room (large group). Prior to table work, provide a brief period for self-reflection to ensure that the individual work receives attention.

- Find the balance between giving people enough information to get smart and having them exchange ideas about what they heard, know, think, and believe. Follow presentations with small group discussion of what they heard. Ask for their reactions and the questions they need answered to deepen their understanding of the presenter's message.

- After people have stretched their thinking to the maximum in small group work, it is time to "get whole," that is, provide opportunities for everyone to gain a whole system perspective. One option includes a roomwide call-out where, on a rotating basis, a spokesperson from each table voices the group's agreed-on question or response to the topic being discussed. Another option is a "walk-about" activity, where everyone walks around and reads the small group responses recorded on flip charts. A voting step (dots or check marks) may be added to gain a collective sense of the most critical issues or next steps.

Principle 3: Evoke the Right Conversations in Large Groups to Be Sure All Voices in the Room Are Heard and Considered

Conversation is an avenue that leads to constructing a common picture of where we are. Reality often lies somewhere between the way you see something and the way I see the same thing. We often ask participants in large group meetings to "listen to see the world through the eyes of the speaker." Our experience is that in listening this way, we begin to see realities other than our own.

The art of evoking the right conversations in a large group meeting has several components. The conversation must:

- *Be purpose driven.* For every meeting we facilitate, we have a purpose statement for the meeting: How will our world be different because we had this meeting? This purpose statement then drives every conversation during the meeting. We are constantly asking ourselves and our client, "How will *this* conversation lead us to achieving our meeting purpose?"

- *Be theory based.* A key theoretical model that we based on the work of Beckhard and Harris (1987) and use in designing conversation for large group meetings is DVF: *Dissatisfactions × Vision × First Steps > Resistance* (Dannemiller Tyson Associates, 2000). As we design the meeting, we ask ourselves how this conversation will help build a shared dissatisfaction, a shared vision of the future, and the right first steps to lead us forward. We know that resistance is normal and that a group with a shared picture of DVF can overcome the normal resistance that comes with change.

- *Build toward a common database.* The more that meeting participants all know what everyone else knows, the better the chance is that the large group will be able to move toward a collective vision of success. Each conversation needs to contribute to the large group's shared understanding of the world they work in.

- *Build the team.* Whether we have participants seated in functional or cross-functional teams, we always strive to build a better team. In designing conversations, this means ensuring that the conversation encourages the inclusion of everyone's voice. In the workings of the team, this means rotating roles such as facilitator, recorder, and reporter so that the team builds its capacity to run good meetings while sharing the load for keeping the conversation on track.

- *Be empowering.* When I feel smart about my contribution to a conversation, I feel empowered. Following this thought, we do not ask participants to provide their thoughts on a draft strategic plan without first having conversations to ensure that participants have a shared understanding of the environment in which they work, that is, giving them a firsthand opportunity to hear from and then ask questions of customers, senior leaders, or other key stakeholders to see the world they see.

- *Allow for appropriate risk.* We all know the difference between a healthy stretch in exercising and a stretch that is too much too fast. It is the same with conversations. When we first meet someone, we are less willing to be open—we feel more vulnerable—than we are once we get to know that person. At the beginning of a large group meeting, the conversations should be less risky than they might be at the end of the meeting when we are asking people to commit to specific actions or new behaviors.

Principle 4: Plan for Emergent Design Throughout the Meeting to Use Information Gathered as the Meeting Progresses

Even with a good agenda based on a planning team's purpose, outcomes, and design recommendations, large group meeting facilitators need to be prepared to change the design throughout the meeting. We call this *emergent design.* Unlike small group meetings, in a large group meeting there is no luxury of having a whole room conversation about "how this is going." Instead, we make sure we have a process for continually gathering data and redesigning the agenda as indicated by those data. This is a simple example of action research in motion.

We manage emergent design in a number of ways—for example:

- Never work alone. Large group meetings require two facilitators to manage the meeting in the moment while looking ahead at the design. Include the logistics coordinator in the redesign conversations.

- Stay flexible and attuned to what is happening in the moment. Continuously reexamine the upcoming agenda items for the meeting. Ask the planning team to huddle at the end of each day and at other times during the meeting to discuss questions such as, "What's happening at your table? What are we seeing in the whole room? Are we where we would expect to be, given our meeting purpose and outcomes? Is the energy the right energy? What are we learning from these observations? Given that, and our meeting's purpose, do we need to change our agenda [meeting process, facilitation, energy, or something else]?"

- Include leadership in this huddle. Leaders learn from the discussion in the planning team.

- Avoid getting hooked by the feedback of a single person (even if it is the leader). When approached by a meeting participant who sees something that is not working, we listen intently and recommend, "Let's pull together some of our planning team members [or talk to a few more people] and get their impression."

- End each meeting day with a written evaluation from each participant. Ask a few simple questions that reflect where you expect participants to be at that point in the agenda. End with asking for "advice for tomorrow." On the last day's evaluation, create questions that link back to the meeting purpose and solicit comments on follow-up. Members of the planning team, as well as leaders and meeting sponsors responsible for the outcome of the meetings, play an important role in reviewing participant feedback at the end of each day and help to formulate changes, if necessary, in the design for the following day.

- The next day, share what you and the planning team learned from the written evaluations and how the data have influenced the day's agenda. This sharing reinforces that the meeting results and process are everyone's responsibility.

- When we are redesigning, we practice a principle that Kathie Dannemiller, cofounder of Dannemiller Tyson Associates and Whole-Scale processes, instilled in us: "Don't do anything for the individual that hurts the whole, and don't do anything for the whole that hurts the individual." We do not hold back the whole room so one or two tables can finish their work. And we do not rush the rest of the room because one or two tables are finished.

- If we are behind the original schedule, we adjust the timing for upcoming activities. We do not eliminate or shorten a break or lunch.

- We stay optimistic about what is happening ("It ain't over 'til it's over"), and we simply will not let it fail.

Principle 5: Prepare the Logistics to Make the Meeting Details Appear Seamless to Participants

As the number of meeting participants increases, the logistical planning for the meeting becomes more critical to its success. We have found that having a detailed logistics plan and an organized, well-briefed logistics team to carry out the behind-the-scenes activities ensures a seamless meeting for the participants. Remember that the devil is in the details.

The work of the logistics team includes administrative planning prior to the meeting (such as making facility arrangements, specifying room setups, and assembling supplies and equipment) and getting everything set up and ready to go the day before the meeting. The role of the facilitators before the large group meeting is to oversee the preparation of the logistics plan and make sure that everyone on the team has a good understanding of their role before and during the meeting. During the actual meeting, the facilitators work through the logistics team leader to coordinate all communication, work, and assignments for the logistics team and facility staff.

Some other logistical tips for managing large group meetings include these:

- Make sure logistic team members understand that logistics work is often menial but nevertheless important, demanding, and fast-paced.
- Before the meeting begins, hold a staging session with the logistics team to ensure that all the logistics details are handled, in the actual meeting room if possible. The more complex the meeting is, the longer the staging session needs to be.
- Make sure a logistics coordinator who is internal to the client organization receives enough help to prevent him or her from becoming overwhelmed.
- Keep the logistics team leader informed before and during the large group meeting about any changes in the design of the meeting or in logistics needs.
- Provide real-time feedback to the logistics team leader about the performance of the team.
- Make sure the logistics team is acknowledged for their contribution to a successful meeting.
- Schedule a lessons-learned session with the logistics team after the large group meeting to learn what could have been done differently or better from their perspective.

Principle 6: Develop a Follow-Up Strategy to Maintain Momentum

After every meeting, action needs to occur to continue what was started in the meeting. For example, continuation after a strategic planning meeting may include the finalization of the plan or the beginning of executing the plan. Continuation after a business meeting could involve action by those attending to build commitment throughout the organization to the decisions made at the session.

Large group meetings can take on a life of their own. The preparation, the unusual nature of bringing many people together, and the excitement of the meeting can all contribute to making the meeting an isolated happening. The collective sigh of relief after the meeting can contribute to a letdown; people go back to work with the intention of following up, but the crush of the everyday routine gets in the way. Intended actions get put off, and the overall effectiveness of the meeting may slip away.

Here are some of the ways to help ensure that momentum continues after a large group meeting:

- Make certain that the purpose of the meeting describes a worthwhile difference that the meeting will make. A bland purpose or merely a set of activities in a meeting can result in no momentum to maintain.

- Start planning for continuation before the meeting begins, that is, in the planning process for the meeting itself. Although you cannot always predict the specific outcomes of a meeting, you often know enough about what will happen in the meeting to anticipate needed follow-up activities. For example, planning team members might anticipate the need for communication of results or establishment of work groups to execute decisions made. This helps to anticipate the resources that may need to be committed, as well as the structures that may need to be put into place to ensure follow-up. If nothing else, schedule a follow-up meeting with the planning team or leadership group (or both) shortly after the large group meeting. Schedule it well in advance.

- Create as much of the documentation of the meeting as possible during the meeting. The longer you wait, the colder the information is that was generated, and accurate recording may be lost. Having the results and decisions set down before you leave a meeting is a powerful message to everyone that there is a sense of urgency to move forward.

- Be clear about actions and accountabilities before people leave the meeting. If people do not know their responsibilities, they will not act.

- Quickly communicate the results of the meeting, especially the decisions made to those affected by those decisions, to begin to enlist their commitment to the decisions and their execution.

- Find and achieve quick successes that result from the meeting actions. Give credit to those who made them happen, and publicize the results to show that progress is being made.

Principle 7: Balance the Multiple Roles of Facilitation to Ensure That Nothing Falls Through the Cracks

This a huge job for facilitators of large group meetings since they wear many hats, often simultaneously. The key is in knowing which hats to wear and when to wear them. The seasoned facilitator has the ability to be in tune with the conscience of the group as it changes and to shift gears to achieve breakthrough. Kathie Dannemiller described this as taking in the DNA of a group and enabling what wants to happen next to actually happen. Facilitators must keep their antennas up and bring to bear everything they know about group dynamics, human interaction, and good design by watching the flow of the meeting as the design unfolds, taking a reading on the energy of the group, and knowing when to intervene. Above all, the facilitator is the guardian of the purpose statement; any on-the-spot changes to the design must be in the service of achieving the stated purpose of the meeting. Through a combination of art and science, the skilled facilitator knows which roles need to come to the foreground at any given moment and can seamlessly integrate all roles to dance to the beat of the group.

The facilitator begins wearing multiple hats before the meeting begins and continues wearing some of the hats after the meeting is over. Below are the roles that the facilitator plays during the actual meeting. The challenge is simultaneously to be the time cop, shepherd, and Picasso of the large group meeting:

- *Coach.* It is important to coach leaders on the role they should play during the meeting, including hints for presentations they will make and their participation throughout the meeting. All speakers need coaching to understand the purpose of their presentations and how the information they are imparting fits into the overall design.

- *Coordinator.* The facilitation team must remain in synch at all times. One of the facilitators needs to ensure that the entire team is involved in decisions regarding changes to the design. The logistics team leader must be involved in all changes to the design, such as changes in timing, sequence of activities, and the addition of or deletion of activities. It is critical that the activities of the logistics team be performed with precision and in a seamless manner.

- *Designer.* The facilitators must anticipate changes that need to happen to the design before they need to happen. Decisions need to take into account the purpose statement and participant needs. Planning team members need to be included in decisions regarding major shifts in the design.

- *Facilitator.* The facilitators need to ensure that participants make smooth transitions from one activity to another. For example, because we cannot repeat instructions to a large group, clear framing for each activity is necessary to launch the participants to successful work. Facilitation of small groups may also be required in the planning and the actual meeting.

Principle 8: Manage the Energy to Maintain Focus and Forward Movement Throughout the Meeting

We have all experienced enervating meetings that steal the energy of everyone present. When we leave those meetings, we are often tired and unmotivated to take further action. Sometimes we do not care about or cannot even remember what happened. When large groups meet, the cumulative energy is significant and can pull a group in one of two directions; the potential for both energy loss and energy gain is great. Our goal when facilitating these meetings is to have participants leave with a great deal of individual and collective energy to move forward and continue the work started in the meeting. In order to accomplish this goal, we strive to ensure that the meeting design addresses both individual and group energy needs, enabling the necessary work to get done and the desired outcomes to be achieved.

Our experience tells us that the key ingredient for managing energy is active participation by all participants throughout the meeting. When participants have a chance to respond to what they hear in the moment and share their individual ideas with people who are really listening, they begin to own more of the system's issues and build greater commitment to action.

Below are some thoughts to keep in mind for managing energy in a large group meeting:

- Ensure that during most of the meeting, participants are working on activities or engaged in discussions versus listening to lectures and watching PowerPoint presentations. Having discussions and accomplishing meaningful tasks together in small groups creates energy.

- Alternate between passive listening (presentations that make people smart) and active participation (opportunities to build energy by acting on what people have heard).

- Limit individual presentations to fifteen to twenty minutes and multiple sequential presentations to thirty minutes total.

- If possible, avoid slide presentations. Often slides are illegible, and put the participants into a passive state that saps energy.

- Provide opportunities for physical movement throughout the meeting. When people get out of their chairs and move around, for example, to visit booths or participate in different small group meetings, they become more alert. (Activities requiring movement help overcome the lethargy that often follows a big lunch.)

- Insert short stand-up huddles to help get the blood flowing after a long stretch of listening to speakers or intense discussions at the table.

- Schedule frequent breaks to help people renew their energy and take care of physical and work issues that may distract them from full participation.

- Put energy in your voice and your body when giving assignments. Frame each activity so that participants understand that it is doable and is the right thing to be doing at that moment.

Principle 9: Practice the Art of Precise Language to Evoke Energy and Action

Often the way we see and explore an issue is determined by the words we use to describe it. Words paint a picture for the listener based on how she or he perceives them. Practicing the art of language involves making conscious choices about the spoken and written words we use and the images and energy we want them to evoke. The language we use is critical in setting up each activity—what we refer to as framing the assignments. Besides giving directions, framing also includes creating the context and the energy for people to do the work that needs to be done.

When we give instructions to a small group of twenty, we can tell by facial expressions and actual questions whether participants understand what to do next. With a large group, it is much harder to recover if directions are not clear. Whether for twenty, two hundred, or two thousand participants, the words we use matter.

What is key for us as the facilitators of large groups in particular is the need to be authentic and aware of our choice of words, to know and understand the audience, and to understand the emotional tone of the group. If we are using language effectively, it serves many functions:

- *It is an invitation.* We always treat participants as adults who have choices, so our language is an invitation for them to participate—an invitation they can choose to accept or not.

- *It enables diverse perspectives.* Each individual has a unique view of the system, and his or her truth needs to be accepted rather than judged. Our goal is to allow each person's perspective to be heard, resulting in a rich and diverse common database.

- *It opens rather than closes possibilities.* The only way for organizations and communities to address the challenging issues they face today is to expand their thinking with new possibilities that come from all key stakeholders.

- *It empowers participants.* We often do an organization diagnosis in which we ask participants to share their experience and perceptions on a specific topic or process, such as communication. We intentionally choose language that triggers the appropriate ego state. For example, we might ask, "What makes you glad, sad, and mad about the communication that has taken place in the last year?" The choice of "glad, sad, mad" invites participants to step into their emotions about the topic; it gives voice to their emotions, and this creates an empowering experience.

- *It builds relationships.* One of the key advantages of a large group meeting is that it brings people from diverse parts of the system together to learn from each other. The language we use, spoken and written, sets the tone for building stronger relationships—for example, "Listen to see the world this person sees."

- *Make every word count.*

Principle 10: Facilitate from an Egoless Presence to Keep the Spotlight on the Meeting, Not the Facilitator

When designing and facilitating meetings of all sizes, we always bear in mind that each meeting must be about the participants, not us. In large group meetings in particular, it is essential to create processes that enable participants sitting at tables to engage in conversation with one another rather than direct their remarks to a facilitator leading roomwide conversations from the front of the room. This requires that the facilitator be in a healthy, adult state and willing to gain satisfaction from the work of the group rather than being a star, often characterized by behaviors that exhibit respect, responsibility, and partnership. (See also Chapter Thirty-Two.)

As facilitators, examining our own value system and beliefs about people and ourselves is essential. First and foremost, we must be in touch with our personal purpose and individual control issues, ensuring that we always serve the client's needs, not our own. We act out of our belief that the real wisdom in any organization is in the people, and we are driven to employ processes that uncover that wisdom. This belief is based on the characteristic of living systems to self-organize. When each part of the system sees the system as a commonly directed whole, they find the answers and know what to do in order to meet their purpose (Capra, 1996; see also Chapter Fourteen). To that end, we make a conscious effort to ensure that every interaction we have with the client system builds empowerment in its members. We seek to help connect the wisdom within the system rather than give the system our diagnosis and answers.

Standing in front of one hundred or more people can give one a great sense of importance and power. However, the kind of facilitation we are talking about involves facilitators' being subtle enablers in the room—that is, intentionally creating clear, brief framings for assignments that help meeting participants engage with one other and then stepping out of the way. When our joy and affirmation come from helping people achieve their desired results, then we hope to hear participants say as they walk out the door, "That was exactly the meeting we needed to have right now. We need to do this more often," instead of, "You are a very good facilitator to handle a crowd like this!"

Here are some additional considerations to keep in mind in developing an egoless presence:

- Never work alone. Ask and trust a partner to hold up a mirror for you regarding your facilitation.

- Be curious. When you listen to clients, listen to see the world they see. If you are arguing with clients or complaining to others about them, it might be a clue that you believe you have the answer. In order to be of service to clients, we need to love and respect them, especially when we do not agree with them.

- Create self-sufficiency. Build participants' competencies in listening, speaking, recording, and facilitating throughout the meeting.

- Consult with your planning team when things are not going as expected.

- Base meeting evaluations on whether desired outcomes were achieved rather than how well participants liked the meeting or the facilitator.

- Admit when you are wrong, and learn from your mistakes.

CONCLUSION

Facilitating a meeting that gets results every time can become more predictable (and energizing for everyone) when you truly believe that the wisdom is in the people and that when connected around the right purpose and activities, they will find the answers.

As you integrate these principles into your own knowledge, experience, and style, stay alert to the fact that each client is unique, and adjust each engagement to meet that client's specific requirements. Listen to the advice of the planning team members. Together with the meeting sponsor and planning team, agree that the meeting design has a clear purpose, a shared set of the right information that makes the system whole and wise so participants make and execute informed decisions, and structured processes to support the conversations and activities that must take place in order to accomplish the desired meeting outcomes.

Facilitating Communication in Group Decision-Making Discussions

Dennis S. Gouran
Randy Y. Hirokawa

Facilitation, broadly construed, is any activity that makes the accomplishment of tasks easier than would be the case in its absence, as even a casual examination of the essays in Lawrence Frey's book dealing with group facilitation (1995) in natural settings makes abundantly clear. However, for the specific context to which this chapter relates, we find the precise and appropriate sort of focus necessary for the ideas we develop in Schwarz's characterization (2002) of facilitation as helping "a group improve its process for solving problems and making decisions so that the group can achieve goals and increase overall effectiveness" (p. 57).

Although Schwarz appears to be more concerned with external parties who engage in facilitation, he does not preclude their performance by group members themselves, the agents to whom most of our attention has been directed in the years we have been writing about the role of communication in group decision-making discussions. Our treatment of the subject of facilitation, then, relates primarily to what members can do to overcome problems they may have a hand in creating and for which no sort of external agent may be available to provide assistance when the problems arise.

Finally, we think that it is important to acknowledge that our concerns lie largely in the realm of intentional behavior. We recognize that group members may engage in communicative acts that have facilitative influence without any conscious design on their part. However, in this chapter, we deal with problematic situations requiring awareness and activities having the deliberate aim behind them of altering those situations in positive ways, not incidental forms of behavior that may have such consequences.

Since 1983, we have been developing a perspective on group process, as related to decision making and problem solving, now commonly referred to as the functional theory of communication in decision-making groups (Gouran and Hirokawa, 1983, 1996, 2003). The central proposition of the theory is as follows. The likelihood that a decision-making or problem-solving group will make appropriate choices among the options it considers relates directly to the extent to which members' communicative behavior ensures that they satisfy the requirements of their task. The theory also acknowledges that in the course of executing such tasks, and depending on the sorts of constraints that exist, group members frequently, if not always, encounter an array of obstacles that may be of a substantive (or task-related), relational, or procedural nature. (See Chapter Nine for more about these terms.) It is within such arenas that we see the need for skill in facilitation.

In this chapter, we briefly review the basic features of the functional theory of communication in decision-making groups, identify some of the problems that arise and that reveal a need for facilitation, and then provide an overview of some ways of furthering group members' ability to manage such problems. The result will not be so much a repertoire of facilitation strategies and tactics on which he facilitators can mechanically draw, but rather an expanded awareness of the types of situations in which they can play a facilitative role, an improved understanding of how that role can aid in enhancing the performance of decision-making groups, and a knowledge of some general ways of addressing situations in which facilitation may be necessary if a group is to perform well in discharging its task.

THE FUNCTIONAL THEORY OF COMMUNICATION IN DECISION MAKING

The basic propositions of the functional theory of communication in decision making rest on certain assumptions, including five of particular importance: (1) the members of a group seek to make good choices; (2) the collective resources of the group, with respect to the task at hand, exceed those of any single member; (3) the best choice is not obvious in the absence of relevant information and thoughtful processing of it; (4) the requirements of the task are specifiable; and (5) the members have the intellectual skills necessary to satisfy these requirements (Gouran and Hirokawa, 1996). Task requirements include (1) "showing correct understanding of the issue to be resolved"; (2) "determining the minimal characteristics any alternative, to be acceptable, must possess"; (3) "identifying a relevant and realistic set of alternatives"; (4) "examining carefully the alternatives in relationship to each previously agreed-upon characteristic of an acceptable choice"; and (5) "selecting the alternative that analysis reveals to be most likely to have the desired characteristics" (pp. 76–77).

This model is in line with others in the classical economics and reflective thinking traditions, for example, the one Bazerman (2002) presents. In Bazerman's characterization, the task consists of defining the problem, identifying and weighting criteria, generating alternatives, assessing each alternative in the light of each criterion, and "computing" the optimal decision—by which he means determining the one with the highest "expected value" (see Beach, 1997, for a similar description). This description is consistent with the vigilance model that Janis and Mann (1977) introduced more than twenty-five years ago. Vigilance, according to these scholars, entails surveying the objectives to be fulfilled, canvassing alternative actions, searching intensively for information to be used in evaluating alternatives, reconsidering possible consequences of alternatives initially rejected, considering the comparative risks and benefits of initially preferred alternatives, choosing, making provisions for implementation, and monitoring the chosen course of action.

When the members of groups satisfy the requirements mentioned, whether in the form we have stated or an equivalent one, such as that of Bazerman (2002) or Janis and Mann (1977), the likelihood that their choices will be appropriate, if not optimal, is considerably greater than if they fail to satisfy them. From the perspective of functional theory, communication is instrumental in ensuring that such requirements are met.

Unfortunately, participants also encounter obstacles that interfere with their communication serving this function. The obstacles are often a product of three kinds of constraints, to which Janis (1989) applied the labels *cognitive*, *affiliative*, and *egocentric* and on which we focus in this chapter. We discuss each of these, identify some of the inhibiting influences to which they frequently give rise in various domains of group interaction, and suggest the sorts of facilitative interventions that can one can apply.

OBSTACLES TO APPROPRIATE CHOICE MAKING AND FACILITATIVE RESPONSES

Cognitive Constraints

Cognitive constraints, according to Janis (1989), consist of "all the salient external factors that restrict cognitive inputs . . . as well as internal factors that restrict the amount and quality of cognitive activity" (p. 17) in which decision makers engage. These include limited time, lack of expertise, multiple tasks, and ideological commitments. When the members of a group have fallen victim to a cognitive constraint, they are likely to experience feelings of psychological discomfort resulting from their perceptions concerning the amount of time available for completing their task, a lack of suitable information (or a way to integrate massive amounts of it), their ability to perform the task successfully, and conflicts with particular values to which they subscribe and that predispose them to some choices over others. Under these sorts of conditions, communication can serve to reinforce and intensify such perceptions and lead to one or more of the members' taking the sort of mental shortcuts to choice that Nisbett and Ross (1980) refer to as heuristics.

According to Janis (1989), cognitive heuristics manifest themselves in a variety of forms, for example, concluding that the first alternative that appears on its face to be appropriate is the one to endorse, resorting to a standard operating procedure in the face of uncertainty, or analogizing and subsequently selecting the alternative that appears most strongly to resemble one that has worked under other circumstances. Decision-making and problem-solving groups, under the grip of severe cognitive constraints, may also display a pattern of avoidance and fail to choose while seeming at a superficial level to be concerned about the impact of their actions and thorough in their deliberations (Janis and Mann, 1977).

The consequences of allowing cognitive constraints to dominate the efforts of decision-making and problem-solving groups to make appropriate, informed choices can pose both substantive and procedural obstacles for members to overcome. Of course, a reliance on heuristics does not inevitably lead the members of a group to make poor choices. However, it can increase the likelihood of their doing so. At the very least, resorting to such mental shortcuts and rules reduces a group's chances for making the best choice. In the case of avoidance, moreover, it is clear that leaving the issue under consideration unresolved can be undesirable, as when a deadline is near but a decision does not appear to be forthcoming and the group therefore endorses the status quo by default or agrees to the least objectionable, but far from best, alternative. As a result, when a member of a group senses that a cognitive constraint has come into play in a potentially injurious way, he or she should attempt to intervene.

We do not wish to imply that making decisions quickly or avoiding doing so are inevitably in opposition to the interests of good decision making. Our concern is with the effects of the heuristics and rules to which decision makers resort that provide no assurance of sound judgment or reasoned choice.

When a cognitive constraint is operative and is adversely affecting a group's ability to satisfy the requirements of its task, useful facilitation may consist initially of simply pointing that out, for example, "I think that we may be rushing toward a decision when I am not convinced we are ready to choose or that we need to at this point." Having focused attention on the fact that one or more cognitive constraints are operative and exerting possibly unhealthy influences on how the group is performing, one could then easily shift into a different mode, for instance, proposing that the group halt its work until the members are able to acquire more information, suggesting that the group ask for an extension in the time allowed to complete its task, or offering reassurances that the members have the ability to perform competently if they go about the task in a thorough and vigilant manner (such as using a more powerful analytical framework to manage and integrate the available information). In the case of a group whose members are displaying avoidance behavior, a participant functioning in the role of facilitator could share his or her perception that this, rather than the nature and requirements of the task, may be the reason for their apparent inability to achieve closure and then proceed to identify what would constitute a reasonable or realistic effort to satisfy the requirements, putting the task into perspective.

Clues for how one might address situations stemming from the presence of cognitive constraints derive from work in the area of leadership. For instance, the life cycle theory of leadership (Blanchard, 1985; Hersey and Blanchard, 1993) suggests that when individuals who are in fact competent to perform a task do not see themselves as competent, a supportive style of leadership has value in motivating them to perform in a more productive manner. Borrowing from this insight, by implication, a facilitator who adopts a supportive posture and style of interaction in a group whose members, under a particular set of circumstances, doubt their competence or ability to choose appropriately presumably could be of considerable assistance in convincing them to the contrary, and thereby freeing them from any felt need or reflexive tendency to resort to any of the various cognitive heuristics in Janis's inventory (1989).

Affiliative Constraints

If the constraint taking hold in the discussion of a decision-making or problem-solving group qualifies as affiliative, the members are likely to be experiencing some sort of difficulty that reflects a conflict between what may be necessary to make an appropriate choice and relationships among the members. In such situations, it often, if not usually, is the case that a desire to maintain positive relationships or have a strong identification with a group has a distorting influence on how one or more members see their task and go about performing it. The preoccupation with relational needs can predispose those experiencing it to the well-known phenomenon that Irving Janis (1972, 1982) introduced under the heading of groupthink, a syndrome that can in some manifestations be a source of substantive, relational, and procedural obstacles to making optimal choices, or even reasonably good ones, in situations in which such choices may be of considerable importance. (See Chapter Seven for more information concerning groupthink.)

As in the case of cognitive constraints, when an affiliative constraint is exerting a powerful influence on the members of a group, they are likely to resort to heuristics rather than persist in a vigilant approach to the performance of their task. Among the rules that are operative, according to Janis (1989), are ones he characterizes as "avoid punishment" (a form of going along to get along), "preserve group harmony," and, in the case of possible power struggles, "follow the party line," "exercise one-upmanship," and "rig meetings to suppress the opposition." The last two aim to prevent unwanted sources of contention relating to initially preferred alternatives from even surfacing.

Janis (1982) has described various approaches to counteracting harmony-preserving heuristics in the face of affiliative constraints. These include such activities as suggesting that the group establish the role of critical evaluator and rotate it among members, that those who have strong preferences absent themselves from portions of discussions, and that members discuss the options under consideration with knowledgeable individuals who are not members of the group. Along similar lines, in playing a facilitative role, one might recommend that a group consider adopting formal procedures, such as devil's advocacy and dialectical inquiry (see Meyers, 1997; Schweiger, Sandburg, and Rechner, 1989), that force the members of groups to think about issues and positions on them in ways that run counter to their initial inclinations and choice-making proclivities.

Other approaches include "establishing resistance to authority [including majorities] in ways that are nonthreatening," "trying to restore a focus on substantive concerns" when efforts to promote harmony seem to be dominating, and "looking for overarching goals" that accommodate the interests of parties who might be in dispute (see Gouran, 2003b, pp. 177–178). However, first and foremost is the need to realize, and acknowledge in a public way, that relationships, rather than issues and pertinent information, are driving the interaction. Otherwise the possibilities of overcoming these problems may be limited.

A significant challenge is to find ways to acknowledge and respect members' needs for affiliation without permitting them to sacrifice the interests of informed choice. In this vein, various aspects of the path-goal theory of leadership (House, 1971, 1996; House and Dessler, 1974) are instructive. Of particular importance is the style of interaction that best suits one's affiliative needs while also allowing sufficient attention to task requirements.

Just as a supportive style can be helpful to group members lacking confidence in their ability, so too can such a style enhance the performance of the members of groups who have pronounced needs for affiliation. However, such support should aim at reinforcing members' behavior that satisfies task requirements rather than behavior that promotes positive relations. Another style that House and Dessler identify as participative can be of value as well. In short, one can contribute to the satisfaction of other group members' affiliative needs by inviting their active involvement in a discussion, not pandering to their desires to be liked and accepted by others.

Egocentric Constraints

Egocentric constraints are present when personal needs of a controlling nature surface and influence choice making. According to Irving Janis (1989), these needs typically involve efforts "to realize personal ambitions, to counteract frustrations, to avoid damage to self-esteem, and 'to cope with the anxiety, fear, or guilt, that they experience from time to time' when dealing with decisional dilemmas" (p. 18). Because needs of the types mentioned are often emotionally arousing, members of groups are given to a reliance on emotion-based rules or heuristics. Among these, Janis identifies the "rely-on-gut-feelings," "retaliate!" and "can do! [that is, audacity]" rules.

When egocentric constraints activate such emotion-based rules, control and coping with personal needs, as opposed to making good choices, become the motives for action, as well as interaction. When this is the case, the likelihood that the affected group members will display vigilance is sharply reduced. They are much more likely to exhibit any of three patterns: defensive avoidance, essentially not making a choice; hypervigilance, or seizing on an alternative in a less-than-thoughtful manner; or bolstering, that is, endorsing whichever alternative appears to be least objectionable at the moment (Janis and Mann, 1977). We have already discussed the first two of these in connection with cognitive constraints and as responses stemming from perceptions of inadequacy and a corresponding inability to make optimal decisions. In the context here, these response mechanisms represent means of influencing interaction in ways that work to one's perceived advantage, or what Folger, Poole, and Stutman (2001) portray as forms of dominance and issue control, and in the process to address concerns that are more compelling to them at the time than the quality of judgment and choice. In short, the parties under the influence of egocentric constraints frequently eschew the use of high-quality procedures in return for the realization of self-serving ends. To the extent that there is a relationship between the quality of procedures that groups use (Herek, Janis, and Huth, 1987), resorting to self-serving rules for making choices can be detrimental to the interests of effective decision making.

In addition, because those applying egocentrically based rules do so primarily, if not exclusively, out of self-interest, their disregard for the views and feelings of others can contribute to relational difficulties. When this occurs, discussion can become a contest of wills, in which the participants are enmeshed in either of the destructive cycles of escalating hostility or withdrawal, about which Folger, Poole, and Stutman (2001) have so convincingly written.

Facilitating groups under conditions in which powerful egocentric constraints are operative can be a daunting task. But neither is one helpless in this regard. Janis (1989) mentions several measures on which one can draw. First, a group member enacting the role of facilitator can simply note that the subject is one that invites individuals to pursue self-serving interests and then make salient the norms and conventions of the group that seemingly proscribe such activity. Gouran (1982) has made much the same point for dealing with the idiosyncratic tendencies of higher-status members of decision-making and problem-solving groups. Janis (1989) further suggests either expressing moral disapproval or having private conversations with those who appear to be placing their concerns for self above the interests of the group and especially of making a good choice. On the face of it, the latter approach seems to be preferable, at least as a first effort. As yet another approach, a would-be facilitator, sensing that self-serving interests have taken hold, might recommend deferring action to give the group as a whole a possibly needed respite from undesirable pressures and, consequently, an opportunity to shift back to a more vigilant posture.

In addition to the kinds of measures that Janis recommends, since conflict can easily arise when egocentric constraints are at work, a facilitator could recommend adoption of consensus-seeking rules along the lines of those formulated by Hall and Watson (1970). These rules, if endorsed and adopted, obligate group members to avoid arguing for their own positions, pursuing distributive (win-lose) approaches, changing their minds only to avoid conflict, and suppressing conflict. The rules also encourage participants to view differences of opinion as natural and initial agreements as suspect. It is helpful if the members of groups agree to such rules in public, as we have long known that public utterances tend to commit those who make them to what they have said (Hovland, Janis, and Kelley, 1953).

Finally, a person attempting to facilitate discussion in the presence of egocentric constraints might recommend to fellow participants that they adopt formal procedures, such as Volkema's problem-purpose expansion technique (1983), which has as its central aim to show that better choices are likely to be made if the parties to a discussion concentrate on understanding the larger ends that they have in mind and for which their preferred position may be less suitable than others. This can sometimes help strong advocates of particular positions to see that there may be superior means of accomplishing what they might hope though implementation of their positions.

KNOWLEDGE AND SKILLS TO ENHANCE FACILITATION

For any member of a decision-making group who attempts to facilitate the other members' performance along constructive lines, various types of knowledge and related capabilities are of significant value. Within the scope of this chapter, we can offer only a general catalogue extracted from a much more extensive discussion by Gouran (2003a).

It almost goes without saying that to be successful in facilitating groups, the facilitator must possess some knowledge of the matters under consideration, relational influences on interaction, and the processes most conducive to the making of informed choices. The last type of knowledge, without the former types, is not likely to leave one well enough equipped to be of help to members in overcoming the sorts of obstacles they may encounter.

Given the kinds of knowledge noted, as well as the ways in which the categories of constraints discussed already can be manifested in substantive, relational, and procedural dimensions of group interaction, Gouran (2003a) sees three types of skills as enhancing the prospects for a group's success in its choice-making activities. In the category of task-related skills, specific ones of interest include problem recognition and framing, inference drawing, idea generation, and argument. Regarding relational skills, ability in leadership, climate building, and conflict management, particularly from the perspective of a neutral third party, can be very helpful when problematic aspects of the relationships among the members are standing in the way of their ability to choose judiciously. Finally, with respect to procedural skills, adeptness in planning and process enactment can help a facilitator to prevent the members of a group from going astray, or at least limit the probability that they will. Because a facilitator never knows when he or she may feel a need to intervene in a decision-making discussion, we feel that everyone who participates in such discussions would be well advised to make an active effort to cultivate these types of skills.

CONCLUSION

Although professional facilitators can render invaluable service, circumstances do not always allow this type of intervention in sufficient time to bear fruit. As a result, we have addressed situations in which obstacles arise in the course of a group's interaction and require immediate attention. To that end, we have considered obstacles posed the types of constraints—cognitive, affiliative, and egocentric—under which members of groups may be functioning and that also reduce their prospects for satisfying the requirements for making appropriate choices. For each category, we described some general approaches that a member acting in the role of facilitator can take to help members overcome the difficulties they face. Finally, we have mentioned particular kinds of knowledge and skills that better equip the members of groups to enact the role of facilitator if and when they should need to do so.

Consensus Building

Strategies for Resolving Disagreement

Michael Wilkinson

There are only three reasons people disagree. We have found that every disagreement in the world can be classified as level 1 (information), level 2 (experience or values), or level 3 (outside factors). As facilitators, we need to understand these types of disagreements and the approaches for resolving them. For, if you try to resolve a level 3 disagreement using a level 1 approach, you will likely fail. This chapter looks at the three reasons people disagree and three specific techniques for helping a group to reach consensus. For simplicity, I will be using examples of disagreements that involve two people. The same principles and techniques are adaptable for disagreements that involve groups as well. Where there is a significant distinction in the techniques for two-way and group disagreements, I highlight the distinction.

Consider the following scenario:

> Pat and Chris work for the same organization. Pat is a manager in human resources and Chris works in operations in one of the field offices. They are the first from their organization to attend a facilitation training course:

Note: The material for this chapter is largely adapted from Chapter Ten of Michael Wilkinson, *The Secrets of Facilitation* (San Francisco: Jossey-Bass, 2004).

Pat: I think this training course is excellent. The methodology is sound; the way it is taught is interactive; the techniques can bring results in a wide range of situations. In total, this stuff will make us more effective. I think everyone in our organization should take this course.

Chris: Everyone? That's a little extreme, don't you think? I could see having key managers take the course. At least they will actually have an opportunity to do something with it.

Pat: No, we can't limit this to managers. Everyone needs these skills. Everyone should take the course.

Chris: This is a business, Pat. You folks in HR sometimes forget this. We can't have everyone away from work for stuff they might not use. Only key managers.

Pat: I know this is a business, Chris. I'm not stupid. If you folks in the field were just more open to empowering your people, you might get better than mediocre results.

Pat and Chris are well on their way to a bitter argument. What started out as a friendly, enthusiastic comment to a colleague seems to have transformed somewhere along the way into a deep philosophical disagreement that has gotten quite personal.

Although this is a fictitious scenario, it is an example of the types of disagreements that happen frequently in business, community, and personal interactions around the world. Disagreements such as these can be constructively addressed when a facilitator or the participants understand the three levels of disagreement and techniques for addressing each level.

UNDERLYING PRINCIPLES: WHY PEOPLE DISAGREE

Our work with literally hundreds of groups over the past decade has led us to categorize disagreements into three basic types or levels.

Level 1 Disagreement: Lack of Shared Information

In a level 1 disagreement, the people disagreeing have not clearly heard or understood each other's alternative and the reasons for supporting it. Level 1 disagreements are often a result of assumed understanding of what the other person is saying or meaning. They are often referred to as disagreements based on facts.

To solve a level 1 disagreement, the facilitator must use techniques that slow down the conversation to encourage careful listening, explicit sharing of information and explanations, testing for shared meaning, and comprehension. When the disagreement is due solely to a lack of shared information, the parties quickly learn that they were not actually in disagreement at all and were just not hearing each other (literally), misunderstanding one another, or had not shared relevant information.

I use the term *violent agreement* to describe a level 1 disagreement. The parties really agree, but they do not know it, so they continue to argue. One of the common statements that one hears following the resolution of a level 1 disagreement is, "Oh, is that what you meant? Why didn't you say that?"

Level 2 Disagreement: Different Values or Experiences

In a level 2 disagreement, the parties have fully heard and understand one another's alternatives. However, they have had different experiences or hold different values that result in their preferring one alternative to another.

Political parties often have level 2 disagreements. The parties typically fully understand each other's platforms and initiatives. They often fundamentally disagree on how a country, state, city, township, or tribe should be run.

In Australia, for example, the Labour party values social democracy and ensuring social justice, especially for low-income earners. Therefore, party adherents tend to believe that the government should intervene to provide more equitable outcomes. In contrast, the Liberal party values social conservatism and encourages a free market. In general, party adherents tend to support business expansion and a limited welfare safety net.

Marriages are also a place where level 2 disagreements are common. My wife and I agree on a lot of things. But every once in a while, we have significant level 2 disagreements, as illustrated in planning a vacation:

Sherry: I'm been thinking about our vacation for next year, and I've got it! There's a ten-day tour of Italy that takes us to eight cities, including Rome, Venice, Milan, and Florence. It's perfect. What do you think?

Michael: That does sound like a wonderful tour. But I have really been looking forward to going to the beach this year.

Sherry: Oh, come on, snookums [that's what my wife calls me when she really wants something]. Let's go to Italy. We haven't been there before.

Michael:	Oh, sweetheart, darling, baby (*in my best impression of the deep baritone of singer Barry White*). Let's go to the beach. It'll be quiet and restful.
Sherry:	Now, Michael, you've been out of town a lot this year, which has left me home to do both my job and take care of the kids solo, so we really should do what I want to do. Let's do Italy.
Michael:	You are right, Sherry. I have been out of town a lot this year, and it has worn me out. I really need a break. Let's go to the beach.
Sherry:	No, we are going to Italy.
Michael:	No, we are going to the beach.
Sherry:	Italy!
Michael:	Beach!
Sherry:	Italy!

Clearly, my wife loves to travel. She values vacations that allow her to see many things and have new and different experiences. For her, the ten-day, eight-city tour is ideal. I, however, live out of a suitcase for major parts of the year. Therefore, the last thing I want to do when I am on vacation is to pack every morning to go visit another city. I want the quiet, sandy beach. I want to be able to sleep late most mornings, get up when I want to get up, and do nothing if I want to do nothing.

Notice that we understand each other's alternatives and reasons for supporting them. I understand that my wife values new and varied experiences, and she understands that I value rest and relaxation—a classic level 2 disagreement.

The key to solving a level 2 disagreement is to isolate the underlying values and create alternatives that combine the values. In the example, my wife and I have both taken positions. If the argument stays at the position level (Italy versus the beach), one of us is going to win (more likely my wife!) and one of us is going to lose.

However, the real issue is not the positions but the reasons for supporting them. If, in consensus building, we can get beyond the positions and focus on the real issues, *or interests* (Fisher, Ury, and Patton, 1991), we may be able to create solutions that satisfy everyone's most important needs.

Think of it much like an iceberg. The tip of the iceberg, that is, the part that you see, is the position. But what is below the surface is what really matters, and these are the critical issues that we have to identify.

To identify the key underlying values, facilitators ask questions such as: Why is that important to you? What benefit do you get from doing this? Working with the answers, we can often help the group identify solutions that provide key benefits to, and satisfy the key interests of, all parties. (At the end of the chapter, you will see how we resolved the vacation dilemma.)

Level 3 Disagreement: Outside Factors

A level 3 disagreement is based on personality, past history, or other outside factors that have nothing to do with the alternatives. Sometimes a disagreement is not at all related to the discussion. Consider this situation about a nominating committee:

Tom:	One of the things I think we can do to improve our board governance is to add one or two board members with strong financial backgrounds. This way we can better understand the financial ramifications of some of the proposals we are considering.
Frank:	That won't work.
Tom:	Sure it will. We just need to make sure we get the right people.
Frank:	No, it won't work.
Facilitator:	Help us understand, Frank. Why won't that work?
Frank:	It just won't work.
Facilitator:	Okay. . .Well, how might we improve it?
Frank:	There's no way to improve it. It just won't work.
Facilitator:	Help us understand, Frank, why you are so convinced it won't work.
Frank:	It just won't work. *He* thought of it. It won't work!

This is an extreme example, to be sure. (More realistically, Frank might retain his objection but without revealing this reason.) Frank clearly does not want to have anything to do with this idea, but his reason is not related to the idea. As it turns out, Frank learned some time ago that when he was nominated to the board, Tom was one of the few people who spoke against him. Since then, Frank has sought to block all of Tom's suggestions.

A disagreement based on personality or past history (level 3) often calls for a deeper intervention and cannot be resolved in a typical session. Therefore, it is important to determine the source of the disagreement as quickly as possible to avoid wasting time.

Level 3 disagreements appear to be irrational. The arguments do not seem to make logical sense, and in many cases, the arguer does not offer any rationale for the position. In addition, in a level 3 disagreement, one or more of the parties show no interest in resolving the disagreement, considering alternatives, or convincing the other side. Since the disagreement is not based on the issue, there is little desire to focus on the issue.

If you are in a facilitated session when an important level 3 disagreement is discovered, consider taking a break and meeting with the parties together privately to indicate to them you do not believe the issue can be solved in the session. Seek to gain their agreement to go to a higher source together for resolution outside the session. In essence, let a higher level in the organization make the decision by having both parties go to the source together to explain the issue.

We recommend not attempting level 3 resolution unless the session was specifically designed for that purpose. Typically, issues based on personality or past history require more time than the group has agreed to give or that you can give, based on your contractual arrangement.

Sessions designed specifically to bring parties together to address level 3 issues (conflict resolution) are beyond the scope of this chapter. (For additional information on this topic, see Deutsch and Coleman, 2000.) Briefly, however, we recommend that level 3 conflict resolution sessions should, at a minimum, include the following steps:

1. An opportunity for each party individually to identify and speak about the various issues, concerns, past actions, and existing situations that have had a negative impact on working together

2. Agreement that all parties want a better working partnership

3. Identification of the benefits of a better working partnership to each party individually and all parties collectively

4. Agreement by all parties that all important issues, concerns, past actions, and existing situations have been identified

5. Interactive presentation and discussion of best practices for working together (this step brings outside insights on partnerships into the room)

6. Development of a set of strategies and partnering principles that will govern how all parties will interact to address past issues, prevent future issues, and resolve issues should they occur

7. A method for monitoring and intentionally making adjustments along the way.

Identifying the Level of Conflict

Let us go back to the conflict Pat and Chris were having concerning the training course. Take a minute to review it again and decide the type of disagreement. Is it level 1, 2, or 3?

Given the tone at the end, one could easily conclude it is a level 3 disagreement. The tone is becoming harsh, and tempers appear ready to surge. However, recall that the two signs of a level 3 disagreement are irrational logic regarding the issues at hand and a lack of commitment to reaching agreement. Both Pat and Chris appear to have reasonable arguments (everyone needs the skills versus taking everyone away from work for "stuff" they might not use). In addition, both seem to be attempting to convince the other of the validity of their position. We conclude that this is not a level 3 disagreement.

This scenario certainly sounds as if it could be a level 2 disagreement: Pat seems to value disseminating basic skills throughout the organization, and Chris seems to value minimizing disruption to the organization's day-to-day operation by training only those who really need the skills. Yet as you will see, this very easily could be a level 1 disagreement. They may think they understand each other's alternatives, but they may find they do not understand them at all.

BUILDING A TOOL BOX OF CONSENSUS TECHNIQUES

If you conclude that a disagreement is level 3, we recommend that you take it to a higher source for decision making. However, once you have ruled out level 3 as the disagreement type, there are several techniques for achieving consensus.

Fisher, Ury, and Patton (1991) cite four bases for negotiating agreement: people, interest, options, and criteria:

- Separate the people from the method.

- Focus on interests, not positions.

- Invent options for mutual gain.

- Insist on using objective criteria.

In *Decisions, Decisions: The Art of Effective Decision Making* (2002), Welch gives nine steps to effective decision making:

1. Identify your objective.

2. Do a preliminary survey of your options.

3. Identify the implicated values.

4. Assess the importance of the decision.

5. Budget your time and energy.

6. Choose a decision-making strategy.

7. Identify your options.

8. Evaluate your options.

9. Make your choice.

Welch suggests that we think of decisions as investment. The more time and energy "you invest in making a decision, the more likely it is that you will make the best possible decision. But sometimes the difference between the best possible decision and the worst possible decision is not very great, or the stakes in the decision are not very high. In such a case, you certainly do not want to invest much in the choice" (Welch, 2002, p. 32).

In contrast, Russo and Shoemaker (2002) advise, "Decision-makers ought to use the simplest technique sufficient for the task at hand" (p. 134). They advocate four types of decision-making techniques:

- Intuition
- Rules of thumb
- Decision weighting
- Value analysis

Marcum, Smith, and Khalsa (2002) take a different approach. They establish seven rules for decision making:

1. Check your ego at the door.

2. Create curiosity.

3. Move off the solution.

4. Get evidence.

5. Calculate the impact.

6. Explore the ripple effect.

7. Slow down for yellow lights.

8. Find the cause.

From these various approaches, we will look at three of the most common techniques, identified in Exhibit 22.1:

Technique 1: Delineation

Technique 2: Strengths and weaknesses

Technique 3: Merge

Technique 1: Delineation

After ruling out outside factors as the source of the disagreement, you will want to take the steps to determine if it is a level 1 disagreement. In essence, you want to make sure each party clearly understands the other's alternatives. We call the process *delineation*. The purpose is to delineate the facts. Delineation has six steps:

Step 1: Start with Agreement   Starting with agreement helps both parties see that they already have something in common. This initial agreement can serve as a bridge for constructing the final solution.

Facilitator: Let me make sure I'm understanding what I'm hearing. You seem to both agree that this is a valuable course. Is that right?

Pat: Oh, yeah.

Chris: Sure, I can agree with that.

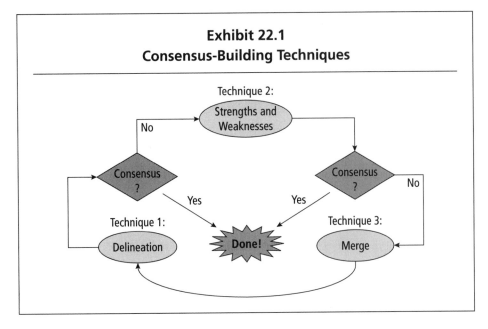

**Exhibit 22.1
Consensus-Building Techniques**

Step 2: Confirm the Source of the Disagreement   Identifying the source of the disagreement shows the parties that they are not far apart, despite the fact that the discussion may have become somewhat strained:

Facilitator:	Where you seem to disagree is on who should take the course.
Pat:	Yes.
Chris:	That's right.

Step 3: Identify the Alternatives Under Discussion and Create New Ones
Once the source of the disagreement is confirmed, you then identify the alternatives that have been discussed and ask the participants to create any new ones that come to mind. If there are two alternatives, we recommend creating a two-column chart and labeling the columns with the name of each alternative. If there are more than two alternatives, you will have as many columns as you have alternatives.

Facilitator:	So, Pat, you are saying everyone should take the course.
Pat:	That's right. [Facilitator labels the first column "Everyone."]
Facilitator:	And Chris, you are saying something different?
Chris:	Yes. I think only key managers should take the class. [Facilitator labels the second column "Key Managers."]

Step 4: Ask Specific Delineating Questions to Each Party   For each alternative, direct specific questions at the supporter of the alternative, and record the responses on the flip chart. For most disagreements, the questions should result in the group's understanding the following: how much it will cost, how long it will take, what is involved, and who is involved.

Facilitator:	Pat, you said everyone would take the course. How many people is that?
Pat:	All five hundred of our employees.
Facilitator:	Would each one take the full three-day course?
Pat:	Yes, that's right.
Facilitator:	How many people would be in each class?
Pat:	I understand that the vendor permits up to sixteen people per class. So let's assume that we will have fourteen to sixteen people per class.

Facilitator:	So, to get all five hundred people, does that mean that there will be about thirty-five classes?
Pat:	That sounds right.
Facilitator:	How would people be assigned to particular classes? Would you go department by department, have people sign up when available, or use some other method?
Pat:	I would have people sign up when they were available.
Facilitator:	What are the out-of-pocket costs for the class?
Pat:	I think the vendor charges ten thousand dollars per class. We would use our facilities, so there would be no out-of-pocket costs for this. There would not be travel costs or any other major expenses.
Facilitator:	And how often would you offer the class?
Pat:	Probably two classes per month.
Facilitator:	Well, that gives us a pretty good idea of how that would work. Now, Chris, you said that you were for only key managers taking the class. How many people would that be?
Chris:	Eighty key managers.
Facilitator:	Who would choose the eighty?
Chris:	The executive team would select the eighty. But for the most part, I think it would be all of the vice presidents, directors, and managers who have other managers reporting to them.
Facilitator:	Would they also take the three-day course?
Chris:	Yes, they would.
Facilitator:	Would you also have fourteen to sixteen people per class?
Chris:	Yes.
Facilitator:	So, to get the eighty key managers trained, would that be five classes?
Chris:	No, I think we would need seven. We would schedule each manager for one of the first five classes, but I know that we would need at least two makeup classes for managers who missed the first round.
Facilitator:	Would the out-of-pocket costs be the same?
Chris:	Yes. Ten thousand dollars would be right.
Facilitator:	And how often would you offer the class?

Chris: Probably one class per month.

Facilitator: Okay, I think I've gotten all that down.

Step 5: Summarize the Information   After getting the details for each alternative, summarize the key points at the bottom of the flip chart:

Facilitator: Let's summarize the information that we've learned. With the key managers alternative, we would have eighty people trained, it would take about seven months, and we would have about $70,000 in out-of-pocket costs. For the alternative in which we train everyone in the organization, we would have five hundred people trained, and it would take eighteen months at a cost of $350,000.

The results from the delineation are shown in Exhibit 22.2.

Step 6: Take a Consensus Check   Once each alternative is delineated and summarized, check to determine if consensus has been reached. If it has been reached, you will be able to move on. If it has not been reached, you will want to move to the next consensus-building technique:

Exhibit 22.2
Results of Technique 1: Delineation

Everyone	Key Managers Only
Five hundred people	Eighty people
Sign up when available	Executives select managers
Three-day class	Three-day class
Fourteen to sixteen/class	Fourteen to sixteen/class
Thirty-five classes	Seven classes
Two classes/month	One class/month
$10,000/class	$10,000/class

Summary	
Five hundred people	Eighty people
Eighteen months	Seven months
$350,000	$70,000

Facilitator: I know that we've only talked about the logistical and cost details without looking at some of the other issues. But it would be helpful to get a sense of what people are thinking at this point. Based on the information we've talked about so far, how many people would be in favor of the first alternative: having everyone trained? And how many would be in favor of the second alternative: having only key managers trained? *(pause)* Well, it is clear we do not have consensus yet.

There are several points to remember when delineating alternatives:

- Delineation encourages people to listen to each other. Prior to the facilitator's stepping in, Pat and Chris were talking at each other. The facilitator used a simple technique for getting Pat and Chris to listen. The facilitator took control of the conversation and then directed all of the questions at one person, Pat. This encouraged Chris to be quiet and listen. Then the facilitator turned and directed all of the questions at Chris, and it was Pat's turn to listen.

- When asking the delineation questions (step 4), rather than ask the direct question (for example, "How much does this alternative cost?"), ask instead the questions that provide the information needed to answer the direct question. For example, when the facilitator wanted to know the total cost of the alternative, the facilitator first asked the questions that would help the person figure out the number of classes needed and the cost of each class. This made it much easier to figure out the total cost. In situations in which the components of cost might be complicated, it can be helpful to ask the cost question directly in the following way: "Let's talk about costs. If we wanted to determine the costs of this alternative, what are the various components we would have to price?"

- The delineation questions focus on facts only. There are no evaluation questions (for example, "Why is that important?") during this stage.

- I recommend waiting until you have gathered information for all alternatives before summarizing. If you summarize following each alternative, participants tend to focus on trying to ensure that their alternative "beats" the summary for the other alternatives.

Recall that delineation is designed to provide the information needed to resolve level 1 disagreements. Could this issue with Pat and Chris have been a level 1 disagreement? Certainly. For example, the discussion could have gone as follows:

Facilitator:	Pat, you said everyone would take the course. How many people is that?
Pat:	All five hundred of our employees.
Facilitator:	Would each one take the full three-day course?
Pat:	No. I would want the vendor to create a special one-day class for our people so they wouldn't have to spend so much time away from work.
Chris:	A one-day course? Why didn't you say that? I have no problem with that.

In this case, Pat and Chris would have been in "violent agreement." They were in agreement but did not know it. If the disagreement is truly level 1, delineation will likely resolve it by encouraging participants to take the time to understand one another.

Technique 2: Strengths and Weaknesses

If consensus has not been reached through delineation, I recommend identifying the strengths and weaknesses of each alternative.

Step 1: Identify the Strengths   With delineation, the focus is on just the supporter of each alternative. With strengths and weaknesses, the entire group is involved:

Facilitator:	Now that Pat and Chris have delineated the alternatives, let's all identify the strengths and weaknesses of each one. This will help us better understand the alternatives and the reasons for supporting them. Let's start with the first alternative: having everyone trained. Think about this alternative compared to the other. There are particular strengths of taking this alternative over the other one. There are particular benefits to this alternative that the other one doesn't have. Let's list them. What are the strengths of having everyone trained?
	What about the second alternative: having only key managers trained? What are the key strengths of this alternative?

Step 2: Identify the Weaknesses   Once the strengths of each alternative have been identified, have the entire group discuss the weaknesses of each alternative. The results from the strengths and weaknesses discussion are shown in Exhibit 22.3.

Exhibit 22.3
Results of Technique 2: Strengths and Weaknesses

Everyone	Key Managers
Strengths	*Strengths*
• Common language	• Less expensive
• Everyone benefits	• Completed more quickly
• Skills throughout the organization	• Less time away from work
	• Training focused on those who need it
Weaknesses	*Weaknesses*
• More expensive	• Focuses only on higher levels in the organization
• Takes longer	• Skills and language not shared
• More time away from the organization	

Step 3: Take a Consensus Check   Once the strengths and weaknesses have been identified for each alternative, check to determine if consensus has been reached. If consensus has been reached, you will be able to move on. If consensus has not been reached, you will move to the next consensus-building strategy.

There are several points to remember when using the strengths and weaknesses technique:

- It's very important to get the strengths of all alternatives first before discussing the weaknesses.

- This method gives value to each alternative before the participants devalue either through the weaknesses discussion.

- For many disagreements, especially when there are only two alternatives, the weaknesses of one alternative are equivalent to the strengths of the competing alternative. Notice in our example how the weaknesses of the "everyone" alternative reflect the strengths of the "key managers only" alternative. Once the group identifies this relationship, you can save time discussing the weaknesses.

- If there are only two people involved in the discussion, we recommend having them give the strengths of the alternative they oppose. This approach encourages active listening and helps the parties see the other side. The supporter of each alternative then adds any additional strengths that may have been missed.

- Recall that a level 2 disagreement is based on different experiences or values. When you ask people the strengths of an alternative, their responses typically represent the values they hold that result in their preferring one alternative over the other. For example, those who prefer the "everyone" alternative place greater value on common language and everyone benefiting. Those who prefer the "key managers only" alternative place greater value on saving dollars and limiting time away from the operation. Even if consensus is not reached at this stage, identifying these underlying values will provide the group with a clear basis for moving forward.

Technique 3: Merge

If the group does not reach consensus through strengths and weaknesses, the next technique we recommend is merge. Through merging, the group creates a third alternative, which combines the key strengths of the prior alternatives.

Step 1: Identify Key Strengths   Start the merge process by identifying the most important strengths of each alternative:

Facilitator: Now that we have identified the strengths and weaknesses of each alternative, let's see if we can use this information to help us come to consensus. For those who prefer the first alternative, would you raise your hand? I'm going to read through each of these strengths. When I'm done, I would like you to tell me what are the one or two most important strengths. (*Reads through the strengths; places an asterisk next to the one or two most important identified by the group.*) For those who prefer the second alternative, let's do the same.

Exhibit 22.4 shows the strengths, with asterisks indicating the key strengths.

Step 2: Create One or More New Alternatives   Have the group focus on the key strengths to create one or more alternatives that combine the strengths:

Facilitator: Is there a way to create a new alternative that combines these strengths? Is there an alternative that is . . . ? (*reads the strengths and draws a single circle around all the key strengths*)

Exhibit 22.4
Results of Technique 3: Key Strengths Identified

Everyone	Key Managers
Strengths	*Strengths*
• Common language*	• Less expensive*
• Everyone benefits	• Completed more quickly
• Skills throughout the organization*	• Less time away from work*
	• Training focused on those who need it

Note: Asterisks indicate the key strengths.

Pat:	Chris, I can see how having only the key managers take the class limits the time away from work. But I would still want everyone to be exposed to the skills. What do you think of having all managers hold a two- or three-hour briefing for the members of their staff to focus on the skills they learned in the workshop?
Chris:	That can work, especially if we can get the vendor to develop a briefing packet for the managers to use.
Facilitator:	I've written that alternative. Are there other alternatives we should consider?

Step 3: Delineate the Top Alternative   Have the group select the new alternative with the most promise, and delineate it:

Facilitator:	Of these additional alternatives, is there one in particular that we might focus on first?
Chris:	I think having the managers brief the rest of the staff is the way to go. It focuses the training on the most important group and provides a means for getting the training communicated throughout our organization.
Facilitator:	Other thoughts? We seem to have strong consensus around the briefing approach. So let's delineate this alternative to make sure we all understand how it would work.

Step 4: Take a Consensus Check   Once the group has delineated the merged alternative, check to determine if consensus has been reached. If consensus has been reached, you will be able to move on. If consensus has not been reached, you will want to move to another consensus-building strategy.

There are several points to remember when using the merge technique:

- Through merge, the group creates an alternative that combines the key values of the participants. Typically, we use the three techniques in sequence. You may find, however, that the group is ready to create a short-cut through the process early and create new alternatives right away.

- Be sure to delineate the new alternative before assuming consensus. The delineation will ensure that all participants understand how the new alternative will work.

Additional Consensus Processes

Facilitators may find other techniques helpful as well.

Five-Finger Consensus   This method achieves consensus-based decision making without resulting in watered-down decisions. It is often appropriate with cross-functional teams and community groups in which there is a wide variety of interests and the desire for full consensus can potential erode the quality of the decision (Wilkinson, 2004).

With five-finger consensus, once an alternative is proposed and discussed and the group is ready to check for agreement, the facilitator explains that on the count of three, each person should hold up between one and five fingers indicating the level of support for the recommendation on the table:

5: Strongly agree

4: Agree

3: Can see pluses and minuses, but willing to go along with the group

2: Disagree

1: Strongly disagree and can't support

If everyone shows a 5, 4 or 3, consensus has been reached, and we can move ahead. If there are any 1s or 2s, there is further discussion, and the originator of the alternative has the option to make adjustments to the alternative.

Then the facilitator tests five-finger consensus again. If everyone shows a 5, 4, 3, or 2, the decision is made, and we move ahead. If there are any 1s, there is further discussion, and the originator of the alternative again has the option to make adjustments to the alternative. In the final review, majority rules. The decision is made based on the majority of the participants.

Weighted Score   This process seeks to reach consensus by scoring alternatives across a set of criteria. The weighted score approach is most appropriate when there are multiple discrete criteria that need to be assessed in order to evaluate the relative value of the alternatives (Leadership Strategies, 2003). With weighted score, the facilitator steps the participants through this process:

1. Identifying criteria

2. Weighting the criteria—for example, 1 for criteria that are low in importance, 2 for criteria with medium importance, and 4 for criteria with high importance

3. Scoring the alternatives against the criteria—for example, 10 for the most favorable alternative for each criterion, with the other alternatives scored from 1 to 10 relative to the most favorable one

4. Applying the weights by multiplying the score by the criterion weight

5. Summing the weighted scores to arrive at a value for each alternative

Converge   This process seeks to reach consensus through a "least change" method. When there are many parties involved and agreement from all parties is required to move forward, the converge technique can address a situation in which a small number of people are not in agreement with the majority (Leadership Strategies, 2003).

In this method, the facilitator asks each person not in agreement, "What is the least amount of change we could make to the most favored alternative for it to be acceptable to you?" Of course, some changes may cause others to disagree with the alternative. The facilitator continues to ask the question, and changes continue to be made until the group converges on a solution that all parties are willing to accept.

CONCLUSION

This chapter has focused on three consensus-building strategies: delineation, strengths and weaknesses, and merge. These techniques can help you move a group past disagreement to creating solutions for moving forward. As always, a facilitator must take care to understand the needs of the group and the nature of the disagreement to apply the appropriate consensus building strategy.

Remember the Italy/beach challenge for my wife and me? These days our favorite vacations are cruises. She gets the different ports of call; I get to sleep late most mornings. Consensus building works.

Quality Without a Name

Reinhard Kuchenmüller
Marianne Stifel

Visual facilitation is a rather new discipline, and we introduce our specific approach to it in this chapter. We find it exciting to sail on the great ocean of visual culture with our small ship, called *Visuelle Protokolle* (the name of our company), and visit the manifold Visual Islands. If we are lucky, we shall sail into the harbor called "quality without a name."

Note: This chapter, with full-color illustrations, is reproduced in its entirety on the CD-ROM accompanying this book.

Christopher Alexander, who for decades has done research in the field of human behavior and well-being, writes: "There is a central quality which is the root criterion of life and spirit in a man, a town, a building, or a wilderness. This quality is objective and precise, but it cannot be named" (1979, p. 19). He continues, "The search which we make for this quality, in our own lives, is the central search of any person. . . . It is the search for those moments and situations when we are most alive" (p. 41).

Such moments occur in our visual work with people when the group feels whole and alive. Nobody can pinpoint the quality we experience together, so we refer to it as a *quality without a name.*

AN ILLUSTRATIVE STORY

OVERVIEW

HISTORY MAPPING

Ancient Origins

Twenty thousand years ago, humans created the first cultic cave paintings, images with which they retained and transported information (Horn, 1998). Images thus existed long before the recording of languages. Between fifteen hundred and three thousand years ago, spoken languages, which often were rich in imagery, were gradually recorded in scripts. Particularly in Egypt and China, ideographic scripts originated with integrated word and picture elements (Horn, 1998).

The ancient world was the birthplace of the spoken language. Until about five hundred years ago in Europe, most written documents (books and scrolls) were skillfully scribed and illustrated by specialists. With the invention of the letterpress, pictures were pushed further into the background as a general means of communication. They retained their significance in the cultural areas of art and religion and gained importance in special fields such as the mapping of discoveries on land and sea maps.

Modern Developments

The development of comics, photography, and film in the nineteenth century and animation, television, and electronic transmission of data in the twentieth opened a whole new world of pictures, inundating our private and public lives, without, however, crushing the predominance of words. What has been scarcely noticed is that a third language has slowly developed that links verbal and visual elements into a visual language.

Visual Language

Robert E. Horn (1998) defines *visual language* as "the integration of words, images and shapes into a single communication unit [and] the use of words and images or words and shapes to form a single communication unit" (p. 8).

For fifty years, visual techniques to support the work of groups have been developing at different locations independent of one another and with little cross-influence.

Around 1950, the architects William M. Peña and William W. Caudill from CRSS in Houston, Texas (Peña, Parschall, and Kelly, 1987), began capturing the statements of their clients graphically on small cards for analysis, communication, and documentation. The aim of this method was to gather quantitative data for building programs. When it reached Germany in the 1980s, we modified the aim toward gathering of mainly qualitative data to support group processes, and this became the starting point for our spectrum of services.

In 1972, a turbulent development in group graphics began to take place in San Francisco when David Sibbet met with other innovative people. A broad scope of visualizers emerged in which the work of Sibbet, backed up by the philosophy of Arthur Young and the theory of models, occupies a special position. (See Chapter Ten.) With regard to more image-accentuated developments, we mention Nancy Margulies and Nusa Maal, who combine visualization and the technique of mind mapping (Margulies and Maal, 2002; Buzan, 1996).

These developments offer a new language that touches people directly and in their entirety. It can be used straightaway in visualization, and everyone understands it.

BUSINESS WORLD MAPPING

Work

About two hundred years ago, the business world was invented in the form as we know it today: organized work, based on the principle of the division of labor, in increasingly greater units, extending to the point of globalization. It is apparent to many that this has not been good for humans. The Gallup organization, for example, regularly examines job satisfaction and engagement of employees, with alarming results.

As many as two-thirds of employees are dissatisfied to the point of being aggressive. Gallup compares eleven nations worldwide: none can count on more than 27 percent of employees who are loyal, productive, and psychologically committed to their work. The resulting deficit costs for the world economy are staggering. Gallup speaks of $350 billion per annum for the United States alone ("The High Cost of Disengaged Employees," 2002).

There is something basically wrong in the relationship of people and work—a gap. We do not believe that employees will become satisfied through higher wages or shorter working hours, or even by the occasional exhilarating event at work. We have to understand the demand for another quality of business life.

Birgitt Williams got it right: "There is one WHOLE organization and if we can eliminate the divide, it functions at optimal performance. . . . In a holistic and integrated approach, one pulls together the multi-dimensions of the organization—spiritual, physical, mental and emotional" (e-mail to R. Kuchenmüller Dec. 23, 2003).

Meetings as a Model

Companies around the world conduct 11 million business meetings daily (Horn, 1998). What does it mean when millions of largely dissatisfied people meet and one of their tasks is to diminish dissatisfaction? This absurd situation is the playing field for facilitators. And working with images helps to pinpoint meetings in a holistic sense.

The difference that facilitators can make in this mass of meetings is to slowly change the way people meet with and experience each other.

In preparation for a meeting, sixteen employees were interviewed in advance. Their statements were noted visually on cards, made anonymous, and rearranged according to themes. Their manager arrived to look at the images prior to the meeting. He looked at the images for "leadership behavior" for a particularly long time. When the visualizer inquired curiously, "If somebody had said this to you personally," he replied loudly, "I would have been furious!!!"

In fact, he did not get angry and was courageous enough to open the meeting using the images, a meeting that turned out to be unusually productive.

It clearly is easier to attack and offend using words than images. Visual language delivers the message directly to the heart.

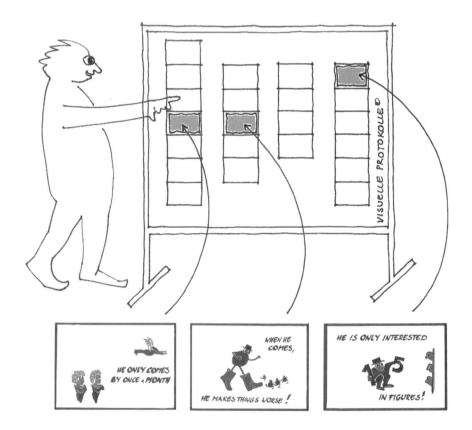

VERBAL AND VISUAL FACILITATORS

 The International Association of Facilitators (IAF), founded in 1994, is composed largely of verbal facilitators. Nevertheless, visualizers have participated in its conferences on several occasions and conducted events. This is a first step in the professional interlinking of verbal and visual facilitation.

No More Flip Charts?

A facilitator recently posed the provocative question: "The flip chart is declared illegal. What are other types or methods for collecting and/or displaying 'group memory?'" (D. Driver, e-mail to the Electronic Discussion on Group Facilitation, Nov. 14, 2003). The answers were: stenographer, electronic meeting system, time line, blackboard, photos, sticky walls, cards on which participants write/draw, draw on the walls, and graphic art.

In the place of flip charts, visualizers offer large murals or small cards, both drawn simultaneously during the meeting, that contain images and texts in different mixtures, prefabricated templates to draw and write into, techniques to encourage people to do the drawing themselves, white boards, and computers one can draw on and project simultaneously. There is great diversity in reproducing the results; they can be printed on paper as booklets, posters, and wallpaper, or digitalized and put on the Web. Above all, the visualizer integrates visual language into the process. Visual facilitation is thus more than facilitation plus some pictures.

Benefits of Visual Language for Facilitation

The participants of visualized events observe what they are saying much better than on handwritten flip charts and are able to look at the issues directly. Central themes become clearer, and boring text protocols become at least partially superfluous. Decisions are made more rapidly. One can present the content of a day-long meeting within a matter of minutes to someone who has not participated, and people remember the content many times better than they do text (Horn, 1998). A visual group memory emerges that is the basis for further steps in the process. All of this enriches the group process and saves time and costs as well.

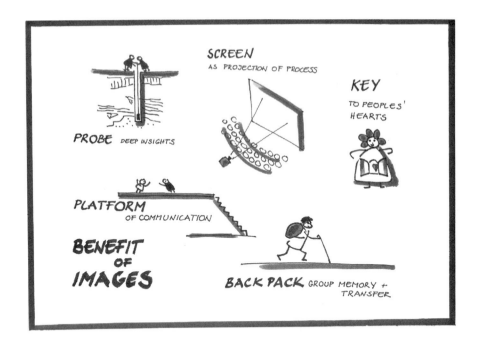

The Visualizers

There are thousands of people who have learned to visualize and at least hundreds who practice it professionally in different ways. The core of this group is driving the increasing professionalism of this field.

As shown in Exhibit 23.1, the range of services that visualizers provide goes hand in hand with various descriptions of the activities involved, such as scribing, graphic recording, visual practitioning, visual coaching, visual repatterning, graphic facilitation, and visual facilitation. (See "Key Terms and Definitions" at the end of the chapter.)

The IAF Statement of Values and Code of Ethics for Group Facilitators also applies to the work of visual facilitators. So the growing field of visual facilitation belongs in the broader family of group facilitation as represented by IAF.

Roles

Is it possible for a single individual to guide the group process and visualize at the same time? Based on our experience, this happens only in exceptional cases. As a rule, two facilitators that are well suited to one another should act in combination: one to guide the group and one to visualize on its behalf.

For any cooperation to occur, it is important to clarify the roles. They must be precisely defined in coordinating the responsibility for the images and the process up to the joint development of new methods.

Exhibit 23.1
Visualizer Services Range

From	To
Documentation of the content	Reflection of the process
Result oriented	Process oriented
Emphasis on writing	Emphasis on images
Silent servant	Process guide
Assisting given methods	Own models, procedures, and methods
Visualizes alone	Stimulates participants' visualizations
Passive	Interactive

OUR WORK BASE

 Our methods are different from those of many other visualizers. As this chapter does not strive for an overall description, we will concentrate on our method.

We focus on our coworkers who carry every company. Our facilitating work serves to give these people a voice in their organization as a way to involve them and at the same time to honor them.

Just as images are older than texts and every child processes images before words, we work in the same sequence, always starting with images. Images are culturally universal, archaic, emotional, and open to various interpretations. They represent patterns and archetypes. With images, we gather the essence of a process.

Words are younger than pictures, culturally specific, more precise, rational, logical, and mainly used for communication limited by rules. Adding some words, we anchor the image in the specific situation. We use the advantages of both words and images to foster communication, synthesize the process, and form our specific dialect of the visual language.

We all have our own wealth of internalized images that we have collected over the years, and they slumber within us. When we work with organizations by externalizing the group's images, we reopen the emotional entrance to their internal world.

Methods

Live visualization is the metaphorical trunk of our tree. Over the years, it has grown branches in different directions, mainly connected with group meetings and ongoing processes. Today, we define our work in three stages: preparing images, live process images, and summary images. These are the elements from which we compose our specific services in order to satisfy customers' needs. To pass on our knowledge, we offer seminars and coaching.

Preparing Images

To support events, we have developed a variety of methods and techniques, such as informative documents (agendas, posters), motivating material (complex company games, hand-drawn films), didactic products (metaphorical sea, land, and road maps; illustrations of messages; fairy tales), and live interviews.

For these methods, we use common drawing and painting techniques and formats, such as pastel and crayon, on huge wall paper, friezes, and collages. The visual language we choose is customized for each client.

Live Process Images

In general, images drawn live on site during the facilitating process are a visible recording of what is happening during the session. Our technique is very simple and has not changed much over the years. We use small cards and felt-tip pens. The small cards are easy to handle and accommodate one idea or thought, each one a basic truth; one is forced to avoid unnecessary details. They have the freshness of a small sketch and are thus easy to comprehend. When we work with these cards, we follow exact rules:

- Using seven selected colors (we eliminated black), we first draw the image and then add a word or brief text in a specified script. White boards and touch screens present new possibilities.

- The visualizer links these individual images together with tape to form a picture wall. In doing so, he gives the process a face, which interacts with the participants.

- The cards that form a picture wall can be interchanged or regrouped easily. At all times, they give an account of the status of the debate at a glance.

In the case of large groups, we recommend presenting the images using a projector and perhaps background music. As a group memory and a basis for further processes or as a document for others, the images can be digitalized, printed, or used in the Web.

Drawing Actions

Another important tool we use live during meetings is large group drawing action. The participants (as many as six hundred people) draw images on "templates" in answering important questions while observing definite rules. With this method, the group gives answers on issues regarding the group process that were not known before.

Summarizing Images

After most meetings, people often stand empty-handed and often forget very quickly what transpired at the meeting. Visual products, in contrast, support the sustainability of the group work. We produce result maps, images of an anticipated future, steps of progress (for repeat sessions), summary films, and even visual workbooks.

Afterward, all images get digitalized and reproduced on paper (for example, as posters, brochures, folding postcards, and calendars) or as virtual image walls to be displayed on-line.

We have gained thousands of images from live process visualization. Because of their general nature, they have the potential to be used anew in other contexts.

QUALITY MAPPING

 The quality of image-oriented visualization affects the satisfaction, humanity, and truthfulness of meetings, and it touches the participants of the group. It is this last quality that we are repeatedly surprised to encounter. We view it as the main secret of our visualization.

How Images Evolve

Visualization begins with listening. In the process of live visualization, the inner ear perceives not only the words but also their meaning, intent, and often the unspoken intent. Body language, the mood in the room, reactions of the group, and even unconscious content flow into the image.

The visualizer draws and lives and breathes with the group and is supported by it. The more directly one gets to the point, the more the observer feels he is being understood.

The pure image can be interpreted in several ways. Therefore, we add an accompanying word or sentence to anchor it in its context. If we were to reverse this process, we would end up illustrating our own text. When a word or sentence is added, the image emerges in relation to the situation, to the process, and takes on its own special meaning. There are parallels here to interpretation in a psychoanalytical context.

Images Tell Stories

Images meet up with stories. According to the script model, each of us has a treasure of stories saved in our memory. We all use stories that have already been experienced, which give rise to "narrative answers" and are the only way of keeping memories alive (Schank and Abelson, 1995). Stories thrive on metaphors and are therefore of special significance for our work. Metaphors evoke visual images: *brainstorming, springboard, floating on a sea of papers, letting off steam.*

By combining uncensored truths with humor, our role sometimes resembles that of the medieval court jester. By means of images and stories, it may be possible to gradually approach the heart of an organization, to come closer, little by little, to its main theme and its corporate story.

The Effect of Images

When we discuss the effect of images, we find ourselves at the borderline of art therapy, psychoanalysis, neurobiology, creativity theory, art psychology, and system theory. Each of these plays a role and mingles with our everyday experiences.

The visualizer offers himself as a container for the situation and content. He transforms the absorbed data and develops something qualitatively new. The image evolves in an unconscious process of symbol forming. In the words of Albert Einstein, "Intuition is a divine gift, the reasoning mind is a faithful servant. It is a paradox that we have begun nowadays to admire the servant and to profane the divine gift."

In this spontaneous production of the image, the visualizer makes himself available as the medium, the collector. He draws the first image that appears without reflecting on it.

Without taking sides and judging, the visualizer acts like an empty mirror, transparent for what is happening. The "thinking hand" absorbs everything without filtering it and then reproduces it.

We avoid repeating in words what has already been expressed by the image. So we create a fruitful friction between words and images.

Patterns and Repatterning

The images achieve their entire effect in their affiliation for patterns. Christopher Alexander has recognized "the extraordinary degree of agreement in people's feelings (not opinions) about patterns" (Alexander, Ishikawa, and Silverstein, 1977, p. 292). "A pattern which is real makes no judgments about the legitimacy of the forces of the situation. By seeming to be unethical, by making no judgments about individual opinions, or goals, or values, the pattern rises to another level of morality" (p. 304).

When a pattern emerges in the group and shows itself, ranging from extremely individual to archetypal, the visualizer then expresses this pattern as "the unthought known," that is, the implicit knowledge held by the group, heretofore unrepresented and unexpressed. When the visualizer's outer images meet the world of participants' inner images, we assume that they arrange them into patterns. We call this process of inner arrangement and ordering *repatterning*.

The Third Level

If two parties each stay on separate levels of arguments and feelings, they will never meet. Seen through a third eye offered by visual language, both alternatives become equally good or bad, since they are part of the whole. At this level, the level of the heart, new possibilities arise; hidden themes and taboos can be addressed and dissolved. In the illustration here, management, as the company head, demands; workers, as the company's belly, reject; but both find some understanding on the third level, the heart, through images.

Whether and how such processes take place is dependent on company spirit, the readiness of the group, the atmosphere, and the personal sensitivity of the visualizer. When inner and outer readiness converge, when inner and outer images meet, the group achieves quality without a name.

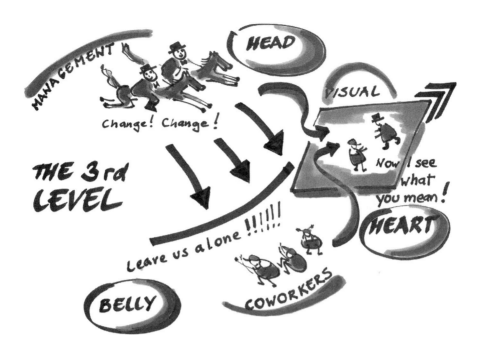

CASE STUDIES

 Based on about two hundred projects, we present some typical examples.

Preparing Images: Map Making

Following a merger, a regional information technology organization was being re-structured. The dynamic manager seized this opportunity to involve the employ-ees actively in the change process. They were to display entrepreneurial reasoning, work on a common definition of goals, and support the actions emotionally. She commissioned an external facilitator to accompany the process in the department for a period of nine months.

The facilitator searched for a creative and playful medium to visualize the process. He turned to us with the initial question: "Can you develop an interac-tive, flexible, visual medium?"

Process   We conceived of the idea of a large sea map on which the employees were able to continually test new details of their method in the metaphorical world of seafaring. The first image shows the relationship of central and regional locations of the organization, customer territory, currents of emotional sensitivities (*Verändern* and *Bewahren,* translated as "change" and "preservation"), and much more.

The first version was drawn and experienced by the employees using children's plastic ships. The image here shows the detail with the boat, which is the new department ship, sailing by Woman's Island (*Fraueninsel*). The sea map was brought up to date on a regular basis with newly acquired insights. The final version was created and complemented by a peninsula with a depiction of the future.

At the conclusion, the head of the department, the facilitator, and the visualizer met for a day to process the feedback. This evaluation showed that the sea map had been a great help to employees in understanding and learning how to steer and control and how to anchor the process emotionally.

Product The colorful walkable sea map, measuring 5 × 1.8 meters, was full of islands and bays, currents and harbors that had specific names tailored to the process. In addition, it also had integrated board games and individually developed card games such as "pirate poker." Finally the map was printed as a desk pad and given to each employee to keep the experience alive.

Remarks   Land and sea maps incorporate the charm and the secrets of hundreds of years of map making. They are suited for representing and documenting many types of journeys, such as organization development, change and merger processes, and company stories (the way from the "old country" to the vision), and they can be used for interactive games as well.

They will be a success if management opens the space, if visualizers find the fitting visual language, and if the employees dare to jump into the map's world.

Preparing Images: Fairy Tale

Two banks had decided to merge and consolidate their information technology departments. The employees, who feared the loss of their technology as well as changes in where they worked, were to be informed at a general meeting and motivated. The manager of the internal change process addressed us: "Can you put our vision into pictures for a kick-off meeting?"

Process   Two visualizers went on site, spent a day visually recording the discussions of the project group and the two top managers, mirrored the images back that had evolved, and received the commission to create and visualize an appropriate story. On their way home, the story line suddenly sprang from the images: the fusion of two ocean harbors. An old lighthouse keeper finally convinced the reluctant harbor masters to accept the challenge together.

We formulated the story (the fairy tale of the Northern Harbor) in close coordination with the company, illustrated it in a series of fourteen images that depicted the phases of the merger, and created the dramaturgy with the organization's events department. It was not easy to give equal consideration in the story to the pride of both companies.

Two months later when the kick-off meeting took place, the colorful images hung on the walls. Accompanied by seafaring music, they were then projected on a large screen. The top managers stood at the front wearing sailor shirts and read the story aloud. They stuttered a little, but the employees were personally touched and understood their message.

Product   We provided the dramaturgy and the illustrated story on CD and on three picture friezes, each 11 meters long. Each of the two hundred participants received the illustrations in the form of a notebook cover, and in the evening each person received a poster depicting the new harbor.

Remarks   Fairy tales can encapsulate the corporate culture and reality to make identification possible. With supportive upper management, the employees sense immediately that the intentions are genuine.

The elaborate pictures serve as permanent representations of the messages; after a year, they are still hanging in the corridors. The harbor metaphor is alive and is used for other events.

Preparing Images: Company Game

Following an unstable past, a public utilities company with twelve regional branches was taken over by an international group. Its economic situation was extremely difficult. But instead of closing down the company, the group sent in two top managers, who were successful in returning the company to the black. These managers approached us with the initial question: "Can you transpose a master plan so that all the employees understand it?"

Our charge was to help the workers, many of them without much formal education, understand the past, including all the poor decisions that had nearly ruined the company. It was also to help them understand how the international managers had accomplished the turnaround that saved the company. Finally, it was to show that German management was to be put into a position, enabling them to run the company successfully from this point with the commitment of all the workers.

Process   Only gradually did we realize the enormity of the challenger. It took four months before we found the solution, which had been preceded by discussions on numerous proposals (fairy tale, film, different story lines): a corporate game that was to be played in all the regional branches. The company was very male oriented, which gave rise to the metaphor of a car rally like the Paris–Dakar race through the desert. We and the managers immersed ourselves in business reports and the company's plans in order to transcribe the relevant information into the phases of the rally. The route went up hill and down dale through the past, present, and future, with each phase represented on an individual road map. Together with the managers, we discovered strategies for interactive involvement that would make the game realistic and exciting.

It was the far-sightedness of the managers, that made the game a sweeping success. They gave the game the space it needed and appointed two long-time employees to be the game leaders and supervise the content and course of the game.

The game leaders got down to work and developed the optimum dramaturgy, selected pieces of music for each episode, procured equipment, and dressed up in costumes; in short, they created an unbelievable mélange consisting of the glaringly poor figures of the company, the excitement of the rally, and the motivation of all the participants.

They played the game for three hours in each of the regional branches. The emotional outcome of the game and its lasting effect surpassed all expectations; it created a new corporate culture. Today, the company is financially sound and once again a leading player in the market.

Product   Our final product was a collage of photographs and paintings developed as a triptych of three road maps (approximately 1.40 by 3.00 meters), with thirty movable picture elements that were printed two hundred times and packed in suitable bags for transport, together with a description of the game.

Remarks   A game such as this, not a common occurrence, can change the corporate culture. The playing of the game must arouse respect among the players with regard to the idea and implementation. It thus has to be perfect in its design, dramaturgy, and content. Even years later, it should still be a topic of conversation in the company.

Live Process Images: Basis for Building Project

Two automobile development centers that employed over eight thousand workers were scheduled to merge. An internal team was in charge of the project management and commissioned external facilitators. Its initial question was, "Can you develop a method of providing the ideas and demands of the employees for the design and planning process in the shortest time possible?" We proposed to conduct a series of interviews and record the ideas, concepts, and visions of a large number of workers visually.

Process   We interviewed 174 workers divided into twenty-five thematic groups; the topics had been developed by the internal team. Each interview session was limited to one to two hours, and definite rules had to be followed:

- The goal of the session was discussed for five minutes and then codified in writing.
- The groups, each with about eight participants, then carried on an open discussion; all of their statements were recorded by three visual facilitators on small cards.
- The cards, with their image and word combinations, were presented as a picture wall and discussed briefly.
- Each group was sent a folder containing its images and requested to make corrections and approve them by signature.

The participants valued the opportunity to voice their opinions anonymously and directly through the images. The interview series was a hot topic of conversation in the company and was taken very seriously, also owing to the support from upper management.

From the twenty-five interviews, thirteen hundred images emerged. An additional record in writing proved unnecessary.

In the following weeks, the visualizers analyzed the huge accumulation of images and condensed and grouped them into clusters. This process resulted in thirty-six cluster themes.

Three general thematic groups evolved: human sensitivities, urgent pending decisions, and technical information and clarification. The documentation was complemented by brief verbal introductions.

Product Eight hundred remaining images grouped in three categories were summarized as a report in three volumes and provided to both the management and the commissioned architects in a ceremony. They had never before seen such an insightful "X-ray" of the company.

Three of the eight hundred images were proposals for recreation areas, a mixing of blue- and white-collar employees, and connections joining the separate buildings.

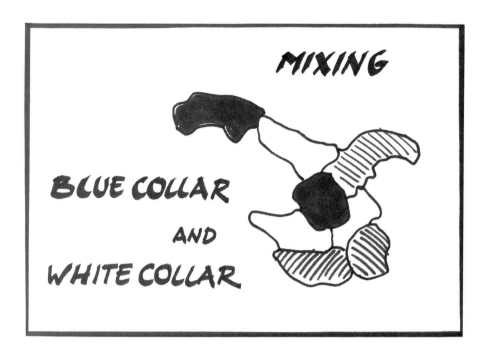

Remarks   We are not aware of another method of gathering the opinions of so many people within only six weeks and making them available in a way that everybody understands and can use.

The method combined strict top-down elements: the structure, the given themes, the selection of the participants, and unusual freedom during the interviews, which were conducted similarly to groups in open space technology without a leading figure. Subsequently, both aims were met: gathering a broad range of information, facts, and emotions relevant for the workers and for the project, and guaranteeing their direct use in the planning process.

It was not easy for top management to risk this process. Now, ten years later, the company wants to apply the same method again to make a retrospective evaluation of the process as well as to add a research department to its development center.

Live Process Images: Emotional Organigram

One year after the merger of a large insurance company, another drastic savings scheme was announced. The board of directors decided to travel to the main office and inform the employees in nine individual meetings. The initial question posed to us was: "Can you capture the participants' immediate reactions in the coffee break and make them visible directly after the presentation by the board?"

Process.   After the chairman announced the cutbacks, the employees left the room, many of them furious, frustrated, or paralyzed. The visualizer invited the employees to express their views and their feelings. The reactions were intense and emotional, as were the resulting images.

The visualizer drew their reactions (in less than one minute per image) and displayed them for all to see. The plenum gathered again. The chairman fetched the most critical images, took them to the platform, held them up, and commented on them with great seriousness.

Product In each of the nine meetings, a picture wall was created depicting the heated topics. All nine picture walls together formed an emotional organigram, that is, a graphic chart showing the interrelationships in the organization.

Remarks The fact that the images found their way to the chairman so quickly and that he responded to them immediately and honestly was most unusual. The brain of the board and the worker's belly had found a way to connect with one another. The images served as a barometer of public opinion. Communication had begun.

Small and flexible image cards are well suited to record reactions and opinions at lightning speed and present them on site for interaction purposes.

Live Process Images: Large Group Drawing Action

One hundred fifty international facilitators from sixteen countries were expected for the IAF annual conference near Amsterdam. The initial question from the conference design team to us was: "How can the conference attendees get to know one another and, at the same time, make their expectations of the conference known?" We proposed a guided drawing action, which we had successfully tested in other large groups.

Process The participants sat in groups of eight around "What Do You Expect" templates (which are shown here); they were laughing and holding broad felt-tip pens in their hands. The templates had been designed and printed in advance by the visual facilitators.

The visual facilitators supervised the drawing activity and explained the rules. Each person was to jot down his or her expectations of the conference on a sticky note and attach it to the template. Each group then had twenty minutes to think of an idea for a jointly drawn picture. The sticky notes were removed from the templates, and off they went with their drawing (another twenty minutes). In conclusion, the group was to give the picture a short title and write it on the template.

Directly following the drawing, the completed pictures were mounted at designated places. The individual pictures were then explained by the members of the conference design team who had not painted themselves.

"Oh, you did such a wonderful opening for the IAF! You could just see people coming to life as they discussed their expectations and thought of ways to image them. It created the right feeling for starting the conference. So this is a big hug and thank you!" said Maureen Jenkins, representing the conference design team.

Product   Within one hour, twenty posters were created that made the expectations of the conference visually clear in a most impressive fashion.

Remarks   Guided drawing actions allow a large group to focus on an important question and answer it within one hour. But there is a caution here: trivial or rhetorical questions result in trivial pictures and cause irritation in the under-challenged groups.

Hundreds of participants can be activated at the same time and make use of the wisdom in the groups. It is important to develop a specific template as well as to acknowledge the finished product. Also important are the room conditions, space, lighting, and display area.

The drawings are a good representation of the group results and keep the process vivid in the minds of those involved, as well as sustaining the results.

The area of application is large. We have led drawing actions for a change process kickoff with 300 information technology specialists, target development with 130 scientists, and a strategy conference with 600 railroad labor unionists, all of whom initially said, "I cannot draw!"

HOW TO LEARN

When we started visualizing years ago, everything was simple. Somebody explained the rules: "First, a quick, roughly sketched image, one picture per thought; then brief text in uppercase letters!" We took the colored felt-tip pens and off we went. You see, one can visualize immediately—but not everybody can do it.

Once we needed several visualizers and tested the staff of an architect's office. Several efficient architects failed. They were not able to sort out the colors, could not cope with the speed, and wrote too much text. Their knowledge was a hindrance to them (ambitious artists often fail in the same manner). But a young Kurd, intuitive, quick, filled with images, was a born visualizer.

We learned that everybody can draw and express themselves by means of pictures. But not everybody can mirror group processes through images. Only some have the talent, the inner willingness, and the courage to do this.

There is no formal educational program available for visual facilitators. Yet each individual can try. Simply take cards and pens into a meeting and draw. If you enjoy it, we, like other visual facilitators, offer workshops and seminars (that are influenced by the respective method of working). We also recommend sitting in on visualization sessions.

Perhaps a passion will arise. Then it means practice, practice, and practice again. When it starts becoming professional, you will enter your own visual world.

IAF board member Jon Jenkins calls a visual facilitator a specialized species, comparing him to a cardiologist. Is visual facilitating really more than the ability to draw fast and nicely? Yes. "It is only with the heart that one can see rightly; what is essential is invisible to the eye" (Saint-Exupéry, 1991, p. 68).

In the foreground, visual facilitating requires the courage to be spontaneous and risk a quick stroke of the pen; in the background, it requires listening, intuition, love, sensitivity, creativity, knowledge, and experience.

THE PUSH OF LIFE FORCE

CONCLUSION

In extending and deepening our main points of focus and discovering new possibilities, we have not yet met any limits. This should go on for a lifetime. We would like to encourage others to become involved in this process.

A development has begun in which the pioneering work of some individuals has started to develop into professional networking. We are curious how this development will influence the IAF. When "visual" and "verbal" meet and touch, whether in the person of a facilitator, whether on a team, whether in the entirety of the professional field, it should make facilitation more complete and thus make a contribution to a more holistic and human working world.

Thousands of visual facilitators are needed, from nursery school through college to firms and organizations, to enable the rediscovery of visual culture in all of our lives.

KEY TERMS AND DEFINITIONS

Archetype: Original pattern.

Cluster: A classification technique for grouping items by making comparisons of multiple characteristics (cluster analysis).

Communication graphics, graphic facilitation, graphic recording, graphic transla-tion, group graphics, information architects, interactive graphics, mirroring, re-flective graphics, scribing, social architects, visual facilitation, visual synthesis, visual thinking, Visuelle Protokolle: Terms for visualizers and their work in groups.

Didactic illustrations: Messages transformed into metaphorical images.

Emotional organigram: Visual representation of the emotional state of a group or company.

Facility programming: Developing a building program according to people's needs.

Graphic recorder: A visualizer, with emphasis on the content of a meeting (passive, off-to-the-side scribing approaches).

Large group drawing action: Structured drawing action with large groups to answer important questions visually.

Image: Here, a hand-drawn picture serving as a visual graphic representation, a symbolic map.

International Forum of Visual Practitioners: Emerging network of visualizers; a registered association since 2003.

Live process images: Images visualized simultaneously during group sessions.

Mapping: To make a survey for the purpose of making and drawing a map. Here, mapping inner themes of groups, organizations, and companies using maps as metaphors.

Metaphor: Figurative language; application of term to object or action to which it is imaginatively, but not literally, applicable.

Mural: A mural work of visualization, normally on paper.

Pattern: A discernible, coherent system based on the interrelationship of component parts. Here, it applies mainly to visual elements.

Pattern language: According to Christopher Alexander, development of a structure of patterns describing problems and solutions to create buildings and towns that are alive.

Preparing images: Images of all kinds drawn in preparation for a session.

Scribing: Old term for the production of artifacts, for example, illustrated handwritings.

Sea, land, or road map: Here, a metaphorical map drawn to communicate business themes.

Summary images: Visual documents showing process results.

Visual coaching: Coaching using visualization tools.

Visual dialogue tools: Pictures and images or templates produced to support visual communication and facilitation in group processes.

Visual facilitation: Facilitation using visual tools in interactive, highly facilitated approaches. Also referred to as *graphic facilitation.*

Visual practitioning: Using visual tools and methods as a practitioner (www.visualpractitioner.org).

Visualization: The forming of an image in the mind of something that is not actually existent, of the abstract. The formulation and communication in images; here, making visible and adapting thoughts, content, and processes. The formulation of something that cannot be said or written.

Visualizer: The visualizing person.

Visual repatterning: Reordering intrapersonal images to patterns by the means of outer images.

Visual language: "1. the integration of words, images, and shapes into a single unit. 2. the use of words and images or words and shapes to form a single communication unit" (Horn, 1998, 8). Horn comprehends images as "visible shapes that resemble objects in the perceivable world," and shapes as "abstract forms that . . . do not resemble objects in the natural world" like lines, points, arrows" (Horn, 1998, p. 72).

RESOURCES

Bion, W. R. *Learning from Experience.* London: Heinemann, 1962.

Bion, W. R. *Elements of Psychoanalysis.* London: Heinemann, 1963.

Blake, A.G.E. *Intelligence Now.* Gloucestershire, U.K.: Blake, 1973.

Cowan, J. *A Mapmaker's Dream.* London: Shambala, 1996.

Lundin, S. C. *Fish! A Remarkable Way to Boost Morale and Improve Results.* New York: Hyperion, 2000.

Sibbet, D. *Best Practices for Facilitation.* San Francisco: Grove Consultants, 2002a.

Sibbet, D. *The Purpose and Potential of Leading Group Process.* San Francisco: Grove Consultants, 2002b.

Sueddeutsche Zeitung. "Deutsche Unternehmen." May 2003. [http://www.sueddeutsche.de/wirtschaft/artikel/302/11291/].

Whyte, D. *The Heart Aroused.* New York: Doubleday, 1996.

Wilson, F. R. *The Hand. How Its Use Shapes the Brain, Language and Human Culture.* New York: Vintage, 1999.

Facilitating Participatory Evaluation Through Stories of Change

Terry D. Bergdall

Increasingly, facilitators are being asked to play an enabling role in participatory evaluations, that is, the review and assessment of organizational activities by people who are involved in their implementation. At least two major factors contribute to this. First, there is growing awareness of the importance of organizational learning. Whereas evaluation was once primarily seen as a management tool to inform top decision makers, there is now greater recognition of the relationship between active participation of key stakeholders and organizational effectiveness. Many people today see participatory evaluation as a practical mechanism for expanding learning opportunities among those directly involved in and affected by particular activities.

Second, organizations that invest in facilitated processes are increasingly interested in learning more about the ultimate impact of such processes. This can be a major challenge because many of the anticipated benefits associated with facilitation—such as team effectiveness, group initiative and responsibility, capacity for problem solving, transparency in decision making, creativity, and self-confidence—are intangible and are difficult to quantify. Participatory evaluation is not only consistent with the underlying values and principles of facilitation, it can offer an effective means for understanding organizational and social change, including the role of facilitation itself, in ways that more conventional evaluation methods cannot.

This chapter provides facilitators with an overview of participatory evaluations and is divided into two parts. It first introduces and then focuses on a particular approach to participatory evaluation based on stories of change. This approach systematically engages stakeholders in a dialogue about outcomes. Although it is illustrated through experiences gained in international development projects, suggestions are made for how it might be applied in connection with any facilitated process.

AN OVERVIEW OF PARTICIPATORY EVALUATION
Professional Program Evaluation

New initiatives, interventions, and innovations—programs in the broadest sense of the word—are planned and implemented in most sectors of organized life: education, social services, public health, private business, community and organizational development, and many others. When time and money are invested in planned activities, it is reasonable to expect that people want to know the results. Over the years, a profession of program evaluation has evolved with established values, norms, and practices for accomplishing this (Rossi, Freeman, and Lipsey, 2003; Wholey, Hatry, and Newcomer, 1994).

Participatory evaluation is a relatively new feature that has emerged within this larger environment. Before venturing forth to do participatory evaluation, it is advisable for new facilitators to gain some basic familiarity with the professional turf that they are about to enter. Terms and concepts are a good place to start. *Summative evaluations* provide information to decision makers about the impact and worth of particular programs. They typically occur at the end of a program cycle when curtailment, extension, or expansion is being considered. The primary clients for these evaluations tend to be policymakers or funders. *Formative evaluations* support an ongoing program. They are normally commissioned by, and delivered to, people who have the power to make improvements—often program managers. They are primarily concerned with furthering a program's effectiveness.

In both types of evaluation, professional evaluators usually rely on comparisons as the basis for drawing conclusions. This is usually seen as the foundation of all program evaluation. One approach is to compare actual program outcomes to planned targets. For example, a program might have planned to deliver 20 workshops to 400 attendees but in actuality delivered 15 workshops to 225 attendees. Another approach is to compare key outcome measures in two different locations: one that received the program and one that did not. An example is comparing the number of drunk driving violations in two communities: one in which teens participated in drunk-driver workshops and one in which there were no such workshops. A third approach is to compare costs and benefits—for example, comparing the amount of money spent on training employees in new procedures with the savings realized afterward by the use of these procedures. The purpose of these comparisons is to enable reasoned analysis about the results and effectiveness of program activities.

Many professional evaluators have stressed the importance of producing findings that have the greatest possible practical use. They ask, "Who will be the primary consumers of the evaluation findings, and what information do they need about the program? What are the particular aims and objectives of these users?" This approach, known as *utilization evaluation,* suggests that since different users have different needs, the design of any evaluation should be tailored to meet the needs of specific users (Patton, 1997). The range of potential users includes public policymakers, private donors, program managers, project staff, and other stakeholders. The purposes of evaluation are as varied as the users. Besides the broad categories of summative and formative evaluation, the evaluation objectives include impact assessment, project management and planning, and public accountability. Because there is no one simple approach to evaluation that can satisfy all users and all purposes, utilization evaluators argue for a wide range of methodologies that can be selectively applied to diverse situations.

Debates about objectivity and subjectivity within evaluations have an intense history among professional evaluators. The difference between objectivity and subjectivity was primarily seen as a distinction between the use of quantitative and qualitative methodologies. Although this debate still exists, it has largely subsided. Most evaluators today would agree that both qualitative and quantitative methods are valuable and that most evaluations benefit from a mix of the two. Still, experienced evaluators recognize the importance of clearly acknowledging points of vulnerability where subjectivity, or the appearance of subjectivity, might inadvertently creep into an evaluation and take measures to counterbalance it. Such vulnerabilities, and prescribed actions for addressing them, are then described in the methodology section of an evaluation report.

Although the particular approaches of program evaluation vary infinitely depending on the needs of particular users, almost all follow a basic generic format. The following five steps provide an overview for the evaluation process:

1. Define the agenda and identify the key evaluation questions to be answered.
2. Design a plan, identify data sources, select methods, and set a schedule.
3. Collect relevant information according to the evaluation design.
4. Analyze and interpret data to draw conclusions and make recommendations.
5. Disseminate findings.

Program evaluation is typically viewed as an activity to be planned and carried out by external professionals brought in from outside the program. Monitoring is often seen as an internal formative process that is usually carried out by program staff to provide information for ongoing internal assessments. A recent development has been to involve program participants, or beneficiaries, along with other interested stakeholders, in the monitoring process. Participatory monitoring and evaluation (PM&E) is the term that includes this monitoring function (Estrella and Gaventa, 1998). The acronym PM&E is also often used as a shorthand synonym for the more general term *participatory evaluation.*

Participatory Monitoring and Evaluation

Participatory monitoring and evaluation refers to stakeholder involvement in assessing the effectiveness and efficiency of activities planned and carried out by organizations or groups to realize particular goals. Stakeholder involvement usually builds upward from those who are most directly involved in a program or innovation, for example, primary implementers and direct beneficiaries, to others who were less directly involved in the ongoing work being evaluated, for example, personnel who sit at different levels of an implementing agency far away from the actual delivery of program activities.

There is a wide spectrum of approaches for doing PM&E. Variations largely depend on different aims and objectives. A distinction made by some observers divides PM&E into two basic types of evaluation: practical and transformative (Cousins and Whitmore, 1998).

Practical participatory evaluation is based on a utilization perspective that stakeholder participation is the best way to enhance evaluation relevance, ownership, and stakeholder adoption (Patton, 1997). Four outcomes are usually anticipated as a result of practical PM&E activities:

- An increase in stakeholder understanding of the program and insights about its effective implementation
- Enhanced capacity of stakeholders to engage further in future evaluation processes and other program activities
- A greater sense of ownership of the evaluation findings and therefore an increased likelihood that stakeholders will be committed to act on recommendations
- Accountability to other stakeholders by providing information about the degree to which project objectives have been met and resources used

Professional evaluators in most cases will carry out the technical aspects of such evaluations. These tasks include overall responsibility for designing the process, selecting methods, facilitating data collection, overseeing the analysis of data, and writing and presenting the final report. Potential roles for stakeholders might include defining the evaluation topic and interpreting data. Also, evaluators may train stakeholders and involve them directly in the collection of data.

Participatory evaluations are undertaken in all sectors of society, including private business, and they are extensively used in social programs. Based on needs assessments, most social programs are designed to deliver basic services to targeted beneficiaries. Traditionally, staff and management are seen as the primary actors in these programs, while target groups are more or less objects of an intervention. Practical participatory evaluation provides a tool for allowing recipients to become more connected to the program through their involvement in the evaluation process. However, decisions about the degree of beneficiary involvement in the evaluation usually remain in the hands of program management.

Transformative participatory evaluation is a more ideologically driven approach and is fundamentally concerned with issues of control and power. Its intellectual roots include action research originating primarily, but not exclusively, in the developing world. Its aims are far different from those of practical PM&E. Rather than merely improving service delivery within a program, transformative PM&E employs participatory principles for the sake of democratizing social change. It attempts to turn relationships upside down. In transformative PM&E, the beneficiaries—those who are often seen as the "objects" of an intervention—are the primary stakeholders and actors responsible for the evaluation process. Although they may be dependent on professional evaluators and facilitators for training in the initial phases, it is envisioned that as they become more familiar with and sophisticated in the process, they will control all aspects of evaluation, including the generation, ownership, and dissemination of resulting knowledge. This also includes decision making regarding project change and implementation of new strategies. Indeed, it is sometimes difficult within this perspective to distinguish evaluation activities from other ongoing development work.

Rhetoric about transformative PM&E often exceeds its practice. Rather than an either-or relationship, it is perhaps more helpful to see practical and transformative aspects of PM&E on a continuum of aims and objectives. An example is a particular approach called empowerment evaluation (Fetterman, Kaftarian, and Wandersman, 1996) that clearly envisions PM&E in transformative terms. It begins by building on utilitarian aims—increased understanding, sense of ownership, and enhanced capacity among stakeholders—and then moves toward developing the abilities of participants to continue assessment on their own. This is an important step toward realizing, as Fetterman calls it, "participant liberation," that is, release from preexisting roles and constraints. In addition to facilitating the PM&E process, Fetterman encourages evaluators to play a direct advocacy role with policymakers and donors on behalf of a program and its stakeholders. Liberation and advocacy are transformative aims that clearly move well beyond the utilitarian purposes of most practical evaluation.

The degree to which professional facilitators are involved in the practical or transformative facets of participatory evaluation will largely depend on their personal values, priorities, and opportunities. However, these distinctions between practical and transformative facets are important because they help facilitators become more self-conscious as they make decisions about the overall design and underlying purpose of their PM&E activities.

Resources and Methods for PM&E

If determining the aims of a participatory evaluation is the first step in the process, selecting appropriate methods is the second. Many traditional evaluation methods, such as surveys, questionnaires, group interviews, participant observation, and document reviews, are also used in participatory evaluation (Wholey, Hatry, and Newcomer, 1994; Herman, Morris, and Fitz-Gibbon, 1987). The methods themselves are rather neutral in regard to PM&E. Their "participatory" nature largely depends on the degree of stakeholder involvement in their selection, application, and analysis.

There are, however, a number of methods that have been specifically created for use in participatory evaluations. A Venn diagram is one and therefore provides a good example of a PM&E method (Donnelly, 1997). Venn diagrams use overlapping circles to analyze relationships within institutions or between organizations and stakeholders. They can show, for example, different participant perceptions about accessibility or restrictions to resources. Circles of various sizes are cut out of paper and given to participants, who are then asked to use the circles to represent different institutions, groups, or departments, with the size of the circle indicating its perceived importance. By overlapping them or placing them at far distances from each other, they show the degree of contact and interaction between institutions or groups. Reflective discussions with the group after the exercise can then help generate additional qualitative data that are documented for the evaluation.

A Venn diagram is only one of a countless number of methods that are appropriate for conducting participatory evaluations and is mentioned here only as an example. Facilitators can draw on numerous others. An especially valuable resource that describes a large number of unusually innovative methods is *Creative Evaluation* (Patton, 1987). (Though out of print, it is worth a trip to the library or a search on the Internet.) It has an abundance of ideas that will help facilitators design evaluation processes and help stimulate other fresh ideas. Participatory rapid appraisal methods are often used in evaluations (Robinson, 2002). The International Institute of Environment and Development (IIED) has published a series of manuals and workbooks on participatory assessment tools (originally the PLA Notes series and now Participatory Learning and Action series) since 1988. Although these are primarily intended for use in the developing world, they illustrate a large variety of methods that might be adapted to other contexts. The Kellogg Foundation (1998) and UNDP (Donnelly, 1997) have also published valuable resources describing various methods that are especially appropriate for participatory evaluations.

PARTICIPATORY EVALUATION THROUGH STORIES OF CHANGE

The particular approach to PM&E explored here, as applied within different community development programs, consists of a system that has four basic aims and is built around five design features. Central to this system is the identification of stories of change originating with local stakeholders. Exhibit 24.1 provides an example of such stories. Before jumping directly to the stories, however, brief descriptions about the underlying intentions of the programs involved and their relationship to social change set the foundation for the broader context in which these evaluations took place.

Exhibit 24.1
School Renovation in Ovsište: An Example of Stories of Change

Ovsište is a small farming village in the rural municipality of Topola in central Serbia located about 100 kilometers south of Belgrade. According to the municipality census figures of 2002, its population consisted of 628 people and 268 households. Thirty-two children between the ages of six and twelve were registered at the local elementary school in 2002. Based on priorities determined by the community at a local planning meeting in November 2002, a decision was made to renovate the school building. All three classrooms and the administrative office were renovated over a two-month period, with completion occurring in March 2003. This involved floor repair (133 square meters), repair and refinishing of walls (470 square meters), installation of new wall paneling (135 square meters), hanging of five new doors, installation of new rain gutters (125 meters), and renovation of the school's entire electrical system. The total cost was €12,130; €1,180 was raised in cash by the community, €5,450 came from the municipality, and €5,500 came from Topola Rural Development Program (TRDP). The community local action group selected the four most significant changes as a result of this project.

The following stories were discussed and agreed on by the community residents at a quarterly review meeting in March 2003 (Opto International, AB 2003). Effort was made to maintain the original voice of community members.

For the first time in ten years, Ovsište has successfully completed a development project. Several different projects had been started in during the past ten years, but not one of them was ever completed: repair to the water system, renovation of the access road, maintenance work on the health clinic, repairs to the church. Money was even collected from residents for doing many of these things, but still every one of them ended in failure. This time we successfully organized all of the work and properly managed the donations so that the school renovation could be completed. We started and we finished! If someone can't visit our school to see it for themselves, then photographs of the "completion ceremony" are proof of our success.

Importance of this change as viewed by the community: We have pride in what we have accomplished. It makes us think about other things we want to do.

Children now have a more conducive environment for learning. Before, children were easily distracted from their studies because of the condition of the building. Moving their desks to avoid dripping rainwater became a game. The school was full of noise and laughter when they should have been attending to their lessons. The students were also careless about the use of the building and of their educational materials; they simply tracked mud into the building with little regard to the mess it made. Since books and other materials were always becoming wet, students didn't take very good care of them. Now, children are much more careful and remove their muddy shoes before coming in and put their books away. They are no longer distracted and are better able to focus their attention on their studies.

Importance of this change as viewed by the community: Anything that encourages children to be more serious about their studies is important for parents.

We learned practical details about supervising projects during renovation of the school. We were very poor supervisors in the past. Though we contributed money, we did not adequately give attention to how it was used or where it went. Then in the end we were disappointed. In doing this project, we learned a lot of things about making good preparation plans, attracting good contractors, and then overseeing their work. The tender [contractual] guidelines were especially valuable for us since we had never had that kind of experience before. Everyone knew exactly what was happening and why.

Importance of this change as viewed by the community: Without good supervision, nothing happens. We know because we had a lot of past failures due to poor supervision!

Confidence has been gained for launching new development activities. Several years ago we tried to improve our church. When the money we collected disappeared, we became discouraged and quit. Completion of the school has encouraged us to try again on the church. Work is underway now. We are applying lessons learned from the school work; we only pay part of the money at the beginning and will make full payment only after work is completed.

Importance of this change as viewed by the community: People are now ready to do more things together.

Asset-Based Community Development

The PM&E system discussed here is drawn directly from work with three innovative development programs that built on local assets. The first was the Community Empowerment Program (CEP) in central Ethiopia. It involved 309 villages across five districts during a three-and-a-half-year period of operation and was funded by Sida, the Swedish International Development Cooperation Agency (Bergdall and Powell, 1996). The second was the Governance and Local Democracy (GOLD) program in the Philippines. It was funded by the U.S. Agency for International Development (USAID) and involved hundreds of local communities in numerous districts across the country (Bergdall, 1997). Third was the Topola Rural Development Program (TRDP) in central Serbia. It was a municipal development program, also funded by Sida, that included development activities in thirty-two small, outlying rural communities (Opto International AB, 2003).

Asset-based community development focuses on the capacities and strengths of communities and rests on the conviction that sustainable development emerges from within, not from outside, by mobilizing and building on existing resources (Kretzmann and McKnight, 1993). This is in contrast to many community development programs that might be characterized as needs based, that is, focusing on problems and deficiencies and following strategies for injecting various forms of external support. This tends to reinforce a sense of needy people being either passive clients waiting to receive services or hapless victims dependent on the generosity of outsiders for assistance and help. Asset-based development fosters a sense of community residents being active agents of their own development (Giddens, 1987, 1990). This is a role of an engaged citizenship whereby people take charge themselves for planning and initiating proactive steps to respond to the challenges that confront them.

A shared intention in all three programs was to enable a shift in community participation from passive involvement to active engagement. All were about catalyzing change. The PM&E system that emerged from those programs is envisioned as a complement for continuing the transformative process.

Images and the Dynamics of Change

If change and transformation are primary aims of social programs and participatory monitoring and evaluation, then it is important to have a framework for understanding how change occurs.

Behavior, the way people act, is directly connected to how they see themselves in the world, which is a matter of self-perception, self-story, self-image. These are all ways of saying the same thing and are based on a constructionist view of knowledge (Long and Long, 1992). Many have conceptualized such constructions as that of an image (Tye, 1991; Beach, 1990; Cooperrider, 1990; Lazarus, 1977; Polak, 1973). Kenneth Boulding's book, *The Image,* remains a seminal work on the subject (1956). Images are ways of understanding the world and envisioning one's place in it. They occur in connection with multiple reference points: time, space, nature, society, personal relationships, and emotions. "Knowledge, perhaps, is not a good word for this. Perhaps one would rather say my *image* of the world. Knowledge has an implication of validity, of truth. What I am talking about is what I believe to be true; my subjective knowledge" (Boulding, 1956, p. 2). Images, however, are also relevant to presumed scientific truth.

> The scientific method merely stands as one among many of the methods whereby images change and develop. The development of images is part of the culture or subculture in which they are developed, and it depends upon all the elements of that culture or subculture. Science is a subculture among subcultures. It can claim to be useful. It may rather more dubiously claim to be good. It cannot claim to give validity [Boulding, 1956, p. 6].

Images are constructed by individuals; they are also constructed by groups when images are collectively shared and acted on among individuals. These images include self-perceptions that account for attitudes, opinions, ideas, beliefs, and customs. Boulding maintains that the construction of images largely governs the behavior of individuals and groups. This is the second proposition of his image theory: people act in accordance with the images they have of themselves and their place in the world.

Images go through a continual process of change and reconstruction. Most involve minor adjustments as new pieces of information, or "messages" as Boulding calls them, are aligned with an existing image. Messages come in many forms: verbal, visual, and experiential. They also come in varying degrees of strength. For example, while one might read about the negative health effects of fatty foods, a heart attack conveys a much stronger message about the need to act on the information. Most change in behavior is incremental as an image is gradually altered through the accumulation of consistent messages. Radical changes in behavior occur when an established image is replaced by a totally new self-understanding.

Boulding's understanding about knowledge and change can be summarized in five points: (1) people live out of images, (2) images control behavior, (3) images are created by messages, (4) images can change, and (5) when images change, behavior changes.

Aims of PM&E Based on Stories of Change

This approach to participatory evaluation has been applied within programs oriented toward asset-based community development in Ethiopia, Serbia, and the Philippines. It is a modification of similar PM&E work done earlier in Bangladesh (Davies, 1998). These programs have shared four basic aims in regard to participatory evaluation:

- *The primary purpose of PM&E is to enable learning.* The emphasis is more on enhancing proactive practices and improving the ability of community residents to become agents of their own development than on attempting to measure long-term impact. While some indications of outcomes are necessary for such learning to occur, they are not the primary driving force.

- *PM&E is a participatory process that is directly useful to beneficiaries.* Initial data collection, analysis, and responsive action take place at the community level. PM&E work is driven first and foremost by the needs of insiders, that is, community residents, rather than by the needs of outsiders, for example, senior managers, donors, and other interested parties external to the local situation.

- *All stakeholders are tied together in one unifying PM&E conversation.* Both outsiders and insiders have legitimate concerns. An effective PM&E system should encourage issues of concern to all stakeholders to be addressed based on a single body of information that is defined and found to be meaningful and useful by all stakeholders. A single, unifying conversation on these PM&E topics should link these different stakeholders.

- *The PM&E system is to remain relatively simple.* Many approaches to PM&E suffer from unrealistically high ambitions, especially during early stages of design, resulting in overly complex systems. A large amount of information is often included on the unspecified possibility that it might be useful to someone eventually. Overloaded with self-imposed demands to gather, manage, and store data, these ambitious systems repeatedly break down and fall into disuse. A good PM&E design intends to avoid this danger.

Design Features for PM&E and Stories of Change

Consistent with these aims and objectives, the PM&E system based on stories of change is built around five basic design features: (1) quarterly PM&E review meetings with community representatives, (2) PM&E meetings with midlevel stakeholders, (3) involvement of higher-level stakeholders, (4) verification, and (5) feedback.

Quarterly PM&E Review Meetings with Community Stakeholders   Regular community review meetings are the foundational activity of this system. The first meeting usually occurs three months after a communitywide planning event. The review meeting follows these steps:

1. Verbal progress reports by community coordinators that provide objective information about local projects previously prioritized by the community

2. Reflections by participants on the current status of each project, for example, identification of success factors, difficulties encountered in project implementation, and suggestions for ways to overcome difficulties

3. Planning of new implementation activities to complete these projects (or planning new projects if any were completed)

4. Identifying significant changes, based on their own criteria, that have occurred during the past three months

The first step, objective information about progress on the local projects, enables the recording of selective quantitative information. This information simply tracks the accomplishments of community projects (for example, number of wells rehabilitated, total meters of terracing completed, number of tree seedlings planted and distributed) based on whatever the community had prioritized as projects.

The last step, identifying significant changes, is the most innovative aspect of this approach. This involves participants' brainstorming changes that have occurred in the community, selecting the four changes they think are most important, and stating their reasons for making these selections. Participants decide for themselves criteria for making their choices.

The photographs in Exhibit 24.2 are related to the stories of change in Exhibit 24.1. They come from a community in Serbia (Ovsište in the Topola municipality) during a PM&E review meeting in March 2003. The photos show stages of progress on the school renovation project in Ovsište. Photos like these are a good way to enhance other participatory evaluation techniques. The final two pictures in the sequence were taken during the community ceremony to celebrate completion of the project. The portrait on the wall is of Radoje Domanović, a famous nineteenth-century Serbian writer and satirist who was born in the village. When renovations were completed, the school was renamed in his honor.

Exhibit 24.2
School Renovation Activities by Ovsište Community Members

Quarterly PM&E Meetings with Midlevel Stakeholders   Building on these community PM&E review meetings (and the selection of significant stories of change), special PM&E meetings are held during a reporting period when key midlevel stakeholders, for example, district or municipal officials, meet together for an hour or so to review data generated by local communities. The review meeting at this level begins with discussion about statistics compiled from project activities. (Two illustrative tables from the Community Empowerment Program in Ethiopia are found in the appendixes at the end of the chapter.) Tables that summarize substantial quantitative data are very important. Without a reliable compilation of such numbers, stories of change are too easily dismissed as being merely anecdotal. Statistics, which are presented before the stories, help build a credible environment for stakeholders to consider community views about change.

After reviewing overall statistics about project activities, stories of change are passed out. Once midlevel stakeholders have a chance to read the documented stories, the facilitator leads a brief discussion by asking a series of questions like these:

- What reported change surprised you?

- What were you pleased to hear?

- What additional information would you like?

- Where do you have doubts about the reliability of some of these reports?

- What do all of these changes add up to? What does it all mean?

- What effect do you think this will have on overall development within the district?

- What can various stakeholders do to support communities in their development process?

After a fifteen- or twenty-minute discussion on these questions, participants are asked to select the four reported changes that they consider to be the most important. They too are asked to state their reasons about why they made the selections they did. The mayor and chairman of the municipal council in Topola reviewed progress reports from five communities on the day they discussed stories of change from Ovsište (a total of twenty stories). They selected "confidence has been gained for launching new development activities" as the change they thought was the most important from Ovsište. The reason for their selection was that "this shows that local action is now taking place as a continuous ongoing activity within the community" (Opto International AB. 2003).

Annual PM&E Meetings with Higher-Level Stakeholders   Changes selected by midlevel stakeholders are then compiled so that the entire process can be repeated at the next level. The selection process ensures that a manageable number of stories, usually about twenty, are presented to a group of stakeholders at any one time. The highest level of stakeholders might eventually include senior managers and representatives from relevant donor organizations. PM&E meetings at this level usually occur only once a year. By the nature of the selection process, the changes filtering up through the different levels are the most significant across the entire program.

The entire selection process from CEP in Ethiopia is provided in Exhibit 24.3. It depicts the relationship of selected stories of change moving from level to level and

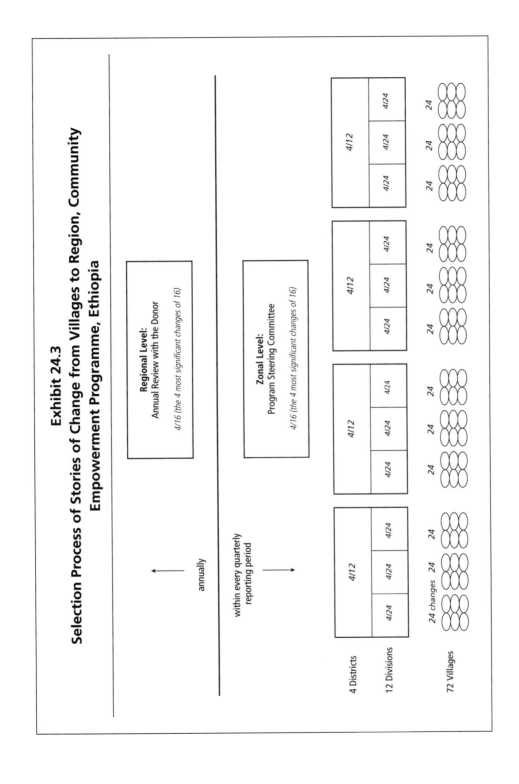

Exhibit 24.3
Selection Process of Stories of Change from Villages to Region, Community Empowerment Programme, Ethiopia

is based on the PM&E in Ethiopia (Bergdall and Powell, 1996). Building from the bottom up, 288 stories of changes (4 per village) were identified by villagers during a single reporting period. They form the foundation for a review process through different levels of stakeholders. The four changes considered to be the most significant at one level are forwarded up to the next level.

Verification   Stakeholders outside the community are also asked to choose reported changes, perhaps only one or two, which they feel need verification. This is especially important if any skepticism remains among these stakeholders. This was the case in Ethiopia, where most government officials firmly believed that "poor peasants" did not have the skills or the motivation to do development activities based on their "meager" resources. Verification visits not only help to build midlevel stakeholders' confidence about the reliability of PM&E reports, they also provide an opportunity for these stakeholders to become directly familiar with events taking place in the field through face-to-face encounters. Similarly, when quantitative information is reported during community PM&E review meetings, physical inspections are made by program staff to verify the numbers reported. Awareness that midlevel stakeholders might eventually select one of their communities for a verification trip tends to ensure accuracy in quantitative data because most staff members want to avoid potential embarrassment.

Feedback   After all stories of change have filtered their way up the PM&E system, feedback begins a journey back down through the chain by the use of memos and group discussions. Selections of the four significant changes made at the higher levels are reported to the communities during the next quarterly community review meetings. This provides a practical learning opportunity for local people in several ways. First, community members come to realize that their initiatives were recognized and that serious attention was paid to their grassroots efforts. Second, they learn what program effects higher-level stakeholders valued most and why. Third, they gain information about what other communities are doing, which enriches their own discussions as they plan future projects. The feedback process thereby closes the monitoring loop, tying together all levels of stakeholders into one unified conversation.

Reflections about PM&E Based on Stories of Change

The PM&E process of regularly reviewing progress on local initiatives, discussing lessons learned, making new plans, and then reflecting together on accomplishments and change can be a deeply profound experience for a community. These PM&E events provide a practical opportunity for groups to become self-conscious about their latent power. This was certainly the case in Ovsište; one can easily imagine their excitement as they rehearsed and reveled in their accomplishment. Such discussions enable groups to build a larger story for themselves about who they are as a group and what they can accomplish through their own concerted efforts. These are all based on strong experiential messages that have the potential to alter images dramatically. Ultimately, this is the key to long-term changes in behavior. Therefore, this PM&E approach, with its emphasis on stories of change, is transformative.

The system uses a highly inductive approach in which indicative changes become the basis for drawing conclusions about results. This is valuable when objectives of community development include ideas like increased participation, self-confidence, local responsibility, capacity for problem-solving, and transparency. Such benefits are extremely difficult to evaluate. Rather than being confined to a narrow range of predetermined indicators, this approach is flexible and adaptive to changing circumstances. Of course, it is in sharp contrast to conventional monitoring approaches that are deductive in orientation, begin with a theoretical idea about intended results identified by experts far from the locus of activity, and then attempt to identify indicators of its occurrence (Davies, 1998).

It gives those closest to the activity being monitored, in this case community residents, the opportunity to guide the process by making their choices and interpretations at the beginning of the process rather than at the end. External officials and senior program managers are put into the position of responding to explanations generated from below. Consistent with the aims of community development, the basic monitoring agenda is thereby established from the bottom rather than the top. However, its participatory nature is not limited to the communities; all stakeholders are effectively tied into a single unifying PM&E conversation.

The retelling of stories about selected changes has a modeling effect within communities. Such changes tend to be stories about success, focusing on positive results rather than negative shortcomings. Through feedback mechanisms, best practices are highlighted and become the primary subject of reflection and appraisal by all stakeholders. The monitoring work thereby becomes a direct contributor to institutional learning at every level of the project.

Possible Uses of Stories of Change in Other Settings

Although this PM&E system has been created and used primarily in international development, it should be easily adaptable to any situation where subgroups are working within a large setting, be they different geographical locations of a company or different departments or sections of a public agency housed in a single building.

Stories of change are also applicable for PM&E of facilitated processes themselves, especially when there is an interest, or a demand, to provide some data on the ultimate impact of such processes. The initial brainstorm about the changes participants have experienced need not be general. In a systematic way, specific topics might be stipulated. Instead of asking a group to come up with four selected changes in an open-ended manner, groups can be asked to make a selection within particular areas—for example, "What are the most important changes that have occurred in the following areas? As a group, choose one change each in the areas of team effectiveness, group initiative and responsibility, capacity for problem solving, transparency in decision making, creativity, and self-confidence?"

By systematically collecting data in these areas, along with stated reasons about why choices were made, a wealth of information is available for drawing conclusions. A mechanism for involving stakeholders from other levels in a review of the stories and providing feedback on their thoughts enables various stakeholders to become involved in a common dialogue. Collective knowledge about the significance of facilitated processes is thereby generated and is shared throughout the organization. PM&E based on stories of change can provide a practical means for enabling institutional learning on any initiative or program.

APPENDIX 24A: PM&E IN THE COMMUNITY EMPOWERMENT PROGRAMME, ETHIOPIA

The Community Empowerment Programme (CEP) took place in five districts, or *woredas,* in central Ethiopia. The only support that CEP offered was the facilitation of community planning workshops (CPW) where members of local *kires,* or

villages, met to discuss issues and plan local projects based exclusively on local resources. The tables are quantitative summaries of work in 309 villages. The story
that follows is one of 288 that was documented during one PM&E reporting
period:

> In Jebukie kire in Legehida . . . prior to the CPW the work on clearing
> springs was done only when clearing was very desperately needed; even
> then only a minimum amount of work was done. Additionally, no
> fences were ever built nor had any repair been done. After the CPW,
> however, we tried to work harder. The work on the springs involved
> both the construction of fences and continuous follow-up. An exam-
> ple of follow-up by the community was when it was noticed that some
> pieces of wood had been stolen from the fences around the spring we
> had built and reported this to the *kire* leader. The *kire* leader then called
> an *afersata* [judicial meeting] to investigate the crime and the crimi-
> nal was found. Then we were able to return back the pieces of wood
> to the *kire* as a result of the *afersata,* and the spring fence was repaired.
>
> *Why selected by the woreda officials:* From this we can see that the
> people understand that they are responsible for their own develop-
> ment. It indicates that they really feel a sense of ownership in what they
> planned and accomplished [Bergdall and Powell, 1996, p. 68].

Community Empowerment Programme Workshop Numbers and Attendance Figures

Final Database Figures, 15 November 1996		Debra Sina	Legambo	Saint	Woreilu and Kelala	Totals
CPW	Number of workshops	76	81	81	71	309
	Attendance	9,493	7,531	10,211	5,099	32,334
F/U-1	Number of workshops	62	70	68	62	263
	Attendance	6,003	3,971	7,438	3,581	20,993

Final Database Figures, 15 November 1996		Debra Sina	Legambo	Saint	Woreilu and Kelala	Totals
F/U-2	Number of workshops	47	55	56	46	204
	Attendance	4,226	2,730	5,843	2,810	15,609
F/U-3	Number of workshops	42	44	47	30	163
	Attendance	3,380	2,054	4,653	1,670	11,757
Totals	Number of workshops	*227*	*250*	*252*	*209*	*938*
	Attendance[a]	23,102	16,286	28,145	13,160	80,693

Source: Bergdall and Powell 1996)

[a]Women 24,543 (30 percent); youth 18,678 (23 percent); men 37,472 (46 percent).

COMMUNITY EMPOWERMENT PROGRAMME QUANTITATIVE ACCOMPLISHMENTS, FINAL DATABASE FIGURES THROUGH 15 NOVEMBER 1996

ACTIVITIES	Debra Sina (76 *kires*)	Legambo (81 *kires*)	Saint (81 *kires*)	Woreilu and Kelala (71 *kires*)	Totals
Tree planting (number)	315,150	1,020,300	419,222	605,500	2,360,172
Terracing (kilometers)	196	67.90	200	11	475
Spring clearing/ protection (number)	428	528	698	228	1,882
Spring development (number)	43	10	9	9	71

ACTIVITIES	Debra Sina (76 *kires*)	Legambo (81 *kires*)	Saint (81 *kires*)	Woreilu and Kelala (71 *kires*)	Totals
Footpath construction (kilometers)	85	7	10	1	103
Footpath maintenance/ repair (kilometers)	69	35	109	26	240
Checkdam construction (kilometers)	68	6	15	1	90
Unabled house construction (number)	28	18	56	14	116
Unabled house repair (number)	14	7	44	12	77
Agricultural assistance for unabled (hectares)	1	12	54	59	126
Diversion canal construction (kilometers)	49	34	32	9	125
Diversion canal maintenance (kilometers)	16	26	21	17	79
New irrigation schemes (hectares)	72	194	97	49	412
New income-generating activities (number)	3	108	102	33	246
Raising local seedlings (number)	253,500	801,110	941,002	884,000	2,879,612
Church/mosque construction/repair (number)	17	11	73	10	111
New pit latrines (number)	0	6	0	33	39
New local savings schemes (number)	0	3	3	0	6

Note: Kires refer to the community groupings in villages that served as the basic operational units around which the Community Empowerment Programme was organized. *Woredas* is the word used in Ethiopia for districts.

Source: Bergdall and Powell (1996).

APPENDIX 24B: AN EXAMPLE OF STORIES OF CHANGE FROM THE PHILIPPINES

Following are the four stories of change that a community in the Philippines identified during a Barangay Development Council meeting in October 1997 (Bergdall, 1997). Barangays are the lowest level of government administration in the Philippines, like a precinct, and are similar to villages. The PM&E exercise was within the Governance and Local Democracy Project (GOLD) funded by USAID. One of the primary aims of GOLD was to conduct communitywide planning workshops so that local communities could collectively prioritize and plan local projects. Instead of a small grants program, GOLD enabled communities to budget small capitalization funds, which were redistributed to local communities from the central government's tax revenues. The following stories of change are from the Nagbitin Barangay of the Villa Verde municipality in the Nueva Vizcaya province.

The community now has a "structured guide" to follow for its planning. In the past, planning was only done by a few leaders and it was often haphazardly based on personal favoritism. Most people in the community did not understand how projects were planned and were not consulted about their views. Now, since the "planning and budgeting workshop," people know about the projects, understand the priorities, and are aware about progress in implementation—or reasons for delay. Consultation has been widespread and everyone now stands behind the community plans. The extraordinary efforts to successfully raise money from community members to complete the multi-purpose slab (that is, a paved area in the center of the community for basketball, which is the national sport in the Philippines, and other community activities) in time for the November fiesta is an example of what has happened because of the new approach to planning: people understood why there were limited community funds and acted to solve the problem.

Reason selected by the community: People have come to realize that everyone can and should be involved in community planning.

Community leaders are serving the community better. Before, community leaders tended to have a narrow political view of their role and often made decisions based more on personal connections than on community-wide development needs. This also often resulted in the chairman being the primary person in charge: he was the one who made major decisions and assigned people to do particular work. If things went wrong, the chairman was always blamed. Now, development priorities planned by the community are the focus of work and many people are assuming responsibility for agreed upon projects—everyone shares in their success or failure. Outside visitors can see this change by reviewing the budget plan and talking to community members about their knowledge of the plans.

Reason selected by the community: Leaders have a better understanding about their proper functions in participatory development planning and are making sacrifices to serve.

Greater transparency in managing development funds has minimized perceptions of corruption. Before, very few people knew details about development money used in the community. They didn't know how much money was available or how it was used. Now, because of the planning, all projects are known as well as the amounts and sources committed for each. Expenditures are reported to the community in ways they can easily understand and appreciate. Evidence of this change can be seen by viewing the written reports and financial records which are now kept in an orderly way at the community office (written records were not kept before).

Reason selected by the community: People can see practical results from the use of development funds.

Improved access to health services. Before, people could not depend upon local health services because they didn't know where or when to go since no regular schedule was maintained. Mothers would have to waste a lot of time and money going to the clinic in town. Construction of the community health center was made a high priority during the "planning and budgeting workshop." Work has since completed and the center was opened in the past year. Now a regular schedule is maintained by health workers: community members know when and where they can go for immunizations and other assistance. Still there are problems with shortages of medicines, but people no longer have to waste time and money to travel long distances for basic health care. This change can be seen by visiting the health center.

Reason selected by the community: Maintaining good health for the family is one of the most important responsibilities a parent has which means the health center has been a high priority for the community.

APPENDIX 24C: FACILITATING GROUPS AND DOCUMENTING STORIES OF CHANGE

The following procedures provide guidelines for facilitating PM&E Review Meetings with communities participating in the Topola Rural Development Program (Opto 2002).

At three intervals—project commencement, project completion, and six months after completion—facilitators will meet with local project management groups to review progress of local initiatives planned by the community and to spell out next steps. The second and third of these meetings will also provide an opportunity for community residents to reflect on changes that have occurred since becoming involved with the Topola Rural Development Program. Four basic steps are involved in this process: 1) a group brainstorm on changes, 2) selecting the four most important changes, 3) deeper "probing" to more fully understand the selected changes, and 4) documenting four selected changes for monitoring and evaluation (M&E) efforts of the project with other stakeholders.

Step 1: A Brainstorm of Changes by the "Project Management Group"

Members of the group are asked to brainstorm "significant changes" which have occurred since the commencement of the project (or since the last time they did a group reflection on "significant change"). Phrasing the question so that it can be easily understood in Serbian language is crucial. By asking this question, we are attempting to enable participants to think about things that have happened which they think are *important*. The question needs to be phrased in order to broaden the group's thinking. Variations in ways to phrase the question might include the following:

- What changes have occurred?
- What have been key accomplishments?
- How have things improved because of the project?
- What difference has the project made in the quality of life for local residents?

In generating the brainstorm, all of these questions can be asked. List these "changes" on a piece of flip chart paper displayed at the front of the room (i.e., a "template").

Step 2: Selecting the Four Most Important Changes

After a list has been created with several ideas, the facilitator then asks the group to select four. However, instead of making general selections, the facilitator provides categories for making choices. What has been the most important change in regards to:

- Decision-making in the community?
- Practical benefits resulting from completion of the particular project?
- Trust and co-operation among people benefiting from the project?
- Any other change (an undesignated category)?

The facilitator lists the four categories on a piece of flip chart paper and explains them all before the group makes its selections. After making this introduction, the group is asked to make it selections (one per category).

Step 3: Deeper "Probing" to More Fully Understand the Selected Changes

After making their four selections, the facilitators need to ask some additional questions to more fully understand the nature of the changes selected and to assist in the documentation. The following questions need to be asked for each of the selected changes:

- What was the situation like *before* this change (or accomplishment)?
- How is the situation different *now*?
- What is an *example* or illustration about this change which you would show (or tell) a visitor as evidence of this change?
- Why is this change important? What is the *reason* for your selection?

A simple template can be created to enable this discussion. It might look like the table on the next page (with the four selected changes placed in the four left-hand boxes).

Step 4: Documenting the Four Selected Changes

At the end of the workshop, the facilitator responsible for documenting the proceedings needs to write paragraphs for each of these four changes. A title phrase or sentence is written to broadly describe the change. A sentence or two then describes the situation "before," a sentence or two describes the situation "now," and a sentence or two describes the "example" of the change. Finally, the reason the community selected this change is added as a separate explanation after the paragraph on "before, now, and an example" of the change.

In writing the paragraph, the facilitator tries to remain as faithful to the actual words used by the community members while also being descriptive enough that other readers outside of the project can understand as much as possible about the perceived importance of the selected change. Once a draft has been prepared, these are reviewed by community residents; modifications are made as needed to accurately reflect the community's views.

Type of Change	Before	Now	Example	Reason Selected
Selected change about decision-making				
Selected change about the benefit of local projects				
Selected change about trust and co-operation				
Selection about another important change				

Assessing the Effectiveness of Group Decision Processes

John Rohrbaugh

The achievement of continuous improvement has become a key goal for many organizations over the past few decades, creating ever greater need for better forms of performance measurement (Friedlob, Schleifer, and Plewa, 2002; Meyer, 2002; Neely, 2002; Poister, 2003). Although the availability of useful information about organizational performance has increased markedly during this period, continuous improvement in the decision-making processes of management teams has lagged. As a result, the redirection of organizational resources for improved performance has been less than optimal, not because of the lack of relevant information but because of ineffective group problem solving.

With considerable attention being devoted to performance at the organizational level, assessment of group decision process effectiveness generally has been overlooked. That organizational performance depends largely on group performance—especially in critical choices about resource reallocations—is frequently overlooked (Rohrbaugh, 1985). In fact, ineffectiveness in group processes can be extremely costly to organizations, not merely because of unproductive meeting time. There also can be substantially larger opportunity costs resulting from the near impossibility of making smart decisions—such as optimal reallocations of organizational resources—while simultaneously coping with the challenges of participant interactions.

Innovative methods for improving resource reallocations by combining the methods of group facilitation and decision science (see, for example, the use of decision conferencing, Milter and Rohrbaugh, 1985; Rohrbaugh, 1992, 2000) have been projected to produce returns on investment of over 1,000 percent (Meyer and Boone, 1987).

GROUP PERFORMANCE MEASUREMENT

Contemporary standards for performance measurement at both the organizational and group levels were well anticipated by the theory-building work of the sociologist Talcott Parsons (1959; Hare, 1976). Parsons proposed that there are four key functions of any collectivity (or system of action): pattern maintenance, integration, adaptation, and goal attainment. The essential nature of these four functions—and their appropriate balance—has been the emphasis of the competing values approach to organizational analysis (Quinn and Rohrbaugh, 1983; Rohrbaugh, 1983). At the group level, in particular, the competing values approach has been used to identify four domains of collective performance that parallel Parsons's functions: consensual, empirical, political, and rational (Rohrbaugh, 1987, 1989). An illustration of this framework is shown in Exhibit 25.1.

The measurement of group performance from a consensual perspective (that is, emphasis on achieving the pattern maintenance function) focuses on full participation in meetings, with open expression of individual feelings and sentiments. Extended discussion and debate about conflicting concerns should lead to collective agreement on a mutually satisfactory solution. As a result, the likelihood of support for the decision during implementation would be increased through such team building. This very interpersonally oriented perspective is dominant in the field of organization development.

Evaluators of collective decision processes who take an empirical perspective (that is, emphasis on achieving the integration function) stress the importance of documentation. Particular attention is directed in this performance measurement approach to the ways in which groups secure and share relevant information and develop comprehensive, reliable databases to provide appropriate forms of decision support. Proponents of this perspective, typically trained in the physical and social sciences (especially management information systems) believe that, to be effective, a group decision process should allow thorough use of evidence and full accountability.

The political perspective (that is, emphasis on achieving the adaptation function) suggests an approach to performance measurement where group flexibility

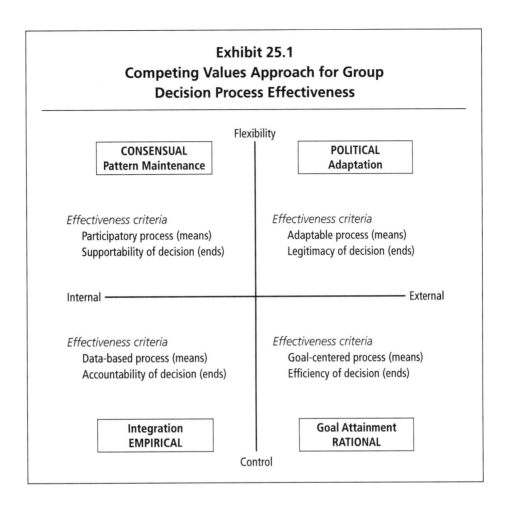

Exhibit 25.1
Competing Values Approach for Group Decision Process Effectiveness

Flexibility

| CONSENSUAL | POLITICAL |
| Pattern Maintenance | Adaptation |

Effectiveness criteria
Participatory process (means)
Supportability of decision (ends)

Effectiveness criteria
Adaptable process (means)
Legitimacy of decision (ends)

Internal ———————————————————— External

Effectiveness criteria
Data-based process (means)
Accountability of decision (ends)

Effectiveness criteria
Goal-centered process (means)
Efficiency of decision (ends)

| Integration | Goal Attainment |
| EMPIRICAL | RATIONAL |

Control

and creativity are the paramount process attributes. Idea generation through brainstorming would be assessed on how attuned participants are to shifts in the problem environment and on how well the standing of the group is maintained or enhanced. The search for legitimacy of the decision—its acceptability to outside stakeholders who are not immediate participants but whose interests potentially are affected by the group's deliberations—would be notable through a fully responsive, dynamic process.

The priority of clear thinking as the primary ingredient for effective decision making is the hallmark of the rational perspective (that is, emphasis on achieving the goal attainment function). From this very task-oriented approach (particularly common in management science and operations research), any decision process should be directed by explicit recognition of organizational goals and objectives. Methods that efficiently assist decision makers as planners by improving the consistency and coherency of their logic and reasoning would yield positive group performance measurements.

A brief diagnostic instrument has been developed and tested rather thoroughly over the past decade that incorporates all four perspectives for group assessment (consensual, empirical, political, and rational) and enables performance measurement at the group level consistent with the four domains of the competing values framework (Reagan and Rohrbaugh, 1990; McCartt and Rohrbaugh, 1995; Wright and Rohrbaugh, 1999). This questionnaire uses thirty-two items to measure such aspects as level of participation, supportability, accountability, adaptability, legitimacy, and efficiency. Thus, the effectiveness of group processes is measured simultaneously against several key—and sometimes competing—performance standards. For example, is the process fully participatory yet efficient? Do participants feel that they can work on a problem flexibly yet maintain full accountability? Effective groups transcend the seemingly competing nature of these performance standards by using facilitation methods that do not require trade-offs but instead accomplish multiple process objectives simultaneously.

The spirit of continuous improvement demands that the measurement of group process effectiveness becomes an ongoing and explicit evaluation by a variety of participants, not just one person, over a variety of decisions, not just one problem (Wright and Rohrbaugh, 1999). Without performance measurement at the group level, organizations will not learn how to reallocate resources better. The avoidance of directly monitoring group process effectiveness by taking a wait-and-see approach that relies solely on subsequent decision outcomes is risky on at least three counts.

First, the time lag required to note any positive or negative consequences of collective action is far too long. Weaknesses in group performance should be remediated quickly, well before long-term results are apparent. Second, it is difficult to establish a causal connection between immediate group decision and subsequent organizational performance. Implementation difficulties that defy anticipation can lead organizations to forgo gains from even the best group decisions, not to mention that external conditions—political and economic—can intervene to worsen outcomes. Conversely, organizational stakeholders can be blissfully unaware of poorly performing executive teams if a temporarily beneficent environment masks even badly flawed processes. Third, any performance assessment based on conse-quences alone gives little or no indication of the process factors that need en-hancement or change. What went wrong in those meetings? We still would need to focus on the strengths and weaknesses of the problem-solving process.

ORGANIZATIONAL CONDITIONS THAT AFFECT GROUP DECISION PROCESSES

Much attention has been given to identifying organizational conditions that are conducive to—or seriously undermine—group decision process effectiveness (see, for example, Hackman, 1990; Senge, 1990; Bennis and Biderman, 1997). Groups do not perform in a vacuum; interaction processes are greatly influenced by their behavioral settings (McGrath, 1984). It may be instructive to consider such key or-ganizational conditions in the context of the competing values framework.

As shown in Exhibit 25.2, the ability of a group to function in pattern mainte-nance requires consensual support. Organizational conditions that undermine pat-tern maintenance are intolerance of alternative perspectives, no belief that the problem is important, conflicts dividing the group into factions, and deceitful and suspicious members. Organizational conditions providing consensual support are genuine openness to others' viewpoints, highly motivated and conscientious participants, constructive use of conflict, and participants who are sincere and pro-mote interpersonal trust.

To function in a more integrated way, groups require empirical support. Orga-nizational conditions that undermine integration are group members who have not taken the time to think about the problem or lack essential expertise, the absence of critically relevant information, and inaccessible or inappropriate information technologies. Organizational conditions providing empirical support are group members with all necessary expertise and a good understanding of the problem, useful information that is readily available, and easy access to appropri-ate information technologies.

Political support is essential for groups to function adaptively. Organizational conditions that undermine adaptation are highly homogeneous group composi-tion, participants who have problem-solving responsibility but no authority (that is, they must always receive directions from superiors), absence of delegated or emergent leadership (that is, no one owns the problem), and too short a time

Flexibility

| CONSENSUAL SUPPORT | POLITICAL SUPPORT |
| Pattern Maintenance | Adaptation |

Genuine openness to others' viewpoints

Highly motivated and conscientious participants

Constructive use of conflict

Sincere participants who promote trust

Presence of a legitimate group leader

Participants who represent diverse stakeholders

Participants who have authority to make decisions

Adequate time to complete all group work

Internal ———————————————————— External

Participants with all of the necessary expertise

Participants who well understand the problem

Useful information that is readily available

Easy access to appropriate information technology

Meeting room environment fostering productivity

A clear definition of the problem

Capacity to use appropriate problem-solving methods

Access to group facilitation expertise

| Integration | Goal Attainment |
| EMPIRICAL SUPPORT | RATIONAL SUPPORT |

Control

period to ensure success. Organizational conditions providing political support are the presence of a legitimate group leader, participants who represent diverse stakeholders, participants who have the authority to make decisions themselves, and adequate time to complete all group work.

Surprisingly, organizations often do not provide even rational support to groups that would allow them to attain their goals. Organizational conditions that undermine goal attainment are uncomfortable meeting rooms with many distractions, poorly defined problems, lack of training about useful problem-solving techniques, and the absence of skillful group facilitation. Organizational conditions providing rational support are a meeting room environment that fosters productivity, a clear definition of the problem, capacity to use appropriate problem-solving methods, and access to group facilitation expertise (Rangarajan and Rohrbaugh, 2003).

CONCLUSION

Performance measurement should be guided by sound theory such as Parsons's articulation of four organizational functions (1959): pattern maintenance, integration, adaptation, and goal attainment. Relatively thorough methods of performance measurement have been developed, tested, and applied to group decision processes over the past twenty years. Continuous improvement in organizational decision making—and, in fact, in the capacity of organizations to reallocate resources optimally—depends on the routine use of these process assessments at the group level.

The difficulties that must be confronted in improving group decision processes often stem from organizational conditions that more broadly undermine group effectiveness. Changing these conditions so that group decision processes are better supported is essential. This chapter has indicated key links between such organizational conditions and the limited or enhanced capacity of groups to perform more effectively, whether one's evaluative perspective is primarily consensual, empirical, political, or rational.

PART FIVE

Build and Maintain Professional Knowledge

1. Maintain a base of knowledge.

- Knowledgeable in management, organizational systems and development, group development, psychology, and conflict resolution
- Understands dynamics of change
- Understands learning and thinking theory

2. Know a range of facilitation methods.

- Understands problem-solving and decision-making models
- Understands a variety of group methods and techniques
- Knows consequences of misuse of group methods
- Distinguishes process from task and content
- Learns new processes, methods, and models in support of client's changing and emerging needs

3. Maintain professional standing.

- Engages in ongoing study and learning related to our field
- Continuously gains awareness of new information in our profession
- Practices reflection and learning
- Builds personal industry knowledge and networks
- Maintains certification

Facilitator Core Competencies as Defined by the International Association of Facilitators

Lynda Lieberman Baker
Cameron Fraser

Modern organizations, whether corporate, government, or nonowned (commonly referred to as nongovernmental organizations or nonprofits), increasingly face the challenge of responding to rapidly changing circumstances. These same organizations are often expected to involve stakeholders in decision-making processes, making any such process more complex and difficult to manage. These two challenges are often at odds with each other, the former requiring speed and agility and the latter requiring time and patience. The increased need for timely collaborative problem solving and participatory decision making in businesses, organizations, and communities worldwide has led to an increase in the use of group facilitators to support those processes.

Note: We acknowledge the tireless efforts of our colleagues who conceived, built, and continue to maintain the IAF professional certification program and also those who gave feedback to us on the early drafts of this chapter.

459

Anecdotally, facilitators are known to increase the efficiency of people working in groups, helping them accomplish more work—in quality or quantity—in a given period of time. In turn, this has led to a growing public awareness of facilitation as a profession. As the profession is coming of age, so too is the need to define its standards of performance. What exactly is the role and function of the group facilitator?

The International Association of Facilitators (IAF), whose mission is to promote, support, and advance the art and practice of facilitation, has undertaken the task of defining the essential qualities of a professional facilitator to help facilitators perfect their practice, as well as serve prospective clients by clarifying expectations of a facilitator's performance. Defining the knowledge, skills, and attitudes that enable a facilitator to function effectively is essential to anyone who wishes to become a competent facilitator as well as to those seeking the services of one. This chapter describes the evolution of the association's system to define and find evidence of facilitator core competencies. In addition, it highlights the current core competency certification process.

DEFINING COMPETENCIES

The word *competency* is derived from the Latin *competere,* meaning "to be suitable." The competency concept, originally developed in the field of psychology to denote an individual's ability to respond to demands placed on him or her by the environment, is now applied in a variety of business contexts (see Rao, 2003). As articulated in the American Society for Training and Development report *Models for Excellence: The Conclusions and Recommendations of the ASTD Training and Development Competency Study* (1983), a competency model portrays the repertoire of skills, abilities, and personal qualities as they relate to the specific demands of a certain job. Once defined, competency assessment refers to the process through which the competencies of an individual are matched to the model.

Malcolm Knowles, often referred to as the father of adult education, provided an overview of several ways in which competency models can be constructed—for example, through research, expert judgment, task analysis, and group participation (Knowles, 1980). All of these methods, to varying degrees, were employed by IAF to define the competency model for group facilitation.

History of IAF Competency Modeling

The IAF, established in 1994, was initiated and created by individuals from the Institute of Cultural Affairs (ICA), a global network of nonprofit organizations implementing social change in thirty-six countries around the world. A core component of their work for more than twenty years has been teaching people how to create a culture of participation through the use of facilitation methods. Consequently, while many facilitators had given thought to competency models as applied to their own training programs of facilitation work, ICA facilitators, consultants, and trainers, along with new IAF members, were among the first to work on clarifying facilitator core competencies across a range of organizations.

Not long after the creation of the professional association, its members set out to define the contemporary professional field of facilitation and the competencies required to practice in it. In June 1995, a task force undertook the initiative. It reviewed the literature, performed task analyses, and obtained feedback from IAF conference attendees, individuals trained in facilitation by the ICA, as well as those qualified to teach ICA's Technology of Participation (ToP) methods. Initially five hundred ideas were synthesized into twenty-seven groups and then further refined into seven areas of competence (J. Nelson, e-mail to the author, Nov. 28, 2003).

IAF's final competency model consisted of eighteen competencies organized in six categories: Engage in Professional Growth, Create Collaborative Partnerships, Create an Environment of Participation, Utilize Multi-Sensory Approaches, Orchestrate the Group Journey, and Commit to a Life of Integrity. Each competency was further detailed with three to four examples of how that competency could be demonstrated. The work of the task force and the resulting competency model was published in 2000 (Pierce, Cheesbrow, and Brau, 2000). In addition, the journal editorial team solicited critical comments from selected individuals involved in facilitator training or active in IAF's professional development activities (Kirk, Schwarz, Tahar, and Wilkinson, 2000).

Competency Certification Launched in the United Kingdom

In 1998, the IAF Professional Development Task Force approved the initiation of a certification scheme under the auspices of a team of IAF members in Europe (see Kirk's comments in Kirk, Schwarz, Tahar, and Wilkinson, 2000).

Using an earlier version of the competencies and through the leadership of active IAF members, Facilitator Accreditation Services Ltd. (FAS) was established in the United Kingdom to develop and manage the certification program for IAF as the certification body.

The IAF program developed by FAS used standard methods of examination for professional certification programs, such as portfolio submission and performance observation in a simulation (National Organization of Competency Assurance, 1996). These techniques were supplemented with face-to-face interviews.

In addition to creating the format for assessing facilitator competencies, a parallel competency model was developed for assessors of those facilitator competencies. As a prerequisite, all of the assessor candidates were required to earn their IAF Certified Professional Facilitator (CPF) designation prior to being considered as assessors. In addition, they demonstrated the distinctly different set of competencies in the areas of conduct of interviews, observation, assessing competency, and documentation, along with a strong value of collaboration. Assessors are required to keep their certification and IAF membership active.

THE COMPETENCIES

The competency assessment program was based on a "pass or defer" threshold rather than a graduated scale of proficiency. Assessors looked for evidence of each of the competencies. In the absence of evidence or in the case of contrary evidence, individuals were deferred rather than failed. Those deferred were provided specific feedback regarding their observed behavior.

Assessors focused on seeking evidence of core, not advanced, levels of competence. The assessment was designed to ensure the candidates were given the best opportunity possible to display their competence and provide feedback to them that might help them improve their future performance. The competencies assessed by the program were Managing the Event, Managing the Process, Managing Groups and Individuals, Managing One's Learning, and Managing Oneself.

After four years, the IAF board of directors decided to manage the certification program internally. They appointed a director of operations from among the accredited assessors and contracted with an administrator to manage the certification program.

In early 2003, all assessors were invited to participate in a program called Project Refresh. The purpose was to create a program that would increase IAF ownership and rights. As a starting point, the assessors referred back to the previously published competencies (Pierce, Cheesbrow, and Brau, 2000). Their work resulted in a revised competency set:

- Create collaborative client relationships.
- Plan appropriate group processes.
- Create and sustain a participatory environment.
- Guide group to appropriate and useful outcomes.
- Build and maintain professional knowledge.
- Model positive professional attitude.

The IAF Facilitator Core Competencies are described in detail in the appendix at the end of the chapter. What do they actually look like in practice? How might a facilitator evidence them?

Create Collaborative Client Relationships

This competency is about effectively establishing and managing the relationship with the client group. An early article by Stanfield (1994), "The Magic of the Facilitator," aptly described this competency as the facilitator's ability to carefully manage the client relationship and prepare thoroughly. This competency includes facilitating planning sessions with the client or planning team; offering a variety of methods or format options for the client to consider; negotiating roles and responsibilities before, during, and after the meeting; and documenting the agreed-on desired outcomes.

Plan Appropriate Group Processes

This competency requires the facilitator to be familiar with a variety of group processes, methods, and techniques; draws on them appropriately to meet specific client needs; and ensure there is adequate time for their implementation.

Create and Sustain a Participatory Environment

Stanfield (1994) describes this competency in terms of the facilitator's ability to evoke participation, appeal to participant imagination, and encourage boldness. This requires creativity on the part of the facilitator as well as a strong belief in the value of participation. "The facilitator knows how to elicit the latent wisdom in the group, involving the whole group in taking responsibility for its own decisions."

Evidence of this competency may include the use of structured activities to engage participation or build rapport. It may also be important to vary the types of activities so that they appeal to people with a wide variety of learning, personality, or communication styles.

Guide the Group to Appropriate and Useful Outcomes

This competency addresses the facilitator's awareness of and responsibility to the group's bottom line. It requires that the facilitator keep an eye on the group's goals and help the group stay focused on the task. At a basic level, this may mean nothing more than managing distraction; at a more sophisticated level, it means managing competing interests and issues unique to each individual in the group. A competent facilitator does so by adapting to a wide variety of unexpected situations to help the group effectively manage interfering issues that might arise along the way.

Build and Maintain Professional Knowledge

This competency is evidenced through training, study, and participation in professional association networks. Knowledge alone is not enough, of course. The question becomes, What does the facilitator know, how does this person act, and, most important, does he or she act consistently with his or her knowledge? In addition, this competency looks at ongoing growth. How does one maintain and expand one's knowledge? (See Chapter Twenty-Eight.)

Model Positive Professional Attitude

This competency can be seen as weaving together the others, since modeling a professional attitude requires knowledge, skills, and behaviors that are aligned with values and ethics. (For more information, see Chapter Thirty.)

One must both understand the values and ethics and act in a manner consistent with them. The goal is to reduce to a minimum the gap between espoused and practiced ethics and values. This requires a sense of maturity and self-awareness to be able to reflect on one's own behaviors and attitudes and assess their potential impact on a group or individual.

CERTIFICATION PROCESS

Candidates seeking professional certification participate in a two-phase assessment during which they demonstrate their competence: through written documentation and then at an in-person assessment that includes interviews and simulations.

(Other systems are under exploration by IAF and may be adopted in the future.) The phases are further delineated in five steps.

Step 1: Documentation

Candidates provide written documentation, which the assessors review. Documentation requirements include the candidate's résumé, a list of seven facilitated events within the past three years, a detailed description of one facilitated event, client references, and documentation of training that developed the competencies. If assessors do not see sufficient evidence of competence to indicate a likelihood of success at the next phase, they will recommend a deferral, including suggested actions for the candidate to pursue before resubmitting documentation for future assessment event. When documentation is sufficient, the candidate is invited to proceed to the on-site event.

Step 2: Simulated Client Interview

To prepare for the on-site certification event, the candidate is asked to participate, often by telephone, in a simulated client interview. The candidate plays the role of the facilitator, and an assessor plays the role of the prospective client. This simulation is in preparation for the in-person simulated event in which the candidate will play the role of the facilitator. No specific competencies are assessed during this interview, as it is conducted with only the candidate and one assessor. Rather, this provides the candidate with the context for the session he or she will run during the assessment day. The assessor may share general impressions of the candidate, based on the interview, with the assessing partner as a way of identifying competencies to explore during the subsequent interviews and simulation during the assessment day.

Step 3: First Candidate Interview

At the day-long, on-site certification event, two assessors interview the candidate. The candidate has the opportunity to demonstrate competencies not yet adequately in evidence (based on the previous two steps).

Step 4: Simulation

With other candidates serving as group participants and assessors in the roles of participants as well as observers, the simulation provides an opportunity for candidates to demonstrate their competencies in action. In addition to looking for evidence of competencies not yet adequately illustrated, assessors look for consistency between espoused and demonstrated behavior.

Step 5: Final Interview

At the close of the day, the candidate has a final opportunity to demonstrate competence. Depending on the outcomes of the initial interview and the simulation, this interview may be used to gather further evidence, clarify any inconsistencies, resolve assessors' concerns, or simply provide feedback. Typically, the session is a debriefing and discussion of the simulation. At this time, the candidates learn the results of their assessment. If the competencies were demonstrated, the candidate passes and is authorized to use the CPF designation. If not, the certification is deferred, and the candidate is invited to participate in another certification event at no additional cost other than personal travel expenses. Substantial advice is provided to those who are deferred in order to support their future certification.

The Costs and Benefits

At the time of this writing (2004), the fee payable to IAF for the certification process is $1,100. This covers venue costs and assessor honoraria and travel. This price is comparable to the fees associated with a day of intensive professional development training in the United States. Additional costs to the candidates vary tremendously depending on the time invested in preparing the documentation and the candidate's travel expenses. As awareness of the program has grown, the number of prospective candidates has increased, and in response to demand, the IAF has been scheduling more assessment events. These are generally run in conjunction with a conference, either international or regional, or in locations where there is sufficient demand to make an event economically viable. In a typical year, four assessment events are held worldwide.

In addition to the use of the Certified Professional Facilitator, Facilitador Profesional Certificado, or Facilitateur Professionnel Accrédité designations, candidates have reported substantial levels of satisfaction with the process for other reasons. Notable benefits include quality professional development as a result of the feedback provided by assessors, a strong sense of collegiality through experiencing the assessment process with other candidates, a renewed commitment to the profession as a result of the rigor of being assessed by their colleagues, and strengthened affiliation with the IAF. Remarkably, even deferred candidates have expressed similar satisfaction with the experience, feedback, and collegiality, and several have returned a second time to complete their designation.

NEXT STEPS

By November 2003, 278 candidates in seventeen countries had received IAF certification at events in the United States, Canada, and the United Kingdom (see Exhibit 26.1). With this certification program firmly in place, IAF is now exploring ways to provide other types and levels of facilitator certifications.

Exhibit 26.1
IAF Certified Professional Facilitators and Active
Accredited Assessors Worldwide, December 2003

Region	Number of Certified Professional Facilitators	Number of Assessors
Barbados	1	
Belgium	2	
Canada	71	3
China	1	
Colombia	2	
Denmark	1	
Germany	1	
Hong Kong	2	
Jamaica	2	
Malaysia	1	
Netherlands	16	2
Slovenia	2	
Taiwan	2	
Turkey	1	
United Kingdom	84	7
United States	88	16
Yugoslavia	1	

Other activities include accrediting training programs whose curricula are designed to develop the core competencies and ensuring that those certified are maintaining their competence through a recertification process. In addition to these expansion efforts, the IAF intends to further develop the certification program where it is currently working well and also expand to other regions of the world where facilitation, IAF, and certification interest are growing.

APPENDIX 26A: IAF FACILITATOR CORE COMPETENCIES

A. Create Collaborative Client Relationships

1. Develop working partnerships

- Clarifies mutual commitment
- Develops consensus on tasks, deliverables, roles and responsibilities
- Demonstrates collaborative values and processes such as in co-facilitation

2. Design and customize applications to meet client needs

- Analyzes organizational environment
- Diagnoses client need
- Creates appropriate designs to achieve intended outcomes
- Predefines a quality product and outcomes with client

3. Manage multi-session events effectively

- Contracts with client for scope and deliverables
- Develops event plan
- Delivers event successfully
- Assesses/evaluates client satisfaction at all stages of the event or project

B. Plan Appropriate Group Processes

1. Select clear methods and processes that . . .

- Fosters open participation with respect for client culture, norms and participant diversity
- Engages the participation of those with varied learning/thinking styles
- Achieves a high quality product/outcome that meets the client needs

2. Prepare time and space to support group process

- Arranges physical space to support the purpose of the meeting
- Plans effective use of time
- Provides effective atmosphere and drama for sessions

C. Create and Sustain a Participatory Environment

1. Demonstrate effective participatory and interpersonal communication skills

- Applies a variety of participatory processes
- Demonstrates effective verbal communication skills
- Develops rapport with participants
- Practices active listening
- Demonstrates ability to observe and provide feedback to participants

2. Honor and recognize diversity, ensuring inclusiveness

- Encourages positive regard for the experience and perception of all participants
- Creates a climate of safety and trust
- Creates opportunities for participants to benefit from the diversity of the group
- Cultivates cultural awareness and sensitivity

3. Manage group conflict

- Helps individuals identify and review underlying assumptions
- Recognizes conflict and its role within group learning/maturity
- Provides a safe environment for conflict to surface
- Manages disruptive group behavior
- Supports the group through resolution of conflict

4. Evoke group creativity

- Draws out participants of all learning and thinking styles
- Encourages creative thinking
- Accepts all ideas

- Uses approaches that best fit needs and abilities of the group
- Stimulates and taps group energy

D. Guide Group to Appropriate and Useful Outcomes

  1. Guide the group with clear methods and processes

- Establishes clear context for the session
- Actively listens, questions and summarizes to elicit the sense of the group
- Recognizes tangents and redirects to the task
- Manages small and large group process

  2. Facilitate group self-awareness about its task

- Varies the pace of activities according to needs of group
- Identifies information the group needs, and draws out data and insight from the group
- Helps the group synthesize patterns, trends, root causes, frameworks for action
- Assists the group in reflection on its experience

  3. Guide the group to consensus and desired outcomes

- Uses a variety of approaches to achieve group consensus
- Uses a variety of approaches to meet group objectives
- Adapts processes to changing situations and needs of the group
- Assesses and communicates group progress
- Fosters task completion

E. Build and Maintain Professional Knowledge

  1. Maintain a base of knowledge

- Knowledgeable in management, organizational systems and development, group development, psychology, and conflict resolution
- Understands dynamics of change
- Understands learning and thinking theory

  2. Know a range of facilitation methods

- Understands problem solving and decision-making models
- Understands a variety of group methods and techniques

- Knows consequences of misuse of group methods
- Distinguishes process from task and content
- Learns new processes, methods, and models in support of client's changing/emerging needs

3. Maintain professional standing
   - Engages in ongoing study/learning related to our field
   - Continuously gains awareness of new information in our profession
   - Practices reflection and learning
   - Builds personal industry knowledge and networks
   - Maintains certification

F. Model Positive Professional Attitude

1. Practice self-assessment and self-awareness
   - Reflects on behavior and results
   - Maintains congruence between actions and personal and professional values
   - Modifies personal behavior/style to reflect the needs of the group
   - Cultivates understanding of one's own values and their potential impact on work with clients

2. Act with integrity
   - Demonstrates a belief in the group and its possibilities
   - Approaches situations with authenticity and a positive attitude
   - Describes situations as facilitator sees them and inquires into different views
   - Models professional boundaries and ethics (as described in ethics and values statement)

3. Trust group potential and model neutrality
   - Honors the wisdom of the group
   - Encourages trust in the capacity and experience of others
   - Is vigilant to minimize influence on group outcomes
   - Maintains an objective, non-defensive, non-judgmental stance

Operational Dimensions of the Profession of Facilitation

Jon C. Jenkins

*Meet the situation without tenseness yet not recklessly. Your spirit
settled yet unbiased. Even when your spirit is calm do not let your
body relax, and when your body is relaxed do not let your spirit
slacken. Do not let your spirit be influenced by your body, or your
body be influenced by your spirit. Be neither insufficiently spirited
nor over spirited. An elevated spirit is weak and a low spirit is weak.*

Miyamoto Musashi (1982)

The practice of group facilitation takes place in the context of a set
of spectra that determine the type of products, how the facilitator intervenes, and what processes are used in a group event. Types of
interventions and processes have their own language and understanding of how groups interact and make decisions. Every facilitated
event can be plotted between several sets of polarities. This chapter
discusses a number of spectra: content versus process, instrumental versus developmental, prestructured versus self-organizing, scripted
versus emergent, and small groups versus large groups.

In some of the spectra, the facilitator chooses where he or she will stand. In other cases, the client and the client's requirements predetermine the location between these polarities. For example, the size of the group can be expressed in a spectrum between very small and very large scale. Some clients want workshops for groups of two to eight people and never larger than ten. Other clients cater to workshops of as many as five thousand members. Techniques also limit the size of groups. Goal Oriented Project Planning ("The Massachusetts Institute of Technology Upgrading Urban Communities: A Resource for Practitioners," 2001; GOPP Moderators Association, 2000), a method widely used in the European Community, is optimal when used in groups of around twenty people. Open Space Technology (Owen, 1997) as a methodology works quite well with several hundred people, but I believe it is less than optimal when used with small groups.

The operating style of the facilitator also determines his or her approach to facilitation. Some places on the spectrum are determined by the particular style, training, and expertise of the facilitator. Some facilitators are interested in, even require, more personal contact with each individual in a group. They tend to limit the group size to fewer than twenty people. Others are more comfortable with larger groups.

Each of the spectra has methodological, personal, and client boundaries that define exactly what kind of facilitation will be done and the style of the facilitator. In order to understand these spectra and the dynamic interaction among them, something needs to be said about the context in which facilitation takes place: organizational and behavioral change.

CHANGE

Facilitation is about enabling change—change in organizations, teams, and individuals. To understand facilitation, something needs to be said about the nature of change in groups. Among the many models of change, the one I have chosen for the purposes of this chapter is based on the work of Peter Senge (1990; Senge and others, 1994, 1999), W. Brian Arthur (2000), Joseph Jaworski (Jaworski and Scharmer, 2000), and others (Arthur and others, 2000). While this model is evolving in a number of directions, the draft of Claus Otto Scharmer (2000) is the most useful from my perspective.

Exhibit 27.1 "depicts five levels of organizational reality and, accordingly, of coping with change. The five levels of organizational reality are similar to an iceberg, in which most reorganization takes place 'below the waterline.' The *action* (at level 0) is 'above the waterline' and leads to four underlying levels of reorganization and change. The four underlying levels of reorganization are *restructuring* (level 1), *redesigning* core processes (level 2), *reframing* mental models (level 3), and *regenerating* common will (level 4)" (Scharmer, 2000).

Level 0, reacting, is the normal day-to-day business of operating within the organization's environment. A problem or opportunity is perceived, and an action is prepared and implemented. All of this takes place within the existing organizational framework, processes, thinking, and purposes.

Level 1, restructuring, is what is often called organizational change. Departments are created, eliminated, or put together in new ways; new lines of communication are instituted; and new responsibilities are given to and taken from managers. One might see this as rearranging the furniture in a home: change but not deep change.

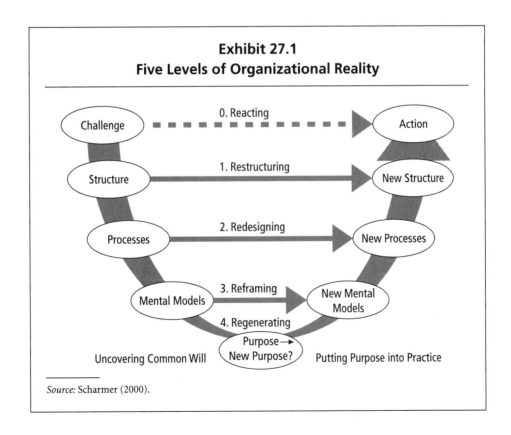

Exhibit 27.1
Five Levels of Organizational Reality

0. Reacting — Challenge ▸ Action

1. Restructuring — Structure ▸ New Structure

2. Redesigning — Processes ▸ New Processes

3. Reframing — Mental Models ▸ New Mental Models

4. Regenerating — Purpose → New Purpose?

Uncovering Common Will   Putting Purpose into Practice

Source: Scharmer (2000).

The redesigning of processes, level 2, is where business process reengineering takes place. The core processes, from initial contact with the client to customer care and follow-up, are reviewed and improved where possible. The organization becomes leaner and more efficient, in theory at least.

Whereas facilitation helps in the change processes of levels 0 to 2 (and many facilitators specialize in these areas), the following processes cannot be accomplished without facilitation.

Reframing mental models (level 3) looks at the assumptions, cognitive constructions, and operating understandings of what the organization is, its purpose, the environment in which it operates, and why it operates the way it does. In reference to the American automobile industry, Senge points to the need for reframing mental models: "Because they remained unaware of their mental models, the models remained unexamined. Because they were unexamined, the models remained unchanged. As the world changed, a gap widened between Detroit's mental models and reality, leading to an increasingly counterproductive actions" (Senge, 1990, p. 176).

Level 4 is regenerating common will. Even if an organization is operating out of the same set of assumptions and images, the change process may fail. This failure often occurs because of the lack of a shared purpose and a common will. The process of aligning the collective will requires an atmosphere of trust. People have to be able to express what they feel and what they believe without fear of negative consequences. Free choice has to operate. At the end of the process, individuals may leave because they disagree with the direction in which the organization is going, but they do so freely.

Scharmer (2000) writes, "Level 4 regenerating means allowing for flexibility in action, structure, processes, and mental models (levels 0, 1, 2, and 3) by focusing on redefining purpose and uncovering common will. . . . Shifting from level 3 to level 4 involves shifting from reflective learning (Type I: learning from the experiences of the past) to generative learning (Type II: learning from emerging futures). The primary issue at this stage is the need for a sound methodology that takes a team from the reflective space (level 3) to the space of deep intention of will (level 4)."

Scharmer, in a refinement of Peter Senge's five disciplines (1990), suggests the following disciplines: systems thinking, dialogue, process consulting, parallel learning structures, personal mastery, and presencing. Both dialogue (see Chapter Thirteen) and process consulting (Schein, 1999) can be considered disciplines of facilitation. Certainly systems thinking is frequently done as a facilitated process (Vennix, 1996). Thus, every manager of a company, governmental department, or nongovernmental organization needs these disciplines in order to manage change. If this is so, why is a profession of facilitation necessary?

Perhaps a metaphor would be useful. The vast majority of health care and prevention takes place in the home without recourse to a medical professional. First aid is done by mom; colds and fevers are fed and starved; basic sanitation (wash your hands before dinner) and nutrition (eat your broccoli; it's good for you) all take place within the family setting. When the family cannot deal with a medical problem, usually they go to a general practitioner who, using a wider range of skills and technology, diagnoses the problem and offers a cure from a much more inclusive set of possibilities. If the family doctor cannot find a solution, a specialist is brought in. The specialist brings to bear an even more sophisticated array of skills, technologies, and insights to the issue.

Much of this is also true of the future of facilitation. Most meetings, groups, teams, conferences, and town meetings are run and should be run by the manager, team leader, or a team member. Although not all of these people have a rich array of group management skills or an up-to-date understanding of how group decisions are made, they should be able to manage the vast majority of group processes. At this level, the manager is a facilitator (Weaver and Farrell, 1997) who uses basic group planning, development, or interaction skills.

Sometimes a meeting is expected to be more difficult than usual or a special problem needs to be dealt with. Occasionally the person who would normally lead the meeting should or would like to participate without the added burden of facilitating. Some teams have what could be called annual checkups, where a facilitator is called in not to solve a problem the group could not solve but to bring a fresh set of skills to lead the meeting. This is the "family doctor" function of facilitation.

When a group requires more than the normal facilitator can offer, there are specialists who can be called on. These specialties are still being developed; some are emerging. For example, meetings of very large groups require different approaches than small groups do.

Whether a specialist, general practitioner, or someone who is responsible for leading meetings, these people make choices about design, types of interaction with the group, kinds of results, and types of audiences. These choices determine the results of the meeting.

SPECTRA OF FACILITATION

Martin Luther King (1981, p. 13) describes the necessary polarities for creating a spectrum when he said, "A French philosopher said, "No man is strong unless he bears within his character antitheses strongly marked.' The strong man holds in a living blend strongly marked opposites. Not ordinarily do men achieve this balance of opposites. The idealists are not usually realistic, and the realists are not usually idealistic. The militant are not generally known to be passive, nor the passive to be militant. Seldom are the humble self-assertive, or the self-assertive humble. But life at its best is a creative synthesis of opposites in fruitful harmony."

In March 2000, a discussion took place on the GRP-FACL listserv (Electronic Discussion on Group Facilitation Process Expertise for Group Effectiveness) on models of facilitation. In this discussion, attempts were made to describe the different aspects of facilitation. James Murphy suggested a series of metaphors (e-mail to Group Facilitation, Mar. 22, 2000). Jim Rough added suggestions (e-mail message to Group Facilitation, Mar. 23, 2000). In the process of this discussion, Ned Ruete (e-mail to Group Facilitation, Mar. 22, 2000) and I (e-mail to Group Facilitation, Mar. 22, 2000) developed an eight-dimensional model of facilitation.

I became aware that frequently, the perspectives held by facilitators could be seen as a spectrum between various sets of polarities. Some argue, for example, that it is necessary and correct to offer content suggestions while acting as a facilitator, and others argue that facilitation works only at the process level. While examining my own practice, I discovered that I fell somewhere between these various sets of extremes. I often facilitate meetings dealing with topics that I have no knowledge about at all (for example, four-dimensional seismic imaging, or pictures of geological formation over time) and I have no content to suggest. Yet in areas where I have some expertise, I might share information that does not seem to be available to the group.

As the discussions continued, it occurred to me that a number of polarities existed; in this chapter, I present sixteen. The spectra that inform the profession of facilitation can be categorized as follows:

Approaches to design: prestructured versus self-organizing, scripted versus emergent, serial threads versus parallel threads

Scale of the problem: one off versus long term, narrow versus wide scope, and symptomatic versus causal

Type of interventions used by facilitators: process versus content, implicit rules versus explicit rules

Types of products: verbal versus visual, idea based versus story based, instrumental versus developmental, and facilitator-owned product versus group-owned product

Types of audiences: monochromatic versus polychromatic, large groups versus small groups, single party versus multiple party, and hierarchical versus egalitarian

Approaches to Design

One of the issues facing a facilitator is how group process will be designed. I present three spectra having to do with design: prestructured versus self-organizing, scripted versus emergent, and serial threads versus parallel threads.

Prestructured versus Self-Organizing   Structured, or perhaps more accurately, prestructured facilitation occurs when the facilitator designs the meeting or workshop usually in consultation with the client before the workshop begins. In self-organizing designs, the participants determine the content, usually in relation to a focused question, and create the process by which the meeting is done.

Examples of prestructured designs are the Institute of Cultural Affairs (ICA) Technology of Participation (ToP) Methods (Spencer, 1989; Stanfield, 2002) and Joint Applications Development (Rottmann, 2001). In each of these approaches, the facilitator, in discussion with the client, determines the sequence of the workshops or meetings, prepares specific interventions beforehand, and trusts the process. A facilitator who trusts the process understands that the sequence of steps planned for in the workshop will enable the group to come to an effective conclusion without modification during the meeting. Not trusting the process leads to trusting your feelings or immediate impressions or intuitions and using personal concerns as a basis of intervening. The facilitator then follows the planned sequence of the process of the meeting regardless of things seemingly going wrong. This does not imply that things will not go wrong or that the facilitator will never change the process, but generally the planned procedures result in the desired outcome.

Examples of self-organizing designs are Open Space Technology (Owen, 1997), Dynamic Facilitation by Jim Rough (2003), and the ICA's Problem Solving Units

("PSU Manual," 1996). In these approaches the participants determine during the session the specific topics, how they are treated, and who deals with each one.

Scripted versus Emergent   Scripted facilitation occurs when the facilitator or a design team writes out a script for the facilitator. The emergent design approach usually begins with an exercise or icebreaker or some other way of engaging the group. Then, depending on how the group responds, the facilitator (perhaps in consultation with the group) proceeds based on intuitions about what the group needs.

Several facilitators seem to be emergent, but when they are observed over several workshops, their process does not vary. They are, in fact, scripted without the burden of writing.

The ICA's ToP Methods were scripted at their inception. In the strategic planning method ("Convoy Course: Lecture One," 1996; "NINS," 1996), word-for-word scripts were written for the facilitator. While ToP facilitators today have great latitude in revising the process on the spot, they still tend to let the process carry the group through difficult moments. They also have a number of memorized "short courses" that they can draw on, if necessary. These "short courses" are contexts, additional explanations, instructions, and even funny stories making some point. These facilitators seldom intervene outside the script. The advantage of scripted programs is that all of the dynamics of the process are thought through in great detail beforehand. This helps bring high intentionality to the process. The disadvantage of this approach is that being too tied to a script can prevent responding sensitively to the group.

Dynamic Facilitation is probably the best-known emergent form of facilitation. The introduction phase of Open Space Technology is quite standard: the facilitator explains four principles and one law. The principles are: "Who ever comes is the right people. Whatever happens is the only thing that could have, Whenever it starts is the right time. When it is over, it's over" (Owen, 1997, p. 95). The one law is "the Law of Two Feet, which says that if, during the course of the gathering, any person finds him or herself in a situation where they are neither learning nor contributing, they must use their two feet and go to some more productive place" (Owen, 1997, p. 98). The actual work is more emergent because after the topics are determined and rooms and times allocated, there is no further guidance from the facilitator. The advantage of this approach is that the immediate requirements of the group can be met. The disadvantage of this kind of approach is that if poor meeting practices are the norm in the group, they will continue in the small groups. Disadvantages of facilitator-directed emergent forms are that it requires a great deal of skill, discipline, and experience and a huge repertoire of techniques.

Serial Threads versus Parallel Threads   Some facilitated meetings have a single topic or "thread." Although there may be several stages and preliminary or intermediary products, the meeting has a single focus and results in a single, integrated product. A serial thread meeting might have several threads in a sequence. Parallel thread meetings take on several topics or intermediary products simultaneously.

Open Space Technology is an example of parallel thread facilitation. Topics are identified in a plenary session, and times and locations are posted. All of the work on these topics takes place at the same time. After the work is done, reports are presented in a plenary session (Owen, 1997). Serial thread methods can be used in a parallel way. I have used After Action Review, a method for debriefing an event, project, or campaign (M. Jenkins, 2002; Hoskins, 2002; Signet Consulting Group, 2000) for multiple threads. The whole group was instructed in the five steps of the After Action Review process: (1) What did we intend? (2) What actually happened? (3) What did we learn? (4) What will we do differently next time? (5) Who should we tell? Individuals then volunteered to work on one of several topics, and the groups reported conclusions from their workshops.

Some techniques use a combination of single- and multiple-thread thinking. In the grassroots community improvement planning sessions, Human Development Project Launch Workshops, six intermediate products were created in the course of five days: vision, contradictions, proposals, tactics, implementaries, and organization. During the last five of these stages, each of the five teams worked on different topics that came from the product of the previous stage. A vision, for example, might have twelve elements, and each specialist team would be given two or three to look for blocks to their realization.

Scale of the Problem

Although not all facilitation is problem solving in intent, the vast majority of planning sessions are located within some understanding of the scale of the problem being faced. Each decision-making process occurs in a set of boundaries that determine how much of the group's organization is to be dealt with in the process.

There are three dimensions to this. One-off events versus long-term series of interventions are about how far into the future the interventions will be planned for. Narrow versus wide scope is about how much of the organization or social unit will be within the mandate of the meeting. Symptomatic versus causal is about how deep into root causes the group will look.

One Off versus Long Term   Most approaches to facilitation focus on a single event. These often operate out of the assumption that single events can result in long-term, sustainable change. A project to select and introduce a new telephone system can lead to lasting and more effective communications. Other facilitators understand that in doing one-off events, they are creating temporary solutions that are not sustainable and in fact may be detrimental to sustainable change. The event may be a strategic planning session or a single team-building or planning day (in Europe, often called an away day), or some other relatively short-term program. It can last from three to four hours to several days. These events can be planned well in advance and followed up weeks or even months later.

Long-term approaches to change recognize that a great deal of time is needed. Planning for major infrastructure developments takes into account that decades may pass before even beginning to implement a plan and the goal is realized. In some cases, the change process itself may take a long time. Collins (2001) points our that companies that make the transition from good to great companies take years before the change process is noticeable from the outside.

One-off methods include Future Search, Strategic Forum, and SimuReal (Holman and Devane, 1999). In each case, a planning process ranging from a few days to six months is required before the event. The follow-up ranges from none to preparing facilitators, follow-up events, and tracking changes in the organization. Regardless of whether the planning and follow-up is brief or extensive, these methods focus on a single event.

The Whole System Approach and appreciative inquiry are examples of methods that are designed specifically for long-term change. (See Chapter Twelve for additional insight regarding long-term change.)

Narrow versus Wide Scope   The breadth of the issue that the meeting is dealing with also affects what approach the facilitator needs to take. Narrow-scope planning looks at some part of the work of an organization or community. It could be an implementation plan for a project or planning how to increase repeat sales for a particular retail outlet. Wide scope would look at comprehensive community development issues or a complete redefinition of a company's direction. Somewhere in the middle of the spectrum is strategic planning.

The scope of the problem sets boundaries for what can and cannot be discussed. Assumptions about where the discussion can start in a narrow scope are different than with a wide scope. The narrow-scope project planning methods assume that the project itself is valid and its goal is fixed and not to be challenged. Changes in scope can be made but normally are not. Project planning methods such as JAD and ToP Action Planning are more useful in a narrow-scope planning process.

In wide-scope projects, everything imaginable can be discussed. For example, in a community development project week-long planning event I helped lead in Vogar, Manitoba, one idea that was seriously considered was to move everyone to Winnipeg and destroy the community. Methodologies such as Future Search, the ToP Environmental Analysis (Spencer, 1989), and the Human Development Project Planning (Mathews, 1996) process of the ICA would tend to be more effective in a wide-scope program.

Symptomatic versus Causal   Another spectrum that has to do with the scale of the problem could be called symptomatic versus causal or shallow versus deep. In treating a common cold, it is often most effective to simply reduce the symptoms of the cold while the natural immune system deals with the infection. In many cases, the client only wants or has a mandate to deal with the symptoms.

In-depth organizational or community transformation looks at processes of eliciting a collective will, developing shared universes of discourse, building individual and corporate capacity, and changing behavior. In these cases, no single intervention or type of intervention is sufficient.

Dealing with causes requires a rather complex diagnostic model such as systems thinking. Morgan (1986) suggests three approaches to systems thinking: autopoiesis, mutual causality, and dialectic change. The two systems most used by facilitators are mutual causality, advocated by Peter Senge (1990), and dialectic change, which can be traced back to Taoism through to Hegel and Marx. Process consulting often uses systems thinking. One example of dialectic change is contradictions, as used by the ICA in its strategic planning process, which was developed from Mao Ze Dong's book *On Contradiction* (1999). Other diagnostic tools that are of use to facilitators are the Social Process Triangles and its derivatives (Jenkins and Jenkins, 1997) and Motorola's Six Sigma (I Six Sigma, 2000).

An alternative to sophisticated diagnostic tools are methods that provide enough insight into the underlying causes of issues, such as DMAIC (Define, Measure, Analyze, Improve, Control), an incremental process improvement method using Six Sigma tools. Five Whys (I Six Sigma, 2000) and the fishbone method, when appropriately applied, can develop insights into underlying causes.

Type of Interventions Facilitators Use

A third set of spectra has to do with the kinds of interventions the facilitator will make in delivering the process. The process versus content continuum has to do with the division between the sequence of activities used by the group to process information and to make decisions and the actual content of the discussions and decisions. The second spectrum, implicit rules versus explicit rules, assumes that there are rules governing behavior. The question is how explicit those rules should be.

Process versus Content   The process versus content discussion is perhaps the most frequent one among facilitators. When should a facilitator act as a content expert? While few facilitators would suggest that a facilitator should be a pure content expert, many would share their thinking about the topic of the meeting or provide information that is not otherwise available to the group.

As soon as the facilitator supports or promotes a position, whether it is his own or the position of a faction within the group, he has become a consultant or advocate. A common way to deal with this situation is for the facilitator to announce that he is stepping out of his role as facilitator and stepping into a role as content expert.

Pure process facilitators never make content suggestions; they work only with the meeting process. They manage information flow and treatment, idea generation, development and evaluation, group and individual emotions, decision making, and group spirit.

It can be argued that all facilitators make some content interventions. They ask questions about content such as, "Could you say more about that?" or "Could you give an example of what you mean?"

Implicit Rules versus Explicit Rules   Implicit rules assume that the existing principles of behavior operating within the group are of a standard such that the group can function in a healthy way. Few formal methods advocate relying on implicit rules, but many facilitators operate this way in practice.

Explicit rules are the basis of a model of effective behavior. Without them, it is not possible to add value to the client. They are also the basis of diagnostic models and models of intervention. They provide a structure within which more important issues can be discussed. They also enable the group to hold the facilitator accountable to them (R. Schwarz, e-mail to Group Facilitation, May 23, 2003). Explicit rules of participation and interacting in the meeting are usually agreed to and posted in the meeting room. There are three approaches to this: rules that are agreed to in the contracting process, rules that the facilitator suggests to the group, and rules that are created by the people in the meeting. Both implicit and explicit rules expect the facilitator to model behavior that is consistent with the rules.

Some methods use explicit rules (Schwarz, 2002). In this method, the rules are required by the facilitator and agreed to before the meeting. Owen (1997) uses four principles and one law. Most methods that I am familiar with do not require a specific set of rules, but when rules are made explicit, the participants in the meeting create them. (See Chapter Nineteen.) One approach that does not use ground rules is Dynamic Facilitation by Jim Rough, who argues that rules prevent transformation: "Ground rules evoke critical thinking and encourage self-censorship, both of which are an anathema to creativity and transformation" (Rough, e-mail to Group Facilitation, May 24, 2003).

One of the issues that facilitators face is how to "enforce" the rules. Part of the process of enforcement has to do with calling attention to someone who is ignoring the rules. This intervention is often sufficient to correct the behavior. If it is not, the facilitator (or the group) must decide if the infraction warrants an additional intervention; finally, the intervention is carried out. Some facilitators leave enforcement in the hands of the group.

Types of Products

The products produced by facilitators vary quite a bit. The verbal versus visual spectrum ranges from written reports to a series of drawings. A list of interrelated concepts results at one end of the idea-based versus story-based spectrum and a number of individual or collective narratives at the other end. In the instrumental versus developmental spectrum, the products range from a concrete artifact to improved group dynamics. The "owner" of the product is considered in the facilitator-owned product versus group-owned product spectrum.

Verbal versus Visual   By far, most facilitators at least begin as verbal facilitators. They use flip charts, cards, or computers to record and process the ideas that emerge in the meetings. The reports are written; no pictures, drawings, or other visual images are used. There is a trend toward visual facilitation. Horn (1998) argues that a new international visual language is emerging that includes shapes and images. Facilitators in cross-cultural situations or multilingual workshops can use this visual language.

Pure visual facilitators use only drawings. Some facilitators toward this end of the spectrum use a single word or a phrase to help participants recall the context in which the picture was drawn. An example of this end of the spectrum is the work of Reinhard Kuchenmüller and Marianne Stifel (n.d.) of Visuelle Protokolle of Munich, Germany (see Chapter Twenty-Three). They begin with drawings and then add text if it is needed. Nearer the text end of the spectrum but still visual are graphic facilitators like David Sibbet (Grove Consultants International, 2003), who uses a predrawn image on which text is recorded (see Chapter Ten). Somewhere in the middle is the work of Gareth Morgan (1993). He uses visual metaphors to develop self-awareness. This approach can act as a bridge from verbal to visual.

A trend toward using other senses in the facilitation process is also developing. For example, Lego Serious Play is another visual and tactile approach to facilitating team building, strategic and project planning, product development, and innovation and branding strategy. Participants use Lego pieces to create a visual image of the answer to a question posed: Opportunity or challenge? (To see the way Lego pieces are used in planning, go to http://www.seriousplay.com/.)

Music is often used at the beginning, end, and during breaks to create an atmosphere. Some discussions have been held between Imaginal Training (verbal facilitators) and Visuelle Protokolle (a visual facilitation company) to experiment with using music as an integral part of the facilitation process. The combination of music, images, and concepts seeks to deepen the thinking and enhance the creativity of a group.

Idea Based versus Story Based   Stories and storytelling are increasingly being recognized as an important tool in business. Stories are being used in induction training (Ransdell, 2000), knowledge management (Brown, 2001), and problem solving (Watkins and Mohr, 2001). Story-based facilitation is growing in importance.

Idea-based facilitation focuses on discrete concepts being developed by the group. Story-based facilitation uses the personal narratives of the participants to create an understanding of the focus issues. Insights into issues and possibilities are gathered by drawing lessons and developing interpretations from the individual narratives (Denning, 2001).

Most facilitation methods—JAD, ToP, and GOPP—are idea-based methods. Cards, flip charts, and white boards are used to capture concepts. In some cases, these concepts are combined into higher levels of abstraction. In other cases, one or more are selected to be further refined.

Appreciative inquiry is a good example of a story-based facilitation method: "Appreciative Inquiry asks people to tell their stories about what works, to share their connections with others where they have been at their best, to talk about what is life giving and equitable. It assists people to imagine their organizations and communities in more affirming ways and to envision policies, practices and behaviours that promote equity and that enhance the life giving forces in relationships" (Stewart, 1995). Based on the way the stories describe an organization's present situation and its perception of the future, the appreciative inquiry facilitator helps create verbal images for the new organization. Yet even these images are always accompanied by the images and language used in the stories (Watkins and Mohr, 2001).

Instrumental versus Developmental   Instrumental facilitation focuses on producing a concrete product. It is task oriented. Developmental facilitation focuses on improving the interaction, communication skills, and decision-making skills of the participants. Roger Schwarz's work includes basic facilitation (instrumental facilitation) and developmental facilitation. With instrumental facilitation, the group uses a facilitator to temporarily improve decision-making processes to solve a concrete problem, such as developing a project plan. When the plan is developed, the facilitator's work is completed. The diagnostic tools used in this kind of facilitation ask, "Is the group accomplishing the goal of the meeting?" Interventions are aimed at enabling the group to make the best decision possible. Interpersonal relations are dealt with only when they are blocking the realization of the task.

A number of methods lie at the instrumental facilitation end of the spectrum. GOPP, ToP, Future Search, and JAD have already been cited. The vast majority of facilitation is task oriented. The growing demand for facilitator training has increased public awareness that facilitation is a necessary skill for leading meetings and may well result in a growth of interest and a diversity of new techniques for developmental facilitation.

Developmental systems of facilitation focus in part on the sociopsychological dynamics in the group processes, asking participants about their feelings and motives while sharing observations about relationships and communications within the group. The facilitator may suggest exercises to practice new ways of interacting. In these approaches, interpersonal relationships are seen as the key to long-term group effectiveness. Their aim is to reduce dependency on external facilitators over the long term. While accomplishing the task is important in these systems, the group's work is secondary to improvement in the group's dynamics. (For a fuller description, see Schwarz, 2002.)

A Dutch method of developmental facilitation is *intervisie,* or peer consultation teams (Werkgroep Docenten Onderwijszaken, 2000), which tends to be oriented toward personal growth in the working environment. It is used for team and personal development and for sharing learning in a number of Dutch companies.

Another aspect of this is the difference between workshops and dialogues. Workshops in the sense that I am using the term have concrete products, such as a plan, model, or set of priorities. The goal of the workshop is a product. Dialogue sessions often result in new understandings or awareness but little that is tangible. The goal of a dialogue is the dialogue itself. "Usually people gather either to accomplish a task or to be entertained, both of which can be categorized as predetermined purposes. But by its very nature dialogue is not consistent with any such purposes beyond the interest of its participants in the "unfoldment" and revelation of the deeper collective meanings that may be revealed. These may on occasion be entertaining, enlightening, lead to new insights or address existing problems. But surprisingly, in its early stages, the dialogue will often lead to the experience of frustration" (Bohm, Factor, and Garrett, 1991). Factor (1994) would even argue that having a facilitator in a dialogue is problematic. (For a different view of the dimensions of task and relation in group process, see Chapter Nine.)

Also, concern for task versus relationship can be viewed as a function of the group's cultural context. (For more information regarding this perspective, see Chapter Sixteen.)

Facilitator-Owned Product versus Group-Owned Product   In some meetings, the group serves as a source of ideas. The facilitator may be the team leader or manager. The facilitator is responsible for the product, usually to her boss, and is using group facilitation to reach that objective. In group-owned products, the group is using the facilitator as a tool to reach some objective for which they are jointly responsible. In these cases, any of many methods of facilitation can be used.

The primary difference between these two kinds of ownership is the problem of detachment (Jenkins and Jenkins, 2002). While all facilitators have to be careful to remain neutral in any of the meetings they facilitate, the problem multiplies when the facilitator is the manager or team leader. The end product reflects on the effectiveness of his or her work. The manager also understands the problems and has opinions—sometimes strong ones about the topic. By being manager, she is responsible for the content and results, and by being the facilitator, she is responsible for the process. The capacity to let go of the content and the results is a difficult discipline. Some managers choose not to put themselves in this kind of position, but many have to, and many just do. In order to be effective facilitators, these managers need to develop skills such as maintaining detachment.

All facilitators have the problem of maintaining some professional stance while leading a group. Facilitator ownership can cause some conflicts with the ethical requirements of being a facilitator. The IAF Code of Ethics states:

> *We practice stewardship of process and impartiality toward content.* While participants bring knowledge and expertise concerning the substance of their situation, we bring knowledge and expertise concerning the group interaction process. We are vigilant to minimize our influence on group outcomes. When we have content knowledge not otherwise available to the group, and that the group must have to be effective, we offer it after explaining our change in role (International Association of Facilitators, 2004; see Chapter Thirty).

Types of Audiences

The final set of spectra has to do with the kind of group that is being facilitated. Some groups talk one at a time, and some speak all at once. This is considered in the monochromatic versus polychromatic section. Groups as large as five thousand participants pose one set of issues for the facilitator that are different from groups of three or four. This is looked at in the section on large groups versus small groups. The single-party versus multiple-party spectrum refers to the differences between relatively homogeneous groups committed to the same values and goals and ones with differing interests, intentions and understandings of the issues. Finally, the differences in facilitation groups that are highly hierarchical and groups with a flat hierarchy are dealt with in the hierarchical versus egalitarian spectrum.

Monochromatic versus Polychromatic   This spectrum is closely related to that of serial versus parallel threads, which is the result of the combination of choices of the assignment giver, the group, and the facilitator. In this spectrum, it is a cultural difference. In some groups, one person at a time speaks; they follow a logical progression of ideas and become uncomfortable when a meeting becomes "disorganized." Other groups are uncomfortable with linear thinking and the convention of one speaker at a time. They deal with all issues, solutions, constraints, and anything else all at once.

Methods that work well with monochromatic audiences are the ones that have a lot of structure and follow an obvious process, such as ToP, JAD, and After Action Review. Polychromatic audiences appreciate methods that can take into account more chaotic situations, like Dynamic Facilitation and Open Space Technology.

It is possible to use methods that are more suited to monochromatic audiences with polychromatic ones. I was part of a team of facilitators facilitating a community development project in the Abruzzi region of central Italy. I was leading the economic development team and was being assisted by a businessman from Milan, who was also translating. When we posed the first question to our team, thirty people stood up and began shouting. I looked at my colleague, and he rolled his eyes as if to say, "Don't ask me; you're the facilitator." We agreed that as the shouting was going on, we would capture as much as we could on flip charts and stop the group every few minutes and summarize what we had captured and ask for more. It was a chaotic meeting, but in the end, it worked.

Large Groups versus Small Groups   Large group facilitation faces four issues: the dilemma of voice, the dilemma of structure, the egocentric dilemma, and the contagion of affect. The dilemma of voice is that only a few can talk and many are silent, resulting in the experience of not being recognized or heard. Some people may feel intimidated by the number of people. To succeed in large groups, the facilitator needs to use small group technology in creative ways. The dilemma of structure is that if the group experiences too little structure, things seem chaotic, out of control. If there is too much structure, however, members of the group feel manipulated and their behavior controlled. Sophisticated use of structuring subgroups, discussions, and reporting at an effective minimum is required. The egocentric dilemma is that, on one hand, people tend to believe that their own perception is reality. On the other hand, larger groups tend to offer interaction between many more diverse, contradictory perspectives than do small groups. The facilitator needs to manage the team composition, reporting formats, and group reflections to realize effective products (Bunker and Alban, 1997).

The differences between facilitating large and small groups are mostly in the areas of logistics, visibility, group dynamics, and facilitator skills. A few examples may be helpful:

- Moving 250 people from one plenary room to small subgroup rooms takes much more time than moving 20 people.
- Microphones need to be accessible to everyone, or else the facilitator needs to repeat every comment.
- Electronic projectors or very large printing is needed if everyone in a plenary session is to be able to read the brainstormed items or to follow a presentation.
- Effective use of individual, small group, and plenary dynamics is critical. Special care is needed to ensure that everyone has an opportunity to participate and to experience that their contribution has been heard and considered if not used.
- The facilitator's capacity to listen to the whole group rather than a few is important. In small groups, it is possible to intervene directly with an individual. In large groups, this is not possible, leaving interventions to be focused on representatives of types of participants or stakeholders.
- Ground rules may not be necessary in managing the behavior of a group of 10. With 250 people, they are much more important.

Open Space Technology, Real Time Strategic Change (Holman and Devane, 1999), and ToP Methods have successfully been used in large groups. These are "methods for involving the whole system, internal and external, in the change process. . . . The key similarity is that these methods deliberately involve a critical mass of people affected by change, both inside the organization (employees and management) and outside it (suppliers and customers)" (Bunker and Alban, 1997, p. xv).

GOPP is limited to about thirty people. *Intervisie* is usually limited to a maximum of six people. The reason is that every participant is expected to use a minimum of thirty minutes in the discussion, so a six-person meeting requires more than three hours.

(For more information on facilitating large groups, see Chapter Fifteen.)

Single Party versus Multiple Party   Single homogeneous work groups share a common task and common starting points. They have shared values and goals. Teams have a foundation to build agreement on in the meeting. Multiple stakeholder groups are made up of different vested interests, values, and often organizations. In these types of groups, a common ground needs to be built first.

The ICA's project planning method, ToP Action Planning, assumes concrete agreement about the goals of the project. The method enables the group to work through how it will be accomplished. The focus of the workshop is developing the actions to do the project.

Two dangers of all group decision making but especially single-party groups are groupthink and the Abilene paradox. The facilitator has a responsibility to the group to help them prevent both.

Groupthink is the result of the normal process of seeking conformity and unity. The group sacrifices good sense in order to maintain internal peace; the result is poor decision making. A classic example of groupthink is the process of giving approval for launching the space shuttle *Challenger* on January 28, 1986, which exploded shortly after take-off (Rounds, 2000).

"When organizations blunder into the Abilene paradox, they take actions in contradiction to what they really want to do and therefore defeat the very purposes of what they try to accomplish. It is a symptom of the inability to manage agreement—not the inability to manage conflict" (Cunningham, 2004).

GOPP is especially designed for multiple stakeholder groups. It is used to create agreement between different parties about what is to be accomplished by the project and what activities will be carried out to achieve the project's goals. The danger in multiple stakeholder groups is that individuals or subgroups fix on positions and refuse to find ways to reach agreement. (For more information on this topic, see Chapter Eight.)

Hierarchical versus Egalitarian   Groups that are very hierarchical may have difficulty in developing a dynamic of free-flowing ideas. Members often defer to more senior members of the group or wait until their seniors have expressed their opinions. The way the meeting is conducted in these situations depends on the nature of input needed and desired by all participants. A format in which the senior individual defines the problem at the beginning of the workshop, then leaves the group to work out suggestions, and returns to hear their reports is common in our experience of this type of situation. It is important for the person in authority to inform the group what she has done with their input.

Groups that are more hierarchical need to be facilitated with care by those from more egalitarian cultures. In some situations, the boss needs to give permission to participate. I did a strategic planning workshop at a vodka distillery in Poland in which all of the workers were reluctant to suggest anything other than agreeing with the factory manager and one or two other managers. At the suggestion of my Polish cofacilitator, we asked the senior manager to tell people that he expected them to contribute their own ideas during the workshop. Although this did not change the hierarchy, it did result in lots of participation on the part of the workers.

Other methods are available to the facilitator when facilitating more hierarchical groups. When dividing the group into teams, for example, put the senior people in one group and less senior members in others. The facilitator can ask the most senior member to make a presentation supporting the workshop and evaluate the work at the end of the program. And in cross-cultural situations, it is wise to check with people who can provide a bridge between the two cultures.

In groups with little power distance among the participants, the decision-making process is necessarily more participatory in nature. Here, individuals must be consulted about a decision, whether in its general direction or sometimes even the details. In extreme examples of this kind of group, every individual needs to speak about every issue even if the person's point has been made more than once before. Here the facilitator has to devise a process for managing a great deal of input and ongoing group reflection. The facilitator's job is to enable everyone to have time to speak, which is usually best done in small groups. When asking for additions, it is good to suggest that you want ideas that have not been presented before. More care than normal needs to be paid to timekeeping.

CONCLUSION

The spectra suggested in this chapter have several uses. Facilitators can reflect on each of these spectra and consider in what range they normally operate. This offers them the opportunity to decide in what directions they would like to develop. Some facilitators might want to develop from one end of the spectrum toward the other. By doing this between several polarities, they gain greater flexibility in their capacity to work with clients. A wider range of clients is then available, as well as a wider range of services for current clients.

Trainers of facilitators can gear their training in more flexible ways. Facilitators can be evaluated based on this system of spectra. Specific skill sets and competencies can then be more accurately targeted for trainees. Specialist facilitators can deepen their skills around a specific set of locations within sets of spectra. These specialists, such as visual or large group facilitators, can develop markets around specific benefits to clients. These spectra also offer organizations a way of selecting what kind of facilitator with which they would like to work. And a facilitator's selection of methodologies can be done with greater sensitivity by determining where on these spectra an upcoming program needs to be located.

Change is what facilitation is about: transformation, participation, and process. It is about altering the way decisions are made and who makes them. The old hierarchical worldview is giving way to a more inclusive, less arbitrary one. Responsibility for decisions is being driven further down the social and organizational hierarchies in the hope that decisions can be made more quickly and more in line with operational requirements. The problems facing organizations and communities are far too complex to be dealt with by a single person. Alignment of the members of a group is becoming an important factor in raising the quality of their decisions. The profession of facilitation is one of emerging disciplines responding to and giving shape to these trends.

In these sixteen spectra, the breadth of the discipline of facilitation is obvious. My hope is that these spectra will offer a way of defining what facilitation is about.

How to Build Your Expertise in Facilitation

Kristin J. Arnold

In the early days of facilitation, pioneers in the field learned from experience, practice, and reflection with their peers. They spread their knowledge and skills through apprenticeships, training, reference materials, and formal and informal networks. (For an account of early notions and development of group facilitation, see Maier, 1967; Keltner, 1989.)

Today, much of the foundation groundwork is already established. This book is a testament to the great thinking around facilitation that already exists. Yet facilitation is not a rote subject easily learned. Because of the diverse nature of groups, facilitation is more an intuitive art form than a science. Every situation is unique and requires a masterful facilitator to be flexible and adaptable, serving the needs of the group.

For most seasoned practitioners, facilitation is not just something they do; it is a state of being. They see opportunities to facilitate human interactions all the time: in the workplace, community groups, church meetings, youth organizations—anytime a group of people gets together to accomplish a specific goal.

Facilitators are on a continuing journey to expand their skills through various means, such as training, reference materials, Internet learning, observation of

Note: All of the lists provided in this chapter are the opinions of the survey respondents and not a recommendation from the author or the publisher.

others, practice, feedback, teaching, and publishing their ideas within the facilitation community.

This chapter shares many strategies that seasoned practitioners use to build their facilitation expertise. These strategies are based on the answers to an informal electronic survey sent once in October 2003 to practicing facilitators from three communities: (1) those who earned the Certified Professional Facilitator (CPF) designation from the International Association of Facilitators (IAF; see Chapter Twenty-Six), (2) those who participate in the Professional Experts Group on Facilitation through the National Speakers Association (NSA), and/or (3) those who participate in the IAF-sponsored electronic discussion group. In all, there were 250 CPFs, 132 NSA members, and 800 electronic discussion group participants. There was some duplication of names within these three communities, for an estimated total of 700 potential respondents. These communities were selected because of my personal knowledge of the quality and caliber of the respondents and easy access to the e-mail list. The candidates were solicited only once by e-mail, with two weeks to respond to the survey. (The complete survey text is in Appendix 28A at the end of the chapter.)

A total of 125 practicing facilitators responded to the survey, which consisted of thirty-eight questions. The survey drew extensively on Parisse and others (2003). This chapter discusses each of the major strategies identified in the survey. Interspersed in the findings are quotations from individual respondents (primarily from North America) whose comments were particularly insightful or reflective of the comments submitted in general. (The overall results can be accessed at http://www.surveymonkey.com/Report.asp?U=29145365059.)

TRAINING

On average, seasoned facilitators attend a formal training, course, or workshop once a year. Typically, they attend formal training more frequently in the early stages of their practice and then tend to taper off as they became more experienced and comfortable in their role. After a while, they attend only sessions that are of specific interest, are geographically desirable, or complement their existing skills, often including different disciplines. One facilitator said, "I take on workshops I have never done before. I try not to use the same old approaches every time (although, trouble is, they usually work!) . . . and I transfer skills from other disciplines e.g. clinical psychology, family and group systems, conflict resolution."

Many facilitators prefer "hands-on, interactive seminars that present new methods and techniques and provide useful materials." When attending training, they come prepared to engage the instructor as well as participants and may have very specific learning objectives that may (or may not) be published in the course brochure. They do not leave until their personal objectives are fulfilled.

Many have established a practice to reinforce the learning. For example, one facilitator writes a "mini retrospective after each workshop. I note the key learning points for myself and put it in my Palm [to review later]." Another said, "I try to find ways of using them in events that I facilitate as soon after as possible."

Classroom Training Providers

The following organizations were cited the most often as offering "the best training/seminars" in facilitation (the entries in this and other lists are cited in the order in which they were most often mentioned):

Community at Work (www.communityatwork.com)

Community Store (www.thecommunitystore.com)

Franklin-Covey (www.franklincovey.com)

ICA Associates (www.ica-associates.ca)

Interaction Associates (www.interactionassociates.com)

Goal/QPC (www.goalqpc.com)

Grove Consultants International (www.grove.com)

Roger Schwarz and Associates (www.schwarzassociates.com)

H. H. Owen and Company (www.openspaceworld.com)

Participative Dynamics (www.participative-dynamics.com)

Electronic Media

With the advent of high-speed Internet connectivity, facilitation training providers are turning to electronic media to deliver their programs remotely. They range from fairly simple technology such as teleclasses (training conducted using conference call capability), video teleconferencing (VTC), Web-based seminars (often referred to as Webinars), and live Web-based training (WBT). Regardless of the specific format, electronic media eliminate travel for participants and the facilitator, increase access beyond typical participants, consume less time away from daily activities, and offer easier and less expensive follow-on sessions to increase the transfer of training.

One facilitator extols the virtues of electronic media: "Many facilitators live in remote locations and do not have the luxury of time and/or money to travel to conventions or trainings across the country. Teleclasses and Webinars offer a viable alternative."

Because facilitators highly value face-to-face interaction, it is absolutely crucial to choose a training provider who is substantially skilled in facilitating interaction in the electronic medium.

National and Regional Conferences

Facilitators attend national and regional conferences, workshops, and sessions to enhance their professional development and learning. The respondents most often attend those sponsored by:

International Association of Facilitators (www.iaf-world.org)

Canadian Institute of Cultural Affairs (www.icacan.ca)

American Society for Training and Development (www.astd.org)

OD Network (ww.odnetwork.org)

International Federation for Professional Speakers (www.iffps.org)

Association for Quality and Participation (ww.aqp.org)

American Society for Quality (www.asq.org)

Association for Conflict Resolution (www.acrnet.org).

Professional Organizations

In addition to attending national conferences and workshops, many facilitators also participate in these professional organizations at the national, regional, and local levels. Participation ranges from simply attending the meetings to holding a leadership position within the organization; presenting at a local, regional or national program; and chairing a national or regional event.

Many facilitators participate in regional professional organizations or networks as well. While this list is ever growing and changing, some of the more steadfast North American networks are:

Arizona Association of FacilitatorsBay Area Facilitators Guild

Boston Facilitators Roundtable

Mid-Atlantic Facilitators Network

Minnesota Facilitators Network

OD Network of Ottawa

Southeast Association of Facilitators

Southern Ontario Facilitators Network

Southwest Facilitators' Network

IAF updates this information online (www.iaf-world.org).

REFERENCE MATERIALS

Seasoned facilitators are avid readers of books, publications, magazines, articles, and other published works. They read reference materials devoted to facilitation, as well as other works in various disciplines, such as education, cognitive science, psychology, change management, and personal growth.

Most set aside time that they commit to professional reading. For example, one facilitator reads for one hour each day while exercising. Another takes her professional reading with her while traveling. Several facilitators "peruse facilitation books every time I get ready for a session."

Books

The typical facilitator reads at least one or two books on facilitation each year. They frequently review their favorites—for inspiration or to garner new ideas for a specific session—and have a small library of books and other reference materials. The top twelve "best books on facilitation" cited most often by survey respondents were:

Bens, I. *Facilitating with Ease!* San Francisco: Jossey-Bass, 2000.

Doyle, M., and Straus, D. *How to Make Meetings Work.* New York: Berkley Publishing Group, 1982.

Gottesdiener, E. *Requirements by Collaboration: Workshops for Defining Needs.* Reading, Mass.: Addison-Wesley, 2002.

Heron, J. *The Facilitator's Handbook.* London: Kogan Page, 1990.

Hunter, D., and others. *The Art of Facilitation.* Auckland: Tandem Press, 1992.

Justice, T., and Jamieson, D. W. *The Facilitator's Fieldbook.* New York: AMACOM, 1999.

Kaner, S. *Facilitator's Guide to Participatory Decision-Making.* Philadelphia: New Society Publishers, 1996.

Owen, H. *Open Space Technology: A User's Guide.* San Francisco: Berrett-Koehler, 1997.

Schwarz, R. M. *The Skilled Facilitator.* San Francisco: Jossey-Bass, 1994.

Senge, P. *The Fifth Discipline Fieldbook: Strategies and Tools for Building a Learning Organization.* New York: Currency, 1994.

Sibbet, D. *Principles of Facilitation* and *Best Practices for Facilitation.* San Francisco: Grove Consultants International, 2002.

Stanfield, R. B. *The Art of Focused Conversation: One Hundred Ways to Access Group Wisdom in the Workplace.* Philadelphia: New Society Publishers, 2000.

Other Publications

Most facilitators tend to be voracious readers, and not just about facilitation. They tend to read widely, enjoying a variety of publications that shed insight into the client, topic, and environment, as well as process. They typically read journals published by professional organizations such as ACR's *Conflict Resolution Quarterly,* AQP's *Journal for Quality and Participation,* ASQ's *Quality Management Journal,* ASTD's *Training and Development,* IAF's *Group Facilitation: A Research and Applications Journal,* and OD Network's *Practicing.* The periodicals most often chosen by respondents were:

Training (www.trainingmag.com)

Harvard Business Review (www.hbr.com)

Harvard Management Communication Letter (www.hbr.com)

Fast Company (www.fastcompany.com)

Fortune (www.fortune.com)

Business 2.0 (www.business2.com)

Many facilitators also read journals specific to the fields in which they specialize. For example, one facilitator who works in the software development field reads technical journals e appropriate for the work she is doing with her clients. An anthropologist reads "tons of theory literature and [tries] to construct tools that benefit from the latest and greatest research and theory of human interaction."

Newsletters

There were also several newsletters and e-zines that facilitators read on a regular basis:

Facilitator (www.thefacilitator.com)

3M Meeting News (www.3m.com/meetingnetwork)

Master Facilitator Journal (www.masterfacilitatorjournal.com)

Extraordinary Team (www.qpcteam.com)

Creative Training Techniques (www.vnulearning.com)

Effective Meetings (www.effectivemeetings.com)

Better Meetings Newsletter (www.janakemp.com)

Leadership Strategies Newsletter (www.leadstrat.com)

ThinkPeople's Monthly Workout (www.thinkpeople.com)

One facilitator said he reads "anything fun and thought provoking that stimulates ideas on how to keep my clients coming back for more and to continue to remind them the value we can bring!"

INTERNET LEARNING

With the explosion of the Internet, most facilitators use the World Wide Web for networking with colleagues and searching for best practices in facilitation.

Electronic Discussion Groups

Many professional organizations sponsor an e-mail list—a listserv or e-mail conversation—for their members. Over half of the survey respondents participated in the IAF-sponsored list (www.iaf-world.org). With over eight hundred facilitators from thirty-three countries, this list provides a running commentary among facilitators all over the world. Each e-mail can be delivered to your in-box, or you can choose to receive daily summaries. The list engages the facilitation community and provides an opportunity for facilitators to learn from each other. "I try to read the majority of the messages that come via the list as I find most of the information shared to be wise and practical. I appreciate the expertise that people so generously share." (Refer to www.iag-world.org/about/iaflistserv.cfm for more information about the IAF listserv and additional electronic discussion groups sponsored by other organizations.)

World Wide Web Searches

Many facilitators search the World Wide Web at least quarterly for best practices in facilitation, updates, new ideas, and team activities and warm-up exercises. Ask them for their favorite sites, and they ask, "What did you have in mind?" for the field is wide and varied. Many facilitators keep a "favorites list" in their Web browser, organized by topic, in order to access these sites quickly. One facilitator says he tends to "surf the Web just before the wave breaks to try and get a little extra edge when I start or have been at it for a while with a group."

OBSERVATION OF OTHERS

Most facilitators truly enjoy watching others in action. By seeing someone else facilitate a group discussion in any setting, a particular technique may be recognized and reinforced. Not only do we "observe things that are and aren't valuable," but we get a sense for different facilitation styles. "By being aware of human behaviors and reactions in everyday situations, we recognize our best teachers are those with styles different from our own." As we observe others, we expand our horizons and learn more about ourselves and our possibilities.

Other Facilitators

Facilitators are exposed to myriad options and possibilities by observing other facilitators in action. They can watch others lead sessions, observe students try facilitation techniques during a role-play, or be "a participant in facilitated sessions to ensure that I understand facilitation from a participant's perspective." Another facilitator discovered that being an CPF assessor "allowed me opportunities to see different approaches and techniques" that CPF candidates used during the assessment process.

Other Settings

Recognizing that any time a group of people gets together presents an opportunity to observe others in action, seasoned facilitators look for facilitation techniques and nuances in other settings. One respondent noted that he makes a point of watching the "process-interaction dynamics of someone else's dialogue. How is the conversation initiated? What is the initial conditions-context? How do ideas move in and out of the discussion? How do participants know when they agree or disagree?" Another facilitator explained, "I remain open to alternative sources of information and skill development. I look for behavior that affects human interaction . . . wherever I find it. It might be a workshop, a film, a book, an article, or a dinner party."

Films

A favorite learning activity is to watch a full-length feature film and extract lessons in team dynamics, visioning, change management, diversity, decision making, and related areas. Although not specifically requested in the survey, a few facilitators mentioned the importance of films in developing their skills. Some of the favorite films cited in the IAF Listserv resource files are *A Few Good Men, Apollo 13, Babe, The Big Chill, Blue Collar, The Breakfast Club, Cat on a Hot Tin Roof, The Commitments, The Dirty Dozen, The Englishman Who Went Up a Hill But Came Down a Mountain, Erik the Viking, From Earth to the Moon, The Hunt for Red October, Lean on Me, Lord of the Flies, The Man in the Gray Flannel Suit, Mission Impossible, Norma Rae, One Flew over the Cuckoo's Nest, Remember the Titans, The Shawshank Redemption, To Sir with Love, Twelve Angry Men,* and *Whale Rider.*

One of my favorite scenes on team problem solving is from the movie *Apollo 13*. On the way to the moon, there is an explosion in the service module affecting the carbon dioxide scrubbers that chemically remove exhaled carbon dioxide from the enclosed capsule. Ground control is given the formidable task to jerry-rig a solution with only the materials onboard or the astronauts will die. With just a few hours of breathable air left, ground control concocts a makeshift solution and saves the day.

Keep in mind that if a video or film clip is used in a facilitated or training environment (regardless of whether you are profit or nonprofit), it is considered a public performance and requires the consent of the original copyright holder or its agent. To obtain information and purchase rights to use movie clips, contact ASCAP (www.ascap.com), BMI (www.bmi.com), or ACF (www.acf-film.com).

APPLICATION

While training and reading are outstanding forms to build facilitation expertise, all respondents agreed on the importance of applying learned knowledge to real-life situations. Similar to the adage about what makes real estate valuable (location, location, location), many facilitators emphasized, "It's all about practice, practice, practice." The average respondent works with groups at least three to four times a month, staying fluent in the art of facilitation.

"I practice all the fundamentals of facilitation in every situation where appropriate, not just when performing professionally. In the university classroom, at Rotary meetings, on boards of directors and so on. In other words, walk the talk in everyday life."

Be Present

A recurring theme for seasoned facilitators is to be present and transparent for the group. "When you facilitate, throw away all of your generalizations and be present to these individuals, this group, here, now." (For another discussion of transparency and related ideas, see Chapter Thirty-Two.)

Experimentation

Most facilitators discover new methods experientially. By "splicing together pieces of different ideas from books and other people," they pick up ideas at conferences and training sessions and from reading, discussion, and observation, and then adapt them to their specific situation. When venturing forth with a new tool or technique, many try it out in a small, safe group such as family, friends, or fellow facilitators.

Relying on a solid base of facilitation skill and understanding, many just "make it up by using what's necessary in the room." One facilitator found that "when I try something new 'on the fly' during facilitation exercises, participants are more willing to 'work without a net' if you create a proper context and support for the group's work." A different facilitator noted that he "creates solutions on a regular basis for clients. They drive my innovations by stretching my capabilities." Another facilitator encourages others to "try new things as often as possible—while honouring your group's needs. Also take some risks. Sometimes challenging yourself with a new method can help the group take some risks as well." Yet another cautioned, "Different groups have different needs. To work with them you will need to try different activities. Once tried, these activities may work in many areas you wouldn't have expected."

When experimenting, one respondent found it useful to tap into the wisdom of individual participants: "Develop relationships with group participants that have some level of facilitation skill and discuss what they observe. I use them as a sounding board." It is always helpful to get another person's perspective.

One caveat to remember when trying out new material with groups is this: "Put yourself in challenging situations regularly but remember people are not your lab. Observe the code of ethics for human experimentation." The IAF Statement of Values and Code of Ethics echoes these sentiments: "We avoid using processes, methods, or tools with which we are insufficiently skilled, or which are poorly matched to the needs of the group." (See also Chapter Thirty.)

Self-Awareness and Reflection

All facilitators engage in "continual reflection on what's working and what's not working," what happened, and why. The seasoned facilitator is on a journey, continually exploring "why we approach group activities as we do and what underlies the choices we make."

This self-reflection is an internal process: "I am very critical after any facilitation, noting what I could have done differently and storing that last session in my memory bank for the future." Another facilitator states he goes through "much personal soul-searching to re-evaluate the session and what might have gone differently or been a more helpful way to address an issue." Another facilitator asks herself, "Did I stay in role? Did I deal effectively with conflict? Did I use tools effectively? Review what I could have done differently."

Said another, "I reflect deeply on every single session that I facilitate, both by myself and with others who will de-brief with me. I ponder the feedback, and I take notes on what happened. I write up each process as a case so that the reflection and design is captured for future use."

Best Practices

Several facilitators commented that they intuitively learn what works and what does not and rely on their memories to keep track of best practices. A few reported that they have a process to capture participant feedback and lessons learned, captured in a personal journal, diary, or log. By documenting each session, seasoned facilitators discern patterns in the responses and make small improvements. For example, I developed a log book to capture lessons learned (as well as document required information for a professional certification). After each session, I note the feedback and write my thoughts in the log (for an example, see www.qpcteam.com/nsa/log.pdf). Over time, I can see trends that show my strengths and areas for improvement.

One facilitator writes a short, but insightful "lessons learned" paper each year that reinforces key learnings from her facilitation projects.

Another way to capture best practices is to keep paper or computer files of team activities, process models, tools, and techniques (noting the origins, so to be able to credit the source). The files are organized for easy access and retrieval of information (which varies from facilitator to facilitator).

FEEDBACK

Seasoned facilitators deliberately search for opportunities to receive feedback from others within both the facilitated group and the larger facilitation community. In the survey, a facilitator acknowledged, "Receiving valuable feedback is one of the weakest spots in my practice and an area that needs improvement." Another facilitator added, "An often-used throw-away line is to 'treat feedback as a gift.' The real trick is to actually do that—no defensiveness—just acceptance, exploration of alternatives and developmental planning."

Group Feedback

Throughout the process, facilitators continually seek feedback from the group and change direction as needed. One respondent advises to "listen hard to what is being said, observing and picking up on group dynamics and body language. . . . Listen to what participants tell you or each other during the session breaks and after the session. . . . Listen for asides and throw-away comments and jokes that might tell you something more than first indicated. . . . Look at their faces, their eyes, listen for sighs or frustrations. . . . They are giving constant feedback—you just have to look and listen for it."

Critiques   In our survey, over 80 percent of respondents either always or frequently conduct a critique where the participants are asked to evaluate the facilitated session. The critique can occur anytime and can range from a casual check-in to a full, formal debriefing either during or after the session. One facilitator noted, "Critiques are for the group, not me, usually trying to bring consciousness to the changes in what they do and how they work together." (For alternative views of evaluation, see Chapters Twenty-Four and Twenty-Five.) Others use the group feedback and their own intuition to reflect and improve their craft.

Formal Debriefs   Many practitioners facilitate a dialogue at the end of a session, using a flip chart to capture "plus/deltas (what went well/what to do differently) or charting the mood and effectiveness across the time frame of the event."

Several respondents indicated that more formal debriefing meetings were also held with their groups, clients, and other stakeholders at key intervals in the process (for example, midway, before entering a key phase, or when the project is finished). A formal debrief typically measures and compares project or session objectives. The debrief also evaluates what worked well and what could have worked better and the degree to which the group dealt with difficult issues, managed conflict, built consensus, solved problems, shared visions, developed synergy, and honored its culture.

Debriefs may also probe into more affectual issues, asking the participants if they felt they had an opportunity to contribute their talents and ideas, as well as express everything they felt necessary; if they felt valued; whether they appreciated the process; made free and informed choices; took ownership of their decisions and actions; and a sensed forward movement. One facilitator creates a "group barometer at the beginning of a session where progress is tracked throughout the session."

After-Action Reviews   One facilitator borrowed the U.S. Army's "after-action review" process that debriefs the success of an engagement by asking specific questions: "(1) What did we plan to do? (2) What actually happened? (3) How did that vary from our plans? (4) What might have been the cause for this? (5) How did we alter our plans and adapt? (6) What can we learn from this situation or event?" (For a description of the U.S. Army's After Action Review process, see Garvin, 2000, or www.mvr.usace.army.mil/PublicAffairsOffice/2003AnnualReport/DistrictHighlights/AAR%20Guide.doc.)

Follow-Ups   Many facilitators also follow up "a day or two later and check if the bloom is still on the rose and to see if there's something that came to them that I might need to know and to find out how they plan to move forward." Others follow up "a few weeks later to discuss the impact of the intervention on the group/organization." Another facilitator sends out a "simple post-workshop evaluation form or survey about four to eight weeks after each session to get additional feedback from the sponsors and to determine if group outcomes were achieved."

Peer Feedback

Between fellow facilitators, feedback is a mutually beneficial exchange of information that can also inspire brainstorming, problem solving, and mutual support. When the relationship is between different skill levels, it is more of a mentoring relationship. And when money or something else of value exchanges hands, it is a professional coaching relationship.

Several seasoned facilitators commented that they tend to get discriminating about whom they seek feedback from. Ultimately they select someone they trust and respect to give specific, candid feedback. One respondent declared, "I receive feedback at this point only from co-facilitators and clients. I'm nearly 60 years old and want collaborative learning rather than critiquing at this point in my career."

Cofacilitation   Occasionally, seasoned facilitators work with partners (not necessarily facilitators) who have different approaches or skills that can complement and expand their learning. One facilitator explained, "Co-facilitating draws on all your skills as a facilitator *and* as a member of a small, interdependent group. It's a microcosm of the world we practice in." Another facilitator cautions, "Co-facilitation works best when it is in the client's interest, not when the only goal is to expand your learning."

Critiques by Another Facilitator   "When I first started, I practiced facilitation skills in front of the mirror, in front of my wife, kids, and anyone who would sit and give me any kind of feedback. Now I ask people I know are good facilitators to regularly give me a tough critique on everything I am doing in front of groups."

One of the best formal methods to obtain substantive feedback is during the CPF process where candidates facilitate a twenty- to thirty-minute session. At the end of the session, the candidates and assessors provide immediate verbal feedback. In addition, the assessors provide written and verbal feedback on the candidate's strengths and areas for improvement.

Informal Collegial Network   Almost all (95 percent) of the respondents said that they "get new ideas from conversations with half a dozen close peers." In this informal network, colleagues ask each other questions, brainstorm ideas, share best practices, and "try out new techniques before using them live and in person."

"Getting feedback can be difficult in a one-person operation. Thus, the informal group is critical to sharing, analyzing, and digging into the real usefulness (or not) of various approaches."

In addition to meeting face to face, some informal, geographically dispersed networks use conference calls, establish e-mail lists, and coordinate an annual gathering among respected colleagues.

Master Mind   Napoleon Hill coined the concept of the "Master Mind" alliance in his book *Think and Grow Rich* (1937). He believed that a group of like-minded, achievement-oriented individuals could dramatically leverage each other's success. It is all about creating the synergy of like-minded professionals to have a safe place to celebrate success, solve pressing issues, offer support and encouragement, unleash creativity, gain valuable insights, and expand and develop their businesses.

A quarter (28 percent) of respondents indicated that they belong to a master mind group or formal peer advisory group. These groups differ from the informal networks in that they are far more structured. They tend to have a broader charter with members, roles and responsibilities, and ground rules, as well as agendas, meeting minutes, and structures that support accountability and follow-through. "I am part of a local facilitator mastermind that meets four to five times a year to share best practices, educate one another, support and refer work to each other."

Mentoring   An overwhelming majority (over 80 percent) of respondents have mentored another facilitator, and half have been mentored themselves. Most of these relationships were informal in nature, formed by bonds of friendship, geography, common interest, or shared values. These relationships were primarily centered around learning and reflection. (For more information on how to mentor and be a good mentor, see Sjodin and Wickman, 1996.)

Professional Coaching   A few facilitators "found professional coaching sessions were very helpful when I seemed stuck." One facilitator suggested using a "skilled psychotherapist to help deal with counter-projections [and to] decide if you are in the field to facilitate or become famous—they are different tracks." Ultimately, the use of a coach or other professional is about understanding who you are and how you show up in the world and with your groups. (See Chapter Thirty-Two.)

TEACH OTHERS

At a certain point, a seasoned facilitator has enough experience to be able to teach others. Over 75 percent of respondents teach facilitation skills at educational institutions, public seminars, corporate seminars, and community groups. In addition to mastering the learning objectives and materials, the instructors "learn a great deal from the participants in my programs." "I find the course participants an endless source of new perspectives. . . . Students' questions are a great way for me to gain greater understanding of what I do." Being an instructor also allows the opportunity to "develop new resources for facilitation and testing in the field."

BE A THOUGHT LEADER

Fifty percent of the surveyed facilitators have contributed "original thought" to the facilitation field. Usually these ideas are a refinement, a new model, framework, perspective, rationale, approach, tool, technique, or experiential exercise. Some facilitators have exchanged facilitation and group process skills with individuals in other countries, helped to design and build the CPF process, and contributed to the development of the IAF professional competencies (see Chapter Twenty-Six) and ethics (see Chapter Thirty). These thought leaders have been published in academic and professional journals, books, internal publications, newsletters, published books, pamphlets, and white papers, and they have compiled papers from international peers.

Most facilitators approach idea development in a collaborative mode "so my original thought gets kind of lost!" There is also a healthy skepticism that nothing is truly original and newly discovered, "but rather re-applications and/or revisions of others' thinking." Regardless, thought leaders take the time to write these ideas down to share them with the larger facilitation community.

PROFESSIONAL STANDING

Every profession has its own credentials, and facilitation is no different. The most prevalent is the CPF designation bestowed by the IAF. Half of the surveyed facilitators earned the CPF as well as several other credentials that complement their practices. Following is a list of the various types of credentials and some examples offered from the survey results:

• Educational. Almost all respondents have at least an undergraduate degree. Around half have graduate degrees, and 13 percent have earned doctoral degrees.

• Certifications from professional organizations in a complementary field. Most professional organizations and societies provide some accredited certification for their profession or standard of practice. Examples are Certified Six Sigma Black Belt (www.asq.org), Certified Management Consultant (www.imcusa.org), Certified Speaking Professional (www.nsaspeaker.org), and Certified Human Resource Professional (www.hria.org).

• Certifications from educational institutions in a complementary field. Many colleges and universities offer certification programs in facilitation skills and other diverse programs such as creativity and innovation and creative problem solving.

• Certification or qualification from an independent organization to perform a specific task or training course. Many organizations offer certifications or qualifications in conjunction with the successful completion of a training program. These titles include Certified Quality Facilitator, Certified Master Facilitator, Certified Training Consultant, Certified Mediator, Master Facilitator, and Certified Team Leader. In addition, many of these certification organizations license the use of a defined, proprietary process, such as Franklin-Covey Certified Trainer and the Myers-Briggs Type Indicator.

• Certifications and qualifications from professional associations within their chosen industry. A few facilitators hold certifications such as Certified Systems Professional (www.microsoft.com), Certified Computing Professional (www.iccp.org), Professional Engineer (www.nspe.org), Certified Association Executive (www.asaenet.org), and Advanced Certified Fundraising Executive (www.afpnet.org).

• Examiners. Not only are seasoned facilitators certified in their particular field, but a few respondents also served on the examining board to evaluate candidates for individual or organizational certification. For example, some respondents were CPF Assessors, Malcolm Baldrige National Quality Award Examiners, and State Productivity Award Examiners.

THE INTENTIONAL PLAN

When collecting the results of the survey, the one theme that distinguishes a master facilitator is the intentionality of his or her actions to build personal expertise. Master facilitators take their craft seriously and strive to improve their ability to effectively facilitate group process.

To develop your own intentional plan, use Exhibit 28.1. The first column lists the strategies presented in this chapter. Place a check mark in the second column if you have *ever used* that strategy as a part of your improving your skills. Place a check mark in the third column if you *currently use* that strategy. Place a check mark in the fourth column if you *intend to use* that strategy in the near future.

After you complete this checklist, reflect on what has been working well for you, and focus on one or two strategies (column 4) you think will make a difference in mastering your craft.

Exhibit 28.1
Strategies to Maintain and Enhance Your Professional Knowledge as a Group Facilitator

Strategy	Ever?	Currently?	Future?
Training			
Attend on-site training			
Use electronic media			
Teleclasses			
Video teleconferencing			
Webinars			
Web-based training			
Attend national and regional conferences			
Participate in professional organizations			
Attend meetings			
Hold a leadership position			
Present a program			
Chair a national or regional event			
Reference materials			
Read books			

Strategy	Ever?	Currently?	Future?
Read publications			
Read newsletters and e-zines			
Internet learning			
Participate in electronic discussion groups			
Search the Internet			
Observation of others			
Other facilitators			
Other settings			
Films			
Application			
Be present			
Experiment			
Self-awareness, reflection			
Capture best practices			
Feedback			
Solicit group feedback			
Conduct group critiques			
Obtain peer feedback			
Facilitate with others			
Be critiqued by another facilitator			
Participate in an informal network			
Belong to a mastermind group			
Mentor another facilitator			
Be mentored by another facilitator			
Be professionally coached			
Teaching			
Teach others how to facilitate			
Be a thought leader			
Publish, share ideas			
Professional standing			
Education			
Certifications			
Examiner of a certification process			

CONCLUSION

This chapter shares several strategies that seasoned facilitators use to build their facilitation expertise. As you strive to improve your ability to facilitate group process effectively, stand on the shoulders of others who have gone before you. Using the strategies and examples presented here, assess your current state, and develop an intentional plan to improve your facilitation expertise.

APPENDIX 28A: SURVEY OF GROUP FACILITATORS: HOW TO BUILD YOUR EXPERTISE

I want to know how you build your expertise as an experienced facilitator. Your ideas will be part of a chapter entitled "How to Build Your Expertise in Facilitation" in *The IAF Handbook of Group Facilitation*. As you take this survey, please keep a few things in mind:

Be realistic. This survey is designed to elicit your actual behaviors in building mastery . . . not what you would like to do, or what you think is a great idea to do. So please answer in complete honesty.

Provide detail. Each question will provide the opportunity for you to provide detail in how you go about accomplishing each item. If you have a great book, magazine, technique or tip to share, we would really appreciate it!

Identify what's missing. This list of "best practices" was culled from responses from the CPF assessment synopses. It is a great list to use to guide your own growth and development as a facilitator, but it is just a starting point. Did we miss something you do/use to build your expertise?

Thanks again for taking the time to complete this survey.
Kristin

1. On average, how often do you attend formal training, course or workshop for the sole purpose of learning a new facilitation skill or enhancing a current skill?

   Once a month
   Once a quarter
   Twice a year
   Once a year
   Once every two years
   Other (please specify)

2. In your opinion, what were the best training/seminars you have taken?

3. Do you attend national conferences to enhance your professional development as a facilitator? Which do you attend and how often?

	Always (every year)	Frequently (2 or 3 times in five years)	Occasionally	Never
ACR				
AQP				
ASQ				
ASTD				
IAF				
IAP				
ICA				
IMC				
ISPI				
NCPCR				
NSA				
OD Network				
Other				

4. Are you involved in any of the following professional organizations to network with other facilitators and for continued skill development?

	Not Involved	Attend Meetings	Held Leadership Position	Presented at Local Program	Presented at National Program	Chaired a National Program
ASQ						
ASTD						
CAPS						
IAF						
IMC						
NSA						
ODN						

5. Please list the local facilitator network/organizations you participate in, if any.

6. On average, how many books on facilitation do you read per year?

   1–2
   2–5
   5–8
   8–11
   Dozen or more
   Don't know

7. In your opinion, what are the best book(s) on facilitation?

8. What publications do you read?

   Business Communication Quarterly
   Conflict Resolution Quarterly
   Decision Sciences
   Group Decision and Negotiation
   Group and Organization Studies
   Group Facilitation: A Research and Applications Journal
   International Journal
   Journal of Applied Behavioral Science
   Journal of Business Communication
   Journal for Quality and Participation
   Management Communication Quarterly
   Management Decision
   Organization Development Journal
   Organizational Behavior and Human Decision Processes
   Quality Progress

Small Group Research
Training and Development
Training
Other (please specify)

9. What newsletters do you read on a regular basis?

3M Meeting News
Harvard Management Communication Letter
Master Facilitator Journal
The Facilitator
None
Other (please specify)

10. Do you participate in grp-facl, the IAF Listserv?

Yes
No
What's that?

11. Do you search the Internet for best practices in facilitation?

Weekly
Monthly
Quarterly
Yearly
Never

12. How do you learn a new tool or technique?

13. What are some of the ways you expand your knowledge and expertise of facilitation beyond those listed above?

14. On average, how often do you facilitate groups?

15. At the end of each session, do you conduct a critique where the participants are asked to evaluate the facilitated session?

    Always
    Frequently
    Occasionally
    Seldom
    Never

16. How do you evaluate group progress/success?

17. How do you evaluate your success as a facilitator?

18. As part of your learning, do you purposefully watch other facilitators in action?

    Always
    Frequently
    Occasionally
    Seldom
    Never

19. Do you ever purposefully co-facilitate with others to enhance your skills?

   Always
   Frequently
   Occasionally
   Seldom
   Never

20. Have you ever had a seasoned facilitator observe your session(s) and provide feedback/coaching afterwards?

   Always
   Frequently
   Occasionally
   Seldom
   Never

21. Have you ever had a facilitator mentor you?

22. Do you have an informal network of colleagues that you can call on when needed?

23. Do you belong to a "mastermind" or formal peer advisory group?

24. Please note any specifics you would like to share about the ways you practice your skills and receive feedback.

25. Do you teach facilitation skills at an academic institution?

No, I don't
K-12
Undergraduate
Graduate (Master's level)
Graduate (Doctoral level)
Other (Please specify)

26. Do you offer courses/training in facilitation?

Public seminars
In-house/corporate seminars
Community service
No, I don't offer any courses
Other (please specify)

27. Have you mentored other facilitators?

Yes
No

28. Have you contributed original thought to the facilitation field, e.g., new models, approaches and/or techniques?

No
Yes (please elaborate)

29. Where have your ideas on facilitation been published?

Not published
Articles
Books
Columns
Internet
Pamphlets
Others (please specify)

30. What professional qualifications have you received?

None
MBTI
DISC
NLP
Kolb's Learning Styles Inventory
Other (please specify)

31. What professional certifications have you earned?

None
CMC—Certified Management Consultant
CPCM—Certified Professional Consultant to Management
CPF—Certified Professional Facilitator
CQM—Certified Quality Engineer
CSP—Certified Speaking Professional
Other—(please specify)

32. Based on your personal experience, please rate the value of the following methods to maintain and enhance your professional knowledge as a group facilitator.

	7 – Great Value	6	5	4	3	2	1 – Little Value	Don't Know; N/A
Training/seminars								
Conferences								
Professional organizations								
Books								
Publications/ newsletters								
Grp-fcl, IAF listserv								
Internet searches								
Practice								
Evaluation								
Self-assessment								
Observation								
Co-facilitation								
Being mentored								
Networking								
Teaching								
Mentoring others								
Writing								
Qualifications								
Certifications								

33. Are there any other ways you enhance your facilitation skills that you'd like to share?

34. What is your gender?

Male

Female

35. What is your highest level of education?

High school
Undergraduate degree
Graduate degree
Doctoral degree

36. How many years have you been facilitating groups?

0–2
3–5
6–9
10–14
15–19
Over 20

37. In your role as a facilitator, are you a

Full-time internal facilitator
Part-time internal facilitator
Full-time external facilitator
Part-time external facilitator
No formal job responsibilities as a facilitator

38. Thanks! Would you like to receive a copy of the chapter?

No; thanks anyway
Yes, please! Here's my e-mail address!

Dimensions of Facilitator Education

Glyn Thomas

The literature on facilitation is primarily focused on describing facilitation skills and models for practice and, to a lesser extent, the theories of facilitation practice. There is, however, considerably less focus on the assumptions and philosophies that underpin facilitation practice. Similarly, there is little discussion about the processes that may help facilitators develop their skills, competence, judgment, and theoretical grounding. Historically, most of the literature on facilitation has not been grounded in empirical research, although recently there has been growth in the research-based facilitation literature within the organization development (OD) field (see Ellinger and Bostrom, 2002; Mongeau and Morr, 1999; Niederman and Volkema, 1999).

This chapter provides a model that differentiates the numerous approaches to facilitator education found in the facilitation literature within an OD context. The model provides a useful interpretive framework to stimulate reflection, discussion,

Notes: This chapter is based on Glyn Thomas, "A Typology of Facilitator Education Processes," *Journal of Experiential Education,* forthcoming.

I acknowledge the guidance of Lorraine Ling from La Trobe University, Melbourne, Victoria. Thanks and appreciation to the workshop participants at the Australasian Facilitators' Network Conference in November 2003 who provided valuable comments on an earlier version of this chapter.

and further research into the theory and practice of facilitator education. The aim here is not to provide an extensive review of the facilitation skills, strategies, models, and theories described in the literature; rather, the focus will be on the assumptions and philosophies underpinning facilitator education as stated or implied in the facilitation literature. We begin with the growing emphasis of facilitation within the OD field.

THE DEMAND FOR FACILITATOR EDUCATION IN ORGANIZATION DEVELOPMENT

The growing need for more facilitative styles of management seems to be commonly accepted in the OD literature even though there is little empirical evidence to support this view. Global economic change continues to put increased pressure on organizations by increased competition for customers, the rapid development of technology, reductions in production costs, and the proliferation of customers who are increasingly sophisticated about choices and pricing (Marsick and Watkins, 1999; Weaver and Farrell, 1997). Hogan (2002) contends that to meet these challenges, there has been an increase in participatory approaches to management, which has boosted the profile of facilitation. Pierce, Cheesebrow, and Braun (2000) also state that "facilitation is increasingly being used as a participatory tool for getting results in group dialogue, analysis, decision making, and planning" (p. 31).

There has been a corresponding shift away from traditional conceptions of management, of command and control, to a new focus on employee involvement, self-managed work teams, and Total Quality Management approaches (Stahl, 1995). The traditional management functions of planning, organizing, leading, and controlling are now shared with nonsupervisory employees at different organizational levels because there is too much to do and not enough time to do it. The effect on managers has been significant: "The pace of work is faster and more furious . . . managers have to deal with a staggering amount of information . . . they have far more responsibilities and fewer resources to get the job done . . . technology is rapidly changing the way people work together . . . it is common for work groups to be geographically dispersed. Meetings frequently take place over the phone, and sales transactions are made via e-mail" (Weaver and Farrell, 1997, p. 2).

Responsive organizations require managers who are genuinely committed to deep change in themselves and in their organizations. These managers lead by developing new skills, capabilities, and understandings, and they come from many places within their organizations (Senge, 1996). Larsen and others (2002, p. 31) state that "group facilitation is often the necessary process that allows organizations to learn and to learn how to change," and managers within organizations are increasingly being expected to act as de facto facilitators (Webne-Behrman, 1998). Despite the lack of empirical research examining the roles and behaviors of leaders and managers and their effect on learning in their organizations, in many organizations today, managers are exhorted to become teachers, educators, developers, leaders of learning, strategic learning managers, and coaches (Ellinger and Bostrom, 2002).

In one of the rare empirical studies on facilitation in an OD context, Ellinger and Bostrom (2002) explored the mental models of exemplary managers as they were serving as facilitators of learning. They found that organizations with new empowerment paradigms needed to focus management development initiatives on more than just behavior (coaching skills); they also needed to focus on the beliefs managers hold. Many managers in progressive organizations have had to shift away from a traditional control model to a facilitator-of-learning model. A supportive organizational culture was mentioned by managers in the study as very important in sustaining and supporting the transition to the facilitator-of-learning role, a process that takes time and presents many challenges (Ellinger and Bostrom, 2002).

Larsen and others (2002) also espouse the importance of the participation of skilled facilitators in the development of the core disciplines of learning organizations as identified by Senge (1990), which include personal mastery, mental models, team learning, shared vision, and systems thinking. In their summary of the literature, Larsen and others (2002) describe the key characteristics of a learning organization as "a belief in the ability of people and organizations to change and become more effective, and that change requires open communication and empowerment of community members as well as a culture of collaboration" (p. 31).

In response to this growing demand for facilitation, the Facilitator Competency Model was developed by the International Association of Facilitators (IAF) and the Institute of Cultural Affairs (ICA) to define the profession, guide facilitators' professional development, provide a framework for those who serve as mentors to other facilitators, provide a system of certification, and be a resource to those developing academic programs specific to facilitation (Pierce, Cheesebrow, and Braun, 2000).

To balance this rosy view of facilitation in OD, Hughes (1999) warns that although the workplace is usually seen as a rich and exciting learning environment, it can also be an extremely hostile one, and it "can be argued that the role of employers and their supervisors as facilitators of learning is also fundamentally problematic because of the hierarchy and conflict of interest that is inherent in the relationships involved" (p. 34).

In summary, although some aspects of facilitation within OD may be problematic, there is no shortage of literature espousing the value of facilitation in this context. However, the facilitation literature is not in full agreement on how managers or consultants may be best educated to fulfill these facilitation roles in OD.

APPROACHES TO FACILITATOR EDUCATION

A range of definitions and conceptualizations of the facilitation process exists within the literature. They typically describe how facilitation should occur, which in turn influences how facilitator education should proceed. This chapter deliberately uses the term *facilitator education* rather than *facilitator training* or *facilitator development* because, as suggested by Hogan (2002), the term *education* implies a deeper level of engagement than *training* or *development* implies.

Many of the approaches to facilitator education in the literature seem to fit into one of the following broad frameworks:

- Technical facilitator education approaches, which are skills based and formulaic in style (see Bendaly, 2000; Hart, 1991, 1992; Havergal and Edmonstone, 1999; Parry, 1995; Sharp, 1992)

- Intentional facilitator education approaches, where practice is grounded in theory and justifications and particular interventions are provided (see Bentley, 1994; Brockbank and McGill, 1998; Heron, 1989, 1993, 1999; Priest, Gass, and Gillis, 2000; Schwarz, 2002; Weaver and Farrell, 1997)

- Person-centered facilitator education approaches, which specifically emphasize the attitudes, personal qualities, and presence of the facilitator (see Hunter, Bailey, and Taylor, 1999; Ringer, 2002; Rogers, 1983, 1989)

- Critical facilitator education approaches, which emphasize awareness of the political nature of facilitation and the effects on all participants (see Kirk and Broussine, 2000).

The above frameworks are forthwith called dimensions; and the relationships between these dimensions are shown in Exhibit 29.1, the Dimensions of Facilitator Education Model. Previously, Thomas (forthcoming) used a typology to describe the differences between approaches to facilitator education in an experiential education context. However, following a workshop at an Australasian Facilitator's Network conference in November 2003, where the typology was discussed, feedback from participants suggested that nested boxes more effectively communicated the relationships among the different approaches to facilitator education. Before describing these dimensions, it is important to clarify two issues.

First, the dimensions portrayed in the larger boxes are considered to be extensions of the dimensions portrayed in the smaller boxes nested inside them. In this respect, the model implies that a dimension portrayed in a larger box covers much (but not necessarily all) of the content or foci of the preceding dimension, but there is also an implied progression in the depth and complexity of the facilitator education process. This is consistent with the way these approaches are described in the literature.

**Exhibit 29.1
Dimensions of Facilitator Education Model**

Critical	**Facilitator**	**Education**	
Person Centered	**Facilitator**	**Education**	Approaches that raise an awareness of the political nature of facilitation
Intentional Facilitator	**Education**	Approaches intentionally emphasizing attitudes, personal qualities, or presence of the facilitator	
Technical Facilitator Education Approaches that are skills based and formulaic	Approaches that are purposively grounded in theory		

Second, although many of the approaches to facilitator education tended to focus primarily on the content and foci of a single dimension portrayed in the model, there were exceptions. Some approaches to facilitator education (see Hogan, 2002, 2003; Hunter, Bailey, and Taylor, 1995, 1999; Pierce, Cheesebrow, and Braun, 2000) emphasized the importance of skills, processes, and knowledge across a number of the dimensions presented in the model.

Technical Facilitator Education Dimension

Approaches to facilitation that may be classified as technical focus on the skills and competencies required to facilitate groups. Implicit within these approaches is the assumption that by mastering a certain set of skills and methods, an individual can learn to facilitate a group's process effectively. However, there is a range of approaches to facilitation even within this dimension. In *The Facilitation Skills Training Kit,* Bendaly (2000) presents twenty skills-focused modules that can be used to help people develop facilitation skills. The delivery of each module is highly structured, inflexible, and outcomes focused. A similar facilitation training resource developed by Hart (1991, 1992), the Faultless Facilitation Method, provides an equally prescriptive training program focused on developing particular facilitation skills. Hart provides detailed lesson plans, examples of course overviews, resources, and evaluation forms. The *Facilitator's Toolkit* by Havergal and Edmonstone (1999) takes a similar approach to facilitator education. All of these authors are deliberately prescriptive about the skills they believe are needed to facilitate effectively.

In an article focusing on the "never-evers" of workshop facilitation, Sharp (1992) provides a list of twenty practical tips for potential facilitators, and all but one (deals with the beliefs or attitudes of the facilitator). Parry (1995) maintains that facilitators, in addition to possessing certain attributes, need a combination of technical skills, behavioral and interpersonal skills, and consultancy skills. Not all the literature within this classification is as formulaic in the way they conceptualize facilitation as the previous examples. Although still emphasizing the need to develop skills, Hackett and Martin (1993) also consider ideas and concepts. Justice and Jamieson (1999) predominantly emphasize the need for skills but also briefly discuss the need to "draw on some knowledge bases useful to facilitation" and to "employ personal characteristics that are helpful to the facilitator role" (p. 5).

In summary, the approaches in this dimension focus on the skills that facilitators need, using what may be described as a competency-based training approach. At this point, it is important to address the difference between a competency-based training approach and the Facilitator Competency Model developed by the IAF and ICA (Pierce, Cheesebrow, and Braun, 2000). The Facilitator Competency Model uses the term *competency* in a much broader sense than is typically used in the competency-based training literature. Some of the "competencies" presented in that model could be more accurately described as values, goals, or commitments of a professional facilitator (Hogan, 2002; Schwarz, 2000). Competency-based training tends to downplay the affective and cognitive dimensions of learning, which means that it may fail to address values and professionalism, conceptual knowledge, underpinning experience, and tacit knowledge (James, 2001). Some sections of the literature within this dimension provide little or no discussion about the theories on which skills or actions are based or about the values, attitudes, and beliefs that are conducive to effective facilitation. Hogan (2002, p. 207) describes these kinds of approaches as having a "'box of tricks' mindset," and she tries to help emerging facilitators become "aware of the complexities of human behavior and the responsibilities of their facilitation roles." Some of the literature within this dimension provides an impression that facilitation is easy if the facilitator follows the recipes provided, which would be fine if the "ingredients" were all the same. Although this kind of thinking may facilitate book sales, approaches to facilitator education that do not move beyond this first dimension belie the true complexity and difficulty of facilitation in many OD contexts. Many of the approaches to facilitator education in the next dimension of the model explain the importance of helping emerging facilitators to move beyond this dimension of technical facilitator education.

Intentional Facilitator Education Dimension

Approaches within this dimension recognize the importance of teaching prospective facilitators suitable methods, skills, and strategies, but also encourage facilitators to be intentional, "in the sense that the facilitator is conscious of what she is doing and why" (Brockbank and McGill, 1998, p. 152). This type of explicit intentionality is demonstrated: in the dialogue used, through an awareness of the process, by making otherwise hidden processes explicit, by encouraging an awareness of personal stances, and by modeling desired behaviors (Brockbank and McGill, 1998).

Weaver and Farrell (1997, p. xiv) are critical of authors who "assume that facilitation is simply having a sufficiently large stock of tools that can be selected when a group becomes bogged down," and they maintain that "effective facilitation reflects a practical set of skills and knowledge that helps people work together better to complete real work." Bentley (1994) states that traditional definitions of facilitation describe an activity—things that people do. However, he argues that it also includes "non-action, silence and even the facilitator's absence" (Bentley, 1994, p. 10). Thus, the intentional facilitator must not only carefully consider how he or she acts and responds but also how and when not to respond.

In one of the rare articles based on empirical research, Ellinger and Bostrom (2002) explored the way that managers frame their roles and beliefs about learners and the learning process. The research used a descriptive qualitative methodology that included semistructured interviews with twelve managers and an adaptation of the Critical Incident Technique (cited in Ellinger and Bostrom, 2002). This technique involved systematic and sequential procedures to record detailed observations of critical incidents in the past. The data were then analyzed using content analysis to establish emerging themes and develop broad psychological principles (Ellinger and Bostrom, 2002). A purposive sampling strategy was used, and the managers who participated came recommended by their employers as exemplary facilitators of learning. Weaknesses in the research design, including problems with the assessment process used to ascertain the participants' status as "exemplary" facilitators and the heavy reliance on memories of critical incidents, do not detract from the findings of this piece of exploratory research.

In the study, it was found that managers perceive their roles as "manager" and "facilitator of learning" distinctly. The findings indicated that managers successfully shift from a traditional managerial controlling role to a facilitator-of-learning role only if their corresponding beliefs are also changed. Ellinger and Bostrom (2002, p. 173) found that "while most management development programs often focus on skill or behavior development, few if any focus on the belief aspects associated with acquired new behaviors." One of the research recommendations for improved facilitation education for managers is that "skill training and interventions that focus on behavioral change must pay attention to beliefs" (Ellinger and Bostrom, 2002, p. 173). The study also highlighted the need for a supportive organizational culture in sustaining and supporting the transition to the facilitator-of-learning role, a process that takes time and presents many challenges. (For additional perspectives on the role of organizational culture in supporting facilitation, see Chapter Twelve.)

In one of the more comprehensive texts on facilitation, Schwarz (2002) outlines the Skilled Facilitator approach, which is based on a set of core values, assumptions, and principles. His systems approach integrates theory and practice and focuses on the internal and external work of facilitation. The first premise on which Schwarz builds his approach to facilitation involves making core values explicit. He explains that "rendering them explicit enables you to understand and evaluate them directly rather than having to infer them from the techniques I describe" (p. 9). The other premise of Schwarz's approach is understanding and establishing ground rules for effective groups, because they function as a diagnostic tool and a teaching tool for developing effective group norms. Schwarz's approach is intentional because, he explains, "you not only need a set of methods and techniques but also an understanding of how and why they work . . . you see the reasoning that underlies each technique and method . . . you can improvise and design new methods and techniques consistent with the core values . . . you can discuss your approach with clients so they can make informed choices about choosing you as a facilitator" (p. 9). (See Chapter Two.)

In a critique of technical approaches to facilitation, Schwarz (2002) states it is "not simply a matter of learning new strategies, tools, or techniques. Your ineffectiveness results from the core values and assumptions you hold" (p. 66). Schwarz warns aspiring facilitators of uncritically borrowing methods and techniques from a variety of other approaches because basing methods and techniques on conflicting values and principles can also lead to ineffectiveness. He explains that simply "changing what you say and how you say it is not sufficient to significantly change the unintended consequences you get" (p. 93). In conditions of low favorability, the facilitator's theory-in-use (see Argyris and Schön, 1996) will override any new behavior that lacks a corresponding change in thinking patterns, which supports his stance that facilitation approaches that teach only techniques will not work in difficult situations.

Heron has published numerous books on the topic of group facilitation over the past few decades (for example, see Heron, 1989, 1993), but his latest book, *The Complete Facilitator* (1999), presents the culmination of his published work on the topic. Heron (1999) creates a matrix of six dimensions of facilitation (planning, meaning, confronting, feeling, structuring, and valuing) and three modes of facilitation (hierarchical, cooperative, and autonomous). Heron is not prescriptive or formulaic with the resulting eighteen combinations of modes and dimensions. Rather, he suggests the matrix can be used to make facilitators aware of the range and subtlety of options, as a self and peer assessment tool to work on strengths and weaknesses, and to devise training exercises to develop skill within particular modes and dimensions. From an intellectual perspective, this matrix provides a finely tuned look at complexities of facilitation; however, from a pragmatic perspective, it is rather cumbersome.

Priest, Gass, and Gillis (2000) encourage facilitators to clarify their own personal belief systems and develop their knowledge of OD theories. They present a pragmatic smorgasbord of facilitation ideas, methods. and models to help facilitators increase their effectiveness, but unlike Heron (1999) and Schwarz (2002), there is not a central model or theory to hold their recommendations together.

Van Maurik (1994) developed a model that summarizes the range of styles that facilitators can also use in a management context. The model outlines four facilitation styles with varying degrees of knowledge input and process input. The model is similar to the Situational Leadership Model developed by Hersey and Blanchard (1993) in that the four styles described use different combinations of emphasis on task behavior and relational behavior. Van Maurik maintains that the challenge is for facilitators to become more consciously aware of and intentional about the style they use. He explains, "The benefits of having models of facilitative behavior to think about are that the facilitator can enact a more deliberate strategy and then look to see how effective it was" (p. 34).

An unresolved issue within this dimension concerns the level of awareness associated with intentionality. The work of Schön (1988, 1995), on how professionals practice, indicates that it is possible for a professional to function effectively without being able to articulate clear rationales for his actions. According to Schön, "There is nothing strange about the idea that a kind of knowing is inherent in intelligent action" and "our bias towards thinking blinds us to the non-logical processes which are omnipresent in effective practice" (1995, p. 52). Proponents of this perspective would argue that facilitators who draw on intuitive processes practice a different kind of intentionality, yet there is little discussion of this kind of practice within the facilitation literature. Hunter, Bailey, and Taylor (1999, p. 76) explain that "being connected with and using your intuition is essential as a facilitator" and that "often you will need to act in the moment, with little time to think." They also maintain that "facilitation is not a bundle of recipes. It is much more subtle and complex than that" (p. 76).

In summary, intentional facilitator education approaches enhance the technical facilitator education dimension by deliberately integrating many of the skills, techniques, and methods with learning about theories, values, and beliefs.

Person-Centered Facilitator Education Dimension

The person-centered approach is also intentional in nature, but rather than emphasizing skills, techniques, methods, and the underpinning theories, facilitator education in this dimension focuses on the qualities of the interpersonal relationships between the facilitator and group. Rogers (1983, 1989) provides a good example of such an approach because he stated that the personal qualities and attitudes of the facilitator are more important that any methods he or she employs. Rogers explained that methods and strategies will be ineffective unless the facilitator demonstrates a genuine desire to "create a climate in which there is freedom to learn" (Rogers, 1983, p. 157). Rogers (1983, 1989) described the essential personal qualities of a facilitator as being real; demonstrating prizing, acceptance, and trust; and practicing empathic understanding.

Also within this dimension, Ringer (2002) advocates a subjectivist view of group leadership and facilitation that frees the facilitator from "the illusion that leaders are in control of the group. We can see our interactions with the group in a new light: as influence rather than control" (p. 62). In this respect, the facilitator is still intentional in his or her approach to facilitation, but the role in a group is aided less by technique and more through the facilitator's presence, which is developed by enhancing a conscious awareness of his or her own subjectivity. Thus, the facilitator's presence also becomes the focus of her intentionality, not just her actions or responses to the group. Ringer's approach, based in psychodynamics, takes the emphasis solely off learning skills and methods, and raises the profile of "maintaining your self fully present with the group and providing appropriate support for the group to achieve its goal" (2002, p. 18). Ringer deliberately avoids providing "algorithmic step-by-step recipes that are intended to substitute for the judgment and experience of the group leader" (Ringer, 2002, p. 38). Ringer (1999) also espouses the need for facilitators to demonstrate suitable levels of psychological and emotional maturity to make sure that group functioning is bounded, purposeful, and safe. He describes the core aspects of this psychological maturity as the ability to reflect on and take responsibility for one's own assumptions;

appropriate levels of involvement with the group; congruence between feelings, actions, and reality; and the ability to tolerate complexity, ambiguity, and contradiction.

Although the model of facilitation competencies identified by the IAF and the ICA (Pierce, Cheesebrow, and Braun, 2000, p. 33) focuses on technical skills and knowledge, these authors also recognize that "in the art and science of guiding a group process, facilitators develop an awareness that they themselves are an important instrument in getting the work done" and that facilitators must also develop personal qualities in order to help groups achieve their purposes. Similarly, Hunter, Bailey, and Taylor (1995) explain that the secret to being an effective facilitator is "more to do with who you are and who you are being for the group you're working with. . . . The relationship you develop with the group is the key" (p. 201). Similarly, Hogan (2002) emphasizes the importance of relationships and the need for facilitators to be fully present and authentic with group members in their approach to facilitator education. (For an example of this approach, see Chapter Thirty-Two.)

In summary, the person-centered facilitator education dimension builds on the previous two dimensions in the model by incorporating the importance of relationships with participants and the presence that the facilitator maintains in the group. In the fourth and final dimension, facilitator education approaches are "specifically concerned with the influences of educational knowledge, and of cultural formations generally, that perpetuate or legitimate an unjust status quo" (Burbules and Berk, 1999, p. 46).

Critical Facilitator Education Dimension

The dominant theme of facilitator educator within this dimension is that facilitators must recognize the political and emotional impact that organizations have on them. These approaches to facilitator education are based on critical theory, which originated with the work of Kant, Hegel, and Marx and was further developed by Habermas and his predecessors in the Frankfurt school (Rasmussen, 1996). Critical theory seeks to expose the operation of power and to bring about social justice by redressing inequalities and promoting individual freedoms within a democratic society (Habermas, 1984, 1991).

The approach to facilitator education that Kirk and Broussine (2000) take neatly fits this dimension because they refute the notion of facilitation as a set of skills and processes that are value free, objective, and neutral. However, they also observe that facilitators are often conceived as people apart, distanced from an organization's political networks, and able to comment and intervene independently and neutrally. They argue that protestations of facilitator neutrality show either naiveté or cleverness because there will always be tensions between those who wish to preserve the system and those who wish to change it. Other authors (Broussine and others, 1998; Cervero and Wilson, 2001) have also identified the difficulty for facilitators in organizations to admit to the emotional and political aspects of their roles.

Hughes (1999) claims that those who espouse the value of facilitation in organizations often assume that there is no conflict of interest between the facilitator and the learner, or they ignore the issue altogether. Consequently, he perceives a fundamental barrier to supervisors' becoming effective facilitators. These conflicts of interest have an impact on both the ability of the supervisor to develop a trusting relationship with their supervisees and his or her ability to foster critical reflectivity that probes for assumptions, values, and beliefs underlying actions. In the related fields of community development and experiential education, several authors espouse the need for a socially critical approach to facilitation. Warren (1998) suggests that socially critical facilitation requires us to "become more conscious of how methods can advance or impede social justice" (p. 21). She is also critical of facilitation lacking in theoretical validation and describes it as "empty attempts to practice without a sound grounding" and that it is particularly irresponsible if facilitators "attempt to 'do the right thing' without an understanding of their own biases or the current anti-bias work theory" (Warren, 1998, p. 23).

White (1999) adopts a socially critical perspective by suggesting that "good facilitators are . . . committed to empowering those who are weaker, more vulnerable, marginalized, oppressed or otherwise disadvantaged" (p. 9). White explains that socially critical facilitation entails unlearning, which requires facilitators to reflect critically on the way they practice and consider how their training and development have influenced and shaped the way they think and practice as a facilitator. White maintains that it is possible for facilitators to inherit a complex set of attitudes, values, beliefs, and practices that unwittingly perpetuate injustices when they facilitate. Similarly, Warren (1998) is critical of facilitation training that focuses only on techniques and suggests that developing facilitators must also focus on the "social and cultural backgrounds of their participants and the way their locations in privilege or marginality affect how they teach and facilitate" (p. 23). Although most facilitation would aim to be emancipatory, "facilitation can become part of a system of oppression and perpetuation of dependent relations, with facilitators becoming unwitting agents of manipulation and managerialism" (Kirk and Broussine, 2000, p. 14).

Kirk and Broussine (2000) identify four positions of facilitator awareness: partial awareness–closed, immobilized awareness, manipulative awareness, partial awareness–open. They recommend practicing from the position of partial awareness–open where the facilitator is "aware of his or her own limited awareness, actively and openly works with what they think is going on in themselves, in the group and wider system . . . realizing their own partiality" (p. 20). To help facilitators practice with authority and confidence, Kirk and Broussine provide some practical suggestions in the context of an increased political awareness. They suggest that facilitators should acknowledge their partial awareness, engage in reflective practice, give attention to their own development, practice reflexivity, acknowledge the complexity of the facilitation role, and exercise care about the process and for the people in the process. The critical thinking integral to this dimension works on the premise that "where our beliefs remain unexamined, we are not free; we act without thinking about why we act, and thus do not exercise control over our own destinies" (Burbules and Berk, 1999, p. 46).

In summary, critical facilitator education approaches go beyond critical thinking to target beliefs, theories, and practices that are repressive, partisan, or implicated in the preservation of an unjust status quo (Burbules and Berk, 1999). It is possible that in so doing, critical facilitator education approaches go dangerously close to prejudging what might be suitable facilitator interventions rather than allowing facilitators to respond to the group and its needs in the moment. However, critical facilitator educators would contend that failure to focus on social injustices under the pretense of impartiality would simply enshrine many conventional assumptions in a manner that intentionally, or unintentionally, maintains political conformity (Burbules and Berk, 1999).

LIMITATIONS OF THE MODEL AND ISSUES FOR FACILITATOR EDUCATION

George Box (1979, p. 202) wrote, "All models are wrong, some are even useful" and in this context, the Dimensions of Facilitator Education Model, like every other model ever developed, fails to conceptualize the literature on facilitator education perfectly.

Although many examples of the literature seem to focus primarily on one dimension of the model, some approaches to facilitator education transcend several dimensions of the model. The approaches taken by Hogan (2002, 2003), Hunter, Bailey, and Taylor (1995, 1999), and the IAF and ICA (Pierce, Cheesebrow, and Braun, 2000) are good examples. This is potentially confusing but reflects the fact that some of the facilitation literature is broader in scope and addresses a range of facilitation competencies, knowledge, values, and beliefs. For other authors, one dimension is enough to classify the approach to facilitator education they present. The model is more user friendly if the boundaries between each dimension are viewed as overlapping or at least blurred.

By definition, the model implies that each new dimension incorporates the elements of previous dimensions and then adds a layer of complexity of facilitator education. The progression is in some respects sequential, but in reality, facilitator education has multiple entry points. For example, a person with knowledge, interest, or experience in critical education (see Freire, 1973) or community development in developing countries (see Phnuyal, Archer, and Cottingham, 1997) may gravitate straight toward a critical facilitator education approach. However, they may also have to double back to previous dimensions to master certain competencies, gain specific knowledge, or develop certain attributes or qualities. Similarly, before an emerging facilitator can truly focus on the approach of a more complex dimension of facilitator education, it could be argued that he or she must first achieve mastery in a preceding dimension of the model.

Literature on the nature of expertise (Chi, Farr, and Glaser, 1988) suggests that experts are often able to function with greater speed and effectiveness because they have mastered, to a level of automaticity (Flor and Dooley, 1998), skills or processes required to perform particular tasks. It is possible that the same is true for facilitators and that they must master previous dimensions to be "fully present" and facilitate using the approaches recommended in other dimensions of facilitator education. It is also important to flag the obvious tension that exists when trying to develop a model that encapsulates the diversity of approaches to facilitator education presented in the literature. Some authors in their description of facilitator education processes never move beyond a technical focus, while other authors are explicitly critical of this practice. The model attempts to provide a fair, respectful, and balanced summary of the approaches to facilitator education contained within the literature. An emerging innovation, used by qualitative researchers to overcome such difficulties, is called multiple voicing. In this approach, researchers provide a rich array of interpretations or perspectives without "pressing them into coherence" (Gergen and Gergen, 2003, p. 580). In the interests of generating further discussion and research, this chapter presents a model designed to advance research and discussion, but it does so with an appropriate level of diffidence.

Second, when the literature on facilitation did not specifically identify processes, rationales, or values concerning facilitator education, judgments about authors' perspectives on facilitator education were made. It is possible that the critical reading of the literature presented in this chapter is flawed or that others may interpret implied meanings differently. In what could be described as a crisis of representation (Denzin and Lincoln, 2003a; Lincoln and Guba, 2003), I accept responsibility for the fact that despite all attempts to portray the literature accurately, some errors in interpretation are unavoidable. In the spirit of collaborative inquiry, I hope that further discussion and research on the model presented in this chapter will lead to a better understanding of facilitator education processes and the development of a better model. It would also be helpful if more authors were explicit about the strategies and techniques that they believe emerging facilitators could use to continue their development.

Another issue that warrants further research is the apparent tension regarding interpretations of intentionality. Some authors advocate an explicit intentionality, and yet there may be a case for a tacit level of intentionality. I hope that further research and discussion will contribute to an increased understanding of the relationship between theory and practice of facilitation in experiential education. Hovenlynck (1998) describes the facilitator education process as a generative process where developing facilitators learn to articulate what makes sense in practice, or their knowing-in-action. In this respect, although Schön's work (1988, 1995) should not be used to justify theoretical laziness, he does balance the view that facilitators could ever hope to reach a state of complete intentionality. Approaches such as action learning and action research (see Carr and Kemmis, 1986; Elliot, 1991; Weinstein, 1999; Winter, 1989) may help lead to an alternative theory-practice relationship, which would be beneficial in facilitator education. The action learning and action research frameworks build on programmed knowledge (preexisting expert knowledge, theories, and personal knowledge) by questioning it, acting on it, and reflecting on it.

Fourth, there are some apparent weaknesses in the facilitation literature at present. Only a small proportion is grounded in empirical research, and although the profession may not be well suited to the positivist paradigm, research using naturalistic approaches within an interpretive paradigm (see Denzin and Lincoln, 2003a, 2003b, 2003c; Erlandson, Harris, Skipper, and Allen, 1993; Ezzy, 2002) would strengthen and deepen our understanding of facilitation and facilitator education, practice, and theory. Methodologies based on critical theory paradigm (see Habermas, 1984, 1991; Kincheloe and McLaren, 2003) would be well suited to exploring the dimension of critical facilitator education.

Finally, while there is ample discussion of the skills, theories, and practice of facilitation, there is less discussion in the literature about the processes and strategies that facilitators can use to develop their skills, understanding and experience. (See Chapter Twenty-Eight for a report on such strategies.) The facilitation literature would also benefit if authors were more explicit about their assumptions or philosophies on how they believe facilitators develop.

CONCLUSION

The Dimensions of Facilitator Education Model presented in this chapter has been developed to provide an interpretive framework for continued research and discussion about facilitator education. I hope that it will contribute to the facilitation profession in an OD context by providing a richer understanding of the assumptions, philosophies, and processes in facilitator education.

PART SIX

Model Positive Professional Attitude

1. Practice self-assessment and self-awareness.

   - Reflects on behavior and results

   - Maintains congruence between actions and personal and professional values

   - Modifies personal behavior and style to reflect the needs of the group

   - Cultivates an understanding of one's own values and their potential impact on work with clients

2. Act with integrity.

   - Demonstrates a belief in the group and its possibilities

   - Approaches situations with authenticity and a positive attitude

   - Describes situations as the facilitator sees them and inquires into different views

   - Models professional boundaries and ethics, as described in the Statement of Values and Code of Ethics for Group Facilitators

3. Trust group potential, and model neutrality.

- Honors the wisdom of the group
- Encourages trust in the capacity and experience of others
- Is vigilant to minimize influence on group outcomes
- Maintains an objective, nondefensive, nonjudgmental stance

Facilitator Values and Ethics

Dale Hunter
Stephen Thorpe

General use of the term *facilitator* makes no distinction between the professional group facilitator who skillfully guides the group process from a basis of cooperative values and ethics and other professionals, such as managers, consultants, and trainers, who use some facilitative techniques but may operate from differing value sets and competencies. To appreciate the values and ethical dilemmas that group facilitators confront, imagine you are faced with the following three scenarios:

Scenario 1: You have been invited to facilitate team building. Your contact is the manager of the team, who will, however, not be attending the team-building sessions. She asks you to report back to her on team progress and keep a special eye on a particular team member who seems to be a disruptive influence on the team. How do you respond to this request?

Scenario 2: You have been hired to facilitate a strategic plan for a business. During the process, you become aware that you have information that vitally affects the competitiveness of the business. You have this information because you facilitated a strategic plan for a competitor a few weeks ago. Do you share this information?

Scenario 3: During a break in a day-long workshop, you are approached by a participant who wants to give you some confidential information about one of the other group members. The participant insists that you need to have this information. What do you do?

The desire to resolve such issues led to a project by members of the International Association of Facilitators (IAF) to develop a professional Statement of Values and Code of Ethics. This chapter documents the process by which the code was developed, which we believe serves as a model collaborative process for a globally dispersed group, explores the key issues that were identified during its development, and touches on some further issues that are now emerging. (The complete version of the code is in Appendix 30A at the end of the chapter.)

IAF VALUES AND COMPETENCIES

The IAF code project builds on previous work by the IAF in the area of the association's values and competencies of group facilitators. The mission of the IAF is to promote, support, and advance the art and practice of professional facilitation through methods exchange, professional growth, practical research, collegial networking, and support services. This is accomplished through peer-to-peer networking, professional development, and annual conferences, which are crucial means for fulfilling the mission and reflecting their core values.

These core values of the association are (IAF, 2004):

- Inclusiveness—Including the full spectrum of personal, professional and cultural diversity in our membership and in the field of facilitation

- Global Scope—Connecting and serving facilitators locally, nationally, and internationally

- Participation—Advocating participative methodologies that generate ownership of decisions and actions

- Celebration—Celebrating life through spirit-filled quality interchange, activities, and events

- Innovative Form—Modeling a participative and flexible organizational structure that promotes growth, change, and learning

- Social Responsibility—Supporting socially responsible change within private, public, and voluntary organizations

In addition, a set of facilitator competencies was developed as an aid to understanding the role and values of facilitators and what they do. The eighteen competencies, which serve as the framework for this book, are grouped into six categories:

engage in professional growth, create collaborative partnerships, create an environment of participation, utilize multisensory approaches, orchestrate the group journey, and commit to a life of integrity (Pierce, Cheesebrow, and Braun, 2000).

DEVELOPMENT OF THE CODE

The project to develop the code was initiated by a small group of IAF members (Sandy Schuman, Roger Schwarz, and Dale Hunter) at the global conference in Toronto in May 2000. Schuman and Hunter subsequently cochampioned the project. The Ethics and Values Think Tank (EVTT), convened after the conference as an on-line group for IAF members, became the primary vehicle for the development of the code. The rationale and purpose of the code project was described as follows:

Rationale

IAF has moved forward in adopting a set of competencies and a certification program for the same. An important complement to competencies is a coherent set of values or ethical standards that guide the application of those competencies. A "code of profession ethics" or "statement of core values" or similar document (hereinafter referred to as "code") will further strengthen the credibility of group facilitation as a profession, enhance the professional identity of group facilitators, and avoid misconceptions of group facilitation by existing and potential customers.

Purpose

To create a "code of professional ethics," "statement of core values" or similar document that can be formally adopted by the IAF and made available for adoption by individual members. Members may then indicate to existing and potential customers that they have agreed to adhere to the code and may provide the customer with a copy of it [Schuman, e-mail to EVTT, Oct. 24, 2000].

Plan

An eleven-point plan outlined the major tasks of the project:

1. Develop a two-year plan for creating and implementing a code.

2. Gather and examine similar documents from other professional organizations.

3. Develop among Think Tank members a draft document. Consult with professional ethicists.

4. Draft a document for review by the Association Coordinating Team ACT [the IAF's board of directors].

5. Revise and make available a draft to all members.

6. Conduct a Think Tank session at IAF Conference 2001.

7. Revise and re-circulate a draft to ACT and make available to all members.

8. Develop training materials.

9. At IAF 2002 present code to ACT (and perhaps to general membership) for formal agreement.

10. Test training materials at Think Tank session at IAF 2002.

11. Finalize training materials and make available to IAF members [Schuman, e-mail to EVTT, Oct. 24, 2000].

The EVTT e-mail group, varying over time between forty-seven and eighty-five people, was assisted at times by a small face-to-face subgroup of five to seven people called the task force. The e-group was facilitated for part of the time by Tony Nash and moderated by Sandy Schuman.

Process

The process used to develop the code followed the plan as described above. Additional in-person forums were held at IAF global and regional conferences in Canada, Bolivia, the United States, Malaysia, Australia, and New Zealand. Agreement on the exact wording of the code was reached on-line on May 4, 2002, and adopted in draft form by the IAF in Texas on May 22, 2002, with the provision that it be reviewed and presented for final adoption in 2004.

Inclusiveness, participation, and global scope are three of the key values for the IAF. By using the on-line medium, many professional facilitators around the world were able to participate in the code's development. Although the on-line dialogue was English speaking, face-to-face discussions at regional conferences involved other languages. Different perspectives were shared from many cultures and facilitation backgrounds. By including as many as possible in the process, wider applicability and greater acceptance of the code was generated.

On-line discussion was useful for generating ideas and for in-depth dialogue over time on key issues and areas of difference. The use of the small face-to-face task force helped with the convergence of ideas. The face-to-face discussion at conference forums provided opportunities for clarification and exploration of differences and misconceptions that had arisen. These forums also provided for relationship building, as people could put a face to the names of others they had previously experienced only through e-mail. At these forums, plans were developed and agreed for the next steps in the process.

The values statement section of the code was agreed to on-line during an intensive conversation between a small number of participants while remaining part of the larger on-line group. A number of other significant amendments were also negotiated on-line toward the end of the development of the final draft. This required commitment and concentration by the participants, who had to keep up with the parallel conversations and not lose the several threads that were unfolding concurrently.

Perhaps the most significant learning regarding the process was that given time, a clear purpose, and a variety of on-line and face-to-face methods, a widely dispersed, internationally diverse group can achieve consensus.

KEY ISSUES

A range of issues was identified and addressed during the EVTT dialogue. In addressing and resolving these key issues, the ethics dialogue played a pivotal role in defining the role of a facilitator.

Facilitator as Process Guide

Facilitators generally agreed their role was that of process expert and process guide who worked with groups to help them be more effective. The preamble to the code begins, "Facilitators are called upon to fill an impartial role in helping groups to become more effective. We act as process guides to create a balance between participation and results."

These first two sentences contain the essential elements of the facilitator role: a facilitator *is impartial*—not taking a position with regard to content. A facilitator *helps groups to become more effective*—focuses primarily on the group and then on individuals and maintains the group's responsibility for its own effectiveness (rather than taking this responsibility for the facilitator). A facilitator *is a process guide*—the focus is on process, not content, and on guiding, not imposing. A facilitator *balances participation and results*—works with both rather than gives precedence to one over the other.

Neutral or Impartial

The facilitator's role is often described as neutral, content neutral, or substantively neutral (Schwarz, 2002a). The facilitator competencies developed in association with the IAF include the term *modeling neutrality* (Pierce, Cheesebrow, and Braun, 2000). The facilitator does not contribute directly to content or take part in decision making (unlike a committee chairperson who has voting rights). The first draft of the code described the role of the facilitator as "objective" and maintaining "neutrality." Some facilitators in the dialogue were, however, concerned about the use of these words to describe the facilitator role, believing that "the facilitator is not and never will be" neutral and that "the neutral facilitator is a myth." In response to these objections, the word *impartial* was substituted. One participant suggested: "We are impartial with regard to potential outcomes. We do not favor one individual or sub-group over another. However we are not impartial in respect to process issues: rather we are process leaders and advocates, exercising our process expertise to help groups achieve their purpose" (Schuman, 2002).

There are problems with the word *impartial* too, as it has a static feel, suggesting plurality—parts and parties—and is more applicable to the role of a mediator. The skills of mediation are allied to those of facilitation (in that both are process guides); however, a mediator works with parties in conflict, assisting them to come to an agreement. Although the facilitator may often also work with conflict, facilitation is associated with collections of individuals in often shifting group configurations, and the systemic context is arguably that of a single group, however large or diverse, such as a community or region with many stakeholders (Hunter, Bailey, and Taylor, 1994).

Relationships or Results

Some facilitators emphasize the importance of encouraging full participation and good relationships within the group, believing that this will strengthen trust and understanding and minimize feelings of lack of inclusion and rejection. With strong, healthy relationships, decisions are made more easily and results tend to flow. Other facilitators believe that relationship building in groups is not a priority within the often tight time frames provided. Such facilitators prefer to concentrate on the issues—on making decisions and obtaining measurable results.

The type of group situation is obviously a factor in deciding the appropriate emphasis, and the debate tends to be based on personal experience. Rather than creating a polarization between participation and results, it was agreed that some kind of balance is needed and this is a matter of judgment by the group and the facilitator.

Trust

Another issue that arose was the meaning of the word *trust*. The dialogue around this included an essay and facilitated discussion by Joan Firkins (2001) on the topic of trust, safety, and equity. The first draft of the code included in the preamble: "We understand that by engaging us, our clients have placed a trust in us. As members of the International Association of Facilitators (IAF), we recognize the importance of defining and making known the ethical principles that will help us act in such a manner that we honor and respect that trust."

Some facilitators wanted further clarity as to the meaning of *trust,* and Firkins (2001) considered that cultural difference in the use of language was involved. Different editions of the *Oxford Dictionary* (U.K. and Australian) were cited. As the dialogue unfolded and understanding of differing perspectives developed, the wording in the various drafts of the preamble was altered first to, "We believe our role is one of trust and that our profession gives us a unique opportunity to make a positive contribution to individuals and society." A more explanatory sentence was used in the final version: "Our effectiveness is based on our personal integrity and the trust developed between ourselves and those with whom we work. Therefore we recognize the importance of defining and making known the values and ethical principles that guide our actions."

Facilitator Values

Discussion took place around the key values that underpin or are inherent in facilitation, and some facilitators expressed the desire for a statement of values as part of the code. In the statement of values, the debate centered on the relationship between the facilitator and the group, including to whom the facilitator is accountable and the importance of consensus decision making.

The first draft of the statement of values stated, "As facilitators we believe in the inherent value of the individual and the collective wisdom of the group *understanding that participants come with varying levels of familiarity, readiness, knowledge, and ability to engage in the process."* This proviso (in italics) implied that individuals and the group may not necessarily be competent and laid open the possibility of dependency on the facilitator and their expertise. This was changed in the final version to: "As facilitators we believe in the inherent value of the individual and the collective wisdom of the group. We strive to help the group make the best use of the contributions of each of its members."

The Group as the Client

The first draft of the code distinguished between "clients" and "participants," creating an opening for these being separate categories. A spirited on-line debate ensued about "who is the client" and to whom the facilitator is accountable. Some facilitators believed that the client was the specific sponsor, project manager, or other individual person who hired the facilitator. One person went as far as to say that only one person could be the client and that identifying this person was part of the preparation for facilitation. Other facilitators were very clear that the client was always and only the group of participants being facilitated. Roger Schwarz wrote a discussion paper on the topic of "Who Is the Client?" which said this, in part:

> Who is the client? I believe that the entire group is the client—not the group leader, the group leader's manager, or some other subset of the group. . . . To inform our conversation about who is the client, I need to explain how I think about what it means to be the client. Being the client means you get to decide whether you want to work with me as the facilitator. It also means that you get to decide what issues will be addressed in the facilitation. Together with me you also get to decide how these issues will be addressed. . . . I believe that the entire group is the client. . . . If you are not a member of the group being facilitated you are not a member of the primary client group [Schwarz 2002b, pp. 325–328].

Schwarz added to his model by naming some subcategories of the client group—contact clients, intermediate clients, and ultimate clients:

> I consider my *primary* client to be the group that has accepted responsibility for working on the issue—the group that I may eventually

facilitate. . . . The *contact* client makes the initial contact with the facilitator. The *contact* client may be a staff member or a secretary who is not a member of the primary client group but has been asked to contact the facilitator on behalf of the primary client. *Intermediate* clients serve as links between contact clients and primary clients and are involved in early parts of contracting. . . . Finally, *ultimate* clients are "stakeholders whose interests should be protected even if they are not in direct contact with the consultant or manager" (Schein, 1987, p. 125). The ultimate clients include the organization as a whole, the customers who use the services of the organization or buy its products, and the larger community or society [Schwarz 2002a, pp. 274–275].

There was a suggestion in response to Schwarz's paper that "we should simply refer to the group as the people we facilitate and the client as the people that hire us, or get us involved" (Marvin, e-mail to EVTT, Mar. 4, 2002). Other e-group members did not agree with this definition.

The final agreed wording was: "Our clients include the groups and those who contract with us on their behalf." It could be argued that there is still work to be done in clarifying this issue.

Consensus Decision Making

Although consensus decision making is closely linked with the practice of facilitation, there are different understandings of what *consensus* means. Papers on consensus were contributed to the dialogue by Freeman Marvin and John Butcher, and they also commented on one another's papers. Marvin considers consensus decision making essential for cooperative groups: "I believe that consensus is at the core, at the heart, and is primary to our profession of facilitation. It is more than a technique. It is more than best practice. It is part of who we are when we facilitate. A facilitated group process without consensus is like inhaling without exhaling" (Marvin and Butcher, 2002, p. 4).

Butcher suggested a "situational approach" and considers consensus to be desirable but not essential for a group to make durable decisions that can be fully implemented. "Making consensus a ground rule for group decisions is unnecessary and may inhibit a group from doing good work. It may create 'false closure' by pressuring participants to publicly agree when it may be equally effective if a dissenter can say: 'I expressed my concerns and they heard me, but the general view was to move forward. Because I respected the significant majority of the group in its wishes, I can still have influence as this decision is implemented'" (Marvin and Butcher, 2002, p. 7).

The difference between these two views is in the definition of *consensus.* Butcher's scenario could be accommodated in a more flexible definition of *consensus,* which includes the option of expressing one's view but not blocking the group from moving forward. Marvin explains this in his response to Butcher. However, Butcher is not fully convinced, believing that "it is not consensus decision making [that] is at the heart of facilitation, as Freeman states, but the creation of an atmosphere that will permit true dialogue among the group's members, and growth in the group's capacity to manage its thinking and its internal relationships" (p. 10).

The wording agreed for the statement of values was: "We believe that collaborative and cooperative interaction builds consensus and produces meaningful outcomes."

Group Autonomy

Underpinning many of the dialogue discussions, such as consensus decision making and the identification of the facilitator's client, was the issue of group autonomy. This issue was inherent in the discussion but not often named. Does a group have rights? How do these relate to individual rights? How do group and individual rights play out in relation to the facilitator? Who is in charge of the facilitated group session: the facilitator, the group, the leader? To whom is a facilitator accountable? Who chooses the facilitator?

The identification of group autonomy as an ethical issue was one of the last clauses added. The group autonomy clause was worded as, "We respect the culture, rights, and autonomy of the group. We seek the group's conscious agreement to the process and their commitment to participate. We do not impose anything that risks the welfare and dignity of the participants, the freedom of choice of the group, or the credibility of its work."

Handling Conflict of Interest

In the initial draft of the code, it was stated in the preamble, "We understand our responsibilities have the potential to be in conflict: responsibilities to the client; to the group participants; to ourselves; to society and to our profession." As well as separating the role of the client and the participants, this wording drew attention to a possible problem, conflict of interest, without giving the facilitator any responsibility for resolving it or even attending to it.

In the final draft, this issue was comprehensively addressed in the code: "We openly acknowledge any potential conflict of interest. Prior to agreeing to work with our clients, we discuss openly and honestly any possible conflict of interest, personal bias, prior knowledge of the organization or any other matter which may be perceived as preventing us from working effectively with the interests of all group members. We do this so that, together, we may make an informed decision about proceeding and to prevent misunderstanding that could detract from the success or credibility of the clients or ourselves. We refrain from using our position to secure unfair or inappropriate privilege, gain, or benefit."

EMERGING ISSUES

Now that the code is in use, new issues are emerging relating to its application in an increasingly diverse context.

Application of the Code

IAF promotes the code on its Web site and in Certified Professional Facilitator materials. Workshops have been held at a number of facilitator conferences to promote the code and educate facilitators on its use. An increasing number of facilitators provide the code to their clients, referring to it in work proposals and contract negotiations.

Nonetheless, there is continuing need for training facilitators in values and ethics. IAF sees the code as a set of strongly recommended guidelines; there is no move at this time to introduce an enforcement process. The draft code was reviewed after the first two years of use and formally adopted by the IAF in June 2004.

On-Line Facilitation

Group dialogue using and mixing telephone, video, and Internet is growing exponentially. A variety of software tools have been designed to assist in these processes on-line, including sorting, polling, and priority-setting tools. Although these technologies for virtual groups are more widely used, much remains to be learned and written about on-line facilitation (Rangarajan and Rohrbaugh, 2003).

As new software is released, more on-line group processes are developed. This process is ongoing.

Many aspects of face-to-face communication such as visual cues, body language, and tone of voice are not always available on-line. Without rich feedback, the facilitation of an on-line group can be challenging, as participants do not always respond and the boundaries of the group are often unclear.

Although the IAF code process was conducted mostly on-line, the focus of the dialogue was mainly around face-to-face issues. The consensus was that on-line facilitation involves substantially the same ethical concerns as face-to-face, but with some specific variations.

One concern relates to privacy. Confidentiality (clause 7 of the code) cannot be guaranteed on-line because written material cannot be secured once it is posted on the Internet. Also, different countries have differing legal requirements for public disclosure, including relating to on-line material.

Another concern relates to participation. Although the importance of matching processes, methods, and tools to the needs and skills of the group is addressed in the code, the wording of clause 4 may not be sufficient for on-line settings where there are limited mechanisms to find out why some participants are "mute" or "invisible" (N. White, E-mail message to EVTT, Jan. 1, 2002).

There are also widespread and endemic world, regional, and societal barriers and inequalities relating to access that must be addressed in any consideration of ethical issues relating to technology and text-based communication.

Diversity and Complexity

While the code has sought to bring together the values and ethics underpinning the breadth of group facilitation practice, diversity and complexity in the field of facilitation has proliferated. As well as the mediums of facilitation, such as on-line facilitation, this diversity also comes from the following factors:

• Growing use of group facilitation worldwide in diverse geographical, cultural, political, and community settings; in organizational sectors (business, public, and nonprofit); and recently in international peacemaking.

• A growing variety of approaches, methods, techniques, and schools of facilitation, including the Interaction Method (Doyle and Straus, 1976), the ToP Method of the Institute of Cultural Affairs (Spencer, 1989), Open Space Technology (Owen, 1992), appreciative inquiry (Cooperrider, Sorensen, Whitney, and Yaeger, 2000), graphic facilitation (see Chapters Ten and Twenty-Three), future search conferencing (Emery, 1993), and the Zenergy co-operacy approach (Hunter, Bailey, and Taylor, 1997). In addition, facilitator accreditation systems have been introduced by the IAF and other bodies.

- The generalized use of the word *facilitation*—group facilitation, meeting facilitation, learning facilitation, self-facilitation, organizational facilitation, community facilitation, facilitation of personal development, facilitation of public consultation, disaster relief facilitation, facilitative management, and facilitative leadership. The list of applications continues to grow.

Are there limits to how the word *facilitation* can be applied without losing its meaning? It is becoming necessary to distinguish between the generic use of the word *facilitation* as a general "easing of the way" and the specific use as a set of professional competencies, skills, and ways of being. Although the code clarifies the domain of facilitation and implicitly distinguishes it from other disciplines, such as management, consultation, training, and mediation, it does not specifically address all the above applications.

CONCLUSION

The IAF Statement of Values and Code of Ethics for Group Facilitators has made a positive contribution to clarifying the role of the group facilitator. In its work, the EVTT demonstrated the application of these values and ethics. As the practice of facilitation grows and develops, there will be further deepening of facilitator values and ethical standards.

Finally, we refer back to the three scenarios described at the beginning of this chapter. In scenario 1, the manager asks you to report back to her on team progress and specifically on the behavior of one participant in team-building sessions. Here you are guided by clauses 5, 7, and 1 of the code. Reflection on these clauses will lead you to decline the request for specific information about a participant's behavior. You may also invite the manager to take part in the team-building session or meet with the team after the session rather than your reporting back to her, even in general terms.

Scenario 2 describes a situation where you have content information from one client interaction that vitally affects a competing client who hires you to facilitate a similar strategic planning process. If you are aware of this situation in advance, clause 2 suggests that you consult with both clients to determine the suitability of your involvement with the second client. You will address with them the possibility of any perceived conflict of interest and misunderstandings that could arise. You may advise the second client to hire another facilitator for this particular piece of work. If you become aware of this situation during the process itself, you will be best guided by clause 7 and observe complete confidentiality of the key information. This situation is especially problematic because clause 6 appears to give conflicting advice. This situation is a potential minefield for the facilitator if any content information is shared, even indirectly.

In scenario 3, a participant in a workshop wants to confidentially share with you information about another participant. Referring to clause 5, you are very likely to decline to hear the information and request that the participant share this concern directly with the participant involved or in the whole group.

Readers may find themselves wanting to debate these interpretations of the code. EVTT is the vehicle through which IAF members are able to do this. (For others, you might like to contact us at zenergy@xtra.co.nz. Note that by our opening up these ethical debates, it is a matter of integrity for us to provide an opportunity for readers to respond.)

APPENDIX 30A: STATEMENT OF VALUES AND CODE OF ETHICS FOR GROUP FACILITATORS

This is the Statement of Values and Code of Ethics of the International Association of Facilitators (2004). The development of this code has involved extensive dialogue and a wide diversity of views from IAF members from around the world. A consensus has been achieved across regional and cultural boundaries.

The code was adopted by the IAF Association Coordinating Team (ACT) in June 2004. The Ethics and Values Think Tank (EVTT) will continue to provide a forum for discussion of pertinent issues and potential revisions of this code.

Preamble

Facilitators are called upon to fill an impartial role in helping groups become more effective. We act as process guides to create a balance between participation and results. We, the members of the International Association of Facilitators

(IAF), believe that our profession gives us a unique opportunity to make a positive contribution to individuals, organizations, and society. Our effectiveness is based on our personal integrity and the trust developed between ourselves and those with whom we work. Therefore, we recognise the importance of defining and making known the values and ethical principles that guide our actions. This Statement of Values and Code of Ethics recognizes the complexity of our roles, including the full spectrum of personal, professional and cultural diversity in the IAF membership and in the field of facilitation. Members of the International Association of Facilitators are committed to using these values and ethics to guide their professional practice. These principles are expressed in broad statements to guide ethical practice; they provide a framework and are not intended to dictate conduct for particular situations. Questions or advice about the application of these values and ethics may be addressed to the International Association of Facilitators.

Statement of Values

As group facilitators, we believe in the inherent value of the individual and the collective wisdom of the group. We strive to help the group make the best use of the contributions of each of its members. We set aside our personal opinions and support the group's right to make its own choices. We believe that collaborative and cooperative interaction builds consensus and produces meaningful outcomes. We value professional collaboration to improve our profession.

Code of Ethics

1. Client Service

We are in service to our clients, using our group facilitation competencies to add value to their work.

Our clients include the groups we facilitate and those who contract with us on their behalf. We work closely with our clients to understand their expectations so that we provide the appropriate service, and that the group produces the desired outcomes. It is our responsibility to ensure that we are competent to handle the intervention. If the group decides it needs to go in a direction other than that originally intended by either the group or its representatives, our role is to help the group move forward, reconciling the original intent with the emergent direction.

2. Conflict of Interest

We openly acknowledge any potential conflict of interest.

Prior to agreeing to work with our clients, we discuss openly and honestly any possible conflict of interest, personal bias, prior knowledge of the organisation or any other matter which may be perceived as preventing us from working effectively with the interests of all group members. We do this so that, together, we may make an informed decision about proceeding and to prevent misunderstanding that could detract from the success or credibility of the clients or ourselves. We refrain from using our position to secure unfair or inappropriate privilege, gain, or benefit.

3. Group Autonomy

We respect the culture, rights, and autonomy of the group.

We seek the group's conscious agreement to the process and their commitment to participate. We do not impose anything that risks the welfare and dignity of the participants, the freedom of choice of the group, or the credibility of its work.

4. Processes, Methods, and Tools

We use processes, methods, and tools responsibly.

In dialogue with the group or its representatives we design processes that will achieve the group's goals, and select and adapt the most appropriate methods and tools. We avoid using processes, methods or tools with which we are insufficiently skilled, or which are poorly matched to the needs of the group.

5. Respect, Safety, Equity, and Trust

We strive to engender an environment of respect and safety where all participants trust that they can speak freely and where individual boundaries are honoured. We use our skills, knowledge, tools, and wisdom to elicit and honour the perspectives of all.

We seek to have all relevant stakeholders represented and involved. We promote equitable relationships among the participants and facilitator and ensure that all participants have an opportunity to examine and share their thoughts and feelings. We use a variety of methods to enable the group to access the natural gifts, talents and life experiences of each member. We work in ways that honour the wholeness and self-expression of others, designing sessions that respect different styles of interaction. We understand that any action we take is an intervention that may affect the process.

6. Stewardship of Process

We practice stewardship of process and impartiality toward content.

While participants bring knowledge and expertise concerning the substance of their situation, we bring knowledge and expertise concerning the group interaction process. We are vigilant to minimize our influence on group outcomes. When we have content knowledge not otherwise available to the group, and that the group must have to be effective, we offer it after explaining our change in role.

7. Confidentiality

We maintain confidentiality of information.

We observe confidentiality of all client information. Therefore, we do not share information about a client within or outside of the client's organisation, nor do we report on group content, or the individual opinions or behaviour of members of the group without consent.

8. Professional Development

We are responsible for continuous improvement of our facilitation skills and knowledge.

We continuously learn and grow. We seek opportunities to improve our knowledge and facilitation skills to better assist groups in their work. We remain current in the field of facilitation through our practical group experiences and ongoing personal development. We offer our skills within a spirit of collaboration to develop our professional work practices.

Facilitation from the Inside Out

John Epps

Facilitation as a professional practice includes a rapidly expanding number of methods and processes. As this book indicates, they represent a wide variety of approaches, and their end is nowhere in sight. Mastery of the entire field is an impossible task.

One might say that these methods and processes represent the outside of the profession, its visible manifestation. The inside, the source of facilitation methods, consists of certain fundamental assumptions about individuals and groups from which the methods are derived. Although there is no facilitator creed (and there should not be one), certain beliefs provide the basis for constantly evolving methods and processes. There is an emerging Statement of Values and Code of Ethics for Group Facilitators, developed by the International Association of Facilitators, and this is a move toward achieving some common standards of practice. It too rests on certain assumptions about individuals and groups. (See Chapter Thirty.)

This chapter is about some of those assumptions that guide facilitators in their practice. In that sense it is a "starter credo," an assertion of fundamental beliefs that many of us have found helpful in facilitation. They are expressed here as practical rather than deeply philosophical tenants; each could be the subject of lengthy philosophical analysis, but the intent here is to illumine facilitation, not to develop a philosophical anthropology.

Facilitation is about calling out the best from a group. It calls forth authentic humanity among participants and assists the group in becoming more than the sum of its parts. It is a task of reconciliation—of people with each other, of people with the organization, and of people with themselves. Facilitation is about helping a group to become the best it can be in carrying out its task.

One underlying assumption that deserves special emphasis, because it sets apart facilitation from other such roles as training, consulting, or managing, is this: everyone has something valuable to contribute, and the primary source of contribution is the group. While other professions may assume that their clients are defective in some way and so need the help of experts, facilitators take a different tack: facilitators assume everyone has a valuable contribution to make, and the best results are achieved when those contributions form the basis of the group consensus.

This assumption, when embodied through appropriate methods, creates vitality and enthusiasm in a group. I watched this happen recently. The session had a number of presentations on various learning methods. They were interesting, clever, and interactive. One presentation demonstrated an immersion method of teaching a foreign language. The group, fascinated to see a skilled trainer "teach" Italian to a group of volunteers in fifteen minutes, asked numerous questions about his techniques. Next on the agenda was a facilitated session in which the group was invited to create a model of trends in training from their own insights and experience. The group's energy level changed markedly. Before, there was interest; now there was involvement. Before, it was interactive; now it was participatory. Before there was one expert; now there were fifty. The interest was evident and the contributions substantial.

People usually come to sessions with the mind-set of a recipient, intent on getting something out of it, whether that be an insight, a skill, a plan, an idea, or even a laugh. This is a default mechanism brought on by years of schooling and training sessions, which teach us to be recipients of a master's wisdom. We evaluate sessions for their take-away value.

Facilitated sessions emphasize a different mode—a contributor mind-set. One of our basic jobs as a facilitator is to help people move into a position in which their insights and experiences create something that did not exist before. We move them from recipient to contributor, a major shift in mind-set that releases immense vitality. Regarding individuals as having something valuable to contribute honors them and generates an energy and commitment that so often is lacking when plans are developed through a different approach.

This assumption does not mean that we necessarily assume expertise among people in our groups. In some situations, that is obviously not the case. Training and consulting are valuable professions. However, in facilitation, our job is not primarily to train but to elicit insights and ask questions that may help group consensus to emerge. We make efforts before the session to ensure that appropriate persons are present and then assume that people have insights and experience that are relevant to the topic at hand. We craft our questions carefully to draw out that wisdom. That approach tends to make group members owners of the results.

There are several additional assumptions that we should examine. They fall into three broad arenas: what facilitators know, what facilitators do, and what facilitators are.

WHAT FACILITATORS KNOW

Facilitators understand some things about life that undergird our sometimes fanatical concern for details that others might regard as unimportant.

Facilitators Know That People Are Moved by Hopes and Dreams

Most of us deny that people are moved by hopes and dreams. We have been so disillusioned and disappointed that no one beyond the age of eight takes Santa seriously. It is not that facilitators are naive. Indeed, most facilitators could give a hardened cynic a case of depression with their lucidity about what is really possible and likely. But facilitators understand that people live in the tension between the desired future and the present condition. Attempting to reduce that tension by negating the future is a common but dehumanizing practice. Even in the midst of knowing what you know, you still dream. People are driven to hope even in hopelessness, and that hope is a driving force in human affairs.

The facilitator dares to draw on vision to elicit unspoken hopes and dreams for the future. He restores tension to life. In helping a group create a vision, she works in an arena that is beyond the simply rational. He works with spirit. And spirit has to do with genuine desires and passion that operate below the conscious level. Vision is not what you do; it is what you dream. We are moved by our dreams.

One job of facilitators is to discern ways of smoking out the real hopes and dreams of participants, to help them get beyond caution and acknowledge their desires, even when it means heightening the tension between vision and reality. Facilitation is not stress relief. It does not mean making people feel good. It means making them own up to the energizing reality of life. Common visions can overcome a wealth of diversity. A group with similar desires for the future is a powerful force for getting things done.

Facilitators Know That Problems Do Not Exist

Obstacles are opportunities through which to realize the future. Calling something a problem puts a negative cast on it and fosters a desire to negate or avoid it. This can seriously limit alternatives for dealing with the situation.

Negative perspectives that close off alternatives often thwart potential resolutions. Full potential is realized only when one perceives that all that is is good. This is a perspective on reality, not a moral judgment; it allows looking deeply and seriously at reality without being threatened by blocks. (For a full discussion of this posture that goes back to St Augustine, see Niebuhr, 1960.) In fact, obstacles, irritations, issues, barriers, frustrations, and constraints are part of life at every point. They are not problems to solve as if it were possible to get away from them; they are opportunities to seize in creating a desirable future.

Facilitators help people get beyond fault finding, excuse making, and blame seeking to the underlying factors we sometimes call contradictions. Sometimes you have to be hard on people both to identify the real contradictions and to regard them in a positive light.

Facilitators Know That People Find Their Fulfillment in Taking Responsibility, Not in Avoiding It

Authentic humanness is not realized only after working hours. The after-hours time is a time for replenishing the energy and perspective required by one's work. One's work, the expenditure of energy, is a place where life can find meaning and fulfillment. Structures, attitudes, and habits that deny this fact of life are major enemies of facilitators.

The hierarchical form of organization, along with top-down decision making, has been an effective form of evading responsibility for all levels in an organization. At the top, people declare they cannot know everything that is going on; at the bottom, people declare that they cannot do anything without permission. For both levels and everywhere in between, the structure provides space to hide from responsibility and authenticity. Being fully human certainly includes a level of responsibility. This may be one reason that people in hierarchies are so intransigent: everyone finds them a comfortable dodge. But the idea that one can avoid responsibility in an organization was exposed as an illusion at the Nuremberg trials. Soldiers are responsible even when they are carrying out orders.

By implication, just following orders does not mitigate responsibility for one's work. Facilitators know that, and they also know that whatever role one plays in however authoritarian an organization, one still has responsibility. Moreover, living out that responsibility is energizing. Facilitators have no hesitation in inviting people to take responsibility for implementing their decisions. Surprisingly, they are often delighted to take on major responsibilities. It is invigorating.

Facilitators Know That Teams Are Tension Filled

The joy and comfort one finds in real teamwork is not serene; it comes in the midst of active struggle with colleagues in a similar cause. The idea that teams must get along well and have good interpersonal relations is an ideal that often does not correspond with reality.

The teamwork that facilitators advocate and generate is not based on mutual affection so much as on mutual commitment to a common task. Startling amounts of diversity of age, sex, culture, ability, and interest can be held within that commitment. And this diversity is tension filled. But it is mitigated by the common concern to get a job done to which each participant contributes. When the tensions are recognized and appreciated, they tend to produce creativity.

Getting a task done is the basis of teamwork. This includes the need for communication and a shared vision of what the task is about and what it is for. Facilitation concentrates on the task as the source of cohesion for the group.

WHAT FACILITATORS DO

The assumptions about what facilitators know give rise to particular actions that, though symbolic, are no less real. These actions have to do with taking exquisite care to be sure the group is honored. Life can be thought of as having the dimension of practicality and the dimension of significance (see the discussion of internal versus external history in Niebuhr, 1954). The practical dimension is enlivened by attention to details that point beyond themselves to significance. Attending to these details constitutes what I mean by symbolic activity, and it directly addresses this world of significance. It has four aspects: space, time, celebration, and role model.

Facilitators Take Care of the Space of Their Gatherings

The facilitator takes ultimate responsibility to clean and set up the space. She inspects the meeting room at least an hour ahead of time, usually rearranging the furniture to provide a venue that announces to the participants as they arrive, "Something significant is about to occur here." Certain room arrangements are more conducive to participation than others, and the facilitator makes sure that the space enhances the process.

This may mean providing decor that highlights the focus of the gathering so that when minds wander, as they surely will, they wander to something related to the topic rather than to something unrelated. And it means straightening up the place during breaks so that on reentry, participants get the same message. It may mean filling the space with sound—music—during breaks to create a mood of relaxation in the midst of work. The facilitator is the profound janitor for the group. (See Chapter Five.)

Facilitators Attend to the Time of Meetings

Nothing dishonors people quite so much as waiting for one or two latecomers to arrive. If it is inevitable that some come late, then the facilitator either begins on time or has activities for the rest of the group as a special treat. Facilitators also attend to the ending time: it further dishonors people to be kept past the time they have agreed to give. If it is absolutely necessary to extend the session, facilitators get the permission of the group. If that permission is not forthcoming, then another time to complete the work is arranged. Starting and ending times set the limits for task completion. Facilitators take them quite seriously. (See Chapter Four.)

Rhythm is also important: the facilitator varies the pace of sessions so that repetition and routine are avoided and people remain attentive to the proceedings. A boring pace can kill a group's participation. The facilitator avoids it. The facilitator senses the rhythm that is most enlivening at the particular time of day and paces the activities so as to capitalize on the beat of the group. For example, physical and high-energy activities may work best just after lunch or later in the day when people tend to be sleepy. Serious and thoughtful deliberations may be best early in the day when energy is still high. Facilitators need to be sensitive to the energy level of the group and pace the activities to take advantage of it. The facilitator is the profound metronome for the group.

Facilitators Celebrate Significant Milestones in the Group's Journey

Birthdays, awards, anniversaries, task completions, payday, winning (or losing) an account—virtually anything can be the basis for a celebration. The point is not so much to have fun as it is to dramatize the significance of the actions that are taking place. People occasionally need to pause in their work and acknowledge their significance. It is like taking a drink from a fountain when you are very thirsty. Celebrations help the group to remember why it is there. And they help group members to appreciate both their task and their colleagues. In ensuring that celebrations take place, the facilitator is the profound clown for the group.

Facilitators Models Authentic Selfhood for the Group

The facilitator plays the role of a model of personal authenticity. He avoids defensiveness even when attacked, listens for the depth of decisions that need to be faced, and speaks only from personal experience, preferring to remain silent rather than giving ungrounded advice. She rejoices in the successes of the group and, by the intensity of her engagement, seems to be of having the time of her life.

This role modeling may involve playing roles that do not come naturally. Facilitation is not about "just being yourself" in front of a group; it is about assisting a group to be its best. If that means hiding particular moods that one has at the moment for the sake of the group, then so be it. In that sense, the facilitator is an accomplished actor improvising in response to the group's need. (See Chapter Seventeen.)

The facilitator can exhibit a variety of behaviors that address the group's emergent needs. One may be serious, probing the depths of unknown puzzles. One may be glad-handed, setting at ease those who are reluctant to participate. One may be distant, causing the group to reflect on its own insights. Or one may be close, sharing one's learning in ways that illuminate the present situation of participants. Since the facilitator has nothing to win or lose, he is totally free to do what is required by the situation to help the group achieve its potential. The facilitator is the profound role model for the group.

WHAT FACILITATORS ARE

We have spoken about what facilitators know and what facilitators do. Now we go further inside to explore how facilitators "be."

Facilitators Are Filled with Wonder

Facilitators, perhaps because of their close contact with groups of people, are in constant wonder at the complexity of social life. Nothing seems without potential awesomeness. Every person, every comment, every method, every organization is a window into the profound mystery that pervades all that is. So facilitators exude appreciation, even while doing fierce battle with the forces that block a group's potential. Strangely, that same appreciation can become an infectious epidemic capable of transforming a workplace into a place of meaning.

Facilitators Are People of Paravocation

The particular work at hand is done with energy, creativity, and enthusiasm, but the real work of the facilitator goes beyond the particular. The facilitator, no less than the spiritual leader, is in the business of mediating between ultimate values and particular situations. Specifically, the facilitator brings the organization, group, and individual into encounter with the profound dimension of life and brings ultimate values down to the practical level. That is what it is all about. Everything else is just the specific assignment within which the facilitator operates.

Facilitators Are Purveyors of Group Absolution

The new physics and chaos theory have made it plain that simple causation is an outmoded category (Gleick, 1987; Herbert, 1985; Senge, 1990; see also Chapter Fourteen). Relations are so complex that no simple cause can be identified for anything. This means that everyone may be blamed for anything, so there is no point to grudges and nothing to gain by pretending righteousness. Blame is not a relevant category for the facilitator, so she lives as though forgiven of character defects, mistakes, weaknesses, and ignorance—not without regrets or apologies, but without the crippling effect of lingering guilt and fears of reprisal. More important, she brings this stance to the group, where it becomes a catalyst of humility and gratitude.

Facilitators Are Agents of Social Change at a Group, Organizational, and Societal Scale

Meaning is the contribution of a particular task to a larger context that the meaning seeker values (Epps, 2003). Facilitation is a meaningful profession, because it contributes far beyond the particular sessions one is conducting.

First, it contributes to the participants by according them respect and honor for their contributions. Sessions are designed to elicit contributions, and the very assumption that people have something to contribute can be deeply honoring. This is often enough to elicit profound and lasting commitment toward a project that participants have helped to develop.

Second, facilitation contributes to the organization it serves. It does this in part by achieving the task-related objectives for which it was designed. In a deeper sense, facilitation demonstrates a new and different style of operation. Organizations are currently undergoing a transition away from the pyramid style of operation, but the new style has not yet appeared. Facilitated sessions provide a clue that a new mode is possible that allows people of great diversity to work together effectively. At a time when organizations are under suspicion of violating trust of the public and corporate governance is a major issue, occasions that demonstrate effective group operation are welcome portents of a positive future.

Third, facilitation contributes to the social context. By demonstrating the possibility of groups of great diversity working together effectively, facilitation offers an alternative to conflict as a means of making decisions. In a time when political, legal, and economic systems are all based on conflict, facilitation provides a different way to proceed.

Facilitation makes a contribution far beyond satisfying a client's expectations. It is a meaningful profession with great significance, noble purpose, and genuine professionalism. Facilitators are confident in their field while taking every opportunity to heighten their competence.

CONCLUSION

Facilitation can be an exhausting role to play. It involves one's beliefs, one's actions, and one's being in bringing the group to its full potential. It is helpful to understand the larger contribution of facilitation to society because at the conclusion of a well-facilitated session, in which the facilitator reached the limit of her ability, the group's response is likely to be, "We did it ourselves!" That is when the facilitator has done well.

The Gift of Self

The Art of Transparent Facilitation

Miki Kashtan

In this chapter, I examine the opportunities and challenges that arise in relation to transparent facilitation—the practice of revealing oneself to a group while facilitating. Revealing oneself may include revealing one's feelings and needs as they unfold, personal stories or reflections, and reasons for making specific choices or decisions regarding facilitation.

When practiced with awareness and care, transparency can contribute to trust, safety, learning, efficiency, productivity, connection, empowerment, and community. Yet transparency is often discouraged, based on a concern for the integrity of the facilitator's role and for the primacy of participants' needs. I argue here that the benefits of transparent facilitation outweigh the risks and propose a practical approach for deciding when and how to be transparent while facilitating.

Responsible transparency requires both a high level of self-awareness and internal mastery, as well as finely tuned communication skills to convey to the group what we choose to share of our inner experience while sustaining the focus on participants' needs. The practical aspects of my approach rely on the skills of nonviolent communication (NVC) to achieve this level of mastery. The most relevant NVC skills for facilitating are the capacity to separate observations from evaluations; the practice of expressing and hearing feelings and needs, especially when tension rises; and consistent clarity about what we want to hear back from the group after expressing ourselves (see Exhibit 32.1).

Exhibit 32.1
Nonviolent Communication: An Explanation

Nonviolent communication (NVC) is a process of communication created by Marshall Rosenberg (1999) based on principles of nonviolence and compassion. NVC aims to contribute to connection and understanding and to support compassionate expression and listening even in times of conflict, so that everyone's needs can be attended to. NVC consists of four components:

Observations: Description of what one sees or hears without any added interpretations, translating evaluative terms into descriptive ones. For example, instead of saying, "She's dishonest," one could say, "She told me she was okay with what I said, yet Paul told me she said she wasn't."

Feelings: One's inner emotions rather than any story or thoughts about what others are doing. For example, instead of saying, "I feel manipulated," which includes an interpretation of another's behavior, one could say, "I feel uncomfortable" or "I feel irritated."

Needs: Feelings are caused by needs, which are universal, ongoing, and independent of other people's actions—for example, "I feel uncomfortable *because I need* direct communication" rather than "I feel uncomfortable *because you* are being dishonest."

Requests: Effective requests are doable, immediate, and stated in positive action language, that is, what we want instead of what we do not want—for example, "Would you be willing to come back tonight at the time we've agreed?" rather than, "Would you make sure not to be late again?" By definition, when we make requests we are open to hearing a no, taking it as an opportunity for further dialogue.

TRANSPARENCY AND NEUTRALITY

Joan is called to facilitate a meeting between two teachers and a class of ninth graders in a church. For almost two hours, her attempts to connect with the class and invite them to express what is in their hearts do not elicit any productive responses. Instead, at any moment, three to five students are talking at once about other things, and the teachers are sitting quietly in the corner. At some point, Joan asks everyone to take turns and express what is alive in them: what they are feeling and what needs of theirs are met or not. The first few students make statements such as, "I am really tired, and I need some sleep," or "I am bored, and I need to have more fun." When Joan's turn arrives, she says, "I am deeply disappointed, because I so much want to contribute to creating safety and space for you to tell us what's really going on in this class." Within a minute or two, the floodgates open, and for the remainder of their time together, students express their concerns and mistrust about the class and the teachers.

As seen in the story above and other examples in this chapter (taken from real-life experiences), transparent facilitation, when practiced effectively, can affirm our essential human bond with a group. By expressing her frustration and care, Joan communicated to the students just how much their experiences mattered to her. Prior to hearing from her, students' experience of life in school could lead them to be suspicious of adults rather than trust that adults would care. They likely did not often notice the essential humanity of the adults who interacted with them. Joan's words conveyed to them in a visceral way that their suffering counted and that she had a human response to their behavior in the class.

Sharing our feelings, however, does not always produce the results we may hope for:

Andy is substituting for the group's usual facilitator, who is older and more experienced but is ill that evening. He invites the group to engage in a personal reflection activity and then share what they discover with the group. The purpose of the exercise is to practice connecting with and articulating one's feelings and needs. Andy feels mild tension and anxiety about his role as substitute facilitator and as part of the exercise chooses to explore and then share these feelings with the group. Later, members of the group express concern about Andy's competence and level of confidence. Participants' concerns arose despite the fact that Andy himself was quite comfortable. Neither having these feelings nor sharing them with the group interfered with his confidence.

How can we make sense of the difference between Joan's sharing, which contributed to safety and connection, and the loss of trust experienced by Andy's group participants? For many of us, the apparent unpredictability of such differences and the level of risk associated with sharing ourselves in a group result in opting for caution and even restraint regarding self-disclosure.

Apparent unpredictability and risk are not the only factors leading us at times to refrain from self-disclosure. Having feelings and expressing them are often seen as nonneutral. Since neutrality is considered a core value in the profession (Webne-Behrman, 1998; Rees, 2001), maintaining neutrality is seen as inconsistent with transparency. In addition, even where no explicit philosophical objection exists about transparency, we may nonetheless avoid disclosing our own experience when we are not skilled at staying present when feelings are up, or at maintaining openness to different outcomes, both important skills necessary for transparent facilitation.

However, even when we choose not to disclose ourselves, what appear to be neutral and objective statements often hide within them expressions of self. For example, Harry Webne-Behrman (1998) describes a moment in a facilitation session as follows: "Rachel [the facilitator] affirmed how important this discussion was for the group. She added encouragement for how they were dealing with their disagreement, to which several others added brief nods of support" (p. 156). Webne-Behrman does not describe Rachel's encouragement as sharing of self, but rather as simply providing feedback to the group. Yet Rachel is taking on the role of authority by deciding what is important. When we express our own impressions and evaluations as if they are pure observations, we consciously or unconsciously disguise the fact that we are expressing our own subjective perceptions and experience.

More recently, the injunction of nondisclosure has been tempered with a growing recognition of the importance and value of transparency in facilitation. Such recognition appears prominently in the context of facilitating participatory processes, as in the collection of articles edited by Shirley A. White (1999). But such references also appear in books designed for more mainstream organizational settings. For example, Glenn Kiser (1998) makes a number of references to the significance of self-disclosure.

Yet despite the growing interest in transparent facilitation, its increased use has not yet yielded a systematic analysis of the value and risks of disclosing oneself in a group or specific guidelines for how to bring oneself into the situation. Thus, for example, Kiser's idea that "used with sufficient forethought, personal disclosure can be a powerful tool for unsticking things" (1998, p. 84) does not aid the reader with what "forethought" would include, what would make it "sufficient," and how it can support "unsticking things."

The art of self-disclosure does not lend itself to hard and fast rules and therefore requires considerable skill and consciousness. Before risking self-disclosure, it is essential to consider elements such as the group's purpose and the capacity of the group to contain expressions from a facilitator.

At the same time, most decision points about whether and how to reveal ourselves to the group do not announce themselves ahead of time. Therefore, a thorough understanding of our relationship to ourselves and the group moment by moment (rather than "once and for all") is also necessary. Indeed, transparent facilitation presupposes a high degree of awareness of our inner experience, a level of self-connection, or conscious awareness of our feelings and needs.

In my own and others' practice of facilitation, I have found the process of NVC to be an invaluable tool for guiding my decision-making process while facilitating. The tools of NVC allow me to quickly assess what is going on inside me, what I am feeling, what is important to me right now, and what my long-term goals and needs might be. In addition, NVC consists of specific communication skills that form a foundation for transparent facilitation. Thus, NVC skills support both my decision-making process about transparency and my choice of how to go about it.

CONDITIONS FOR SUCCESS: KNOW THE MOMENT

Adding transparency to the range of options available to us requires ongoing, quick decision making before choosing what to say and while speaking. Several factors combine to increase the likelihood that sharing ourselves with the group will be productive: clarity about how transparency will contribute to the group, self-knowledge about our capacity to maintain the dual focus on ourselves and the group, monitoring the group's ability to handle our transparency, and ongoing assessment about when to stop.

Clarity of Purpose

Having clarity about what we are trying to achieve or create by revealing an aspect of ourselves to a group is key to successful integration of such expressions with group facilitation. The more rigorously we examine our motivation in speaking, the more likely we are to support the group process rather than hinder it.

If we have not clearly identified the purpose of sharing a part of ourselves, we run the risk of acting on our needs instead of first connecting with our needs and then making conscious choices about what we want to do. To illustrate this point, we will explore Andy's choice in one of the stories that opened this chapter. What would be his purpose in taking full part as a participant in a group exercise and sharing his feelings as part of his participation? If he is not clear about how doing so will contribute to the group, he could explore what needs he is trying to meet and whether those needs are ones he wants to act on while facilitating. As facilitators, we cannot rest with a casual choice like the one Andy made, because in the absence of clarity of purpose, participants may interpret unconscious needs in us even if those needs are not there.

As facilitators, we bring many needs and intentions to our work. Intrinsic to the process of facilitation is a desire to contribute to the group. As facilitators, we might contribute process guidance that helps the group build safety, provide insight and experience that contribute to meaning, and offer suggestions and structures that promote the possibility of resolution and movement in a group. Without wanting to contribute, we will be unlikely to mobilize the heart and skill required to proceed with the task at hand.

We have other needs that can seriously undermine the process if they are not met during facilitation. One key need we have as facilitators is that of self-connection. Without knowing our own inner experience moment by moment, we lose some of our capacity to make choices about facilitation. Kiser reminds us that "the ability to be aware of what is happening both around you and inside you is the primary means by which you determine the appropriate intervention and measure your progress" (1998, 24).

By self-connection, I mean the capacity to be aware of our feelings in each moment and of how the many thoughts, evaluations, and judgments that occupy our consciousness are manifestations of our deeper needs. Being able to notice when a judgment arises and through self-empathy (that is, listening to our own feelings and needs and establishing inner clarity and connection to ground out choice of action) to discover and connect with the feelings and needs that give rise to it is a key entry point into making choices, moment by moment, about our next actions while facilitating. For example, if we think that someone in the group is being "domineering," we are likely to react rather than respond—that is, likely to make a statement to the group coming out of unaware judgment or frustration rather than conscious choice about what would most contribute to the group. In contrast, if we do inquire into the feelings and needs underneath the judgment and engage in a moment of self-empathy, we make room to recognize and own our experience. For example, we may discover that we are irritated because of wanting care and consideration for everyone in the group. Becoming aware of our underlying feelings and needs and allowing ourselves to experience them fully, however briefly, is often all it takes to be able to make a conscious choice. We may then choose to maintain silence, express our irritation and the underlying care it signals, or offer some reflection on group process, for example. The more we know about what needs are alive in us, the more options we have for choosing whether and how to try to meet our needs. Having more options and more awareness benefits the group and its process.

When we learn to tune into our feelings and needs, we are likely to discover many other needs that are not specific to the process of facilitation, such as our needs for acceptance, love, protection, and safety, to name a few. (See Kaplan, 1985, for further discussion of other needs we bring with us to the facilitation task.)

To use one example, White, in her discussion of the challenge of facilitating participation, describes a common occurrence: "You become overwhelmed by the charge to use participatory approaches and soon revert to an 'expert' status for *protection*" (1999, p. 338, emphasis added). Instead of becoming aware of the need for protection and making choices about how to meet it, the facilitator in this example acts on the need without awareness, thereby making choices that likely conflict with her or his own intentions and hopes for the group.

Transparency is most effective when we have made a conscious choice to reveal some of our inner process to the group based on clarity about how doing so will contribute to the group's process. To achieve such clarity requires both self-knowledge and reflection on the connection between what we are about to reveal and the purpose for which the group has gathered.

Again, using Andy's story, having participated in the group exercise, he could have reflected on his feelings and needs during that particular exercise and inquired inside himself whether sharing those feelings with the group at that time would support the group purpose, which was to learn about how to connect with one's own feelings and needs. Such reflection might well have led him to conclude that the specific content of his feelings could easily distract people from that task into anxiety about the content of what he said, and he might have chosen not to take a turn when people shared.

Conversely, Joan's choice of sharing her feelings with the group came from her assessment that the purpose for which she was asked to come was not being served: students were not expressing themselves at the level that she and the teachers had hoped. Joan chose to give voice to her feelings and needs because of her assessment, or hope, that her doing so would bring the conversation to a deeper level.

What makes transparency effective is not necessarily the specific content of what we are transparent about but the relationship of that content to the purpose at hand. For example, I co-led a year-long leadership training program in which we train participants in the skills needed to teach NVC. One of the key facilitation skills in teaching NVC is making conscious choices about the teaching through rigorous self-exploration. In teaching the leadership program, I often share with the group the nuances of my internal process of making decisions moment by moment. For people learning to facilitate, sharing at this level has been a rich and powerful model of what they are trying to learn.

However, if I were working with a group that has a different purpose, my offering the same information about my decision-making process could be enormously confusing and even irritating. Attention to process and content at the same time, the hallmark of facilitation, is most definitely an acquired skill. Participants new to self-reflection or even to being facilitated may lose track of what is going on and feel anxious, confused, distracted, or bored.

Continuing to Hold the Whole While Sharing

The fundamental stance of facilitating is one of split awareness of self and of the group. As facilitators, we need to track what is happening inside us and be attentive to the needs of participants and the dynamics of the group as a whole at the same time. Once we have identified a purpose for self-disclosure, we need to determine our capacity to stay on both of these levels at once even while being transparent. This capacity to maintain split awareness is a large component of what Kaplan refers to when he suggests that we need "to know how to regulate communication" of information about ourselves (1985, p. 472).

Even if we start sharing our inner process with a clearly identified purpose, we can easily get lost while speaking as other needs come alive in us. For example, in expressing her pain and frustration, Joan was hoping to convey to the students the depth of her caring, and thus to contribute to their willingness to come forth and express their concerns. However, once she began to speak, Joan could (although in real life she did not) touch needs for understanding, connection, or acceptance and lose her focus on the purpose of her sharing in an unaware attempt to get those other needs met.

With experience, we can learn how to assess our capacity to remain on two levels at once. We can develop discernment about how much of ourselves we can touch and reveal before losing our capacity to hold the whole. Before and during sharing an inner experience, we can ask ourselves, for example: "Can I talk about this painful feeling in myself and maintain my split awareness, or will I disappear in the feeling and lose my attention to others? Can I tell this story without losing track of the main thread of the moment?"

Tracking Participants' Capacity to Contain Transparency

Whatever our inner experience, however relaxed, confident, and present we are in sharing our experience, we also need to be aware of the capacity of group members to hear our openness and maintain their own focus and sense of safety, trust, and empowerment.

For example, transparency about our decision-making process often serves to build trust and to empower participants. However, with less experienced groups, our attempts to share with participants our process of making decisions might lead to an interpretation of indecision or weakness on our part, and thus to mistrust in our capacity to navigate the group.

Both before and while speaking about ourselves, we need to assess where the group is and whether participants are likely to receive what we are about to share, or what we have already shared, in a way that is consistent with the purpose of sharing. Even if we do not know ahead of time the skill and capacity of group members, our own ability to notice the effects of our sharing on the group will give us information about our next choices. For example, if while sharing his feelings Andy had noticed discomfort in the group, he could have changed course while speaking or taken measures afterward to increase trust in the group.

One particular risk of expressing our own feelings and needs is the possibility that group members may think that they must somehow do something about what we have shared, thereby becoming distracted from paying attention to the purpose at hand. To address this risk, close attention to what we do with what we just shared and what requests we make of the group is paramount. If group members expect neutrality, authority, and self-control from us, they may become quite agitated and nervous when hearing our feelings and seeing our human vulnerability. People who are not accustomed to seeing the humanity of facilitators, or of leaders more generally, may derive part of their sense of safety from having someone whom they trust to be the authority. Such expectations on the part of group members do not mean that we must avoid sharing ourselves altogether. Such expectations do, however, require us to be flexible about how far to go and skillful about how to maintain the sense of safety in the group. With enough awareness and skill, we can prevent outcomes such as the one Andy experienced.

The most challenging feelings to reveal effectively are any fears or anxieties we experience while facilitating. Even if we are relaxed about our fears, we can lose the trust of the group if participants believe that our fear is overwhelming and detracting from our ability to conduct the meeting effectively, as Andy's example illustrates powerfully. With feelings of fear and anxiety in particular, but also more generally, effective use of transparency requires finding a way to bring our inner confidence across so participants can be relaxed about our expressions and trust that we can still handle the situation. Clearly, to convey that confidence requires having it in the first place, based on having enough experience and trust in ourselves to know that we can navigate the situation.

Tracking Myself to Know How Much Is Relevant in This Moment

Having identified our purpose in speaking about ourselves, part of our split awareness involves continually assessing and reassessing how much self-expression is relevant to the purpose at hand and whether what we have said already is enough to accomplish the purpose.

For example, one of the skills I teach in my NVC workshops is self-empathy: the capacity to articulate within myself to myself my own feelings and needs as a way of stepping out of judgments and gaining deeper self-connection. For people new to NVC, this practice is often mysterious, and modeling it supports learning, integration, and understanding for them. When modeling, however, I am careful to choose how deeply to go into my own experience, so that I can share something authentic and yet am able to contain it. At that point I stop, because my purpose of modeling has been accomplished, and going further would shift the focus into my own healing, which is not part of the purpose at hand.

As another example, let us say I have a reaction to something happening in the group, and my assessment is that sharing that reaction will contribute to group process. An example of this transparent facilitation is by calling attention to some dynamics in the group that have not yet been approached. I still need to clarify in my own mind how much of my reaction is relevant to the moment and to the purpose at hand, rather than to my own issues with whatever is happening that I am reacting to. Sharing the latter is no longer likely to support the group; it is in fact likely to derail the group's focus and may even diminish the level of safety in the group.

THE NUTS AND BOLTS OF TRANSPARENCY

Once we make the decision to be transparent about our inner experience, knowing how to express ourselves increases the chances that our purpose will be served and decreases the risk of loss of connection, focus, or trust in the group. NVC supports transparent facilitation, with key skills required for communicating our inner experience effectively.

I have already alluded to the importance of connecting to our feelings and needs as a way of assessing our purpose and our capacity to maintain a dual focus. This capacity is key to making choices, as well as for effective communication of our inner experience.

In addition to communicating our feelings and needs to the group, transparent facilitation includes clearly articulating what we want back from the group and being able to differentiate observations from evaluations. The complete process of self-expression in NVC includes the following four components:

- Purely descriptive observations free of evaluations
- Our feelings, free of judgments and thoughts
- Our needs separate from any specific strategies
- Clear requests about what we want back from the group

The following sections highlight some examples of how these and other skills contribute to transparent facilitation.

Ending Expressions with a Clear Request

When I discussed Andy's experience with him, we quickly realized he did not tell the group what he wanted from them in response to his sharing. Indeed, when he was done speaking, he thought that he did not have any request. When I think I do not want anything back from a group, or do not know what it is, I see it as an indication that my choice is not yet clear enough about why I want to share of myself. In such moments, I wait until I have full clarity about what my purpose is and what response from the group would support me in knowing if my purpose got accomplished.

Further discussion with Andy indicated he knew what he did not want from the group: any reassurance or help around any of his feelings. Saying that to the group would not be enough, however. It is vitally important to find what we do want back rather than only what we do not.

Knowing what to ask from the group offers us an effective feedback mechanism for assessing whether our purpose in disclosure was met already, is still being met, or is not likely to be met at all. Here is what Andy said at the time: "I am feeling a little anxious stepping into Janet's group, because I want to have the confidence that my leading the group tonight will contribute to your learning."

Without asking the group for something after this expression, it is not surprising that his fears were realized. If Andy had taken a moment to consider his purpose in sharing his feelings from the exercise that everyone did, he might have either decided not to share those feelings or found a specific purpose.

Given several observations—that this was Andy's first time with this group, that participants came to learn skills, that this was only their fourth of thirteen weeks in this class, and that the feelings he was about to share were the most challenging for a group to hear (the facilitator's discomfort about her or his facilitation)—I would find it unlikely that any sharing he did in that moment could support the group process.

Still, on reflection, Andy may have found some purpose for expressing his feelings, most likely before or after everyone else shared. For example, he might have considered his sharing to be a way of bringing up any discomfort he might have guessed was present in the room. In that case, once the exercise was complete, he might have expressed himself as follows: "I am feeling a little anxious stepping into Janet's group, because I want to have the confidence that my leading the group tonight will contribute to your learning. Would anyone tell me if you have any concerns about my facilitating instead of Janet?"

This expression, whose beginning is identical to the one above, ends with a specific and clear request. By acknowledging in his request that participants may indeed have concerns about his presence and inviting them to share any they had, Andy communicates to the participants that he is comfortable enough in his role to hear their discomfort if it arises.

Alternatively, Andy may have discovered a different purpose, such as contributing to equality and trust in the group. In that case, he might have said, "During the exercise, I explored some of my feelings of vulnerability. In this moment, I'd like to share what I discovered with you, because I am hoping my doing so will create more trust and equality between us. I'd like to see by a show of hands how many of you would like me to do that now."

In this case, Andy checks with the group before expressing fully his feelings. Once participants are invited to check in and see if they are comfortable with the idea of hearing from him, a level of reflection about his sharing is then present in the room, and proceeding is a joint choice rather than based solely on the discretion of the facilitator. However, this way of expressing himself leaves open important questions Andy would need to consider before choosing to proceed: If only some people raise their hands, what will he do? Is he up for engaging with those who did not raise their hand? If he is not and he chooses after all not to share with the group, will others be disappointed? Once again, reflecting on what he wants back, and whether his request is clear, specific, and doable, will go a long way toward assisting him in choosing whether to express his feelings.

As another example, if I choose to share a story about my own life to illustrate a point, and thus contribute to learning or inspiration, I might end my story by inviting reflection: "I'd like to hear from one or two people your sense of what I was hoping to illustrate by sharing this story."

Developing a habit of ending any of my expressions in the group with a clear request of what I want to hear back contributes to clarity, understanding, and movement in the group. Without it, chances increase that I will make decisions that are not fully serving the needs of the group. This can include losing some people, going in a direction that is not supporting the group without having mechanisms for the group to communicate that to me, or losing the thread of interest and connection, which is vital to the very trust people would have in my facilitation.

Making a practice of ending my expressions with clear requests is useful even when I assess that continuing to reveal myself is no longer contributing to the group. I can still check my intuition with the group by requesting feedback from them about it. What I then say may sound something like this: "I would like to stop what I am doing right now and instead go back to our agenda, because I don't trust that pursuing it further would contribute to the group. Is anyone still incomplete with what I have said so far?"

However, the practice of ending each expression with a clear request is not a rule, and important exceptions exist. For example, in the opening story of this chapter, Joan shared her feelings and needs with the group within the context of a talking circle, and several of the students still had their turn after she was done. That context does not lend itself to making requests. However, Joan can and did state what she wanted even though she did not put it in the form of a request. She simply articulated her strong wish and hope to hear from the students what was really going on.

In addition, I want to be mindful of how often I check in with the group before proceeding with what I want to do next. If I am confident what I am doing is contributing to the group, or if I am confident people will speak up if their needs are not met, I am more likely to continue without checking with the group. Similarly, if I assess that there is not enough safety and trust in the group for people to respond honestly to my requests, or if my requests are likely to trigger a lengthy discussion, I may choose to rely more on my own assessments rather than checking with the group. When and how to make requests of the group is an essential ingredient of the art of facilitation, independent of how much we reveal of ourselves.

Owning Any Feedback We Give to the Group

As Kiser suggests, "Many groups finally get to the heart of an issue only when the facilitator is willing to state what he or she is feeling at that moment" (1998, p. 23). When I facilitate, expressing my feelings is in itself a powerful feedback mechanism for the group, a remarkable mirror, and an opportunity to see the effect of their actions on another. At the same time, depending on the levels of experience and maturity of group members, such expressions may trigger reactions or concerns on the part of group members and have the potential to derail the group process.

Providing feedback to a group entails both observing behaviors and evaluating them. Thus, we need skills for differentiating between observations and evaluations, describing behavior in nonevaluative terms, and taking full responsibility for our evaluations. Without specific competencies in all these areas, participants are much less likely to make use of our feedback and instead take offense, become upset, or withdraw from participation.

Kaplan offers several examples of what he considers to be observations about participant behaviors: "inauthentic, domineering, incongruent, or unassertive" (1985, p. 469). However, I consider these to be evaluations rather than purely descriptive observations. In fact, when presented with this dilemma of describing behavior, many of us are hard-pressed to find concrete observations of behavior that lead us to make our evaluations. What is it that we see someone do or say that we might call "domineering"? Is it that we saw the person start speaking several times in a meeting before others were done? Is it that when someone else puts forth a new idea, she or he expresses disagreement with it? Being able to observe behavior before evaluating it contributes immensely to people's ability to hear our feedback without defensiveness.

Kaplan recommends, when giving feedback, supplementing observations with "a comparison of that behavior with a social norm" (1985, p. 469). His presentation implies that social norms are clear and that we can reach shared agreement about whether a norm is followed. My own assessment is that we compare behavior to our own sense of values and norms, while often assuming that such norms are universally shared. Any time we give feedback to the group that is not a strict observation, we are, in fact, engaged in revealing aspects of our inner life, which may include our feelings and needs as they are known to us, as well as our values or our core beliefs. What this means is that much of what we say involves sharing of ourselves, and the choice we have is whether to be open about it or mask this disclosure with statements that appear to be neutral or objective. For example, when noticing that one of the participants is bringing up a new issue, we might say something like this: "Addressing what Joe said in this moment is taking us away from what we already agreed to do today. Let's stay focused on the task at hand."

This statement seems to be objective, and thus maintains the appearance of neutrality. However, it runs the risk of alienating Joe and possibly others in the group. In addition, opting for this form of feedback misses the opportunity to tap into the group's power of making agreements and then making conscious choices about whether to keep them. To express this feedback in a way that recognizes our subjective experience might sound like this: "I am uncomfortable taking time right now to address what Joe said, because I want to support the group in completing a task as well as in keeping to our agreements. I also want to support your choice in the matter, so I am willing to address Joe's issue if this is what you all want. I'd like to see by a show of hands how many people would like to take more time now to discuss this item."

This expression owns both the feelings (discomfort) and the needs (supporting the group's process), and invites the group to participate in deciding what happens next. Involving groups not only in content decisions but also in ongoing process decisions supports group empowerment, which is one of the key purposes of facilitation. This practice also prepares the group for the challenge of standing up to the facilitator or working together without an experienced facilitator.

Fluidity in Switching Between Expressing Oneself and Reflecting Others

One of the key skills of facilitation not highlighted in this chapter is the skill of reflective, empathic listening. The capacity to discern and check with participants our understanding of the underlying feelings and needs behind their statements is vital to making progress in a group, especially in charged moments. When we also want to bring into our facilitation the practice of sharing more of ourselves, one of the key skills we need to learn is to notice when we are paying attention to ourselves and express that separately from our empathic reflection of what participants are saying. If we mix self-expression and reflective listening, we run the risk that both will lose their potential for greater connection with the group and for contributing to the group. Consider the following example:

Facilitator: Jane, I really understand your concern about long-term effects of this policy proposal and how much you care about patient well-being, and I am worried that taking more time with it right now will not move us toward greater understanding in the team. How about if we come back to it later, after we have addressed the immediate issues of information sharing we are looking at?

When Jane hears this, she is not likely to experience being understood and therefore is very unlikely to be open to hearing the rest of what the facilitator says. Separating the two parts provides an opportunity to connect fully with Jane's concern, and potentially also to gather more information relevant to facilitation choices. Consider this alternative:

Facilitator: Jane, are you concerned about the long-term effects of this policy proposal because of how much you care about patient well-being?

Jane: Yes. There is no point in continuing to discuss any of this now because I don't see how this policy could ever be approved.

At this point the facilitator has more information than before and may choose to change course and stay with Jane's concern, or ask her if she would be willing to hold off until the other issues on the table had been discussed. In the latter case, Jane is much more likely to be willing to wait having already been heard about her concerns.

CONCLUSION

At the root of the injunction to avoid revealing our own inner experience is an assumption that expressing ourselves and supporting others in expressing themselves are mutually exclusive behaviors. Fugelsang, referring to the facilitator as a "communications professional," expressed this assumption in the 1970s as follows: "The true communications professional does not express anything. (S)he helps people to express themselves" (quoted in White, 1999, p. 15).

My premise in this chapter has been that self-expression and support for others' expression can enhance each other *or* interfere with each other depending on how skillfully we navigate the delicate terrain of group facilitation. In particular, I have called attention to the following factors as key to deciding about how transparent we want to be and when:

- Careful consideration of what aspects of self involve more or less risk to group integrity, especially by relating them to our and the group's purpose at hand

- Ongoing attention to the group's responses to our facilitation and transparency, so that we can assess how well our transparency is contributing to the group

- Cultivation of a high level of self-awareness and capacity to maintain and return to our stance of holding the whole, so that we can continue supporting the group even while speaking about ourselves

Awareness alone may not be sufficient to the task. In this chapter, I have described several skills that provide a practical method for attaining these capacities. With these skills in place, the practice of transparent facilitation is likely to support, and to deepen, group process.

Affirmative Facilitation

An Asset-Based Approach
to Process Consultation

James P. Troxel

The purpose of this handbook is to provide those engaged in the field of facilitation with the best practice wisdom from some of its leading professional experts and practitioners. Drawing on and organized around the International Association of Facilitators' own Foundational Facilitation Competencies statement, this handbook has sought to provide its readers with original chapters that represent the best thinking, practices, and tools regarding group process facilitation.

The final part of this book has been tasked with describing the interior qualities that comprise the facilitator's external style. Underlying all quality facilitation is the fundamental belief in the affirmation of life. Facilitators cannot effectively engage in group process unless they believe in the inherent capacity of the group they are working with to be its own best change agents.

This chapter seeks to understand this unique characteristic of facilitators—their grasp that all good facilitation is fundamentally affirmative in nature. This affirmative approach, applied to the group process in both community and organizational planning, can be a breath of life and renewal for communities and residents who are all too accustomed to being talked down to instead of listened to, as well as organizations whose employees are all too often ignored by top management. It is a radical departure from the traditional consultant-as-expert approach to organization and community development.

591

This chapter describes a paradigm shift from deficiency- to potency-based models and methods. It contrasts expert consulting with process consulting, and describes the tenets and applications of affirmative facilitation. The new paradigm is a visionary, empowering frame of reference that underlies a philosophy of positive change for organizations, systems, and communities.

Affirmative facilitation rests on the fundamental belief that the keys to the transformation of a community or an organization are already present (however latent) within the system in question rather than external to it. These keys are the images the members carry within themselves of their own inherent capacities and of the potentials of the situation they find themselves in. Facilitation approaches then focus on uncovering or discovering those images, making them manifest to the organization or community in order to be recognized, harvested, and used as building blocks for the system's future.

The philosophy of affirmative facilitation holds that our communities and organizations have infinite capacities as centers of creativity and incubators of hope—gifts to humanity and all of history. Organizations in particular were invented as a solution to a social problem; companies were created to meet an economic or social need. Recovering the organization's essential nature is a key to forecasting its future.

Affirmative facilitation is predicated on the tenets of image theory, introduced by Polack (1973) and Boulding (1966). Image theory posits that it is the image or mental pictures that in fact determines the current behavior of any individual or organization. The image acts as a field, a sphere of behavioral influence. Behavior consists of gravitating toward the most highly valued part of the field. Also contained within image theory is the notion that the way we observe a situation determines what we observe. (Chapter Twenty-Four explains image theory in more detail.)

BACKGROUND OF AFFIRMATIVE FACILITATION

Affirmative Facilitation is located within the field of organization development (OD), a subset of organizational behavior. OD as a discipline started in the 1940s and 1950s. Its founders looked to the medical model as their metaphorical prototype. OD professionals conducted an examination of problems and dysfunctions using a needs assessment and then applied treatment that they determined most appropriate. Just as a physician considered his patient to be sick, the OD professional considered a client organization or community to be disadvantaged or dysfunctional. On diagnosis, an intervention was performed with the purpose of healing the client.

Frustrated with simply being diagnosticians, OD professionals developed the practice of process consultation, which focused more on the people side of the consultation. Classically espoused in the works of Schein (especially *Process Consultation Revisited*, 1999), this model is based on consultation as a helping relationship. The mutual nature of this relationship, with the consultant working with and not for the client, is key to the process consultation philosophy.

Problem-Focused Consultation versus People-Oriented Consultation

Process consultation is generally contrasted with expert consultation. In practice, however, almost all management consulting involves a mix of both models, with the consultant frequently shifting roles to meet the needs of the situation.

Too often in the field of community and organization development, consultants carry a worldview underpinned by the deficiency model. Problem-focused consultants go into a community or organization assuming that they will find what is lacking and what is needed. They learn about the problems through interviews, focus groups, and brainstorming sessions. They develop action plans for their clients. They tell their clients what they are doing wrong. They propose to provide the solution or "fix" (called an intervention), such as a new software solution, a reengineered business process, or a new training module. Although this is a caricature, it makes the point that all too often, this type of thinking is indicative of the deficiency-based worldview of an outside professional consultant.

Simply conducting a workshop that asks community and organizational members what their needs are sends the message that the people and their situation are needy and deficient in some way. Although techniques of process consultation are being employed, the style of people-oriented consultation is not.

The fundamental difference between expert consulting versus process consulting has to do with the images the consultant has of the community or organization. Simply put, is their cup half-full or half-empty? The consultant's already-held image of the organization determines her behavior. Seeing the organization as half-full propels the consultant to figure out how to release the potentials that are there, however obscure and latent. The half-empty approach leads one to make interventions because the situation one is dealing with is lacking something that the expert consultant needs to bring. The first is about empowering people; the second is about keeping people victimized, however unintentionally, and dependent on circumstances and influences outside themselves.

In people-based process consultation, the consultant maintains the belief that the group holds the keys to its future. To do this, the consultant works with all members of the organization or community to identify what they are already doing well. Consultants allow participants in the change process to accent their strengths and emphasize what they want rather than presupposing what is best and then telling them. People-focused consultation does not ignore problems; it strives to bring about their resolution by helping clients build on their strengths and potentials while at the same time looking at the issues, challenges, and threats. The consultant helps the group imagine viable future scenarios, select the most appropriate ones, and implement them. A people-oriented consultant does not make interventions, but rather releases the latent power of the organization or the community to be their own change agents.

The practice of facilitation is partially an extension of process consultation; affirmative facilitation is the next step in the evolution of this field. Before examining affirmative facilitation in depth, it is instructive to view two parallel people-oriented consulting developments.

Appreciative Inquiry

A breakthrough parallel to affirmative facilitation in OD practice is appreciative inquiry. In the 1980s, Cooperrider and his associates at Case Western Reserve University conducted pioneer work with the Cleveland Clinic and the GTE Corporation in the areas of organizational theory and development (1999). Cooperrider came to believe in the self-fulfilling prophecy with regard to organizations, in other words, that an organization's image of itself is what works toward manifesting change. If its employees believe their organization is vibrant, then they will work toward maintaining and enhancing that vibrancy.

As Cooperrider and others developed the methodology of appreciative inquiry, they established an organizational theory of affirmation, which the tenets of affirmative facilitation parallel. They saw that organizations have in their history, mission, employees, and operations positive elements that can be identified and then used to develop the organization. An organization's vision of itself and the rest of the world is the key to its overall well-being. "Envisioning provocative new futures for an organization relies upon the assumption that human systems . . . exhibit an observable and largely automatic tendency to evolve in the direction of positive anticipatory images of the future" (Cooperrider, 1990, p. 117).

Virtually any pattern of organizational action is open to alteration and reconfiguration. Organizations therefore can transform themselves by replacing unproductive images they have of themselves with those of a new and better future. According to Cooperrider, since organizations have the capacity to create their own realities and futures, the key to an organization's having a hope-filled future is its capacity to be self-reaffirming. Therefore, every organization that wants to change itself needs constant reaffirmation. Creating the conditions for organizationwide appreciation is the single most important action for ensuring conscious evolution of a valued and positive future.

Asset-Based Community Development

A few years ago, researchers at Northwestern University conducted an innovative assessment of a public housing development for the urban poor in Chicago. The researchers rejected the usual expert-dominated, problem-focused approaches for determining needs in crime-ridden, poor communities and instead developed methods for determining the inherent assets within the development and the people who lived in it. Beyond asking residents, "What are the challenges that the people who live in this apartment complex have?" they also asked, "What talents would any of the residents bring to their community?" Four single women, all with children and on public assistance, claimed they were excellent cooks and had dreamed of having their own restaurant. The women were asked to provide food for the lunch meeting where the researchers presented their findings. The lunch was such a great success that with the help of some technical assistance and start-up funds, the women were subsequently able to open their own soul food restaurant.

The researcher's asset-based approach presupposed that given opportunities and encouragement, residents of so-called needy communities had the wherewithal to use their own talents and skills to change their lives and become contributors to the economy and society.

This second development parallel to affirmative facilitation is the asset-based approach to community development. After three decades of community development research, John Kretzmann and John McKnight from Northwestern University established the Asset Based Community Development (ABCD) Institute in 1995 (Kretzmann and McKnight, 1993). Their work has provided convincing evidence that when communities focus on their assets rather than their deficiencies, they can create new business opportunities, improve local health and service delivery, revitalize their housing supply, strengthen their infrastructure, incorporate marginalized citizens into productive community life, and increase their visibility and power within larger community contexts.

AFFIRMATIVE FACILITATION: EMPOWERING THE PEOPLE

The best way for a people-focused process consultant, an asset-based community developer, or an appreciative inquirer to work with a community or organization is by playing the role of facilitator. Effective facilitation embraces the tenets of affirmation that underpin any of the basic approaches just discussed. The driving question for an affirmative facilitator is, "How do I ask questions that lead this group to discover their own power?"

For example, a typical organizational or community change engagement might call for a SWOT analysis—identifying strengths, weaknesses, opportunities, and threats. Typically, expert consultants would interview a series of senior stakeholders within the organization, and perhaps some key external figures, and then compose a written document, following the SWOT scheme (called the situational analysis or current reality) to serve as a basis for further interventions. All too often in this scenario, the client group simply puts the information away and moves ahead with business as usual.

By contrast, an affirmative facilitator would propose that a series of short workshops be conducted throughout the organization (or community) whereby a greater number of the stakeholders of the organization would be allowed to provide their input into the SWOT picture. After contributing to the inventory of strengths, weaknesses, opportunities, and threats, the participants would be asked to identify similar themes or emerging patterns, revealing powerful clusters of concerns that would suggest action.

Note also that the employees (or community members) themselves are doing the work, and it is their view of the organization that is being gathered, affirmed, and analyzed. Their group process helps them build a common story about their situation and strengthen the human relationships between them. The facilitator is relying on the resident experience and wisdom of the stakeholders themselves as the primary source of data and action options. In the process of being asked about their own experiences with the organization, their experiences with it are being affirmed. As their experiences are affirmed, they are readier to participate in the act of responding to their own analysis. The group members become owners of the data and action plans, which deepens their motivation to change far beyond simply being asked for their input in a series of interviews, which are then coalesced and presented back by the expert outside consultant. In my experience as a consultant, no one wholeheartedly implements what others have planned (Troxel, 1993).

In a sense, all good facilitation is about allowing the members of the organization to affirm their experiences as the basis on which change is built. This is why the term *affirmative facilitation* has been used. Affirmative facilitation allows the members of a community or organization to say yes to their situation and embrace it as the basis on which their future will be built.

So, continuing the SWOT example, frequently an affirmative facilitator might ask the group members to probe more deeply and reflect on their results, asking, "What are the vulnerabilities within this list of strengths?" "What are the assets inherent in this list of weaknesses?" Not every workshop led by an affirmative facilitator has the chance to probe beyond the surface, frequently due to the constraints of time and circumstances, but the facilitator is always ready to guide the group deeper.

After a SWOT analysis, is it natural to turn to visioning. Once the participants have painted the current reality, moving into what one would like to see in place in five years provides a vehicle for pent-up hopes and dreams to be expressed. Reading the future is based on a realistic perception of the present. You cannot really see the future until you can clearly see the present. Affirmative facilitation honors the will of the people and capitalizes on their sense of destiny and the well-being of the organization. It assumes that each individual has a hope-filled future vision. Even a cynic is seen as a person whose vision has been thwarted. Beyond that, the individuals in the group build on one another's shared sense of purpose for the organization, affirming the ideas expressed, and enhancing their willingness to act upon the outcome.

Once an organization or community is able to craft a vision of the future for themselves, the participants begin to live their vision and start to put it in place.

Like miners who go deep into the bowels of a mountain to seek the valuable ore that has been lying there for millennia, affirmative facilitators go deep into an organization or community looking for the assets that have often been hidden under daily routine, negative attitudes, and misconceptions. With the assistance of the organization's members, the facilitator mines these assets. Instead of picks, buckets, and screeners, the facilitator's tools are acceptance, honor, realization, comprehension, awareness, and esteem. The mining process consists of skillful questioning that leads the group to its own discovery and appreciation, dreaming and envisioning, designing and coconstructing, and destiny or sustaining. The "ores" that are mined are shared understanding of the past, present, and future and workable solutions accepted by participants with ownership in the mining process.

The facilitator brings the following beliefs to the mining process: concern about changing people's lives as well as changing an organization or community's image, an appreciation of diversity as an asset, a realistic view of life's ambiguities and paradoxes, and the belief that all people, no matter what their position in the organization or community, are valuable to the change process. Typically, the solutions to problems are found to have been in people's minds and hands rather than having to be brought in from the outside.

AFFIRMATIVE SYSTEM DEVELOPMENT IN OTHER DISCIPLINES

Affirmative facilitation is not alone in realizing the power of image, in grasping that the key to being an effective consultant rests on one's view of the reality you are looking and the people you are serving. Throughout the past several decades, people in many other fields, such as education and the sciences, have developed affirmative approaches based on image theory. Following are examples of this new paradigm of affirmative system development in these fields.

Education

In Robert Rosenthal's breakthrough 1968 book, *Pygmalion in the Classroom: Teacher Expectations and Pupils' Intellectual Development,* it is evident that what we expect from one another often turns out to be what we actually get. Even in scientific research, researchers' expectations can become the cause of their results. The Pygmalion effect involves a belief about another person held so strongly and persistently that it becomes a reality. The person believed in, being believed, becomes the person whom he or she is believed to be. Rosenthal's work with teacher expectations, also known as the self-fulfilling prophecy, has been demonstrated in more than three hundred studies.

The sociologist Robert Merton said the self-fulfilling phenomenon occurs when "a false definition of the situation evokes a new behavior which makes the original conception come true" (1968, p. 477). In other words, once an expectation is set, even if it is not accurate, we tend to act in ways that are consistent with that expectation. Surprisingly often, the expected result comes true. In short, one's expectations become reality. So the question of the educator, indeed, even of the parent, is how to harness the power of positive expectation.

Physical and Social Sciences

A similar point has been shown to be the case with the hard sciences as well—with the Heisenberg uncertainty principle. In the field of quantum physics, Werner Heisenberg pioneered the notion that "the more precisely the position of a particle is determined, the less precisely the momentum of that particle is known, and vica versa" (1983, p. 66). Because of the scientific and philosophical implications of the seemingly harmless-sounding uncertainty relations, physicists often have called this more descriptively the "principle of indeterminacy." In lay terms, this means that it is physically impossible to measure both the exact position and the exact momentum of an object at the same time. The more precisely one of the quantities is measured, the less precisely the other is known.

Heisenberg concluded that what we observe is not nature itself but "nature exposed to our method of questioning" (1958, p. 81). One's method of observing reality constructs the reality itself. The observer changes the observed. Michael Shermer (1997) noted that this truth applies for all observations of the world. He recounts how when Columbus arrived in the New World, he had a theory that he was in Asia and proceeded to perceive the New World as such. Such is the power of theory and our preconceived views of the world.

Anthropologists have learned that the act of studying an event can change it. They know that when they study a tribe, the behavior of the members may be altered by the fact that an outsider is observing them. Subjects in a psychology experiment may alter their behavior if they know what experimental hypotheses are being tested.

This means there is no such thing as pure objective observational knowledge of facts in any of the sciences. There are no "facts" as such. The more we know, the less we know. The most amazing aspects of life perpetually elude conventional science. Life is a constant surprise. Furthermore, whatever it is that one observes depends as much on the observer's position as it does on what is being observed. We can never know with certainty that which is possible and that which is impossible.

This has implications for the consultant: we tend to find and realize what we are looking for. This does not mean that there is no real basis to what we find. Rather, it is just that "reality has a tendency to reveal itself in accordance with the perspectives through which it is approached" (Morgan, 1998, p. 8). There is, in the physical world, no objective reality. We literally create our own world. If we refuse to believe in the power that members of communities and organizations have, that power does not exist, and vice versa. What we believe is what comes true.

This opens up the role of the subject of the research, valuing the participant of the research as much as, if not even more than, the researcher itself. It provides further evidence of the importance of involving the members of the organization or community as active participants in the consulting exercise.

Health

This same phenomenon is seen also in the field of health. One of the lessons from the health field is that one can never know the limits of healing, never know with certainty who will live and who will die, who will recover and who will not. What is known is that patients have far more influence over their own well-being than doctors frequently believe. Research has shown that when people recall affirmative moments in their life, their health indicators improve (Mehl-Madrona, 1997).

AFFIRMATIVE FACILITATION: RELEASING FREEDOM

One of the notions in the field of social psychology is the idea of the internal locus of control, which holds the most pertinent parallels for facilitators of organizational change. Having restricted freedom can result from external limitations on freedom, such as being a prisoner in jail, or from internalized limitations, such as being imprisoned by parental teachings that one is a failure. People with restricted freedom, no matter what the cause, have the following options: succumb to their circumstances, rebel against their circumstances, or transform their circumstances by taking a new relationship to them. Their response comes from staring reality in the face and coming to terms with it—or not. Some people whose freedoms are restricted by external limitations develop a sense of internal locus of control, that is, a sense of freedom. In a maximum-security prison, for example, are some inmates with no possibility of parole who have put together a constructive life that includes volunteering as tutors for other inmates, attending twelve-step meetings and church, and working. These inmates find their freedom in how they relate to the situation they find themselves in rather than the externalities of their situation.

People who are internally victimized or sense themselves with restricted freedom have the same options: succumb, rebel, or transform. Those who choose to transform are those whose attitudes about life most closely resemble the tenets of affirmative facilitation. These individuals realize that in spite of all they have experienced, they still have valuable contributions to make to society. By focusing on their internal capacity to have power over their relationship to the past and present, they are able to face the future with hope. They do not find their freedom externally, but rather in an internal locus of control (Rotter, 1966; Lefcourt, 1976). The psychotherapist Victor Frankl described this same phenomenon in his classic book, *Man's Search for Meaning* (1959).

Only those who grasp their own internal locus of control can be an agent of change in their own lives. If one thinks that life's outcomes are determined by forces beyond one's self (fate, the system, "them," the government, and so forth), then one's response to life is passive. Those who grasp that they are their own change agents tend to be more proactive in their responses to life and the situations they find themselves in. They become accountable for their actions because they sense they are able to respond to life's challenges. They avoid excuses for why things do not happen the way they want and instead take responsibility for the outcomes.

The same holds true with organizations and communities as with individuals. After the vision workshop, it is customary to ask the group, "What are the obstacles standing in the way of realizing the vision?" This question probes the underlying barriers—institutional, attitudinal, and so forth—that stand in the way of the organization fulfilling its future.

For example, in a workshop with a municipal agency that I led several years ago, when it came time to title the blocks and barriers to their vision of the future, the titles themselves gave the participants' perspective away. The group wanted to title the first cluster of issues "Uncontrollable Outside Forces" and the second "Federal Bureaucratic Regulations." Implicit within the titles was the view that the members of this agency had no control over their situation. They felt their locus of control was outside themselves. If the planning had ended then, there would have been no need to proceed because the group felt they had no control over actions that would alleviate the barriers to release momentum toward their vision.

The key breakthrough came when they were asked, "How do you participate in perpetuating these forces? How do you take part in keeping this situation intact?" This moved the conversation from the barriers as being outside their control to issues within their control. It was only once they got a handle on the ways in which they perpetuated their own blocks that they were free to consider alternative action plans.

What looked hopeless to them became something possible. Affirmative facilitators see things inside the group (or allows the possibility that they might be there, whether "seen" or not) that the group does not. Facilitators see possibility; to be more precise, they may not actually see it, but they know it is there. With this knowledge, the facilitators skillfully guide the group in workshops to discover this possibility for themselves.

Unfortunately, not every facilitated workshop has such a powerful "aha!" experience when an individual or a group experiences a rush of freedom to be in control over their situation, but when it does happen, it is like a breath of fresh air blowing through the group, releasing new energy in its wake, energy to seize the possibility and put it into action.

THE DISTINCTIVE CHARACTER OF AFFIRMATIVE FACILITATION

In the light of all that we have said thus far, affirmative facilitation holds great promise as a frame of reference for a society that is growing more diverse demographically and economically and that must function in a world that is both globally interdependent and closely connected through interpersonal communications. Affirmative facilitation's frame of reference is holographic, polyphonic, heliotropic and chaordic.

One aspect of the notion of a hologram is that within any part of an organism one can "see" the whole of the organism. A holographic process draws in the whole system, from executive to front-line worker to support staff. The equality of this process makes each person feel valued and necessary to the change process, and establishes connections that are important during the change process. For this reason, an affirmative facilitator desires to have the whole system in the room for the planning session, knowing that the plan with the widest perspective is better than one from a narrow view.

Affirmative facilitation is a polyphonic process, in which all people invited to participate are considered responsible for the result. The word *polyphonic* means "many voices" and is used to describe organizations that effectively hear the voices of all their employees (Andersen, 2001). All members are encouraged to enunciate their ideas, hopes, and visions for their organization or community and to make their opinions and suggestions known. Taking advantage of all of the diversity in the organization is a critical step in bringing about this polyphonic feature. For this reason, affirmative facilitators prefer to mix group process sessions with different parts of the community or organization. As Sandy Schuman has observed, "To believe in the efficacy of groups to solve our most complex and conflictual problems, we must select group members for their diversity, for their unique constructions of reality" (2002, p. 1).

The Greek word *helio* means "toward the light." Affirmative facilitators bring their own positive outlook to the organizations or communities they serve. In doing so, they work with them to develop a corporate ethos that illuminates the heliotropic character of their group. "Organizations are heliotropic in character in the sense that organizational actions have an observable and largely automatic tendency to evolve in the direction of positive imagery" (Cooperrider, Sorensen, Whitney, and Yaeger, 2000, p. 43). With that vision, they have the capacity to create their own realities and futures. For this reason, affirmative facilitators take great pains to deeply explore the pent-up hopes and dreams of every stakeholder of the organization to manifest the already present vision.

According to chaos theory, order emerges out of chaos. A chaordic system is one that "combine[s] chaos and order in ways which interweave . . . infinite variety and self-organizing order" into an entity that is diverse and unique unto itself. What appears to most as chaos, however, upon closer scrutiny, one can recognize a coherent and cohesive pattern (Cooperrider, Sorensen, Whitney, and Yaeger, 2000). In *Birth of the Chaordic Age* (1999), Dee W. Hock, founder and former CEO of VISA International, describes how he first conceived of an electronic global system for the exchange of value. He proposed that the future lies in transforming our notion of organization and embracing the belief that the chaos of competition and the order of cooperation can and do coexist, succeed, even thrive. For this reason, while affirmative facilitators prepare extensively for their workshop sessions with written procedures, they are always prepared to let go of the plan and to go with their trained intuitions as to what works best for this group at this time.

FACILITATING AFFIRMATIVELY

Affirmative facilitation is more a style of facilitation than a separate set of methodologies. It can be used to enhance the delivery of various programs such as Open Space, Technology of Participation, Total Quality Management, and Future Search.

Adopting an Affirmative Facilitation Style

Here are some practical tips for adopting an affirmative facilitation style.

Create an Affirmative Climate   Setting a context is an important first step in any group process, but how you set the context is extremely important. Previous chapters (see, for example, Chapter Five) have already emphasized its importance, so I will add just a couple of additional ideas.

Every time I address any person in the group, I call him or her by name. I practice memorizing everyone's name and use their names frequently. This helps people realize that I am taking them seriously and have taken an extra step to know them. This may seem insignificant, especially if you are going to be with the group only a short time, but I find it critical.

Keeping eye contact with the group is another key to creating an affirmative climate. I try never to look at my prepared notes but rather move my eyes from one person to another. I also avoid looking over the group at the back wall, that is, beyond where they are seated.

I try to use humor as much as I can. Some people are fairly natural at this; others of us have to practice. If you are a newer facilitator, it is okay to experiment with telling a joke near the beginning of your facilitation exercise. I can attest to the power of the release of endorphins in the body's chemistry to release affirmative participation, in balance with adrenalin as well.

Require the Participants' Best   One way to elicit people's best is to challenge them beyond what they think they are capable of. Therefore, sooner or later in every facilitated opportunity, I find myself asking challenging questions to help participants think about things in new ways. For example, if the responses the participants are providing are abstract, I might ask, "If I were to put you on salary to do this, when would I know you've earned a raise?" The idea is to help them think differently about things they might be taking for granted.

Another way to do this is by inviting the participants to join in the work of group process. I used to think that the facilitator had to do all the work of processing information and input. Now, after I have modeled it once, I ask the participants to comment and place their input with the other groups of similar information. This is a modified version of the affinity process many teams are familiar with, so they get the idea pretty quickly. This reduces the dependency on the facilitator and turns the process over to the participants more easily.

Prepare Flexibly/Flexibly Prepare   Although I am prepared for every session, I try never to overprepare, that is, become too attached to my preparation and group process procedures. I try to be open to the teachable moment, those times during most sessions when it seems as if a group is on the verge of a breakthrough and needs to spend more time on a particular topic. Frequently, these might be the moments of biggest enlightenment, but only if the facilitator is willing to allow them to happen.

Sometimes I inadvertently get in the way of group process rather than allowing the group to run itself. This usually happens each time I become attached to a particular set of procedures or a specific planned outcome. The facilitator needs to remember that the participants have to become the owners of the input if they are going to be owners of the output as well. I keep a sign in front of my desk, taking a clue from James Carvell of the Clinton presidential campaign, "It's Their Process, Stupid!" This keeps me focused on the real issues in team development.

Reinforce Everyone's Participation   I give feedback to the group at the end of almost every session I lead. It is like giving them a blessing on their work and themselves as a group. I share with them how I experienced the session myself, sometimes comparing their participation with other successful groups. I give them things to watch out for going forward, especially as they begin implementation on their own. I find groups appreciate these words of wisdom and are willing to accept them freely at the end rather than at the beginning after they have been listened to and able to produce quality results.

I have been critical and even harsh on a couple of occasions when I thought the group was simply going through a game-playing exercise with me and not taking the challenge of their task seriously. Even at this late stage in the process, I am still hopeful that I can arouse the group.

Challenges to the Affirmative Facilitation

The biggest critics of affirmative facilitation are those who view the approaches as Pollyannaish, claiming that new paradigm consultants and facilitators are blind to the tragic life conditions some people experience. They call their criticism "realism." They are more comfortable with problem-focused expert consultation approaches and the use of deficit-based needs assessments and techniques that reinforce their convictions and substantiate the community's need for their services. They sometimes even have a vested interest in maintaining the perspective that a community or organization has no assets. After all, who would really want an outside expert if they felt they already had the wherewithal to improve their own situation by themselves? Affirmative facilitators help organizations move beyond this platitude and require their organizations and communities to not only look at the harsh realities of their situation but to go beyond, to see through them as well.

Deficit-focused consultants consider resistance to change, for example, as a phenomenon to be battled and overcome. They look for causes of the resistance and the resister's need to hold on to it and then expend great amounts of their own and the resister's energy trying to get the resister to accept the consultant's interpretation of the situation. The result is frequently a frustrated consultant and still-angry resister.

The people-oriented facilitator views resistance as a normal and equal energy component to all aspects of the change process and creates an environment in which resistance to change is seen as an energy that can be redirected. The facilitator also respects resistance as an effort on the part of participants to educate him or her; it demands that the facilitator listen more closely to surface an underlying insight on how best to help the participants. Thus, resistance is no longer opposition, but the participant's way of encouraging the facilitator to better understand and serve the participant's needs and issues. Clarification and reframing with honest and respectful inquiry are mechanisms for addressing each person's concerns, ideas, and fear of the unknown. They are strategies that allow participants to offer their own interpretations and expectations. These strategies often remove, reduce, or transform many of the underlying causes of resistance. By responding to the facilitator's tactful exploration, the participants become clearer about the issues and frequently let go of some or all resistance.

CONCLUSION

Affirmative facilitation provides the opportunity for organizations and community members to shed their negative self-images and discover the talents and interests that make up their true selves. Affirmative facilitators assist in and empower this process.

Ascribing to an affirmative worldview when undertaking the transformation of organizations or communities leads to more successful outcomes than basing one's efforts on a deficit—or problem-oriented worldview. The affirmative process of facilitation brings people together in a way that makes them more confident individuals and cohesive team members, thus increasing the likelihood of the success of the overall endeavor.

Affirmative facilitators are like the character Belle in the Disney movie version of the classic story of "The Beauty and the Beast." Belle believed in the Beast so much that he was able to be transformed into a prince.

Trusting the process of affirmative facilitation is more important than directing it as experts. The participants' willingness to question and make provocative proposals is an act of affirmation and faith in the organization or community. People and organizations grounded in the affirmative facilitation worldview are the ones who successfully lead their organizations and local communities into the future.

REFERENCES

Introduction

Barnard, C. *The Functions of the Executive Thirtieth Anniversary Edition.* Cambridge, Mass.: Harvard University, 1968. (Originally published 1938.)

Chapter One

NLP Learning Systems Corporation. *NLP in Action: Personal and Professional Development Workbook/Manual.* Dallas: NLP Learning Systems Corporation, 1993.

Rosenberg, M. *Nonviolent Communication, A Language of Life.* (2nd ed.) Encinitas, Calif.: Puddle Dancer Press, 2003.

Schwarz, R. M. *The Skilled Facilitator.* (2nd ed.) San Francisco: Jossey-Bass, 2002.

Wilson Learning Company. *Versatile Salesperson Reference Handbook.* Eden Prairie: Wilson Learning Company, 1987.

Chapter Two

Argyris, C. *Intervention Theory and Method: A Behavioral Science View.* Reading, Mass.: Addison-Wesley, 1970.

Argyris, C., and Schön, D. A. *Theory in Practice: Increasing Professional Effectiveness.* San Francisco: Jossey-Bass, 1974.

Goleman, D. *Emotional Intelligence.* New York: Bantam Books, 1995.

Kaplan, R. E. "The Conspicuous Absence of Evidence That Process Consultation Enhances Task Performance." *Journal of Applied Behavioral Science,* 1979, *15,* 346–360.

Salovey, P., and Mayer, J. D. "Emotional Intelligence." *Imagination, Cognition, and Personality,* 1990, *9,* 185–211.

Senge, P. M. *The Fifth Discipline: The Art and Practice of the Learning Organization.* New York: Doubleday, 1990.

Chapter Three

Berne, E. *Transactional Analysis in Psychotherapy.* New York: Grove Press, 1961.

Bleandonu, G. *Wilfred Bion: His Life and Works, 1897–1979.* London: Other Press, 1998.

Cini, M. A. "Group Newcomers: From Disruption to Innovation." *Group Facilitation: A Research and Applications Journal,* 2001, *3,* 3–13.

Cooperrider, D. L., and Dutton, J. E. (eds.). *Organizational Dimensions of Global Change— No Limits to Cooperation.* Thousand Oaks, Calif.: Sage, 1999.

Gardner, H. *Multiple Intelligences: The Theory in Practice.* New York: Basic Books, 1993.

Gardner, H. *Intelligence Reframed.* New York: Basic Books, 1999.

Goleman, D. *Emotional Intelligence.* New York: Bantam Books, 1995.

Jung, C. G. *Psychological Reflections.* New York: HarperCollins, 1961.

Katz, D., and Kahn, R. L. *The Social Psychology of Organizations.* (2nd ed.) New York: Wiley, 1978.

Keirsey, D., and Bates, M. *Please Understand Me.* (4th ed.) Del Mar, Calif.: Prometheus Nemesis Press, 1994.

Kotter, J. P. *Leading Change.* Boston: Harvard Business School Press, 1996.

Marston, W. M. *Emotions of Normal People.* London: Kegan, Paul, 1928.

Miscisin, M. *Showing Our True Colors.* Riverside, Calif.: True Colors, 2001.

Ritberger, C. *What Color Is Your Life.* Carlsbad, Calif.: Hay House, 1999.

Rogers, C. R. *Client Centered Therapy: Its Current Practice, Implications and Theory.* London: Constable, 1995. (Originally published 1951.)

Schein, E. *Organizational Culture and Leadership.* (2nd ed.) San Francisco: Jossey-Bass, 1996.

Stern, G. J. *The Drucker Foundation Self-Assessment Tool Process Guide.* (Rev. ed.) San Francisco: Jossey-Bass, 1999.

Tuckman, B. "Developmental Sequence in Small Groups." *Psychological Bulletin,* 1965, *63,* 384–399.

Tuckman, B. W., and Jensen, M. A. "Stages of Small Group Development Revisited." *Group and Organisational Studies,* 1977, *2,* 419–427.

Chapter Four

Block, P. *Flawless Consulting.* San Francisco: Jossey-Bass, 1981.

Gilley, J. W., Boughton, N. W., and Maycunich, A. *The Performance Challenge.* New York: Perseus Books, 1999.

Institute of Cultural Affairs in the U.S.A. *Participatory Strategic Planning* Course Manual. Phoenix, Ariz.: Institute of Cultural Affairs in the U.S.A., 1996.

Institute of Cultural Affairs in the U.S.A. *Group Facilitation Methods Course Manual.* Phoenix, Ariz.: Institute of Cultural Affairs in the U.S.A., 2000.

Pike, R. W. *Creative Training Techniques Handbook.* Minneapolis, Minn.: Lakewood Books, 1989.

Senge, P. M. *The Fifth Discipline: The Art and Practice of the Learning Organization.* New York: Doubleday, 1990.

Spencer, L. J. *Winning Through Participation.* Dubuque, Iowa: Kendall/Hunt Publishing, 1989.

U.S. Department of Commerce, Technology Administration, National Institute of Standards and Technology, Baldrige National Quality Program. *2004 Criteria for Performance Excellence.* Gaithersburg, Md.: U.S. Government Printing Office, 2004.

Chapter Five

Bender, T. *Feng Shui Meditation Journal.* Berkeley, Calif.: Amber Lotus Publishing, 2003.

Bostrom, R., Watson, R., and Kinney, S. (eds.). *Computer Augmented Teamwork: A Guided Tour.* New York: Van Nostrand Reinhold, 1992.

Hickling, A. "'Decision Spaces': A Scenario About Designing Appropriate Rooms for Group Decision Management." In E. Eden and J. Radford (eds.), *Tackling Strategic Problems: The Role of Group Decision Support.* Thousand Oaks, Calif.: Sage, 1990.

Jacobs, R. W. *Real Time Strategic Change.* San Francisco: Berrett-Koehler, 1994.

Senge, P. *The Fifth Discipline: The Art and Practice of the Learning Organization.* New York: Doubleday, 1990.

Spencer, L. J. *Winning Through Participation.* Dubuque, Iowa: Kendall/Hunt, 1989.

Weisbord M., and Janoff, S. *Future Search: An Action Guide to Finding Common Ground in Organizations and Communities.* San Francisco: Berrett-Koehler, 1995.

Williams, D. "Setting the Stage: Aesthetics, Feng Shui, and the Design of the Mediation Room," Unpublished manuscript, 2003.

Wydra, N. *Designing Your Happiness: A Contemporary Look at Feng Shui.* Torrance, Calif.: Heian International, 1995.

Chapter Six

Covey, S. *The Seven Habits of Highly Effective People.* New York: Simon & Schuster, 1989.

Meeker, L., Fischer, S., and Michalak, B. *High Performance Teamwork.* Amherst, Mass.: HRD Press, 1994.

Reina, D., and Reina, M. *Trust and Betrayal in the Workplace.* San Francisco: Berrett-Koehler, 1999.

Shaw, B. *Trust in the Balance.* San Francisco: Jossey-Bass, 1997.

Chapter Seven

Berry, B., and Stewart, G. L. "Composition, Process, and Performance in Self-Managed Groups: The Role of Personality." *Journal of Applied Psychology,* 1997, *82,* 62–78.

Bouchard, T. J. "Personality, Problem-Solving Procedure, and Performance in Self-Managed Groups: The Role of Personality." *Journal of Applied Social Psychology,* 1969, *82,* 62–78.

Bradley, J., White, B. J., and Mennecke, B. E. "Teams and Tasks: A Temporal Framework for the Effects of Interpersonal Interventions on Team Performance." *Small Group Research,* 2003, *34,* 353–387.

Brown, V. R., and Paulus, P. B. "Making Group Brainstorming More Effective: Recommendations from an Associative Memory Perspective." *Current Directions in Psychological Science,* 2002, *11,* 208–212.

Camacho, L. M., and Paulus, P. B. "The Role of Social Anxiousness in Group Brainstorming." *Journal of Personality and Social Psychology,* 1995, *68,* 1071–1080.

Coskun, H. "The Effects of Outgroup Comparison, Social Context, Intrinsic Motivation, and Collective Identity in Brainstorming Groups." Unpublished doctoral dissertation, University of Texas at Arlington, 2000.

Coskun, H., Paulus, P. B., Brown, V., and Sherwood, J. J. "Cognitive Stimulation and Problem Presentation in Idea Generation Groups." *Group Dynamics: Theory, Research, and Practice,* 2000, *4,* 307–329.

Delbecq, A. L., Van de Ven, A. H., and Gustafson, D. H. "Guidelines for Conducting NGT Meetings." In A. L. Delbecq, A. H. Van de Ven, and D. H. Gustafson (eds.), *Group Techniques for Program Planning: A Guide to Nominal Group and Delphi Processes.* Middleton, Wis.: Greenbriar Press, 1986.

Dennis, A. R., and Williams, M. L. "Electronic Brainstorming: Theory, Research, and Future Directions." In P. B. Paulus and B. A. Nijstad (eds.), *Group Creativity.* New York: Oxford University Press, 2003.

Devine, D. J., and Philips, J. L. "Do Smarter Teams Do Better: A Meta-Analysis of Cognitive Ability and Team Performance." *Small Group Research,* 2001, *32,* 507–532.

Diehl, M., and Stroebe, W. "Productivity Loss in Brainstorming Groups: Toward the Solution of a Riddle." *Journal of Personality and Social Psychology,* 1987, *53,* 497–509.

Dugosh, K. L., Paulus, P. B., Roland, E. J., and Yang, H. C. "Cognitive Stimulation in Brainstorming." *Journal of Personality and Social Psychology,* 2000, *79,* 722–735.

Geschka, H., Schaude, G. R., and Schlicksupp, H. "Modern Techniques for Solving Problems." *Chemical Engineering,* Aug. 1973, pp. 91–97.

Grawitch, M. J., Munz, D. C., and Kramer, T. J. "Effects of Member Mood States on Creative Performance in Temporary Workgroups." *Group Dynamics,* 2003, *7,* 41–54.

Janis, I. *Groupthink.* (2nd ed.) Boston: Houghton Mifflin, 1982.

Janis, I., and Mann, L. *Decision Making: A Psychological Analysis of Conflict, Choice, and Commitment.* New York: Free Press, 1977.

John-Steiner, V. *Creative Collaboration.* New York: Oxford University Press, 2000.

Karau, S. J., and Williams, K. D. "Social Loafing: A Meta-Analytic Review and Theoretical Integration." *Journal of Personality and Social Psychology,* 1993, *65,* 681–706.

Kramer, T. J., Fleming, G. P., and Mannis, S. M. "Improving Face-to-Face Brainstorming Through Modeling and Facilitation." *Small Group Research,* 2001, *32,* 533–557.

Larey, T. S., and Paulus, P. B. "Social Comparison and Goal Setting in Brainstorming Groups." *Journal of Applied Social Psychology,* 1995, *25,* 1579–1596.

Lerner, J. S., and Tetlock, P. E. "Accounting for the Effects of Accountability." *Psychological Bulletin,* 1999, *125,* 255–275.

Milliken, F. J., Bartel, C. A., and Kurtzberg, T. R. "Diversity and Creativity in Workgroups: A Dynamic Perspective on the Affective and Cognitive Processes That Link Diversity and Performance." In P. B. Paulus and B. A. Nijstad (eds.), *Group Creativity*. New York: Oxford University Press, 2003.

Nemeth, C. J., and Nemeth-Brown, Z. "Better Than Individuals: The Potential Benefits of Dissent and Diversity for Group Creativity." In P. B. Paulus and B. A. Nijstad (eds.), *Group Creativity*. New York: Oxford University Press, 2003.

Offner, A. K., Kramer, T. J., and Winter, J. P. "The Effects of Facilitation, Recording, and Pauses on Group Brainstorming." *Small Group Research,* 1996, *27,* 283–298.

Osborn, A. F. *Applied Imagination*. New York: Scribner, 1957.

Oxley, N. L., Dzindolet, M. T., and Paulus, P. B. "The Effects of Facilitators on the Performance of Brainstorming Groups." *Journal of Social Behavior and Personality,* 1996, *11,* 633–646.

Paulus, P. B. "Developing Consensus About Groupthink After All These Years." *Organizational Behavior and Human Decision Processes,* 1998, *73,* 362–374.

Paulus, P. B., and Brown, V. "Enhancing Ideational Creativity in Groups: Lessons Learned from Research on Brainstorming." In P. B. Paulus and B. A. Nijstad (eds.), *Group Creativity*. New York: Oxford University Press, 2003.

Paulus, P. B., Larey, T. S., and Ortega, A. H. "Performance and Perceptions of Brainstormers in an Organizational Setting." *Basic and Applied Social Psychology,* 1995, *17,* 249–265.

Paulus, P. B., Nakui, T., and Putman, V. L. "Group Brainstorming, Meetings, and Teamwork: Some Rules for the Road to Innovation." In L. Thompson and H. Choi (eds.), *Creativity and Innovations in Organizational Teams*. Mahwah, N.J.: Erlbaum, forthcoming.

Paulus, P. B., and Nijstad, B. (eds.). *Group Creativity*. New York: Oxford University Press, 2003.

Paulus, P. B., and Yang, H. C. "Idea Generation in Groups: A Basis for Creativity in Organizations." *Organizational Behavior and Human Decision Processes,* 2000, *82,* 76–87.

Paulus, P. B., and others. "Social Influence Process in Computer Brainstorming." *Basic and Applied Social Psychology,* 1996, *18,* 3–14.

Paulus, P. B., and others. "Social and Cognitive Influences in Group Brainstorming: Predicting Production Gains and Losses." *European Social Psychology Review,* 2002, *12,* 299–325.

Siegel, G. B. *Mass Interviewing and the Marshalling of Ideas to Improve Performance: The Crawford Slip Method*. Lanham, Md.: University Press of America, 1996.

Smith, S. "The Constraining Effects of Initial Ideas." In P. B. Paulus and B. A. Nijstad (eds.), *Group Creativity*. New York: Oxford University Press, 2003.

Stasser, G., and Birchmeier, Z. "Group Creativity and Collective Choice." In P. B. Paulus and B. A. Nijstad (eds.), *Group Creativity*. New York: Oxford University Press, 2003.

Sutton, R. I., and Hargadon, A. "Brainstorming Groups in Context: Effectiveness in a Product Design Firm." *Administrative Science Quarterly,* 1996, *41,* 685–718.

Taylor, D. W., Berry, P. C., and Block, C. H. "Does Group Participation When Using Brainstorming Facilitate or Inhibit Creative Thinking?" *Administrative Science Quarterly,* 1958, *3,* 23–47.

Van Gundy, A. *Techniques of Structured Problem Solving.* (2nd ed.) New York: Van Nostrand Reinhold, 1988.

Watson, W. E., Kumar, K., and Michaelson, L. K. "Cultural Diversity's Impact on Interaction Process and Performance: Comparing Homogeneous and Diverse Task Groups." *Academy of Management Journal,* 1993, *36,* 590–602.

Chapter Eight

Kaner, S., Lind, L., Toldi, C., Fisk, S., and Berger, D. *Facilitator's Guide to Participatory Decision-Making.* Gabriola Island, B.C.: New Society Publishers, 1996.

Peck, M. S. *The Different Drum: Community Making and Peace.* New York: Simon & Schuster, 1987.

Rogers, C., and Roethlisberger, F. J. "Barriers and Gateways to Communication." *Harvard Business Review,* 1991, *69*(6), 105–111. (Originally published 1952.)

Tuckman, B. "Developmental Sequence in Small Groups." *Psychological Bulletin,* 1965, 384–399.

Chapter Nine

Benne, K., and Sheats, P. "Functional Roles of Group Members." *Journal of Social Issues,* 1948, *4,* 41–49.

Chilberg, J. "Exploring the Role of the Facilitator: A Typology of Formal Task Group Communication." Paper presented at the Eastern Communication Association Convention, Providence, R.I., 1985.

Chilberg, J. "A Review of Group Process Designs for Facilitating Communication in Problem-Solving Groups." *Management Communication Quarterly,* 1989, *3,* 51–70.

Chilberg, J., and Riley, M. "Brainstorming in a Multicultural World." Paper presented at the Eastern Communication Association Convention, Pittsburgh, Pa., 1995.

Collins, B. E., and Guetzkow, H. *A Social Psychology of Group Processes for Decision Making.* New York: Wiley, 1964.

Delbecq, A. L., Van de Ven, A. H., and Gustafson, D. H. "Guidelines for Conducting NGT Meetings." In A. Delbecq, A. H. Van de Ven, and D. H. Gustafson (eds.), *Group Techniques for Program Planning: A Guide to Nominal Group and Delphi Processes.* Middleton Wis.: Greenbriar Press, 1986.

Doyle, M., and Straus, D. *How to Make Meetings Work.* New York: Wyden, 1976.

Fox, W. M. *Effective Group Problem Solving: How to Broaden Participation, Improve Decision Making, and Increase Commitment to Action.* San Francisco: Jossey-Bass, 1987.

Gibb, J. R. "Defensive Communication." *Journal of Communication,* 1961, *11,* 141–148.

Hackman, J. R. (ed.). *Groups That Work (and Those That Don't): Creating Conditions for Effective Teamwork.* San Francisco: Jossey-Bass, 1990.

Hirokawa, R., and Salazar, A. "Task-Group Communication and Decision-Making Performance." In L. Frey, D. Gouran, and M. S. Poole (eds.), *The Handbook of Group Communication Theory and Research.* Thousand Oaks, Calif.: Sage, 1991.

Jarboe, S. "Group Communication and Creative Processes." In L. Frey, D. Gouran, and M. S. Poole (eds.), *The Handbook of Group Communication Theory and Research.* Thousand Oaks, Calif.: Sage, 1999.

Jensen, A. D., and Chilberg, J. C. *Small Group Communication: Theory and Application.* Belmont, Calif.: Wadsworth, 1991.

Keyton, J. "Relational Communication in Groups." In L. Frey, D. Gouran, and M. S. Poole (eds.), *The Handbook of Group Communication Theory and Research.* Thousand Oaks, Calif., Sage, 1999.

Osborn, A. F. *Applied Imagination.* New York: Scribner, 1982.

Poole, M. S. "Procedures for Managing Meetings: Social and Technological Innovations." In R. A. Swanson and B. O. Knapp (eds.), *Innovative Meeting Management.* Austin, Tex.: 3M Meeting Management Institute, 1991.

Poole, M. S. "Group Communication Theory." In L. Frey, D. Gouran, and M. S. Poole (eds.), *The Handbook of Group Communication Theory and Research.* Thousand Oaks, Calif.: Sage, 1999.

Poole, M. S., and Salazar, A. J. "Group Communication Theory." In L. Frey, D. Gouran, and M. S. Poole (eds.), *The Handbook of Group Communication Theory and Research.* Thousand Oaks, Calif.: Sage, 1999.

Prince, G. M. *The Practice of Creativity.* New York: HarperCollins, 1970.

Sieberg, E. "Confirming and Disconfirming in an Organizational Setting." In J. Owen, P. Page, and G. Zimmerman (eds.), *Communication in Organizational Settings.* St. Paul, Minn.: West, 1976.

Sunwolf, and Seibold, D. "The Impact of Formal Procedures on Group Processes, Members, and Task Outcomes." In L. Frey, D. Gouran, and M. S. Poole (eds.), *The Handbook of Group Communication Theory and Research.* Thousand Oaks, Calif.: Sage, 1999.

Ulschak, F. L., Nathanson, L., and Gillan, P. G. *Small Group Problem Solving.* Reading, Mass.: Addison-Wesley, 1981.

Watzlawick, P., Beavin, J. H., and Jackson, D. D. *Pragmatics of Human Communication: A Study of Interactional Patterns, Pathologies and Paradoxes.* New York: Norton, 1967.

Zarefsky, D. "Does Intellectual Diversity Always Serve Us Well?" *Spectra,* 1993, *29*(4), 2–3.

Chapter Ten

Brunon, J. "Group Dynamics and Visual Thinking." *Journal of Architectural Education,* 1971, *25*(3), 53–54.

Doyle M., and Straus, D. *How to Make Meetings Work.* New York: Jove Books, 1976.

Grove Consultants International. "Grove Facilitation Model." Oct. 2002. [http://www.grove.com/about/model_facil.html].

Halprin, L., and Burns, J. *Take Part: A Workshop Approach to Creativity.* Cambridge, Mass.: MIT Press, 1963.

Horn, R. *Visual Language: Global Communication for the Twenty-First Century.* Bainbridge Island, Wash.: Macro VU Press, 1998.

Margulies, N., and Maal, N. *Mapping Inner Space: Learning and Teaching Visual Mapping.* Tucson, Ariz.: Zephyr Press, 2002.

Miller, G. A. "The Magical Number Seven, Plus or Minus Two: Some Limits on Our Capacity for Processing Information." *Psychological Review,* 1956, *63,* 81–97. [http://www.well.com/user/smalin/miller.html]

Sibbet, D. *Principles of Facilitation.* San Francisco: Grove Consultants International, 2002.

Chapter Eleven

Burson, M. C. "Finding Clarity in the Midst of Conflict: Facilitating Dialogue and Skillful Discussion Using a Model from the Quaker Tradition." *Group Facilitation: A Research and Applications Journal,* 2002, *4,* 23–29.

Cini, M. A. "Group Newcomers: From Disruption to Innovation." *Group Facilitation: A Research and Applications Journal,* 2001, *3,* 3–13.

Frankl, V. E. *Man's Search for Meaning: An Introduction to Logotherapy.* New York: Pocket Books, 1985.

Gergen, K. J. *Realities and Relationships: Soundings in Social Construction.* Cambridge, Mass.: Harvard University Press, 1994.

Janis, I. L., and Mann, L. *Decision Making: A Psychological Analysis of Conflict, Choice, and Commitment.* New York: Free Press, 1977.

Leong, F. L., and Wong, P.T.P. "Optimal Human Functioning from Cross-Cultural Perspectives: Cultural Competence as an Organizing Framework." In W. Bruce Walsh (ed.), *Counseling Psychology and Optimal Human Functioning.* Mahwah, N.J.: Erlbaum, 2003.

Maier, N.R.F. "Assets and Liabilities in Group Problem Solving: The Need for an Integrative Function." *Psychological Review,* 1967, *74,* 239–249.

Maslow, A. *Toward a Psychology of Being.* (Rev. ed.) New York: Van Nostrand Reinhold, 1968.

Maslow, A. *Motivation and Personality.* (Rev. ed.) New York: HarperCollins, 1970.

May, R. *The Springs of Creative Living: A Study of Human Nature and God.* New York: Abingdon-Cokesbury, 1940.

May, R. *Man's Search for Himself.* New York: Norton, 1953.

May, R. *Psychology and the Human Dilemma.* New York: Van Nostrand Reinhold, 1967.

Rogers, C. *Client-Centered Therapy.* Boston: Houghton Mifflin, 1951.

Rogers, C. "The Necessary and Sufficient Conditions of Therapeutic Personality Change." *Journal of Consulting Psychology,* 1957, *21,* 95–103.

Rogers, C. "Carl Rogers on the Development of the Person-Centered Approach." *Person-Centered Review,* 1986, *1,* 257–259.

Schuman, S. "What to Look for in a Group Facilitator." *Quality Progress,* 1996, *29*(6), 69–72.

Schuman, S. P. "Believe in Doubt." *Group Facilitation: A Research and Applications Journal,* 2002, *4,* 1.

Senge, P., and others. *The Fifth Discipline Field Book: Strategies and Tools for Building a Learning Organization.* New York: Doubleday, 1994.

Sibbet, D. *Principles of Facilitation: The Purpose and Potential of Leading Group Process.* San Francisco: Grove Consultants, 2002.

Sue, D. W., and Sue, D. *Counseling the Culturally-Different: Theory and Practice.* (3rd ed.) New York: Wiley, 1999.

Triandis, H. C. *Individualism and Collectivism.* Boulder, Colo.: Westview Press, 1995.

Wong, P.T.P. "Meaning-Centered Counselling." In P.T.P. Wong and P. S. Fry (eds.), *The Human Quest for Meaning: A Handbook of Psychological Research and Clinical Applications.* Mahawah, N.J.: Erlbaum, 1998.

Wong, P.T.P. "Towards an Integrative Model of Meaning-Centered Counselling and Therapy." *International Forum for Logotherapy,* 1999, *22,* 47–55.

Wong, P.T.P. "Logotherapy." In G. Zimmer (ed.), *Encyclopedia of Psychotherapy.* Orlando, Fla.: Academic Press, 2002a.

Wong, P.T.P. "Creating a Positive Meaningful Work Climate: A New Challenge for Management and Leadership." In B. Pattanayak and V. Gupta (eds.), *Creating Performing Organizations: International Perspective for Indian Management.* Thousand Oaks, Calif.: Sage, 2002b.

Wong, P.T.P. "Building Positive Communities." *INPM Positive Living Magazine,* Oct. 2003. [http://www.meaning.ca/articles/presidents_column/community_oct03.htm].

Wong, P.T.P., and Gupta, V. "The Positive Psychology of Transformative Organizations." In V. Gupta (ed.), *Transformative Organizations.* Thousand Oaks, Calif.: Sage, 2004.

Chapter Twelve

Chrislip, D. D. *Collaborative Leadership Fieldbook.* San Francisco: Jossey-Bass, 2002.

Fisher, C. J. "Like It or Not, Culture Matters: Linking Culture to Bottom Line Business Performance." *Employee Relations Today,* 2000, *27,* 46–49.

Schein, E. H. *Organizational Culture and Leadership.* San Francisco: Jossey-Bass, 1985.

Straus, D. *How to Make Collaboration Work: Powerful Ways to Build Consensus, Solve Problems, and Make Decisions.* San Francisco: Berrett-Koehler, 2002.

Vroom, V. H. "Educating Managers for Decision Making and Leadership." *Management Decision,* 2003, *40,* 968–978.

Chapter Thirteen

Aretz, A., Bolen, T., and Devereux, K. "Critical Thinking Assessment of College Students." *Journal of College Reading and Learning,* 1997, *28,* 12–23.

Atlee, T. *The Tao of Democracy.* Cranston, R.I.: The Writer's Collective, 2003.

Bohm, D. *On Dialogue* (L. Nichol, ed.). New York: Routledge, 2003. (Originally published 1996.)

Conflict Research Consortium. *Treating Communication Problems.* Conflict Research Consortium, 1998a. [http://_/_www.colorado.edu/_conflict/_peace/_!treating_overlays.htm.]

Conflict Research Consortium. *Dialogue Projects.* Conflict Research Consortium, 1998b. [http:/_/_www.colorado.edu/_conflict/_peace/_treatment/_dialog2.htm].

Conversation Café. "Come to a Conversation Cafe." 2002. [http://www.conversationcafe. org/join_main.html].

Davis, S. "Build and Maintain a Process Vessel." In S. Davis (ed.), *Selected Articles from the Master Facilitator Journal.* Ridgecrest, Calif.: Master Facilitator Journal, 2003.

Edwards, A. "The Moderator as an Emerging Democratic Intermediary: The Role of the Moderator in Internet Discussions about Public Issues." *Information Polity,* 2002, *7.* [https:/_/_ep.eur.nl/_retrieve/_608/_BSK019.pdf].

Gerard, G., and Ellinor, L. "Dialogue Contrasted with Discussion." 2004. [http://www. thedialoguegrouponline.com/whatsdialogue.html#Contrast].

Heierbacher, S. "What Are Dialogue and Deliberation?" 2004. [http://www.thataway.org/ resources/understand/what.html#deliberation].

Heierbacher, S., and Fluke, A. "What Is Dialogue?" 2001. [http://www.thataway.org/dialogue/ org/org2.htm].

Hunter, D., Bailey, A., and Taylor B. *The Art of Facilitation: How to Create Group Synergy.* Tucson, Ariz.: Fisher, 1995.

International Association of Facilitators. "Statement of Values and Code of Ethics for Facilitators—Draft Adopted May 21, 2002." 2002. [http://www.iaf-world.org/about/iaf/ iafethics.cfm].

Isaacs, W. "Strategies for Team Learning." In P. Senge and others, *The Fifth Discipline Fieldbook: Strategies and Tools for Building a Learning Organization.* New York: Doubleday, 1994.

Isaacs, W. *Dialogue and the Art of Thinking Together: A Pioneering Approach to Communicating in Business and in Life.* New York: Doubleday, 1999.

Jaworski, J. *Synchronicity: The Inner Path of Leadership.* San Francisco: Berrett-Koehler, 1998.

Kirby, G., Goodpaster, J., and Levin, M. *Critical Thinking.* Boston: Pearson, 2003.

Madonik, B. *I Hear What You Say, But What Are You Telling Me? The Strategic Use of Nonverbal Communication in Mediation.* San Francisco: Jossey-Bass, 2001.

Nierenberg, G., and Calero, H. *How to Read a Person Like a Book.* New York: Barnes and Noble, 2003. (Originally published 1971.)

Palmer, P. *The Courage to Teach: Exploring the Inner Landscape of a Teacher's Life.* San Francisco: Jossey-Bass, 1998.

Public Conversations Project. "Distinguishing Debate from Dialogue: A Table." [http://www.publicconversations.org/pcp/uploadDocs/toolbox.pdf]. 1992.

Pyser, S., and Figallo, C. "The 'Listening to the City' Online Dialogues Experience: The Impact of a Full Value Contract." *Conflict Resolution Quarterly,* 2004, *21,* 381–393.

Schoem, D., and others. "Intergroup Dialogue: Democracy at Work in Theory and Practice." In D. Schoem and S. Hurtado (eds.), *Intergroup Dialogue: Deliberative Democracy in School, College, Community and Workplace.* Ann Arbor: University of Michigan, 2001.

Schuman, S. "What to Look for in a Group Facilitator." *Quality Progress,* 1996, *29*(6), 69–72.

Scott, S. *Fierce Conversations: Achieving Success at Work and in Life, One Conversation at a Time.* New York: Viking Penguin, 2002.

Senge, P., and others. *The Fifth Discipline Fieldbook: Strategies and Tools for Building a Learning Organization.* New York: Doubleday, 1994.

Society for Human Resource Management. "What Is the 'Business Case' for Diversity?" 2004. [http://www.shrm.org/diversity/businesscase.asp].

Study Circles Resource Center. "Organizing Community-Wide Dialogue for Action and Change: A Step-by-Step Guide." Pomfret, Conn.: Topsfield Foundation, 2001. [http://www.studycircles.org/pdf/SCRCPG.pdf].

Swain, V. M. "The Sacred Container as a Way to Address the Cycle of Violence." 2001. [http://www.global-leader.org/gl_sacred_container.htm].

Whitney, D., Cooperrider, D., Trosten-Bloom, A., and Kaplin, B. *Encyclopedia of Positive Questions: Using Appreciative Inquiry to Bring Out the Best in Your Organization.* Euclid, Ohio: Lakeshore Communications, 2002.

Zuniga, X., and Nagda, B. "Design Considerations in Intergroup Dialogue." In D. Schoem and S. Hurtado (eds.), *Intergroup Dialogue: Deliberative Democracy in School, College, Community, and Workplace.* Ann Arbor: University of Michigan, 2004.

Chapter Fourteen

Appalachian Center for Economic Networks. *Cooperative Economic Development Strategies Replication Manual.* Athens, Ohio: Appalachian Center for Economic Networks, 1998.

Axelrod, R., and Axelrod, E. *The Conference Model.* Wilmette, Ill.: Axelrod Group, 1993.

Cole, C. R., and others. "Heart-Rate Recovery After Exercise as a Predictor of Mortality." *New England Journal of Medicine,* 1999, *341,* 1351–1357.

Dannemiller, K., and others. *Consultant Guide to Large-Scale Meetings.* Ann Arbor, Mich.: Dannemiller Tyson, 1994.

Dixon, N. *Common Knowledge: How Companies Thrive by Sharing What They Know.* Boston: Harvard Business School Press, 2000.

Eisenhardt, K. M., and Sull, D. M. "Strategy as Simple Rules." *Harvard Business Review,* 2001, *79*(1), 106–116.

Owen, H. *Open Space Technology: A User's Guide.* Potomac, Md.: Abbott Publishing, 1992.

Owen, H. "A Brief User's Guide to Open Space Technology." N.d. [http://www.openspaceworld.com/users_guide.htm].

Stacey, R. D. *Complex Responsive Processes in Organizations: Learning and Knowledge Creation.* London: Routledge, 2001.

Sweeney, L. B., and Meadows, D. *The Systems Thinking Playbook.* Durham, N.H.: University of New Hampshire Institute for Policy and Social Science Research, 2001.

Weisbord, M. *Discovering Common Ground.* San Francisco: Berrett-Koehler, 1992.

World Café Community Foundation. *The World Café.* 2003. [http://www.theworldcafe.com].

Zimmerman, B., Plsek, P., and Lindberg, C. *Edgeware: Insights from Complexity Science for Health Care Leaders.* Cranbury, N.J.: VHA, 1998.

Chapter Fifteen

Agazarian, Y. M. *Systems-Centered Therapy for Groups.* New York: Guilford Press, 1997.

Asch, S. *Social Psychology.* Upper Saddle River, N.J.: Prentice Hall, 1952.

Bertalanffy, L. *General System Theory.* New York: George Braziller, 1968.

Lawrence, P. R., and Lorsch, J. W. *Organization and Environment: Managing Differentiation and Integration.* Cambridge, Mass.: Harvard University Press, 1967.

Lewin, K., Lippitt, R., and White, T. "Patterns of Aggressive Behavior in Experimentally-Created 'Social Climates.'" *Journal of Social Psychology,* 1939, *10,* 271–299.

Marrow, A. J. *The Practical Theorist: The Life and Work of Kurt Lewin.* New York: Teachers College, 1977. (Originally published in 1969.)

Trist, E. L., with Murray, H. *The Social Engagement of Social Science: A Tavistock Anthology.* Philadelphia: University of Pennsylvania, 1990.

Weir, J. "The Personal Growth Laboratory." In K. D. Benne, L. P. Bradford, J. R. Gibb, and R. O. Lippitt (eds.), *The Laboratory Method of Changing and Learning: Theory and Application.* Palo Alto, Calif.: Science and Behavior, 1971.

Weisbord, M., and Janoff, S. *Future Search: An Action Guide.* (2nd ed.) San Francisco: Berrett-Koehler, 2000.

Chapter Sixteen

Abdullah, A. "The Influence of Values on Management in Malaysia." Unpublished doctoral dissertation, Universiti Kebangsaan, Bangi, Malaysia, 2001.

Abdullah, A., and Shephard, P. *The Cross Cultural Game.* Kuala Lumpur, Malaysia: Brain Dominance Technologies, 2000. [http://asma.braindominance.com/game.htm].

Adler, N. *International Dimensions of Organisational Behaviour.* (3rd ed.) Cincinnati, Ohio: International Thomson, 1997.

Ballard, B., and Clanchy, J. *Studying in Australia.* Melbourne, Australia: Longman Cheshire, 1991.

Beasley, C., and Hogan, C. F. *Cultural Dimensions of Australian and Overseas Students.* Perth, Western Australia: Edith Cowan University Staff Development Workshop, 2003.

Blainey, J., Davis, K., and Goodwill, B. *Valuing Diversity: Facilitating Cross Cultural Communication and Conflict Resolution.* French's Forest, New South Wales, Australia: Working Together, 1995.

Bohm, D., Factor, D., and Garrett, P. 1995, *Dialogue: A Proposal.* Nov. 10, 2003. [http://world.std.com/~lo/bohm/0001.html].

Brenson-Lazán, G. "The Evolution of Conflict and the Facilitation of Its Resolution." Paper presented at the Second Chinese Facilitators' Conference, Taipei, Taiwan, Nov. 2003.

Brislin, R. W. *Understanding Culture's Influence on Behavior.* (2nd ed.) Fort Worth, Tex.: Harcourt, 2000.

Burson, M. "Finding Clarity in the Midst of Conflict: Facilitating Dialogue and Skillful Discussion Using a Model from the Quaker Tradition." *Group Facilitation: A Research and Applications Journal,* 2002, *4,* 23–29.

Chakraborty, S. K. *Values and Ethics for Organisations.* New York: Oxford University Press, 1998.

Chang, S. "Cultural Dimensions Workshop Handout." Melbourne, Australia: University of Melbourne, 2002.

de Bono, E. *Six Thinking Hats.* London, England: Penguin, 1985.

de Bono, E. *The CoRT Thinking Process.* London: Pergamon Press, 1987.

Distefano, J. J., and Maznevski, M. L. "Creating Value with Diverse Teams in Global Management." *Organizational Dynamics,* 2000, *29*(1), 45–63.

Gardenswartz, L., Rowe, A., Digh, P., and Bennett, M. *The Global Diversity Desk Reference: Managing an International Workforce.* San Francisco: Pfeiffer, 2003.

Geschka, H., Schaude, G. R., and Schlicksupp, H. "Modern Techniques for Solving Problems." *Chemical Engineering,* 1973, *6*(80), 91–97.

Hall, E. T. *Understanding Cultural Differences,* Yarmouth, Me.: Intercultural Press, 1990.

Hofstede, G. *Culture's Consequences: International Differences in World-Related Values.* Thousand Oaks, Calif.: Sage, 1980.

Hofstede, G. *Cultures and Organizations: Software of the Mind.* New York: McGraw-Hill, 1991.

Hogan, C. F. "Cross-Cultural Communication Workshop." *Training and Management Development Methods,* 1996, *10*(2) 8.01–8.16.

Hogan, C. F. *Understanding Facilitation: Theory and Principles.* London: Kogan Page, 2002.

Hogan, C. F. *Practical Facilitation: A Toolkit of Techniques.* London: Kogan Page, 2003a.

Hogan, C. F. "Using Music to Promote Harmony, Learning and Fun with Groups." Paper presented at the Sixth Annual International Association of Facilitators' Regional Conference, Kuala Lumpur, Malaysia, Sept. 2003b.

Honey, P., and Mumford, A. *Using Your Learning Styles.* Maidenhead, England: Peter Honey, 1986.

Honey, P., and Mumford, A. *The Manual of Learning Styles.* (3rd ed.) Maidenhead, England: Peter Honey, 1992.

Reese, R. "A Proactive-Interactive Approach to Bridging Cultural Differences." Nov. 2001. [http://www.csupomona.edu/~rreese/MULTICULTURAL.html].

Samovar, L. A., and Porter, R. E. *Communication Between Cultures.* (5th ed.) Belmont, Calif.: Thomson Wadsworth, 2004.

Satir, V. *Conjoint Family Therapy.* Palo Alto, Calif.: Science and Behavior Books, 1983.

Schnelle, E. *The Metaplan-Method—Communication Tools for Planning and Learning Groups.* Quickborn, West Germany: Metaplan, 1979.

Teaching and Learning Committee. "Teaching with Diversity Checklist." Perth, Western Australia: University of Western Australia, Nov. 2003. [http://www.acs.uwa.edu.au/csdtl/99TDChecklist.htm].

Trompenaars, F. *Riding the Waves of Culture: Understanding Cultural Diversity in Business.* London: Economist Books, 1993.

Trompenaars, F., and Hampden-Turner, C. *Building Cross-Cultural Competence.* New York: Wiley, 2000.

Tuckman, B. W., and Jensen, M. A. "Stages of Small Group Development Revisited." *Group and Organisational Studies,* 1977, *2,* 419–427.

Verghese, T. "Facilitating Successfully with Culturally Diverse Groups." Paper presented at the Sixth Regional Facilitators' Conference, Kuala Lumpur, Malaysia, Sept. 2003.

Chapter Seventeen

Gesell, I. *Playing Along: Group Learning Activities Borrowed from Improvisation Theater.* Duluth, Minn.: Whole Person Associates, 1997.

Johnstone, K. *Impro: Improvisation and the Theater.* New York: Theater Arts, 1989.

Spolin, V. *Improvisation for the Theater.* Chicago: Northwestern University Press, 1963.

Waldrop, M. M. "Dee Hock on Management." *Fast Company,* Oct.–Nov. 1996, p. 79.

Chapter Eighteen

Anderson, J., Ashraf, N., Douther, C., and Jack, M. "Presence and Usability in Shared Space Virtual Conferencing: A Participatory Design Study." *CyberPsychology and Behavior,* 2001, *4*(2), 287–305.

Attaran, M., and Attaran, S. "Collaborative Computing Technology: The Hot New Managing Tool." *Team Performance Management,* 2002, *8*(1/2), 13–20.

Bal, J., and Teo, P. "Implementing Virtual Teamworking: Part 3-A Methodology for Introducing Virtual Teamworking." *Logistics Information Management,* 2001, *14,* 276–292.

Bradley, L., Wagner-Johnson, D., and Ballantine, R. *Effective Virtual Meetings.* Denton, Tex.: Center for Collaborative Organizations, University of North Texas, 2002.

Connell, J. B. "Organizational Consulting to Virtual Teams." In R. Lowman (ed.), *Handbook of Organizational Consulting Psychology: A Comprehensive Guide to Theory, Skills, Techniques.* San Francisco: Jossey-Bass, 2002.

Creighton, J. L., and Adams, J. W. *Cyber Meeting: How to Link People and Technology in Your Organization.* New York: AMACOM, 1998.

Duarte, D., and Snyder, N. *Mastering Virtual Teams: Strategies, Tools, and Techniques That Succeed.* San Francisco: Jossey-Bass, 2001.

Fels, D., and Weiss, P. "Toward Determining an Attention-Getting Device for Improving Interaction During Video-Mediated Communication." *Computers in Human Behavior,* 2000, *16,* 189–198.

LeMay, E. A. *Virtual Teams: Work Processes, Communication, and Team Development. Dissertation Abstracts International,* 2000, *61*(09), 322A, 2000. (UMI No. 9981350).

Straus, D. *How to Make Collaboration Work.* San Francisco: Berrett-Koehler, 2002.

Whittaker, S. "Rethinking Video as a Technology for Interpersonal Communications: Theory and Design Implications." *International Journal of Human-Computer Studies,* 1995, *42,* 501–529.

Chapter Nineteen

Bens, I. *Facilitation at a Glance.* Salem, N.H.: GOAL/QPC, 1999.

Brassard, M., and Ritter, D. *The Memory Jogger II.* Salem, N.H.: GOAL/QPC, 1994.

Fisher, R., Ury, W. L., and Patton B. *Getting to Yes: Negotiating Agreement Without Giving In.* (2nd ed.) New York: Penguin Books, 1991.

Katzenbach, J. R., and Smith, D. K. *The Wisdom of Teams: Creating the High Performance Organization.* Boston: Harvard Business School Press, 1993.

Marianccio, D. *All I Really Need to Know I Learned from Watching Star Trek.* New York: Crown, 1994.

Napolitano, C. S. "Some Thoughts About the Vision Thing." Notes from presentation at the University of Maryland, University College, Leadership Institute College Park, Md., Aug. 1992.

Smith, G. "Group Development: A Review of the Literature and Commentary on Future Research Directions." *Group Facilitation: A Research and Applications Journal,* 2001, *3,* 14–44.

Tuckman, B. W. "Developmental Sequence in Small Groups." *Group Facilitation: A Research and Applications Journal,* 2001, *3,* 66–81.

Chapter Twenty

Beckhard, R., and Harris, R. T. *Organization Transitions: Managing Complex Change.* (2nd ed.) Reading, Mass.: Addison-Wesley, 1987.

Bunker, B. B., and Alban, B. T. *Large Group Interventions.* San Francisco: Jossey-Bass, 1997.

Cady, S. H., and Dannemiller, K. D. "Whole System Transformation: The Five Truths of Change." In W. Rothwell, R. Sullivan, and G. McLean (eds.), *Practicing OD.* San Francisco: Jossey-Bass/Pfeiffer, 2004.

Capra, F. *The Web of Life: A New Scientific Understanding of Living Systems.* New York: Doubleday, 1996.

Dannemiller Tyson Associates. *Whole-Scale Change: Unleashing the Magic in Organizations.* Berrett-Koehler, 2000.

Dannemiller Tyson Associates. *Whole-Scale Change Toolkit.* Ann Arbor, Mich.: Dannemiller Tyson Associates, 2004.

Gerard, G., and Ellinor, L. *Dialogue at Work: Skills for Leveraging Collective Understanding.* Waltham, Mass.: Pegasus Communications, 2001.

Chapter Twenty-One

Bazerman, M. H. *Judgment in Managerial Decision Making.* (5th ed.). New York: Wiley, 2002.

Beach, L. R. *The Psychology of Decision Making: People in Organizations.* Thousand Oaks, Calif.: Sage, 1997.

Blanchard, K. H. *SLII: A Situational Approach to Managing People.* Escondo, Calif.: Blanchard Training and Development, 1985.

Folger, J. P., Poole, M. S., and Stutman, R. K. *Working Through Conflict: Strategies for Relationships, Groups, and Organizations.* (4th ed.). Reading, Mass.: Addison-Wesley, 2001.

Frey, L. R. (ed.). *Innovations in Group Facilitation: Applications in Natural Settings.* Cresskill, N.J.: Hampton Press, 1995.

Gouran, D. S. *Making Decisions in Groups: Choices and Consequences.* Glenview, Ill.: Scott, Foresman, 1982.

Gouran, D. S. "Communication Skills for Group Decision Making." In J. O. Greene and B. R. Burleson (eds.), *Handbook of Communication and Social Interaction Skills.* Mahwah, N.J.: Erlbaum, 2003a.

Gouran, D. S. "Leadership as the Art of Counteractive Influence." In R. Y. Hirokawa, R. S. Cathcart, L. A. Samovar, and L. D. Henman (eds.), *Small Group Communication Theory and Practice: An Anthology.* (8th ed.) Los Angeles: Roxbury, 2003b.

Gouran, D. S., and Hirokawa, R. Y. (1983). "The Role of Communication in Groups: A Functional Perspective." In M. S. Mander (ed.), *Communications in Transition: Issues and Debates in Current Research.* New York: Praeger, 1983.

Gouran, D. S., and Hirokawa, R. Y. "Functional Theory and Communication in Decision-Making and Problem-Solving Groups: An Expanded View." In R. Y. Hirokawa and M. S. Poole (eds.), *Communication and Group Decision Making.* (2nd ed.). Thousand Oaks, Calif.: Sage, 1996.

Gouran, D. S., and Hirokawa, R. Y. "Effective Decision Making and Problem Solving in Groups." In R. Y. Hirokawa, R. S. Cathcart, L. A. Samovar, and L. D. Henman (eds.), *Small Group Communication Theory and Practice: An Anthology.* Los Angeles: Roxbury, 2003.

Hall, J., and Watson, W. H. "The Effects of a Normative Intervention on Group Decision-Making Performance." *Human Relations,* 1970, *23,* 299–317.

Herek, G., Janis, I. L., and Huth, P. "Decision Making During International Crises: Is Quality of Process Related to Outcome?" *Journal of Conflict Resolution,* 1987, *31,* 203–226.

Hersey, P., and Blanchard, K. H. *Management of Organizational Behavior: Utilizing Human Resources.* (6th ed.) Upper Saddle River, N.J.: Prentice Hall, 1993.

House, R. J. "A Path-Goal Theory of Leader Effectiveness." *Administrative Science Quarterly,* 1971, *16,* 321–328.

House, R. J. "Path-Goal Theory of Leadership: Lessons, Legacy, and a Reformulated Theory." *Leadership Quarterly,* 1996, *7,* 323–352.

House, R. J., and Dessler, G. "The Path-Goal Theory of Leadership: Some Post Hoc and A Priori Tests." In J. G. Hunt and L. L. Larson (eds.), *Contingency Approaches to Leadership.* Carbondale: Southern Illinois University Press, 1974.

Hovland, C. I., Janis, I. L., and Kelley, H. H. *Communication and Persuasion: Psychological Studies of Opinion Change.* New Haven, Conn.: Yale University Press, 1953.

Janis, I. L. *Victims of Groupthink: A Psychological Study of Foreign-Policy Decisions and Fiascoes.* Boston: Houghton Mifflin, 1972.

Janis, I. L. *Groupthink: Psychological Studies of Policy Decisions and Fiascoes.* (2nd ed.). Boston: Houghton Mifflin, 1982.

Janis, I. L. *Crucial Decisions: Leadership in Policymaking and Crisis Management.* New York: Free Press, 1989.

Janis, I. L., and Mann, L. *Decision Making: A Psychological Analysis of Conflict, Choice, and Commitment.* New York: Free Press, 1977.

Meyers, R. A. "Social Influence and Group Argumentation." In L. R. Frey and J. K. Barge (eds.), *Managing Group Life: Communicating in Decision-Making Groups.* Boston: Houghton Mifflin, 1997.

Nisbett, R., and Ross, L. *Human Inference: Strategies and Shortcomings of Social Judgment.* Upper Saddle River, N.J.: Prentice Hall, 1980.

Schwarz, R. *The Skilled Facilitator: A Comprehensive Resource for Consultants, Facilitators, Managers, Trainers, and Coaches.* (2nd ed.). San Francisco: Jossey-Bass, 2002.

Schweiger, D. M., Sandberg, W. R., and Rechner, P. L. "Experiential Effects of Dialectical Inquiry, Devil's Advocacy, and Consensus Approaches to Strategic Decision Making." *Academy of Management Journal,* 1989, *32,* 745–772.

Volkema, R. J. "Problem Formulation in Planning and Design." *Management Science,* 1983, *29,* 639–652.

Chapter Twenty-Two

Deutsch, M., and Coleman, P. *The Handbook of Conflict Resolution: Theory and Practice.* San Francisco: Jossey-Bass, 2000.

Fisher, R., Ury, W., and Patton B. *Getting to Yes: Negotiating Agreement Without Giving In.* (2nd ed.) New York: Penguin Books, 1991.

Leadership Strategies Institute. *The Effective Facilitator.* Atlanta, Ga.: Leadership Strategies Institute, 2003.

Marcum, D., Smith, S., and Khalsa, M. *Businessthink: Rules for Getting It Right—Now and No Matter What.* New York: Wiley, 2002.

Russo, J. E., and Schoemaker, P.J.H. *Winning Decisions: Getting It Right the First Time.* New York: Doubleday, 2002.

Welch, D. A. *Decisions, Decisions: The Art of Effective Decision Making.* Amherst, N.Y.: Prometheus Books, 2002.

Wilkinson, M. *The Secrets of Facilitation.* San Francisco: Jossey-Bass, 2004.

Chapter Twenty-Three

Alexander, C. *The Timeless Way of Building.* New York: Oxford University Press, 1979.

Alexander, C., Ishikawa, S., and Silverstein, M. *A Pattern Language: Towns, Buildings, Construction.* New York: Oxford University Press, 1977.

Buzan, T. *The Mind Map Book: How to Use Radiant Thinking to Maximize Your Brain's Untapped Potential.* New York: Plume, 1996.

De Saint-Exupéry, A. *The Little Prince.* London: Mammoth, 1991.

"The High Cost of Disengaged Employees." *Gallup Management Journal,* Apr. 15, 2002, pp. 1–2.

Horn, R. E. *Visual Language: Global Communication for the Twenty-First Century.* Bainbridge Island, Wash.: MacroVU, 1998.

Margulies, N., and Maal, N. *Mapping Inner Space: Learning and Teaching Visual Mapping.* Tucson, Ariz.: Zephyr, 2002.

Peña, W., Parschall, S., and Kelly, K. *Problem Seeking: An Architectural Programming Primer.* Houston: CRSS, 1987.

Saint-Exupéry, A. *The Little Prince.* (K. Woods, trans.). London: Mammoth, 1991.

Schank, R. C., and Abelson, R. *Scripts, Plans, Goals, and Understanding.* Mahwah, N.J.: Erlbaum, 1977.

Schank, R. C., and Abelson, R. *Knowledge and Memory: The Real Story.* Mahwah, N.J.: Erlbaum, 1995.

Chapter Twenty-Four

Beach, L. R. *Image Theory: Decision Making in Personal and Organization Context.* New York: Wiley, 1990.

Bergdall, T. D. *Baragay Monitoring and Evaluation: Consultant's Report on the Governance and Local Democracy Project.* Manila: ARD, 1997.

Bergdall, T. D., and Powell, C. F. *Beyond Participation: The Final Report of the Community Empowerment Program in South Wollo, Ethiopia.* Addis Abba: Sida, 1996.

Boulding, K. *The Image: Knowledge in Life and Society.* Ann Arbor: University of Michigan Press, 1956.

Cooperrider, D. "Positive Image, Positive Action: The Affirmative Basis of Organizing." In S. Srivastva and D. Cooperrider (eds.), *Appreciative Management and Leadership: The Power of Positive Thought and Action in Organizations.* San Francisco: Jossey-Bass, 1990.

Cousins, J. B., and Whitmore, E. "Framing Participatory Evaluation." In E. Whitmore (ed.), *Understanding and Practicing Participatory Evaluation.* New Directions for Evaluation, no. 80. San Francisco: Jossey-Bass, 1998.

Davies, R. "An Evolutionary Approach to Facilitating Organisational Learning: An Experiment by the Christian Commission for Development in Bangladesh." In D. Mosse, J. Farrington, and A. Rew (eds.), *Development as a Process: Concepts and Methods for Working with Complexity.* London: Routledge/ODI, 1998.

Donnelly, J. (ed.). *Who Are the Question-Makers: A Participatory Evaluation Handbook.* New York: Office of Evaluation and Strategic Planning, UNDP, 1997.

Estrella, M. (ed.). *Learning from Change: Issues and Experiences in Participatory Monitoring and Evaluation.* London: Intermediate Technology, 2000.

Estrella, M., and Gaventa, J. *Who Counts Reality? Participatory Monitoring and Evaluation: A Literature Review.* Sussex: IDS, 1998.

Fetterman, D. M., Kaftarian, S. J., and Wandersman, A. (eds.). *Empowerment Evaluation: Knowledge and Tools for Self-Assessment and Accountability.* Thousand Oaks, Calif.: Sage, 1996.

Giddens, A. *Social Theory and Modern Sociology.* Cambridge: Polity Press, 1987.

Giddens, A. "Structuration Theory and Sociological Analysis." In J. Clark, C. Modgil, and S. Modgil (eds.), *Anthony Giddens: Consensus and Controversy.* Bristol: Falmer Press, 1990.

Herman, J. L., Morris, L. L., and Fitz-Gibbon, C. T. *Evaluator's Handbook.* Thousand Oaks, Calif.: Sage, 1987.

Kellogg Foundation. *Kellogg Foundation Evaluation Handbook.* Battle Creek, Mich.: Kellogg Foundation, 1998.

Kretzmann, J., and McKnight, J. *Building Communities from the Inside Out: A Path Toward Finding and Mobilizing a Community's Assets.* Chicago: ACTA Publications, 1993.

Lazarus, A. *In the Mind's Eye: The Power of Imagery.* New York: Raison, 1977.

Long, N., and Long, A. (eds.). *Battlefields of Knowledge: The Interlocking of Theory and Practice in Social Research and Development.* London: Routledge, 1992.

Opto International AB. *Twenty-One Steps for Preparing a Project: A Manual to Guide the Journey.* Topola: Opto, 2002.

Opto International AB. *Second Bi-Annual Report to Sida for the Topola Rural Development Programme, June-December 2003.* Stockholm: Opto, 2003.

Patton, M. Q. *Creative Evaluation.* Thousand Oaks, Calif.: Sage, 1987.

Patton, M. Q. *Utilization Evaluation: The New Century Edition.* Thousand Oaks, Calif.: Sage, 1997.

Polak, F. *The Image of the Future.* San Francisco: Jossey-Bass, 1973.

Robinson, L. "Participatory Rural Appraisal: A Brief Introduction." *Group Facilitation: A Research and Applications Journal,* 2002. no. 4. [http://iaf-world.org/Docs/CommPub/issue4.cfm].

Rossi, P. H., Freeman, H. E., and Lipsey, M. W. *Evaluation: A Systematic Approach.* (7th ed.) Thousand Oaks, Calif.: Sage, 2003.

Tye, M. *The Imagery Debate.* Cambridge, Mass.: MIT Press, 1991.

Wholey, J. S., Hatry, H. P., and Newcomer, K. E. (eds.). *Handbook of Practical Program Evaluation.* San Francisco: Jossey-Bass, 1994.

Chapter Twenty-Five

Bennis, W. G., and Biderman, P. W. *Organizing Genius: The Secrets of Creative Collaboration.* Reading, Mass.: Addison-Wesley, 1997.

Friedlob, G. T., Schleifer, L. F., and Plewa, F. J. *Essentials of Corporate Performance Measurement.* New York: Wiley, 2002.

Hackman, J. R. *Groups That Work (and Those That Don't): Creating Conditions for Effective Teamwork.* San Francisco: Jossey-Bass, 1990.

Hare, A. P. *Handbook of Small Group Research.* New York: Free Press, 1976.

McCartt, A. T., and Rohrbaugh, J. "Managerial Openness to Change and the Introduction of GDSS: Explaining Initial Success and Failure in Decision Conferencing." *Organization Science,* 1995, *6,* 569–584.

McGrath, J. E. *Groups: Interaction and Performance.* Upper Saddle River, N.J.: Prentice Hall, 1984.

Meyer, M. W. *Rethinking Performance Measurement.* Cambridge: Cambridge University Press, 2002.

Meyer, N. D., and Boone, M. E. *The Information Edge.* New York: Holt, Rinehart and Winston, 1987.

Milter, R. J., and Rohrbaugh, J. "Microcomputers and Strategic Decision Making." *Public Productivity Review,* 1985, *9,* 175–189.

Neely, A. *Business Performance Measurement.* Cambridge: Cambridge University Press, 2002.

Parsons, T. "General Theory in Sociology." In R. Merton, L. Broom, and L. S. Cottrell, Jr. (eds.), *Sociology Today: Problems and Prospects.* New York: Basic Books, 1959.

Poister, T. H. *Measuring Performance in Public and Nonprofit Organizations.* San Francisco: Jossey-Bass, 2003.

Quinn, R. E., and Rohrbaugh, J. "A Spatial Model of Effectiveness Criteria: Towards a Competing Values Approach to Organizational Analysis." *Management Science,* 1983, *29,* 363–377.

Rangarajan, N., and Rohrbaugh, J. "Multiple Roles of Online Facilitation: An Example in Any-Time, Any-Place Meetings." *Group Facilitation: A Research and Applications Journal,* 2003, *5,* 26–36.

Reagan, P., and Rohrbaugh, J. "Group Decision Process Effectiveness: A Competing Values Approach." *Group and Organization Studies,* 1990, *21,* 20–43.

Rohrbaugh, J. "The Competing Values Approach: Innovation and Effectiveness in the Job Service." In R. H. Hall and R. E. Quinn (eds.), *Organizational Theory and Public Policy.* Thousand Oaks, Calif.: Sage, 1983.

Rohrbaugh, J. "Comments for Panel 6: The Productivity Frontier." *Public Productivity Review,* 1985, *9,* 384–388.

Rohrbaugh, J. "Assessing the Effectiveness of Expert Teams." In J. Mumpower, L. Phillips, O. Renn, and V.R.R. Uppuluri (eds.), *Expert Judgment and Expert Systems.* Berlin: Springer-Verlag, 1987.

Rohrbaugh, J. "Demonstration Experiments: Assessing the Process, Not the Outcome, of Group Decision Support." In I. Benbasat (ed.), *Experimental Methods in Information Systems.* Cambridge, Mass.: Harvard Business School, 1989.

Rohrbaugh, J. "Cognitive Challenges and Collective Accomplishments." In R. P. Bostrom, R. T. Watson, and S. T. Kinney (eds.), *Computer Augmented Teamwork: A Guided Tour.* New York: Van Nostrand Reinhold, 1992.

Rohrbaugh, J. "The Use of System Dynamics in Decision Conferencing: Implementing Welfare Reform in New York State." In G. D. Garson (ed.), *Handbook of Public Information Systems.* New York: Marcel Dekker, 2000.

Senge, P. M. *The Fifth Discipline: The Art and Practice of the Learning Organization.* New York: Doubleday, 1990.

Wright, B. E., and Rohrbaugh, J. "Evaluating the Strengths and Weaknesses of Group Decision-Making Processes: A Competing Values Approach." *Group Facilitation: A Research and Applications Journal,* 1999, *1,* 5–13.

Chapter Twenty-Six

American Society for Training and Development. *Models for Excellence: The Conclusions and Recommendations of the ASTD Training and Development Competency Study.* Baltimore, Md.: ASTD Press, 1983.

Kirk, J., Schwarz, R. M., Tahar, M., and Wilkinson, M. "Comments on Facilitator Competencies." *Group Facilitation: A Research and Application Journal,* 2000, *2*(2), 32–37.

Knowles, M. S. *The Modern Practice of Adult Education: From Pedagogy to Andragogy.* (Rev. ed.) Chicago: Association Press, 1980.

National Organization of Competency Assurance. *Certification: A NOCalif. Handbook, Updated.* Washington, D.C.: National Organization of Competency Assurance, 1996.

Pierce, V. Cheesbrow, D., and Brau, L. M. "Facilitator Competencies." *Group Facilitation: A Research and Application Journal,* 2000, *2*(2), 24–31.

Rao, P.U.B. "Competency Profiling." Dec. 4, 2003. [http://www.indiainfoline.com/bisc/imtfac08.html].

Stanfield, R. B. "The Magic of the Facilitator." *Edges: New Planetary Patterns,* Sept. 1994. [http://www.iaf-world.org/i4a/pages/index.cfm?pageid=3439].

Chapter Twenty-Seven

Arthur, W. B., and others, "Illuminating the Blind Spot: Leadership in the Context of Emerging Worlds (Summary Paper on an Ongoing Research Project)." 2000. [http://www.dialogonleadership.org/WhitePaper.html#two].

Bohm, D., Factor, D., and Garrett, P. "Dialogue—A Proposal." 1991. [http://www.muc.de/~heuvel/dialogue/dialogue_proposal.html].

Brown, J. S., Denning, S., Groh, K., and Prusak, L. "Storytelling: Passport to the Twenty-First Century." 2001. [http://www.creatingthe21stcentury.com/JSB.html]

Bunker, B. B., and Alban, B. T. *Large Group Interventions: Engaging the Whole System for Rapid Change.* San Francisco: Jossey-Bass, 1997.

Collins, J. *Good to Great: Why Some Companies Make the Leap . . . and Others Don't.* New York: Random House, 2001.

"Convoy Course: Lecture One." *Golden Pathways*. Chicago: Institute of Cultural Affairs, 1996. CD-ROM.

Cunningham, W. "Abilene Paradox." Jan. 2004. [http://c2.com/cgi/wiki?AbileneParadox].

Denning, S. *The Springboard: How Storytelling Ignites Action in Knowledge-Era Organizations*. Boston: Butterworth Heinemann, 2001.

Factor, D., "On Facilitation and Purpose." 1994. [http://www.muc.de/~heuvel/dialogue/facilitation_purpose.html].

GOPP Moderators Association. "What Is GOPP?" [http://www.gopp.org/gma/gmagopp.htm]. 2000.

"Grove Consultants International." 2003. [http://www.grove.com/index.html].

Harvey, J. B. *The Abilene Paradox and Other Meditations on Management*. San Francisco: Jossey-Bass, 1996.

Holman, P., and Devane, T. (eds.). *The Change Handbook: Group Methods for Shaping the Future*. San Francisco: Berrett-Koehler, 1999.

Horn, R. E. *Visual Language: Global Communications for the Twenty-First Century*. Bainbridge Island, Wash.: MacroVU, 1998.

Hoskins, S. (ed.). *After Action Review Facilitation Guide*. Rijswijk, The Netherlands: Shell International Exploration and Production, 2002.

International Association of Facilitators. "Statement of Values and Code of Ethics for Facilitators." 2004. [http://www.iaf-world.org/about/iaf/iafethics.cfm].

I Six Sigma, "Determine the Root Cause: 5 Whys." 2000. [http://www.isixsigma.com/library/content/c020610a.asp].

Jaworski, J., and Scharmer, C.O., "Leadership in the Digital Economy: Sensing and Actualizing Emerging Futures." 2000. [http://www.dialogonleadership.org/LeadingDigital Econoomy.html].

Jenkins, J. C., and Jenkins M. R. *The Social Process Triangles*. Groningen, The Netherlands: Imaginal Training, 1997.

Jenkins, J. C., and Jenkins M. R., "The Personal Disciplines of a Facilitator." Paper presented at the International Association of Facilitators' Conference 2000, Toronto, Canada, May 2000.

Jenkins, M. R., "Making an Evaluation Without Making a Big Fuss." 2002. [http://www.imaginal.nl/articleEvaluation.htm].

King, M. L., Jr. *Strength to Love*. Philadelphia: Fortress Press, 1981.

Kuchenmüller, R., and Stifel, M., "Simultaneous Process Pictures." N.d. [http://www.visuelle-protokolle.de/eng/index2.html].

"LENS Contextual Charts." *Golden Pathways*. Chicago: Institute of Cultural Affairs, 1996. CD-ROM.

"The Massachusetts Institute of Technology Upgrading Urban Communities: A Resource for Practitioners, Interactive Community Planning: ZOPP: Goal Oriented Project Planning." 2001. [http://web.mit.edu/urbanupgrading/upgrading/issues-tools/tools/ZOPP.html].

Mao Ze Dong. *On Contradiction.* Mao Ze Dong Internet Archive. 1999. [http://www.marxists. org/reference/archive/mao/works/1937/08.htm]. (Originally published 1937.)

Mathews, J. W. "Consult Contextual Spin Kawangware (Nairobi, Kenya) Human Development Project." *Golden Pathways,* Institute of Cultural Affairs, 1996.

Morgan, G. *Images of Organization.* Thousand Oaks, Calif.: Sage, 1986.

Morgan, G. *Imaginization: The Art of Creative Management.* Thousand Oaks, Calif.: Sage, 1993.

Musashi, Miyamoto, *A Book of Five Rings.* (V. Harris, trans.). Woodstock, N.Y.: Overlook, 1982.

"NINS." *Golden Pathways.* Chicago: Institute of Cultural Affairs, 1996. CD-ROM.

Owen, H. *Open Space Technology: A User's Guide.* (2nd ed.) San Francisco: Berrett-Koehler, 1997.

"PSU Manual." *Golden Pathways.* Chicago: Institute of Cultural Affairs, 1996. CD-ROM.

Ransdell, E. "The Nike Story: Just Tell it!" *Fast Company,* 2000, *31,* 24.

Rottmann, D. "Joint Applications Development (JAD)." Nov. 2001. [http://www.umsl.edu/ ~sauter/analysis/488_f01_papers/rottman.htm], Nov. 2001].

Rough, J. "Dynamic Facilitation." May 23, 2003. [http://www.tobe.net/topics/facilitation. html].

Rounds, J. "Group Think." Nov. 13, 2002. [http://www.colostate.edu/Depts/Speech/rccs/ theory16.htm].

Scharmer, C. O. "Presencing: Shifting the Place from Which Leaders Operate: On the Tacit Dimension of Leading Revolutionary Change." Paper presented at the Conference on Knowledge and Innovation, Helsinki, Finland, May 2000.

Schein, E. *Process Consultation Revisited: Building the Helping Relationship.* Reading, Mass.: Addison-Wesley, 1999.

Senge, P. *The Fifth Discipline: The Art and Practice of the Learning Organization.* New York: Doubleday, 1990.

Senge, P., and others *The Fifth Discipline Fieldbook: Strategies for Building a Learning* Organization. London: Nicholas Brealey, 1994.

Senge, P., and others. *The Dance of Change: The Challenges of Sustaining Momentum in Learning Organizations.* London: Nicholas Brealey, 1999.

Signet Consulting Group. "From Post-Mortem to Living Practice: An In-Depth Study of the Evolution of the After Action Review." 2000. [http://www.signetconsulting.com/ aarsum.html].

Spencer, L. J. *Winning Through Participation.* Dubuque, Iowa: Kendall/Hunt, 1989.

Stanfield, R. B. *The Workshop Book, From Individual Creativity to Group Action.* Philadelphia: New Society, 2002.

Stewart, A. "Appreciative Inquiry: A Description." 1995. [http://www.pancultural.com/ aibasicdescrip.html].

Vennix, J. *Group Model Building: Facilitating Team Learning Using System Dynamics.* New York: Wiley, 1996.

Watkins, J. M., and Mohr, B. J. *Appreciative Inquiry: Change at the Speed of Imagination.* San Francisco: Jossey-Bass, 2001.

Weaver, R. G., and Farrell, J. D. *Managers as Facilitators.* San Francisco: Berrett-Koehler, 1997.

Werkgroep Docenten Onderwijszaken, *Collegiale consultatie en intervisie: het stellen van vragen als middel tot probleemverheldering* (Collegial consultation and peer consultation teams: The posing of questions as a means for clarifying problems). Utrecht, NLD: HvU Press, 2000.

Chapter Twenty-Eight

Garvin, D. *Learning in Action: A Guide to Putting the Learning Organization to Work.* Boston: Harvard Business School Press, 2000.

Hill, N. *Think and Grow Rich.* New York: Fawcett, 1960. (Originally published 1937.)

Keltner, J. "Facilitation: Catalyst for Problem Solving." *Management Communication Quarterly,* 1989, *3*(1), 8–32.

Maier, N.R.F. "Assets and Liabilities in Group Problem Solving: The Need for an Integrative Function." *Psychological Review,* 1967, *74*(4), 239–249.

Parisse, A., and others. *The Expertise Imperative: An NSA White Paper on the Future of the Speaking Profession.* Tempe, Ariz.: National Speakers Association, 2003.

Sjodin, T., and Wickman, F. *Mentoring: The Most Obvious Yet Overlooked Key to Achieving More in Life Than You Ever Dreamed Possible.* New York: McGraw-Hill, 1996.

Chapter Twenty-Nine

Argyris, C., and Schön, D. A. *Organizational Learning II: Theory, Method and Practice.* Reading, Mass.: Addison-Wesley, 1996.

Bendaly, L. *The Facilitation Skills Training Kit.* New York: McGraw-Hill, 2000.

Bentley, T. "Facilitation: "Providing Opportunities for Learning." *Journal of European Industrial Training,* 1994, *18*(5), 8–22.

Box, G.E.P. "Robustness in the Strategy of Scientific Model Building." In G. N. Wilkinson (ed.), *Robustness in Statistics.* Orlando, Fla.: Academic Press, 1979.

Brockbank, A., and McGill, I. *Facilitating Reflective Learning in Higher Education.* Bristol, Pa.: SHRE and Open University Press, 1998.

Broussine, M., and others. "The Best and Worst Time for Management Development." *Journal of Management Development,* 1998, *17*(1), 56–67.

Burbules, N. C., and Berk, R. "Critical Thinking and Critical Pedagogies: Relations, Differences, and Limits." In L. Fendler (ed.), *Changing Terrains of Knowledge and Politics.* New York: Routledge, 1999.

Carr, W., and Kemmis, S. *Becoming Critical: Education, Knowledge, and Action Research.* Bristol, Pa.: Falmer Press, 1986.

Cervero, R. M., and Wilson, A. L. *Power in Practice: Adult Education and the Struggle for Knowledge and Power in Society.* San Francisco: Jossey-Bass, 2001.

Chi, M.T.H., Farr, M. J., and Glaser, R. *The Nature of Expertise.* Mahwah, N.J.: Erlbaum, 1988.

Denzin, N. K., and Lincoln, Y. S. "The Discipline and Practice of Qualitative Research." In Y. S. Lincoln (ed.), *The Landscape of Qualitative Research: Theories and Issues.* (2nd ed.) Thousand Oaks, Calif.: Sage, 2003a.

Denzin, N. K., and Lincoln, Y. S. (eds.). *Collecting and Interpreting Qualitative Materials.* (2nd ed.) Thousand Oaks, Calif.: Sage, 2003b.

Denzin, N. K., and Lincoln, Y. S. (eds.). *Strategies of Qualitative Inquiry.* (2nd ed.) Thousand Oaks, Calif.: Sage, 2003c.

Ellinger, A. D., and Bostrom, R. P. "An Examination of Managers' Beliefs About Their Roles as Facilitators of Learning." *Management Learning,* 2002, *33*(2), 147–179.

Elliot, J. *Action Research for Educational Change.* Bristol, Pa.: Open University Press, 1991.

Erlandson, D. A., Harris, E. L., Skipper, B. L., and Allen, S. D. *Doing Naturalistic Enquiry: A Guide to Methods.* Thousand Oaks, Calif.: Sage, 1993.

Ezzy, D. *Qualitative Analysis: Practice and Innovation.* New York: Allen and Unwin, 2002.

Flor, R., and Dooley, K. "The Dynamics of Learning to Automaticity." *Noetic Journal,* 1998, *1*(2), 168–173.

Freire, P. *Education for Critical Consciousness.* New York: Seabury Press, 1973.

Gergen, M. M., and Gergen, K. J. "Qualitative Inquiry: Tensions and Transformations." In Y. S. Lincoln (ed.), *The Landscape of Qualitative Research: Theories and Issues.* (2nd ed.) Thousand Oaks, Calif.: Sage, 2003.

Habermas, J. *The Theory of Communicative Action,* Vol. 1: *Reason and Rationalisation of Society.* (T. McCarthy, trans.). Boston: Beacon Press, 1984.

Habermas, J. *Communication and the Evolution of Society.* (T. McCarthy, trans.). Cambridge: Polity Press, 1991.

Hackett, D., and Martin, C. L. *Facilitation Skills for Team Leaders.* Menlo Park, Calif.: Crisp, 1993.

Hart, L. B. *Faultless Facilitation: An Instructor's Manual for Facilitation Training.* Amherst, Mass.: Human Resource Development Press, 1991.

Hart, L. B. *Faultless Facilitation: A Resource Guide for Group and Team Leaders.* Amherst, Mass.: Human Resource Development Press, 1992.

Havergal, M., and Edmonstone, J. *The Facilitator's Toolkit.* Aldershot, England: Gower, 1999.

Heron, J. *The Facilitators' Handbook.* London: Kogan Page, 1989.

Heron, J. *Group Facilitation: Theories and Models for Practice.* London: Kogan Page, 1993.

Heron, J. *The Complete Facilitator's Handbook.* London: Kogan Page, 1999.

Hersey, P., and Blanchard, K. H. *Management of Organizational Behavior: Utilizing Human Resources.* (6th ed.) Upper Saddle River, N.J.: Prentice Hall, 1993.

Hogan, C. F. *Understanding Facilitation: Theory and Principles.* London: Kogan Page, 2002.

Hogan, C. F. *Practical Facilitation: A Toolkit of Techniques.* London: Kogan Page, 2003.

Hovenlynck, J. "Facilitating Experiential Learning as a Process of Metaphor Development." *Journal of Experiential Education,* 1998, *21*(1), 6–13.

Hughes, C. "Facilitation in Context: Challenging Some Basic Principles." *Studies in Continuing Education,* 1999, *21*(1), 21–43.

Hunter, D., Bailey, A., and Taylor, B. *The Art of Facilitation.* Auckland, New Zealand: Tandem, 1995.

Hunter, D., Bailey, A., and Taylor, B. *The Essence of Facilitation: Being in Action in Groups.* Auckland, New Zealand: Tandem, 1999.

James, P. "The Double Edge of Competency Training: Contradictory Discourses and Lived Experience." *Journal of Vocational Education and Training,* 2001, *53*(2), 301–324.

Justice, T., and Jamieson, D. W. *The Facilitator's Fieldbook.* New York: AMACON, 1999.

Kincheloe, J. L., and McLaren, P. "Rethinking Critical Theory and Qualitative Research. In Y. S. Lincoln (ed.), *The Landscape of Qualitative Research: Theories and Issues.* (2nd ed.) Thousand Oaks, Calif.: Sage, 2003.

Kirk, P., and Broussine, M. "The Politics of Facilitation." *Journal of Workplace Learning: Employee Counselling Today,* 2000, *12*(1), 13–22.

Larsen, K.R.T., and others. "Learning Organizations: A Primer for Group Facilitators." *Group Facilitation: A Research and Applications Journal,* 2002, *4*(1), 30–44.

Lincoln, Y. S., and Guba, E. G. "Paradigmatic Controversies, Contradictions, and Emerging Confluences." In Y. S. Lincoln (ed.), *The Landscape of Qualitative Research: Theories and Issues.* (2nd ed.) Thousand Oaks, Calif.: Sage, 2003.

Marsick, V. J., and Watkins, K. E. *Facilitating Learning Organisations: Making Learning Count.* Aldershot: Gower, 1999.

Mongeau, P. A., and Morr, M. C. "Reconsidering Brainstorming." *Group Facilitation: A Research and Applications Journal,* 1999, *1*(1), 14–21.

Niederman, F., and Volkema, R. "The Effects of Facilitator Characteristics on Meeting Preparation, Set Up and Implementation." *Small Group Research,* 1999, *30*(3), 330–360.

Parry, L. "Effective Facilitators—A Key Element in Successful Continuous Improvement Processes." *Training for Quality,* 1995, *3*(4), 9–14.

Phnuyal, B., Archer, D., and Cottingham, S. "Participation, Literacy and Empowerment: Reflections on Reflect." *Education Action,* 1997, *8,* 27–35.

Pierce, V., Cheesebrow, D., and Braun, L. M. "Facilitator Competencies." *Group Facilitation: A Research and Applications Journal,* 2000, *2*(2), 24–31.

Priest, S., Gass, M., and Gillis, L. *The Essential Elements of Facilitation.* Dubuque, Iowa: Kendall/Hunt, 2000.

Rasmussen, D. M. "Critical Theory and Philosophy." In D. M. Rasmussen (ed.), *The Handbook of Critical Theory.* Oxford: Blackwell, 1996.

Ringer, M. "Two Vital Aspects in the Facilitation of Groups: Connections and Containment." *Australian Journal of Outdoor Education,* 1999, *4*(1), 5–11.

Ringer, M. *Group Action: The Dynamics of Groups in Therapeutic, Educational and Corporate Settings.* London: Jessica Kingsley, 2002.

Rogers, C. R. *Freedom to Learn for the 80s.* Columbus, Ohio: Charles E. Merrill, 1983.

Rogers, C. R. "The Interpersonal Relationship in the Facilitation of Learning." In H. E. Kirschenbaum (ed.), *The Carl Rogers Reader.* Boston: Houghton Mifflin, 1989.

Schön, D. A. *Educating the Reflective Practitioner.* San Francisco: Jossey-Bass, 1988.

Schön, D. A. *The Reflective Practitioner: How Professionals Think in Action.* Aldershot, England: Arena, 1995.

Schwarz, R. "Comments of Facilitator Competencies." *Group Facilitation: A Research and Applications Journal,* 2000, *2*(2), 33–34.

Schwarz, R. *The Skilled Facilitator: A Comprehensive Resource for Consultants, Facilitators, Managers, Trainers, and Coaches.* San Francisco: Jossey-Bass, 2002.

Senge, P. M. *The Fifth Discipline: The Art and Practice of the Learning Organization.* New York: Doubleday, 1990.

Senge, P. M. "Leading Learning Organisations: The Bold, the Powerful, and the Invisible." In R. Beckhard (ed.), *The Leader of the Future.* San Francisco: Jossey-Bass, 1996.

Sharp, P. A. "The 'Never-Evers' of Workshop Facilitation." *Journal of Staff Development,* 1992, *13*(2), 38–40.

Stahl, M. J. *Management: Total Quality in a Global Environment.* Cambridge, Mass.: Blackwell, 1995.

Thomas, G. J. "A Typology of Approaches to Facilitator Education." *Journal of Experiential Education,* forthcoming.

van Maurik, J. "Facilitating Excellence: Styles and Processes of Facilitation." *Leadership and Organisational Development Journal,* 1994, *15*(8), 30–34.

Warren, K. "A Call for Race, Gender, and Class Sensitive Facilitation in Outdoor Experiential Education." *Journal of Experiential Education,* 1998, *21*(1), 21–25.

Weaver, R. G., and Farrell, J. D. *Managers as Facilitators.* San Francisco: Berrett-Koehler, 1997.

Webne-Behrman, H. *The Practice of Facilitation: Managing Group Process and Solving Problems.* Westport, Conn.: Quorum Books, 1998.

Weinstein, K. *Action Learning: A Practical Guide.* (2nd ed.) Aldershot, Hampshire: Gower, 1999.

White, S. A. "Participation: Walk the Talk!" In S. A. White (ed.), *The Art of Facilitating Participation: Releasing the Power of Grassroots Communication.* Thousand Oaks, Calif.: Sage, 1999.

Winter, R. *Learning from Experience: Principles and Practice in Action Research.* Bristol, Pa.: Falmer Press, 1989.

Chapter Thirty

Cooperrider, D. L., Sorensen, P. F. Jr., Whitney, D., and Yaeger, T. F. (eds.). *Appreciative Inquiry: Rethinking Human Organization Toward a Positive Theory of Change.* Champaign, Ill.: Stipes Publishing, 2000.

Doyle, M., and Straus, D. *How to Make Meetings Work: The Interaction Method.* New York: Jove, 1976.

Emery, M. *Participative Design for Participative Democracy.* Canberra: Australian National University, 1993.

Firkins, J. "Trust, Safety and Equity." Jan. 2002. [http://groups.yahoo.com/group/EVTT/files/Discussion on trust.txt].

Hunter, D., Bailey, A., and Taylor, B. *The Art of Facilitation.* Auckland: Tandem, 1994.

Hunter, D., Bailey, A., and Taylor, B. *Co-operacy: A New Way of Being at Work.* Auckland: Tandem, 1997.

International Association of Facilitators. "Mission, Values and Vision." Sept. 2004. [http://www.iaf-world.org/i4a/pages/index.cfm?pageid=3343].

Marvin, F., and Butcher, J. "Essays on Consensus: Consensus Is Primary to Group Facilitation; Consensus Is Situation Dependent." *Group Facilitation: A Research and Applications Journal,* 2002, *4*(Spring) 56–63.

Owen, H. *Open Space Technology: A User's Guide.* Potomac, Md.: Abbott, 1992.

Pierce, V., Cheesebrow, D., and Braun, L. M. "Facilitator Competencies." *Group Facilitation: A Research and Applications Journal,* 2000, *2*(2), 24–31.

Rangarajan, N., and Rohrbaugh, J. "Multiple Roles of Online Facilitation: An Example in Any-Time, Any-Place Meetings." *Group Facilitation: A Research and Applications Journal,* 2003, *5*, 26–36.

Schein, E. *Process Consultation,* Vol. 2: *Lessons for Managers and Consultants.* Reading, Mass.: Addison-Wesley, 1987.

Schuman, S. "The Report of the Ethics and Values Think Tank June 2002." June 2002. [http://groups.yahoo.com/group/EVTT/files/Report of the EVTT 2002.doc].

Schwarz, R. *The Skilled Facilitator: A Comprehensive Resource for Consultants, Facilitators, Managers, Trainers, and Coaches, New and Revised.* San Francisco: Jossey-Bass, 2002a.

Schwarz, R. "Who Is the Client?" Jan. 2002b. [http://groups.yahoo.com/group/EVTT/files/].

Spencer, L. J. *Winning Through Meeting the Challenge of Corporate Change with the Technology of Participation: The Group Facilitation Models of the Institute of Cultural Affairs.* Iowa: Kendall/Hunt, 1989.

Chapter Thirty-One

Epps, J. "The Journey of Meaning at Work." *Group Facilitation: A Research and Application Journal,* 2003, *5*, 17–25.

Gleick, J. *Chaos: Making a New Science.* London: Cardinal, 1987.

Herbert, N. *Quantum Reality: Beyond the New Physics.* New York: Doubleday Anchor, 1985.

Niebuhr, H. R. *The Meaning of Revelation.* New York: Macmillan, 1954.

Niebuhr, H. R. *Radical Monotheism and Western Culture.* New York: HarperCollins, 1960.

Senge, P. *The Fifth Discipline.* New York: Doubleday, 1990.

Chapter Thirty-Two

Kaplan, R. E. "Some Hidden Elements of Control in Group Facilitation: Appreciating the Bounded and Binding Aspects of Openness." *Small Group Behavior,* 1985, *16*, 462–476.

Kiser, A. G. *Masterful Facilitation: Becoming a Catalyst for Meaningful Change.* New York: AMACOM, 1998.

Rees, F. *How to Lead Work Teams: Facilitation Skills.* San Francisco: Jossey-Bass, 2001.

Rosenberg, M. *Nonviolent Communication: The Language of Compassion.* San Diego, Calif.: PuddleDancer Press, 1999.

Webne-Behrman, H. *The Practice of Facilitation: Managing Group Process and Solving Problems.* Westport, Conn.: Quorum Books, 1998.

White, S. A. (ed.). *The Art of Facilitating Participation: Releasing the Power of Grassroots Communication.* Thousand Oaks, Calif.: Sage, 1999.

Chapter Thirty-Three

Andersen, N. A. "Polyphonic Organizations." S-WoBA: Scandinavian Working Papers in Business Administration, 13, 2001.

Boulding, K. *The Image: Knowledge in Life and Society.* Ann Arbor: University of Michigan, 1966.

Cooperrider, D. L. "Positive Image, Positive Action: The Affirmative Basis of Organizing." In S. Srivastva and D. L. Cooperrider (eds.), *Appreciative Management and Leadership.* San Francisco: Jossey-Bass, 1990.

Cooperrider, D. L. "Appreciative Inquiry: New Horizons for a Positive Revolution in Change." Speech at Benedictine University, Lisle, Ill., Nov. 1999.

Cooperrider, D. L., Sorensen, P. F., Whitney, D., and Yaeger, T. F. (eds.). *Appreciative Inquiry: Rethinking Human Organization Toward a Positive Theory of Change.* Champaign, Ill.: Stipes, 2000.

Frankl, V. E. *Man's Search for Meaning: An Introduction to Logotherapy.* New York: Washington Square Press, 1959.

Heisenberg, W. *Physics and Philosophy.* New York: HarperCollins, 1958.

Heisenberg, W. "The Physical Content of Quantum Kinematics and Mechanics." In J. A. Wheeler and H. Zurek (eds.), *Quantum Theory and Measurement.* Princeton, N.J.: Princeton University Press, 1983.

Hock, D. W. *Birth of the Chaordic Age.* San Francisco: Berrett-Koehler, 1999.

Kretzmann, J. P., and McKnight, J. L. *Building Communities from the Inside Out: A Path Toward Finding and Mobilizing a Community's Assets.* Chicago: ACTA, 1993.

Lefcourt, H. M. *Locus of Control: Current Trends in Theory and Research.* Mahwah, N.J.: Erlbaum, 1976.

Mehl-Madrona, L. *Coyote Medicine.* New York: Scribner, 1997.

Merton, R. *Social Theory and Social Structure.* New York: Free Press, 1968.

Morgan, G. *Images of Organization: The Executive Edition.* San Francisco: Berrett-Koehler, 1998.

Polack, F. *The Image of the Future.* New York: Elsevier, 1973.

Rosenthal, R. *Pygmalion in the Classroom: Teacher Expectations and Pupils' Intellectual Development.* New York: Holt, 1968.

Rotter, J. B. "Generalized Expectations for Internal versus External Control of Reinforcement." *Psychological Monographs: General and Applied,* 1966, 80(1), 1–28. Whole No. 609.

Schein, E. *Process Consultation Revisited: Building the Helping Relationship.* Reading, Mass.: Addison-Wesley, 1999.

Schuman, S. P. "Believe in Doubt." *Group Facilitation: A Research and Applications Journal,* 2002, 4, 1.

Shermer, M. *Why People Believe Weird Things.* New York: Holt, 1997.

Troxel, J. P. *Participation Works: Business Cases from Around the World.* Alexandria, Va.: Miles River, 1993.

NAME INDEX

A

Abdullah, A., 263, 267, 269
Abelson, R., 396
Adams, J. W., 297
Adler, N., 256, 261
Agazarian, Y. M., 243, 249, 251
Alban, B. T., 338, 491, 492
Alexander, C., 382, 398, 418
Allen, S. D., 541
Andersen, N. A., 603
Anderson, J., 297
Archer, D., 539
Aretz, A., 216
Argyris, C., 23, 25, 29–30, 533
Arnold, K. J., 495
Arthur, W. B., 474
Asch, S., 250
Ashraf, N., 297
Atlee, T., 208
Attaran, M., 297
Attaran, S., 297
Axelrod, E., 230
Axelrod, R., 230

B

Bailey, A., 205, 528, 530, 534, 536, 539, 550, 557
Baker, L. L., 459
Bal, J., 296
Ballantine, R., 305, 309
Ballard, B., 275
Barnard, C., 1–3
Bartel, C. A., 107
Bates, M., 39
Bazerman, M. H., 353

Beach, L. R., 353, 431
Beasley, C., 271
Beavin, J. H., 136
Beckhard, R., 340
Bell, N., 7
Bendaly, L., 528, 530
Bender, T., 74
Benne, K., 137
Bennett, M., 258
Bennis, W. G., 453
Bens, I., 328
Bentley, T., 528, 532
Bergdall, T. D., 421, 430, 438, 441, 444
Berger, D., 123
Berk, R., 536, 538
Berne, E., 45
Berry, B., 106
Berry, P. C., 103
Bertalanffy, L., 243
Beyerlein, M., 295
Biderman, P. W., 453
Bion, W., 37, 46, 243
Birchmeier, Z., 104
Blainey, J., 264
Blanchard, K. H., 355, 534
Bleandonu, G., 37
Block, C. H., 103
Block, P., 63
Bohm, D., 208, 209, 271, 488
Bolen, T., 216
Boone, M. E., 450
Bostrom, R. P., 84, 525, 527, 532
Bouchard, T. J., 106
Boughton, N. W., 60–61

Elliot, J., 540
Elliott, J., 241
Emery, M., 557
Epps, J., 563, 570
Erlandson, D. A., 541
Estrella, M., 424
Ezzy, D., 541

F

Factor, D., 271, 488
Farr, M. J., 539
Farrell, J. D., 477, 526, 528, 532
Fels, D., 297
Fetterman, D. M., 426
Figallo, C., 215
Firkins, J., 551
Fischer, S., 89, 100
Fisher, C. J., 201–202
Fisher, R., 327, 364, 367
Fisk, S., 123
Fitz-Gibbon, C. T., 426
Fleming, G. P., 111
Flick, D. L., 208
Flor, R., 539
Fluke, A., 209
Folger, J. P., 358
Fox, W. M., 141, 143, 144
Frankl, V. E., 174, 177, 601
Fraser, C., 459
Free, K., 315
Freeman, H. E., 422
Freire, P., 539
Frey, L. R., 351
Friedlob, G. T., 449

G

Gardenswartz, L., 258
Gardner, H., 37, 50–51
Garrett, P., 271, 488
Garvin, D., 507
Gass, M., 528, 534
Gaventa, J., 424
Gerard, G., 207, 337
Gergen, K. J., 178, 540
Gergen, M. M., 540
Geschka, H., 109, 271
Gesell, I., 281
Gibb, J. R., 141
Giddens, A., 430

Gillan, P. G., 146, 147, 148, 149
Gilley, J. W., 60–61
Gillis, L., 528, 534
Glaser, R., 539
Gleick, J., 570
Goleman, D., 34, 37
Goodpaster, J., 213
Goodwill, B., 264
Gouran, D. S., 351, 352, 353, 357, 358, 359, 360
Grawitch, M. J., 113
Guba, E. G., 540
Guetzkow, H., 137
Gupta, V., 184
Gustafson, D. H., 109

H

Habermas, J., 536, 541
Hackett, D., 530
Hackman, J. R., 137, 453
Hall, E. T., 267
Hall, J., 359
Halprin, L., 160
Hampden-Turner, C., 267
Hare, A. P., 450
Hargadon, A., 103
Harris, E. L., 541
Harris, R. T., 340
Hart, L. B., 528, 530
Hatry, H. P., 422, 426
Havergal, M., 528, 530
Heierbacher, S., 207, 208, 209
Heisenberg, W., 599
Heraclitus, 35
Herbert, N., 570
Herek, G., 358
Herman, J. L., 426
Heron, J., 528, 533, 534
Hersey, P., 355, 534
Hickling, A., 78–79
Hill, N., 509
Hirokawa, R. Y., 143, 351, 352, 353
Hock, D. W., 286, 603
Hofstede, G., 267
Hogan, C. F., 255, 256, 261, 271, 272, 277, 278, 526, 528, 530, 531, 536, 539
Holman, P., 482, 491
Honey, P., 259
Horn, R. E., 160, 384, 385, 387, 389, 419, 486
Hoskins, S., 481

Marcum, D., 368
Margulies, N., 160, 385
Marrow, A. J., 243
Marsick, V. J., 526
Marston, W. M., 36–37
Martin, C. L., 530
Marvin, F., 553, 554
Maslow, A., 174, 176
Mathews, J. W., 483
May, R., 176
Maycunich, A., 60–61
Mayer, J. D., 34
Maznevski, M. L., 255, 261–262, 263, 264
McArthur, P., 30
McCartt, A. T., 452
McDonald, J. W., 208
McGill, I., 528, 531
McGrath, J. E., 453
McKnight, J., 430, 596
McLaren, P., 541
Meeker, L., 89, 100
Mehl-Madrona, L., 600
Mennecke, B. E., 106
Merton, R., 599
Meyer, M. W., 449
Meyer, N. D., 450
Meyers, R. A., 357
Michaelson, L. K., 107
Michalak, B., 89, 100
Miller, G. A., 160
Milliken, F. J., 107
Milter, R. J., 450
Miscisin, M., 40
Mohr, B. J., 487
Mongeau, P. A., 525
Morgan, G., 483, 486, 600
Morr, M. C., 525
Morris, L. L., 426
Mumford, A., 259
Munz, D. C., 113
Murphy, J., 478
Murray, H., 243
Musashi, M., 473

N

Nagda, B., 209, 220
Nakui, T., 103, 111, 112
Napolitano, C. S., 329
Nash, T., 548

Nathanson, L., 146, 147, 148, 149
Neely, A., 449
Nelson, J., 86, 461
Nemeth, C. J., 104
Nemeth-Brown, Z., 104
Newcomer, K. E., 422, 426
Niebuhr, H. R., 566, 567
Niederman, F., 525
Nierenberg, G., 215
Nijstad, B., 103
Nisbett, R., 354
Niziol, F., 315
Nurre, S., 7

O

Offner, A. K., 111
Ortega, A. H., 107, 110
Osborn, A. F., 105, 111
Owen, H., 233, 474, 479, 480, 481, 485, 556
Oxley, N. L., 111

P

Palmer, P., 216
Parry, L., 528, 530
Parschall, S., 385
Parsons, T., 450, 455
Patton, B., 327, 364, 367
Patton, M. Q., 423, 425, 427
Paulus, P. B., 103, 104, 105, 106, 107, 108, 109, 110, 111, 112
Peck, M. S., 132
Peña, W., 385
Philbrook, L., 256
Philips, J. L., 106
Phnuyal, B., 539
Pierce, V., 461, 463, 526, 527, 530, 531, 536, 539, 547, 550
Pike, R. W., 71
Plewa, R. J., 449
Plsek, P., 228
Poister, T. H., 449
Polak, F., 431, 592
Poole, M. S., 137, 138, 358
Porter, R. E., 269
Powell, C. F., 430, 438, 441
Priest, S., 528, 534
Prince, G., 148, 150
Putman, V. L., 111, 112

Putnam, R., 30
Pyser, S. N., 205, 215

Q

Quinn, R. E., 450

R

Rangarajan, N., 455, 555
Ransdell, E., 486
Rao, P.U.B., 460
Rasmussen, D. M., 536
Reagan, P., 452
Rechner, P. L., 357
Rees, F., 576
Reese, R., 263, 264, 265
Reina, D., 90
Reina, M., 90
Reynolds, C., 228
Riley, M., 140
Ringer, M., 528, 535
Ritberger, C., 40
Ritter, D., 328, 331
Robinson, L., 427
Rodas-Meeker, M. B., 89
Roethlisberger, F. J., 115
Rogers, C., 37, 115, 174, 175, 528, 535
Rohrbaugh, J., 449, 450, 452, 455, 555
Roland, E. J., 109
Rosenberg, M., 14, 574
Rosenthal, R., 598–599
Ross, L., 354
Rossi, P. H., 422
Rotter, J. B., 601
Rottmann, D., 479
Rough, J., 478, 479, 485
Rounds, J., 492
Rowe, A., 258
Ruete, N., 478
Russo, J. E., 368

S

Saint-Exupéry, A., 415
Salazar, A., 138, 143
Salovey, P., 34
Samovar, L. A., 269
Sandberg, W. R., 357
Satir, V., 277
Saunders, H., 207, 208

Schank, R. C., 396
Scharmer, C. O., 474–475, 476
Schaude, G. R., 109, 271
Schein, E., 38, 49, 192, 476, 553, 593
Schlicksupp, H., 109, 271
Schliefer, L. F., 449
Schnelle, E., 271
Schoem, D., 207
Schoemaker, P.J.H., 368
Schön, D. A., 25, 30, 533, 534, 540
Schuman, S., 1, 171, 178, 215, 547, 548, 550, 603
Schwarz, R. M., 11, 21, 351, 461, 485, 487, 488, 528, 531, 533, 534, 547, 550, 552–553
Schweiger, D. M., 357
Scott, S., 213
Seibold, D., 137, 141, 143, 144, 147
Seiford, B., 335
Senge, P. M., 31, 70, 86, 182, 208, 211, 453, 474, 476, 483, 527, 570
Sharp, P. A., 530
Shaw, B., 94
Sheats, P., 137
Shephard, P., 263, 269
Shermer, M., 599
Sherwood, J. J., 110
Sibbet, D., 155, 162, 178, 385, 486
Sieberg, E., 141
Silber, T., 225
Silverstein, M., 398
Sjodin, T., 509
Skipper, B. L., 541
Smith, D. K., 315, 316
Smith, D. M., 30
Smith, S., 111, 368
Smithe, G., 315
Snyder, N., 296
Sorensen, P. F., Jr., 556, 603
Spencer, L. J., 61, 84, 479, 483, 556
Spolin, V., 286
Stacey, R. D., 227
Stahl, M. J., 526
Stanfield, R. B., 463, 479
Stasser, G., 104
Stern, G. J., 49
Stewart, A., 487
Stewart, G. L., 106
Stifel, M., 381, 486
Stratford, K., 161
Straus, D., 143, 144, 160, 191, 192, 296, 297, 556

SUBJECT INDEX

C

CD-ROM, how to use, 1–2
Celebrations, 182, 569
Certification. *See* Professional certification
Change: behavior, and images, 430–432; dialogue as agent of, 208–209; improvisation as bringing about, 291; and locus of control, 600–602; organizational reality model of, 474–477; small, big effects from, 229; social, facilitators as agents of, 570–571; systemic, of organizations, 192, 194; of thinking, 29–31; trust important for, 94. *See also* Participatory evaluation through stories of change
Chaos, edge of, 229
Chaos theory, 603–604
Chartering bodies, 316
Circles in the Air exercise, 238
Clapping exercise, 260–261
Client-centered approach, 37
Clients: Big Picture approach to relationship with, 7–20; evaluating satisfaction of, 19–20; gathering information about, 58–60; IAF Code of Ethics on, 552–553, 559; needs and expectations of, 17–18, 60–62, 92; thinking about, 16–17; trust between facilitators and, 12, 91–92
Closure on commitments, graphic facilitation, 167–168
Code of ethics. *See* International Association of Facilitators (IAF), Statement of Values and Code of Ethics for Group Facilitators
Cofacilitation: building expertise using, 508; of virtual meetings, 302, 304–305, 309; in visual facilitation, 391
Cognitive constraints on communication, 354–356
Cognitive stimulation, and group brainstorming, 108–110
Collaboration: mutual understanding necessary for, 117; virtual, 296–297. *See also* Multiple-stakeholder collaboration
Collaborative culture. *See* Collaborative environments
Collaborative environments, 195–203; characteristics of, 192–193; conditions for building, 193–194; five-pronged approach to building, 195–202; importance of, 203

Collective Inquiry Model of dialogue, 209, 211
Commitments, closure on, in graphic facilitation, 167–168
Common information bias, as hindrance to group functioning, 104
Communication: functional theory of, in decision-making groups, 351–360; importance of, to group decision making, 136, 138, 151; intentional, in Big Picture approach, 15–16; message dimension of, 136–137; nonviolent (NVC), 573–574, 577, 583; and operating styles, 15–16; to show thinking about client, 17; and thinking styles, 15. *See also* Group communication
Community At Work, multiple-stakeholder collaboration case study from, 116–132
Community development, asset-based, 430, 595–596
Community Empowerment Program (CEP) (Ethiopia), 430, 435, 436–437, 440–443
Competencies: core, IAF's definition of, 213, 461, 463–464, 468–471, 546–547; defined, 460; of facilitators using meaning-centered counseling (MCC) approach, 183–185; IAF's model of, 527, 531. *See also* Professional certification; Skills
Competency-based training, 531
The Complete Facilitator (Heron), 533
Complexity, increase in, 2
Complexity science, 225–240; applied to meeting facilitation, 235–239; on characteristics of complex adaptive systems, 227–230; design principles from, for facilitating meetings, 230–234; general information on, 225–227; resources on, 239–240
Conference Model, 230
Conferences, professional, 498
Confidentiality, IAF Code of Ethics on, 556, 561
Conflict of interest: disclosure of, 91; IAF Code of Ethics on, 554–555, 560
Conflict Research Consortium, 206, 219
Conflict resolution sessions, 366
Consensus building. *See* Consensus decision making
Consensus decision making, 361–380; approaches to, 367–368; converge technique for, 379; danger of groupthink to, 178; delineation technique for, 369–374; five-finger consensus technique for, 378–379; and IAF

Code of Ethics, 553–554; and levels of disagreements, 361–367; merge technique for, 376–378; in Start-Up meetings, 324, 325; strengths and weaknesses technique for, 374–376; weighted score technique for, 379

Consensus rule, interaction method, 146

Consensus-seeking rules, for groups with egocentric restraints, 359

Consultation: expert vs. process, 593–594; focusing on people, 594, 606–607; focusing on problems, 593, 606; peer (*intervisie*), 488, 492

Content interventions, 484

Continuing education. *See* Professional development

Continuous improvement, as goal of performance measurement, 449, 452, 455

Control: giving up, 292–293; locus of, and change, 600–602

Converge technique, consensus decision making, 379

Converge/diverge principle, designing conversations in large group meetings, 338–340

Convergent thinking, 122

Conversation About Conflict, 223

Conversation Café, 219–220, 221

Conversations. *See* Dialogue

Core competencies. *See* Competencies

Core values. *See* Values

Creating an edge, 232–234, 237, 238

Creative Evaluation (Patton), 427

Creative Training Techniques Handbook (Pike), 71

Critical approaches, facilitator education, 528, 529, 536–538

Critical Incident Technique, 532

Critiques: by group members, 507; by other facilitators, 508–509

Cultural iceberg model, 266

Cultural suitcases exercise, 267

Culture: defined, 255–256; focusing on dimensions of, with multicultural groups, 267–277; group, 49–50; mapping, 264–270; organizational, attitude surveys on, 96. *See also* Multicultural groups

D

Dannemiller Tyson Associates, 336, 340

Debate, dialogue vs., 207, 210–211

Debriefs: formal, 507; with improvisation, 289; in meaning-centered counseling approach, 182; of virtual meetings, 309, 311

Decision making, participatory, diamond model of, 124, 131–132. *See also* Consensus decision making; Functional theory of communication in decision-making groups; Group decision making

Decisions, Decisions (Welch), 367–368

Deliberation, dialogue vs., 208

Delineation technique, consensus decision making, 369–374

Denison Organizational Culture Survey, 201–202

Dependency, 23, 37, 46

Design approaches, 479–481; prestructured vs. self-organizing, 479–480; scripted vs. emergent, 480–481; serial threads vs. parallel threads, 481

Developmental facilitation, 24

Diagnosis–intervention cycle, Skilled Facilitator approach, 28

Dialogue, 205–223; Collective Inquiry Model of, 209, 211; Conversation Café model of, 219–220, 221; conversation starters for, 220, 222; debate vs., 207, 210–211; defined, 206, 207; deliberation vs., 208; example of designing, 212–213; framing and asking questions in, 216–218; guidelines for designing and leading, 213–219; history of movement for, 208; planning for, in large group meetings, 338–341; as possible change agent, 208–209; potential opportunities for, 205–206; resources on, 222–223; simple rules for, 233; workshops vs., 488

Differentiation-integration (D/I) theory, 241–254; and designing meetings, 242, 245–246; facilitation based on, 242, 243–245; and managing meetings, 242, 247–252; and managing ourselves, 242, 252–254; theoretical basis of, 243

Difficult behaviors, of group members, 40–46, 175–176

Dimensions of Facilitator Education Model, 528–541; critical dimension of, 528, 529, 536–538; intentional dimension of, 528, 529, 531–535; limitations of, 538–541; person-centered dimension of, 528, 529, 535–536; technical dimension of, 528, 529, 530–531, 533

Disagreements: example of, 361–362; fostered by specialization, 2; identifying level of, 367; level 1 (information), 361, 362–363; level 2 (experience or values), 361, 363–365; level 3 (outside factors), 361, 365–366

DISC Profile, 37, 39

Divergent thinking, 122

Diversity: checklist on, when designing workshops, 257–259; designing dialogue on, 212–213; effect of, on group brainstorming, 107; importance of trust when working with, 90–91. *See also* Multicultural groups

Documentation: of best practices, 506; of large group meetings, 344; of process, 67–68; required for professional certification, 465; of virtual meetings, 309, 311; in visual facilitation, 394–395, 418

Drawing actions, visual facilitation, 394, 411–414

Driver operating style, 15

DVF model, designing conversations in large group meetings, 340

Dynamic Facilitation, 479, 480, 485, 490

E

Edge of chaos, 229

Education. *See* Facilitator education; Professional development

Egocentric constraints on communication, 357–359

Egoless presence, facilitators in meetings, 349–350

Eight Ps approach to preparation, 58–71; people in, 58, 62–63; personal preparation in, 58, 69–71; perspective in, 58–60; place in, 58, 64–67; practice in, 58, 68–69; process in, 58, 67–68; product in, 58, 63–64; purpose in, 58, 60–62

Electronic Discussion on Group Facilitation, 389

Electronic media, facilitation training using, 497–498

Emergent design, managing, in large group meetings, 341–342

Emotional bank account, 98

Emotional intelligence, 37

Emotional organigram technique, visual facilitation, 409–411, 418

Emotional skills, and Skilled Facilitator approach, 33–34

Emotions, readiness associated with, 69–70

The Emotions of Normal People (Marston), 37

Empathetic listening, 13–14, 588

Empowerment: with affirmative facilitation, 596–598; and trust, 97

Ethics: facilitators as role models of, 92; issues regarding, clarified by IAF Code of Ethics, 549–555. *See also* International Association of Facilitators (IAF), Statement of Values and Code of Ethics for Group Facilitators

Ethics and Values Think Tank (EVTT): development of IAF Code of Ethics by, 547–549; ethics issues discussed by, 549–555

Evaluation: of client satisfaction, 19–20; daily written, in large group meetings, 342; and organizational learning, 421; program, 422–424. *See also* Participatory evaluation

Existential/humanistic psychology, and meaning-centered counseling (MCC), 174, 176, 177

Expectations, client, 60–61

Experiences: disagreements based on different, 361, 363–365; facilitation, learning from, 504–506

Experiential learning, as trust-building technique, 100–101

Expert consultation, 593–594

Expressive operating style, 16

F

Facilitation. *See* Group facilitation

The Facilitation Skills Training Kit (Bendaly), 530

Facilitator Accreditation Services Ltd. (FAS), 462

Facilitator Competency Model, 527, 531

Facilitator education, 525–541; areas for research in, 538–541; critical approaches to, 528, 529, 536–538; defined, 528; demand for, in organization development (OD), 526–528; intentional approaches to, 528, 529, 531–535; person-centered approaches to, 528, 529, 535–536; technical approaches to, 528, 529, 530–531, 533. *See also* Professional development

Facilitators: actions of, in multiple-stakeholder collaboration, 131–132; common errors made by, 179–180; competencies and characteristics of, using meaning-centered counseling (MCC) approach, 183–185; criteria for, in Skilled Facilitator approach, 22; critiques by other, 508–509; egoless presence of, in large group meetings, 349–350; increased demand for, 459–460; intervention by, 23; observing other, 502–503; personal preparation by, in Eight Ps approach, 69–71; situations benefiting from, 171–174, 477; trust between clients and, 12, 91–92; trust between groups and, 92–94

Facilitators, roles of: in group brainstorming, 111; in improvisation, 291–292; of large group meetings, 345–346; in meaning-centered counseling (MCC) approach, 187; as process guides, 549–550; in Skilled Facilitator approach, 24; in Start-Up method, 317, 320–321

Facilitator's Toolkit (Havergal and Edmonstone), 530

Fairy tale technique, visual facilitation, 402–404

Faultless Facilitation Method, 530

Feedback: accepting, 71; in affirmative facilitation, 605–606; from group members, 506–508; in meaning-centered counseling approach, 182; owning, in transparent facilitation, 586–588; from peers, 508–510

Feng shui, 74–75

The Fifth Discipline (Senge), 70

Fight-or-flight response, 37, 46–47

Films, learning from, 503–504

Five-finger consensus technique, consensus decision making, 378–379

Flawless Consulting (Block), 63

Flexibility, and trust between facilitator and group, 93

Focus questions, 61–62

Focus rule, interaction method, 144–145

Follow-up: feedback obtained from, 508; for large group meetings, 344–345

Formative evaluations, 422

Forming stage, group development, 37, 47, 315

Four Seasons (personality inventory instrument), 40, 51–53

Framing assignments, large group meetings, 347–348

Functional theory of communication in decision-making groups, 351–360; on affiliative constraints, 356–357; central proposition of, 352; on cognitive constraints, 354–356; on egocentric constraints, 357–359; and knowledge and skills to enhance facilitation, 359–360; overview of, 352–353. *See also* Group communication; Group decision making

The Functions of the Executive (Barnard), 1–2

Future Search, 84, 230, 242, 482, 483, 487, 557

G

Game technique, visual facilitation, 404–406

Gender, and group brainstorming, 107

Goal Oriented Project Planning (GOPP), 474, 487, 492

Governance and Local Democracy (GOLD) program (Philippines), 430, 444–445

Graphic facilitation, 155–169, 557; advantages of, 155, 159–160, 169; case example of, 156–159; and Grove Facilitation Model, 162–164; history of, 160–161; processes benefiting from, 161; products of, 486; skills required of facilitator using, 155–156; steps in, 164–169. *See also* Visual facilitation

Graphic Gameplan, 167–168

Graphic Guides, Inc., 160

Graphic recording, 156, 231

Groan Zone: defined, 123; in diamond model of participatory decision making, 124; group discussion in, 124–125; inevitability of, in multiple-stakeholder collaboration, 132–133; listening in, 126; multiple visits to, 128, 129. *See also* Storming stage

Ground rules: for dialogue, 215; in meaning-centered counseling (MCC) approach, 181; in Skilled Facilitator approach, 26–27; for Start-Up meetings, 318, 324, 326; for virtual meetings, 306–307

Group autonomy, IAF Code of Ethics on, 554, 560

Group brainstorming, 103–114; best practices for, 113–114; factors that hinder, 104–105; factors that improve, 105–112; and nominal group technique (NGT) for idea generation, 109, 146–148; rules for, 111, 233; theory vs. practice of, 112–113

Group communication, 135–151; functions of message behaviors in, 137–138; in interaction method for meetings, 143–146; in nominal group technique (NGT) for generating ideas, 146–148; procedural levels of analysis of, 139–142; in synectics for creative problem solving, 148–151. *See also* Communication; Functional theory of communication in decision-making groups

Group culture, 49–50

Group decision making: communication's importance to, 136, 138, 151; dynamics of, 120, 122–124; and group brainstorming, 112. *See also* Functional theory of communication in decision-making groups; Group communication; Group decision processes

Group decision processes: assessing effectiveness of, 449–455; continuous improvement of, 449, 452, 455; importance of, 449–450; increased efficiency of, with facilitators, 459–460; measurement of, 450–453; organizational conditions affecting, 453–455

Group development: Bion's principles of, 37, 46–47; Tuckman's stages of, 37–38, 46, 47–48, 315

Group dynamics: asking questions about, 63; managing, in meaning-centered counseling approach, 182; origin of term, 243

Group effectiveness model, in Skilled Facilitator approach, 24

Group facilitation: basic vs. developmental, 24; complexity and diversity of applications of, 556–557; defined, 21–23, 351; Grove Facilitation Model of, 162–164; increasing demand for, 526–527; methods vs. process focus in, 35–36; as superlative task, 1–3. *See also* Affirmative facilitation; Cofacilitation; Graphic facilitation; Spectra of facilitation; Transparent facilitation; Visual facilitation

Group Facilitation Methods (Institute of Cultural Affairs), 61

Group members: addition of new, 48–49; as contributors, 564–565; dealing with difficult behaviors of, 40–46, 175–176; diversity of, and brainstorming, 107; empowerment of, with affirmative facilitation, 596–598; feedback from, 506–508; knowledge and

skills of, 106, 359–360; noticing effects of transparency on, 581–582; training to increase collaborative skills of, 198–199. *See also* People

Groups: celebrating milestones in, 182, 569; as clients, 552–553; composition of, and brainstorming, 105–107; large vs. small, 490–492; master mind, 509; psychological theories relevant to process issues in, 36–38; subgroups in, 243, 248–252, 259; trust between facilitator and, 92–94; trust within and between, 94–95; types of, 489–494. *See also* Large group meetings; Multicultural groups

Groupthink, 104, 178, 492

Grove Consultants International, 160, 486

Grove Facilitation Model: applied to graphic facilitation, 164–169; flows in, 162–164

H

Habitat for Humanity, leadership education program, 98

Hewlett Packard, Work Innovation Network (WIN) meetings, 234

How to Make Meetings Work (Doyle and Straus), 160

Human Development Project Planning, 483

Humor, 265, 604

I

I Six Sigma, 484

Ideas: facilitation methods based on, 487; nominal group technique (NGT) for generating, 109, 146–148

The Image (Boulding), 431

Image theory: affirmative approaches based on, 592, 594–596, 598–600; on behavior change, 430–432

Images (in visual facilitation): effect of, 397; evolution of, 396; live process, 394, 406–414, 418; method of working with, 392–395; and patterns, 398; preparing, 393–394, 399–406, 418; stories told by, 396; summary, 394–395, 418

Imaginal Training, 486

Impartiality, vs. neutrality, 550

Improvisation, 281–294; benefits of, 281–282, 288, 293–294; change brought about by,

291; debriefing games of, 286–290; defined, 281; facilitator as energy director with, 291–292; "One Word at a Time" game of, 283–284, 287, 292; paradoxes of, 292–293; resources on, 294; structure of, 282–284, 292; tips on, 294; "yes . . . and" principle in, 284–286

Inferences, low-level, in Skilled Facilitator approach, 28–29

Information: disagreements based on lack of shared, 361, 362–363; drawing out, in graphic facilitation, 166–167; gathering, on client's organization and operating situation, 58–60

Information exchange. *See* Group brainstorming

Information Mapping, 160

Institute of Cultural Affairs (ICA): Facilitator Competency Model, 527, 531; and founding of IAF, 461; Problem Solving Units, 479. *See also* Technology of Participation (ToP) Group Facilitation Methods

Intelligence: emotional, 37; multiple, 37, 50–51

Intentional approaches, facilitator education, 528, 529, 531–535

Interaction Associates, 160

Interaction Method, 143–146, 556

International Association of Facilitators (IAF): competency model of, 527, 531; core competencies as defined by, 213, 461, 463–464, 468–471, 546–547; core values of, 546; establishment of, 461; listserv, 501–502; mission of, 460, 546; professional certification by, 461–462, 464–468; and visual facilitation, 389, 391, 416

International Association of Facilitators (IAF), Statement of Values and Code of Ethics for Group Facilitators: applied to specific scenarios, 545, 557–558; development of, 547–549; emerging issues for, 555–557; ethics issues clarified by, 549–555; on facilitator ownership, 489; text of, 558–561; and visual facilitators, 391, 505

International Forum of Visual Practitioners, 161

International Institute of Environment and Development (IIED), 427

Intersubjectivity: defined, 115; in multiple-stakeholder collaboration, 115–116, 123, 131, 132

Interventions: and dependence on facilitators, 23; and diagnosis–intervention cycle in Skilled Facilitator approach, 28; with implicit vs. explicit rules, 484–485; process vs. content, 484

Interviews: in Big Picture approach, 10–11; eliciting stories in, 98; required for professional certification, 465, 466; visual facilitation technique based on, 406–409

Intervisie (peer consultation teams), 488, 492

Introductions: to create participatory climate, 180; for multicultural groups, 259–261; in Start-Up meetings, 320–321; in virtual meetings, 305–306

J

Joint Applications Development (JAD), 479, 483, 487, 490

Journals, professional, 500–501

K

Keirsey Temperament Sorter (personality inventory instrument), 39

Kellogg Foundation, 427

Key result area (KRA), 197

Kinesthetic thinking style, 15

Knowledge: assumptions underlying, of facilitators, 565–567; to enhance facilitation, 359–360

L

Language: exercise on, for multicultural groups, 264–265; tips on, in large group meetings, 347–348; visual, 385, 388, 389, 419

Large group meetings, 335–350; egoless presence when facilitating, 349–350; follow-up for, 344–345; logistics preparations for, 343; managing emergent design in, 341–342; managing energy in, 346–347; meeting space for, 84; planning for conversations in, 338–341; planning team process for, 336–337; purpose statement for, 337–338; roles of facilitators of, 345–346; tips on language use in, 347–348; visual facilitation techniques for, 399–414; vs. small group meetings, 490–492

Leadership: actions by, to build collaborative environments, 195, 196–198; path-goal theory of, 357; process, 215

Leadership Strategies Institute, 379
Learning: experiential, as trust-building technique, 100–101; leveraging, in graphic facilitation, 169; mutual learning model, 30; names, 261, 604; organizational, evaluation's role in, 421
Lego Serious Play, 486
Let's Talk America, 223
Listening: authentic, to build trust, 92; building mutual understanding through, 126–128, 133; empathetic, 13–14, 588; lack of, in group discussions in Groan Zone, 124–125; in multiple-stakeholder collaboration, 124–125, 126–128, 133
Live process images, visual facilitation, 394, 406–414, 418
Locus of control, and change, 600–602
Logotherapy, and meaning-centered counseling (MCC), 174, 177

M

Managers, facilitator education for, 532
Man's Search for Meaning (Frankl), 601
Map making technique, visual facilitation, 402
Mapping, cultural, 264–267
Mapping, bridging, and integrating (MBI) model, 261–264
Master mind groups, 509
Meaning-centered counseling (MCC) approach: characteristics of effective facilitators using, 185–187; competencies needed by facilitators using, 183–185; creating positive participatory climate in, 179–182; overview of, 174, 177–179; situations appropriate for, 188–189; theoretical basis of, 174–177
Measurement, of trust, 95–96. *See also* Evaluation; Performance measurement
Meeting space, 73–88; adapting, 87–88; arrangement of furnishings in, 75–76, 79–84; blocking vs. inviting participation, 75–76, 80, 81; checking out, 64, 66–67, 86–87; creating inviting environment in, 85–86; determining requirements for, 65; in Eight Ps approach to preparation, 58, 64–67; electronic meeting support arrangements in, 84–85; and feng shui, 74–75; importance of carefully considering, 73–74, 88; responsibility for, 568; size

and shape of, 77–79; specifications for, 82–84; for Start-Up meetings, 318–320; for very large groups, 84
Meetings: complexity science applied to, 230–239; differentiation-integration (D/I) theory applied to, 242, 247–254; diversity checklist for designing, 257–259; participative, 75–76; time issues with, 67, 219, 568. *See also* Large group meetings; Start-Up meetings; Virtual meetings
Mentoring, 509
Merge technique, consensus decision making, 376–378
Methods: defined, 36; experimenting with, 504–505. *See also* Spectra of facilitation; *specific methods and techniques*
Microsoft Corporation, virtual collaboration technology, 297
Mirroring process, 277–278
Mission: of International Association of Facilitators (IAF), 460, 546; of organizations with collaborative cultures, 195–197, 201; statement of, in Start-Up meetings, 329–331
Models for Excellence (American Society for Training and Development), 460
Monitoring progress: in graphic facilitation, 168–169; when building collaborative environments, 200–202
Motivation, level of, and group brainstorming, 107–108
Multicultural groups, 255–280; and cultural differences, 256; cultural mapping exercises for, 264–267; diversity checklist for designing workshops for, 257–259; focusing on cultural dimensions with, 267–277; and mapping, bridging, and integrating (MBI) model, 261–264; mirroring process for, 277–278; tips on facilitating, 279–280; warm-ups and energizers for, 259–261
Multiple intelligences, 37, 50–51
Multiple-stakeholder collaboration, 115–133; building mutual understanding for, 117, 126–128, 132, 133; case study of, 116–132; diamond model of participatory decision making in, 123, 124, 131–132; facilitator actions in, 131–132; frames of reference of participants in, 120, 121; intersubjectivity problem in, 115–116, 123, 131, 132;

potential danger in, 492–493; pseudo-solution in, 118–120

Music, 261, 486, 568

Mutual learning model, 30

Mutual understanding: building, through listening, 126–128, 133; as necessary for multiple-stakeholder collaboration, 117, 132

Myers-Briggs Type Indicator, 37, 39

N

Names: and affirmative facilitation style, 604; and graphic facilitation, 165; in multicultural groups, 261

National Coalition for Dialogue and Deliberation, 222

National Organization of Competency Assurance, 462

Needs, client: clarifying, 60–61; and trust between facilitator and client, 92; understanding, in Big Picture approach, 17–18

Neutrality: competencies in maintaining, 184; with group members having offensive values and attitudes, 175–176; transparent facilitation and, 574–577; vs. impartiality, 550

Newsletters, professional, 501

NLP Learning Systems Corporation, 15

No-attack rule, interaction method, 146

Nominal group technique (NGT), 109, 146–148

Nonviolent communication (NVC): components of, 574, 583; as tool for transparent facilitation, 573–574, 577

Nonviolent Communication (Rosenberg), 14

Norming stage, group development, 38, 48

O

On-line facilitation, and IAF Code of Ethics, 555–556. *See also* Virtual meetings

"One Word at a Time" game, 283–284, 287, 292

Open Space Technology, 233, 474, 479, 480–481, 490, 491, 556

Operating styles, 15–16

Opto International AB, 430, 436, 445

Organization development (OD): appreciative inquiry (AI) method from, 99, 487, 556, 594–595; demand for facilitator education in, 526–528; history of, 592–593

Organizational Profile, Baldrige National Quality Program, 59

Organizational psychology, 38

Organizations: attitude surveys on culture of, 96; collaborative, 191–192; conditions in, affecting group decision processes, 453–455; developing demographic profile of, 63; increasing complexity of, 2; level of trust in, 96–97; organizational reality model of change in, 474–477; professional, 498–499; systemic change of, 192, 194

Outdoor training, as trust-building technique, 100

Outside factors, disagreements based on, 361, 365–366

P

Pairing, in group development, 37, 46

Paraphrasing, in empathetic listening, 13

"Parking Lot" technique, 320, 321

Participation: assumption about, by group members, 564–565; creating positive climate for, 179–182; ensuring, in large group meetings, 346–347; meeting space inviting vs. blocking, 75–76, 80, 81

Participative Strategic Planning, 84

Participatory evaluation, 421–427; defined, 424; methods used in, 426–427; practical, 424–425; and program evaluation, 422–424; reasons for increased interest in, 421–422; resources on, 427; transformative, 425–426. *See also* Participatory evaluation through stories of change

Participatory evaluation through stories of change, 427–448; asset-based community development as origin of, 430; and Community Empowerment Program (CEP) (Ethiopia), 430, 435, 436–437, 440–443; design features for, 433–439; example of stories of change, 428–429; goals of, 432; and Governance and Local Democracy (GOLD) program (Philippines), 430, 444–445; possible applications of, 440; reflections on, 438–440; and relationship between images and change, 430–432; and Topola Rural Development Program (TRDP) (Serbia), 430, 433–435, 436, 445–448

Participatory monitoring and evaluation (PM&E). *See* Participatory evaluation

Participatory Strategic Planning (Institute of Cultural Affairs), 61

procedure for, 464–466; initial IAF program for, 461–462; number of facilitators with, 467; types of, held by facilitators, 511

Professional coaching, 510

Professional development, 495–523; by being thought leaders, 510; from feedback, 506–510; IAF Code of Ethics on, 561; intentional plan for, 512–513; by learning from facilitation experiences, 504–506; by observing others, 502–504; and professional standing, 511; publications for, 499–501; survey on, 496, 514–523; by teaching others, 510; training opportunities for, 496–499; using Internet for, 501–502. *See also* Facilitator education

Professional organizations, 498–499

Program evaluation: basic format for, 424; types of, 422–423

Projection, 248, 253–254

Pseudo-solutions, 118–120

Psychological theories: and differentiation-integration (D/I) theory, 243; and meaning-centered counseling (MCC), 174–177; and process issues in facilitation, 36–51; and Start-Up meetings, 315

Public Conversations Project, 223

Publications, professional, 499–501

Purpose: clarity of, in transparent facilitation, 577–580; in Eight Ps approach to preparation, 58, 60–62; statement of, for large group meetings, 337–338

Pygmalion in the Classroom (Rosenthal), 598

Q

Quality: achieved in visual facilitation, 381–382, 395–399; importance of, in Big Picture approach, 14–15

Questions: dialogue, techniques for, 216–218; focus, 61–62; as tool in facilitation, 10–11

R

Real-Time Strategic Change, 84, 230, 491

Relationships: building, between facilitators and groups, 31; client, Big Picture approach to, 7–20; as focus in person-centered facilitator education, 536; focus on, vs. on results, 550–551

Resistance, people-based vs. problem-based view of, 606

Responsiveness, as important to trust between facilitator and group, 93

Role models: facilitators as, 69, 92, 569; organizational leaders as, 196–197

Roots of Change (ROC) advisory board, graphic facilitation use by, 156–159

Ropes courses, as trust-building technique, 100

Rules: for brainstorming, 111, 233; implicit vs. explicit, 484–485; with interaction method, 144–146; simple, 228, 231–232, 233, 236. *See also* Ground rules

S

Satisfaction, evaluating client, 19–20

Scale of problem, 481–484; narrow vs. wide scope, 482–483; single event vs. long-term approach, 482; symptomatic vs. causal, 483–484

School discipline policy, case study of multiple-stakeholder collaboration to develop, 116–132

Self-actualization, 176

Self-differentiation, 243–244

Self-disclosure. *See* Transparent facilitation

Self-organization, 227–228

Self-reflection, 505

The Seven Habits of Highly Effective People (Covey), 98

Signet Consulting Group, 481

SimuReal, 482

Situational Leadership Model, 534

Skilled Facilitator approach, 21–34; changing thinking in, 29–31; core values of, 25–26; diagnosis–intervention cycle process in, 28; emotional skills developed with, 33–34; facilitator's role in, 24; ground rules in, 26–27; group effectiveness model in, 24; intentionality of, 533; key elements of, 23; low-level inferences in, 28–29; overview of, 34; process for building facilitator-group relationship in, 31; as systems approach, 31–33; usefulness of, in range of roles, 25

The Skilled Facilitator (Schwarz), 11

Skills: emotional, and Skilled Facilitator approach, 33–34; to enhance facilitation, 359–360; facilitation education based on developing, 530–531; of graphic facilitators, 155–156; increasing collaborative, of workforce, 198–199; teaching, to group members, 182. *See also* Competencies

Small groups, large groups vs., 490–492

Social loafing, as hindrance to group functioning, 104

Society for Human Resource Management, 212, 213

Socrates, 256

Space. *See* Meeting space

Specialization, misunderstandings fostered by, 2

Spectra of facilitation, 478–494; and approaches to design, 479–481; choice of, 474, 494; and organizational reality model of change, 474–477; and scale of problem, 481–484; and types of audiences, 489–494; and types of interventions used, 484–485; and types of products produced, 485–489

SRI International, 160

Stakeholders: defined, 61; identifying, 62–63; participatory evaluation involving, 424, 433–438. *See also* Multiple-stakeholder collaboration

Start-Up meetings, 315–333; benefits of, 333; conducting, 320–333; consensus decision making in, 324, 325; creating vision in, 328–329; developing mission statement in, 329–331; drafting work plan in, 331–332; ending, 332–333; gathering data in, 322–323; ground rules for, 318, 324, 326; identifying interests in, 326–328; objectives of, 316; preparing for, 317–320; terms used in, 316–317; theoretical context of, 315

Statement of values. *See* International Association of Facilitators (IAF), Statement of Values and Code of Ethics for Group Facilitators

Stories: facilitation methods based on, 486–487; as trust-building technique, 98–99. *See also* Participatory evaluation through stories of change

Storming stage, group development, 37, 46, 47. *See also* Groan Zone

Strategic Forum, 482

Strategic planning, as prerequisite for cultural change effort, 195–197

Strengths and weaknesses technique, consensus decision making, 374–376

Study Circles Resource Center, 212, 223

Subgroups: cross-cultural, 259; and differentiation-integration (DI) theory, 243, 248–252

Summary images, visual facilitation, 394–395, 418

Summative evaluations, 422

Survey, on professional development, 496, 514–523

Synectics, procedural communication analysis of, 148–151

Systemic change, of organizations, 192, 194

Systems: complex adaptive, 227–230; facilitating whole, 241–254; as focus of Skilled Facilitator approach, 31–33; groups as, 38

T

Task force on human rights, unsuccessful functioning of, 172–174

Team leaders, 316

Team sponsors, 316

Team Start-Up meetings. *See* Start-Up meetings

Teamness, 317

Teams: defined, 315; importance of trust in building, 95; as tension filled, 567; virtual (VTs), 296–297. *See also* Planning team

Technical approaches, facilitator education, 528, 529, 530–531, 533

Technology: electronic, to support meetings, 84–85, 108–109; for virtual meetings, 297, 298, 300, 307–309

Technology of Participation (ToP) Group Facilitation Methods, 479, 480, 487, 490, 491, 556; Action Planning, 483, 492; Environmental Analysis, 483; resources for learning, 61

Theories. *See* Psychological theories

Thinking: about clients, in Big Picture approach, 16–17; changing, in Skilled Facilitator approach, 29–31; critical, by facilitator leading dialogue, 216; divergent vs. convergent, 122; styles of, 15

Tool rule, interaction method, 145–146

SYSTEM REQUIREMENTS

PC with Microsoft Windows 98SE or later
Mac with Apple OS version 8.6 or later

USING THE CD WITH WINDOWS

To view the items located on the CD, follow these steps:

1. Insert the CD into your computer's CD-ROM drive.

2. A window appears with the following options:

   Contents: Allows you to view the files included on the CD-ROM.

   Software: Allows you to install useful software from the CD-ROM.

   Links: Displays a hyperlinked page of websites.

   Author: Displays a page with information about the Author(s).

   Contact Us: Displays a page with information on contacting the publisher or author.

   Help: Displays a page with information on using the CD.

   Exit: Closes the interface window.

If you do not have autorun enabled, or if the autorun window does not appear, follow these steps to access the CD:

1. Click Start ⇨ Run.

2. In the dialog box that appears, type d:<\\>start.exe, where d is the letter of your CD-ROM drive. This brings up the autorun window described in the preceding set of steps.

3. Choose the desired option from the menu. (See Step 2 in the preceding list for a description of these options.)

IN CASE OF TROUBLE

If you experience difficulty using the CD-ROM, please follow these steps:

1. Make sure your hardware and systems configurations conform to the systems requirements noted under "System Requirements" above.

2. Review the installation procedure for your type of hardware and operating system.

It is possible to reinstall the software if necessary.

To speak with someone in Product Technical Support, call 800–762–2974 or 317–572–3994 M–F 8:30 a.m. – 5:00 p.m. EST. You can also get support and contact Product Technical Support through our website at www.wiley.com/techsupport.

Before calling or writing, please have the following information available:

• Type of computer and operating system

• Any error messages displayed

• Complete description of the problem

It is best if you are sitting at your computer when making the call.